TELL ME NO LIES

*Investigative Journalism
and Its Triumphs*

BY JOHN PILGER

The Last Day

Aftermath: The Struggle of Cambodia and Vietnam
(with Anthony Barnett)

The Outsiders
(with Michael Coren)

Heroes

A Secret Country

Distant Voices

Hidden Agendas

The New Rulers of the World

TELL ME NO LIES

*Investigative Journalism
and Its Triumphs*

Edited by

JOHN PILGER

JONATHAN CAPE
LONDON

Published by Jonathan Cape 2004

4 6 8 10 9 7 5 3

First published in Great Britain in 2004 by
Jonathan Cape
Random House, 20 Vauxhall Bridge Road,
London SW1V 2SA

Random House Australia (Pty) Limited
20 Alfred Street, Milsons Point, Sydney,
New South Wales 2061, Australia

Random House New Zealand Limited
18 Poland Road, Glenfield,
Auckland 10, New Zealand

Random House South Africa (Pty) Limited
Endulini, 5A Jubilee Road, Parktown 2193, South Africa

The Random House Group Limited Reg. No. 954009
www.randomhouse.co.uk

A CIP catalogue record for this book
is available from the British Library

ISBN 0–224–06288–3

Papers used by The Random House Group Limited are natural,
recyclable products made from wood grown in sustainable forests;
the manufacturing processes conform to the environmental
regulations of the country of origin

Typeset by Palimpsest Book Production Limited, Polmont, Stirlingshire
Printed and bound in Great Britain by William Clowes Ltd, Beccles, Suffolk

To the memory of Paul Foot

CONTENTS

viii CONTENTS

ACKNOWLEDGEMENTS

I would like to thank Jörg Hensgen of Jonathan Cape, who not only gave me the idea for this book, but whose superb and unstinting editorial work made it possible. I also owe my appreciation, as ever, to my editor Jane Hill; to Andrew Howard for his very fine jacket design; to Jacqueline Korn, Ann Cunningham, Eric Herring, John Manthorpe, Vicki Robinson, Sarah Barlow, Mandy Greenfield and Kate Worden.

NOTE ON THE TEXT

Some of the extracts and articles collected in this book have been abridged, and notes and references have been omitted. A deletion of text is indicated by a one-line space; a two-line space indicates a section break in the original, or the place where a new chapter originally occurred. Readers who would like to read the full text of an extract, or a book in its entirety, are referred to the bibliographical information in the Sources.

Unless marked 'Author's footnote', the footnotes have been added by the editor to provide the reader with explanatory detail or background information.

INTRODUCTION

John Pilger

Disobedience, in the eyes of anyone who has read history, is man's original virtue.

Oscar Wilde

Printed on the back of this book is a favourite quotation of mine by the American journalist T. D. Allman: 'Genuinely objective journalism', he wrote, is journalism that 'not only gets the facts right, it gets the meaning of events right. It is compelling not only today, but stands the test of time. It is validated not only by "reliable sources", but by the unfolding of history. It is journalism that ten, twenty, fifty years after the fact still holds up a true and intelligent mirror to events.'

Allman wrote that as a tribute to Wilfred Burchett, whose extraordinary and often embattled career included what has been described as 'the scoop of the century'. While hundreds of journalists 'embedded' with the Allied occupation forces in Japan in 1945 were shepherded to the largely theatrical surrender ceremony, Burchett 'slipped the leash', as he put it, and set out on a perilous journey to a place now engraved in the human consciousness: Hiroshima. He was the first Western journalist to enter Hiroshima after the atomic bombing, and his front-page report in the London *Daily Express* carried the prophetic headline, 'I write this as a warning to the world'.

The warning was about radiation poisoning, whose existence was denied by the occupation authorities. Burchett was denounced, with other journalists joining in the orchestrated propaganda and attacks on him. Independently and courageously, he had exposed the full horror of nuclear warfare; and his facts were validated, as T. D. Allman wrote when Burchett died in 1983, 'by the unfolding of history'. His dispatch is reprinted on page 10.

Allman's tribute can be applied to all those whose work is collected in these pages. Selecting them has been an immense privilege for me. The opportunity to honour the 'forgotten' work of journalists of the calibre of Wilfred Burchett, Martha Gellhorn, James Cameron and Edward R. Murrow is also a reminder that one of the noblest human struggles is against power and its grip on historical memory. Burchett on the meaning of Hiroshima, Gellhorn on genocide, Cameron on resistance: each work, together with that of contemporaries such as Paul Foot, Robert Fisk, Linda Melvern and Seumas Milne, not only keeps the record straight but holds those in power to account. This is journalism's paramount role.

The reference to investigative journalism in the title needs explaining, even redefining. T. D. Allman's description is a sure starting point, rescuing 'objectivity' from its common abuse as a cover for official lies. The term, investigative journalism, did not exist when I began my career; it became fashionable in the 1960s and 1970s and especially when Bob Woodward and Carl Bernstein exposed the Watergate scandal. In making my selection, I have applied a broader definition than detective work and included journalism that bears witness and investigates ideas. Thus, Phillip Knightley's account of the London *Sunday Times*'s tortuous disclosure of the scandal of the drug thalidomide, which caused terrible foetal malformations in the 1950s and 1960s, sits easily alongside historian, poet and satirist Eduardo Galeano's exposé of the propaganda of war, consumerism and mass impoverishment.

I have preferred the great mavericks, whose work continues to inspire, over those perhaps more celebrated and whose inclusion would merely commemorate their fame. Although Seymour Hersh's exposé of the My Lai massacre in Vietnam helped make his name, it is his consistent work over forty years, calling power to account, that has earned his place in these pages.

I hasten to say that, in making this selection (with 1945 as an arbitrary starting year), I have had to leave out some remarkable work rather than further reduce the length of each essay. I apologise to those who could rightly expect to see their names included here. In my original list was I. F. Stone's investigation into the 'hidden history' of the Korean War (1952), which demonstrates that the fraudulent reasons for the Anglo-American attack on Iraq in 2003 were not the first of their kind. Inexplicably, Jeremy Stone refused to allow the inclusion of this landmark work of his father 'Izzy', who fought censorship all his life.

The best investigations are not always the work of journalists. In the section on Iraq, Joy Gordon, an academic, contributes an essay (see page 541) that draws on her study of a tragedy many journalists avoided and still suppress: the effects of the United Nations sanctions imposed on Iraq between 1990 and 2003. This medieval-style siege cost the lives of up to a million people, many of them young children. Compared with the misdeeds of Saddam Hussein, whose devilry was, for a time, a headline a day, this epic crime of 'our' side is little known.

My other favourite quotation belongs to the great Irish muckraker Claud Cockburn. 'Never believe anything,' he wrote, 'until it is officially denied.' That the state lies routinely is not what the media courses teach. If they did – and the evidence has never been in greater abundance – the cynicism that many young journalists believe ordains them as journalists would not be directed at their readers, viewers and listeners, but at those in false authority.

Secretive power loathes journalists who do their job: who push back screens, peer behind façades, lift rocks. Opprobrium from on high is their badge of honour. When the BBC refused to show James Cameron's filmed report from wartime North Vietnam, Cameron said, 'They whispered that I was a dupe, but what really upset them was that I was not *their* dupe.' In these days of corporate 'multimedia' run by a powerful few in thrall to profit, many journalists are part of a propaganda apparatus without even consciously realising it. Power rewards their collusion with faint recognition: a place at the table, perhaps even a Companion of the British Empire. At their most supine, they are spokesmen of the spokesmen, de-briefers of the briefers, what the French call *functionnaires*. It is the honourable exceptions who are celebrated here, men and women whose disrespect for authoritarianism has allowed them to alert their readers to vital, hidden truths.

In his superb exposé of the secret government and media role in the attack on Arthur Scargill and the National Union of Mineworkers, (page 284), Seumas Milne identifies the subtle collaboration of journalism with power in the 'dogmatic insistence' of many mainstream journalists

that events are largely the product of an arbitrary and contingent muddle . . . a chronic refusal by the mainstream media in

Britain – and most opposition politicians – to probe or question
the hidden agendas and unaccountable, secret power structures
at the heart of government . . . The result is that an entire dimension of politics and the exercise of power in Britain is habitually left out of standard reporting and analysis. And by refusing
to acknowledge this dimension, it is often impossible to make
proper sense of what is actually going on. Worse, it lets off the
hook those whose abuse of state authority is most flagrant . . .

The Indian writer Vandana Shiva had this in mind when she celebrated 'the insurrection of subjugated knowledge' against the 'dominant knowledge' of power. For me, that describes the work in this
collection. Each piece stands outside the mainstream; and the common
element is the journalist's 'insurrection' against the 'rules of the game':
Burchett in Japan, Cameron in Vietnam, Melvern in Rwanda, Max du
Preez and Jacques Pauw in apartheid South Africa, Greg Palast and
David Armstrong in the United States, Günter Wallraff in Germany,
Amira Hass in Gaza, Anna Politkovskaya in Chechnya, Fisk in Lebanon
and Iraq.

Thus, Paul Foot's eleven-year investigation of the sabotage of Pan
Am 101 over the Scottish town of Lockerbie in 1989 and the injustice of the subsequent trial and judgement concludes with these
words of outrage:

> The judgement and the verdict against Megrahi [one of two
> Libyans accused] were perverse. The judges brought shame and
> disgrace, it is fair to say, to all those who believed in Scottish
> justice, and have added to Scottish law an injustice of the type
> which has often defaced the law in England. Their verdict was
> a triumph for the CIA, but it did nothing at all to satisfy the
> demands of the families of those who died at Lockerbie – who
> still want to know how and why their loved ones were murdered.

Why is journalism like this so important? Without it, our sense of
injustice would lose its vocabulary and people would not be armed
with the information they need to fight it. Orwell's truth that 'to be
corrupted by totalitarianism, one does not have to live in a totalitarian
country' would then apply. Consider the hundreds of journalists who
have been persecuted and murdered in Guatemala, Nigeria, the
Philippines, Algeria, Russia and many other oppressive states because

their independence and courage are feared. When the Turkish parliament responded to the overwhelming public opposition to Turkey joining the invasion of Iraq in 2003 and voted against the demands of Washington and the Turkish generals, this unprecedented show of real democracy in a country of murderous shadows was due, in no small part, to those journalists who have often led the way in exposing the criminality of the state, particularly the repression of the Kurds. Ocar Isik Yurtcu, the editor of *Ozgur Gundem* (Free Agenda), is currently serving fifteen years for breaking a law which classifies all reporting of the oppression and rebellion in Turkey as either propaganda or 'incitement to racial hatred'. His case is emblematic of laws used against those who challenge the state and the military; and he and dozens of other independent journalists are an inspiration.

In Europe, the United States, Canada and Australia, journalists generally do not have to risk their lives. The writer Simon Louvish recounts the story of a group of Russians touring the United States at the height of the Cold War. They were astonished to find, after reading the newspapers and watching television, that all the opinions on the vital issues were more or less the same. 'In our country,' they said, 'to get that result we have a dictatorship, we imprison people, we tear out their fingernails. Here you have none of that. So what's your secret? How do you do it?'

In his unpublished introduction to *Animal Farm*, Orwell described how censorship in free societies was infinitely more sophisticated and thorough than in dictatorships because 'unpopular ideas can be silenced and inconvenient facts kept dark, without any need for an official ban'. It is more than half a century since he wrote that, and the essential message remains the same.

None of this is to suggest a 'conspiracy', which in any case is unnecessary. Journalists and broadcasters are no different from historians and teachers in internalising the priorities and fashions and propriety of established power. Like others with important establishment responsibilities, they are trained, or groomed, to set aside serious doubts. If scepticism is encouraged, it is directed not at the system but at the competence of its managers, or at popular attitudes as journalists perceive them.

From the Murdoch press to the BBC, the undeclared rules of the modern media club vary not a great deal. The invisible boundaries of 'news' allow false premises to become received wisdom and official deceptions to be channelled and amplified. The fate of whole societies is reported according to their usefulness to 'us', the term frequently used for Western power, with its narcissism, dissembling language and public omissions: its good and bad terrorists, worthy and unworthy victims. This orthodoxy, wrote Richard Falk, professor of international relations at Princeton University, is conveyed 'through a self-right-eous, one-way moral/legal screen [with] positive images of Western values and innocence portrayed as threatened, validating a campaign of unrestricted political violence'. This is so 'widely accepted' that 'law and morality [are] irrelevant to the identification of rational policy.'

It seems exquisitely ironic that as media technology advances almost beyond our imagination, it is not just the traditional means of jour-nalism that are becoming obsolete, but its honourable traditions. What of Edmund Burke's concept of the press as a 'fourth estate', as a counter to the state and its 'interests'? The question is perhaps answered in the country where I was apprenticed, Australia, which has a rich history of fierce, independent journalism, yet today offers a microcosm of the demise of a free media in a relatively free society. In its 2003 index of press freedom, the press monitoring organisation Reporters Without Borders listed Australia in 50th place, ahead of only autocracies and dictatorships. How did this come about? And what does it tell us?

To most Australians, the name Edward Smith Hall will mean nothing; yet this one journalist did more than any individual to plant three basic liberties in his country: freedom of the press, representative government and trial by jury. In 1826, he launched his weekly, eight-page, eight-penny Sydney *Monitor* by giving prominence to a letter from a reader who described the function of the journalist as 'an invet-erate opposer [rather] than a staunch parasite of government'.

The measure of Hall's principled audacity can be judged by the times. He started his newspaper not in some new Britannia flower-ing with Georgian liberalism, but in a brutal military dictatorship run with convict slave labour. The strong man was General Ralph Darling; and Hall's defiance of Darling's authority in the pages of his news-paper, his 'insurrection', brought down great wrath and suffering on him. His campaigns for the rights of convicts and freed prisoners and his exposure of the corruption of officials, magistrates and the Governor's hangers-on made him a target of the draconian laws of criminal libel. He was routinely convicted by military juries, whose members were selected personally by General Darling. He spent more than a year in prison, where, from a small cell lit through a single grate and beset by mosquitoes, he continued to edit the *Monitor* and to campaign against official venality. When Darling was recalled to London and free speech took root in Australia, it was the achievement of Edward Smith Hall and independent journalists like him.

When Hall died in 1861, there were some fifty independent newspapers in New South Wales alone. Within twenty years this had risen to 143 titles, many of which had a campaigning style and editors who regarded their newspapers as, in Hall's words, 'the voice of the people . . . not the trade of authority'. The Australian press then, wrote Robert Pullan, was 'a medley of competing voices'. Today, the medley is an echo chamber. Of twelve principal newspapers in the capital cities, Rupert Murdoch controls seven. Of the ten Sunday newspapers, Murdoch has seven. In Adelaide, he has a complete monopoly; he owns everything, including all the printing presses. He controls almost 70 per cent of principal newspaper circulation, giving Australia the distinction of the most concentrated press ownership in the Western world.

In the 1970s and 1980s, one remarkable newspaper, the *National Times*, bore Edward Smith Hall's legacy. The editor, Brian Toohey, refused to subvert his paper's journalism to the intimidation and manipulations of politicians and their corporate 'mates'. Toohey had suitcases of leaked documents hidden all over Sydney (see some of them in 'The Timor Papers' on page 174). His small editorial team, in exposing a catalogue of Australia's darkest secrets, posed a real threat to political corruption and organised crime. Although owned by the establishment Fairfax family, which then controlled a newspaper, radio and television empire, the *National Times* had limited resources and was vulnerable to libel actions, and political intimidation.

In the mid-1980s, the Labor Party Prime Minister Bob Hawke and his Treasurer Paul Keating openly campaigned for the paper's demise, accusing its journalists of distortion. Finally removed from the editorship, Toohey wrote a seminal piece that described 'a new Australia forged by a new type of entrepreneur [whose] fortunes are built on deals where nobbling official watchdogs or bribing union bosses eliminates much of the risk . . . [where] tax cheats become nation builders'. Hawke and Keating, he wrote, 'do more than enjoy the company of the new tycoons: they share their values while the sacrifices are being made by the battlers for whom they once fought.' The article was never published.

As a small media pond inhabited by large sharks, Australia today is a breeding ground for censorship by omission, the most virulent form. Like all his newspapers throughout the world, Murdoch's harnessed team in Australia follows the path paved with his 'interests' and his world view (which is crystallised in the pages of his *Weekly Standard* in Washington, the voice of America's 'neo-conservatives'). They echo his description of George W. Bush and Tony Blair as 'heroes' of the Iraq invasion and his dismissal of the 'necessary' blood they spilt, and they consign to oblivion the truths told by history, such as the support Saddam Hussein received from the Murdoch press in the 1980s. One of his tabloids invented an al-Qaida training camp near Melbourne; all of them promote the Australian élite's obsequiousness to American power, just as they laud Prime Minister John Howard's vicious campaign against a few thousand asylum-seekers, who are locked away in camps described by a United Nations inspector as among the worst violations of human rights he had seen.

The Australian experience is what the British can expect if the media monopolies continue to grow in Britain and broadcasting is completely deregulated in the name of international 'competitiveness' (profit). The Blair government's assault on the BBC is part of this. The BBC's power lies in its dual role as a publicly-owned broadcaster and a multinational business, with revenues of more than $5 billion. More Americans watch BBC World than Britons watch the main BBC channel at home. What Murdoch and the other ascendant, mostly American, media barons have long wanted is the BBC broken up and privatised and its vast 'market share' handed over to them. Like godfathers dividing turf, they are impatient.

In 2003, Blair's ministers began to issue veiled threats of 'reviewing' the whole basis of licence fee funding of the BBC which, with this source taken away, would soon diminish to a version of its progeny, the Australian Broadcasting Corporation, which relies on direct government grants and is frequently intimidated. Indeed, privatisation was almost certainly on the hidden agenda behind Blair's spin master's attack on the BBC over one radio report by the journalist Andrew Gilligan, who exposed the government's manipulation of the evidence and intelligence reports in a dossier that sought to give credence to the 'threat' posed by Saddam Hussein's non-existent weapons of mass destruction.

The genesis for this is not hard to trace. In 1995, Rupert Murdoch flew Tony and Cherie Blair first class to Hayman Island, off the Queensland coast. In the tropical sunshine and standing at the blue News Corp. lectern, the future British prime minister effused about his 'new moral purpose in politics' and pledged safe passage of the media from 'heavy-handed regulation' to the 'enterprise' of those like his host, who applauded and shook his hand warmly. The next day, in London, satire died once again when Murdoch's *Sun* commented: 'Mr Blair has vision, he has purpose and he speaks our language on morality and family life.'

Until recently, these matters were rarely discussed in the media pages of British newspapers, which preferred the arcane manoeuvres of media executives and their cleverness in securing generous rewards for themselves. There was the usual hypocritical tut-tutting over tabloid intrusions into the lives of the rich and famous. Critical ideas about journalism were mentioned in passing, or defensively, if at all. The publication of Lord Hutton's now notorious report in January 2004, attacking the BBC and absolving the government in the Gilligan affair, has broken the silence, though for how long, we shall have to see. Certainly, his lordship's service to establishment cover-up presents one of the clearest threats to free journalism in my memory.

With the exception of Edward R. Murrow's radio broadcasts, the journalism in this book was published, not broadcast. It is only thirty years since newspapers relinquished their mantle to television as the main source of public information. The power of broadcast journalism's immediacy brought a form of censorship that the press had never known: insidious and subtle, dressed in terms that were often euphemisms, such as 'impartiality', 'balance' and 'objectivity'.

A pioneer of a very different kind of visual journalism was Peter Watkins, whose astonishing work *The War Game* created on film the effects of a nuclear attack on Britain: the celluloid equivalent of Wilfred Burchett's 'warning to the world'. Commissioned in 1965 by the BBC, it was immediately banned. The BBC's director-general, Sir Ian Trethowan, said it would disturb those of 'limited mental capacity and the elderly living alone'. What the public were not told was that the then chairman of the BBC Board of Governors, Lord Normanbrook, formerly Secretary to the Cabinet, had already written to his successor in Whitehall, Sir Burke Trend, inviting the government to censor the film. *The War Game*, he wrote,

> is not designed as propaganda: it is intended as a purely factual statement, and is based on careful research into official material. I have seen the film and I can say that it has been produced with considerable restraint. But the subject is, necessarily, alarming; and the showing of the film on television might have

a significant effect on public attitudes towards the policy of the nuclear deterrent. In these, I doubt whether the BBC ought alone to take the responsibility of deciding whether this film ought to be shown.

So they agreed, and *The War Game* was suppressed for twenty-one years, and when it was finally shown, the studio presenter, Ludovic Kennedy, merely said it had been 'too shocking and too disturbing' to show when it was made, and the deception remained.

What Watkins's film showed was the danger to the population of a country which had more nuclear bases per head of population and per square mile than anywhere on earth. So complete was the suppression of this that between 1965 and 1980 Parliament did not once debate the nuclear arms race, arguably the most urgent and dangerous issue facing humanity. A parallel silence existed in the media, buttressed by the 'lobby system'. Journalists were either put off the scent or given briefings that were exercises in outright lying. There were twelve bases, said the Ministry of Defence, 'and no more'. This was not challenged until 1980 when Duncan Campbell, a *New Statesman* journalist, revealed that Britain was host to 135 bases, each presumably targeted by the Soviet Union.

The Falklands War in 1982 gave the game away. Journalists who had defended their objectivity as 'a matter of record' were, on their return from the South Atlantic, outspoken in their praise of their own subjectivity in the cause of Queen and Country, as if the war had been a national emergency, which it was not. If they had any complaint it was that they had not been allowed to be sufficiently 'on side' with the British military so they could win 'the propaganda war'. (The same complaints were heard following the 1991 Gulf War and the 1999 NATO attack on Yugoslavia.)

During the Falklands conflict, the minutes of the BBC's Weekly Review Board showed that the coverage was to be shaped to suit 'the emotional sensibilities of the public' and that the weight of the BBC's coverage would be concerned with government statements of policy and that an impartial style was felt to be 'an unnecessary irritation'. This was not unusual. Lord John Reith, the BBC's founder, established 'impartiality' as a principle to be suspended whenever the establishment was threatened. He demonstrated this, soon after the BBC began broadcasting in the 1920s, by secretly writing propaganda for the Baldwin Tory government during the General Strike.

Some eighty years later, in 2003, the traditional right-wing press renewed its refrain, together with the Blair government, that the BBC's journalism was 'anti-war'. Such irony, for the opposite was true. In its analysis of the coverage of the invasion and occupation of Iraq by some of the world's leading broadcasters, the Bonn-based media institute Media Tenor found that the BBC had permitted less coverage of dissent than all of them, including the US networks. News of anti-war demonstrations, which reflected views held by the majority of the British public, accounted for merely 2 per cent of the BBC's reporting.

The honourable exceptions stand out. The often inspired *Independent*, the intermittent *Guardian* and a reborn *Daily Mirror* exposed the unprovoked and bloody nature of Bush's and Blair's attack. The *Mirror*'s support for the two million who filled London in protest, the largest demonstration in British history, was a phenomenon, as was its bold, informed and thoughtful coverage. The very notion of the tabloid as a real newspaper was reclaimed from the Murdoch *Sun*, which looked feeble and out of step by comparison. However, when Baghdad fell, the *Mirror* stumbled too. 'Patriotic' readers had raised objections, it was said, the circulation had faltered, and a new corporate management ordered the paper's return to the realm of faithless butlers and witless celebrities, with its refound glory revisited only now and then.

During the invasion of Iraq, a new euphemism appeared: 'embedding', invented by the heirs of the Pentagon's language assassins who had dreamt up 'collateral damage'. 'Embedding' was not just true of journalists in the field. Standing outside 10 Downing Street, the BBC's political editor reported the fall of Baghdad as a kind of victory speech, broadcast on the evening news. Tony Blair, he told viewers, 'said they would be able to take Baghdad without a bloodbath, and in the end the Iraqis would be celebrating. And on both these points he has been proved conclusively right.' Studies now put the death toll as high as 55,000, including almost 10,000 civilians, a conservative estimate. One of Robert Fisk's pieces in this collection is his investigation in September 2003 that showed that at least 500 Iraqis die or are killed every week as a result of the Anglo-American occupation (page 566). And this apparently does not constitute a 'bloodbath'. Would the same have been said about the massacre of 3,000 people in New York on September 11, 2001? What distinguishes the honourable exceptions from other journalists is, above all, the equal value they place on life, wherever it is. Their 'we' is humanity.

In the United States, which has constitutionally the freest media in the world, the suppression of the very idea of universal humanity has become standard practice. Like the Vietnamese and others who have defended their homelands, the Iraqis are unpeople: at worst, tainted; to be abused, tortured, hunted. 'For every GI killed,' said a letter given prominence in the New York *Daily News*, '20 Iraqis must be executed.' The *New York Times* and *Washington Post* might not publish that, but each played a significant role in promoting the fiction of the threat of Saddam Hussein's weapons arsenal.

Long before the invasion, both newspapers cried wolf for the White House. The *New York Times* published front-page headlines such as '[Iraq's] SECRET ARSENAL: THE HUNT FOR GERMS OF WAR', 'DEFECTOR DESCRIBES IRAQ'S ATOM BOMB PUSH', 'IRAQI TELLS OF RENOVATIONS AT SITES FOR CHEMICAL AND NUCLEAR ARMS' and 'DEFECTORS BOLSTER US CASE AGAINST IRAQ, OFFICIALS SAY'. All these stories turned out to be crude propaganda. In an internal email (published in the *Washington Post*), the *New York Times* reporter Judith Miller revealed her principal source as Ahmed Chalabi, an Iraqi exile and convicted embezzler who ran the Washington-based and CIA-funded Iraqi National Congress (INC). A Congressional inquiry concluded that almost all the 'information' provided by Chalabi and other INC exiles was worthless.

In July 2003, as the occupation was unravelling, both the *Times* and the *Post* gave front-page prominence to the administration's carefully manipulated 'homecoming' of twenty-year-old Private Jessica Lynch, who was injured in a traffic accident during the invasion and captured. She was cared for by Iraqi doctors, who probably saved her life and risked their own lives in trying to return her to American forces. The official version, that she bravely fought off Iraqi attackers, is a pack of lies, like her 'rescue' from an almost deserted hospital, which was filmed with night-vision cameras by a Hollywood director. All this was known in Washington, and some of it was reported.

This did not deter the best of American journalism from uniting to help stage-manage Private Lynch's beatific return to Elizabeth, West Virginia, with home-town imagery and locals saying how proud they were. The *Post* lamented that the whole affair had been 'muddied by conflicting media accounts', which brought to mind Orwell's description of 'words falling upon the facts like soft snow, blurring their outlines and covering up all the details'.

In Washington, I asked Charles Lewis, the former CBS *60 Minutes* star, about this. Lewis, who now runs an investigative unit called the Center for Public Integrity, said, 'You know, under Bush, the compliance and silence among journalists is worse than in the 1950s. Rupert Murdoch is the most influential media mogul in America; he sets the standard, and there is no public discussion about it. Why do the majority of the American public still believe Saddam Hussein was behind the attacks of 9/11? Because the media's constant echoing of the government guarantees it.'

I asked him, 'What if the freest media in the world had seriously challenged Bush and Rumsfeld and investigated their claims, instead of channelling what turned out to be crude propaganda?' He replied, 'If the media had been more aggressive and more tenacious towards getting the truth, there is a very, very good chance we would not have gone to war in Iraq.'

It is hardly surprising that outstanding foreign reporting from Iraq, such as Fisk's, is eagerly read on internet websites. Jane Harman, a rare dissenting voice in the US Congress, said of the invasion: 'We have been the victims of the biggest cover-up manoeuvre of all time.' But that, too, is an illusion. What is almost never reported in the United States is the pattern of American colonial interventions. Only 'anti-Americans', it seems, refer to the hundreds of illegal 'covert operations', many of them bloody, that have denied political and economic self-determination to much of the world.

This has been suppressed by a voluntary system of state-sponsored lies that began with the genocidal campaigns against Native Americans and the accompanying frontier myths; and the Spanish-American War, which broke out after Spain was falsely accused of sinking an American warship, the *Maine*, and war fever was whipped up by the newspapers of Randolph Hearst, the Murdoch of his day; it lived on in the 1960s, in the non-existent North Vietnamese attack on two American destroyers in the Gulf of Tonkin for which the media demanded reprisals, giving President Johnson the pretext he wanted to bomb North Vietnam.

In the late 1970s, a free, silent media allowed President Carter to arm the Indonesian dictatorship as it slaughtered the East Timorese, and to begin secret support for the mujaheddin in Afghanistan, from which came the Taliban and al-Qaida. In the 1980s, an absurdity, the 'threat' to the United States from popular movements in Central America, notably the Sandinistas in tiny Nicaragua, allowed President Reagan to arm and support the bloodthirsty terrorists known as the

Contra, leaving an estimated 70,000 dead. That George W. Bush's administration gives refuge to hundreds of Latin American torturers, favoured murderous dictators and anti-Castro hijackers, terrorists by any definition, is almost never reported in the mainstream media. Neither is the work of a 'training school' at Fort Benning, Georgia, the School of the Americas, where manuals teach methods of intimidation and torture and the alumni include Latin America's most notorious oppressors.

'There never has been a time,' said Tony Blair in his address to Congress in 2003, 'when the power of America was so necessary or so misunderstood or when, except in the most general sense, a study of history provides so little instruction for our present day.' He was warning us off the study of imperialism, for fear that we might reject the 'manifest destiny' of the United States and his embrace of an enduring, if subordinate, imperial role for Britain.

Of course, he cannot warn off anybody without the front pages and television and radio broadcasts that echo and amplify his words. By discarding its role as history's 'first draft', journalism promotes, directly and by default, an imperialism whose true intentions are rarely expressed. Instead, noble words and concepts like 'democracy' and 'freedom' and 'liberation' are emptied of their true meaning and pressed into the service of conquest. When journalists allow this corruption of language and ideas, they disorientate, not inform; or, as Edward S. Herman put it, they 'normalise the unthinkable for the general public'.

In June 2002, before an audience of robotically cheering West Point military cadets, George W. Bush repudiated the Cold War policy of 'deterrence' and said that the United States would take 'pre-emptive action' against potential enemies. A few months earlier, a leaked copy of the Pentagon's Nuclear Posture Review had revealed that the administration had contingency plans to use nuclear weapons against Iran, North Korea, Syria and China. Following suit, Britain has announced for the first time that it will 'if necessary' attack non-nuclear states with nuclear weapons. There has been almost no reporting of this, and no public discussion. This is as it was fifty years ago when British intelligence warned the government that the United States was ready to wage a 'preventative' atomic war against the Soviet Union, and the public knew nothing about it.

Neither did the public know, according to declassified official files from 1968, that Britain's most senior Cold War planners were convinced the Russians had no intention of attacking the West. 'The Soviet Union will not deliberately start general war or even limited war in Europe,' advised the British chiefs of staff, who described Soviet policy as 'cautious and realistic'. This private truth was in stark contrast to what the press and the public were told.

'When truth is replaced by silence,' the Soviet dissident Yevgeni Yevtushenko said, 'the silence is a lie.' There is a surreal silence today, full of the noise of 'sound-bites' and 'grabs' of those with power justifying their deception and violence. This is presented as news, though it is really a parody in which journalists, variously embedded, gesture cryptically at the obvious but rarely make sense of it, lest they shatter the 'one-way moral screen', described by Richard Falk, between 'us' and the consequences of political actions taken in our name. Never has there been such a volume of repetitive 'news' or such an exclusiveness in those controlling it.

In 1983, the principal media were owned by fifty corporations. In 2002, this had fallen to nine transnational companies. Rampant de-regulation has ended even a semblance of diversity. In February 2004, Rupert Murdoch predicted that, within three years, there would be just three global media corporations and his company would be one of them. On the internet, the leading twenty websites are now owned by the likes of Fox, Disney, AOL Time Warner, Viacom and a clutch of other giants; just fourteen companies attract 60 per cent of all the time Americans spend online. Theirs is a global ambition: to produce not informed, free-thinking citizens, but obedient customers.

It is fitting that *Tell Me No Lies* ends with a selection of the work of Edward Said. Prophetically, he wrote in *Culture and Imperialism*, 'We are beginning to learn that de-colonisation was not the termination of imperial relationships but merely the extending of a geo-political web which has been spinning since the Renaissance. The new media have the power to penetrate more deeply into a "receiving" culture than any previous manifestation of Western technology.' Compared with a century ago, when 'European culture was associated with a white man's pres-ence, we now have in addition an international media presence that insinuates itself over a fantastically wide range.'

Recent events in Venezuela illustrate this. Since he swept to power with a popular vote, the reformist President Hugo Chavez has had to defend himself and his government in an all-out war waged by the huge corporations that control the country's media. 'While Chavez respected the rules of democracy,' wrote Ignacio Ramonet, the director of *Le Monde Diplomatique*, 'the media, in the hands of a few magnates, used manipulation, lies and brainwashing [and] abandoned any role as a fourth estate. Their function is to contain demands from the grass roots and, where possible, also to seize political power.' This is how the Chilean press helped ignite events that led to a coup against Salvador Allende in 1973. Should the governments of Ecuador, Brazil and Argentina attempt to make genuine popular reforms, they, too, are ripe for a media 'dirty war'.

It is more than 400 years since the first great battle for the freedom of the press was fought by dissenters, dreamers and visionaries, who begged to differ from the established guardians of society. They suffered terrible penalties. Thomas Hytton was executed for selling books by William Tyndale, who translated the Bible into English. Richard Bayfield, John Tewsbury and other booksellers were burned at the stake. For the crime of printing Puritan books in Holland, John Lilburne, the Leveller, was given 500 lashes in the streets of London, pilloried and fined the fortune of £500.

'What is deeply ironic,' wrote David Bowman in *The Captive Press*,

is that, having thrown off one yoke, the press should now be falling under another, in the form of a tiny and ever-contracting band of businessmen-proprietors. Instead of developing as a diverse social institution, serving the needs of a democratic society, the press, and now the media, have become or are becoming the property of a few, governed by whatever social, political and cultural values the few think tolerable . . . you could say that what we are facing now is the second great battle of the freedom of the press.

Never has free journalism been as vulnerable to subversion on a grand, often unrecognisable scale. Giant public relations companies, employed by the state and other powerful vested interests, now account for much of the editorial content of the media, however insidious their methods and indirect their message. Their range is ideological: from corporatism to war. This is another kind of 'embedding', known in military circles as 'information dominance', which in turn is part of 'full spectrum dominance': the global control of land, sea, air, space and information, the stated policy of the United States. The aim, as the media analyst David Miller has pointed out, is that eventually 'there is no distinction between information control and the media'.

'How do we react to all of this? How can we defend ourselves?'

asks Ignacio Ramonet. 'The answer is simple. We have to create a new estate, a fifth estate, that will let us pit a civic force against this new coalition of [media] rulers.' He proposes an international association of journalists, academics, newspaper readers, radio listeners and television viewers that operates as a 'counterweight' to the great corporations, monitoring, analysing and denouncing them. In other words, the media, like governments and rapacious corporations and the international financial institutions, itself becomes an issue for popular action.

My own view is that the immediate future lies with the emerging *samidzat*, the word for the 'unofficial' media during the late Soviet period. Given the current technology, the potential is huge. On the worldwide web, the best 'alternative' websites are already read by an audience of millions. The courageous reporting of Jo Wilding from besieged Iraq is a striking example (page 573). She is not an accredited journalist, but one of a new breed of 'citizen reporters'. In the United States, independent newspapers, like the Toledo *Blade*, to name just one, flourish alongside popular independent community-based radio stations, such as Pacifica Radio and Democracy Now.

It is this network that has helped raise the consciousness of millions; never in my lifetime have people all over the world demonstrated greater awareness of the political forces ranged against them and the possibilities for countering them. 'The most spectacular display of public morality the world has ever seen,' was how the writer Arundhati Roy described the outpouring of anti-war anger across the world in February 2003. That was just a beginning and the cause for optimism. For the world has two superpowers now: the power of the military plutocracy in Washington and the power of public opinion. The latter ought to be the constituency of true journalists. This is not rhetorical; human renewal is not a phenomenon; a movement has arisen that is more diverse, more enterprising, more internationalist and more tolerant of difference than ever and growing faster than ever. I dedicate this collection to the best of my fellow journalists, who are needed now more than ever.

John Pilger
June 2004

MARTHA GELLHORN

Dachau

1945

When he sent me to report the war in Vietnam in 1966, Hugh Cudlipp, then editor-in-chief of the *Daily Mirror*, handed me an article by Martha Gellhorn. 'We are fighting a new kind of war,' it began. 'People cannot survive our bombs. We are uprooting the people from the lovely land where they have lived for generations; and the uprooted are not given bread but stone. Is this an honourable way for a great nation to fight a war 8,000 miles from its safe homeland?'

The piece was published in the *Guardian*; in the United States, no newspaper would touch such an exposé of American methods and motives. The Johnson administration quietly saw to it that Martha was never allowed back into South Vietnam. To Cudlipp, here was a war reporter who had finally made sense of the war. 'All I did,' she later told me, 'was report from the ground up, not the other way round.'

Martha and I corresponded for almost a decade before we met and became close friends. In scribbled notes, often written in transit in places of upheaval, we agonised over the gulf between the morality in ordinary people's lives and the amoral and immoral nature of power: a distinction she believed journalists were duty-bound to understand. 'Never believe governments,' she wrote, 'not any of them, not a word they say; keep an untrusting eye on all they do.'

Martha was born in St Louis, Missouri; her father was a doctor of powerful liberal instinct and her mother a campaigner for female suffrage. The family was well-connected; Eleanor Roosevelt, the president's wife, was a friend. During the Depression years in the 1930s, Harry Hopkins, who ran the Federal Emergency Relief Administration, sent her across the United States to report on how people were surviving. With her beauty, intelligence and disrespect for authority, she caused her first stir when she encountered the suffering of poverty and demanded that officials all the way up to President Roosevelt do something about it. Her book *The Trouble I've Seen*, a collection of her reports, led her naturally to journalism.

She learned her craft in Spain during the Civil War, feeling, along with many of her contemporaries, that here was the place to stop fascism: the battleground of democracy. Her dispatches to *Collier's* magazine set an intense style that was both humane and sparse, firing bullets from the heart. It was here that she met up with Ernest Hemingway, her future husband. She was audacious, incorrigible and very brave. In 1944, with women banned from the front line, she stowed away in a hospital ship heading for the Normandy beaches and landed with the troops. A year later, she was one of the first to enter the Nazi death camp at Dachau.

She made Britain her base after the war. During the miners' strike in 1985, at the age of seventy-five, she drove into the Welsh valleys and went from pit village to pit village, listening. She phoned me from a telephone box in Newbridge and said, 'Listen, you ought to see what the police are doing here. They're beating the hell out of people at night. Why isn't that being reported?' I suggested she report it. 'I've done it,' she replied.

At the age of eighty, she flew to Panama in the wake of the American invasion in pursuit of its former client, General Noriega. The death toll of civilians was said to be in the hundreds. In the *barrios* of Panama City, Martha went from door to door, interviewing the survivors; she reported that the true number of dead was close to 8,000. She, an American, was accused of 'anti-Americanism', to which she replied, 'The truth is always subversive.' She told me:

I used to think that people were responsible for their leaders, but not any more . . . individuality and the courage and bravery of people is amazing, isn't it? In El Salvador just now some young people are running a thing called the commission on human rights. They're kids, and they work in a shack behind an office collecting information on murder, torture, kidnapping and disappearances connected with government security forces. It's the most dangerous work possible. Nobody rewards them, and the moral and physical guts to do this are colossal. They are the best of human beings. We must always remember not only that they exist but they guard the honour of all of us.

Such words make her following dispatch from Dachau, taken from her book of reportage, *The Face of War,* all the more remarkable. Few pieces of journalism are finer.

DACHAU

We came out of Germany in a C-47 carrying American prisoners of war. The planes were lined up on the grass field at Regensburg and the passengers waited, sitting in the shade under the wings. They would not leave the planes; this was a trip no one was going to miss. When the crew chief said all aboard, we got in as if we were escaping from a fire. No one looked out the windows as we flew over Germany. No one ever wanted to see Germany again. They turned away from it, with hatred and sickness. At first they did not talk, but when it became real that Germany was behind for ever they began talking of their prisons. We did not comment on the Germans; they are past words, there is nothing to say. 'No one will believe us,' a soldier said. They agreed on that; no one would believe them.

'When were you captured, miss?' a soldier asked.

'I'm only bumming a ride; I've been down to see Dachau.'

One of the men said suddenly, 'We got to talk about it. We got to talk about it, if anyone believes us or not.'

Behind the barbed wire and the electric fence, the skeletons sat in the sun and searched themselves for lice. They have no age and no faces; they all look alike and like nothing you will ever see if you are lucky. We crossed the wide, crowded, dusty compound between the prison barracks and went to the hospital. In the hall sat more of the skeletons, and from them came the smell of disease and death. They watched us but did not move; no expression shows on a face that is only yellowish, stubby skin, stretched across bone. What had been a man dragged himself into the doctor's office; he was a Pole and he was about six feet tall and he weighed less than a hundred pounds and he wore a striped prison shirt, a pair of unlaced boots and a blanket which he tried to hold around his legs. His eyes were large and strange and stood out from his face, and his jawbone seemed to be cutting through his skin. He had come to Dachau from Buchenwald

on the last death transport. There were fifty boxcars of his dead travelling companions still on the siding outside the camp, and for the
last three days the American Army had forced Dachau civilians to
bury these dead. When this transport had arrived, the German guards
locked the men, women and children in the boxcars and there they
slowly died of hunger and thirst and suffocation. They screamed and
they tried to fight their way out; from time to time, the guards fired
into the cars to stop the noise.

This man had survived; he was found under a pile of dead. Now
he stood on the bones that were his legs and talked and suddenly he
wept. 'Everyone is dead,' he said, and the face that was not a face
twisted with pain or sorrow or horror. 'No one is left. Everyone is
dead. I cannot help myself. Here I am and I am finished and cannot
help myself. Everyone is dead.'

The Polish doctor who had been a prisoner here for five years said,
'In four weeks, you will be a young man again. You will be fine.'

Perhaps his body will live and take strength, but one cannot believe
that his eyes will ever be like other people's eyes.

The doctor spoke with great detachment about the things he had
watched in this hospital. He had watched them and there was nothing
he could do to stop them. The prisoners talked in the same way –
quietly, with a strange little smile as if they apologised for talking of
such loathsome things to someone who lived in a real world and
could hardly be expected to understand Dachau.

'The Germans made here some unusual experiments,' the doctor
said. 'They wished to see how long an aviator could go without
oxygen, how high in the sky he could go. So they had a closed car
from which they pumped the oxygen. It is a quick death,' he said. 'It
does not take more than fifteen minutes, but it is a hard death. They
killed not so many people, only eight hundred in that experiment. It
was found that no one can live above thirty-six thousand feet alti-
tude without oxygen.'

'Whom did they choose for this experiment?' I asked.

'Any prisoner,' he said, 'so long as he was healthy. They picked
the strongest. The mortality was one hundred per cent, of course.'

'It is very interesting, is it not?' said another Polish doctor.

We did not look at each other. I do not know how to explain it,
but aside from the terrible anger you feel, you are ashamed. You are
ashamed for mankind.

'There was also the experiment of the water,' said the first doctor.

'This was to see how long pilots could survive when they were shot down over water, like the Channel, let us say. For that, the German doctors put the prisoners in great vats and they stood in water up to their necks. It was found that the human body can resist for two and a half hours in water eight degrees below zero. They killed six hundred people in this experiment. Sometimes a man had to suffer three times, for he fainted early in the experiment, and then he was revived and a few days later the experiment was again undertaken.'

'Didn't they scream, didn't they cry out?'

He smiled at that question. 'There was no use in this place for a man to scream or cry out. It was no use for any man ever.'

A colleague of the Polish doctor came in; he was the one who knew about the malaria experiments. The German doctor, who was chief of the army's tropical medicine research, used Dachau as an experimental station. He was attempting to find a way to immunise German soldiers against malaria. To that end, he inoculated 11,000 prisoners with tertiary malaria. The death rate from the malaria was not too heavy; it simply meant that these prisoners, weakened by fever, died more quickly afterwards from hunger. However, in one day three men died of overdoses of Pyramidon, with which, for some unknown reason, the Germans were then experimenting. No immunisation for malaria was ever found.

Down the hall, in the surgery, the Polish surgeon got out the record book to look up some data on operations performed by the SS doctors. These were castration and sterilisation operations. The prisoners were forced to sign a paper beforehand, saying that they willingly understood this self-destruction. Jews and gypsies were castrated; any foreign slave labourer who had had relations with a German woman was sterilised. The German women were sent to other concentration camps.

The Polish surgeon had only his four front upper teeth left, the others on both sides having been knocked out by a guard one day, because the guard felt like breaking teeth. This act did not seem a matter of surprise to the doctor or to anyone else. No brutality could surprise them any more. They were used to a systematic cruelty that had gone on, in this concentration camp, for twelve years.

The surgeon mentioned another experiment, really a very bad one, he said, and obviously quite useless. The guinea pigs were Polish priests. (Over 2,000 priests passed through Dachau; 1,000 are alive.) The German doctors injected streptococci germs in the upper leg of the prisoners, between the muscle and the bone. An extensive abscess formed, accompanied by fever and extreme pain. The Polish doctor knew of more than 100 cases treated this way; there may have been more. He had a record of thirty-one deaths, but it took usually from two to three months of ceaseless pain before the patient died, and all of them died after several operations performed during the last few days of their life. The operations were a further experiment, to see if a dying man could be saved; but the answer was that he could not. Some prisoners recovered entirely, because they were treated with the already known and proved antidote, but there were others who were now moving around the camp, as best as they could, crippled for life.

Then, because I could listen to no more, my guide, a German Socialist who had been a prisoner in Dachau for ten and a half years, took me across the compound to the jail. In Dachau, if you want to rest from one horror you go and see another. The jail was a long clean building with small white cells in it. Here lived the people whom the prisoners called the NN. NN stands for *Nacht und Nebel*, which means night and mist. Translated into less romantic terms, this means that the prisoners in these cells never saw a human being, were never allowed to speak to anyone, were never taken out into the sun and the air. They lived in solitary confinement on water soup and a slice of bread, which was the camp diet. There was of course the danger of going mad. But one never knew what happened to them in the years of their silence. And on the Friday before the Sunday when the Americans entered Dachau, 8,000 men were removed by the SS on a final death transport. Among these were all the prisoners from the solitary cells. None of these men has been heard of since. Now in the clean empty building a woman, alone in a cell, screamed for a long time on one terrible note, was silent for a moment, and screamed again. She had gone mad in the last few days; we came too late for her.

In Dachau if a prisoner was found with a cigarette butt in his pocket he received twenty-five to fifty lashes with a bullwhip. If he failed to stand at attention with his hat off, six feet away from any SS trooper who happened to pass, he had his hands tied behind his back and he was hung by his bound hands from a hook on the wall for an hour. If he did any other little thing which displeased the jailers he was put in a box. The box is the size of a telephone booth. It is so constructed that being in it alone a man cannot sit down, or kneel down, or of course lie down. It was usual to put four men in it together. Here they stood for three days and nights without food or water or any form of sanitation. Afterwards they went back to the sixteen-hour day of labour and the diet of water soup and a slice of bread like soft grey cement.

What had killed most of them was hunger; starvation was simply routine. A man worked those incredible hours on that diet and lived in such overcrowding as cannot be imagined, the bodies packed into airless barracks, and woke each morning weaker, waiting for his death. It is not known how many people died in this camp in the twelve years of its existence, but at least 45,000 are known to have died in the last three years. Last February and March, 2,000 were killed in the gas chamber, because, though they were too weak to work, they did not have the grace to die; so it was arranged for them.

The gas chamber is part of the crematorium. The crematorium is a brick building outside the camp compound, standing in a grove of pine trees. A Polish priest had attached himself to us and as we walked there he said, 'I started to die twice of starvation but I was very lucky. I got a job as a mason when we were building this crematorium, so I received a little more food, and that way I did not die.' Then he said, 'Have you seen our chapel, Madame?' I said I had not, and my guide said I could not; it was within the zone where the 2,000 typhus cases were more or less isolated. 'It is a pity,' the priest said. 'We finally got a chapel and we had Holy Mass there almost every Sunday. There are very beautiful murals. The man who painted them died of hunger two months ago.'

Now we were at the crematorium. 'You will put a handkerchief over your nose,' the guide said. There, suddenly, but never to be believed, were the bodies of the dead. They were everywhere. There were piles of them inside the oven room, but the SS had not had time to burn them. They were piled outside the door and alongside the building. They were all naked, and behind the crematorium the ragged clothing of the dead was neatly stacked, shirts, jackets, trousers, shoes, awaiting sterilisation and further use. The clothing was handled with order, but the bodies were dumped like garbage, rotting in the sun, yellow and nothing but bones, bones grown huge because there was no flesh to cover them, hideous, terrible, agonising bones, and the unendurable smell of death.

We have all seen a great deal now; we have seen too many wars and too much violent dying; we have seen hospitals, bloody and messy as butcher shops; we have seen the dead like bundles lying on all the roads of half the earth. But nowhere was there anything like this. Nothing about war was ever as insanely wicked as these starved and outraged, naked, nameless dead. Behind one pile of dead lay the clothed healthy bodies of the German soldiers who had been found in this camp. They were shot at once when the American Army entered. And for the first time anywhere one could look at a dead man with gladness.

Just behind the crematorium stood the fine big modern hothouses. Here the prisoners grew the flowers that the SS officers loved. Next to the hothouses were the vegetable gardens, and very rich ones too, where the starving prisoners cultivated the vitamin foods that kept the SS strong. But if a man, dying of hunger, furtively pulled up and gorged himself on a head of lettuce, he would be beaten until he was unconscious. In front of the crematorium, separated from it by a stretch of garden, stood a long row of well-built, commodious homes. The families of the SS officers lived here; their wives and children lived here quite happily, while the chimneys of the crematorium poured out unending smoke heavy with human ashes.

The American soldier in the plane said, 'We got to talk about it.' You cannot talk about it very well because there is a kind of shock that sets in and makes it almost unbearable to remember what you have seen. I have not talked about the women who were moved to Dachau three weeks ago from their own concentration camps. Their crime was that they were Jewish. There was a lovely girl from Budapest, who somehow was still lovely, and the woman with mad eyes who had watched her sister walk into the gas chamber at Auschwitz and been held back and refused the right to die with her sister, and the Austrian woman who pointed out calmly that they all had only the sleazy dresses they wore on their backs, they had never had anything more, and that they worked outdoors sixteen hours a day too in the long winters, and that they too were 'corrected', as the Germans say, for any offence, real or imaginary.

I have not talked about how it was the day the American Army arrived, though the prisoners told me. In their joy to be free, and longing to see their friends who had come at last, many prisoners rushed to the fence and died electrocuted. There were those who died cheering, because that effort of happiness was more than their bodies could endure. There were those who died because now they had food, and they ate before they could be stopped, and it killed them. I do not know words to describe the men who have survived this horror for years, three years, five years, ten years, and whose minds are as clear and unafraid as the day they entered.

I was in Dachau when the German armies surrendered unconditionally to the Allies. The same half-naked skeleton who had been dug out of the death train shuffled back into the doctor's office. He said something in Polish; his voice was no stronger than a whisper. The Polish doctor clapped his hands gently and said, 'Bravo.' I asked what they were talking about.

'The war is over,' the doctor said. 'Germany is defeated.'

We sat in that room, in that accursed cemetery prison, and no one had anything more to say. Still, Dachau seemed to me the most suitable place in Europe to hear the news of victory. For surely this war was made to abolish Dachau, and all the other places like Dachau, and everything that Dachau stood for, and to abolish it for ever.

WILFRED BURCHETT
The Atomic Plague
1945

I have not known anyone like Wilfred Burchett. He was a war correspondent of the old school; he relished his 'scoops' and would endure
almost anything to get them. But reporting was not enough for him:
if he saw an act of injustice, he would try personally to remedy it;
for this much loved, and at times reviled, man, the roads of good and
evil, right and wrong were discernible, and he was never in doubt
about which one to take.

A harsh Australian upbringing prepared him. He was born into an
impoverished rural community, Poowong in the state of Victoria, in
a family devastated by two depressions. In his autobiography, *At the
Barricades,* he describes watching his father's face 'become ashen' as
the bank manager orders them out of their home. It was the 1930s,
and the young Wilfred spent the rest of his youth 'on the road', looking
for work where there was none. He was adopted by a gang of cane-
cutters, whose spirit of one-for-all-and-all-for-one meant that they
shared their earnings equally. 'It was their real mateship that left a
lasting impression on me,' he told me.

Shortly before the outbreak of war in 1939, and incensed by the
appeasement of Hitler, he travelled to Europe, where he took part in
a daring mission rescuing Jews from Germany; and it was this that
led him to journalism. On his return to Australia, he wrote letter upon
letter to newspapers, warning of the spread of fascism. 'I knew the
only way I could get a real journalist's job was to go where war was
about to happen,' he said. In China, then under siege by the Japanese,
he was appointed correspondent of the London *Daily Express.*

In 1945, he wrote what has been described as the 'scoop of the century'. He was the first correspondent to enter Hiroshima after the atomic bombing. On 11 September 1945, the Brisbane *Courier-Mail* reported: 'A pocket-handkerchief-sized Australian, Wilfred Burchett, left all other correspondents standing in covering the occupation of Japan. Armed with a typewriter, seven packets of K rations, a Colt revolver and incredible hope, he made a one-man penetration of Japan and was the first correspondent into Hiroshima. [He then] embarked on his one-man liberation tour of prison camps . . . even before official rescue parties reached them.'

Wilfred's dispatch, which filled the front page of the *Express*, began, 'I write this as a warning to the world . . .' (To his lifelong bemusement, his byline was mistakenly published as 'Peter Burchett'.) He described an 'atomic plague', which was the effects of nuclear radiation. The occupation authorities categorically denied this; people had died only as a result of the blast, said a military spokesman. This 'official truth' was widely accepted; the *New York Times* reported on its front page: 'No Radioactivity in Hiroshima Ruin'. Wilfred had his press accreditation withdrawn and was threatened with expulsion from Japan. Strict censorship was introduced; the hospitals he had visited were declared out of bounds to the guided press party that followed in the wake of his reports. Japanese film of the hospitals was confiscated and not released until 1968.

'Hiroshima changed my life in two senses,' he told me. 'It confirmed that there is no equivalent or substitute for reporting at first hand, and I became very conscious of what would happen in the event of a new world war. From that moment on, I became active on the question of nuclear disarmament . . . It was not possible to stand by.'

He went on to report the Cold War from the 'other side'. During the Korean War, he was smeared terribly when he was falsely accused of taking part in the interrogation of Australian prisoners-of-war in a North Korean camp. Although he sued his detractors in the Australian courts and proved his innocence, he was subjected to a McCarthyism as virulent as that across the Pacific. The government in Canberra refused to renew his passport and for many years he was forced to travel on a variety of documents, including a Cuban passport, a North Vietnamese permit and a 'laissez-passer', an enormous document that filled an attaché case. In 1972, one of the first acts of the reforming Labor government of Gough Whitlam was to give Wilfred Burchett back his nationality.

I remember him fondly in Vietnam: the cans of beer and his laundry straddling the wheezing air-conditioner in his Hanoi hotel room, his graciousness towards everyone. On my wall in London is a photograph of a rotund figure covered in a camouflage of leaves, about to ride a bicycle down the 'Ho Chi Minh Trail' and into danger. He wrote more than forty books, but never made more than a living wage, sometimes a great deal less.

In 1983, I took him and his dear friend James Cameron, another great correspondent, to lunch in London. When Jimmy was out of the room, Wilfred whispered to me, 'I'm worried about him. He doesn't look good. Too much whisky, I reckon.' He laughed, and died a few months later.

THE ATOMIC PLAGUE

On 6 August 1945, I was shuffling along in the chow line for lunch with fifty or so weary US marines at a company cookhouse on Okinawa. The radio was crackling away with no one paying much attention to it – as usual. A note of excitement in the announcer's voice as the cook's aide dumped a hamburger and mash on my tray prompted me to ask what was new.

'He's going on about some big new bomb we just dropped on the Japs. A lotta good that'll do us here!' (It was taken for granted that after Okinawa was 'secured', the next job for those same units, and many more, would be the unimaginably costly invasion of the Japanese home islands.) Only by straining my ears was it possible to pick up a few snatches from the radio and learn that the world's first A-bomb had been dropped on a place called Hiroshima. I made a mental note that Hiroshima would be my priority objective should I ever get to Japan.

As details of the destructive power of the new bomb were released, I thought of conversations a few months earlier with the American playwright Robert Sherwood. During the invasion of Iwo Jima, Bill McGaffin[1] and I had shared the (absent) admiral's suite on the *Bennington* with Sherwood, then a member of President Roosevelt's

---

[1] A reporter for the Chicago *Daily News*.

brains trust. A companionable and witty man, Sherwood managed to turn every conversation to the question of the reaction if some terribly lethal new weapon was used to shorten the war against Japan.

This was not just with McGaffin and me, but with senior and junior officers, carrier pilots, and ordinary seamen. The consensus was certainly 'Anything to wind it up', accompanied by very uncomplimentary references to the enemy as the justification for using any weapon at all. It was generally felt that Sherwood must be referring to poison gas.

Opinion in naval circles at that time as to how the war would ever be ended was very gloomy. The admirals thought in terms of their own very considerable expertise: sea power, air power, marines admirably trained for swift, bitter assaults to secure beachheads or overrun islands. But even if Japan was occupied – and this was considered feasible if the Allies, principally the United States, were willing to pay the cost – how were the Japanese ever to be dislodged from their well-entrenched positions in China? By developing the raw materials and heavy industry in Manchuria (North-East China) and exploiting the inexhaustible Chinese manpower, they could hang on for ever. Thus, the idea of using some new, war-winning weapon was as welcome as the flowers of spring.

Stalin had promised his wartime allies at the Yalta Conference in February 1945 that Soviet forces would attack the Japanese in mainland China 'within two or three months of the German surrender'. Three months would expire on 8 August 1945, and on that date the Soviet Far Eastern Army attacked Japan's formidable Kwantung Army in Manchuria, forty-eight hours after the A-bomb was dropped on Hiroshima. Before both events the Soviet Union had relayed to Washington information that Japan was ready to quit the war. Revelation of this later raised questions as to the motive in dropping the A-bombs when the war was practically won.

In any case, Japan announced on 14 August its decision to quit, and a few days later I was aboard the troop transport the USS *Millett*, with part of the vanguard marine unit which was to be the first to land at the Yokosuka naval base. My objective was Hiroshima. One of my most precious possessions was a little Japanese phrase book which I hoped would help me find my way about by putting questions that would require simple yes and no answers. Having landed with the first wave of marines, McGaffin and I made straight for the Yokosuka railway station, where we jumped aboard the first Tokyo-bound train. We created something of a sensation. The surrender had not been signed.

Although the train was packed, passengers cleared a space around us, gazing at us with a mixture of fear and curiosity, but not, we felt, with hostility. One who spoke English asked where we were going, and as the only place we could think of in Tokyo was the Imperial Hotel, he counted off the number of stops before we should get off. From the time the train passed through Yokohama, we travelled three or four miles through devastation which we thought must be without parallel in modern times. It was mainly the result of General Curtis Le May's B-29 fire raids. Mile after mile the train rattled through districts which had been among the world's most densely populated, mainly houses of wood and paper. There was nothing left but flat acres with some green poking through the ashes. Factories were reduced to pulverised concrete, twisted girders, and rusty, shattered machinery. We began to feel nervous, surrounded by people who were still technically our enemies, with the evidence of what our air power had done wherever we looked. But passengers stared stolidly at the ruins, showing no resentment at our presence.

We discovered that some colleagues, who had landed with MacArthur's airborne troops a few hours ahead of the marines, were installed at the Imperial, so we went to the Dai Ichi, the only other nearby hotel still standing. The manager, gazing at us as if we had dropped from the moon, explained that the hotel was full and 'uncomfortable'. When we insisted, he pointed out that we would be the only foreigners in a hotel full of Japanese, many of them 'hotheads'. Later he produced forms for us to fill in as if we had just arrived on a Cook's tour. He was nonplussed when he found we had neither passports nor visas.

Tokyo, in those first couple of days, was an example of how the people accepted anything – even surrender – from the emperor. A few days earlier every able-bodied male was armed – even with bamboo spears and old swords – to deal with invaders. But the emperor had told the people to behave and not 'cause incidents' when the foreigners arrived. Now a handful of enemy journalists, without any occupation troops to protect them, could wander around and register at hotels without molestation.

McGaffin's and my interests now diverged. He had flown out specially from Chicago for the surrender-signing ceremony aboard the battleship *Missouri* on 2 September. I was still bent on getting to Hiroshima. With the aid of my phrase book I was able to get to the Japanese official news agency (Domei in those days) and found that a train still went to where Hiroshima used to be. This was a great surprise because journalists had been briefed for months that the Japanese railway system had been brought to a halt by Le May's efforts. The journey would be long, difficult to say how long. Nobody, I was warned, went to Hiroshima. Domei received messages from its correspondent there by Morse code, but the correspondent had no way of receiving messages from Tokyo.

If I insisted on going, my English-speaking Domei man said, he would give me a letter to the local correspondent, asking him to show me around and to transmit my messages to the Tokyo office. All this could be arranged if I would take some food to the Domei man in Hiroshima. Back at Yokosuka a US Navy public relations officer cheerfully dispensed a week's rations for me and a fortnight's for the Domei man, delighted at the prospect that one of its correspondents might get to Hiroshima ahead of one accredited to the Army. From there I went to Yokohama, where Henry Keys[2] had arrived with a cable from the *Express* urging one of us to get to Hiroshima. Henry agreed to maintain contact with Domei's Tokyo office in case my madcap plan came off. The night before I left he gave me his .45 pistol and wished me luck. In the small hours of 2 September, while some 600-odd newsmen were on their way to the *Missouri* for the surrender ceremony, I was on my way to Tokyo to board at 6 a.m. a train which would theoretically land me in Hiroshima within some fifteen to thirty hours.

The train was carrying elements of the Japanese Imperial Army away from their Tokyo barracks. Officers, big swords dangling between their legs, occupied the seating accommodation. I squeezed in among some ordinary soldiers on a platform – standing room only – at the end of a compartment. Having stuffed my military cap, pistol and belt among my rations and purchased an umbrella to give an impression of civilian status, I was still clad in jungle greens. The soldiers were very sullen at first, chattering – obviously about me – in a hostile way. They brightened up when I handed around a pack of cigarettes. Several then offered me bits of dried fish or hard-boiled eggs in exchange. A major breakthrough came when I showed them the impressive scar on my leg, managing to get the idea across that it came from a Japanese plane in Burma, and that I was a journalist – my battered Hermès portable was evidence.

---

[2] Another correspondent of the *Daily Express*.

From then on it was smiles and friendship, more cigarettes against bits of fish – and even a drop of sake. They all had enormous bundles, and I understood later that they had just been demobilised, allowed to take from their barracks as much food and drink as they could carry, as well as their weapons, wrapped in blankets.

My fellow travellers, after the first few hours, started dropping off at various stops. After six hours I managed to get into the compartment and find a seat among the officers. Here the hostility was total. Among the passengers was an American priest, accompanied by armed guards. He had been brought to Tokyo from internment to broadcast to American troops on how they should behave in Japan to avoid friction with the local population, he explained, warning me in veiled tones that the situation in our compartment was very tense and that a false move might cost our lives. The officers were furious and humiliated at their defeat. Above all, I must not smile as this would be taken as gloating over what was happening aboard the *Missouri*. Watching those glowering officers toying with the hilts of their swords and the long samurai daggers that many of them wore, I felt no inclination to smile, especially since the train was in complete darkness when we passed through what seemed like endless tunnels.

At Kyoto, which the priest explained, as he was escorted off the train, was roughly halfway to Hiroshima in terms of time, the situation seemed bleaker than ever. After many more hours had passed and the interior of the train was pitch-black, I poked my head out of the window each time the train stopped and said, 'Kono eki-wa nanti i meska?' According to my phrase book, this meant: 'What is the name of this station?' I thus avoided my pronouncing the name of Hiroshima for fear of the effect it might have on my sword-toting fellow passengers. Dozing off between stations, I managed to awaken at each stop to repeat the question. In the meantime, a few civilians came aboard; one of them accepted a cigarette from me and offered me a welcome swig of sake. He must have guessed my destination. As the train started slowing down for another stop, he said, 'Kono eki-wa Hiroshima eki desu.' Since the compartment platform was crammed again, I climbed out the window, and he threw my knapsack after me.

The station, on the extreme outskirts of the city, was an empty shell, with an exit of improvised wooden gates. There two black-uniformed guards – with swords – grabbed me, probably assuming that I was a runaway POW. Trying to explain that I was a *shimbun kisha* ('journalist'), I opened my typewriter as proof, but they took me to a flimsy shelter and gave me to understand that I was 'locked up'. Because it was two in the morning, I had been twenty hours on the train, and it was just twenty-four hours since I had left Yokohama, I was in no mood to argue. A woman heated some water to drink and gave me some peanutlike small beans, so I felt things were not going too badly. After sunup the guards read the letter addressed to the Domei correspondent, Mr Nakamura, and my status obviously improved. No attempt was made to detain me as I stepped outside and returned to the railway station to get my bearings. It was on the fringe of the belt of heavy destruction. The central hall was intact but with roof and windows badly damaged. The rest – offices, waiting rooms and ticket barriers – had been swept away. By then Mr Nakamura had turned up, together with a Canadian-born Japanese girl who spoke excellent English. We followed a tramline towards buildings a mile or two distant.

There was devastation and desolation and nothing else. Lead grey clouds hung low over the city, vapours drifted up from fissures in the ground, and there was an acrid sulphurous smell. The few people to be seen in this former city of half a million hurried past each other without speaking or pausing, white masks covering mouths and nostrils. Buildings had dissolved into grey and reddish dust, solidified into ridges and banks by the frequent rains and heavy winds, as I learned later.

It was just less than a month since the bomb had exploded, and there had been no time for greenery to cover the wounds. Trees lay on their sides, roots sticking up into the air like legs of dead cows, yawning pits where roots had once been. Some younger trees were still standing, but leaves and smaller branches had been stripped off. Mr Nakamura related what had happened:

We had an alarm early in the morning, but only two aircraft appeared. We thought they were reconnaissance planes, and no one took much notice. The 'all clear' sounded, and most people set off for work. Then, at eight-twenty, one plane came back. It was taken for another photo plane, and the alarm was not even sounded. I was just wheeling out my bicycle to ride to the office when there was a blinding flash – like lightning. At the same time I felt scorching heat on my face, and in a tornadolike blast of wind I was knocked to the ground and the house collapsed around me. As I hit the ground, there was a booming explosion as if a powerful bomb had exploded alongside. When I peered out, there was a tremendous pillar of black smoke, shaped like a parachute but drifting upwards, with a scarlet thread in the middle. As I watched, the scarlet thread expanded, diffusing through the billowing cloud of smoke until the whole thing was glowing red. Hiroshima had disappeared, and I realised that something new to our experience had occurred. I tried to phone the police and fire brigade to find out what had happened, but it was impossible even to raise the exchange.

In the centre of the city I found that the buildings seen from the distance were only skeletons, having been gutted by the fire which swept through after most of the city had disappeared in a great swirling pillar of dust and flame. In the burned-out Fukuoka department store (now rebuilt on the same spot) a temporary police headquarters had been installed. It was there that we went to explain who I was and what I wanted. The atmosphere was very tense and the police looked at me with cold hostility. (Visiting Tokyo-Hiroshima thirty-five years later, I met Mr Nakamura, who had miraculously survived the consequences of atomic radiation. He recalled that some of the policemen wanted us both summarily shot.) In the end it was the head of the Thought Control police, Kuniharo Dazai – who outranked the others – who accepted my explanation, as had Nakamura immediately, that I wanted to report to the world what had happened in Hiroshima. It was he who arranged a police car to drive through the debris and to the only hospital which was still functioning. (Until he retired in 1974, Kuniharo Dazai was subsequently deputy minister at Japan's Ministry of Welfare and Public Health.)

From the third floor of the Fukuoka department store, as I looked in every direction, there was nothing to be seen but flat acres of ground, a few young trees, and some factory chimneys. Among the few gutted buildings still standing near the former department store was a church which, closer inspection revealed, had jumped into the air to return, practically intact, but crazily athwart its foundations. Low-level concrete bridges had also jumped off their piles, some spans landing back again, others dropping into the river. All balustrades and stone facings had disappeared from the bridges. There were no remnants of broken walls, no large chunks of rubble or blocks of stone and concrete, no craters, as one usually finds in

a bombed city. It was destruction by pulverisation followed by fire.
The reason that some buildings were still standing in the centre,
according to the police, was that they were in the epicentre of the
explosion, directly under the bomb as it parachuted down and thus
in a relative safety zone as the explosive force expanded outward
from the epicentre.

Our small group in an ancient car, piloted by one of the police
officers, drove slowly across the city to the Communications Hospital
in the outskirts. It was the only hospital to survive. If the evidence
of the material destruction of the city was horrifying, the effects
on humans I saw inside the hospital wards were a thousand times
more so.

Stretched out on filthy mats on the floor of the first ward I entered
were a dozen or so people in various stages of physical disintegration, from what I later knew to be atomic radiation. The head of the
hospital, Dr Gen Katsube (whom I was also able to meet during my
visit thirty-five years later), assured me they all would die unless
American scientists sent them some antidote for the terrible wasting
disease that had stricken thousands of people since the bomb was
dropped. In ward after ward it was the same. Patients were terribly
emaciated and gave off a nauseating odour which almost halted me
at the first door. Some had purplish burns on the face and body;
others had bunched, blue-black, blistery marks on the neck. Dr Katsube
said he was completely at a loss how to treat them.

At first we treated burns as we would any others, but patients
just wasted away and died. Then people without a mark on
them, including some not even here when the bomb exploded,
fell sick and died. For no apparent reason their health began to
fail. They lost their appetite, head hair began to fall out, bluish
spots appeared on their bodies, and bleeding started from the
nose, mouth and eyes.

The symptoms were of severe general debility and vitamin defi-
ciency. We started giving vitamin injections, but the flesh rotted
away from the puncture caused by the needle. And in every case
the patient dies. We now know that something is killing off the
white corpuscles, and there is nothing we can do about it. There
is no known way of replacing white corpuscles. Every person
carried in here as a patient is carried out as a corpse.

I asked about the masks people were wearing, and the doctor explained that at first, because of the vapours issuing from the ground and the vile sulphurous odour, plus the fact that people who had not been in the city when the bomb was dropped were stricken, it was thought that some type of poisonous gas had been used and still clung to the ground. So people were advised to wear primitive gauze masks. 'Now we know it is not gas, but people are probably comforted psychologically by wearing them, so we have not discouraged this.'

Around each patient squatted a few women, some with children, following my movements with hate-filled eyes. The patients were also mainly women and children, some bleeding from the nose, mouth and eyes, others with halos of black hair, lying where it had fallen on their rough pillows. Others had large suppurating third-degree burns. I asked if anything could be done to improve hospital conditions. 'We have no nurses,' replied Dr Katsube. 'Most of them were killed immediately; others died through handling the patients; still others just left – went back to their villages. Now we can't admit patients unless relatives stay to look after them. We can only keep the wounds clean and try to provide vitamin-rich food.'

The assistant city health officer, on a visit to the hospital, explained that those who sickened after the raid were, in most cases, those who had been digging in the ruins for bodies of relatives or household belongings. It was thought that some sort of rays had been released into the soil, so it was now prohibited to dig among the ruins. 'We estimate there are still thirty thousand bodies under the rubble and dirt,' he said. 'They must remain unburied until we know how to deal with the main disease. This may result in other epidemics, but at least they will be of a kind we know how to deal with.'

At one point Dr Katsube, who was under great strain, asked me to leave. In good English, he said, 'I can no longer guarantee your safety. These people are all doomed to die. I also. I can't understand it. I was trained in the United States; I believed in Western civilisation. I'm a Christian. But how can Christians do what you have done here? Send, at least, some of your scientists who know what it is so that we can stop this terrible sickness.'

I could only explain that as a journalist I would faithfully report what I had seen, and that although not American, but attached to the Allied forces, I would do my best to get scientists who 'knew' to be sent to Hiroshima as soon as possible. Japanese scientists, dissecting corpses in the hospital basement, confirmed that nothing they had discovered so far gave any clue to the origin of the disease or how to treat it.

Back in the centre of the city I sat on a rare block of concrete that had escaped pulverisation and typed my story. Some of the more blood-chilling details were deleted from my original text, but it appeared in the 6 September 1945 edition of the *Daily Express*, substantially as written, with the following headlines and introduction:

THE ATOMIC PLAGUE
I Write This as a Warning to the World
DOCTORS FALL AS THEY WORK
Poison gas fear: All wear masks
Express Staff Reporter, Peter Burchett was the first Allied staff reporter to enter the atom-bomb city. He travelled 400 miles from Tokyo alone and unarmed [incorrect but the *Daily Express* could not know that], *carrying rations for seven meals – food is almost unobtainable in Japan – a black umbrella, and a typewriter. Here is his story from –*

HIROSHIMA, *Tuesday.*

In Hiroshima, thirty days after the first atomic bomb destroyed the city and shook the world, people are still dying, mysteriously and horribly – people who were uninjured by the cataclysm – from an unknown something which I can only describe as atomic plague.

Hiroshima does not look like a bombed city. It looks as if a monster steam-roller had passed over it and squashed it out of existence. I write these facts as dispassionately as I can, in the hope that they will act as a warning to the world. In this first testing ground of the atomic bomb, I have seen the most terrible and frightening desolation in four years of war. It makes a blitzed Pacific island seem like an Eden. The damage is far greater than photographs can show.

I picked my way to a shack used as a temporary police headquarters in the middle of the vanished city. Looking south from there I could see about three miles of reddish rubble. That is all the atomic bomb left of dozens of blocks of city streets of buildings, homes, factories and human beings.

There is just nothing standing except about twenty factory

chimneys – chimneys with no factories. I looked west. A group
of half a dozen gutted buildings. And then again nothing . . .

The dispatch then went on to describe the scenes in the hospital
wards and what Dr Katsube had said. I must have expressed myself
even more strongly because Arthur Christiansen, the prestigious editor
of the *Daily Express* in those days, wrote in his memoirs, *Serving My
Time*, that 'poor Peter' had been so overcome by the horror of it all
that he (Christiansen) had personally taken a hand in editing the story.
To his credit, despite some inserted errors, he used my 'warning to
the world' phrase in the headline. It was the main message I wanted
to get across, but given the euphoria in the West about the monopoly
possession of such a war-winning weapon, plus the justifiably strong
feelings against the Japanese for their methods of conducting the war
and treating Allied prisoners, it was not certain that I would succeed.

It was miraculous that the story got through as quickly and
completely as it did. After my departure for Hiroshima, Tokyo had
been placed out of bounds by General MacArthur. Allied personnel
were forbidden to go beyond the Yokohama defence perimeter. Henry
Keys was twice pulled off the Tokyo-bound train on his way to the
Domei office. He then hired a Japanese courier to sit in the Domei
office and rush any message from me to him at Yokohama. The
greatest miracle of all was that Nakamura in Hiroshima so faithfully
and accurately tapped out that long dispatch on his hand-operated
Morse set to his Tokyo office.

My return trip was interrupted by finding at Kyoto station some
pale ghosts of Australian POWs, who insisted that I should visit their
camps in the Kyoto-Tsuruga area to persuade the inmates that the
war was really over. 'You must come and tell the others,' one of them
said. 'Our mates are dying every hour. If you just show yourself and
tell them what you've told us, you'll save lives. You'll give them that
extra bit of strength to hold on.' Their expressions, even more than
their words, were very eloquent. I decided in their favour.

My belongings were collected, and I set out with them – first to the
Domei office, easily located because one of the POWs had picked up a
knowledge of Japanese. There I was able to confirm that my story from
Hiroshima had indeed been received in Tokyo and handed over to the
Express. The next few days were spent in a morale-boosting tour of
the POW camps, where I was able – by freely using the name of General
MacArthur – to persuade the Japanese authorities to improve food and

other conditions. (I wore my correspondent's cap and strapped on Henry Keys's pistol for the occasion.)

By the time I arrived back Tokyo was in bounds, General MacArthur having received sufficient reinforcements to include Tokyo in his defence perimeter – but not enough to liberate the POW camps! From the station I had set out for the Dai Ichi hotel when I ran into a colleague who urged me to come with him to a press conference at the Imperial Hotel being given by some high-ranking American officers on the bombings of Hiroshima and Nagasaki, also A-bombed on 9 August. Grimy, unshaved, and dishevelled as I was, I accompanied him. The conference was nearing its end, but it was clear that the main purpose was to deny my dispatch from Hiroshima, which the *Daily Express* had made available to the world press, that people were dying from after-effects of the bomb. A scientist in brigadier general's uniform explained that there could be no question of atomic radiation – which could cause the symptoms I had described – because the bombs had been exploded at such a height as to obviate any risk of 'residual radiation'.

There was a dramatic moment as I got to my feet, feeling that my scruffiness put me at a disadvantage with the elegantly uniformed and bemedalled officers. My first question was whether the briefing officer had been to Hiroshima. He had not, so I was off to a good start. I described what I had seen – and asked for explanations. It was very gentlemanly at first, a scientist explaining things to a layman. Those I had seen in the hospitals were victims of blast and burn, normal after any big explosions. Apparently the Japanese doctors were incompetent to handle them or lacked the right medications. He discounted the allegation that any who had not been in the city at the time of the blast were later affected. Eventually the exchanges narrowed down to my asking how he explained the fish still dying when they entered a stream running through the centre of the city.

'Obviously they were killed by the blast or by the overheated water.'

'Still there a month later?'

'It's a tidal river, so they would be washed back and forth.'

'But I was taken to a spot in the city outskirts and watched live fish turning their white stomachs upwards as they entered a certain stretch of the river. After that they were dead within seconds.'

The spokesman looked pained. 'I'm afraid you've fallen victim to Japanese propaganda,' he said, and sat down. The customary 'Thank you' was pronounced, and the conference ended. Although my radiation story was denied, Hiroshima was immediately put out of bounds, and I was whisked off to a US Army hospital for tests, following which I was informed that my white corpuscle count was down. I was also informed that General MacArthur was expelling me for having 'gone beyond the bounds of "his" military occupation'. The diminution of my white corpuscles, which could have been a symptom of radiation, was finally put down to antibiotics given earlier for a knee infection. The expulsion order was rescinded because I was able to prove – with hilarious support by the Navy – that I had landed as an accredited correspondent to the US Pacific Fleet, and it had set no restrictions on correspondents' movements.

By one of those extraordinary coincidences which diligent journalists have the right to expect from time to time, I learned, while revising this chapter, how lucky I was to have got my Hiroshima story through to London. George Weller, noted war correspondent of the Chicago *Daily News*, passing through Paris after his paper ceased publication in mid-1978, telephoned me. Our trails had crossed many times, but we had never met. To my surprise – after all, it was thirty-three years after the event – he congratulated me on my Hiroshima story. Why? Because he had done a far more thorough job on Nagasaki at the same time, but his series of articles never saw the light of day. When I told him what I was working on at that very moment, he dictated over the telephone from his Paris hotel what had happened. The gist was that he managed to get into Nagasaki alone and stayed there for three days, 'looking at everything, interviewing eyewitnesses including doctors and other medical people. I wrote twenty-five thousand words, and as a good, loyal correspondent I sent it back to MacArthur's headquarters for forwarding – and the censors killed the lot.'

After the Nagasaki episode George had not gone back to headquarters, but went off on a ship somewhere and was immobilised with a leg injury. After some time, astonished at not getting any acknowledgement of what had been a most commendable bit of journalistic enterprise, he queried his paper and discovered the articles had never arrived. They had remained at MacArthur's headquarters. (I did not know until a Washington reunion with Henry Keys in December 1979 that the censors also tried to kill my story. Henry, who is as tough as any in the profession, insisted that as the war was over, so was censorship. He refused a plea of 'special case' and actually stood over the telex operator while it was transmitted.)

There was no real confirmation of deaths from atomic radiation for many months after my report was published in the *Daily Express*. General MacArthur's capacity for suppressing inconvenient truth was very great. (According to the Japanese Council Against A and H bombs, the Hiroshima bomb had accounted for 130,000 to 140,000 deaths by the end of 1945, that at Nagasaki 60,000 to 70,000. By 1950 the figure had risen to 300,000 for the two cities. During my visit to Hiroshima in June 1980, Dr Kiyoshi Kuramoto, vice director of the Hiroshima Atomic Bomb hospital, informed me that there were still 370,000 A-bomb victims officially recognised as such by the Japanese Government. 'This is far short of the real number,' he explained, 'because the Government requires that two persons, not related to the victims, must testify that the affected person was in one of the two A-bombed cities at the time of the explosions, or were there within the two weeks that followed. For many of those affected, it is impossible to provide witnesses.'

'Recognition' carries with it free medical care and in extreme cases a disability pension. As for the genetic effects, Dr Kuramoto said the full consequences could only be known after fifty to one hundred years.)

EDWARD R. MURROW
The Menace of McCarthyism
1947–54

It is difficult to imagine the Columbia Broadcasting System, America's famous CBS, as it was in Ed Murrow's time. At the age of twenty-seven, Murrow was 'director of talks' in the department of educational broadcasting. It was the 1930s; there was no television, and newspapers dominated radio. Current affairs programmes, with 'live' eyewitness reports and interviews, were unknown. From 1937, Murrow and his colleague William Shirer pioneered a form of broadcast journalism they called 'being there'.

Murrow made his reputation in 1940, the year of the Battle of Britain. From London, he broadcast 'live' to the United States, at 12.15 a.m. and 3.45 a.m., usually when the bombs were falling and most Americans were listening. This is a typical Murrow report on the Blitz:

> It was like a shuttle service, the way the German planes came up the Thames, the fires acting as a flight path. Often they were above the smoke. The searchlights bored into the black roof but couldn't penetrate it. They looked like long pillars supporting a black canopy. Suddenly all the lights dashed off and a blackness fell right to the ground. It grew cold. We covered ourselves with hay. The shrapnel clicked as it hit the concrete road nearby. And still the German bombers came.

His baritone voice, gentle and even and always calm, is still thrilling to hear. He has been described as 'the ultimate witness'; his live broadcast from an RAF Lancaster bomber during the night raids over Germany is spine-tingling. Indeed, his evocative power is credited with helping to bring America into the war. However, his reports were generally uncritical and it was only after the war, when he teamed up with a young producer, Fred Friendly, that he began to produce a type of programme that is virtually extinct now. It was an early inspiration of mine; he called it *See It Now*.

See It Now began in 1951, when America was consumed by the anti-communist witch hunts of Senator Joseph McCarthy, who had set out to 'expose' communists and fellow-travellers in government, the universities, Hollywood and the media. McCarthy found not a single communist in government; his assault on traditional liberalism was a means of furthering his second-rate political career. Murrow, who was a Quaker and cared deeply about civil liberties, grew to loathe McCarthy and his permanent Senate investigating committee that had assumed powers usurping the constitutional right to free speech.

Murrow's first attack on McCarthyism was a *See It Now* about a junior air force officer threatened with demotion because his father 'read communist newspapers'. Such was the nervousness of CBS executives that they refused to advertise the programme. So Murrow and Friendly paid $1,500 of their own money for a single advertisement in the *New York Times*, which left off the CBS logo. As Murrow disclosed, the officer's father merely read Serbian newspapers from his home town in Yugoslavia. As a result of the programme, the son was 'cleared'.

The McCarthy period was marked by the compliance and silence of many journalists, who feared the lying, ranting thug and his 'hearings'. In the face of this, Murrow sought to educate the American public that dissent was as much a right as McCarthy's bullying was wrong. His *See It Now*, 'A Report on Senator Joseph R. McCarthy', broadcast on 9 March 1954, let McCarthy hang himself with his own lies and distortions. The programme ended with Murrow calling on Americans to break their silence. (Again, he and Friendly had to buy their own advertising.)

Murrow himself believed he should have made this programme earlier, and he was probably right, as McCarthy was already on the slide, having made the fatal mistake of accusing the US Army brass of being communist-infiltrated. You get a sense of the lingering atmosphere of intimidation by the extremely cautious tone adopted by Murrow, who seems to be going out of his way to be 'fair' to the bully: perhaps, one might argue, too fair. Yet, there is no doubt that this one

programme by Murrow, who enjoyed establishment respect, accelerated the political demise of McCarthy by giving others the courage to
attack him. In a touching passage in his autobiography, he describes
walking to work the morning after the broadcast and shaking the hands
of hundreds of well-wishers, as if a pall had lifted. Would that happen
today, as another form of McCarthyism infests America? Glimpse
American television and the answer is self-evident, alas.

Of three pieces I have selected, the first is from a broadcast of
Murrow's on 27 October 1947 about the House Un-American Activities
Committee investigation into Hollywood. The second, from 9 June
1949, shows how fears of treason and subversion damaged American
society and its democratic traditions. The third, from 1954, is the script
of the celebrated *See It Now* on McCarthy.

THE MENACE OF McCARTHYISM

I want to talk for a few minutes about the Hollywood investigation
now being conducted in Washington. This reporter approaches the
matter with rather fresh memories of friends in Austria, Germany and
Italy who either died or went into exile because they refused to admit
the right of their government to determine what they should say, read,
write or think. (If witnessing the disappearance of individual liberty
abroad causes a reporter to be unduly sensitive to even the faintest
threat of it in his own country, then my analysis of what is happening
in Washington may be out of focus.) This is certainly no occasion for
a defence of the product of Hollywood. Much of that product fails
to invigorate me, but I am not obliged to view it. No more is this an
effort to condemn congressional investigating committees. Such
committees are a necessary part of our system of government and
have performed in the past the double function of illuminating certain
abuses and of informing congressmen regarding expert opinion on
important legislation under consideration. In general, however,
congressional committees have concerned themselves with what individuals, organisations or corporations have or have not done, rather
than with what individuals think. It has always seemed to this reporter
that movies should be judged by what appears upon the screen, newspapers by what appears in print, and radio by what comes out of the
loudspeaker. The personal beliefs of the individuals involved would

not seem to be a legitimate field for inquiry, either by government or by individuals. When bankers, or oil or railroad men, are hauled before a congressional committee, it is not customary to question them about their beliefs or the beliefs of men employed by them. When a soldier is brought before a court-martial he is confronted with witnesses, entitled to counsel and to cross-questioning. His reputation as a soldier, his prospects of future employment, cannot be taken from him unless a verdict is reached under clearly established military law.

It is, I suppose, possible that the committee now sitting may uncover some startling and significant information. But we are here concerned only with what has happened to date. A certain number of people have been accused either of being Communists or of following the Communist line. Their accusers are safe from the laws of slander and libel. Subsequent denials are unlikely ever to catch up with the original allegation. It is to be expected that this investigation will induce increased timidity in an industry not renowned in the past for its boldness in portraying the significant social, economic and political problems confronting this nation. For example, Willie Wyler,[1] who is no alarmist, said yesterday that he would not now be permitted to make *The Best Years of Our Lives* in the way in which he made it more than a year ago.

Considerable mention was made at the hearings of two films, *Mission to Moscow* and *Song of Russia*. I am no movie critic, but I remember what was happening in the war when those films were released. While you were looking at *Mission to Moscow* there was heavy fighting in Tunisia. American and French forces were being driven back; Stalin said the opening of the Second Front was near; there was heavy fighting in the Solomons and New Guinea; MacArthur warned that the Japanese were threatening Australia; General Hershey announced that fathers would be called up in the draft; Wendell Willkie's book *One World* was published. And when *Song of Russia* was released, there was heavy fighting at Cassino and Anzio; the battleship *Missouri* was launched, and the Russian newspaper *Pravda* published, and then retracted, an article saying that the Germans and the British were holding peace talks. And during all this time there were people in high places in London and Washington who feared

[1] French-born US film director whose films include *Mrs Miniver* (1942), *The Best Years of Our Lives* (1946) and *Ben-Hur* (1959).

lest the Russians might make a separate peace with Germany. If these pictures, at that time and in that climate, were subversive then what comes next under the scrutiny of a congressional committee? Correspondents who wrote and broadcast that the Russians were fighting well and suffering appalling losses? If we follow the parallel, the networks and the newspapers which carried those dispatches would likewise be investigated.

Certain government agencies, such as the State Department and the Atomic Energy Commission, are confronted with a real dilemma. They are obligated to maintain security without doing violence to the essential liberties of the citizens who work for them. That may require special and defensible security measures. But no such problem arises with instruments of mass communication. In that area there would seem to be two alternatives: either we believe in the intelligence, good judgement, balance and native shrewdness of the American people, or we believe that government should investigate, intimidate and finally legislate. The choice is as simple as that.

The right of dissent – or, if you prefer, the right to be wrong – is surely fundamental to the existence of a democratic society. That's the right that went first in every nation that stumbled down the trail towards totalitarianism.

I would like to suggest to you that the present search for Communists is in no real sense parallel to the one that took place after the First World War. That, as we know, was a passing phenomenon. Those here who then adhered to Communist doctrine could not look anywhere in the world and find a strong, stable, expanding body of power based on the same principles that they professed. Now the situation is different, so it may be assumed that this internal tension, suspicion, witch hunting, grade labelling – call it what you like – will continue. It may well cause a lot of us to dig deep into both our history and our convictions to determine just how firmly we hold to the principles we were taught and accepted so readily, and which made this country a haven for men who sought refuge. And while we're discussing this matter, we might remember a little-known quotation from Adolf Hitler, spoken in Königsberg before he achieved power. He said, 'The great strength of the totalitarian state is that it will force those who fear it to imitate it.'

27 October 1947

Now this is one reporter's comment upon the subject that has been assailing your eyes and your ears for the past several weeks – the whole area of espionage, treason and subversive activity. Mr Truman indicated at his news conference today, as he has done before, that a great deal of it is just 'headline hunting'. While it must be admitted that some of the headlines are so blown up that they appear to have been shot with a big telescopic sight, it seems to me that the situation that obtains in this country today merits careful and cool consideration. We are probably already well launched in a new era. We have abundant testimony from diplomats, military men, educators and statesmen that this 'time of tension' will continue. It is no passing phase; it is not just the psychological and emotional turbulence in the wake of war.

This conflict with the Soviet Union presents us with a new dilemma. The present situation cannot fairly be compared to the one that existed after the First World War, because then the Communist concept was not supported and sustained by any considerable body of power. Now it is. The secretive, clandestine nature of Communist operations has induced both fear and suspicion. It is in the mainstream of American tradition for us to differ with our neighbours, to suspect their motives, to denounce their policies or their political beliefs. But to suspect them of treason, of allegiance to a foreign power and ideology is probably more widespread now than at any time in our national history. That there is danger of Communist espionage and infiltration cannot be denied. That there is need for legal, constitutional methods of protection would seem to be equally obvious. But the current sensations which assail us on all sides shouldn't blind us to the fact that espionage, propaganda and infiltration have been employed by every tribe and state since the beginning of history. The Chinese, two centuries before Christ, spelled out techniques and methods of operation that are still valid today.

If this contest is to continue indefinitely we must, as in war, have a care for the morale of the home front. Fear of the unknown, fear of depression, should not blind us to the fact that this country represents the greatest conglomeration of power in the world today. It may be that it is a mechanistic, materialistic civilisation; a nation of headline readers, as some of our critics claim. But the fact is that the climate for the development of Communism in this country is less salubrious than any other in the world. We have more material goods; we live in luxury compared with the rest of the world. And yet we are worried and apprehensive. We are also an impatient people, anxious for quick solutions, often intolerant, always desirous of action. I think that if we are going to sweat out successfully this continuing crisis, without losing our liberties while trying to defend them, we are going to have to do it in the old-fashioned way in spite of jet planes and television and all the wonders of science. We will have to remain conscious of our own good fortune as well as our strength.

The individual's independence of judgement must be protected. He can't be protected against sensational headlines or irresponsible broadcasters. But, so far as I know, nobody in this country ever lost his liberty through those instruments. We sometimes forget that the thing that makes this country what it is isn't our size or our racial mixture, or anything else, but the fact that this is a nation that lives under law; where we have the right to believe that any law is a bad law and agitate for its repeal; where with few exceptions a man cannot be convicted unless the rules of evidence are followed. This very fact makes it difficult to apprehend and convict Communist agents because a trial in open court may mean divulging information that would be damaging to the national security. I believe there have been cases where the government would have proceeded against individuals had it not been for this fact. It may be that we require new laws. I am not certain about that. It is deplorable that we have come to suspect each other more than we did before. It is regrettable that individuals and some organs of opinion are disposed to convict people by association or before they have been tried. If this tendency is accelerated, it may induce widespread fear and endanger the right of dissent. But so long as neither the state nor an individual can take punitive action against a citizen except through due processes of law, we shall have in our hands the weapons to defend our personal liberty and our national security.

During the darkest days of the war in England I remarked the frequent use of a simple word, one which is often effective with horses *and* with men. The word was 'steady'. In spite of the surface signs, hysteria and suspicion, it seems to me we aren't doing too badly. At least we haven't yet reached the point where we must follow, in fear, the advice once given by Will Rogers, who said, 'So live that you wouldn't be ashamed to sell the family parrot to the town gossip.'

9 June 1949

A Report on Senator Joseph R. McCarthy

MURROW: Good evening. Tonight *See It Now* devotes its entire half hour to a report on Senator Joseph R. McCarthy, told mainly in his own words and pictures.

(*Commercial*)

MURROW: Because a report on Senator McCarthy is by definition controversial we want to say exactly what we mean to say and I request your permission to read from the script whatever remarks Murrow and Friendly may make. If the senator believes we have done violence to his words or pictures and desires to speak, to answer himself, an opportunity will be afforded him on this programme. Our working thesis tonight is this question:

'If this fight against Communism is made a fight between America's two great political parties the American people know that one of those parties will be destroyed and the republic cannot endure very long as a one-party system.'

We applaud that statement and we think Senator McCarthy ought to. He said it, seventeen months ago in Milwaukee.

McCARTHY: The American people realise this cannot be made a fight between America's two great political parties. If this fight against Communism is made a fight between America's two great political parties the American people know that one of those parties will be destroyed and the republic cannot endure very long as a one-party system.

MURROW: Thus on 4 February 1954, Senator McCarthy spoke of one party's treason. This was at Charleston, West Virginia, where there were no cameras running. It was recorded on tape.

McCARTHY: The issue between the Republicans and Democrats is clearly drawn. It has been deliberately drawn by those who have been in charge of twenty years of treason. The hard fact is – the hard fact is that those who wear the label, those who wear the label Democrat wear it with the stain of a historic betrayal.

MURROW: Seventeen months ago candidate Eisenhower met Senator

McCarthy in Green Bay, Wisconsin, and he laid down the ground rules on how he would meet Communism if elected.

EISENHOWER: This is a pledge I make. If I am charged by you people to be the responsible head of the executive department it will be my initial responsibility to see that subversion, disloyalty, is kept out of the executive department. We will always appreciate and welcome congressional investigation but the responsibility will rest squarely on the shoulders of the executive and I hold that there are ample powers in the government to get rid of these people if the executive department is really concerned in doing it. We can do it with absolute assurance.

(*Applause*)

This is America's principle: trial by jury, of the innocent until proved guilty, and I expect to stand to do it.

MURROW: That same night in Milwaukee, Senator McCarthy stated what he would do if the general was elected.

McCARTHY: I spent about a half hour with the general last night. While I can't – while I can't report that we agreed entirely on everything – I can report that when I left that meeting with the general, I had the same feeling as when I went in, and that is that he is a great American, and will make a great president, an outstanding president. But I want to tell you tonight, tell the American people as long as I represent you and the rest of the American people in the senate, I shall continue to call them as I see them regardless of who happens to be president.

MURROW: 24 November 1953.

McCARTHY: A few days ago I read that President Eisenhower expressed the hope that by election time in 1954 the subject of Communism would be a dead and forgotten issue. The raw, harsh, unpleasant fact is that Communism is an issue and will be an issue in 1954.

MURROW: On one thing the senator has been consistent . . . Often operating as a one-man committee, he has travelled far, interviewed many, terrorised some, accused civilian and military leaders of the past administration of a great conspiracy to turn the country over to

Communism, investigated and substantially demoralised the present State Department, made varying charges, of espionage at Fort Monmouth. (The army says it has been unable to find anything relating to espionage there.) He has interrogated a varied assortment of what he calls 'Fifth Amendment Communists'.[2] Republican Senator Flanders of Vermont said of McCarthy today:

'He dons war paint; he goes into his war dance; he emits his war whoops; he goes forth to battle and proudly returns with the scalp of a pink army dentist.'

Other critics have accused the senator of using the bullwhip and smear. There was a time two years ago when the senator and his friends said he had been smeared and bullwhipped.

MR KEEFE: You would sometimes think to hear the quartet that call themselves 'Operation Truth' damning Joe McCarthy and resorting to the vilest smears I have ever heard. Well, this is the answer, and if I could express it in what is in my heart right now, I would do it in terms of the poet who once said:

> Ah 'tis but a dainty flower I bring you,
> Yes, 'tis but a violet, glistening with dew,
> But still in its heart there lies beauties concealed
> So in our heart our love for you lies unrevealed.

McCARTHY: You know, I used to pride myself on the idea that I was a bit tough, especially over the past eighteen or nineteen months when we have been kicked around and bullwhipped and damned. I didn't think that I could be touched very deeply. But tonight, frankly, my cup and my heart is so full I can't talk to you.

MURROW: But in Philadelphia, on Washington's birthday, 1954, his heart was so full he could talk. He reviewed some of the General Zwicker[3] testimony and proved he hadn't abused him.

---

[2] The Fifth Amendment to the Constitution of the United States (adopted in 1791) guarantees a grand-jury trial for serious crimes, protects against double jeopardy and prohibits compelling testimony of a defendant against himself.

[3] During an investigation of alleged espionage at Fort Monmouth, New Jersey, Senator McCarthy had interrogated General Ralph Zwicker, who refused to disclose the names of those responsible for the promotion of an army dentist accused of Communist leanings. In a personal attack McCarthy had announced that the general 'does not have the brains of a five-year-old'.

McCARTHY: Nothing is more serious than a traitor to this country in the Communist conspiracy. Question: Do you think stealing $50 is more serious than being a traitor to the country and a part of the Communist conspiracy? Answer: That, sir, was not my decision.

Shall we go on to that for a while? I hate to impose on your time. I just got two pages. This is the abuse which is . . . the real meat of abuse, this is the official reporter's record of the hearing. After he said he wouldn't remove that general from the army who cleared Communists, I said: 'Then general, you should be removed from any command. Any man who has been given the honour of being promoted to general, and who says, "I will protect another general who protects Communists," is not fit to wear that uniform, general.'

(*Applause*)

'I think it is a tremendous disgrace to the army to have to bring these facts before the public but I intend to give it to the public, general, I have a duty to do that. I intend to repeat to the press exactly what you said so that you can know that and be back here to hear it, general.'

And wait 'til you hear the bleeding hearts scream and cry about our methods of trying to drag the truth from those who know, or should know, who covered up a Fifth Amendment Communist major. But they say, 'Oh, it's all right to uncover them but don't get rough doing it, McCarthy.'

MURROW: But two days later, Secretary Stevens[4] and the senator had lunch, agreed on a memorandum of understanding, disagreed on what the small type said.

STEVENS: I shall never accede to the abuse of army personnel under any circumstance, including committee hearings. I shall not accede to them being browbeaten or humiliated. In the light of those assurances, although I did not propose cancellation of the hearing, I acceded to it. If it had not been for these assurances, I would never have entered into any agreement whatsoever.

[4] Army Secretary Robert T. Stevens.

MURROW: Then President Eisenhower issued a statement that his advisers thought censured the senator, but the senator saw it as another victory, called the entire Zwicker case 'a tempest in a teapot'.

McCARTHY: If a stupid, arrogant or witless man in a position of power appears before our committee and is found aiding the Communist Party, he will be exposed. The fact that he might be a general places him in no special class as far as I am concerned. Apparently – apparently, the president and I now agree on the necessity of getting rid of Communists. We apparently disagree only on how we should handle those who protect Communists. When the shouting and the tumult dies the American people and the president will realise that this unprecedented mud-slinging against the committee by the extreme left-wing elements of press and radio were caused solely because another Fifth Amendment Communist was finally dug out of the dark recesses and exposed to the public view.

MURROW: Senator McCarthy claims that only the left-wing press criticised him on the Zwicker case. Of the fifty large circulation newspapers in the country, these are the left-wing papers that criticised. These are the ones which supported him. The ratio is about three to one against the senator. Now let us look at some of these left-wing papers that criticised the Senator.

The *Chicago Tribune*: McCarthy will better serve his cause if he learns to distinguish the role of investigator from the role of avenging angel.

The *New York Times*: The unwarranted interference of a demagogue – a domestic Munich.

The *Times Herald*, Washington: Senator McCarthy's behaviour towards Zwicker is not justified.

The *Herald Tribune* of New York: McCarthyism involves assault on Republican assets.

Milwaukee Journal: The line must be drawn and defended or McCarthy will become the government.

The *Evening Star* of Washington: It was a bad day for everyone who resents and detests the bully-boy tactics which Senator McCarthy often employs.

The *New York World Telegram*: Bamboozling, bludgeoning, distorting.

St Louis Post-Dispatch: Unscrupulous bullying. What tragic irony – the President's advisers keep him from doing whatever decent instinct must command him to do.

That is the ratio from three to one of the left-wing press.

There was one other interesting quote on the Zwicker controversy, and it came from the senator himself.

McCARTHY: May I say that I was extremely shocked when I heard that Secretary Stevens told two army officers they had to take part in the cover-up of those who promoted and coddled Communists. As I read his statement, I thought of that quotation 'On what meat doth this, our Caesar, feed?'

MURROW: And upon what meat does Senator McCarthy feed? Two of the staples of his diet are the investigations (protected by immunity) and the half truth. We herewith submit samples of both. First, the half truth. This was an attack on Adlai Stevenson at the end of the '52 campaign.[5] President Eisenhower, it must be said, had no prior knowledge of it.

McCARTHY: I perform this unpleasant task because the American people are entitled to have the coldly documented history of this man who says he wants to be your president. But strangely, Algen – I mean Adlai . . . but let's move on to another part of the jigsaw puzzle. While you may think that there can be no connection between the debonair Democrat candidate and a dilapidated Massachusetts barn, I want to show you a picture of this barn and explain the connection. Here is the outside of the barn. Give me the picture of the inside of the barn. Here is the outside of the barn at Lee, Massachusetts. It looks as though it couldn't house a farmer's cow or goat. Here's the inside. (*Showing picture*) A beautiful, panelled conference room with maps of the Soviet Union. What way does Stevenson tie up with that?

My – my investigators went out and took pictures of the barn after we had been tipped off what was in it. Tipped off that there was in

[5] Adlai F. Stevenson, the Democratic candidate in the 1952 presidential campaign, who had attacked McCarthy. He lost the election to the Republican candidate, Dwight D. Eisenhower.

this barn all the missing documents from the Communist-front IPR.[6] The IPR which was named by the McCarran Committee[7] – named before the McCarran Committee as a cover-up for Communist espionage. Let's take a look at the photostat of the document taken from the Massachusetts barn. One of those documents which was never supposed to see the light of day. Rather interesting it is. This is a document which shows that Alger Hiss[8] and Frank Coe recommended Adlai Stevenson to the Mount Tremblant Conference which was called for the purpose of establishing foreign policy – post-war policy in Asia. As you know, Alger Hiss is a convicted traitor, Frank Coe is a man who has been named under oath before the congressional committee seven times as a member of the Communist Party. Why, why do Hiss and Coe find that Adlai Stevenson is the man they want representing them at this conference? I don't know. Perhaps Adlai knows.

MURROW: But Senator McCarthy didn't permit his audience to hear the entire paragraph. This is the official record of the McCarran hearings and anyone could have bought it for two dollars. Quote: 'Another possibility for the Mount Tremblant Conferences on Asia is someone from Knox' office or Stimson's office.' (Frank Knox was our wartime secretary of the navy; Henry Stimson our secretary of the army, both distinguished Republicans.) Coe and Hiss mentioned Adlai Stevenson, one of Knox' special assistants and Harvey Bundy, former assistant secretary of state under Hoover, and now assistant to Stimson because of their jobs.

We read from this documented record not in defence of Mr Stevenson, but in defence of truth. Specifically, Mr Stevenson's identification with that red barn was no more, no less than that of Knox, Stimson or Bundy. It should be stated that Mr Stevenson was once a member of the Institute of Pacific Relations. But so were such other loyal Americans as Senator Ferguson, John Foster Dulles, Paul

[6] Institute of Pacific Relations.

[7] The McCarran Act of Internal Security of 1950 required that all Communist organisations register the names of their members with the federal government. Working closely with the FBI, McCarran's Senate Inquiry Security Subcommittee conducted hearings for the next twenty-five years.

[8] In August 1948, Alger Hiss, who had been one of President Roosevelt's closest advisers in the State Department, was accused before the House Un-American Activities Committee of being a Soviet agent. Hiss denied the accusation but after a controversial trial he was proclaimed guilty in 1950 and sentenced to five years in prison.

Hoffman, Henry Luce and Herbert F. Hoover. Their association carries with it no guilt, and that barn has nothing to do with any of them.

Now a sample investigation. The witness was Reed Harris, for many years a civil servant in the State Department directing the information service. Harris was accused of helping the Communist cause by curtailing some broadcasts to Israel. Senator McCarthy summoned him and questioned him about a book he had written in 1932.

McCARTHY: Mr Reed Harris, your name is Reed Harris?

REED HARRIS: That's right.

McCARTHY: You wrote a book in '32, is that correct?

REED HARRIS: Yes, I wrote a book and as I testified in executive session –

McCARTHY: At the time you wrote the book – pardon me, go ahead, I'm sorry, proceed.

REED HARRIS: – at the time I wrote the book the atmosphere in the universities of the United States was greatly affected by the great depression then in existence. The attitudes of students, the attitudes of the general public were considerably different than they are at this moment, and for one thing there certainly was no awareness to the degree that there is today of the way the Communist Party works.

McCARTHY: You attended Columbia University in the early thirties, is that right?

REED HARRIS: I did, Mr Chairman.

McCARTHY: Will you speak a little louder, sir?

REED HARRIS: I did, Mr Chairman.

McCARTHY: And you were expelled from Columbia?

REED HARRIS: I was suspended from classes on 1 April 1932. I was later reinstated and I resigned from the university.

McCARTHY: You resigned from the university. Did the Civil Liberties Union provide you with an attorney at that time?

REED HARRIS: I had many offers of attorneys and one of those was from the American Civil Liberties Union, yes.

McCARTHY: The question is: did the Civil Liberties Union supply you with an attorney?

REED HARRIS: They did supply an attorney.

McCARTHY: The answer is yes?

REED HARRIS: The answer is yes.

McCARTHY: You know the Civil Liberties Union has been listed as a front for and doing the work of the Communist Party?

REED HARRIS: Mr Chairman, this was 1932.

McCARTHY: I know it was 1932. Do you know they since have been listed as a front for and doing the work of the Communist Party?

REED HARRIS: I do not know that they have been listed so, sir.

McCARTHY: You don't know they have been listed?

REED HARRIS: I have heard that mentioned or read that mentioned.

McCARTHY: You wrote a book in 1932. I'm going to ask you again: at the time you wrote this book did you feel that professors should be given the right to teach sophomores that marriage 'should be cast off of our civilisation as antiquated and stupid religious phenomena'? Was that your feeling at that time?

REED HARRIS: My feeling was that professors should have the right to express their considered opinions on any subject, whatever they were, sir.

McCARTHY: I'm going to ask you this question again.

REED HARRIS: That includes that quotation. They should have the right to teach anything that came to their mind as being a proper thing to teach.

McCARTHY: I'm going to make you answer this.

REED HARRIS: I'll answer yes, but you put an implication on it and you feature this particular point out of the book which of course is quite out of context, does not give a proper impression of the book as a whole. The American public doesn't get an honest impression of even that book, bad as it is, from what you are quoting from it.

McCARTHY: Then let's continue to read your own writings.

REED HARRIS: Twenty-one years ago again.

McCARTHY: Yes, we shall try and bring you down to date if we can.

REED HARRIS: Mr Chairman, two weeks ago Senator Taft took the position that I taught twenty-one years ago, that Communists and Socialists should be allowed to teach in the schools. It so happens nowadays I don't agree with Senator Taft as far as Communist teachers in the schools is concerned because I think Communists are in effect a plainclothes auxiliary of the Red Army, the Soviet Red Army, and I don't want to see them in any of our schools teaching.

McCARTHY: I don't recall Senator Taft ever having any of the background that you have got.

REED HARRIS: I resent the tone of this inquiry very much, Mr Chairman. I resent it not only because it is my neck, my public neck that you are I think very skilfully trying to wring, but I say it because there are thousands of able and loyal employees in the federal government of the United States who have been properly cleared according to the laws and the security practices of their agencies as I was, unless the new regime says no. I was before.

McCARTHY: Do you think this book you wrote then did considerable harm? Its publication might have had adverse influence on the public by an expression of views contained in it?

REED HARRIS: The sale of that book was so abysmally small, it was so unsuccessful that a question of its influence, really you can go back to the publisher, you'll see it was one of the most unsuccessful books he ever put out. He's still sorry about it, just as I am.

McCARTHY: Well, I think that's a compliment to American intelligence, I will say that.

MURROW: Senator McCarthy succeeded only in proving that Reed Harris had once written a bad book which the American people had proved twenty-two years ago by not buying it, which is what they eventually do with all bad ideas. As for Reed Harris, his resignation was accepted a month later with a letter of commendation. McCarthy claimed it was a victory. The Reed Harris hearing demonstrates one of the senator's techniques. Twice he said the American Civil Liberties Union was listed as a subversive front. The attorney general's list does not and has never listed the ACLU as subversive, nor does the FBI or any other government agency. And the American Civil Liberties Union holds in its files letters of commendation from President Eisenhower, President Truman and General MacArthur.

Now let us try to bring the McCarthy story a little more up to date. Two years ago Senator Benton of Connecticut accused McCarthy of apparent perjury, unethical practice and perpetrating a hoax on the senate. McCarthy sued for two million dollars. Last week he dropped the case saying no one could be found who believed Benton's story. Several volunteers have come forward saying they believe it in its entirety.

Today Senator McCarthy says he's going to get a lawyer and force the networks to give him time to reply to Adlai Stevenson's speech. Earlier, the senator asked, 'upon what meat does this our Caesar feed.' Had he looked three lines earlier in Shakespeare's *Caesar* he would have found this line, which is not altogether inappropriate: 'The fault, dear Brutus, is not in our stars, but in ourselves.'

No one familiar with the history of this country can deny that congressional committees are useful. It is necessary to investigate before legislating, but the line between investigation and persecuting is a very fine one and the junior senator from Wisconsin has stepped over it repeatedly. His primary achievement has been in confusing the public mind as between internal and the external threat of Communism. We must not confuse dissent with disloyalty. We must remember always that accusation is not proof and that conviction depends upon evidence and due process of law. We will not walk in fear, one of another. We will not be driven by fear into an age of unreason if we dig deep in our history and our doctrine, and remember that we are not descended from fearful men, not from men who feared to write, to speak, to associate and to defend causes which were for the moment unpopular.

This is no time for men who oppose Senator McCarthy's methods to keep silent, or for those who approve. We can deny our heritage and our history but we cannot escape responsibility for the result. There is no way for a citizen of a republic to abdicate his responsibilities. As a nation we have come into our full inheritance at a tender age. We proclaim ourselves, as indeed we are, the defenders of freedom, what's left of it, but we cannot defend freedom abroad by deserting it at home. The actions of the junior senator from Wisconsin have caused alarm and dismay amongst our allies abroad and given considerable comfort to our enemies, and whose fault is that? Not really his, he didn't create this situation of fear, he merely exploited it and rather successfully. Cassius was right, 'The fault, dear Brutus, is not in our stars, but in ourselves.'

Good night, and good luck.

9 March 1954

JESSICA MITFORD

The American Way of Death

1963

Jessica Mitford, the youngest daughter of Lord and Lady Redesdale, was born in 1917 into a privileged family which, until the 1930s, had not been so eccentric by English upper-class standards as to be notorious. The Mitford sisters were to change all that. In the first volume of her autobiography, *Hons and Rebels,* Jessica writes: 'To my father, outsiders included not only Huns, Frogs, Americans, blacks and all other foreigners, but also other people's children . . . in fact, the whole teeming population of the earth's surface.'

Her sisters, Unity and Diana, embraced this view of humanity: Unity became a Nazi and joined Hitler's circle in Germany, and Diana married British fascist leader Oswald Mosley. Nancy, the eldest, was a novelist who 'skipped through the dark life of the family with flashes of laughter and more than a little brilliance', wrote Jessica, whose own very different instincts appeared early; as a child she would ask her mother why all the money in England could not be divided up equally among everybody, thus putting an end to poverty.

It was this radicalism that shaped her life and powered her journalism. Having settled in the United States, 'to escape the suffocation of the English class system', she devoted herself to writing and politics. She joined the Communist Party, then left it in 1956 in protest against the Soviet invasion of Hungary. Her first major magazine series, an investigation into the American prison system, established a provocative, fluent style of relentless curiosity and dark wit.

In 1963, she published *The American Way of Death*. It is one of the most important investigative books ever written, exposing the exploitation of the American funeral business, whose profiteering was, until then, an apparently untouchable scandal. The idea came from her second husband, Bob Treuhaft, a labour lawyer and founder, in the late 1950s, of the Bay Area Funeral Society, which provided funerals at a fraction of the going rate and campaigned for better pay and conditions for funeral workers. When a magazine article she wrote on the subject ('St. Peter, Don't You Call Me') had a huge public response, she decided to write a book about the funeral business.

The American Way of Death became an instant bestseller in 1963. It not only made funerals a fashionable media topic, but caused membership in the non-profit funeral societies to leap from 17,000 to almost a million. This was the 'Mitford Syndrome', according to the trade press, which condemned her work as a Red plot. As Jessica wrote, 'They found an ally in Congressman James B. Utt of California [who] read a two-page statement about my subversive background into the *Congressional Record.* As for the purpose of my book, "she is really striking another blow at the Christian religion. Her tirade against morticians is simply the vehicle to carry her anti-Christ attack." His statement ended with the ringing words, "I would rather place my mortal remains, alive or dead, in the hands of any American mortician than to set foot on the soil of any communist nation." (In 1970, Mr Utt exercised that option)'.

The book led to legal reforms, including new Federal Trade Commission regulations on funerals. It also provoked more than one offer of a 'free funeral' for the author from less than grateful undertakers.

When I met Jessica some twenty years later, I found her still chuckling over trade magazines called *Mortuary Management* and her favourite, *Concept – The Journal of Creative Ideas for Cemeteries.* 'Well, there was this whole wonder world of the mortuary I hadn't known existed,' she said. 'You could have a choice of foam-rubber or inner-spring mattress in your eternal sealer casket, for God's sake . . . You see, the industry knew they couldn't beat me, so they resigned themselves to me. I still get *Mortuary Management* and my name is in every copy; they call me Jessica, which I always think is the height of fame, like being Za Za or Marilyn. And they seem to think I invented cremations; after the book came out, cremations increased by eight per cent. Why it terrifies them is because unlike any other industry their market is inelastic: one to a customer. There was a terribly sad article in *Mortuary Management* saying that due to the national speed limit being reduced and due to medical advances, the death rate is falling. Terrible! I mean, *you can see their plight.*'

She kept her family pet name, 'Decca', and her cut-glass accent remained during a lifetime of exile. Carl Bernstein, the Watergate reporter, described her as 'looking very much the picture of a slightly dotty English lady' with 'her winsome manner' distracting her prey from an 'unfailing ear and instinct for the jugular'.

Shortly before her death in 1996, she completed an updated edition, *The American Way of Death Revisited*, from which the following passages are taken.

THE AMERICAN WAY OF DEATH

A funeral is not an occasion for a display of cheapness. It is, in fact, an opportunity for the display of a status symbol which, by bolstering family pride, does much to assuage grief. A funeral is also an occasion when feelings of guilt and remorse are satisfied to a large extent by the purchase of a fine funeral. It seems highly probable that the most satisfactory funeral service for the average family is one in which the cost has necessitated some degree of sacrifice. This permits the survivors to atone for any real or fancied neglect of the deceased prior to his death . . .

National Funeral Service Journal

O death, where is thy sting? O grave, where is thy victory? Where, indeed. Many a badly stung survivor, faced with the aftermath of some relative's funeral, has ruefully concluded that the victory has been won hands down by a funeral establishment – in a disastrously unequal battle.

Much fun has been poked at some of the irrational 'status symbols' set out like golden snares to trap the unwary consumer at every turn. Until recently, little has been said about the most irrational and weirdest of the lot, lying in ambush for all of us at the end of the road – the modern American funeral.

If the Dismal Traders (as an eighteenth-century English writer calls them) have traditionally been cast in a comic role in literature, a universally recognised symbol of humour from Shakespeare to Dickens to Evelyn Waugh, they have successfully turned the tables in recent years to perpetrate a huge, macabre and expensive practical joke on the American public. It is not consciously conceived of as a joke, of course; on the contrary, it is hedged with admirably contrived rationalisations.

Gradually, almost imperceptibly, over the years the funeral men have constructed their own grotesque cloud-cuckoo-land where the trappings of Gracious Living are transformed, as in a nightmare, into the trappings of Gracious Dying. The same familiar Madison Avenue language, with its peculiar adjectival range designed to anaesthetise sales resistance to all sorts of products, has seeped into the funeral industry in a new and bizarre guise. The emphasis is on the same desirable qualities that we have been schooled to look for in our daily search for excellence: comfort, durability, beauty, craftsmanship. The attuned ear will recognise, too, the convincing quasi-scientific language, so reassuring even if unintelligible.

So that this too too solid flesh might not melt, we are offered 'solid copper – a quality casket which offers superb value to the client seeking long-lasting protection', or 'the Colonial Classic beauty – 18-gauge lead-coated steel, seamless top, lap-jointed welded body construction'. Some are equipped with foam rubber, some with inner-spring mattresses. Batesville offers 'beds that lift and tilt'. Not every casket need have a silver lining, for one may choose among a rich assortment of 'colour-matched shades' in non-abrasive fabrics. Shrouds no longer exist. Instead, you may patronise a grave-wear couturière who promises 'handmade original fashions – styles from the best in life for the last memory-dresses, men's suits, negligees, accessories'. For the final, perfect grooming: 'Nature-Glo – the ultimate in cosmetic embalming'. And where have we heard that phrase 'peace-of-mind protection' before? No matter. In funeral advertising, it is applied to the Wilbert Burial Vault, with its $3/_8$-inch pre-cast asphalt inner liner plus extra-thick, reinforced concrete – all this 'guaranteed by Good Housekeeping'. Here again the Cadillac, status symbol par excellence, appears in all its gleaming glory, this time transformed into a sleek funeral hearse. Although lesser vehicles are now used to collect the body and the permits, the Cad is still the conveyance of choice for the Loved One's last excursion to the grave.

You, the potential customer for all this luxury, are unlikely to read the lyrical descriptions quoted above, for they are culled from *Mortuary Management* and other trade magazines of the industry. For you there are the ads in your daily newspaper, generally found on the obituary page, stressing dignity, refinement, high-calibre professional service and that intangible quality, sincerity. The trade advertisements are, however, instructive, because they furnish an important clue to the frame of mind into which the funeral industry has hypnotised itself.

A new mythology, essential to the twentieth-century American funeral rite, has grown up – or rather has been built up step-by-step – to justify the peculiar customs surrounding the disposal of our dead. And just as the witch doctor must be convinced of his own infallibility in order to maintain a hold over his clientele, so the funeral industry has had to 'sell itself' on its articles of faith in the course of passing them along to the public.

The first of these is the tenet that today's funeral procedures are founded in 'American tradition'. The story comes to mind of a sign on the freshly sown lawn of a brand-new Midwestern college: 'There is a tradition on this campus that students never walk on this strip of grass. This tradition goes into effect next Tuesday.' The most cursory look at American funerals of past times will establish the parallel. Simplicity to the point of starkness, the plain pine box, the laying out of the dead by friends and family who also bore the coffin to the grave – these were the hallmarks of the traditional American funeral until the end of the nineteenth century.

Secondly, there is the myth that the American public is only being given what it wants – an opportunity to keep up with the Joneses to the end. 'In keeping with our high standard of living, there should be an equally high standard of dying,' says an industry leader. 'The cost of a funeral varies according to individual taste and the niceties of living the family has been accustomed to.' Actually, choice doesn't enter the picture for average individuals faced, generally for the first time, with the necessity of buying a product of which they are totally ignorant, at a moment when they are least in a position to quibble. In point of fact, the cost of a funeral almost always varies, not 'according to individual taste' but according to what the traffic will bear.

Thirdly, there is an assortment of myths based on half-digested psychiatric theories. The importance of the 'memory picture' is stressed – meaning the last glimpse of the deceased in an open casket, done up with the latest in embalming techniques and finished off with a dusting of make-up. Another, impressively authentic-sounding, is the need for 'grief therapy', which is big now in mortuary circles. A historian of American funeral directing hints at the grief-therapist idea when speaking of the new role of the undertaker – 'the dramaturgic role, in which the undertaker becomes a stage manager to create an appropriate atmosphere and to move the funeral party through a drama in which social relationships are stressed and an emotional catharsis or release is provided through ceremony'.

Lastly, a whole new terminology, as ornately shoddy as the rayon satin casket liner, has been invented by the funeral industry to replace the direct and serviceable vocabulary of former times. 'Undertaker' has been supplanted by 'funeral director' or 'mortician'. Even the classified section of the telephone directory gives recognition to this; in its pages you will find 'Undertakers – see Funeral Directors'. Coffins are 'caskets'; hearses are 'coaches' or 'professional cars'; flowers are 'floral tributes'; corpses generally are 'loved ones', but mortuary etiquette dictates that a specific corpse be referred to by name only – as 'Mr Jones'; cremated ashes are 'cremains'. Euphemisms such as 'slumber room', 'reposing room' and 'calcination – the kindlier heat' abound in the funeral business.

If the undertaker is the stage manager of the fabulous production that is the modern American funeral, the stellar role is reserved for the occupant of the open casket. The decor, the stagehands, the supporting cast are all arranged for the most advantageous display of the deceased, without which the rest of the paraphernalia would lose its point – *Hamlet* without the Prince of Denmark. It is to this end that a fantastic array of costly merchandise and services is pyramided to dazzle the mourners and facilitate the plunder of the next of kin.

The sellers of funeral service have, one gathers, a preconceived, stereotyped view of their customers. To them, the bereaved person who enters the funeral establishment is a bundle of guilt feelings, a snob and a status seeker. Funeral directors feel that by steering the customer to the higher-priced caskets, they are administering the first dose of grief therapy. In the words of the *National Funeral Service Journal*: 'The focus of the buyer's interest must be the casket, vault, clothing, funeral cars, etc. – the only tangible evidence of how much has been invested in the funeral – the only real status symbol associated with a funeral service.'

Whether or not one agrees with this rather unflattering appraisal of the average person who has suffered a death in the family, it is nevertheless true that the funeral transaction is generally influenced by a combination of circumstances which bear upon the buyer as in no other type of business dealing: the disorientation caused by bereavement, the lack of standards by which to judge the value of the commodity offered by the seller, the need to make an on-the-spot decision, general ignorance of the law as it affects disposal of the dead, the ready availability of insurance money to finance the transaction. These factors predetermine to a large extent the outcome of the transaction.

The funeral seller, like any other merchant, is preoccupied with price, profit, selling techniques. Mr Leon S. Utter, a former dean of the San Francisco College of Mortuary Science, has written, 'Your selling plan should go into operation as soon as the telephone rings and you are requested to serve a bereaved family . . . Never preconceive as to what any family will purchase. You cannot possibly measure the intensity of their emotions, undisclosed insurance or funds that may have been set aside for funeral expenses.'

The selling plan should be subtle rather than high-pressure, for the obvious 'hard sell' is considered inappropriate and self-defeating by industry leaders. Two examples of what not to say to a customer are given in the *Successful Mortuary Operation Service Manual*: 'I can tell by the fine suit you are wearing, that you appreciate the finer things, and will want a fine casket for your Mother', and 'Think of the beautiful memory picture you will have of your dear Father in this beautiful casket.'

At the same time, nothing must be left to chance. The trade considers that the most important element of funeral salesmanship is the proper arrangement of caskets in the selection room (where the customer is taken to make his purchase). The sales talk, while preferably dignified and restrained, must be designed to take maximum advantage of this arrangement.

The uninitiated, entering a casket-selection room for the first time, may think he is looking at a random grouping of variously priced merchandise. Actually, endless thought and care are lavished on the development of new and better selection-room arrangements, for it has been found that the placing of the caskets materially affects the amount of the sale. There are available to the trade a number of texts devoted to the subject, supplemented by frequent symposiums, seminars, study courses, visual aids, scale-model selection rooms complete with miniature caskets that can be moved around experimentally. All stress the desired goal: 'selling consistently in a bracket that is above average'.

The relationship between casket arrangement and sales psychology is discussed quite fully by Mr W. M. Krieger, former managing director of the influential National Selected Morticians Association, in his book *Successful Funeral Management*. He analyses the blunder of placing the caskets in order of price, from cheapest to the most expensive, which he calls the 'stairstep method' of arrangement. As he points out, this plan 'makes direct dollar comparisons very easy'. Or, if the caskets are so arranged that the most expensive are the first ones the buyer sees, he may be shocked into buying a very cheap one. A mistake to be avoided is an 'unbalanced line' with too many caskets in the low price range: 'The unbalanced line with its heavy concentration of units under $300 made it very easy for the client to buy in this area with complete satisfaction.'

In developing his method of display, Mr Krieger divides the stock of caskets for convenience into four 'quartiles', two above and two below the median price, which in his example is $400. The objective is to sell in the third, or just above median, quartile. To this end the purchaser is first led to a unit in this third quartile – about $125 to $150 *above* the median sale, in the range of $525 to $550. Should the buyer balk at this price, he should next be led to a unit providing 'strong contrast, both in price and quality', this time something well below the median, say in the $375 to $395 range. The psychological reasons for this are explained. They are twofold. While the difference in quality is demonstrable, the price is not so low as to make the buyer feel belittled. At the same time, if the buyer turns his nose up and indicates that he didn't want to go *that* low, now is the time to show him the 'rebound unit' – one priced from $25 to $50 above the median, in the $425 to $450 bracket.

Mr Krieger calls all this the 'Keystone Approach', and supplies a diagram showing units 1, 2 and 3 scattered with apparent artless abandon about the floor. The customer, who has been bounced from third to second quartile and back again on the rebound to the third, might think the 'Human Tennis Ball Approach' a more appropriate term.

Should the prospect show no reaction either way on seeing the first unit – or should he ask to see something better – the rebound gambit is, of course, 'out'. 'In' is the Avenue of Approach. It seems that a Canadian Mountie once told Mr Krieger that people who get lost in the wild always turn in a great circle to their right. Probably, surmises Mr Krieger, because 85 per cent of us are right-handed. In any event, the Avenue of Approach is a main, wide aisle leading to the right in the selection room. Here are the better-quality third- and fourth-quartile caskets.

For that underprivileged, or stubborn, member of society who insists on purchasing below the median (but who should nevertheless be served 'graciously and with just as much courtesy and attention as you would give to the buyer without a limit on what he can spend'), there is a narrow aisle leading to the *left*, which Mr Krieger calls 'Resistance Lane'. There is unfortunately no discussion of two possible hazards: what if an extremely affluent prospect should prove to be among the 15 per cent of left-handed persons, and should therefore turn automatically into Resistance Lane? How to extricate him? Conversely, what if one of the poor or stubborn, possibly having at some time in his past been lost in Canada, should instinctively turn to the broad, right-handed Avenue of Approach?

The Comprehensive Sales Program Successful Mortuary Operation is designed along the same lines as Mr Krieger's plan, only it is even more complicated. Everything is, however, most carefully spelled out, beginning with the injunction to greet the clients with a warm and friendly handshake and a suggested opening statement, which should be 'spoken slowly and with real sincerity: "I want to assure you that I'm going to do everything I can to be helpful to you!"'

Having made this good beginning, the funeral director is to proceed with the arrangement conference, at each stage of which he should 'weave in the service story' – in other words, impress upon the family that they will be entitled to all sorts of extras, such as ushers, cars, pallbearers, a lady attendant for hairdressing and cosmetics, and the like – all of which will be included in the price of the casket, which it is now their duty to select. These preliminaries are very important, for 'the Arrangement Conference can *make* or *break* the sale'.

The diagram of the selection room in this manual resembles one of those mazes set up for experiments designed to muddle rats. It is here that we are introduced to the Triangle Plan, under which the buyer is led around in a triangle, or rather in a series of triangles. He is started off at position A, a casket costing $587, which he is told is 'in the $500 range' – although, as the manual points out, it is actually $13 short of $600. He is informed that the average family buys in the $500 range – a statement designed to reassure him, explain the authors, because 'most of the people believe themselves to be above average'. Suppose the client does not react either way to the $587 casket. He is now led to position B on the diagram – a better casket priced at $647. However, this price is not to be mentioned. Rather, the words 'sixty dollars additional' are to be used. Should the prospect still remain silent, this is the cue to continue upwards to the most expensive unit.

Conversely, should the client demur at the price of $587, he is to be taken to position C – and told that 'he can save a hundred dollars by choosing this one'. Again, the figure of $487 is not to be mentioned. If he now says nothing, he is led to position D. Here he is told that 'at sixty dollars additional, we could use this finer type, and all of the services will be just exactly the same'. This is the crux of the Triangle Plan; the recalcitrant buyer has now gone around a triangle to end up unwittingly within forty dollars of the starting point. It will be noted that the prices all end in the number seven, 'purposely styled to allow you to quote as "sixty dollars additional" or "save a hundred dollars".'

Some grieving families will be spared this tour altogether, for a sales technique of the 1990s is to sell caskets by catalogue only. One might not think of a casket as 'photogenic', but morticians exclaim with enthusiasm that families are choosing more expensive caskets when they don't have to look at the real thing. The buyer is not likely to have caught the significance of this guided tour, whether it be through the catalogue or the display room. As a customer, he finds himself in an unusual situation, trapped in a set of circumstances peculiar to the funeral transaction. His frame of mind will vary, obviously, according to the circumstances which brought him to the funeral establishment. He may be dazed and bewildered, his young wife having just been killed in an accident; he may be rather relieved because a crotchety old relative has finally died after a long and painful illness. The great majority of funeral buyers, as they are led through their paces at the mortuary – whether shaken and grief-stricken or merely looking forward with pleasurable anticipation to the reading of the will – are assailed by many a nagging question: what's the *right* thing to do? I am arranging a funeral, but surely this is no time to indulge my own preferences in taste and style; I feel I know what she would have preferred, but what will her family and friends expect? How can I avoid criticism for inadvertently doing the wrong thing? And, above all, it should be a nice, decent funeral – but what is a nice, decent funeral?

Which leads us to the second special aspect of the funeral transaction: the buyer's almost total ignorance of what to expect when he enters the undertaker's parlour. What to look for, what to avoid, how much to spend. The funeral industry estimates that the average individual has to arrange for a funeral only once in fifteen years. The cost of the funeral is the third-largest expenditure, after a house and a car, in the life of an ordinary American family. Yet even in the case of the old relative whose death may have been fully expected and even welcomed, it is most unlikely that the buyer will have discussed the funeral with anybody in advance. It just would not seem right to go around saying, 'By the way, my uncle is very ill and he's not expected to live; do you happen to know a good, reliable undertaker?'

Because of the nature of funerals, the buyer is in a quite different position from the one who is, for example, in the market for a car. Visualise the approach. The man of prudence and common sense who is about to buy a car consults a Consumers' Research bulletin or seeks the advice of friends; he knows in advance the dangers of rushing into a deal blindly.

In the funeral home, the man of prudence is completely at sea, without a recognisable landmark or bearing to guide him. It would be an unusual person who would examine the various offerings and then enquire around about the relative advantages of the Keystone casket by York and the Valley Forge by Batesville. In the matter of cost, a like difference is manifest. The funeral buyer is generally not in the mood to compare prices here, examine and appraise quality there. He is anxious to get the whole thing over with – not only is he anxious for this, but the exigencies of the situation demand it.

The third unusual factor which confronts the buyer is the need to make an on-the-spot decision. Impulse buying, which should, he knows, be avoided in everyday life, is here a built-in necessity. The convenient equivocations of commerce – 'I'll look around a little and let you know', 'Maybe I'll call you in a couple of weeks if I decide to take it' – simply do not apply in this situation. Unlike most purchases, this one cannot be returned in fifteen days and your money refunded in full if not completely satisfied.

In 1994 the FTC[1] amended the Funeral Rule to prohibit under-takers from charging a special 'casket-handling fee' to customers who purchased caskets from the store-front discount outlets that were beginning to make their appearance. In the few years since, there has been an explosion of these outlets, and one may now even shop for a casket on the Internet. But just as most funeral buyers feel barred by circumstances from shopping around for a casket, they are like-

[1] Federal Trade Commission.

wise barred by convention from complaining afterwards if they think they were overcharged or otherwise shabbily treated. The reputation of the TV repairman, the lawyer, the plumber is public property, and their shortcomings may be the subject of dinner-party conversation. The reputation of the undertaker is relatively safe in this respect. A friend, knowing I was writing on the subject, reluctantly told me of her experience in arranging the funeral of a brother-in-law. She went to a long-established, 'reputable' undertaker. Seeking to save the widow expense, she chose the cheapest redwood casket in the establishment and was quoted a low price. Later, the salesman called her back to say the brother-in-law was too tall to fit into this casket, she would have to take one that cost 100 dollars more. When my friend objected, the salesman said, 'Oh, all right, we'll use the redwood one, but we'll have to cut off his feet.' My friend was so shocked and disturbed by the nightmare quality of this conversation that she never mentioned it to anybody for two years.

Popular ignorance about the law as it relates to the disposal of the dead is a factor that sometimes affects the funeral transaction. People are often astonished to learn that in no state is embalming required by law except in certain special circumstances, such as when the body is to be shipped by common carrier.

The funeral men foster these misconceptions, sometimes by coolly misstating the law to the funeral buyer and sometimes by inferentially investing with the authority of law certain trade practices which they find it convenient or profitable to follow. This free and easy attitude to the law is even to be found in those institutions of higher learning, the colleges of mortuary science, where the fledgling undertaker receives his training. For example, it is the law in most states that when a decedent bequeaths his body for use in medical research, his survivors are bound to carry out his directions. Nonetheless, an embalming textbook, *Modern Mortuary Science,* disposes of the whole distasteful subject in a few misleading words: 'Q: Will the provisions in the will of a decedent that his body be given to a medical college for dissection be upheld over his widow? A: No . . . No one owns or controls his own body to the extent that he may dispose of the same in a manner which would bring humiliation and grief to the immediate members of his family.'

I had been told so often that funeral men tend to invent the law as they go along (for there is a fat financial reward at stake) that I decided to investigate this situation first hand. Armed with a copy of the California Code, I telephoned a leading undertaker in my community

with a concocted story: my aged aunt, living in my home, was seriously ill – not expected to live more than a few days. Her daughter
was coming here directly; but I felt I ought to have some suggestions,
some arrangements to propose in the event that . . . Sympathetic monosyllables from my interlocutor. The family would want something very
simple, I went on, just cremation. Of course, we can arrange all that,
I was assured. And since we want only cremation and there will be
no service, we should prefer not to buy a coffin. The undertaker's
voice at the other end was now alert, although smooth. He told me,
calmly and authoritatively, that it would be 'illegal' for him to enter
into such an arrangement. 'You mean, it would be against the law?'
I asked. Yes, indeed. 'In that case, perhaps we could take a body
straight to the crematorium in our station wagon?' A shocked silence,
followed by an explosive outburst: 'Madam, the average lady has
neither the facilities nor the inclination to be hauling dead bodies
around!' (Which was actually a good point, I thought.)

I tried two more funeral establishments and was told substantially
the same thing: cremation of an uncoffined body is prohibited under
California law. This was said, in all three cases, with such a ring of
conviction that I began to doubt the evidence before my eyes in the
state code. I reread the sections on cremation, on health requirements;
finally I read the whole thing from cover to cover. Finding nothing,
I checked with an officer of the Board of Health, who told me there
is no law in California requiring that a coffin be used when a body
is cremated. He added that indigents are cremated by some county
welfare agencies without benefit of coffin.

It was just this sort of tactic described above that moved the FTC
to rule in 1984 that morticians may no longer lie to the public.

The fifth unusual factor present in the funeral transaction is the availability to the buyer of relatively large sums of cash. The family accustomed to buying every major item on time – car, television set, furniture – and spending to the limit of the weekly pay cheque, suddenly
finds itself in possession of insurance funds and death-benefit payments,
often from a number of sources. It is usually unnecessary for the
undertaker to resort to crude means to ascertain the extent of insurance
coverage; a few simple and perfectly natural questions put to the
family while he is completing the vital statistics forms will serve to
elicit all he needs to know. For example, 'Occupation of the deceased?'
'Shall we bill the insurance company directly?'

The undertaker knows, better than a schoolboy knows the standings of the major-league baseball teams, the death-benefit payments of every trade union in the community, the Social Security and workmen's compensation scale of death benefits: Social Security payment, $255; if the deceased was a veteran, $300 more and free burial in a national cemetery; an additional funeral allowance of up to $5,000 under some state workers' compensation laws if the death was occupationally connected; and so on and so on.

The undertaker has all the information he needs to proceed with the sale. The widow, for the first time in possession of a large amount of ready cash, is likely to welcome his suggestions. He is, after all, the expert, the one who knows how these things should be arranged, who will steer her through the unfamiliar routines and ceremonies ahead, who will see that all goes as it should.

At the lowest end of the scale is the old-age pensioner, most of whose savings have long since been spent. He is among the poorest of the poor. Nevertheless, most state and county welfare agencies permit him to have up to $2,500 in cash; in some states he may own a modest home as well, without jeopardising his pension. The funeral director knows that under the law of virtually every state, the funeral bill is entitled to preference in payment as the first charge against the estate. There is every likelihood that the poor old chap will be sent out in high style unless his widow is a very, very cool customer indeed.

The situation that generally obtains in the funeral transaction was summed up by former Surrogate Court Judge Fowler of New York in passing upon the reasonableness of a bill which had come before him: 'One of the practical difficulties in such proceedings is that contracts for funerals are ordinarily made by persons differently situated. On the one side is generally a person greatly agitated or overwhelmed by vain regrets or deep sorrow, and on the other side persons whose business it is to minister to the dead for profit. One side is, therefore, often unbusinesslike, vague and forgetful, while the other is ordinarily alert, knowing and careful.'

The guiding rule in funeral pricing appears to be 'from each according to his means', regardless of the actual wishes of the family. A funeral director in San Francisco says, 'If a person drives a Cadillac, why should he have a Pontiac funeral?' The Cadillac symbol figures prominently in the mortician's thinking. This kind of reasoning is peculiar to the funeral industry. A person can drive up to an expensive restaurant in a Cadillac and can order, rather than the $40 dinner, a $2 cup of tea and he will be served. It is unlikely that the proprietor will point to his elegant furnishings and staff and demand that the Cadillac owner order something more commensurate with his ability to pay so as to help defray the overhead of the restaurant.

There is, however, one major difference between the restaurant transaction and the funeral transaction. It is clear that while the Cadillac owner may return to the restaurant tomorrow with a party of six and order $40 dinners all around, this will not be true of his dealings with the undertaker. In the funeral business it's strictly one to a customer. Very likely many a funeral director has echoed with heartfelt sincerity the patriotic sentiments of Nathan Hale: 'I only regret that I have but one life to lose for my country.'

There was a time when the undertaker's tasks were clear-cut and rather obvious, and when he billed his patrons accordingly. Typical late-nineteenth-century charges, in addition to the price of merchandise, are shown on bills of the period as: 'Services at the house (placing corpse in the coffin), $1.25', 'Preserving remains on ice, $10', 'Getting permit, $1.50'. It was customary for the undertaker to add a few dollars to his bill for being 'in attendance', which seems only fair and right. The cost of embalming was around $10 in 1880. An undertaker, writing in 1900, recommends these minimums for service charges: washing and dressing, $5; embalming, $10; hearse, $8 to $10. As Robert W. Habenstein and William M. Lamers, the historians of the trade, have pointed out, 'The undertaker had yet to conceive of the value of personal service offered professionally for a fee, legitimately claimed.' Well, he has now so conceived with a vengeance.

When weaving in the story of service as it is rendered today, spokesmen for the funeral industry tend to become so carried away by their own enthusiasm, so positively lyrical and copious in their declarations, that the outsider may have a little trouble understanding it all. There are indeed contradictions. Preferred Funeral Directors International has prepared a talk designed to inform people about service: 'The American public receive the services of employees and proprietor alike, nine and one half days of labour for every funeral handled, they receive the use of automobiles and hearses, a building including a chapel and other rooms which require building maintenance, insurance, taxes and licences, and depreciation, as well as heat in the winter, cooling in the summer, light and water.' The writer goes on to say that while the process of embalming takes only about three hours, 'it would be necessary for one man to work two forty-hour weeks to complete a funeral service. This is coupled with an additional forty hours of service required by members of other local allied professions, including the work of the cemeteries, newspapers and, of course, the most important of all, the service of your clergyman. These some 120 hours of labour are the basic value on which the cost of funerals rests.'

Our informant has lumped a lot of things together here. To start with 'the most important of all, the service of your clergyman': the average religious funeral service lasts no more than twenty-five minutes. Furthermore, it is not, of course, paid for by the funeral director. The 'work of the cemeteries' presumably means the opening and closing of a grave. This now mechanised operation, which takes fifteen to twenty minutes, is likewise not billed as part of the funeral director's costs. The work of 'newspapers'? This is a puzzler. Presumably, reference is made here to the publication of an obituary notice on the vital statistics page. It is, incidentally, surprising to learn that newspaper work is considered an 'allied profession'.

Just how insurance, taxes, licences and depreciation are figured in as part of the 120 man-hours of service is hard to tell. The writer does mention that his operation features '65 items of service'. In general, the funeral salesman is inclined to chuck in everything he does under the heading of 'service'. For example, in a typical list of 'services' he will include items like 'securing statistical data' (in other words, completing the death certificate and finding out how much insurance was left by the deceased), the 'arrangements conference' (in which the sale of the funeral to the survivors is made) and the 'keeping of records', by which he means his own bookkeeping work. Evidently, there is some confusion here between items that properly belong in a cost-accounting system and items of actual service rendered in any given funeral. In all likelihood, the idle time of employees is figured in and prorated as part of the 'man-hours'. The up-to-date funeral home operates on a twenty-four-hour basis, and the prepared speech contains this heartening news:

The funeral service profession of the United States is proud of the fact that there is not a person within the continental limits of the United States who is more than two hours away from a licensed funeral director and embalmer. That's one that even the fire-fighting apparatus of our country cannot match.

While the hit-or-miss rhetoric of the foregoing is fairly typical of the prose style of the funeral trade as a whole, and while the statement that 120 man-hours are devoted to a single funeral may be open to question, there really is a fantastic amount of service accorded the dead body and its survivors.

Having decreed what sort of funeral is right, proper and nice, and having gradually appropriated to himself all the functions connected with it, the funeral director has become responsible for a multitude of tasks – beyond the obvious one of 'placing corpse in the coffin' recorded in our nineteenth-century funeral bill. His self-imposed duties fall into two main categories: attention to the corpse itself, and the stage-managing of the funeral.

The drama begins to unfold with the arrival of the corpse at the mortuary.

Alas, poor Yorick! How surprised he would be to see how his counterpart of today is whisked off to a funeral parlour and is in short order sprayed, sliced, pierced, pickled, trussed, trimmed, creamed, waxed, painted, rouged and neatly dressed – transformed from a common corpse into a Beautiful Memory Picture. This process is known in the trade as embalming and restorative art, and is so universally employed in the United States and Canada that for years the funeral director did it routinely, without consulting corpse or kin. He regards as eccentric those few who are hardy enough to suggest that it might be dispensed with. Yet no law requires embalming, no religious doctrine commends it, nor is it dictated by considerations of health, sanitation or even of personal daintiness. In no part of the world but in North America is it widely used. The purpose of embalming is to make the corpse presentable for viewing in a suitably costly container; and here too the funeral director routinely, without first consulting the family, prepares the body for public display.

Is all this legal? The processes to which a dead body may be subjected are, after all, to some extent circumscribed by law. In most states, for instance, the signature of next of kin must be obtained before an autopsy may be performed, before the deceased may be cremated, before the body may be turned over to a medical school for research purposes; or such provision must be made in the decedent's will. In the case of embalming, permission is required (under Federal Trade

Commission rules) only if a charge is to be made for the procedure. Embalming is not, as funeral providers habitually claim, a legal requirement even when the body of the deceased is to be on display in an open casket. A textbook, *The Principles and Practices of Embalming,* comments on this: 'There is some question regarding the legality of much that is done within the preparation room.' The author points out that it would be most unusual for a responsible member of a bereaved family to instruct the mortician, in so many words, to 'embalm' the body of a deceased relative. The very term 'embalming' is so seldom used that the mortician must rely upon custom in the matter. The author concludes that unless the family specifies otherwise, the act of entrusting the body to the care of a funeral establishment carries with it an implied permission to go ahead and embalm.

Embalming is indeed a most extraordinary procedure, and one must wonder at the docility of Americans who each year pay hundreds of millions of dollars for its perpetuation, blissfully ignorant of what it is all about, what is done and how it is done. Not one in 10,000 has any idea of what actually takes place. Books on the subject are extremely hard to come by. You will not find them in your neighbourhood bookshop or library.

In an era when huge television audiences watch surgical operations in the comfort of their living rooms, when, thanks to the animated cartoon, the geography of the digestive system has become familiar territory even to the nursery-school set, in a land where the satisfaction of curiosity about almost all matters is a national pastime, surely the secrecy surrounding embalming cannot be attributed to the inherent gruesomeness of the subject. Custom in this regard has within this century suffered a complete reversal. In the early days of American embalming, when it was performed in the home of the deceased, it was almost mandatory for some relative to stay by the embalmer's side and witness the procedure. Today, family members who might wish to be in attendance would certainly be dissuaded by the funeral director. All others, except apprentices, are usually barred by law from the preparation room.

A close look at what actually does take place may explain in large measure the undertaker's intractable reticence concerning a procedure that has become his major *raison d'être*. Is it possible he fears that public information about embalming might lead patrons to wonder if they really want this service? If the funeral men are loath to discuss the subject outside the trade, the reader may, understandably, be equally loath to go on reading at this point. For those who have the stomach for it, let us part the formaldehyde curtain. Others should skip a few pages.

The body is first laid out in the undertaker's morgue – or, rather, Mr Jones is reposing in the preparation room to be readied to bid the world farewell.

The preparation room in any of the better funeral establishments has the tiled and sterile look of a surgery, and indeed the embalmer/restorative artist who does his chores there is beginning to adopt the term 'dermasurgeon' (appropriately corrupted by some mortician-writers as 'demi-surgeon') to describe his calling. His equipment – consisting of scalpels, scissors, augers, forceps, clamps, needles, pumps, tubes, bowls and basins – is crudely imitative of the surgeon's, as is his technique, acquired in a nine- or twelve-month post-high-school course at an embalming school. He is supplied by an advanced chemical industry with a bewildering array of fluids, sprays, pastes, oils, powders, creams, to fix or soften tissue, shrink or distend it as needed, dry it here, restore the moisture there. There are cosmetics, waxes and paints to fill and cover features, even plaster of Paris to replace entire limbs. There are ingenious aids to prop and stabilise the cadaver: a VariPose Head Rest, the Edwards Arm and Hand Positioner, the Repose Block (to support the shoulders during the embalming), and the Throop Foot Positioner, which resembles an old-fashioned stocks.

Mr John H. Eckels, president of the Eckels College of Mortuary Science, thus describes the first part of the embalming procedure: 'In the hands of a skilled practitioner, this work may be done in a comparative short time and without mutilating the body other than by slight incision so slight that it scarcely would cause serious inconvenience if made upon a living person. It is necessary to remove the blood, and doing this not only helps in the disinfecting, but removes the principal cause of disfigurements due to discoloration.'

Another textbook discusses the all-important time element: 'The earlier this is done, the better, for every hour that elapses between death and embalming will add to the problems and complications encountered . . .' Just how soon should one get going on the embalming? The author tells us, 'On the basis of such scanty information made available to this profession through its rudimentary and haphazard system of technical research, we must conclude that the best results are to be obtained if the subject is embalmed before life is completely extinct – that is, before cellular death has occurred. In the average case, this would mean within an hour after somatic death.' For those who feel that there is something a little rudimentary, not to say haphazard, about this advice, a comforting thought is offered by another writer. 'Speaking of fears entertained in the early days of premature burial,' he points out, 'one of the effects of embalming by chemical injection, however, has been to dispel fears of live burial.' How true; once the blood is removed, chances of live burial are indeed remote.

To return to Mr Jones, the blood is drained out through the veins and replaced by embalming fluid pumped in through the arteries. As noted in *The Principles and Practices of Embalming*, 'Every operator has a favourite injection and drainage point – a fact which becomes a handicap only if he fails or refuses to forsake his favourites when conditions demand it.' Typical favourites are the carotid artery, femoral artery, jugular vein and subclavian vein. There are various choices of embalming fluid. If Flextone is used, it will produce a 'mild, flexible rigidity. The skin retains a velvety softness, the tissues are rubbery and pliable. Ideal for women and children.' It may be blended with B. and G. Products Company's Lyf-Lyk tint, which is guaranteed to reproduce 'nature's own skin texture . . . the velvety appearance of living tissue'. Suntone comes in three separate tints: Suntan; Special Cosmetic Tint; moderately pink.

About three to six gallons of a dyed and perfumed solution of formaldehyde, glycerin, borax, phenol, alcohol and water is soon circulating through Mr Jones, whose mouth has been sewn together with a 'needle directed upwards between the upper lip and gum and brought out through the left nostril', with the corners raised slightly 'for a more pleasant expression'. If he should be buck-toothed, his teeth are cleaned with Bon Ami and coated with colourless nail polish. His eyes, meanwhile, are closed with flesh-tinted eye caps and eye cement.

The next step is to have at Mr Jones with a thing called a trocar. This is a long, hollow needle attached to a tube. It is jabbed into the abdomen and poked around the entrails and chest cavity, the contents of which are pumped out and replaced with 'cavity fluid'. This done, and the hole in the abdomen having been sewn up, Mr Jones's face is heavily creamed (to protect the skin from burns which may be caused by leakage of the chemicals), and he is covered with a sheet and left unmolested for a while. But not for long – there is more, much more, in store for him. He has been embalmed, but not yet restored, and the best time to start the restorative work is eight to ten hours after embalming, when the tissues have become firm and dry.

The object of all this attention to the corpse, it must be remembered, is to make it presentable for viewing in an attitude of healthy repose. 'Our customs require the presentation of our dead in the semblance of normality . . . unmarred by the ravages of illness, disease or mutilation,' says Mr J. Sheridan Mayer in his *Restorative Art*. This is rather a large order since few people die in the full bloom of health, unravaged by illness and unmarked by some disfigurement. The funeral industry is equal to the challenge: 'In some cases the gruesome appearance of a mutilated or disease-ridden subject may be quite discouraging. The task of restoration may seem impossible and shake the confidence of the embalmer. This is the time for intestinal fortitude and determination. Once the formative work is begun and affected tissues are cleaned or removed, all doubts of success vanish. It is surprising and gratifying to discover the results which may be obtained.'

The embalmer, having allowed an appropriate interval to elapse, returns to the attack, but now brings into play the skill and equipment of sculptor and cosmetician. Is a hand missing? Casting one in plaster of Paris is a simple matter. 'For replacement purposes, only a cast of the back of the hand is necessary; this is within the ability of the average operator and is quite adequate.' If a lip or two, a nose or an ear should be missing, the embalmer has at hand a variety of restorative waxes with which to model replacements. Pores and skin texture are simulated by stippling with a little brush, and over this cosmetics are laid on. Head off? Decapitation cases are rather routinely handled. Ragged edges are trimmed, and head joined to torso with a series of splints, wires and sutures. It is a good idea to have a little something at the neck – a scarf or high collar – when time for viewing comes. Swollen mouth? Cut out tissue as needed from inside the lips. If too much is removed, the surface contour can easily be restored by padding with cotton. Swollen neck and cheeks are reduced by removing tissue through vertical incisions made down each side of the neck. 'When the deceased is casketed, the pillow will hide the suture incisions . . . [A]s an extra precaution against leakage, the suture may be painted with liquid sealer.'

The opposite condition is more likely to present itself – that of emaciation. His hypodermic syringe now loaded with massage cream, the embalmer seeks out and fills the hollowed and sunken areas by injection. In this procedure, the backs of the hands and fingers and the under-chin area should not be neglected.

Positioning the lips is a problem that recurrently challenges the ingenuity of the embalmer. Closed too tightly, they tend to give a stern, even disapproving expression. Ideally, embalmers feel, the lips should give the impression of being ever so slightly parted, the upper lip protruding slightly for a more youthful appearance. This takes some engineering, however, as the lips tend to drift apart. Lip drift can sometimes be remedied by pushing one or two straight pins through the inner margin of the lower lip and then inserting them between the two front upper teeth. If Mr Jones happens to have no teeth, the pins can just as easily be anchored in his Armstrong Face Former and Denture Replacer. Another method to maintain lip closure is to dislocate the lower jaw, which is then held in its new position by wire run through holes which have been drilled through the upper and lower jaws at the midline. As the French are fond of saying, *il faut souffrir pour être belle*.

If Mr Jones has died of jaundice, the embalming fluid will very likely turn green. Does this deter the embalmer? Not if he has intestinal fortitude. Masking pastes and cosmetics are heavily laid on, burial garments and casket interiors are colour-correlated with particular care, and Jones is displayed beneath rose-coloured lights. Friends will say, 'How *well* he looks.' Death by carbon monoxide, on the other hand, can be rather a good thing from the embalmer's viewpoint: 'One advantage is the fact that this type of discoloration is an exaggerated form of a natural pink coloration.' This is nice because the healthy glow is already present and needs but little attention.

The patching and filling completed, Mr Jones is now shaved, washed and dressed. A cream-based cosmetic, available in pink, flesh, suntan, brunette and blond, is applied to his hands and face, his hair is shampooed and combed (and, in the case of Mrs Jones, set), his hands manicured. For the horny-handed son of toil, special care must be taken; cream should be applied to remove ingrained grime, and the nails cleaned. 'If he were not in the habit of having them manicured in life, trimming and shaping is advised for better appearance – never questioned by kin.'

Jones is now ready for casketing (this is the present participle of the verb 'to casket'). In this operation his right shoulder should be depressed slightly 'to turn the body a bit to the right and soften the appearance of lying flat on the back'. Positioning the hands is a matter of importance, and special rubber positioning blocks may be used. The hands should be cupped slightly for a more lifelike, relaxed appearance. Proper placement of the body requires a delicate sense of balance. It should lie as high as possible in the casket, yet not so high that the lid, when lowered, will hit the nose. On the other hand, we are cautioned, placing the body too low 'creates the impression that the body is in a box'.

Jones is next wheeled into the appointed slumber room, where a few last touches may be added – his favourite pipe placed in his hand, or, if he was a great reader, a book propped into position. (In the case of little Master Jones, a teddy bear may be clutched.) Here he will hold open house for a few days, visiting hours 10 a.m. to 5 p.m.

All now being in readiness, the funeral director calls a staff conference to make sure that each assistant knows his precise duties. Mr Wilber Krieger writes: 'This makes your staff feel that they are a part of the team, with a definite assignment that must be properly carried out if the whole plan is to succeed. You never heard of a football coach who failed to talk to his entire team before they go on the field. They have been drilled on the plays they are to execute for hours and days, and yet the successful coach knows the importance of making even the bench-warming third-string substitute feel that he is important if the game is to be won.' The winning of *this* game is predicated upon a glass-smooth handling of the logistics. The funeral director has notified the pallbearers, whose names were furnished by the family, has arranged for the presence of a clergyman, organist and soloist, has provided transportation for everybody, has organised and listed the flowers sent by friends. In *Psychology of Funeral Service*, Mr Edward A. Martin points out: 'He may not always do as much as the family thinks he is doing, but it is his helpful guidance that they appreciate in knowing they are proceeding as they should . . . The important thing is how well his services can be used to make the family believe they are giving unlimited expression to their own sentiment.'

The religious service may be held in a church or in the chapel of the funeral home; the funeral director vastly prefers the latter arrangement, for not only is it more convenient for him, but it affords him the opportunity to show off his beautiful facilities to the gathered mourners. After the clergyman has had his say, the mourners queue up to file past the casket for a last look at the deceased. The family is not asked whether they want an open-casket ceremony; in the absence of instruction to the contrary, this is taken for granted. Consequently, well over 68 per cent of all American funerals in the mid-1990s featured an open casket – a custom unknown in other parts of the world. Foreigners are astonished by it. An Englishwoman living in San Francisco described her reaction in a letter to the writer:

> I myself have attended only one funeral here – that of an elderly fellow worker of mine. After the service I could not understand why everyone was walking towards the coffin (sorry, I mean casket), but thought I had better follow the crowd. It shook me rigid to get there and find the casket open and poor old Oscar lying there in his brown tweed suit, wearing a suntan make-up and just the wrong shade of lipstick. If I had not been extremely fond of the old boy, I have a horrible feeling that I might have giggled. Then and there I decided that I could never face another American funeral – even dead.

The casket (which has been resting throughout the service on a Classic Beauty Ultra Metal Casket Bier) is now transferred by a hydrauli- cally operated device called Porto-Lift to a balloon-tyred, Glide Easy casket carriage which will wheel it to yet another conveyance, the Cadillac Funeral Coach. This may be lavender, cream, light green. Black, once de rigueur, is coming back into fashion. Interiors, of course, are colour-correlated, 'for the man who cannot stop short of perfection'.

At graveside, the casket is lowered into the earth. This office, once the prerogative of friends of the deceased, is now performed by a patented mechanical lowering device. A 'Lifetime Green' artificial grass mat is at the ready to conceal the sere earth, and overhead, to conceal the sky, is a portable Steril Chapel Tent ('resists the intense heat and humidity of summer and the terrific storms of winter . . . available in Silver Grey, Rose or Evergreen'). Now is the time for the ritual scattering of the earth over the coffin, as the solemn words 'earth to earth, ashes to ashes, dust to dust' are pronounced by the officiating cleric. This can today be accomplished 'with a mere flick of the wrist with the Gordon Leak-Proof Earth Dispenser. No grasping of a handful of dirt, no soiled fingers. Simple, dignified, beautiful, reverent! The modern way!' The Gordon Earth Dispenser is of nickel-plated brass construction. It is not only 'attractive to the eye and long wearing';

it is also 'one of the "tools" for building better public relations' if presented as 'an appropriate non-commercial gift' to the clergy. It is shaped something like a saltshaker.

Untouched by human hand, the coffin and the earth are now united.

It is in the function of directing the participants through this maze of gadgetry that the funeral director has assigned to himself his relatively new role of 'grief therapist'. He has relieved the family of every detail, he has revamped the corpse to look like a living doll, he has arranged for it to nap for a few days in a slumber room, he has put on a well-oiled performance in which the concept of *death* has played no part whatsoever – unless it was inconsiderately mentioned by the clergyman who conducted the religious service. He has done everything in his power to make the funeral a real pleasure for everybody concerned. He and his team have given their all to score an upset victory over death.

JAMES CAMERON

Through the Looking-Glass

1966

Soon after I arrived in 'Fleet Street', the physical and spiritual home of British journalism, I wrote to one of its heroes, the foreign correspondent James Cameron, asking him to come to a party in my bolt-hole of a flat in Covent Garden market. 'You can't miss it,' I wrote, 'there's a truck full of cabbages parked at the front door.' All this was bravado; he wouldn't come, of course. But he did: standing at my door, clutching a bottle of Johnnie Walker. 'I'm Cameron,' he said.

That was 1965, and 'Jimmy' Cameron had not long returned from North Vietnam, where he was the first Western journalist to report from Ho Chi Minh's side of America's fast expanding war in Indo-China. President Lyndon Johnson had begun 'Operation Rolling Thunder', the most sustained aerial bombardment in the history of warfare, and the first divisions of American combat troops had landed in the south.

After years of 'hammering at the increasingly unresponsive door of the North', Cameron, a film cameraman and a photographer were given visas to Hanoi. To ensure their independence, he insisted they pay their own way, and although their movement was restricted, they were allowed to report freely from Hanoi and the front line near the border with South Vietnam. Cameron also secured rare interviews with President Ho Chi Minh and Prime Minister Pham Van Dong.

Unlike many of his colleagues in the south, who saw Vietnam not as a human community but as a battlefield to be 'won' or 'lost' by 'us', Cameron's reporting concentrated on the *people* of Vietnam, their vulnerability, endurance and resilience beneath the barrage of a new range of 'anti-personnel' bombs: white phosphorus that caused fire-storms and 'pellet bombs' that showered needles. He and Wilfred Burchett and the American Harrison Salisbury were the first reporters to let ordinary peasants and soldiers in North Vietnam, and politicians, speak to the West; and what emerged was the antithesis of the Asian Prussians portrayed in the myths of the time. 'Once you turn all the political value judgements into terms of people,' Cameron wrote, 'they become both simpler and more difficult.'

He expressed this vividly in the dedication of his book *Witness*. 'I have never dedicated a book to anyone before,' he wrote, 'but I would like to present this one to an old lady who lives in the village of Nanh Nganh, in the Thanh Hoa province of North Vietnam, which is unfortunately near to a strategically important bridge. The bridge, as far as I know, still stands, but the old lady had her left arm blown off by one of the bombs that went somewhat astray. She was more fortunate than her daughter, who was killed. She said, "I suppose there is a reason for all this, but I do not understand what it is. I think I am too old now ever to find out."'

When his dispatches appeared in the London *Evening Standard* and the *New York Times*, he was attacked for his 'lack of objectivity'; *Time* magazine called him a 'conduit for the North Vietnamese Communists'. Cameron responded with characteristic dryness: 'My definition of "conduit", in common with that of a dictionary, is a "channel". I noted down and recorded what diverse people in North Vietnam told me . . . thereafter I printed it in newspapers exactly as noted. It is true that I did not intersperse this record with descriptions of [Prime Minister] Pham Van Dong as a slant-eyed, evasive, yellow-skinned and doubtless anti-American example of Asian Communism; I merely put down what he said. I have no objection to that being defined as the behaviour of a "conduit" or channel . . . If the function of a reporter is not that of a channel, I am at a loss to know what his function is, unless it be that of writing for *Time*.'

What upset his critics was that he had illuminated the Americans' biggest mistake in Vietnam and which led to their defeat. They had completely failed to understand the Vietnamese, whom they dismissed as 'gooks' and 'slits' in thrall to their worldwide nemesis, communism. They refused to recognise that the Vietnamese were fighting an anticolonial struggle against *them*, just as the same people had fought and expelled the French. That the leadership in Hanoi was communist was beside the point; Ho Chi Minh had long regarded the Chinese communists as being almost as threatening as the Americans.

Cameron's conclusion was that the war was as 'imbecile' as it was brutal. His humane common sense, however, went too far for the BBC, which bought cameraman Malcolm Aird's film of their visit, then suppressed it as 'unacceptable in the current circumstances'. In the following extract from *Witness*, Cameron's descriptive power shows that which television would not.

THROUGH THE LOOKING-GLASS

One felt extremely alone in Hanoi. Among its 600,000 inhabitants there seemed to be nobody like oneself – nor was there, nor had there been for years. It had been far from easy to get there; the thing was virtually unprecedented, and felt it. This was not a place where non-Communist Westerners were welcomed, since recently the only ones who had come had arrived in B-50s and F-105s and blown things up, like bridges and people, which was not agreeable when you saw it, nor indeed very persuasive. My European face was accepted so long as I was taken to be a Russian technician or a Czech diplomat; when they learned who I was the reaction was astonishment, curiosity and doubt.

But one was through the looking-glass at last, in the capital of North Vietnam, in Hanoi, which the Americans will say is full of demons and the Communists will say is full of heroes. It seemed to me, on the contrary, to be very full of people, largely indistinguishable from those of Saigon except in the bleak austerity of their condition.

The important thing was that one was now *through* the looking-glass, and everything outside – home and London and New York; everything – was now a sort of mirror-image, where black was white and white was black, good was bad and bad was good, defence was aggression, military efficiency was wanton cruelty, right was wrong. It was not the first time this had happened to me, but more strikingly now than ever before. Once you turn all the political value-judgements into terms of people, they become both simpler and more difficult.

North Vietnam was littered with broken bridges and pulverised roads, but the bridge over the vast Song Hong was intact, spanning the mile-wide Red River that is, indeed, red: a great warm stream of tomato soup. The waters were receding in the dry season; as the banks of silt appeared the peasants descended on them, and cultivated them; they could get a crop off them before the rains returned and drowned the plots.

In the pretty parks by the lakeside were glass showcases of pictures from what are called the 'other comrade countries'. Their names read oddly, transliterated into the tonal monosyllables of Vietnamese: Hun-ga-ri, Ro-ma-ni, Bun-ga-ri, Cu-ba, Ce-sko-wak.

But the centrepiece was the board – in a fanciful way it was like a cricket score-board – that announced the daily figure of US planes shot down. That day they claimed no fewer than ten – in one day, could it be possible? The design on the board was the ubiquitous one of the peasant girl laying down her reaping-hook and pointing her rifle dauntlessly at the sky. One knew it wasn't all done by rifles, but the gesture is important.

I found the figure hard to swallow. Ten in a day! 'J'espère qu'ils sont des prisonniers.' 'Pourquoi?' 'Parce que – je suppose qu'on a eu assez de la mort.' We stared at the score-board, turning war into mathematics, as we did twenty-five years ago in England in the days when it was our turn. It is part of this oblique fantasy that the Vietnam-ese word for aircraft, when it is not officially 'rabid-imperialist-aggressor', is almost coquettish: *may bay*.

Civil defence rehearsals happen all the time. I saw them in the fields of the farm co-operatives, where the alarm was given drama-tically on a drum; in the car-repair factory, where it was sounded on a very old empty French bomb.

The constant emphasis on rifle-drill had a serious purpose obvi-ously not wholly connected with shooting down US planes. The idea that an F-4B Phantom bomber flying at 1,500 mph can be vulner-able to a pretty little peasant girl with a musket is so implausible that serious Vietnamese dislike debating the subject. Doubtless in the early days after 'escalation' some US pilots took the risks too lightly and dawdled somewhat over these harmless paddy-fields, and certainly were destroyed with rifle fire. The necessarily steep angle of dive-bombing also makes them a momentarily good target for a very intrepid machine-gunner.

But clearly a great number of the stricken planes were destroyed by sophisticated anti-aircraft equipment, and the Russian-installed surface-to-air missiles which dot the countryside, serviced by the Soviet technicians one occasionally met on their rare binges in the city. Twice I passed these things, shrouded in the darkness. No one discussed them.

The endless rifle-talk was certainly psychological. It consoled the peasant into a sense of positive activity, of sharing; it was an invaluable means of channelling off his frustration. It was a powerful part of civilian morale. Every Village Committee Room had its Aircraft Recognition Charts, the outlines of the B-52, the A-40, the F-105; the weapon-identifications: 'roccet', 'bom', 'na-pom'. And when the arms-drills were signalled they were taken deadly seriously; there were no larks.

The Farming Co-operatives were five years old, and about 40 per cent of the peasants were involved, I was told – about 150 households per unit in the delta, fifty in the mountains. Every member claimed, naturally, to be unquestionably better off. But for a Vietnamese peasant to own a blanket and a mat and a mosquito net is to be well off.

In Hanoi virtually no private motor-traffic existed, but what did exist was, like all military transport, heavily camouflaged under piles of branches, palm-fronds, banana-leaves. Even in the towns this phenomenon continued, cars and lorries buried in greenery; Birnam Wood forever coming to Dunsinane.

The people, too – every citizen went for his military exercises with a cape of vegetation hanging about his shoulders. It was, perhaps, taken slightly to excess: the cult of camouflage had become in a way modish, and the new standard hat for everyone of importance was, paradoxically, a sort of topi of marked old-fashioned colonial appearance, garnished with little fronds of green cloth. The buses had rationalised the whole thing by being spray-painted in a formal pattern of foliage, like Oriental wallpaper.

Maybe the thing had become a little theatrical – but whom could it be supposed to impress, in a place that sees almost no strangers? This was a land where everyone considered it necessary to live in disguise, to inhabit their own country pretending they were not there, but invisible, resentfully. Rifles abounded in the most improbable places. There was a strong analogy of the early days of Israel, the same sense of wariness and never-ending siege.

You could call it what you liked, but it was a war, an enduring war and a special war, a dedicated and, within the limits of workable society, a complete one. There might be many arguments about its righteousness; they came as a rule from people 10,000 miles away.

I just happened to be where few of the politicians or the soldiers or the statesmen who talked about North Vietnam had ever been – that is, in North Vietnam.

Through the hours of daylight practically nothing whatever moved on four wheels on the roads of North Vietnam: hardly a car or a truck; from the air, in the sunlight, it must have looked as though the country had no wheeled transport at all. That, of course, was the idea. It was the roads and the bridges that were being bombed; it was held to be no longer safe, after sunrise, to be near either. Furthermore it was the illusion that was important; there was a kind of aesthetic importance in creating illusions, and there were, of course, two. One was that the North of Vietnam is a growing and progressive industrial nation. The other was that, between sunrise and sunset, it was inhabited by nobody at all.

In the paddy-fields in the sunlight the farmers were reaping their third harvest of the year, which had been especially abundant. I know nothing of the craft, but it seemed to me odd, in that here one could see every successive process of agriculture in train at the same time: within a mile people were ploughing the fields, sowing the seed, reaping the crop and threshing the harvest. They moved among the rice with their sickles – snick, snick, grasp; snick, hold and turn over; snick and fold; the wonderfully economical and accomplished peasant movement; what would a time-and-motion operator make of this? They moved among the rice bowed under a shawl of foliage, the camouflage that gave everyone a kind of carnival air, like so many Jack-o'-the-Greens. At the corners of every field stood what looked like sheaves of iron corn, and which were stacks of rifles. The roads stretched long and empty, leading from nowhere to nowhere. One could have taken it for a charade; in this land does *nothing* travel from place to place?

Then the sun went down, and everything started to move.

At dusk the roads became alive. From a thousand arbours and copses and the shelter of trees the traffic materialised; the engines were started and the convoys emerged from invisibility, began to grind away through the darkness behind the pinpoints of masked headlights. There were miles of them – heavy Russian-built lorries, anti-aircraft batteries of guns, all deeply buried under layers of branches and leaves; processions of huge green haystacks. By day

North Vietnam is abandoned; by night it thuds and groans with movement. It was an excessively fatiguing routine for those of us who were trying to capture this peculiar picture: moving always by night, and working always by day.

In this fashion I drove down to what is called the 'fighting area' in the central province of Thanh Hoa.

It is not a 'fighting area' at all, in the sense that every province of South Vietnam is a 'fighting area'; in North Vietnam no battles take place, no guerrillas resist, no American soldiers aggress; north of the 17th Parallel there is no ground-bound war. This is merely the neighbourhood most vulnerable, and most attacked by the air-raiders.

It was far from easy to get permission to go. Permits were held back – and I imagine reasonably – simply because it was held to be an unsafe part of the country, and nobody was particularly anxious to have me killed. I cannot for a moment imagine that anyone in North Vietnam would have felt personally bereaved at my disappearance, but I can understand that to have observed this dubious Westerner going to his maker under a stick of American high-explosive would, at this juncture, have been an embarrassment – not without its own especial ironies, but a confounded nuisance. Repeatedly I was asked to appreciate the importance of their responsibility. It seemed to me most excessive. The manager of the hotel in Hanoi, who was very small but one of the most bloodthirsty men I ever met, kept darting forth and saying: 'Now you will understand the truth. Now you will see for yourself. Whomh, whomh – then you will know. Try some suffering, monsieur; how splendid.'

I thought of saying that I had probably had a good deal more whomh, whomh in my life than he had in his, and from a greater variety of sources, since for a number of years that had been my imbecile trade, but it seemed to serve little purpose. I was in any case dependent on this ebullient little patriot to supply me with enough food to last me the journey.

So in this fashion I drove down to the 'fighting area', in the central province of Thanh Hoa. How many nights I was to spend in this way, bouncing around in a Russian jeep, buried in iron-clad technical luggage, my knees overlain by Mr Thing, praying for the dawn.

It was a landscape of almost wildly theatrical beauty. The moon was full. We cleared the city checkpoint – no one leaves Hanoi by road without a clearance – and rumbled down through the Vietnamese countryside which, in certain conditions, is wholly bizarre. It is a

plain studded with strange little precipitous mountains, as though a
shower of enormous meteorites had become embedded in the land;
it is a geological phenomenon I do not understand; once before I had
seen it, in the South Chinese province of Kwangsi; in the light of the
full moon it is eerie beyond expression; it is like living in the heart
of a seventeenth-century Oriental water-colour.

Two hours out of Hanoi we were stopped; all the convoys were
halted. Everybody got out and smoked cigarettes, and relaxed on the
little stacks of rice-straw that had been left to dry beside the road. A
couple of hours earlier there had been a raid, a clean hit on the
highway, and the road was for the time being impassable. It was, they
said, happening all the time.

By and by we got on the move again; by the time we inched through
the darkness to the bombed area it seemed it was already passable,
though only with difficulty. It was hard to see in the darkness what
was happening – though later, after many such experiences, I came
to know: great multitudes of women had somehow been recruited or
accumulated from the neighbourhood and were filling in the holes
and reconstituting some sort of a surface for the road, out of the piles
of stones and gravel that were permanently kept by the roadside, I
assume for just this purpose. It was impossible to count the number
of women, but there were several hundred. This, they said, happened
frequently; almost every major road in the country was in a semi-
permanent condition of running repair.

Two main bridges on the road ahead were gone long since; they
had been destroyed in the early raids; they had been replaced with
pontoons of bamboo rafts. Usually the replacement was a ferry; North
Vietnam is a wilderness of ferries in the delta region; they take up a
tremendous proportion of travelling time. Some were manipulated by
a motor-launch that nudged them across from alongside; some were
manhandled over by crews of men pulling them over by a fixed cable.
For anyone obliged to drive much through the nights of the Red River
delta they were a terrible bore. Sometimes a pontoon-bridge was alter-
nated with a ferry, to cause confusion among the American recon-
naisance aircraft. Frequently with the makeshift bridges, when daylight
came and traffic stopped, one end of the floating bridge was detached,
so that the whole structure could drift down and lie parallel with the
bank, and become invisible. There never was a place where such
importance was attached to invisibility.

But the great showplace of the province of Thanh Hoa was the famous Ham Rong bridge. This, too, has almost become part of the folklore of Vietnam. It was not an especially impressive bridge, though it carried a road and a railway, but it had become a dedi-cated object of American attention. It had been attacked – they said, when I got there – more than 100 times, by at least 1,000 aircraft. It was scarred and pitted and twisted; its girders were deeply burned and marked, and the area around it was in a terrible mess, but the bridge endured, and still carried both the road and the railroad. It lay in a kind of ravine between two very steep little hills; it was probably extremely hard to hit; it would require a very steep, oblique and difficult bombing-approach.

It was my impression, and I am not wholly ignorant of the processes of tactical bombing, that the United States' attacks on North Vietnam had been, as they claimed, aimed generally at what they could define as military objectives – that is to say, bridges and roads. Whether a great power can claim justification for the arbitrary blowing up of the bridges and roads of an alien state against whom they have not invoked the civility of even declaring war is a separate question. It is no particular secret that I, personally, am vehemently and explicitly against the whole thing; I am obliged to insist that I am vigorously opposed to anybody bombing anybody, but especially against this, which seems to me to be as wanton as it is useless; both militarily silly and individually cruel. At the same time it is fatuous to define the United States assault on North Vietnam as 'terror bombing'; the strikes have been against objects that I suppose some obtuse and pedantic commander could define as legitimate, in his limited sense. The difficulty is, with a society that did not build itself in the image of a fortress, that people tend to accrete and establish themselves in the neighbourhoods of roads and bridges, for reasons of convenience, and that in consequence their habitations tend to suffer when such things are bombed, especially when they are bombed by operators who are not only rather poor shots, but have no particular reason to care about the secondary effects of their performance, and who may reason that in a place like Vietnam any moderately substantial building must have some military function.

I do not believe that the Americans set out to bomb homes and hospitals; if they had wished to do so it would have been extremely easy to do so. Nevertheless it is a fact that homes and hospitals have been destroyed by their bombs. I do not think the strategic thinkers of the United States Air Force intended to wage war on the peasants of North Vietnam; nevertheless they managed to kill quite a few.

The *New York Times* estimated that in the ten months before my visit more than 18,000 bombing sorties had been flown against the North – an average of about sixty a day – with a total of some 36,000 tons of bombs. The North Vietnam estimate is a great deal higher.

In the vicinity of the Ham Rong bridge was the only bombed hospital I saw: a tuberculosis clinic that had taken a loose stick of bombs on both sides; it was blasted and deserted. Its equipment had been taken away, or such of it as was worth taking away; a group of old men were desultorily salvaging beams and panels that looked as though they might be of use elsewhere. The houses of the village beside it were shells, deserted.

In the nearby co-operative of Xoan Hanh the villagers, threshing the rice with very medieval-looking flails beside a stacked pile of modern Czech automatic rifles, recalled that the hospital had gone three months earlier. They were not especially dramatic about it; there had been only three casualties, they said; it was largely an out-patient clinic. Why, I asked, had not something been done about repairing it? The neighbourhood, they replied, was raided so frequently it would hardly be worth it; instead the institution had been rebuilt miles away, they had no idea where.

The province of Thanh Hoa is the biggest in the north of Vietnam – it has about 10,000 square kilometres, and a population of two million. It is described as the first line of resistance for the North, and the rear of the revolution of the National Liberation Front.

'Is there much interchange of people? Do you get southerners crossing up here; do you send men down there?'

'Not much through here. We understand most of that traffic goes down the western border. But like everyone else in North Vietnam, many of us have relatives in the South, and the other way round; there are thousands of relatives who have never managed to see each other for ten years.'

Since the 'escalation' Thanh Hoa has been the province that has been worst hit of all in the North. They claimed to have logged more than 400 United States sorties, involving about 1,500 aircraft. They also claimed to have shot down just rather more than 100; this was of course uncheckable.

There was a rather curious *façon de vivre* in Thanh Hoa, involving a daily removal. We arrived in the hours of darkness, as one can do no other in the peculiar circumstances of contemporary North Vietnam transport, and were bedded in what seemed a quite new if rather austere State Guest House. At dawn we were obliged, as they called it, to 'evacuate' it. It was held to be unsafe by daylight; it was too near the celebrated bridge. We then drove a dozen miles or so and set up headquarters in another, smaller, infinitely tattier and more engaging establishment, a four-roomed thatched bungalow with no amenities whatsoever but with a great deal of broken-down charm. Its thatch was inhabited by great numbers of bats, who emerged at dusk in whirling squadrons. The night air crepitated to the sound of cicada, the anthem of South-East Asia. To some this noise, like the sound of an unstoppable sewing-machine, is tiresome and exasperating; I find it the most soothing sound on earth.

But we still had to return to establishment number one to take our bath; huge pans of boiling water ladled into tubs in unlit bathrooms; there is an interesting sensual satisfaction in bathing in the darkness which may repay further experimentation.

This was the first opportunity I had had of seeing the countryside by daylight. How much more attractive is all of South-East Asia outside its towns! Here was the Far East of the conventional imagination, of the scroll paintings and the silken screens; a composition of waters and mountainsides and mists, curious trees and amber lighting; in some inexplicable way at the same time both empty and vitally inhabited.

I think most Westerners have some difficulty in really comprehending the extraordinary intensity of effort necessary even for subsistence in many of these Asian lands, where for so long a man could be tipped over almost to starvation by some quite marginal circumstance – by a poor harvest, by a rain failure, by the caprice of his local taxation officer, even by the hazard of a funeral or a wedding, and the ensuing load of debt. Work was so exhaustingly hard it left little energy to spill over into politics, and government, local or colonial, had been something remote, a factor to be avoided by every stratagem, especially at times of tax collection and war.

How odd that one should have invented the myth that the Asians are fatalists, that they are 'passive' – the Asians who live in a land so incessantly exacting, where a man must wield a scoop all day to irrigate his fields, that must be forever preserved from attack and nourished with the products of his own body, that demands every sort of quality *except* fatalism.

Here were the villages, and the mud bricks drying in the sun – the villages that grew out of the land, were made from the land, that crumbled back into the land to make more bricks for more villages; the endless cycle that had little enough to do with the 'state of war'.

But each one had its little earthen strongpoint, its foxholes, its stack of rifles. You could not escape anything anywhere.

In the village of Nanh Ngang, hard by the famous bridge, I was presented to Miss Nguyen Thi Hanh, who was famous, they said, in song and story. Miss Hanh was a quite attractive twenty-eight-year-old, with the indefinable air of resolution and authority that in other climes marks out the Girl Guide leader or the Captain of Games. She was offered as a Labour Hero and a People's Hero, and wore small decorations to prove it. She was clearly adjusted to a measure of local celebrity as the local Resistance pin-up. She had once been on a delegation to Moscow. Pictures of her from several patriotic magazines decorated the walls of her very simple, austere and impeccably tidy room.

The point about Miss Hanh was that she was the commander of the local militia. In order to dispel any impression that she was a Boadicea, however, she began on our arrival to go through a sequence of activities that were unmistakably feminine: she poured tea with grace and skill, she combed her hair; at one moment she even produced a doll and played with it, in a somewhat off-hand way. I gained the impression, from the casual skill with which she adjusted her attitude to the camera, holding the gesture for exactly the right moment, and the accomplished manner in which she delivered her lines on cue, that she was not wholly unfamiliar with the experience of being Exhibit A of the province of Thanh Hoa. As it subsequently turned out, there has been scarce a foreign visitor to these parts of North Vietnam who has not had the opportunity of meeting Miss Hanh.

Miss Hanh admitted she had been a volunteer for some time; her ambition had always been to dedicate herself to the people's welfare and the defence of the nation, because President Ho had this very much at heart and therefore, she felt, so should she. It seemed an unexceptional sentiment.

By and by we moved outside to the riverside, and Miss Hanh obligingly put her women's corps of the militia through their paces. I was in time to grow rather familiar with these 'mock fights', as they were called – the air-raid drills and rehearsals that had become embodied in the North Vietnam way of life. They were called regularly, or impromptu; there was no doubt at all that this routine did in fact keep the people both in the city factories and in the country very much on the alert.

Miss Hanh's demonstration was less persuasive than many – a covey of pretty little girls dressed in leaves popping into foxholes and pointing their rifles at the sky, with Miss Hanh gesturing dramatically upwards, exactly as in her many photographs.

She also had a little model aircraft carved from wood, about a foot long, which was brandished through the air at the end of a long pole, while everybody aimed their empty guns at it. (This may in fact be a tactic of anti-aircraft training that is of greater usefulness than it appears to be; at first I thought Miss Hanh's property toy bomber was a piece of rather nonsensical stagecraft, until I saw variations of this model-device being put to use all over the place. The Vietnamese are not usually given to fooling themselves over something so elementary.)

It all seemed so palpably make-believe, however – the vital great steel bridge defended by a chorus of pretty little girls; I felt awkward and rueful. One said: 'Yes, very nice; well done, ladies', as though it had been a folk-dance contest.

And then – very suddenly, as I was walking back broodily from the riverside to the village – the alarm went in all truth, with a thumping of a great barrel-drum somewhere, and the war-game was real after all, with the sighing howl of the jets overhead, the thud of anti-aircraft fire from somewhere around and, for all I know, a tiny volley from Miss Hanh's young ladies in the foxholes.

But on this occasion the planes were not after us, but streaking homewards south from some unknown enterprise in the interior. For a while the high air ached with the bitter whine of the engines, but there is a special tenor, hard to define, that marks the sound of bombers that have one's own position in mind and those that are high-tailing it back for the base. The village took cover philosophically, but by the time the children had been herded into the earth dugouts the flight was doubtless far away.

There were several such alerts while I moved around the country, and it is fair to try to analyse one's reaction. It is not easy. The first, obviously, was simple interest – in watching the manner in which the children materialised from nowhere in small crocodiles, and were shepherded into the dugouts; the tension that gripped everyone in a visible moment of truth: the hands that shot out to indicate the position of the planes, the bubble of excited chatter that would spontaneously burst at the same moment from every watching group, the dead silence when it seemed an attacking run was on and the bombs might fall, the low-pitched communal sigh when it was all over, a relaxation that was almost palpable.

Then what supervened, I think, was not the emotion of fear (for I was at no time in any particular danger, except from accident) nor was it high-minded horror at this intolerable breach of the rule of law. There was somehow a sense of outrage against civility; what an impertinence, one felt, what arrogance, what an offence against manners, if nothing else; by what right do these airmen intrude over a country they do not recognise, with which they are not formally at war; who gave these people the sanction to drop their bombs and rockets on other people's roads and bridges and houses, to blow up the harvest, to destroy people of whom they know absolutely nothing?

The crews up there were almost certainly decent American young men, but from down below one felt of their behaviour as not so much wicked, or tyrannical; but as wholly insolent, and in its way futile. These people in Vietnam were hardly angelic; in many cases they were troublesome, unmanageable, awkward; but they were friendly and shy people, and very poor; any pilot up there made more in a week than most of these people did in a year. Would this sort of thing blow Communism out of their heads?

Apart from the cadres and the politicians, who indeed could be truculent and demanding, most of these people never wanted anything in their lives but to be let alone, to get on with their lives, which have always been hard, to see that the crop was got in and the children got enough to eat. From down below, the raids seemed not so much a 'rabid Imperialist aggression', but just a crude and inexcusable imposition, a vulgar demonstration of the strong against the weak.

One thing already appeared to be sure: if the bombing of North Vietnam had been designed either to terrorise the people into submission or to crush their economy into ruin, its effect on both counts seemed to me precisely the reverse.

So far from terrorising and disrupting the people, the bombings seemed to me to have stimulated and consolidated them. By the nature of the attacks so far, civilian casualties had not been very great, but they had been great enough to provide the government of the Vietnam Republic with the most totally unchallengeable propaganda they could ever have dreamed of. A nation of peasants and manual workers who might have felt restive or dissatisfied under the stress of totalitarian conditions had been obliged to forget all their differences in

the common sense of resistance and self-defence. From the moment
the United States dropped its first bomb on the North of Vietnam,
she welded the nation together unshakeably. Every bomb since was
a bonus for Ho Chi Minh.

Nor is this an economy that can be easily wrecked by high-explosive. This was a peasant, agrarian society; immensely resilient. The
Pentagon's thought-processes seemed to me considerably those of a
highly developed and sophisticated Western society; even in their own
interests the US planners failed to recognise the realities of a society
like this. A bomb here, a bomb there; a family eliminated here or
there; a rice-field churned into swamp – these were troublesome, infuriating; they were not disabling.

The destruction of a bridge or a road – in Western terms it could
be disastrous. Here, it was a nuisance. The people would mend it, or
they would go some other way. When I drove to Haiphong it took
three hours along the country's most important road. While I was
away the road was cut. It took seven hours to return – but we
returned; in Vietnam there is always another way.

If the day came when the industries were bombed and destroyed,
it would be a grievous setback to a nation that is only just beginning
to grope among the problems and advantages of industry – but it
would make, fundamentally, very little difference to them. Every single
industrial enterprise in the country could be ruined – and it would
directly affect about 5 per cent of the working population. Vietnam
is not Detroit, nor even Washington or London. Its people can survive
the inconveniences of destruction, dismay and death. They have learned
how, over twenty-five years.

I fear we have learned less.

SEYMOUR M. HERSH

The Massacre at My Lai

1970

'We have smashed the country to bits,' wrote Telford Taylor, chief United States prosecutor at the Nuremberg trials, 'and we will not even take the trouble to clean up the blood and rubble.' He was referring not to Germany, but to Vietnam.

During more than a decade in the 1960s and 1970s, the United States dispatched its greatest ever land army to Vietnam, dropped the greatest tonnage of bombs in the history of warfare, pursued a military strategy deliberately designed to force millions of people to abandon their homes while killing as many of them as possible (the 'kill ratio'), and used chemicals in a manner that profoundly changed the environmental and genetic order, leaving a once beautiful land petrified. At least three million people lost their lives and many more were maimed and otherwise ruined; 58,022 were Americans and the rest were Vietnamese. President Reagan called this a 'noble cause'.

It is one of the enduring myths of the Vietnam war that journalists exposed all this. On the contrary, most journalists covering the war supported the 'noble cause' while criticising the efficiency of its execution. Shortly after the war, General Winant Sidle, the American military's chief spokesman in Vietnam at the height of the war, told me: 'A lot of what we did just wasn't considered newsworthy. Take "collateral damage" [killing civilians] . . . and "search and destroy" [killing mostly civilians] . . . the reporters and the military men using those terms knew what they meant . . . gee, war is hell, and if a civilian doesn't want to get killed in the battle zone, he should leave.'

Shortly before 8 o'clock on the morning of 16 March 1968, C-Company, First Battalion, Twentieth Infantry, Eleventh Brigade,

Americal Division of the US Army, entered the hamlet of My Lai on a 'search and destroy' operation. By noon, almost every living thing the troops could find was dead; up to 500 women, children and old men had been systematically murdered.

For more than a year, a discharged GI, Ron Ridenhour, who had heard about the massacre, tried to interest the American press at home and those based in Saigon, notably *Newsweek*, without success. Finally, the story was broken not by any of the 600 accredited correspondents in Vietnam, but by a young freelancer in the United States, Seymour Hersh, who regarded the murder of unarmed civilians by American soldiers as shocking.

In November 1969, Hersh had spotted a small press agency item that one Lieutenant William Calley had been charged with the murder of 109 'Oriental human beings' and that had gone unnoticed. He tracked Calley down to Fort Benning in Georgia, where he interviewed him. He then set out on a journey in the United States of, he esti- mates, more than 50,000 miles, finding and interviewing more than fifty members of Charlie Company. In 1970, he wrote a reconstruc- tion of the atrocity for the little-known Dispatch News Service. When *Newsweek* finally acknowledged his scoop, its banner headline said, 'An American Tragedy'. This set the tone for the coverage of My Lai as an aberration that called for sympathy for Americans, not the Vietnamese – even though other atrocities were now being revealed.

In the following extract from his book, *My Lai 5: Report on the Massacre and Its Aftermath*, mark the way Hersh catalogues the casual way the My Lai atrocities are committed and the callousness of GIs who murdered even tiny babies, clingling to their dead mothers in the ditch. Then he adds an almost heretical dimension: he makes sure the reader understands there was nothing 'aberrant' about this, just busi- ness as usual for the brutalised men ravaging a faraway country for their criminal superiors.

Seymour Hersh is, in my view, America's greatest reporter. Apart from My Lai, his scoops include the 'secret' bombing of Cambodia, the illegal use of the CIA to spy on Americans at home, key events in the Watergate scandal, notably the secret White House phone-tapping records, and the pivotal role of the CIA and Henry Kissinger in the bloody overthrow of Salvador Allende in Chile. Since September 11, 2001, he has broken story after story. In 2004, his exposé of an American regime of torture in Iraq promises to change the course of the occupation.

A colleague once described 'Sy' Hersh at work as 'this unkempt dervish of a man emitting rapid bursts of strongly worded questions into a telephone with his hair flopping and his arms going in nine different directions at once.' He is what an investigative journalist ought to be: an outsider who knows how to mine on the inside, who protects his sources and is proud of his enemies. Whenever he produces a scoop, someone will say, 'You know, Hersh has gone too far this time.' And indeed he has.

THE MASSACRE AT MY LAI

Nobody saw it all. Some, like Roy Wood, didn't even know the extent of the massacre until the next day. Others, like Charles Sledge, who served that day as Calley's radioman, saw more than they want to remember.

But they all remember the fear that morning as they climbed onto helicopters at LZ Dotti for the assault on Pinkville. They all remember the sure knowledge that they would meet face-to-face for the first time with the enemy.

Calley and his platoon were the first to board the large black army assault helicopters. They were heavily armed, each man carrying twice the normal load of rifle and machine-gun ammunition. Leading the way was Calley, who had slung an extra belt of M16 rifle bullets over his shoulder. There were nine helicopters in the first lift-off, enough for the first platoon – about twenty-five men – and Captain Medina and his small headquarters unit of three radiomen, some liaison officers and a medic. It was sunny and already hot when the first helicopter started its noisy flight to My Lai 4. The time was 7.22 a.m.; it was logged by a tape recorder at brigade headquarters. A brief artillery barrage had already begun; the My Lai 4 area was being 'prepped' in anticipation of that day's search-and-destroy mission. A few heavily armed helicopters were firing thousands of small-calibre bullets into the area by the time Calley and his men landed in a soggy rice paddy 150 metres west of the hamlet. It was harvest season; the green fields were thick with growth.

The first platoon's mission was to secure the landing zone and make sure no enemy troops were left to fire at the second wave of helicopters – by then already airborne from LZ Dotti. As the flight of helicopters hovered over the landing area, the door gunners began spraying protective fire to keep the enemy – if he were there – busy. One of the helicopter's pilots had reported that the LZ was 'hot', that is, Vietcong were waiting below. The first platoon came out firing. But after a moment some men noticed that there was no return fire. 'I didn't hear any bullets going past me,' recalled Charles Hall, a machine-gunner that day. 'If you want to consider an area hot, you got to be fired on.'

The platoon quickly formed a perimeter and secured the landing zone. Sergeant Cowen spotted an old man. Sledge was a few yards to Cowen's right: 'We came to a well and there was a VC. We thought it was a VC. He was standing and waving his arms. Cowen fell back and said, "Shoot the so-and-so." I fired once, and then my [rifle] magazine fell out.' Paul Meadlo noted that 'the gook was standing up shaking and waving his arms and then he was shot'. Allen Boyce saw it a little differently: 'Some guy was in a rice-field, doing something to a rice plant. He looked up and he got it. That was the most confused operation I ever went on. Just everything was screwed up.'

By this time those Vietcong who were in the area had slipped away. Some local supporters of the guerrillas also left, but they did not go too far. They watched as Charlie Company went through My Lai 4.

After about twenty minutes the second flight of helicopters landed, and the fifty men of the second and third platoons jumped off. Gary Garfolo heard the helicopter blades make sharp crackling sounds as they changed pitch for the landing. 'It was a "pop, pop, pop" sound like a rifle. Lots of us never even heard a hot LZ before. We knew we were going into a hot place. This got their adrenalin going.' The men were quickly assembled. Calley's first platoon and Lieutenant Stephen Brooks' second platoon would lead the sweep into the hamlet – Calley to the south, and Brooks to the north. The third platoon, headed by Lieutenant Jeffrey La Crosse, would be held in reserve and move in on the heels of the other men. Captain Medina and his headquarters unit would move with the third platoon and then set up a command post (CP) inside to monitor the operation and stay in touch with other units. Charlie Company was not alone in its assault; the other two companies of Task Force Barker set up blocking positions to the north and south. They were there to prevent the expected Vietcong troops from fleeing.

The My Lai 4 assault was the biggest thing going in the Americal Division that day. To get enough airlift, Task Force Barker had to borrow helicopters from other units throughout the division. The air lanes above the action were carefully allotted to high-ranking officers for observation. Barker monitored the battle from the 1,000-foot level. Major General Samuel Koster, commanding general of the division, was allotted the air space at 2,000 feet. His helicopter was permanently stationed outside his door at division headquarters twenty-one miles to the north, waiting to fly him to the scene of any action within minutes. Oran K. Henderson, commander of the 11th Brigade, was given the top spot – at 2,500 feet. All of the helicopters were to circle anticlockwise over the battle area. Flying low, beneath the 1,000-foot level, would be the gunships, heavily armed helicopters whose mission was to shoot down any Vietcong soldiers attempting to escape.

Brigade headquarters, sure that there would be a major battle, sent along two men from the army's 31st Public Information Detachment to record the event for history. Jay Roberts of Arlington, Virginia, a reporter, and photographer Ronald L. Haeberle of Cleveland, Ohio, arrived with the second wave of helicopters and immediately attached themselves to the third platoon, which was bringing up the rear.

The hamlet itself had a population of about 700 people, living either in flimsy thatch-covered huts – 'hootches', as the GIs called them – or in solidly made red-brick homes, many with small porches in front. There was an east–west footpath just south of the main cluster of homes; a few yards further south was a loose-surface road that marked a hamlet boundary. A deep drainage ditch and then a rice paddy marked the eastern boundary. To the south of My Lai 4 was a large centre, or plaza area – clearly the main spot for mass meetings. The foliage was dense: there were high bamboo trees, hedges and plant life everywhere. Medina couldn't see thirty feet into the hamlet from the landing zone.

The first and second platoons lined up carefully to begin the hundred-metre advance into My Lai 4. Walking in line is an important military concept; if one group of men gets too far in front, it could be hit by bullets from behind – those fired by colleagues. Yet even this went wrong. Ron Grzesik was in charge of a small first-platoon fire team of riflemen and a machine-gunner; he took his job seriously. His unit was supposed to be on the right flank, protecting Calley and his men. But Grzesik's group ended up on Calley's left.

As Brooks' second platoon cautiously approached the hamlet, a few Vietnamese began running across a field several hundred metres on the left. They may have been Vietcong, or they may have been civilians fleeing the artillery shelling or the bombardment from the helicopter gunships. Vernado Simpson, Jr, of Jackson, Mississippi, saw a man he identified as a Vietcong soldier running with what seemed to be a weapon. A woman and a small child were running with him. Simpson fired . . . again and again. He killed the woman and the baby. The man got away. Reporter Roberts saw a squad of GIs jump off a helicopter and begin firing at a group of people running on a nearby road. One was a woman with her children. Then he saw them 'shoot two guys who popped up from a rice-field. They looked like military-age men . . . when certain guys pop up from rice-fields, you shoot them.' This was the young reporter's most dangerous assignment. He had never been in combat before. 'You're scared to death out there. We just wanted to go home.'

The first two platoons of Charlie Company, still unfired upon, entered the hamlet. Behind them, still in the rice paddy, were the third platoon and Captain Medina's command post. Calley and some of his men walked into the plaza area in the southern part of the hamlet. None of the people was running away; they knew that US soldiers would assume that anyone running was a Vietcong and would shoot to kill. There was no immediate sense of panic. The time was about 8 a.m. Grzesik and his fire team were a few metres north of Calley; they couldn't see each other because of the dense vegetation. Grzesik and his men began their usual job of pulling people from their homes, interrogating them, and searching for Vietcong. The villagers were gathered up, and Grzesik sent Meadlo, who was in his unit, to take them to Calley for further questioning. Grzesik didn't see Meadlo again for more than an hour.

Some of Calley's men thought it was breakfast time as they walked in; a few families were gathered in front of their homes cooking rice over a small fire. Without a direct order, the first platoon also began rounding up the villagers. There still was no sniper fire, no sign of a large enemy unit. Sledge remembered thinking that 'if there were VC around, they had plenty of time to leave before we came in. We didn't tiptoe in there.'

The killings began without warning. Harry Stanley told the CID that one young member of Calley's platoon took a civilian into custody and then 'pushed the man up to where we were standing and then stabbed the man in the back with his bayonet . . . The man fell to the ground and was gasping for breath.' The GI then 'killed him with another bayonet thrust or by shooting him with a rifle . . . There was so many people killed that day it is hard for me to recall exactly how some of the people died.' The youth next 'turned to where some soldiers were holding another forty- or fifty-year-old man in custody'. He 'picked this man up and threw him down a well. Then [he] pulled the pin from an M26 grenade and threw it in after the man.' Moments later Stanley saw 'some old women and some little children – fifteen or twenty of them – in a group around a temple where some incense was burning. They were kneeling and crying and praying, and various soldiers . . . walked by and executed these women and children by shooting them in the head with their rifles. The soldiers killed all fifteen or twenty of them . . .'

There were few physical protests from the people; about eighty of them were taken quietly from their homes and herded together in the plaza area. A few hollered out, 'No VC. No VC.' But that was hardly unexpected. Calley left Meadlo, Boyce and a few others with the responsibility of guarding the group. 'You know what I want you to do with them,' he told Meadlo. Ten minutes later – about 8.15 a.m. – he returned and asked, 'Haven't you got rid of them yet? I want them dead.' Radioman Sledge, who was trailing Calley, heard the officer tell Meadlo to 'waste them'. Meadlo followed orders: 'We stood about ten to fifteen feet away from them and then he [Calley] started shooting them. Then he told me to start shooting them. I started to shoot them. So we went ahead and killed them. I used more than a whole clip – used four or five clips.' There are seventeen M16 bullets in each clip. Boyce slipped away, to the northern side of the hamlet, glad he hadn't been asked to shoot. Women were huddled against their children, vainly trying to save them. Some continued to chant, 'No VC.' Others simply said, 'No. No. No.'

Do Chuc is a gnarled forty-eight-year-old Vietnamese peasant whose two daughters and an aunt were killed by the GIs in My Lai 4 that day. He and his family were eating breakfast when the GIs entered the hamlet and ordered them out of their homes. Together with other villagers, they were marched a few hundred metres into the plaza, where they were told to squat. 'Still we had no reason to be afraid,' Chuc recalled. 'Everyone was calm.' He watched as the GIs set up a machine-gun. The calm ended. The people began crying and begging. One monk showed his identification papers to a soldier, but the American simply said, 'Sorry.' Then the shooting started. Chuc was wounded in the leg, but he was covered by dead bodies and thus spared. After waiting an hour, he fled the hamlet.

Nguyen Bat, a Vietcong hamlet chief who later defected, said that many of the villagers who were eating breakfast outdoors when the GIs marched in greeted them without fear. They were gathered together and shot. Other villagers who were breakfasting indoors were killed inside their homes.

The few Vietcong who had stayed near the hamlet were safely hidden. Nguyen Ngo, a former deputy commander of a Vietcong guerrilla platoon operating in the My Lai area, ran to his hiding place 300 metres away when the GIs came in shooting, but he could see that 'they shot everything in sight'. His mother and sister hid in ditches and survived because bodies fell on top of them. Pham Lai, a former hamlet security guard, climbed into a bunker with a bamboo top and heard but did not see the shootings. His wife, hidden under a body, survived the massacre.

By this time, there was shooting everywhere. Dennis I. Conti, a GI from Providence, Rhode Island, later explained to CID investigators what he thought had happened: 'We were all psyched up, and as a result, when we got there the shooting started, almost as a chain reaction. The majority of us had expected to meet VC combat troops, but this did not turn out to be so. First we saw a few men running . . . and the next thing I knew we were shooting at everything. Everybody was just firing. After they got in the village, I guess you could say that the men were out of control.'

Brooks and his men in the second platoon to the north had begun to systematically ransack the hamlet and slaughter the people, kill the livestock and destroy the crops. Men poured rifle and machine-gun fire into huts without knowing – or seemingly caring – who was inside.

Roy Wood, one of Calley's men who was working next to Brooks' platoon, stormed into a hut, saw an elderly man hiding inside along with his wife and two young daughters: 'I hit him with my rifle and pushed him out.' A GI from Brooks' platoon, standing by with an M79 grenade launcher, asked to borrow his gun. Wood refused, and the soldier asked another platoon mate. He got the weapon, said, 'Don't let none of them live', and shot the Vietnamese in the head. 'These mothers are crazy,' Wood remembered thinking. 'Stand right in front of us and blow a man's brains out.' Later he vomited when he saw more of the dead residents of My Lai 4.

The second platoon went into My Lai 4 with guns blazing. Gary Crossley said that some GIs, after seeing nothing but women and children in the hamlet, hesitated: 'We phoned Medina and told him what the circumstances were, and he said just keep going. It wasn't anything we wanted to do. You can only kill so many women and children. The fact was that you can't go through and wipe out all of South Vietnam.'

Once the first two platoons had disappeared into the hamlet, Medina ordered the third platoon to start moving. He and his men followed. Gary Garfolo was caught up in the confusion: 'I could hear heavy shooting all the time. Medina was running back and forth everywhere. This wasn't no organised deal.' So Garfolo did what most GIs did when they could get away with it. 'I took off on my own.' He ran south; others joined him. Terrified villagers, many carrying personal belongings in wicker baskets, were running everywhere to avoid the carnage. In most cases it didn't help. The helicopter gunships circling above cut them down, or else an unfortunate group ran into the third platoon. Charles West sighted and shot six Vietnamese, some with baskets, on the edge of My Lai 4: 'These people were running into us, away from us, running every which way. It's hard to distinguish a mama-san from a papa-san when everybody has on black pajamas.'

West and his men may have thought that these Vietnamese were Vietcong. Later they knew better. West's first impression upon reaching My Lai 4: 'There were no people in the first part . . . I seen bodies everywhere. I knew that everyone was being killed.' His group quickly joined in.

Medina – as any combat officer would do during his unit's first major engagement – decided to move his CP from the rice paddy. John Paul, one of Medina's radiomen, figured that the time was about 8.15 a.m. West remembered that 'Medina was right behind us' as his platoon moved inside the hamlet. There are serious contradictions about what happened next. Medina later said that he did not enter the hamlet proper until well after 10 a.m. and did not see anyone kill a civilian. John Paul didn't think that Medina ever entered the hamlet. But Herbert Carter told the CID that Medina did some of the shooting of civilians as he moved into My Lai 4.

Carter testified that soon after the third platoon moved in, a woman was sighted. Somebody knocked her down, and then, Carter said, 'Medina shot her with his M16 rifle. I was fifty or sixty feet away and saw this. There was no reason to shoot this girl.' The men continued on, making sure no one was escaping. 'We came to where the soldiers had collected fifteen or more Vietnamese men, women and children in a group. Medina said, "Kill every one. Leave no one standing."' A machine-gunner began firing into the group. Moments later one of Medina's radio operators slowly 'passed among them and finished them off'. Medina did not personally shoot any of them, according to Carter, but moments later the captain 'stopped a seven-teen- or eighteen-year-old man with a water buffalo. Medina told the boy to make a run for it,' Carter told the CID. 'He tried to get him to run but the boy wouldn't run, so Medina shot him with his M16 rifle and killed him . . . I was seventy-five or eighty metres away at the time and I saw it plainly.' At this point in Carter's interrogation, the investigator warned him that he was making very serious charges against his commanding officer. 'What I'm telling is the truth,' Carter replied, 'and I'll face Medina in court and swear to it.'

If Carter was correct, Medina walked first into the north side of My Lai 4, then moved south with the CP to the hamlet plaza and arrived there at about the time Paul Meadlo and Lieutenant Calley were executing the first group of villagers. Meadlo still wonders why Medina didn't stop the shooting, 'if it was wrong'. Medina and Calley 'passed each other quite a few times that morning, but didn't say anything. I don't know if the CO gave the order to kill or not, but he was right there when it happened . . . Medina just kept marching around.'

Roberts and Haeberle also moved in just behind the third platoon. Haeberle watched a group of ten to fifteen GIs methodically pump bullets into a cow until it keeled over. A woman then poked her head out from behind some brush; she may have been hiding in a bunker. The GIs turned their fire from the cow to the woman. 'They just kept shooting at her. You could see the bones flying in the air chip by chip.' No one had attempted to question her; GIs inside the hamlet also were asking no questions. Before moving on, the photographer took a picture of the dead woman. Haeberle took many more pictures that day; he saw about thirty GIs kill at least a hundred Vietnamese civilians.

When the two correspondents entered My Lai 4, they saw dead animals, dead people, burning huts and houses. A few GIs were going through victims' clothing, looking for piastres. Another GI was chasing a duck with a knife; others stood around watching a GI slaughter a cow with a bayonet.

Haeberle noticed a man and two small children walking towards a group of GIs: 'They just kept walking towards us . . . you could hear the little girl saying, "No, no . . ." All of a sudden the GIs opened up and cut them down.' Later he watched a machine-gunner suddenly open fire on a group of civilians – women, children and babies – who had been collected in a big circle: 'They were trying to run. I don't know how many got out.' He saw a GI with an M16 rifle fire at two young boys walking along a road. The older of the two – about seven or eight years old – fell over the first to protect him. The GI kept on firing until both were dead.

As Haeberle and Roberts walked further into the hamlet, Medina came up to them. Eighty-five Vietcong had been killed in action thus far, the captain told them, and twenty suspects had been captured. Roberts carefully jotted down the captain's statistics in his notepad.

The company's other Vietnamese interpreter, Sergeant Duong Minh, saw Medina for the first time about then. Minh had arrived on a later helicopter assault, along with Lieutenant Dennis H. Johnson, Charlie Company's intelligence officer. When he saw the bodies of civilians, he asked Medina what happened. Medina, obviously angry at Minh for asking the question, stalked away.

Now it was nearly nine o'clock and all of Charlie Company was in My Lai 4. Most families were being shot inside their homes, or just outside the doorways. Those who had tried to flee were crammed by GIs into the many bunkers built throughout the hamlet for protection – once the bunkers became filled, hand grenades were lobbed in. Everything became a target. Gary Garfolo borrowed someone's M79 grenade launcher and fired it point-blank at a water buffalo: 'I hit that sucker right in the head; went down like a shot. You don't get to shoot water buffalo with an M79 every day.' Others fired the weapon into the bunkers full of people.

Jay Roberts insisted that he saw Medina in My Lai 4 most of the morning: 'He was directing the operations in the village. He was in the village the whole time I was – from nine o'clock to eleven o'clock.'

Carter recalled that some GIs were shouting and yelling during the massacre: 'The boys enjoyed it. When someone laughs and jokes about what they're doing, they have to be enjoying it.' A GI said, 'Hey, I got me another one.' Another said, 'Chalk up one for me.' Even Captain Medina was having a good time, Carter thought: 'You can tell when someone enjoys their work.' Few members of Charlie Company protested that day. For the most part, those who didn't like what was going on kept their thoughts to themselves.

Herbert Carter also remembered seeing Medina inside the hamlet well after the third platoon began its advance: 'I saw all those dead people laying there. Medina came right behind me.' At one point in the morning one of the members of Medina's CP joined in the shooting. 'A woman came out of a hut with a baby in her arms and she was crying,' Carter told the CID. 'She was crying because her little boy had been in front of their hut and . . . someone had killed the child by shooting it.' When the mother came into view, one of Medina's men 'shot her with an M16 and she fell. When she fell, she dropped the baby.' The GI next 'opened up on the baby with his M16'. The infant was also killed. Carter also saw an officer grab a woman by the hair and shoot her with a .45-calibre pistol: 'He held her by the hair for a minute and then let go and she fell to the ground. Some enlisted man standing there said, "Well, she'll be in the big rice paddy in the sky."'

In the midst of the carnage, Michael Bernhardt got his first good look at My Lai 4. Bernhardt had been delayed when Medina asked him to check out a suspicious wood box at the landing zone. After discovering that it wasn't a booby trap, Bernhardt hurried to catch up with his mates in the third platoon. He went into the hamlet, where he saw Charlie Company 'doing strange things. One: they were setting fire to the hootches and huts and waiting for people to come out and then shooting them. Two: they were going into the hootches and shooting them up. Three: they were gathering people in groups and shooting them. The whole thing was so deliberate. It was point-blank murder and I was standing there watching it. It's kind of made me wonder if I could trust people any more.'

Grzesik and his men, meanwhile, had been slowly working their way through the hamlet. The young GI was having problems controlling his men; he was anxious to move on to the rice paddy in the east. About three-quarters of the way through, he suddenly saw Meadlo again. The time was now after nine. Meadlo was crouched, head in his hands, sobbing like a bewildered child. 'I sat down and asked him what happened.' Grzesik felt responsible; after all, he was supposed to be a team leader. Meadlo told him Calley had made him shoot people. 'I tried to calm him down,' Grzesik said, but the fire-team leader couldn't stay long. His men still hadn't completed their sweep of My Lai 4.

Those Vietnamese who were not killed on the spot were being shepherded by the first platoon to a large drainage ditch at the eastern end of the hamlet. After Grzesik left, Meadlo and a few others gathered seven or eight villagers in one hut and were preparing to toss in a hand grenade when an order came to take them to the ditch. There he found Calley, along with a dozen other first platoon members, and perhaps seventy-five Vietnamese, mostly women, old men and children.

Not far away, invisible in the brush and trees, the second and third platoons were continuing their search-and-destroy operations in the northern half of My Lai 4. Ron Grzesik and his fire team had completed a swing through the hamlet and were getting ready to turn around and walk back to see what was going on. And just south of the plaza, Michael Bernhardt had attached himself to Medina and his command post. Shots were still being fired, the helicopters were still whirring overhead, and the enemy was still nowhere in sight.

One of the helicopters was piloted by Chief Warrant Officer Hugh C. Thompson of Decatur, Georgia. For him, the mission had begun routinely enough. He and his two-man crew, in a small observation helicopter from the 123rd Aviation Battalion, had arrived at the area around 9 a.m. and immediately reported what appeared to be a Vietcong soldier armed with a weapon and heading south. Although his mission was simply reconnaissance, Thompson directed his men to fire at and attempt to kill the Vietcong as he wheeled the helicopter after him. They missed. Thompson flew back to My Lai 4, and it was then, as he told the Army Inspector General's office in June 1969, that he began seeing wounded and dead Vietnamese civilians all over the hamlet, with no sign of an enemy force.

The pilot thought that the best thing he could do would be to mark the location of wounded civilians with smoke so that the GIs on the ground could move over and begin treating some of them. 'The first one that I marked was a girl that was wounded,' Thompson testified, 'and they came over and walked up to her, put their weapon on automatic and let her have it.' The man who did the shooting was a captain, Thompson said. Later he identified the officer as Ernest Medina.

Flying with Thompson that day was Lawrence M. Colburn, of Mount Vernon, Washington, who remembered that the girl was about twenty years old and was lying on the edge of a dyke outside the hamlet with part of her body in a rice paddy. 'She had been wounded in the stomach, I think, or the chest,' Colburn told the Inspector

General (IG). 'This captain was coming down the dyke and he had men behind him. They were sweeping through and we were hovering a matter of feet away from them. I could see this clearly, and he emptied a clip into her.'

Medina and his men immediately began moving south towards the Vietcong sighted by Thompson. En route they saw the young girl in the rice paddy who had been marked by the smoke. Bernhardt had a ground view of what happened next: 'He [Medina] was just going alone ... he shot the woman. She seemed to be busy picking rice, but rice was out of season. What she really was doing was trying to pretend that she was picking rice. She was a hundred metres away with a basket ... if she had a hand grenade, she would have to have a better arm than me to get us ... Medina lifted the rifle to his shoulder, looked down the barrel and pulled the trigger. I saw the woman drop. He just took a potshot ... he wasn't a bad shot. Then he walked up. He got up real close, about three or six feet, and shot at her a couple times and finished her off. She was a real clean corpse ... she wasn't all over the place, and I could see her clothing move when the bullets hit ... I could see her twitch, but I couldn't see any holes ... he didn't shoot her in the head.' A second later, Bernhardt remembered, the captain 'gave me a look, a dumb shit-eating grin'.

By now it was past 9.30 a.m. and the men of Charlie Company had been at work for more than two hours. A few of them flung off their helmets, stripped off their heavy gear, flopped down and took a smoke break.

Hugh Thompson's nightmare had only begun with the shooting of the girl. He flew north back over the hamlet and saw a small boy bleeding along a trench. Again he marked the spot so that the GIs below could provide some medical aid. Instead, he saw a lieutenant casually walk up and empty a clip into the child. He saw yet another wounded youngster; again he marked it, and this time it was a sergeant who came up and fired his M16 at the child.

Larry Colburn, who was just eighteen years old at the time, noticed that 'the infantrymen were killing everything in the village. The people didn't really know what was happening. Some of them began walking out of there and the GIs just started going up to them and shooting them all in the back of the head.' He added, 'We saw this one woman hiding there. She was alive and squatting; she looked up when we flew over. We dropped a smoke marker. When we came back she was in the same position – only she was dead. The back of her head was blown off. It had to be point-blank.'

Thompson was furious. He tried unsuccessfully to radio the troops on the ground to find out what was going on. He then reported the wild firings and unnecessary shootings to brigade head-quarters. All the command helicopters flying overhead had multi-channel radios and could monitor most conversations. Lieutenant-Colonel Barker apparently intercepted the message and called down to Medina at the CP just south of the plaza. John Kinch of the mortar platoon heard Medina answer that he 'had a body count of three hundred and ten'. The captain added, 'I don't know what they're doing. The first platoon's in the lead. I am trying to stop it.' A moment later, Kinch said, Medina called Calley and ordered, 'That's enough for today.'

Harry Stanley was standing a few feet away from Calley near some huts at the drainage ditch when the call came from Medina. He had a different recollection: 'Medina called Calley and said, "What the fuck is going on?" Calley said he got some VC, or some people that needed to be checked out.' At this point Medina cautioned Calley to tell his men to save their ammunition because the operation still had a few more days to run.

It is not clear how soon or to whom Medina's order was given, but Stanley told the CID what Calley did next: 'There was an old lady in a bed and I believe there was a priest in white praying over her . . . Calley told me to ask about the VC and NVA[1] and where the weapons were. The priest denied being a VC or NVA.' Charles Sledge watched with horror as Calley pulled the old man outside: 'He said a few more words to the monk. It looked like the monk was pleading for his life. Lieutenant Calley then took his rifle and pushed the monk into a rice paddy and shot him point-blank.'

Calley then turned his attention back to the crowd of Vietnamese and issued an order: 'Push all those people in the ditch.' Three or four GIs complied. Calley struck a woman with a rifle as he pushed her down. Stanley remembered that some of the civilians 'kept trying to get out. Some made it to the top . . .' Calley began the shooting and ordered Meadlo to join in. Meadlo told about it later: 'So we pushed our seven to eight people in with the big bunch of them. And

[1] North Vietnamese Army.

so I began shooting them all. So did Mitchell, Calley . . . I guess I shot maybe twenty-five or twenty people in the ditch . . . men, women and children. And babies.' Some of the GIs switched from automatic fire to single-shot to conserve ammunition. Herbert Carter watched the mothers 'grabbing their kids and the kids grabbing their mothers. I didn't know what to do.'

Calley then turned again to Meadlo and said, 'Meadlo, we've got another job to do.' Meadlo didn't want any more jobs. He began to argue with Calley. Sledge watched Meadlo once more start to sob. Calley turned next to Robert Maples and said, 'Maples, load your machine-gun and shoot these people.' Maples replied, as he told the CID, 'I'm not going to do that.' He remembered that 'the people firing into the ditch kept reloading magazines into their rifles and kept firing into the ditch and then killed or at least shot everyone in the ditch'. William C. Lloyd of Tampa, Florida, told the CID that some grenades were also thrown into the ditch. Dennis Conti noticed that 'a lot of women had thrown themselves on top of the children to protect them, and the children were alive at first. Then the children who were old enough to walk got up and Calley began to shoot the children.'

One further incident stood out in many GIs' minds: seconds after the shooting stopped, a bloodied but unhurt two-year-old boy miraculously crawled out of the ditch, crying. He began running towards the hamlet. Someone hollered, 'There's a kid.' There was a long pause. Then Calley ran back, grabbed the child, threw him back in the ditch and shot him.

Moments later Thompson, still in his helicopter, flew by. He told the IG what happened next: 'I kept flying around and across a ditch . . . and it . . . had a bunch of bodies in it and I don't know how they got in the ditch. But I saw some of them were still alive.' Captain Brian W. Livingston was piloting a large helicopter gunship a few hundred feet above. He had been monitoring Thompson's agonised complaints and went down to take a look for himself. He told a military hearing: 'There were bodies lying in the trenches . . . I remember that we remarked at the time about the old biblical story of Jesus turning water into wine. The trench had a grey colour to it, with the red blood of the individuals lying in it.'

By now Thompson was almost frantic. He landed his small helicopter near the ditch, and asked a soldier there if he could help the people out: 'He said the only way he could help them was to help them out of their misery.' Thompson took off again and noticed a group of mostly women and children huddled together in a bunker near the drainage ditch. He landed a second time. 'I don't know,' he explained, 'maybe it was just my belief, but I hadn't been shot at the whole time I had been there and the gunships following hadn't . . .' He then saw Calley and the first platoon, the same group that had shot the wounded civilians he had earlier marked with smoke. 'I asked him if he could get the women and kids out of there before they tore it [the bunker] up, and he said the only way he could get them out was to use hand grenades. "You just hold your men right here,"' the angry Thompson told the equally angry Calley, '"and I will get the women and kids out."'

Before climbing out of his aircraft, Thompson ordered Colburn and his crew chief to stay alert. 'He told us that if any of the Americans opened up on the Vietnamese, we should open up on the Americans,' Colburn said. Thompson walked back to the ship and called in two helicopter gunships to rescue the civilians. While waiting for them to land, Colburn said, 'he stood between our troops and the bunker. He was shielding the people with his body. He just wanted to get those people out of there.' Colburn wasn't sure whether he would have followed orders if the GIs had opened fire at the bunker: 'I wasn't pointing my guns right at them, but more or less towards the ground. But I was looking their way.' He remembered that most of the soldiers were gathered alongside a nearby dyke 'just watching. Some were lying down; some of them were sitting up, and some were standing.' The helicopters landed, with Thompson still standing between the GIs and the Vietnamese, and quickly rescued nine persons – two old men, two women and five children. One of the children later died en route to the hospital. Calley did nothing to stop Thompson, but later stormed up to Sledge, his radioman, and complained that the pilot 'doesn't like the way I'm running the show, but I'm the boss'.

Gregory Olsen, who had watched the encounter from his machine-gun position a few dozen metres away, said that 'the next thing I knew Mitchell was just shooting into the ditch'. At this point Grzesik and his fire team came strolling into the area; they had gone completely through the hamlet, had a break, and were now returning. It was about ten o'clock. Grzesik saw bodies all over the north-eastern quarter of My Lai 4. He glanced at the ditch. Suddenly Mitchell yelled, 'Grzesik, come here.' He walked over. Calley then

ordered him to go to the ditch and 'finish off the people'. Grzesik
had seen the helicopter carrying some wounded Vietnamese take off
from the area a moment earlier; much later he concluded that Calley
– furious with Thompson's intervention – wanted to make sure there
were no more survivors in the ditch. Calley told Grzesik to gather
his team to do the job. 'I really believe he expected me to do it,'
Grzesik said later, with some amazement. Calley asked him again,
and Grzesik again refused. The lieutenant then angrily ordered him
to take his team and help burn the hootches. Grzesik headed for
the hamlet plaza.

Thompson continued to fly over the ditch and noticed that some
of the children's bodies had no heads. He landed a third time after
his crew chief told him that he had seen some movement in the mass
of bodies and blood below. The crew chief and Colburn began walking
towards the ditch. 'Nobody said anything,' Colburn said. 'We just
got out.' They found a young child still alive. No GIs were in the
immediate area, but Colburn was carrying a rifle. The crew chief
climbed into the ditch. 'He was knee-deep in people and blood,'
Colburn recalled. The child was quiet, buried under many bodies.
'He was still holding onto his mother. But she was dead.' The boy,
clinging desperately, was prised loose. He still did not cry. Thompson
later told the IG, 'I don't think this child was even wounded at all,
just down there among all the other bodies, and he was terrified.'
Thompson and his men flew the baby to safety.

In other parts of My Lai 4, GIs were taking a break, or loafing. Others
were systematically burning those remaining houses and huts and
destroying food. Some villagers – still alive – were able to leave their
hiding places and walk away. Charles West recalled that one member
of his squad who simply wasn't able to slaughter a group of children
asked for and received permission from an officer to let them go.

West's third platoon went ahead, nonetheless, with the killing.
They gathered a group of about ten women and children, who huddled
together in fear a few feet from the plaza, where dozens of villagers
already had been slain. West and the squad had finished their mission
in the north and west of the hamlet, and were looking for new targets.
They drifted south towards the CP. Jay Roberts and Ron Haeberle,
who had spent the past hour watching the slaughter in other parts
of the hamlet, stood by – pencil and cameras at the ready. A few

men now singled out a slender Vietnamese girl of about fifteen. They tore her from the group and started to pull at her blouse. They attempted to fondle her breasts. The old women and children were screaming and crying. One GI yelled, 'Let's see what she's made of.' Another said, 'VC Boom, Boom', meaning she was a Vietcong whore. Jay Roberts thought that the girl was good-looking. An old lady began fighting with fanatical fury, trying to protect the girl. Roberts said, 'She was fighting off two or three guys at once. She was fantastic. Usually they're pretty passive . . . They hadn't even gotten that chick's blouse off when Haeberle came along.' One of the GIs finally smacked the old woman with his rifle butt; another booted her in the rear.

Grzesik and his fire team watched the fight develop as they walked down from the ditch to the hamlet centre. Grzesik was surprised: 'I thought the village was cleared . . . I didn't know there were that many people left.' He knew trouble was brewing, and his main thought was to keep his team out of it. He helped break up the fight. Some of the children were desperately hanging onto the old lady as she struggled. Grzesik was worried about the cameraman. He may have yelled, 'Hey, there's a photographer.' He remembered thinking, 'Here's a guy standing there with a camera that you've never seen before.' Then somebody said, 'What do we do with them?' The answer was, 'Waste them.' Suddenly there was a burst of automatic fire from many guns. Only a small child survived. Somebody then carefully shot him, too. A photograph of the woman and child, with the young Vietnamese girl tucking in her blouse, was later published in *Life* magazine. Roberts tried to explain later: 'It's just that they didn't know what they were supposed to do; killing them seemed like a good idea, so they did it. The old lady who fought so hard was probably a VC.' He thought a moment and added, 'Maybe it was just her daughter.'

West was annoyed at the photographer: 'I thought it was wrong for him to stand up and take pictures of this thing. Even though we had to do it, I thought, we didn't have to take pictures of it.' Later he complained personally to Haeberle about it.

Most of the shooting was over by the time Medina called a break for lunch, shortly after eleven o'clock. By then Roberts and Haeberle had grabbed a helicopter and cleared out of the area, their story for the day far bigger than they wanted. Calley, Mitchell, Sledge, Grzesik and a few others went back to the command post west of My Lai 4 to take lunch with Captain Medina and the rest of his headquarters' crew. Grzesik recalled that at that point he'd thought there couldn't be a survivor left in the hamlet. But two little girls showed up, about ten and eleven years old. John Paul said they came in from one of the paddies, where they apparently had waited out the siege. 'We sat them down with us [at the command post],' Paul recounted, 'and gave them some cookies and crackers to eat.' When a CID interrogator later asked Charles Sledge how many civilians he thought had survived, he answered, 'Only two small children who had lunch with us.'

In the early afternoon the men of Charlie Company mopped up to make sure all the houses and goods in My Lai 4 were destroyed. Medina ordered the underground tunnels in the hamlet blown up; most of them already had been blocked. Within another hour My Lai 4 was no more: its red-brick buildings demolished by explosives, its huts burned to the ground, its people dead or dying.

Michael Bernhardt later summarised the day: 'We met no resistance and I only saw three captured weapons. We had no casualties. It was just like any other Vietnamese village – old papa-sans, women and kids. As a matter of fact, I don't remember seeing one military-age male in the entire place, dead or alive. The only prisoner I saw was in his fifties.'

The platoons pulled out shortly after noon, rendezvousing in the rice paddies east of My Lai 4. Lieutenant Brooks' platoon had about eighty-five villagers in tow; it kept those of military age with them and told the rest to begin moving south. Following orders, Medina then marched the GIs north-east through the nearly deserted hamlets of My Lai 5 and My Lai 6, ransacking and burning as they went. In one of the hamlets, Medina ordered the residents gathered, and then told Sergeant Phu, the regular company interpreter, to tell them, as Phu later recalled, that 'they were to go away or something will happen to them – just like what happened at My Lai 4'.

By nightfall the Vietcong were back in My Lai 4, helping the survivors bury the dead. It took five days. Most of the funeral speeches were made by the Communist guerrillas. Nguyen Bat was not a Communist at the time of the massacre, but the incident changed his mind. 'After the shooting,' he said, 'all the villagers became Communists.'

When army investigators reached the barren area in November 1969, in connection with the My Lai probe in the United States, they found mass graves at three sites, as well as a ditch full of bodies. It was estimated that between 450 and 500 people – most of them women, children and old men – had been slain and buried there.

Specialist 5 Jay Roberts carried his reporter's notepad and a pencil with him when he took the helicopter from 11th Brigade headquarters at Duc Pho early that morning. But whatever he wrote could not be used. The army had decided the night before that the Vietcong were in My Lai 4; nothing that happened in the next twenty-four hours officially changed that view.

A Saigon report of Charlie Company's battle sent to the Pentagon the night of 16 March noted that initial 'contact with the enemy force' occurred at 7.50 a.m., about the time Lieutenant Calley and his platoon had secured the landing zone and shot an unarmed old man. The military message added that a second combat company had been airlifted into the area by 9.10 a.m. and that both units reported 'sporadic contact' with the enemy as they moved towards a rendezvous. The companies had support from 'Army artillery and helicopter gunships'.

Roberts – who had been out of My Lai 4 since 11 a.m. – learned from Colonel Barker in the early afternoon that the final body count for Task Force Barker that day was 128, with three enemy weapons captured. He had no idea how, or why, that total was reached. There was great excitement at LZ Dotti: the 128 body count was the largest for the Task Force since it had begun operations forty days earlier.

The official brigade account of the Task Force operation gave Charlie Company direct credit for only fifteen of the 128 enemy kills, and also said that none of the company's victims was inside My Lai 4 at the time. 'The infantry company led by Captain Ernest Medina engaged and killed fourteen VC and captured three M-1 rifles, a radio and enemy documents while moving towards the village,' the report said, adding that one Vietnamese had been killed earlier at the landing zone. It said firefights in the surrounding areas were responsible for most of the enemy deaths. Six victims were killed by the helicopter gunships from the 123rd Aviation Battalion and 174th Aviation Company, which were flying support for the mission. Those six, according to Roberts' version, were the only Vietnamese who were killed inside My Lai 4. Barker was quoted in the story as saying, 'The combat assault went like clockwork. We had two entire companies on the ground in less than an hour.' The story added that 'the swiftness with which the units moved into the area surprised the enemy. After the battle, the 11th Brigade soldiers moved into the village, searching each hut and tunnel.'

A report of the My Lai 4 invasion, based on the official version supplied to newsmen in Saigon, was published on the front page of the *New York Times*, as well as in many other newspapers, on 17 March. It said that two Americal Division companies had caught a North Vietnamese unit in a pincer movement, killing 128 enemy soldiers. 'The United States soldiers were sweeping the area . . .' the *Times* said. 'The operation is another American offensive to clear enemy pockets still threatening the cities. While the two companies of United States soldiers moved in on the enemy force from opposite sides, heavy artillery barrages and armed helicopters were called in to pound the North Vietnamese soldiers.' The report said two American GIs were killed and ten wounded during the day-long fight six miles north-east of Quang Ngai, even though Medina's company had sustained only one casualty – Carter. There was no mention of civilian casualties.

Charlie Company's apparent victory did not go unnoticed. A few days after the battle, General William C. Westmoreland, then commander of US forces in Vietnam, sent the following message: 'Operation Muscatine [the code name for the My Lai 4 assault] contact north-east of Quang Ngai City on 16 March dealt enemy heavy blow. Congratulations to officers and men of C-1–20 [Charlie Company, 1st Battalion, 20th Infantry] for outstanding action.'

*

The first public hint of the My Lai 4 massacre was a blandly worded news release issued to the Georgia press on Friday afternoon, 5 September, by the public information office at Fort Benning. It said, in full:

1LT William L. Calley, Jr, is being retained on active duty beyond his normal release date because of an investigation being conducted under Article 32 of the Uniform Code of Military Justice.

1LT Calley, who was to have been separated from the Army on 6 Sep. 69, is charged with violation of Article 118, murder, for offences allegedly committed against civilians while serving in Vietnam in March 1968.

Whether the matter will be referred to trial by court-martial will be determined by the Commanding General Fort Benning, upon completion of the Article 32 investigation. In order not to prejudice the continuing investigation and the rights of the accused, it is not appropriate to report further details at this time.

The press release did not state that six specifications of murder had been laid against the young lieutenant, nor did it state that he was accused of murdering, by deliberately shooting with a rifle, 109 Vietnamese civilians. There is nothing in military law that precluded the release of such information. The army said that publication of the specific charges would jeopardise Calley's rights.

As released, the fact that Calley was being kept in the service because of pending murder charges was a routine story. A reporter in Georgia for the Associated Press asked for more information and was referred to the Pentagon, where he was told that no further details were available. The AP's subsequent dispatch did no more than repeat the essential facts as released by Fort Benning. The wire service story was published in dozens of newspapers over the weekend, but none gave it prominence. The *New York Times*, for example, published an edited version of the AP story at the bottom of page 38 of its 8 September editions.

Calley's plight received more attention in Columbus, Georgia, where the local newspapers published it on page 1. Charles Black, military writer for the morning *Columbus Enquirer*, went to visit Calley – the only reporter in the nation to do so at that time – but the young lieutenant refused to discuss the case.

In Miami, Calley's home town, an editor of the *Miami Herald* assigned an experienced reporter, Arnold Markowitz, to follow up the story. Markowitz quickly dug out some old clips about Calley's problems as a railroad switchman, and telephoned Colonel Douglas Tucker, an information officer at Fort Benning, to see if the Calley who had disrupted rush-hour traffic in Fort Lauderdale, Florida, was the same Calley who was now accused of murder. Tucker checked, and called back to say they were indeed the same. 'Listen, is it one, or two, or three – how many did he kill?' Markowitz abruptly asked the officer. 'No comment' was the answer. The reporter later said that 'I wasn't thinking of any guys doing anything like this [My Lai 4]. I just wanted to know if he shot up a gin mill in Saigon, or what.' Markowitz's story was published on page 9 the next morning.

Officers in the Pentagon were prepared for a flood of questions that weekend from all news media – but it didn't come. 'I was amazed that it didn't get picked up – just amazed,' said one colonel. Secretary of Defense Melvin A. Laird later revealed that he had ordered the news wires monitored to see if the announcement would spark immediate controversy. He was informed that the Associated Press ran its story on Calley sixty-two minutes before its main competitor, United Press International.

Five days after the original announcement, the news of Calley's arrest was telecast on the Huntley-Brinkley nightly evening news show. Robert Goralski, NBC's Pentagon correspondent, told the millions of viewers that Calley 'has been accused of premeditated murder of a number of South Vietnamese civilians. The murders are alleged to have been committed a year ago and the investigation is continuing. A growing number of such cases is coming to light and the army doesn't know what to do about them.'

For weeks there was nothing more in the press about Calley, but the army continued to gather evidence for his court-martial. Paul Meadlo, the most important prosecution witness, was interviewed for a third time by CID agents on 18 September at his home in Terre Haute. And Captain Lewellen decided at about that time to turn over his tapes of the radio traffic above My Lai 4 to the prosecution at Fort Benning. He kept a few copies for himself, however.

Ridenhour, meanwhile, became convinced that the army's failure to publicise details of the case against Calley meant not only that 'Calley was going to get hung as a scapegoat' but higher-ranking officers who passed down the order to Calley would get off without a reprimand. He also suspected that the army would make a deal with Calley, through his lawyers, 'to keep him quiet'. On 13 October the army again wrote Ridenhour, telling him that Calley's Article 32 hearing on the murder charges would begin that month, and noting: 'It is not appropriate to report details of the allegations to news media. Your continued cooperation in this matter is acknowledged.'

Ridenhour, of course, continued to urge his agent to help tell the whole story, but on 22 October Michael Cunningham wrote Ridenhour, conceding defeat: 'Quite frankly, Ron, I am doubtful of my ability to be of much more help. I honestly feel that matter is best handled at this stage by waiting until your next response from the army.' At this point Ridenhour decided to give his file to a newspaper reporter. He got the name of Ben Cole, a Washington reporter for the Phoenix, Arizona, *Republic* through Congressman Udall's office. 'They said he had gotten wind of the thing and was interested,' Ridenhour said. 'I called the guy in DC and explained it to him and said, "Are you interested? Will you put it in the paper?" and he said, "Yeah, yeah, yeah."'

By then, in late October, there was another reporter who also had dug up many of the important details of the Calley case. Charles Black of the *Columbus Enquirer* had noticed that Calley was wearing the patch of the Americal Division when Black had interviewed him in September; Black continued to piece together information from former Vietnam veterans of that division who were stationed at Fort Benning. But Black, who had gone to Vietnam five times for his newspaper, decided not to print anything until the army spoke out about the case. He didn't want to embarrass the army. 'Next to Jim Lucas [of the Scripps-Howard newspaper syndicate], I guess I'm the army's favourite newspaperman,' he said later.

Cole missed the story because, as he recalled, he just didn't have time to begin research on it. 'Ridenhour gave it to me just before I came down with a bad cold in October . . . I was a sick baby.' When Ridenhour telephoned a few weeks later to find out why the story hadn't broken, Cole was irritated. 'He just sat on the goddamn thing,' Ridenhour said.

Details of the charges against Calley were now known to dozens of officials – Senator John C. Stennis and his shocked Senate Armed Services Committee were given a private briefing that fall – yet nothing reached the press. Despite the widespread official knowledge of the Calley case, a few Pentagon officers actually thought Calley could be court-martialled without attracting any significant public attention. The opinion was far from unanimous, however. Perhaps anticipating a future furore over My Lai 4, General Westmoreland included these unusual words during a speech on 14 October to the annual meeting of the Association of the US Army in Washington: 'Recently, a few individuals involved in serious incidents have been highlighted in the news. Some would have these incidents reflect on the army as a whole.

They are, however, the actions of a pitiful few. Certainly the army cannot and will not condone improper conduct or criminal acts – I personally assure you that I will not.'

The Calley case remained dormant as far as the press was concerned until the inevitable Washington tipsters got to work. The *New York Times* heard something about a massacre case being tried at Fort Gordon, Georgia. It was the right case, but the wrong base. The *Washington Post* queried the Pentagon about some officer's being charged with more than 150 civilian murders in connection with a Vietnam operation. One *Post* reporter even managed to locate George W. Latimer, Calley's attorney, at his Salt Lake City office, and ask him about the case. Latimer begged off, saying, 'I'm hoping maybe we can come up with some kind of resolution that won't make it necessary for this to be public. I can't see it would do any good to anybody.' No news story was written.

I, the author of this book, was in the midst of completing research for a book on the Pentagon when I received a telephone tip on 22 October. 'The army's trying to court-martial some guy in secret at Fort Benning for killing seventy-five Vietnamese civilians,' the source said. At that time, in fact, the army had done nothing more than prefer charges, and it was still trying to keep any word about the events at My Lai 4 out of the newspapers. It took two days and twenty-five telephone calls before somebody told me about the AP story on Calley. From there, it was a short step to Latimer, and on 29 October, a Monday, I flew from Washington to Salt Lake City to interview the lawyer. Before leaving Washington, I had received confirmation of the essential facts of the story from a government source. Latimer confirmed them, adding that: 'Whatever killing there was was in a firefight in connection with an operation. To me,' Latimer said, 'the thing that's important is this: why do we prosecute our own people while on a search-and-destroy mission and they kill some people, be they civilian or not? Is there a point in the chain of command at which somebody could be tried? I think not.'

On 11 November, a Tuesday, I decided to fly down to Fort Benning and find Calley. But Calley's name did not appear anywhere in the Fort Benning telephone book, nor did the file of tenants in the bachelor officers' quarters list him. It was ten hours afterwards and very late at night before I found a warrant officer, who was a downstairs neighbour of Calley's, at one of the officers' quarters. As we were talking, he suddenly hollered at a slight young man walking towards us – 'Rusty, come over here and meet this guy.' Impatient, I began to leave. 'No, wait a second,' the officer said. 'That's Calley.'

Calley was apprehensive. All he wanted in life was to stay in the army and be a good soldier. He reminded me of an earnest freshman one might find at an agricultural college, anxious about making a fraternity. We went to a party at a friend's apartment and had some drinks. I wanted to leave. Calley wanted me to stay. He knew what was coming and he knew I was the last reporter to whom he would talk, and drink with, for many months. He told me, that evening, a little bit about the operation; he also told me how many people he had been accused of killing. I flew back to Washington the next day and began to write my story. I did it somewhat hesitantly, my thought being that Calley, perhaps, was as much of a victim as those infants he and his men murdered at My Lai 4.

The first story began: 'Lieutenant William L. Calley, Jr, twenty-six, is a mild-mannered, boyish-looking Vietnam combat veteran with the nickname of "Rusty". The army says he deliberately murdered at least 109 Vietnamese civilians during a search-and-destroy mission in March, 1968, in a Vietcong stronghold known as "Pinkville".'

Once I had completed my research on My Lai 4, I tried to get it published. *Life* and *Look* magazines weren't interested. With some hesitation, I turned over my story to the Dispatch News Service, a small Washington news agency managed by David Obst. He was twenty-three years old, but his enthusiasm more than made up for his lack of experience. Fifty newspapers were offered the initial Dispatch story by cable on 12 November; more than thirty – including many of the leading newspapers in the nation – published it the next day, a remarkably high number.

Even more remarkable, however, was the fact that only the *New York Times* chose to pursue the story at its most logical point – South Vietnam. Most newspapers contented themselves with printing a later AP dispatch saying only that 'Army officials say they have completed an investigation into charges of multiple murder of Vietnamese civilians by a young American lieutenant, but that a decision whether to try him remains to be made'. The Pentagon refused to comment on the Dispatch story.

In Saigon, Henry Kamm, the *Times*' roving correspondent in South-East Asia, was assigned to locate the victimised village, which was identified only as 'Pinkville' in the first Dispatch account. Kamm bribed his way onto a commercial flight to Da Nang, and ended up in Quang Ngai City a few hours later. But he couldn't find out which hamlet was 'Pinkville'. On the next day he drove to the Americal Division headquarters at Chu Lai, and ran into André C. R. Feher, an investigator for the CID, who 'lectured me in a heavy German accent as to why he couldn't tell me anything'. By Saturday, 15 November, the army gave in to the inevitable and flew Kamm, along with representatives from *Newsweek* magazine and the American Broadcasting Corporation, to a relocation hamlet in Song My village where some My Lai 4 survivors were living.

The newsmen were given only one hour on the ground, and their interviews with the villagers were taped by a public information officer from the Americal Division. Kamm borrowed a typewriter, banged out a dispatch in which he quoted survivors as saying that 567 Vietnamese men, women and children were massacred by the Americans, and telephoned it to the *Times*' Saigon bureau in time for it to make page 1 of Monday's paper. Later Kamm tried unsuccessfully to get interviews with US Ambassador Ellsworth Bunker and General Creighton Abrams, the military commander for Vietnam. He did get to see a public information officer in Saigon, who 'treated me very coolly. He apparently felt that I had ratted on our side.'

Kamm's report was also treated coolly by the *Times*' main competitor, the *Washington Post*, which chose to publish a Pentagon statement describing Kamm's story as exaggerated. This denial was placed on page 16. Other newspapers were similarly sceptical about My Lai, and initially, few commented editorially on the massacre.

The press was also cautious about Ron Ridenhour's role in exposing the incident. Ben Cole of the *Arizona Republic*, writing a day after other newspapers published the massacre story, told about Ridenhour for the first time, and revealed that the Pentagon had confirmed it was Ridenhour's letter that had started the investigation. The AP picked up a few lines of Cole's story, and one of its reporters in California called Ridenhour for a brief interview. 'Viet Slaying Tipster Sees More Involved' was the headline a San Francisco paper put over the subsequent wire service story.

I flew out to California on 17 November to interview Ridenhour at Claremont College. No other newsman had yet taken the trouble to visit him. Ridenhour, delighted that his story had finally been made public, gave me a copy of his original letter, and his subsequent correspondence with the army and Congress. Most important, he also supplied me with the names and addresses of Michael Terry and

Michael Bernhardt. I left Ridenhour in the early afternoon, drove back to Los Angeles International Airport and took an evening flight to Salt Lake City. From there, it was a ninety-minute drive over snowy mountain passes to Orem, Utah, and to the home of Michael Terry. I knocked at the door of the darkened house. A younger brother let me in; he woke up Terry and the ex-GI came out to talk. I told him who I was and what I wanted. He thought a second, then asked, 'Do you want me to tell you the same thing I told Colonel Wilson?'

I got to Bernhardt at Fort Dix, New Jersey, the next afternoon, came back to Washington, and wrote the second Dispatch story based on the eyewitness accounts of My Lai 4 for newspapers of 20 November. Another revelation about that day was also in the works by that time.

On Tuesday, 18 November, Joseph Eszterhas, a general assignment reporter for the *Cleveland Plain Dealer*, received a phone call from an old schoolmate, an ex-GI named Ron Haeberle, who said he had photographs of the massacre. Haeberle had picked Eszterhas because the reporter had edited the newspaper at a school both had attended. Eszterhas was properly cautious: he conducted hours of taped interviews with Haeberle at the newspaper's office, trying to put together a full account of the photographer's involvement. And on the nineteenth he telephoned the Pentagon, seeking confirmation that Haeberle was indeed at My Lai 4 on 16 March 1968. He did not get it immediately. Later in the day Haeberle was called at home by Captain Aubrey Daniels of Fort Benning, then directing the prosecution against Calley, and was asked not to publish his pictures. Daniels warned that the photos would 'inflame public opinion' and might seriously jeopardise the rights of Calley and the others. Haeberle told Eszterhas about the call, and the reporter, still reluctant to release the story without official confirmation of Haeberle's mission that day, telephoned Fort Benning and received the same warning that Haeberle got from Daniels. The *Plain Dealer* now knew the photographs were authentic. The interview with Haeberle – and some of his photographs, depicting slaughtered women and children – were published on 20 November, the same day my interviews quoting Bernhardt and Terry were made available.

The articles and photographs had an immediate shock effect in England, where the My Lai 4 massacre reports pushed news of the second US landing on the moon off front pages on eight of Britain's nine morning newspapers. 'The Story That Stunned America' headlined the conservative *Daily Mail*. The equally conservative *Daily Sketch*, in a front-page editorial, wrote that 'the Americans were dragged down to the level of terrorism practised by the Vietcong. From today the Vietnam war is over . . . the President will have to pull out.' The *Daily Sketch*'s main headline read: 'War Crime. If This Can Happen, America Has Lost.' Eyewitness accounts of the massacre were prominently displayed on page 1 of the influential London *Times*. George Brown, former Foreign Secretary and a leader of Britain's ruling Labour Party, added to the furore when he told a radio audience that he wished Americans would 'stop weeping and get on with winning the war'. Thirty-two fellow members of the Labour Party demanded Brown's resignation, while others applauded his statement during bitter debate in the House of Commons. A group of demonstrators staged a noisy protest over My Lai 4 in front of the American embassy; a memorial monument to President John F. Kennedy at Runnymede was defaced by a Nazi swastika.

The reaction to the revelations about My Lai 4 in Great Britain was profound compared to that of the United States. In America, perhaps because of the less prominent newspaper coverage, the public was unable to comprehend the full significance of the incident. The impact of Haeberle's photographs and Bernhardt and Terry's eyewitness reports was partially diminished by the *Washington Post*, for example, in a story suggesting that the hardships suffered by Charlie Company might be responsible for its actions. 'For Company C, in March 1968,' said one *Post* story, 'the Pinkville rice paddies and battered hamlets were a nightmare of booby traps and mines.' One Associated Press dispatch attempting to explain the atmosphere in Vietnam included the following in its fourth paragraph: 'In Vietnam the killing of civilians was a practice established by the Vietcong as a major part of the war long before the first US ground troops were committed in March 1965.' The statement, though factual, was not relevant to what Charlie Company did on that 16 March.

On 25 November the army formally announced that Calley had been ordered to stand trial at a general court-martial for the premeditated murder of 109 Vietnamese civilians. Charges against Sergeant David Mitchell had been announced a few days earlier; he was accused of assaulting thirty Vietnamese civilians with intent to commit murder.

The newspapers continued being cautious. Most of them still refrained from commenting editorially. Air Force Lieutenant-General (Retired) Ira C. Eaker, a conservative columnist on military affairs for the *Detroit*

News, wrote how officers in Vietnam were bitter over what they saw as the press's failure to report Vietcong atrocities. 'I asked one of the Joint Chiefs of Staff why the Pentagon did not release any more Red atrocity stories,' Eaker wrote on 22 November. 'He said it was against Administration policy, since this might build up a war psychology in the country which would pressure our leadership to use more force than it wanted to use in this limited conflict.' Two days later, however, army officers in Saigon made available 'newly found' captured Vietcong documents showing that Communist troops killed nearly 2,900 Vietnamese during the Hue offensive in February 1968. Officers said the documents went unnoticed in US military files for nineteen months until a correspondent's questions about Hue brought them to light. 'I know it sounds incredible, but that's the truth,' one official said.

As yet there was little investigative reporting on the part of the American press to determine exactly what had happened, perhaps because newspapers did not try to locate former members of Charlie Company. By Friday, 21 November, I had found Paul Meadlo in Terre Haute, Indiana. Meadlo agreed to tell his story on television, and David Obst and the Dispatch lawyers arranged to produce him – for a fee – on the CBS evening news with Walter Cronkite. His confession, later published in newspapers around the world, stunned the nation. 'Many of us sat in sheltered living rooms,' wrote columnists Richard Harwood and Laurence Stern of the *Washington Post*, 'perhaps starting in on a dinner martini as Meadlo's face showed on the screen ... From the vantage point of those living rooms Meadlo was the American "gook" – the scapegoat and the buffer between the torn bodies in open graves at My Lai and ourselves.' That Sunday the *Post* devoted three full pages to the story.

The disclosure of the My Lai massacre cleared the way for published accounts of previously witnessed American atrocities in South Vietnam. Suddenly reporters were finding out that their newspapers were eager to print stories about the shooting of civilians in Vietnam. On 5 December 1969, an AP reporter told of an incident he had witnessed four years earlier: 'Frustration and fear ... were at work on a group of American Marines I accompanied into a village south of Da Nang in 1965. A half squad, out of a regimental-size force, went on a brief rampage, killing a group hiding in a civilian air-raid shelter. One marine called out, "Whoosh, I'm a killer today. I got me two."

Another said, "Kill them, I don't want anyone moving."' Three days later another AP dispatch reported that 'it was a rising storm of criticism from civilian province advisers against tough tactics by the US Army's 9th Infantry Division that resulted in that unit being the first to go home when President Nixon decided on troop withdrawals. The 9th Division prided itself on killing 100 Vietcong a day, every day. Civilian Americans in the provinces often complained to newsmen that innocent civilians were sometimes included in the totals.' Both stories could have been written and published much earlier. But few reporters would have dared to file such copy, and few newspapers would have dared to publish it.

At the least, Meadlo's CBS appearance made the American press finally face up to the fact that something very terrible had indeed happened at My Lai 4. Newspapers across the country began making judgements about the massacre, and they were uniformly harsh. John S. Knight, president of the Knight newspaper chain, wrote that 'the indiscriminate killings at Song My may now dramatise the larger question of why we remain in Vietnam'. The *Philadelphia Inquirer* described My Lai 4 as 'the kind of atrocity generally associated with the worst days of Hitler and Stalin and other cruel despotisms'. The *Washington Star* noted that 'when all is said, however, it is simply appalling to think of American soldiers gunning down helpless civilians, especially children and women, as the latter sought in vain to shield their offspring'.

Even conservative columnists were no longer able to dismiss My Lai 4. Columnist Ray Cromley of the Newspaper Enterprise Association suggested in all seriousness that America could begin to repay its debt to the Vietnamese by 'sending packages of those small things that poor Vietnamese villagers require to live . . . We can make certain that doctors and surgeons are available to remedy so far as is possible the permanent disfigurement of survivors . . . The Vietnamese people are a very humble people. They respond above all to men and women who accept personal responsibility. They live in a harsh world and know that terrible things happen. So they are amazingly forgiving when men and women personally show their desire to make friends.'

Even after acknowledging the facts of My Lai 4, many conservative newspapers struggled to evade its implications. 'Americans should not be deceived,' wrote the *Chicago Tribune* on 29 November, 'by the contemptible lamentations that we are all guilty and that our troops in

Viet Nam have been brutalised by the war and are just as inhuman as the Communists.' The *National Observer*, after noting that the massacre stories could not be dismissed, added these words of protest: 'It is not the "system", whatever its shortcomings, or the policy, whatever its failings, that are to blame . . . The full story must be learned . . . and when it is learned, individual responsibility must be fixed.'

No matter what private feelings the men of Charlie Company might have shared, most of them went back to their old jobs – in construction, as auto mechanics, hauling garbage in a big city, selling shoes – and tried to forget everything about Vietnam. The men coped with their emotions simply by burying them; but it would all resurface in November 1969, as the nightly TV news and daily newspapers reported about My Lai 4. Almost all of Charlie Company, despite warnings by military officials and civilian lawyers, talked about it in interviews. There was a persistent feeling of shame. 'Don't mention my name,' one GI asked after an interview. 'I don't want people around here pointing to me when I walk down the street, saying, "There goes that storm trooper."'

Robert J. Lee of Oshkosh, Wisconsin, was one of Charlie Company's medics at the time of My Lai 4; the GIs called him 'Doc'. Now he works as a hospital orderly in his home town, and he doesn't want to talk – or think – about what happened. 'I just want to forget it; I don't want to remember,' he said. His sense of remorse – heightened perhaps by his training – was strong. 'It was the worst thing that ever happened to me. Only my wife and parents know about it – that's all I've told.' The other medic in Charlie Company, Nicholas Capezza of New York, was attached to Medina's command post on 16 March 1968. He insisted he saw nothing unusual that day and complained that the news media was 'blowing it all out of proportion. To me, it was just like another day in Vietnam. Something like this is always happening. If you really wanted to find stories, you could find fifteen or twenty that could make this look like a nursery rhyme.'

Henry Pedrick also insisted during a long interview that there was nothing unusual that day. 'I didn't think very much about it,' he kept saying. 'I didn't have feelings towards it one way or another.' He became disturbed, however, when he was told that the Haeberle photographs would be published in *Life* magazine. 'They shouldn't do that, they shouldn't do that,' he said.

Gregory Olsen told the CID when they quizzed him in late August: 'It was a lot to bottle up and I feel better now that I have talked about it. Even if I was not involved in the killing, I still have a feeling of guilt for not stopping it or not reporting it to Colonel Barker . . . without a doubt I feel Lieutenant Calley was responsible for the shooting. Either him or the army for letting him go through OCS.[2] I do not condone the shooting of the civilians by members of Company C. They should have refused. To this day I do not know what came over them by not refusing.'

For one ex-GI, there was near-tragedy. After glibly telling newsmen about his role in the massacre, he lost his job, left his home and one morning attempted to swallow a bottle of aspirins. He was hospitalised and recovered.

Others didn't need reminders in daily newspapers. 'I knew it wasn't right,' Rennard Doines said, 'but over there it makes no difference. I've thought about it since I got back.' For a while William Wyatt just stopped believing everything he had seen in Vietnam. 'When you come back, it's just like there was some sort of fantasy-land over there.' But even so, he added, 'I know it wasn't like it was supposed to be.'

Charles West wasn't troubled by My Lai 4 while he was in uniform. 'Now that I'm a civilian,' he said later, 'I think like a civilian. I knew that after we got in there and didn't meet resistance, that the mission should have been stopped.'

A few GIs – only a few – seemed totally unmoved by the massacre, even in retrospect. 'I haven't let it bother me,' John Smail insisted. 'I never wanted to go there [Vietnam] in the first place. I hated those people, I really did.' A member of the third platoon, he had arrived at the hamlet moments after most of the shooting was over, he said. 'You know what I thought? Good. I didn't care nothing about the Vietnamese.'

Smail also was one of the few Charlie Company members to talk frankly about rape. Most of the company knew there were rapes that day in March, but remained reluctant to talk about them – in war, rape is never justifiable. 'That's an everyday affair,' Smail said. 'You can nail just about everybody on that – at least once. The guys are human, man.' By mid-March 1970, at least three members of Charlie Company were formally accused of rape in connection with the massacre.

[2] Officer Candidate School.

Lieutenant Calley nearly broke down after Sergeant Mitchell was charged with assault with intent to murder. He wanted to take the full responsibility, in public, for all of the crimes being laid against Charlie Company, if it would help his commanding officer and his men and exonerate the army. 'He's giving me fits,' his attorney, George Latimer, said later. 'He's loyal. He doesn't want to embarrass the army, and it wants to hang him.' Calley's attitude didn't change even after the army stripped him of his Vietnam decorations, including two Bronze Stars, and shifted him from a training job to a meaningless clerical task at base headquarters. He remained loyal as the court-martial neared and Latimer was unsuccessful in a series of legal manoeuvres, in January and February 1970, to get the case dismissed. 'He wants to hang,' an officer friend said. The lieutenant was showing increasing signs of tension. He lost weight, and another friend was shocked when, while drinking beer, Calley suddenly dashed into a bathroom and vomited blood. He explained that he hadn't been able to keep food in his stomach for days and had been drinking beer instead.

For a few GIs, the experience at My Lai 4 changed their former outlook on life; they became increasingly critical about the way the war was being conducted. 'I was a candidate for the Minutemen before this,' Michael Bernhardt said. 'Now I'm all turned around.' He had felt no remorse for the Vietnamese civilians while watching them get slaughtered, but he had thought that perhaps he was the odd one. 'Maybe this was the way wars really were,' he later explained. 'Maybe what we saw in the movies and on TV wasn't so, that war was running around and shooting civilians and doing this kind of thing. Maybe all along everybody else knew. I felt like I was left out, like maybe they forgot to tell me something, that this was the way we fought wars and everybody knew but me.'

Herbert Carter shot himself in the foot, perhaps to get out of My Lai 4. For him, there was no later sense of personal shame, only a feeling of amazement and irony at the response to the event. 'I still wonder why human beings claim to be human beings but still conduct themselves as savages and barbarians,' he said. 'The United States is supposed to be a peace-loving country; yet they tell them to do something and then they want to hang them for it.'

As far as he was concerned, Carter said, what happened at My Lai 4 was not a massacre, but a logical result of the war in Vietnam: 'The people didn't know what they were dying for and the guys didn't know why they were shooting them.'

JOHN PILGER
Year Zero
1979

'It is my duty,' wrote the correspondent of *The Times* at the liberation of Belsen, 'to describe something beyond the imagination of mankind.' That was how I felt in Cambodia in the summer of 1979. The ghostliness of Phnom Penh, the deserted houses, the flitting figures of skeletal orphaned children, like tiny phantoms, the millions of dollars in Cambodian banknotes washing through the empty streets in the monsoonal downpour, the stench of death from wells jammed with bodies and the nightly chorus of distress: these are indelible.

The following piece is drawn from many dispatches and chapters in my books, *Heroes* and *Distant Voices*. It covers more than twenty years: from the American bombing of the early 1970s, to 'Year Zero' in 1975, to the overthrow of Pol Pot in 1979 and the United Nations-sponsored 'peace' in 1992. Cambodia consumed much of my life. Apart from written work, I made four documentary films, beginning with *Year Zero: The Silent Death of Cambodia* (1979), which told of a dark age in South-East Asia, in which Pol Pot's infamy was shared with 'our' governments.

My reports first appeared in the *Daily Mirror* on 12 and 13 September 1979. The 12 September issue was devoted almost entirely to Cambodia: thousands of words and eleven pages of Eric Piper's historic photographs; a feat of tabloid design. It was one of the few *Mirrors* ever to sell out completely. Within twenty-four hours of publication, more than £50,000 arrived at the *Mirror* offices, a vast sum then and most of it in small amounts. I calculated that this was more than enough to pay for two fully-laden relief aircraft, but no insurance company would underwrite a flight to Cambodia. A Miami charter company with one old propeller-driven Convair agreed to fly, then the owner rang back to say the pilot had suffered a heart attack. British Midland Airways was considering the lease of a Boeing 707 when an executive phoned me to say the company had been 'warned off' by the Foreign Office, which had claimed that relief aircraft might face 'a hostile reception by Vietnamese troops'. This was disinformation; the Vietnamese had been asking for international help. Finally, an Icelandic company, Cargolux ('Fly anything anywhere'), had a DC-8 available. On 28 September, filled with enough penicillin, vitamins and milk to restore an estimated 69,000 children, the aircraft took off from Luxembourg, all of it paid for by *Mirror* readers.

My documentary *Year Zero* was shown on television soon afterwards. Forty sacks of post arrived at Associated Television (ATV): 26,000 first-class letters in the first twenty-four hours. A million pounds was reached quickly and, once again, most of it came from those who could ill afford to give. 'This is for Cambodia,' wrote an anonymous bus driver, enclosing his week's wage. An eighty-year-old woman sent her pension for two months. A single parent sent her entire savings of £50. People stopped me in the street to write cheques and came to my home with toys and letters, and petitions for Thatcher and poems of indignation for Pol Pot, Nixon and Kissinger. The BBC children's series *Blue Peter* announced an appeal to help the children of Cambodia, the first time the BBC had responded to a programme broadcast by its commercial rival. Within two months, children throughout Britain had raised an astonishing £3,500,000.

Following *Year Zero*'s showing around the world, more than $45 million was raised for Cambodia. This paid for medicines, the rebuilding of schools and clinics and the restoration of water supply. I was in Phnom Penh when the first textile factory making brightly coloured clothing was re-opened; under the Khmer Rouge, everybody had to wear black. Pushed into action by a cataract of letters, telegrams, phone calls and petitions, the British Government became the first Western government to 'de-recognise' the Pol Pot regime, although Britain continued to vote for the seating of Pol Pot's man at the United Nations (who was eventually given asylum in the United States, where he now lives in luxurious retirement).

For many people, as disturbing as the harrowing images in *Year Zero* was the revelation that, for Cold War geo-political reasons, the American and British governments were sending humanitarian aid only to Cambodian refugees in Thailand while denying it to the majority in Cambodia itself. Eleven months after the overthrow of Pol Pot, the total Western aid sent to Cambodia through the Red Cross and the United Nations Children's Fund amounted to 1,300 tons of food: effectively nothing.

Moreover, both governments had secretly joined with Pol Pot's principal backer, China, in punishing both the Cambodian people and their liberators, the Vietnamese. An embargo, reminiscent of the economic siege that was to devastate Iraq in the 1990s, was imposed on both countries, whose governments were declared Cold War enemies.

Two subsequent films of mine, *Year One* and *Year Ten,* disclosed that the Reagan administration was secretly restoring the Khmer Rouge as a military and political force in exile in Thailand, to be used as a weapon against Vietnam, and that British SAS troops were training them in bases along the border. 'You must understand,' Margaret Thatcher had said, 'there are *reasonable* Khmer Rouge.'

YEAR ZERO

The aircraft flew low, following the unravelling of the Mekong River west from Vietnam. Once over Cambodia, what we saw silenced all of us on board. There appeared to be nobody, no movement, not even an animal, as if the great population of Asia had stopped at the border. Whole towns and villages on the riverbanks were empty, it seemed, the doors of houses open, chairs and beds, pots and mats in the street, a car on its side, a mangled bicycle. Beside fallen power lines was a human shadow, lying or sitting; it had the shape of a child, though we could not be sure, for it did not move.

Beyond, the familiar landscape of South-East Asia, the patchwork of rice paddies and fields, was barely discernible; nothing seemed to have been planted or be growing, except the forest and mangrove and lines of tall wild grass. On the edge of towns this grass would follow straight lines, as though planned. Fertilised by human compost, by the remains of thousands upon thousands of men, women and children, these lines marked common graves in a nation where perhaps as many as two million people, or between one-third and a quarter of the population, were 'missing'.

Our plane made its approach into what had been the international airport at Phnom Penh, towards a beaconless runway and a deserted control tower. At the edge of the forest there appeared a pyramid of rusting cars, the first of many such sights, like objects in a mirage. The cars were piled one on top of the other; some of the cars had been brand new when their owners were forced to throw away the ignition keys and push them to the pile, which also included ambulances, a fire engine, police cars, refrigerators, washing machines, hairdriers, generators, television sets, telephones and typewriters, as if a huge Luddite broom had swept them there. 'Here lies the consumer society,' a headstone might have read, 'Abandoned 17 April, Year Zero'.

From that date, anybody who had owned cars and such 'luxuries', anybody who had lived in a city or town, anybody with more than a basic education or who had acquired a modern skill, such as doctors, nurses, teachers, engineers, tradespeople and students, anybody who knew or worked for foreigners, such as travel agents, clerks, journalists and artists, was in danger; some were under sentence of death. To give just one example, out of a royal ballet company of 500 dancers, a few dozen survived; of the others, some escaped abroad, some starved to death or succumbed to illness related to extreme deprivation, and some were murdered.

My previous trip to Cambodia had been twelve years earlier. I had flown across from wartime Saigon, exchanging venality and neurosis for what Western visitors invariably saw as the innocence of a 'gentle land' whose capital, Phnom Penh, had a beauty only the French could contrive. On Sundays the parade down Monivong Avenue was a joy: the parasols, the beautiful young women on their Hondas, the saffron robes, the platoons of well-fed families, the ice-cream barrows, the weddings, the hustlers. You awoke at the cavernous Hotel Royale, switched on your radio and, in all probability, heard the squeaky voice of Prince Norodom Sihanouk berating you or another foreign journalist for writing about the financial excesses of the royal family. This might be followed by a summons to the royal palace and an instruction to listen to the Prince's collection of jazz recordings, usually Oscar Peterson. Sihanouk, 'God-king' and a relic of the French empire, was his country's most celebrated jazz musician, film director, football coach, and juggler of apparently impossible options in Indo-China's cockpit of war. Such was his kingdom: feudal, unpredictable, preposterous and, in relation to events in the region, at peace.

The Cambodia which foreigners romanticised (myself included) belied a recent history of savagery between warring groups, such as those loyal to Sihanouk and the 'Issaraks', who were anti-French and anti-royalty but sometimes no more than murderous bandits. The atrocities which emerged from some of their skirmishes from the 1940s to the 1960s were of a ritual nature later associated with the Pol Pot period, but were probably common enough in a peasant world that few foreigners saw and understood. Sihanouk himself was a capricious autocrat whose thugs dispensed arbitrary terror when Westerners were not looking, or did not wish to look; and his authoritarianism undoubtedly contributed to the growth of an extreme communist party, or Khmer Rouge. Certainly his 'Popular Socialist Community', which he set up in the 1950s, had little to do with socialism and everything to do with creating suitably benign conditions for the spread and enrichment of a powerful mandarinate in the towns and ethnic Chinese usurers in the rural areas. However, hunger was rare; indeed, so bountiful seemed the Khmers' lush, under-populated land that the Chinese coined a superlative: 'As rich as Cambodia!'

In 1959, a United States Defense Department report described the Khmers as a nation of people who could not be easily panicked, whose horizons were limited to village, pagoda and forest, who knew of no other countries, who respected their government, and feared ghosts, and 'cannot be counted upon to act in any positive way for the benefit of US aims and policies'.

Cambodia then was regarded as 'neutral'; that is, it was allied to no bloc. However, Sihanouk later allowed Ho Chi Minh's Vietnamese to run their supply routes through his territory, which gave a general called Lon Nol a pretext to stage a coup in 1970. The CIA denied having anything to do with it; but 1970 was the year Richard Nixon and his national security adviser, Henry Kissinger, were conducting their 'secret bombing' of Cambodia, aimed at Vietnamese 'sanctuaries'. US Air Force pilots were sworn to secrecy and their operational logs were falsified or destroyed. During 1969–70 the American public and Congress knew nothing about it. During one six-month period in 1973, B-52s dropped more bombs in 3,695 raids on the populated heartland of Cambodia than were dropped on Japan during all of the Second World War: the equivalent, in tons of bombs, of five Hiroshimas.

In 1977, a former member of Kissinger's staff, Roger Morris, described the way in which the President's foreign-policy advisers, known as 'the Wise Men', prepared the ground for the final destruction of Indo-China:

Though they spoke of terrible human suffering reality was sealed off by their trite, lifeless vernacular: 'capabilities', 'objectives', 'our chips', 'giveaway'. It was a matter, too, of culture and style. They spoke with the cool, deliberate detachment of men who believe the banishment of feeling renders them wise and, more important, credible to other men . . . [Of Kissinger and Nixon] They neither understood the foreign policy they were dealing with, nor were deeply moved by the bloodshed and suffering they administered to their stereotypes.

On the eve of an American land invasion of 'neutral' Cambodia in April 1970, according to Morris, Nixon said to Kissinger, 'If this doesn't work, it'll be your ass, Henry.'

It worked, in a fashion. The bombing and invasion provided a small group of fanatical Maoists, the Khmer Rouge, with a catalyst for a revolution which had no popular base among the Khmer people. What is striking about the rise of Pol Pot, Khieu Samphan and other principals in the Khmer Rouge is their medievalism, which their ideological pretensions barely concealed. Pol Pot and Khieu Samphan were both left-wing students in Paris in the 1950s, when and where other colonial revolutions were reputedly conceived; but neither admitted the existence of a Marxist-Leninist or communist organisation until 1977, by which time they were prime minister and head of state respectively of 'Democratic Kampuchea'. Indeed, in the movement they led, all ideology, authority and 'justice' flowed from 'Angkar Loeu', literally the 'Organisation on High', which 'has the eyes of a pineapple; it sees everything'.

Angkor was the capital of a Khmer empire at its zenith between the tenth and the thirteenth centuries. It reached from Burma to the South China Sea and was interrupted only by what is now central Vietnam; the equally nationalist Vietnamese had not long freed themselves from a thousand years of Chinese rule. Angkor, the place, was a tribute to the riches, energy and chauvinism of the dynasty, with its series of temples conceived as a symbolic universe according to traditional Indian cosmology, and built by slaves. There was an absolute monarch, a pharaoh-style figure, a bureaucracy organised by Brahmins, and a military leadership; and, like Egypt and Rome, the empire duly collapsed under the weight of its monuments and megalomanias, as well as its changing patterns of trade. The celebrated temples of Angkor Wat are all that remain of its glory.

'If our people can build Angkor Wat,' said Pol Pot in 1977, 'they can do anything!' This was the year Pol Pot probably killed more of his people than during all of his reign. Xenophobic in the extreme, he might have modelled himself on a despotic king of Angkor, which would explain his ambition to reclaim that part of the Mekong Delta, now southern Vietnam and known as Kampuchea Krom, over which the Khmer kings had once ruled. He was also an admirer of Mao Tse-tung and the Gang of Four; and it is not improbable that just as Mao had seen himself as the greatest emperor of China, so Pol Pot saw himself as another Mao, directing his own red guards to purify all élites, subversives and revisionists and to create a totally self-reliant state and one sealed off from the 'virus' of the modern world.

Cambodia is 90 per cent villages and the worsening imbalance in the relationship between peasant and town-dweller was one which Pol Pot and his 'men in black' were able to exploit almost with impunity. The French had created Phnom Penh in their own remote image and had brought in Chinese and Vietnamese bureaucrats and traders. Those in power in the capital took from and taxed the peasants as if by divine right; and when three years of American bombing killed or wounded or dislocated hundreds of thousands of Khmer peasants and created many more as refugees, the Khmer Rouge, now operating from enclaves, swept into a power vacuum in the bloodied countryside.

To understand the opportunities which the American bombing gave to the Khmer Rouge, one need not look beyond the story of Neak Long, a Mekong River town thirty miles from Phnom Penh. In August 1973, a B-52 unloaded its bombs on Neak Long and more than a hundred villagers were killed and several hundred wounded. The fate of the village was promoted in Washington as a 'lesson learned'. Ostentatiously, the bombing was described as a 'mistake' and a crew member was fined $700. The American ambassador to Cambodia, Emory Swank, went to the village and handed $100 bills to each grieving family as 'compensation'. Throughout Cambodia, hundreds of villages suffered terribly without Ambassador Swank's largesse.

At 7.30 on the morning of 17 April 1975, the Khmer Rouge entered Phnom Penh. They marched in Indian file along the boulevards, through the still traffic. They wore black and were mostly teenagers, and people cheered them nervously, naïvely, as people do when war seems to be over. Phnom Penh then had a swollen population of about

two million. At one o'clock the 'men in black' decreed that the city
was to be abandoned by all except for a few thousand who would
maintain its skeleton. The sick and wounded were ordered and dragged
at gunpoint from their hospital beds; surgeons were forced to leave
patients in mid-operation. On the road out through the suburbs a
procession of mobile beds could be seen, with their drip-bottles swinging
at the bedpost; a man whose throat and mouth had been torn away
by a rocket explosion was pushed along by his aged father. The old
and crippled fell beside the road and their families were forced to move
on. Crippled and dying children were carried in plastic bags. Women
barely out of childbirth staggered forward, supported by parents.
Orphaned babies, forty-one by one estimate, were left in their cradles
at the Phnom Penh paediatric centre without anybody to care for them.

'Don't take anything with you,' broadcast the young troops through
loudspeakers. 'The Angkar is saying that you must leave the city for
just three hours so that we can prepare to defend you against bombing
by American aircraft.'

For once, there was no bombing, and even among those on the
road who knew it to be a lie, defeatism, fear and exhaustion seemed
to make them powerless. The haemorrhage lasted two days and two
nights, then Cambodia fell into shadow. When, on 7 January 1979,
the Vietnamese Army came up the Mekong and drove into Phnom
Penh, they found the city virtually as it had been left on the first day
of 'Year Zero'.

This was how I found it when I arrived with photographer Eric
Piper, film director David Munro, cameraman Gerry Pinches and
sound recordist Steve Phillips of Associated Television (ATV). In the
silent, oppressive humidity it was like entering a city the size of
Manchester or Brussels in the wake of a nuclear cataclysm which
had spared only the buildings. Houses, flats, office blocks, schools,
hotels stood empty and open, as if vacated by their occupants that
day. Personal possessions lay trampled on a front path, a tricycle
crushed and rusted in the gutter, the traffic lights jammed on red.
There was electricity in the centre of the city; elsewhere there was
neither power nor a working sewer nor water to drink. At the railway
station trains stood empty at various stages of interrupted departure.
Pieces of burned cloth fluttered on the platform, and when we
enquired about this it was explained that on the day they fled before
the Vietnamese Army the Khmer Rouge had set fire to carriages in
which wounded people lay.

When the afternoon monsoon broke, the gutters of the city were suddenly awash with what looked like paper, but it was money. The streets ran with money, much of it new and unused banknotes whose source was not far away. The modern concrete building of the National Bank of Cambodia looked as if it had sustained one mighty punch. As if to show their contempt for the order they replaced, the Khmer Rouge had blown it up and now with every downpour a worthless fortune sluiced from it into the streets. Inside, cheque books lay open on the counter, one with a cheque partly filled out and the date 17 April 1975. A pair of broken spectacles rested on an open ledger; money seemed to be everywhere; I slipped and fell hard on a floor brittle with coins; boxes of new notes were stacked where they had been received from the supplier in London.

In our first hours in Phnom Penh we shot no film and took no photographs; incredulity saw to that. I had no sense of people, of even the remnants of a population; the few human shapes I glimpsed seemed incoherent images, detached from the city itself. On catching sight of us, they would flit into the refuge of a courtyard or a cinema or a filling station. Only when I pursued several, and watched them forage, did I see that they were children. One child about ten years old – although age was difficult to judge – ran into a wardrobe lying on its side which was his or her refuge. In an Esso station, an old woman and three emaciated children squatted around a pot containing a mixture of roots and leaves, which bubbled over a fire fuelled with paper money: thousands of snapping, crackling brand-new *riel*: such a morbid irony, for money could no longer buy everything these people needed.

The first person we stopped and spoke to was a man balancing a load on his head and an arm on his son's shoulder. He was blind and his face was pitted from what might have been smallpox. His son was fifteen years old, but so thin that he might have been nine. The man spoke some French and said his name was Khim Kon and his son was Van Sok and that 'before Pol Pot' he had been a carpenter. 'This boy', he said, touching his son with affection, 'is my only child left. Because we came from the city, we were classified "new people". We had to work from three in the morning until eleven at night; the children, too. My wife and three others are all dead now.' I asked him how he had lost his sight. 'I was always blind in one eye,' he said. 'When my family started to die I cried, so they took out my other eye with a whip.' Of all the survivors I would talk to in the coming weeks, that man and his son, who had lost four members of their immediate family, were the least damaged.

My memory of Phnom Penh from twelve years before now told me where I was; I was in the middle of Monivong Avenue, facing the Roman Catholic cathedral. But there was no cathedral. In the constitution of Pol Pot's 'Democratic Kampuchea', article twenty stated that all Khmers had 'the right to worship according to any religion and the right not to worship according to any religion', but religion that was 'wrong' and 'reactionary' and 'detrimental' was prohibited. So the Gothic cathedral of Phnom Penh, a modest version of the cathedral at Rheims, a place where the 'wrong' religion was practised, was dismantled, stone by stone. Only wasteland was left.

I walked across Monivong Avenue to the National Library which the 'men in black' had converted into a pigsty, apparently as a symbol, since all books published prior to Year Zero were also 'detrimental'. The library's books and documents had been burned, looted by the returning city dwellers, discarded as rubbish, or thrown into the street. Next door stood the Hotel Royale, whose stuffed crocodiles offered a kind of greeting; they at least had not been considered detrimental, although the garden aviary was empty and overgrown and the swimming-pool was festering and stagnant. I had swum in it long ago; now it was a cesspit.

Our billet was in the former Air France residence, a functional white building which a family of banana palms seemed to be reclaiming by the hour. Beneath many of these palms had been discovered human remains which, it was claimed, were used as human fertiliser. Like almost everywhere else in Phnom Penh, to enter this house was to intrude upon ghosts; an initialled pen, an opened packet of tobacco, a used air ticket lay in a drawer. David Munro unknowingly bedded down beside a nest of rats which gnawed through our supply of candles in the night. The water in the shower ran yellow and the drains smelt rotten; corpses had been found wedged in wells. Whatever we touched, it seemed, had been polluted by the past. We heated our cans and boiled our water on a Primus stove in what had been somebody's sitting room. We ate little and spoke rarely and I found myself gulping neat whisky, without effect. On 15 August David Munro wrote in his diary: 'I don't know what to do to film what we're seeing, because all we're seeing is silence . . . and this smell. No one is going to believe us.'

For a fleeting moment, the normal and mundane would seem to

return. One morning our interpreter, Sophak, was laughing with Eric Piper when she suddenly stopped and spoke, as if to no one, this horrific *non sequitur*: 'Can you imagine they take away friendship?' she said, still smiling. 'A young boy who used to be a student was taken away and beaten to death because he smiled at me while we husked the rice. He smiled at me, that's all.'

Sophak had been forced to live in a communal camp where people were fed according to how 'productive' they were. Those who fell sick were left where they lay in the fields or were attended, she said, by bogus 'doctors', usually teenage boys who would dispense tablets made from roots or give injections with filthy syringes. The 'serum' would leave their patients writhing in pain and often would kill them. Sophak said these 'doctors' would also perform 'operations' during which incisions were made with unsterilised instruments and without anaesthetic of any kind. Sometimes an organ would be removed and 'examined' on the grass while the victim screamed. These young 'doctors' earned food, which was also the reward for boys recruited as spies. The boys, said Sophak, would listen at night for 'detrimental' laughter or sorrow, and would report those falling asleep during a midnight 'ideological study'. Even the word 'sleep' itself was banned; from Year Zero there would be 'rest'. Only the camp controller could sanction marriage and people were married in large groups, having been directed to whom they might 'choose' as a partner; husbands and wives were allowed to sleep together only once a month. At the age of seven, children were put to work; at twelve, they were 'sent away'. There were, said Sophak, 'no families, no sentiment, no love or grief, no holidays, no music, no song'.

On another day, when we were filming several hundred Khmer Rouge prisoners at a barracks outside the city, I said to Sophak, 'Ask him how many people he killed.' In front of us was a man in his thirties who had an almost casual air. She put the question, he answered it briskly and she turned to me and said, 'In his group they kill two hundred and fifty.'

'How many were in his group?' I asked.

'Eight persons in each group,' she said.

'So eight of them killed two hundred and fifty people,' I said.

'Yes,' she said, 'but this man over here says he killed fifty people on his own.'

We moved across to the second man, and when I asked Sophak to ask him who were the fifty people he had killed, she gave as his answer, 'Most of them were men, women and children from the city class, the middle class.'

'Has he children of his own?' I asked.

'He has one child,' she said, 'and that child is very well.' She walked away and, out of sight, she vomited.

Two months earlier Eric Piper and I had followed Pope John Paul on his return to Poland, where we had seen Auschwitz for the first time. Now, in South-East Asia, we glimpsed it again. On a clear, sunny day with flocks of tiny swifts, the bravest of birds, rising and falling almost to the ground, we drove along a narrow dirt road at the end of which was a former primary school, called Tuol Sleng. During the Pol Pot years this school was run by a Khmer gestapo, 'S-21', which divided the classrooms into an 'interrogation unit' and a 'torture massacre unit'. People were mutilated on iron beds and we found their blood and tufts of their hair still on the floor. Between December 1975 and June 1978 at least 12,000 people died slow deaths here: a fact not difficult to confirm because the killers, like the Nazis, were pedantic in their sadism. They photographed their victims before and after they tortured and killed them and horrific images now looked at us from walls; some had tried to smile for the photographer, as if he might take pity on them and save them. Names and ages, even height and weight, were recorded. We found, as at Auschwitz, one room filled to the ceiling with victims' clothes and shoes, including those of many children.

However, unlike Auschwitz, Tuol Sleng was primarily a political death centre. Leading members of the Khmer Rouge Army, including those who formed an early resistance to Pol Pot, were murdered here, usually after 'confessing' that they had worked for the CIA, the KGB or Hanoi. Whatever its historical model, if any, the demonic nature of Tuol Sleng was its devotion to human suffering. Whole families were confined in small cells, fettered to a single iron bar. They were kept naked and slept on the stone floor, without blanket or mat, and on the wall was a school blackboard, on which was written:

1. Speaking is absolutely forbidden
2. Before doing something, the authorisation of the warden must be obtained.

'Doing something' might mean only changing position in the cell, but without authorisation the prisoner would receive twenty to thirty strokes with a whip. Latrines were small ammunition boxes left over from Lon Nol's army, labelled 'Made in USA'. For upsetting a box of excrement the punishment was licking the floor with your tongue, torture or death.

When the Vietnamese discovered Tuol Sleng they found nineteen mass graves within the vicinity of the prison and eight survivors, including four children and a month-old baby. Tem Chan was one of them. He told me, 'For a whole week I was filled with water, then given electric currents. Finally, I admitted anything they wanted. I said I worked for the KGB. It was so ridiculous. When they found out I was a sculptor the torture stopped and I was put to work making busts of Pol Pot. That saved my life.'

Another survivor was Ung Pech, an engineer, whose fingers had been crushed in a vice. He wept as he told me, 'My wife, my sons, my daughter . . . all are gone. I have only one child left. Five children dead. They gave them nothing to eat.'

The days now passed for the five of us as if in slow motion. Anxiety and a certain menace did not leave us. At Siem Reap, in the north-west, after trudging through a nightmarish mass grave filled with skulls, many of which had been smashed, Eric and Steve fell ill and worked most of the time in agony from dysentery. David's exceptional organising skills were much in evidence; he established a routine and saw everybody gently through it.

Two concerns preoccupied us. Was it possible, we asked ourselves, to convey the evidence of what we had seen, which was barely credible to us, in such a way that the *enormity* of the crime committed in Cambodia might be recognised internationally and the survivors helped? And, on a personal level, how could we keep moving *away* from the sounds which pursued us? The initial silence had broken and now the cries of fleshless children tormented us almost everywhere.

This was especially so when we reached the town of Kompong Speu where 150,000 people were said to be 'missing'. Where there had been markets, houses and schools, there was bare land. Substantial buildings had been demolished, *erased* like the cathedral. The town's hospital had disappeared; Vietnamese engineers had erected a temporary one and supplied a doctor and some drugs. But there were few beds and no blankets and antiseptic was splashed urgently on our hands every few yards we walked; many of the people lying on the stone floor were dying from plague and anthrax, which is passed through the meat of diseased cattle and takes about a month to kill.

It can be cured by penicillin, but there was no penicillin, except that brought by two French doctors, Jean Yves Follezou and Jean Michel Vinot, who had travelled down from Phnom Penh with us. The human sounds here, I recall vividly, had a syncopation, a terrible prosody: high and shrill, then deep and unrelenting, the rhythm of approaching death. In the 'orphan's war', the children sat and leaned and lay on mats, impassive, looking directly at us and at the camera lens. When a young girl died after begging us for help, I felt the depths of shame and rage.

Similarly, in the 'hospital' of an orphanage in Phnom Penh, laid out like a First World War field station in the Gothic shell of an abandoned chapel, there were children who had been found wandering in the forest, living off treebark, grass and poisonous plants. Their appearance denied their humanity; rows of opaque eyes set in cloth-like skin. Here Gerry put his camera on the ground, walked away and cried.

One of several adults in charge at the orphanage was Prak Sarinn, a former teacher, who had survived the Pol Pot years by disguising himself as a peasant. 'It was the only acceptable class,' he said. 'I changed my personality, and I shall not be the same again. I can no longer teach; my head is filled with death and worry.' I asked him what had happened on 17 April 1975. He said, 'I was in my classroom when they burst in. They looked like boys, not even thirteen. They put their guns on us and told us all to march north into the countryside. The children were crying. I asked if we could first go home to join our families. They said no. So we just walked away, and most of the little ones died from exhaustion and hunger. I never saw my family again.'

With Mr Sarinn interpreting I spoke to one of the children lying still on a mat in the chapel and asked him his age.

'I remember,' said the child. 'I am twelve years old.'

'What is your name?' I asked.

'I forget,' he replied.

'Where are your parents?'

'I forget . . . I think they died.'

In the main hospital of Phnom Penh, where modern equipment had been vandalised and destroyed and the dispensary was bare, 'No. 23' on a bare iron bed was Kuon, a ten-year-old who seemed to diminish by the hour; he was too ill to eat the crude rice for which the ration was then four pounds per person per month. On the day we were there he might have been saved; antibiotics and milk were all he needed, but there was not an aspirin. When we returned the next morning, his name, along with the names of five other dead children, was chalked on a blackboard in the hospital yard, beside a poster which read, 'The United Nations wishes to remind you that 1979 is the International Year of the Child'. The poster was put there by Dr Follezou 'much more in anger than in sorrow', he said. The United Nations recognised the ousted Pol Pot regime and the United Nations Children's Fund (UNICEF) had sent no relief.

My favourite symbol of international inaction was a large red cross on the roof of the hospital, remaining from the days when ladders of bombs from B-52s fell not far away. The red cross is, of course, the universal mark of humanitarianism and is said to transcend politics and frontiers. At this hospital it might have served to ward off evil spirits; no doctors or nurses of the International Red Cross (ICRC) had come, and the driblets of Red Cross-supplied medicines had evaporated.

Shortly after our arrival in Phnom Penh, two men representing ICRC and UNICEF were preparing to leave. The UNICEF man, Jacques Beaumont, suitcase in hand, was in an emotional state and my interview with him was interrupted several times while he composed himself. I asked him how many people were threatened by famine.

He replied, 'The government [in Phnom Penh] has requested help for 2,250,000 people ... this is the dimension of the problem ... you see, eighty-five per cent of the women have stopped menstruating. Where is the next generation coming from? In Kompong Speu, in one of the very poor barracks with practically nothing, there were fifty-four children dying. I will always remember that I did not do anything for these children, because we had nothing.'

During the interview I asked Beaumont why UNICEF and ICRC had done so little. At this, he walked away from the camera, took David and me by the arm and led us to a Red Cross man sitting alone in the foyer of the Hotel Royale. 'He will explain,' he said. 'Tell them what the truth is, François.'

François Bugnion, of ICRC in Geneva, was clearly distraught. He asked, 'What nationality are you? What government are you?' I told him I was an Australian national and a journalist.

'So you must have contacts in the Australian Government,' he said. 'So you must go to them now please, and get them to send one C-130 Hercules aircraft here. The Hercules is important because all the forklifts at the airport have been destroyed. This plane can unload itself and one consignment of a truck, food and drugs will save thousands ... The Australians have done this thing before. They paint out the military markings, and there is no problem. But you must not say this request has come from me ... Geneva must not find out I have asked you to do this.'

I asked him why the Red Cross itself did not approach the Australian Government; why was there this need for subterfuge?

'I am desperate,' he replied. 'In Geneva they are still studying the framework of a plan of relief for Cambodia, but the situation cannot wait. People are dying around us. *They* can't wait for the politics to be ironed out and for Geneva to say go.'

Bugnion tore a page from a yellow legal pad and laboriously wrote the names of those in the ICRC hierarchy responsible for 'Asia and Oceania'. 'Here', he said, 'are the people you will need to persuade.'

These raw interviews, conducted in Phnom Penh at a time of historic emergency for the Khmer people, are a guide to why this stricken society had to wait so long for Western relief to arrive. There were subsequent attempts, in Bangkok, Geneva and New York, to damage the credibility of both Beaumont and Bugnion; they were variously described as 'unreliable' and drunks. These were among the first of many smears mounted against those who told a truth unpalatable to some Western governments, to sections of the Western media and to the secular missionaries of the established aid industry.

To understand this peculiar bigotry, which persists today, it is necessary to go back to the early spring of 1979 when the first refugees fleeing in advance of the Khmer Rouge crossed the border into Thailand. The Thai regime's immediate response was to describe the refugees as 'illegal immigrants' and to repatriate them forcibly into enclaves held by the Khmer Rouge. In one night in June 1979, the Thais 'pushed back' between 35,000 and 40,000 Cambodian refugees, many of them hungry and sick. They forced them down a hill and across a minefield. Some were killed or injured by the mines, although most were rescued by Vietnamese troops. Many of those who tried to cross the border again were beaten and shot by Thai soldiers.

The reason for this stemmed from the fact that Cambodia's liberators had come from the wrong side of the Cold War. The Vietnamese, who had driven the Americans from their homeland, were not to be acknowledged in any way as liberators, and they and the Khmer people would suffer accordingly. This charade was played out in the

United Nations, where the British Government voted to legitimise the defunct regime of Pol Pot. A majority of the UN credentials committee, including almost all the Western democracies, supported a Chinese motion that Pol Pot's 'Democratic Kampuchea' continue to be recognised as the government of Cambodia. As the American representative, Robert Rosenstock, rose from his seat after voting for Pol Pot, somebody grabbed his hand and congratulated him. 'I looked up and saw it was Ieng Sary [Pol Pot's foreign minister],' he recalled. 'I felt like washing my hands.'

International 'legitimacy' would thus be denied to the new government in Cambodia which the Vietnamese had brought to power, regardless of the fact that it had freed the Khmers from their charnel house and governed 90 per cent of the country. By contrast, the pro-Washington Lon Nol government, which the Americans had sustained from 1970 to 1975, controlled only the towns and main roads, yet had received full international recognition. The cynicism was such that had the Thais, the right people on the right side, liberated their Khmer neighbours under the auspices of the Americans, the sky over Phnom Penh would have been crowded with American relief aircraft and Pol Pot's man would not have taken Cambodia's seat in the world assembly.

The UN vote for Pol Pot meant that stricken Cambodia was denied almost the entire international machinery of recovery and assistance: the United Nations Development Programme, the Asian Development Bank and the World Bank could not legally help. At the World Health Assembly in Geneva, the British delegate, Sir Henry Yellowlees, voted for Pol Pot's man to take Cambodia's seat. This meant that the resources of WHO, the World Health Organisation, were now denied to Cambodia. Shortly after the Geneva meeting, a WHO official telephoned me. 'That picture with your Cambodia story of the pock-marked man,' he said, 'can you tell us if that was caused by smallpox?' I said I did not know, but if smallpox had reappeared during Pol Pot's time, surely a WHO investigator should go to Cambodia to find out. 'We can't do that,' he said. 'They're not recognised.'

By January 1980, the game had become grotesque. The United States had begun secretly funding Pol Pot. The extent of this support – $85 million from 1980 to 1986 – was revealed six years later in correspondence between congressional lawyer Jonathan Winer, counsel to

a member of the Senate Foreign Relations Committee, and the Vietnam
Veterans of America Foundation. Winer said the information had come
from the Congressional Research Service. When copies of his letter
were circulated, the Reagan administration was furious. Then, without
adequately explaining why, Winer repudiated the statistics, while not
disputing that they had come from the Congressional Research Service.
However, in a second letter to Noam Chomsky, Winer repeated the
original charge, which, he told me, was 'absolutely correct'.

As a cover for its secret war against Cambodia and its liberator,
Vietnam, Washington set up the Kampuchean Emergency Group,
known as KEG, in the American embassy in Bangkok and on the
border. KEG's job was to 'monitor' the distribution of Western humanitarian supplies sent to the refugee camps in Thailand and to ensure
that Khmer Rouge bases were fed. Although ostensibly a State
Department operation, its principals were intelligence officers with
long experience in Indo-China.

Two American relief aid workers, Linda Mason and Roger Brown,
later wrote, 'The US Government insisted that the Khmer Rouge be
fed . . . the US preferred that the Khmer Rouge operation benefit
from the credibility of an internationally known relief operation.'
Under American pressure, the World Food Programme handed over
$12 million worth of food to the Thai Army to pass on to the Khmer
Rouge. '20,000 to 40,000 Pol Pot guerrillas benefited,' according to
former Assistant Secretary of State Richard Holbrooke.

I witnessed this. In 1980, a film crew and I travelled in a UN
convoy of forty trucks, seventeen loaded with food, seventeen with
seed and the rest with 'goodies', which was the term UN people used
for their assorted largesse. We headed for Phnom Chat, a Khmer
Rouge operations base set in forest just inside Cambodia and bunkered
with land-mines. The UN official leading the convoy, Phyllis Gestrin,
a University of Texas psychology professor, was worried and clearly
disliked what she was doing. 'I don't want to think what this aid is
doing,' she said. 'I don't trust these blackshirts.' She could barely
suppress her fear and demonstrated it by driving her Land Rover
across a suspected minefield and into a tree. 'Oh man,' she said, 'this
place gives me the creeps. Let's get it over with.' At that, she turned
the Land Rover around and pointed it back along the track. 'We
always position it so we can get out fast,' she said.

After the trucks had dropped their 'goodies' in a clearing, Phyllis
solicited the signature of a man who had watched in bemused silence

from a thatched shelter. 'Well, I guess what I've got here is a receipt,' she said, with a nervous laugh. 'Not bad, from a butcher like him . . .' The 'butcher' was the base commander, who demanded that the foreign aid people address him as '*Monsieur le Président*'. In 1979, I had seen in Siem Reap province the mass grave of several thousand people shortly after it was unearthed. Many of the corpses had been beaten to death, as their splintered skulls clearly showed. Now, smiling before me was Pol Pot's governor of the province at the time of that mass murder. His name, he told me, was Nam Phann, which was a military alias. He was eager to confirm that Western aid had nourished and restored the Khmer Rouge. 'Thank you very much,' he said, 'and we wish for more.' I asked him whom he regarded as his allies in the world. 'Oh,' he replied, 'China, the ASEAN[1] nations . . . and the United States.'

Working through 'Task Force 80' of the Thai Army, which had liaison officers with the Khmer Rouge, the Americans ensured a constant flow of UN supplies to bases like Phnom Chat. The Kampuchean Emergency Group (KEG) was run by Michael Eiland, whose career underscored the continuity of American intervention in Indo-China. In 1969–70, he was operations officer of a clandestine Special Forces group code-named 'Daniel Boone', which was responsible for the reconnaissance of the American bombing of Cambodia. By 1980, Colonel Eiland was running KEG from the American embassy in Bangkok, where it was described as a 'humanitarian' organisation. He was also responsible for interpreting satellite surveillance pictures of Cambodia and in that capacity was a valued informant of a number of resident members of Bangkok's Western press corps, who referred to him in their reports as a 'Western analyst'. Eiland's 'humanitarian' duties subsequently led to his appointment as Defense Intelligence Agency (DIA) chief in charge of the South-East Asia Region, one of the most important positions in American espionage.

In November 1980, direct contact was made between the Reagan White House and the Khmer Rouge when Dr Ray Cline, a former deputy director of the CIA, made a secret visit to a Khmer Rouge operational headquarters inside Cambodia. Cline was then a foreign policy adviser on President-elect Reagan's transitional team. Within a year, fifty CIA agents were running America's Cambodia operation from Thailand.

---

[1] Association of South-East Asian Nations.

The dividing line between the international relief operation and the American war became more and more confused. A Defense Intelligence Agency colonel was appointed 'security liaison officer' between the United Nations Border Relief Operation (UNBRO) and the Displaced Persons Protection Unit (DPPU). In Washington, he was revealed as a link between the US Government and the Khmer Rouge.

By 1981, a number of governments had become decidedly uneasy about the United Nations' continued recognition of Pol Pot. This was dramatically demonstrated when a colleague of mine, Nicholas Claxton, entered a bar at the United Nations in New York with Thaoun Prasith, Pol Pot's representative, whom he was hoping to interview. 'Within minutes,' said Claxton, 'the bar had emptied.'

Clearly, a new mask was required. In 1982, the United States and China, supported by Singapore, invented the Coalition of the Democratic Government of Kampuchea, which was, as Ben Kiernan pointed out, neither a coalition, nor democratic, nor a government, nor in Kampuchea. It was what the CIA calls 'a master illusion'. Prince Norodom Sihanouk was appointed its head; otherwise little had changed. The two 'non-communist' members, the Sihanoukists and the Khmer People's National Liberation Front (KPNLF), were dominated by the Khmer Rouge. The urbane Thaoun Prasith – a personal friend of Pol Pot, who had called on Khmer expatriates to return home in 1975, whereupon many of them 'disappeared' – continued to speak for Cambodia.

The United Nations was now the instrument of Cambodia's punishment. Not only was the new government in Phnom Penh denied the UN seat, but Cambodia was barred from all international agreements on trade and communications, even from the World Health Organisation. In all its history, the United Nations had withheld development aid from only one Third World country: Cambodia. In the United States, church groups were refused export licences for books and toys for orphans. A law dating from the First World War, the Trading with the Enemy Act, was applied to Cambodia and Vietnam. Not even Cuba and the Soviet Union were treated in this way.

By 1987, KEG had been reincarnated as the Kampuchea Working Group, run by the same Colonel Eiland of the Defense Intelligence Agency. The Working Group's brief was to provide battle plans, war material and satellite intelligence to the so-called 'non-communist' members of the 'resistance forces'. The non-communist fig leaf allowed Congress, spurred on by an anti-Vietnamese zealot, Stephen Solarz, to approve both 'overt' and 'covert' aid estimated at $24 million to the 'resistance'. Until 1990, Congress accepted Solarz's specious argument that US aid did not end up with or even help Pol Pot and that the mass murderer's American-supplied allies 'are not even in close proximity with them [the Khmer Rouge]'.

While Washington paid the bills and the Thai Army provided logistics support, Singapore, as middle man, became the main 'conduit' for Western arms. Former Prime Minister Lee Kuan Yew was a major backer of American and Chinese insistence that the Khmer Rouge be part of a settlement in Cambodia. 'It is journalists', he said, 'who have made them into demons.'

Weapons from Germany, the United States and Sweden were passed on directly by Singapore or made under licence by Chartered Industries, owned by the Singapore Government; the same weapons have been captured from the Khmer Rouge. The Singapore connection allowed the administration of George Bush Senior to continue its secret aid to the 'resistance', even though this flouted a law passed by Congress in 1989 banning even indirect 'lethal aid' to Pol Pot. In August 1990, a former member of the US Special Forces disclosed that he had been ordered to destroy records that showed American munitions in Thailand ending up with the Khmer Rouge. The records, he said, implicated the National Security Council, which advised the president.

Until 1989, the British role in Cambodia had remained secret. The first reports appeared in the *Sunday Telegraph*, written by the paper's diplomatic and defence correspondent, Simon O'Dwyer-Russell, who had close professional and family contacts with the highly secretive Special Air Services, the SAS. O'Dwyer-Russell disclosed that the SAS were training Cambodian guerrillas allied to Pol Pot. Oddly, for such a major story, it was buried in the paper. 'I could never understand why,' O'Dwyer-Russell told me. 'When I filed the copy, I had the clear impression I had a page one lead. I never received an adequate explanation.' Shortly afterwards, *Jane's Defence Weekly* published a long article alleging that Britain had been training Cambodian guerrillas 'at secret bases in Thailand for more than four years'. The instructors were from the SAS, '. . . all serving military personnel, all veterans of the Falklands conflict, led by a captain'.

One result of the British training, reported *Jane's*, was 'the creation of a 250-man KPNLF sabotage battalion [whose] members were taught how to attack installations such as bridges, railway lines, power lines and sub-stations. Their first operations were conducted in Cambodia's Siem Reap province in August 1986.'

Other diplomatic correspondents were able to confirm the *Jane's* report; but little appeared in print. In November 1989, after evidence of British involvement was revealed in my film *Cambodia Year Ten*, Britain's complicity in Cambodia's international isolation and civil war became an urgent public issue. Some 16,000 people wrote to Prime Minister Thatcher, seeking an explanation.

Cambodia Year Ten showed an interview the Prime Minister had given shortly before Christmas 1988 to the BBC children's programme, *Blue Peter* (which had raised large sums for Cambodia). The interview had slipped past public attention. Thatcher was asked what her government could do to help stop Pol Pot coming back to power. 'Most people agree', she said, 'that Pol Pot himself could not go back, nor some of his supporters, who were very active in some of the terrible things that happened.' She then said, 'Some of the Khmer Rouge of course are *very* different. I think there are probably two parts to the Khmer Rouge: those who supported Pol Pot and then there is a much, much more *reasonable* group within the Khmer Rouge.'

At this, the interviewer was taken aback. 'Do you really think so?' she asked, to which Thatcher replied, 'Well, that is what I am assured by people who know . . . so that you will find that the more *reasonable* ones in the Khmer Rouge will have to play some part in a future government . . .'

This suggested a kind of de-nazification and raised questions, which I put to a Foreign Office minister, Lord Brabazon of Tara, in a filmed interview for *Cambodia Year Ten*. I asked him to explain Thatcher's statement that there were 'reasonable' Khmer Rouge. Who were they? I asked. 'Um,' he replied, 'the ones that Prince Sihanouk can work with.' When I asked for their names, a Foreign Office minder stepped in front of the camera and said, 'Stop this *now*. This is *not* the way that we were led to believe the line of questioning would go.'

The minder, Ian Whitehead, had earlier taken me aside and urged me to 'go easy on him'. Now he refused to allow the interview to proceed until he had approved the questions. As for the minister, he had fled the interviewing chair and could not be persuaded to return. The head of the Foreign Office News Department later claimed that my director, David Munro, had given an 'assurance' that Whitehead's intervention would not be shown. No such assurance had been given. This was a taste of the kind of Foreign Office disinformation of which a great deal more was to come. What the episode demonstrated was that the government was keenly aware that its policy on Cambodia was indefensible.

British special military forces have been in South-East Asia since the Second World War. Britain has supplied advisers to the Royal Thai Army since the 1970s, along with the Americans, in what is known as Operation Badge Torch. In 1982, when the American, Chinese and ASEAN governments contrived the 'coalition' that enabled Pol Pot to retain Cambodia's UN seat, the United States set about training and equipping the 'non-communist' factions in the 'resistance' army. These were the followers of Prince Sihanouk and his former minister, Son Sann, the leader of the KPNLF, mostly irregulars and bandits. The resistance was nothing without Pol Pot's 25,000 well-trained, armed and motivated guerrillas, whose leadership was acknowledged by Prince Sihanouk's military commander, his son, Norodom Ranariddh. 'The Khmer Rouge', he said, are the 'major attacking forces' whose victories were 'celebrated as our own'.

The guerrillas' tactic, like the *Contra* in Nicaragua, was to terrorise the countryside with ambushes and the seeding of minefields. In this way, the government in Phnom Penh would be destabilised and the Vietnamese trapped in an untenable war: their own 'Vietnam'. For the Americans, in Bangkok and Washington, the fate of Cambodia was tied to a war they had technically lost seven years earlier. 'Bleeding the Vietnamese white on the battlefields of Cambodia' was an expression popular with the US policy-making establishment. Overturning the government in Hanoi was the ultimate goal: 'winning' the war they had lost.

The British provided jungle training camps in Malaysia and in Thailand; one of them, in Phitsanulok province, is known as 'Falklands camp'. In 1991, I filmed an interview with a Cambodian guerrilla who had been trained by the British in Malaysia. Although a member of the KPNLF, he had worked under cover as a Khmer Rouge. He described a journey by train and covered truck from Thailand to an unknown destination. He was one among troops from all three Cambodian groups, including the Khmer Rouge. 'The Khmer Rouge were much more experienced and older,' he said. 'We eventually arrived in a camp in Malaysia, run by the Malaysian Army, where the instructors were British and Americans in uniform. Although we slept and ate separately from the Khmer Rouge, we wore the same uniforms and trained together with the same equipment as one army. We were all taught exactly the same. The British taught us about laying mines and setting booby traps.'

The Cambodian training became an exclusively British operation after the 'Irangate' arms-for-hostages scandal broke in Washington in 1986 and threatened the political life of the Reagan administration. 'If Congress had found out that Americans were mixed up in clandestine training in Indo-China, let alone with Pol Pot,' a Whitehall source told Simon O'Dwyer-Russell, 'the balloon would have gone right up. It was one of those classic Thatcher–Reagan arrangements. It was put to her that the SAS should take over the Cambodia show, and she agreed.'

In high secrecy, seven-man SAS teams arrived from Hong Kong and the SAS base in Hereford. Did Western correspondents based in Bangkok know? Several did, but nothing was reported for at least four years. That British soldiers were training Cambodians to kill and maim each other was not a 'story'. Neither was Operation Badge Torch considered newsworthy, nor Pol Pot himself, who could commute from his headquarters at Trat to his beach house at Bang Saen without hindrance from curious journalists, let alone the Thai authorities. The military hospital in Bangkok where he was treated regularly for haemorrhoids was but a few minutes from the bar of the Foreign Correspondents Club. When Pol Pot slipped into the beach resort of Pattaya in June 1991, his presence was not reported.

The revelation of Britain's training of Pol Pot's allies caused an uproar in Parliament; the government's embarrassment was acute. Copies of a parliamentary statement by Foreign Secretary Douglas Hurd were sent to people who wrote to the prime minister or to their MP. 'We have never given', it said, 'and will never give support of any kind to the Khmer Rouge.' This was false. From 1979 to 1982, the British Government voted in the United Nations for Pol Pot's defunct regime to occupy Cambodia's seat. Moreover, Britain voted with the Khmer Rouge in the agencies of the UN, and not once did it challenge the credentials of Pol Pot's representative.

The Hurd statement caused one of those curious disturbances in the House of Commons when government MPs have to deal with postbags overflowing with letters on a subject they wish would go away. Minister after minister denied that Britain was indirectly backing the Khmer Rouge – until William Waldegrave, then a junior Foreign Office minister, made a slip and gave what the opposition interpreted as a 'tacit admission' that the SAS were indeed in Cambodia.

A group of Labour MPs now demanded the government withdraw the SAS, and threatened to identify the Secret Intelligence Service (MI6) official who ran the British operation from the embassy in Bangkok. As a result, the SAS operation was hurriedly invested with greater secrecy or, as they say in Whitehall, given 'total deniability'. The official at the embassy was withdrawn and the training was 'privatised'; that is, the instructors were no longer to be serving personnel. In operational terms that made no difference whatsoever, as SAS personnel normally 'disappear' from army records whenever they go on secret missions. What was important was that the government could now deny that British servicemen were involved. 'Britain', announced Foreign Office minister Tim Sainsbury, 'does not give military aid *in any form* to the Cambodian factions.' 'I confirm', Margaret Thatcher wrote to Neil Kinnock, 'that there is no British Government involvement of any kind in training, equipping or co-operating with Khmer Rouge forces *or those allied to them.*' (My italics.) The deception was breathtaking.

For most of 1990 David Munro and I – together with Simon O'Dwyer-Russell of the *Sunday Telegraph* – pursued an investigation into Western support for the Khmer Rouge in Europe, the United States and South-East Asia. Our sources were in the Ministry of Defence and in 'R' (reserve) Squadron of the SAS. One of them, himself a former SAS trainer in Thailand, told us,

> We first went to Thailand in 1984. Since then we have worked in teams of four and eight and have been attached to the Thai Army. The Yanks [Special Forces] and us worked together; we're close like brothers. We trained the Khmer Rouge in a lot of technical stuff – a lot about mines. We used mines that came originally from Royal Ordnance in Britain, which we got by way of Egypt, with markings changed. They are the latest; one type goes up in a rocket and comes down on a parachute and hangs in the bushes until someone brushes it. Then it can blow their head off, or an arm. We trained them in Mark 5 rocket launchers and all sorts of weapons. We even gave them psychological training. At first they wanted to go into the villages and just chop people up. We told them how to go easy . . .
>
> Some of us went up to 100 miles inside Cambodia with them on missions. There are about 250 of us on the border at any one time and a lot of those would change sides given half the

chance. That's how pissed off we are. We hate being mixed up with Pol Pot. I tell you: we are soldiers, not child murderers. It costs half a million quid to train one of us. Putting us in the service of a lunatic like Pol Pot makes no sense. There is no insurgency in Cambodia that threatens us.

O'Dwyer-Russell interviewed two SAS trainers whose military background he knew well. They described in detail how they had taught Khmer Rouge troops mine-laying and mines technology. One man told how he had laid anti-personnel and off-route mines, 'which were detonated automatically by the sound of people moving along the track'. The mines, although not necessarily British-made, were supplied by Britain and fired 'thousands of pellets into the air and once they bed themselves in people's bodies are incredibly difficult to find . . .'

The British Government's response was swift. In the *Independent* of 12 October, a front-page headline said, 'Hurd rejects Pilger's Cambodia allegations'. Inside, half a page was devoted to a long riposte under Hurd's name, an unusual step for a foreign secretary. 'The brutality and murder of the Pol Pot regime shocked the world,' wrote Hurd. 'The British Government took the lead in denouncing it at the UN.' This, of course, was false. The government to which Hurd belonged had taken the lead in *supporting* Pol Pot's claim on Cambodia's seat at the United Nations.

In 1991, Pol Pot was given, in effect, an assurance he would not be brought to justice by the 'international community'. This was clear in the decision by the UN Human Rights Sub-commission to reject a draft resolution on Cambodia that referred to 'the atrocities reaching the level of genocide committed in particular during the period of Khmer Rouge rule'. No more, the UN body decided, should member governments seek to 'detect, arrest, extradite or bring to trial those who have been responsible for crimes against humanity in Cambodia'. No more are governments called upon to 'prevent the return to government positions of those who were responsible for genocidal actions during the period 1975 to 1978'.

This 'deal' was part of the UN 'peace plan' which was drafted by the permanent members of the Security Council: that is, by the United States. So as not to offend Pol Pot's principal backers, the Chinese, the plan dropped all mention of 'genocide', replacing it with the euphemism: 'policies and practices of the recent past'. On this, Henry Kissinger, who played a leading part in the mass bombing of Cambodia in the early 1970s, was an important influence; it was Kissinger who, in July 1989, urged Bush Senior to give the Beijing regime 'most favoured nation' trading status in spite of the bloody events in Tiananmen Square only weeks earlier. Kissinger regarded the Chinese leadership as a 'moderating influence' in South-East Asia.

At the first Cambodian 'peace conference' in Paris in August 1989, American delegates demonstrated their desire to rehabilitate China and, if necessary, its Khmer Rouge client. American and other Western diplomats entertained Chinese and Khmer Rouge representatives in private; and it was in this atmosphere that the word 'genocide' was quietly declared 'impolitic'. In a briefing document bearing the handwriting of the Australian minister for foreign affairs, Gareth Evans, a 'specific stumbling block' was 'identified' as 'whether it is appropriate or not to refer specifically to the non-return of the "genocidal" practices of the past'.

De-nazification was almost complete.

On 28 February 1991, the White House issued a statement on Cambodia which it clearly hoped would be ignored or lost by a media overwhelmed by the day's other news: 'victory' in the Gulf War. President Bush, it said, had admitted to Congress that there had been 'tactical military cooperation' between the American-supported 'noncommunist' Cambodian forces and Pol Pot's Khmer Rouge.

On 25 June 1991, the British Government admitted that which the Foreign Secretary had vehemently denied eight months earlier and which my films had disclosed: that the SAS had been secretly training the allies of Pol Pot since 1983, in collusion with mass murderers.

The eradication of public memory was now crucial. 'Public opinion' had proven a potent force in the defence of Cambodia's human rights, as thousands of letters to Downing Street had demonstrated. The three stages of Cambodia's holocaust were all within memory: the American bombing, the Pol Pot period and the American-led blockade against the survivors of stages one and two, and which had maintained Cambodia in a state of physical ruin, disease and trauma. That the holocaust had begun not with the Khmer Rouge but with the American bombing, and that the Khmer Rouge was now being rehabilitated

– diplomatically, politically and militarily – was kept from the public. (In their pioneering work on the media, *Manufacturing Consent*, Noam Chomsky and Edward S. Herman provide an insight into this contrived 'silence'.)

Diminishing Western culpability is, of course, standard media practice in most global matters. However, support for those who put to death a fifth of the Cambodian population presented a challenge. In this, Pol Pot himself provided a lead. 'We must', he said in 1988, 'focus attention on the Vietnamese aggression and divert attention from our past mistakes.' Discrediting Cambodia's liberators was an essential first step. This began with propaganda likening an act of self-defence (Pol Pot's forces had attacked Vietnam for almost two years) to an 'invasion', and with unsubstantiated accusations of Vietnamese 'atrocities' and 'subtle genocide', the latter a claim by William Shawcross in Washington and discredited by journalists in Cambodia. However, the Carter and Reagan administrations took their cue. Once Pol Pot's communists could be equated with Vietnam's communists, regardless of the fact that one group was guilty of genocide and the other was not, in propaganda terms almost anything was possible.

Numerous initiatives by the Vietnamese to extricate themselves from Cambodia were dismissed or went unreported, and the attempts by others to broker their withdrawal were derided. When the Australian foreign affairs minister, Bill Hayden, tried in 1983, he was vilified in the press as a 'communist dupe' and his efforts were dismissed as 'stupid' by the US secretary of state, George Schultz.

By 1985, Vietnam's only condition for the withdrawal of its troops was that the Khmer Rouge be prevented from returning to power. This was welcomed by several South-East Asian governments, and rejected by the United States. On 13 July 1985, the *Bangkok Post* reported, 'A senior US official said that [Secretary of State] Schultz cautioned ASEAN to be extremely careful in formulating peace proposals for Kampuchea because Vietnam might one day accept them.' When the Vietnamese withdrew unconditionally from Cambodia in 1989, Western support for the Khmer Rouge – justified as necessary *realpolitik* as long as Vietnamese troops remained in Cambodia – actually increased.

While the Vietnamese were fulfilling their 'aggressor' function in Western eyes, the Khmer Rouge were being regarded very differently. From 1979, the American far right began to rehabilitate Pol Pot. Douglas Pike, a prominent Indo-China specialist, described Pol Pot as a 'charismatic' and 'popular' leader under whom 'most' Cambodian peasants 'did not experience much in the way of brutality'. Pike argued that the Khmer Rouge should share political power in Cambodia; this was the essence of the UN 'peace plan'.

In 1980, the CIA had produced a 'demographic report' on Cambodia, which softened Pol Pot's reputation by denying that he had carried out any executions during the last two years of his regime. In fact, in 1977–8, more than half a million people were executed. During congressional hearings in November 1989, Assistant Secretary of State Richard Solomon repeatedly refused to describe Pol Pot's crimes as genocidal – thus denying his own department's earlier unequivocal position.

Journalists whose reporting reflected the US administration line received the highest commendation. Nate Thayer, an Associated Press reporter, was described as 'brilliant' by Congressman Stephen Solarz, one of the architects of US policy. Richard Solomon called the following Thayer commentary 'the most sober-minded and well-informed assessment of that issue I've seen'.

In Thayer's view the 'good news' in Cambodia struggled to be heard above the din of the 'tales of terror'. Writing in the *Washington Quarterly*, he described the one-and-a-half million people who died during the Khmer Rouge years as 'displaced'. Using the official euphemism, Thayer distinguished 'the policies and practices of the Khmer Rouge' from what he called the 'violence and misery that preceded and succeeded them'. He wrote that, while Pol Pot did implement some 'objectionable policies' these were 'largely perpetrated only on a certain section of the population . . . to which journalists, scholars and other foreign observers have had access'. Thayer claimed that 'perhaps 20 per cent of Cambodians support the Khmer Rouge'. The source for this? Why, Pol Pot himself! The author made no further mention of the 15 per cent Pol Pot had already 'displaced'.

In Britain, the rehabilitation was similar. In June 1990, the *Independent* published a major report by its South-East Asia correspondent, Terry McCarthy, headlined: 'Whatever the crimes committed by Pol Pot's men, they are on the road to power. The West must stop moralising and learn to deal with them.' McCarthy called on the West to 'reach out' to the Khmer Rouge. The 'genocide issue', as he put it, had been 'exploited to the full'. The point was, the Khmer Rouge had changed. They were now 'respected' for their 'discipline' and 'honesty' and 'admired' for having 'qualities that most spheres of Cambodian society lack'. Moreover, they had 'considerable support' in the countryside because 'many' peasants 'do not have particularly bad memories' of Pol Pot. He offered no real evidence of this 'support' among a rural population of which 15 per cent had perished during the Pol Pot years. He advocated increased aid to the Khmer Rouge to 'entice them back into the real world of human politics'. It is time, he wrote, 'to face up to the fact that the Khmer Rouge embodies some deeply entrenched traits of the Cambodian people . . .'

These 'traits' became a popular theme in the revised explanation for Cambodia's suffering. Forget the actions of Pol Pot, Washington and Beijing; the ordinary people of Cambodia had allowed these horrors to happen because that was the way they were, genetically. According to Michael Fathers in the *Independent*, 'Cambodians are a neurotic people with an intense persecution complex . . .'

Meanwhile, reported *The Times*, Pol Pot had ordered the Khmer Rouge 'to protect the country's wildlife'. Cambodians were 'not to poach birds and animals, and to refrain from killing them for any reason' because they were 'an important part of Cambodia's heritage'. And the source for this nonsense? 'Western intelligence sources' no less, inviting us to believe that Pol Pot had ordered his most trusted general to 'sentence' anyone found poaching rare birds. This general, according to the same disinformation, was himself 'hot on ecology issues and protection of endangered species'. And who might this 'green' Khmer Rouge general be? None other than the notorious Mok, who between 1975 and 1979 was credited with the deaths of thousands of members of the human species. In Cambodia today, he is still known as 'The Butcher', though Western journalists prefer to call him 'Ta Mok'. *Ta* gives him the affectionate sobriquet of 'Grandfather'.

In the same spirit, *The Times* announced that another leading henchman of Pol Pot had asked for 'another chance'. The redemption seeker in this case was Mok's boss, Son Sen, Pol Pot's defence minister. He explained to *The Times* that he 'did not deny the past [but] we have to think about the present and the future'. Son Sen stands accused of the murder of 30,000 Vietnamese villagers in 1977. Under his authority, Tuol Sleng extermination centre in Phnom Penh tortured and murdered some 20,000 people.

On 28 November 1991, the leader writer of the *Independent* proffered the following memorable advice to the people of Cambodia: 'The promise of a return to respectability of the Khmer Rouge is the wormwood baked into the cake. It makes it hard to swallow for those who will always be haunted by the horrors of that regime. If Cambodia is to find peace, then swallowed it must be, *and in its entirety*.' (My italics.)

Few dissenting voices were heard above this. In Britain, one of the most informed and courageous belonged to Oxfam, which in 1979 had defied government pressure and gone to help stricken Cambodia. In 1988, Oxfam published *Punishing the Poor: The International Isolation of Kampuchea*, by Eva Mysliwiec, Oxfam's senior representative in Phnom Penh and the doyenne of voluntary aid workers in Cambodia. Marshalling her facts, most of them gained at first hand, she presented a picture of a people who had suffered more than most and were now being punished by so-called civilised governments for being on the 'wrong side'; she identified the roots of their suffering in the American invasion of Indo-China.

In 1990, an American-funded extreme right-wing lobby group, the International Freedom Foundation, presented an 'Oxfam file' to the Charity Commission in London. Its author was a young Tory activist, Marc Gordon, who had made his name a few years earlier by 'joining' the Nicaraguan *Contra*. His complaint of 'political bias' was supported by several backbench Conservative MPs. Gordon told me, 'All the incidents we cited in our submission to the inquiry were upheld.' I asked an official at the Commission if this were true and he would neither confirm nor deny it. 'A fact is a fact,' he said boldly. Oxfam was never told officially who its accusers were, or the precise nature of the evidence that would prove so damaging.

In 1991, the Charity Commission publicly censured Oxfam for having 'prosecuted with too much vigour' its campaign against Pol Pot's return. Threatened with a loss of its charity status, Oxfam soon fell quiet and withdrew from sale *Punishing the Poor*. Its boldest Cambodia 'firemen' were sidelined or left. As Yun Yat, Pol Pot's minister of information, said, in boasting that Buddhism had been virtually eradicated from Cambodia and that the monks had 'stopped believing' (most of them had been murdered): 'The problem becomes extinguished. Hence there is no problem.'

As each of the principal speakers rose from his chair in the ornate Quai d'Orsay, a silver-headed man a dozen feet away watched them carefully. His face remained unchanged; he wore a fixed, almost petrified smile. When Secretary of State James Baker declared that Cambodia should never again return to 'the policies and practices of the past', the silver head nodded. When Prince Sihanouk acknowledged the role of Western governments in the 'accords', the silver head nodded. Khieu Samphan, Pol Pot's face to the world, was being anointed a statesman, a peacemaker; and this was as much his moment as Sihanouk's; for without his agreement – that is, Pol Pot's agreement – there would be no 'accords'. A French official offered his hand, and Pol Pot's man stood, respectful, fluent in diplomatic small-talk and effusive in his gratitude – the same gratitude he had expressed in the two letters he had written to Douglas Hurd congratulating the British Government on its policy on Cambodia.

It was Khieu Samphan who, at one of Pol Pot's briefing sessions for his military commanders in Thailand, described his diplomatic role as 'buying time in order to give you comrades the opportunity to carry out all your [military] tasks'. In Paris, on 23 October 1991, he had the look of a man who could not believe his luck.

Some 6,000 miles away, on the Thai side of the border with Cambodia, the Khmer people of Site 8 had a different view of the world being shaped for them. Although supplied by the United Nations Border Relief Operation, this camp had long been a Khmer Rouge operations base and, since 1988, had been made into a showcase by Pol Pot. Its leadership was elected; the Red Cross and selected journalists were allowed in. Whisky was produced. Faces smiled, much as Khieu Samphan smiled. The object of this image-building exercise was clear: to persuade Western governments that the Khmer Rouge have 'changed', are now following a 'liberal capitalist line' and could be legitimised as part of a 'comprehensive settlement'.

As Khieu Samphan raised his glass in Paris, a nightmare began for the people of Site 8. The gates were closed, and foreigners told to stay away. A few days earlier the camp's leaders had been called to a 'meeting' with senior Khmer Rouge officials and were not seen again. The camp library, central to the showpiece, was closed and people were told they must no longer be 'poisoned by foreign ideas' as they prepared to return to the 'zones'. From here and in the 'closed camps' run by the Khmer Rouge along the border, the forcible, secret repatriation of hundreds, perhaps thousands of refugees had begun.

They crossed minefields at night and were herded into 'zones of free Kampuchea' in malarial jungles without UN protection, food or medicine. Even as the UN High Commission for Refugees announced that an orderly return of all 370,000 refugees was under way, there were as many as 100,000 refugees in Khmer Rouge border camps and more were trapped in the 'zones', to which UN inspectors had only limited access or none at all.

If the 'peace process' was proving a theatre of the macabre, Prince Sihanouk provided his own theatre of the absurd. As decided in Paris, he returned to Phnom Penh in November 1991 to head the transitional Supreme National Council, made up of representatives of his followers, the KPNLF, the Hun Sen Government and the Khmer Rouge. 'I am returning to protect my children,' he said. 'There is *joie de vivre* again. Nightclubs have reopened with taxi dancers. I am sure soon there will be massage parlours. It is our way of life: it is a good life.' He brought with him four chefs, supplies of pâté de foie gras hurriedly acquired from Fauchon, one of Paris's most famous gourmet shops, a caravan of bodyguards and hangers-on, including two sons with dynastic ambitions.

Many Cambodians were pleased to see the 'god-king', and the elderly struggled to kiss his hand. It seemed the world had again located Cambodia on the map. The cry 'Sihanouk is back' seemed to signal a return to the days before the inferno of the American bombing and the rise of the Khmer Rouge. Sihanouk's presence even suggested to some that the Khmer Rouge had surrendered. For them the Paris 'accords' meant that the United Nations would protect them. They could be pardoned for failing to comprehend the perversity of an agreement which empowered the United Nations to protect the right of the genocidists to roam the cities and countryside free from harm and retribution, and which had appointed two of Pol Pot's henchmen to a body, the Supreme National Council, on which they could not be outvoted. This was described by Congressman Chet Atkins, one of the few American politicians to speak up for the Cambodian people, as 'the consequence of a Faustian pact' with Pol Pot.

At one of his many press conferences, Sihanouk was asked about the Khmer Rouge. 'In their hearts', he said, 'they remain very cruel, very Maoist, very Cultural Revolution, very Robespierre, very French Revolution, very *bloody* revolution. They are monsters, it is true . . . *but* since they decided to behave as normal human beings, we have to accept them . . . naughty dogs and naughty Khmer Rouge, they need to be caressed.' At this, he laughed, and most of the foreign press laughed with him. His most important statement, however, caused hardly a ripple. 'Cambodians', he said, 'were forced by the five permanent members of the UN Security Council . . . to accept the return of the Khmer Rouge.'

The following day Khieu Samphan arrived to join the prince on the Supreme National Council. Suddenly, the gap between private pain and public fury closed. Within a few hours of landing at Pochentong Airport, Pol Pot's emissary was besieged on the top floor of his villa. Crouched in a cupboard, with blood streaming from a head wound, he listened to hundreds of people shouting, *'Kill him, kill him, kill him.'* They smashed down the doors and advanced up the stairs, armed with hatchets. Many of them had lost members of their families during the years that he was in power, at Pol Pot's side. One woman called out the names of her dead children, her dead sister, her dead mother – all of them murdered by the Khmer Rouge. The mob may have been encouraged by the caretaker government of Hun Sen, but its actions were heartfelt. Khieu Samphan and Son Sen (who had escaped the attack) were bundled into an armoured personnel carrier and taken to the airport, and flown back to Bangkok.

What happened to Khieu Samphan, in the streets he helped to terrorise and empty, was a catharsis, and only the beginning. Now, when he and Son Sen were in Phnom Penh, their stays were brief and secret, and they were guarded behind the walls of a UN compound, the protected wards of the international community, the esteemed enemies of Vietnam, the humiliator of America.

The punishment of the Cambodian people for their 'wrong' liberation mocked the Charter of the United Nations. A prime example was the denial of all development aid by the UN Development Programme (UNDP) between the critical years of 1979 and 1992 as a direct result of pressure from the United States, China, Britain and Singapore. No single decision better ensured that Cambodia would remain broken and impoverished, at best a service economy for foreigners.

Development aid provides the tools of reconstruction: resources, materials and expertise, with which poor countries can make a start at developing themselves and thereby strengthening their sovereignty and independence. It should provide such essentials as a clean water supply and decent sanitation. Ten years after liberation, less than 5 per cent of Cambodia's drinking water was uncontaminated. In 1988, the British company Thames Water sent a team to Phnom Penh and reported that when the level of water in the city's pipes rose and fell, it spilled into the streets and drew in drainage and raw sewage. The company's engineers recommended that an entirely new system be installed immediately; their study, submitted to the British Government, was never heard of again. In a poignant passage, they noted that 'most of Cambodia's engineers were killed or still missing'. In any other Third World country, the UNDP would have given priority to funding such a need. When I put this to a UNDP official in Phnom Penh – whose immediate concern was for the state of his air conditioning – he said: 'It's embarrassing, isn't it?'

In 1988, a senior diplomat at the British embassy in Bangkok told Oxfam's Eva Mysliwiec: 'Cambodia is a country of about seven million people. It's of no real strategic value. As far as Britain is concerned, it's expendable.' Cambodia's expendability, and punishment, are exemplified by its children. Whenever I returned, I visited the National Paediatric Hospital in Phnom Penh, the most modern hospital in the country; I invariably found seriously ill children lying on the floors of corridors so narrow there was barely room to step over them. A relative would hold a drip; if the child was lucky, he or she would have a straw mat. Most of them suffered from, and many would die from, common diarrhoea and other intestinal ailments carried by parasites in the water supply. In hospital after hospital children died like that, needlessly and for political reasons.

The international embargo ensured that hospital drug cupboards were depleted or bare; there were no vaccines; sterilisation equipment was broken, X-ray film unobtainable. At Battambang Hospital in the north-west I watched the death of an eleven-month-old baby, while her mother looked on. 'Her name is Ratanak,' she cried. Had there been a respirator and plasma, the child would have lived. A light was kept shining on her face to keep her temperature up. Then the hospital's power went down and she died.

Today, in the north-west, most of the children still fall prey to epidemics of mosquito-carried diseases – cerebral malaria, Japanese encephalitis and dengue fever. 'Our particular tragedy', Dr Choun Noothorl, director of Battambang Hospital, told me, 'is that we had malaria beaten here before 1975. In the 1970s the World Health Organisation assisted us with training, medicines and funding. I remember the statistics for April 1975; we had only a handful of malaria cases; it was a triumph.'

In April 1975, when Pol Pot came to power, Battambang Hospital was abandoned, its equipment and research files destroyed and most of its staff murdered. When the Vietnamese drove out the Khmer Rouge, the World Health Organisation refused to return to Cambodia. Malaria and dengue fever did return, along with new strains which the few surviving Cambodian doctors were unable to identify because they no longer had laboratories. In 1992, two-and-a-half million people, or a quarter of the population, were believed to have malaria. The same was true of tuberculosis, which was also beaten in 1975. Most of them were children.

All this was preventable, beginning with the American bombing of Cambodia that killed an estimated 600,000 people and led to the rise of the Khmer Rouge. Had America, China and Britain kept their distance following the defeat of Pol Pot in 1978, there is little doubt that a solution could have been found in the region. In 1980, the Indonesian and Malaysian Governments – fearful of Pol Pot's chief backer, China – acknowledged that the Vietnamese had 'legitimate concerns' about the return of Pol Pot and the threat from China. In 1985, Australian Foreign Affairs Minister Bill Hayden was told by Cambodian premier Hun Sen, 'We are ready to make concessions to Prince Sihanouk and other people if they agree to join with us to eliminate Pol Pot.' Four years later, reported *The Economist* from Paris, a Sihanouk–Hun Sen alliance against the Khmer Rouge was 'torpedoed' by the US State Department.

Perhaps the most alluring promise of peace came when Thailand's elected prime minister, Chatichai Choonhaven, invited Hun Sen to Bangkok, and Thai officials secretly visited Phnom Penh with offers of development aid and trade. Defying their own generals, the reformist Thais proposed a regional conference that would exclude the great powers. Prime Minister Chatichai's son and chief policy adviser, Kraisak Choonhaven, told me in 1990, 'We want to see the Khmer Rouge kicked out of their bases on Thai soil.' He called on 'all Western powers and China to stop arming the Cambodian guerrillas'.

This represented an extraordinary about-turn for America's most reliable client in South-East Asia. In response, Washington warned the Chatichai government that if it persisted with its new policy it would 'have to pay a price' and threatened to withdraw Thailand's trade privileges under the Generalised Special Preferences. The regional conference never took place. In March 1991, the Chatichai government was overthrown and the new military strongman in Bangkok, Suchinda Krapayoon, described Pol Pot as a 'nice guy', who should be treated 'fairly'. (It was Suchinda who turned the army on pro-democracy demonstrators in Bangkok, killing hundreds.)

At the same time, in a rare initiative, the Japanese Government proposed the establishment of a special commission to investigate the crimes of the Khmer Rouge. US Assistant Secretary of State Richard Solomon rejected this out of hand, describing it as 'likely to introduce confusion in international peace efforts'.

When I drove into Phnom Penh in June 1980, the year after the end of the Pol Pot stage of the holocaust, the tinkling of bells I heard on hundreds of pony traps carrying people and food and goods was a new sound. Compared with the emptiness of the year before, Phnom Penh was a city transformed. There were two bus routes, restaurants, raucous markets, re-opened pagodas, telephones, a jazz band, a football team and currency. And there were freedoms, uncoerced labour, freedom of movement and freedom of worship. I had never seen so many weddings, neither had I ever received as many wedding invitations – four in one day. Marriage had become a mark of resilience, of freedom restored, and was celebrated with as much extravagance as was possible in the circumstances, with long skirts and brocade tops and hair piled high with flowers, and the men bearing gifts of precious food arranged on leaves, their necks craning from unaccustomed collars and ties. There were electricity and re-opened factories – some of them paid for by the British viewers of *Year Zero*. An estimated 900,000 children had been enrolled in rudimentary schools and 19,000 new teachers given a two-month crash course, replacing an entire professional class who were 'missing'.

The tenuous nature of this 'normality' was demonstrated to me during a 'disco night' I attended one Saturday at the Monorom Hotel. The women and children sat on one side of the room, *palais*-style, the men on the other. It was a lot of fun, especially when a competing jazz band next door struck up with 'Stompin' at the Savoy'. But when a cassette of the much-loved Khmer singer, Sin Sisamouth, was played, people stopped dancing and walked to the windows and wept. He had been forced to dig his own grave and to sing the Khmer Rouge anthem, which is about blood and death. After that, he was beaten to death. It brought home to me that the efforts of the Cambodian people to recover from their nightmare of bombs and genocide and blockade ought to be the object of our lasting admiration: at the very least the willingness of our representatives to help them, not hurt them.

GÜNTER WALLRAFF

Lowest of the Low (*Ganz unten*)

1985

Günter Wallraff is Germany's most famous journalist. Since 1966, his undercover reporting in defence of those working and subsisting at the bottom of the industrial heap has demonstrated the power of investigative journalism when the journalist is prepared to go to extraordinary personal lengths. Taking on false identities, Wallraff has infiltrated industry, government and the media in order to expose corruption and malpractice. His quarry has been the German establishment – the playwright Heiner Müller described him as a 'postmodern Robin Hood' – but after decades of being hounded himself by lawyers, officials and the right-wing Axel Springer media, he has exiled himself in Holland.

In researching his book *Der Aufmacher* ('Lead Story', 1977), Wallraff joined the staff of *Bild-Zeitung*, Germany's biggest tabloid, the equivalent of Rupert Murdoch's *Sun*. Working under a pseudonym, he exposed the way the paper worked and revealed the many personal tragedies that lay behind its ruthless sensationalism. *Bild* abused him as a 'terrorist sympathiser', a common accusation in the political climate in Germany in the mid-1970s. (Other prominent victims of the same witch hunt included the novelist and Nobel laureate Heinrich Böll.)

Wallraff's most celebrated work is *Ganz unten* ('Lowest of the Low', 1985), which succeeded in placing the suffering of Germany's immigrant workers on the mainstream political agenda. For his undercover investigation, he disguised himself as a Turkish worker and penetrated Germany's illegal labour market. He recorded his experiences of working at the 'bottom of the heap': in a Thyssen steel factory, a McDonald's and as a human guinea pig in the pharmaceutical industry.

His book was the most successful in German publishing history, selling more than two million copies in less than five months. On publication day in 1985, people queued outside bookshops, and the ensuing national debate about working conditions and racism, specifically German attitudes to 'guest workers', was unprecedented. Translated into more than thirty languages, it was published in English in 1988. (A selection of reports by Wallraff had previously been published in English under the title *The Undesirable Journalist*.)

As a result, German prosecutors and tax officials raided the offices of Remmert and Thyssen, which Wallraff had exposed, looking for evidence that both companies were breaking the law regulating and protecting contract workers. In the state of North Rhine Westphalia – the setting of Wallraff's exposé – the Social Democratic government moved to stamp out 'lease' labour, a kind of bond slavery. Throughout Germany more than 13,000 criminal investigations were instigated, and penalties were increased ten-fold.

However, Wallraff is cautious in assessing his achievements. 'I don't believe that [reporting] can change social reality directly [but it is] a catalyst and its explosive power is often revealed only many years later.' The following is an extract from *Lowest of the Low*.

LOWEST OF THE LOW

Metamorphosis

I put off playing this role for ten years, probably because I'd had a sense of what lay ahead. To put it simply, I was frightened.

Stories told to me by friends, and many different publications, gave me a picture of the lives of foreigners in West Germany. I knew that almost half of young foreigners suffered from some kind of mental illness. The simple fact is that they can no longer *digest* the demands made upon them. They hardly have a chance in the labour market. Having grown up here, they don't really have a way back to their country of origin. They are homeless.

The intensification of asylum law, xenophobia, increasing ghettoisation – I knew about it but I had never experienced it.

In March 1983 I put the following advertisement in various newspapers:

Foreigner, strong, seeks work, any kind, even very heavy and dirty work, even for low wages. Offers to 358 458.

I didn't have to do much to find myself out in the cold, to belong to an ostracised minority, to be *right at the bottom*. A specialist made me two thin, very dark contact lenses that I was able to wear day and night. 'Now you have the piercing gaze of a southerner,' the optician said admiringly. Normally his customers only ever ask for blue eyes.

I knotted a black hairpiece to my own thinning hair. It took a good few years off me, and allowed me to pass for someone between the ages of twenty-six and thirty. I got work that I wouldn't have been offered if I'd given my true age (I'm forty-three). It meant that I looked younger, fresher and more able-bodied, but at the same time I became an outsider, the *lowest of the low*. The 'foreigner's German' that I spoke throughout my metamorphosis was so uncouth and clumsy that anyone who had ever taken the trouble to listen properly to a Turk or a Greek living in this country would have been sure to spot that something wasn't quite right. I just left off a few final syllables, inverted my sentence construction, or spoke in a slightly broken Cologne dialect. Given that, the effect was all the more startling: no one suspected a thing. Those minor changes were enough. The result of my play-acting was that people told me honestly and directly what they thought of me. My simulated stupidity made me cleverer, giving me insights into the icy small-mindedness of a society that saw itself as clever, superior, definitive and just. I was the fool to whom people told the unvarnished truth.

Of course I wasn't really a Turk. But you have to disguise yourself in order to unmask your society, you have to deceive and play-act to get at the truth.

I still don't know *how* a foreigner deals with the daily humiliations, the hostilities and the hatred. But I now know *what* he has to endure, and the level of contempt for humanity that people can reach in this country. There is a piece of apartheid at work among us – in our *democracy*. My experiences went far beyond all my expectations, and in a negative sense. Here in the Federal Republic of Germany I have experienced the kind of conditions that you usually only find described in history books about the nineteenth century.

As filthy and wearing as the work was, however much it might have drained your last reserves, whatever the level of humiliation and general contempt for humanity that I experienced, it didn't only damage me, in another way it actually built me up in a psychological sense. In the factories and on the building sites, I made friends and experienced solidarity. Friends to whom I couldn't expose my true identity for safety reasons.

Now, shortly before the publication of the book, I have drawn some of them into my confidence. And none of them has rebuked me for adopting my disguise. On the contrary, they understood me and also felt that the provocation involved in my role was liberating. Nonetheless, in order to protect my colleagues, in this book I have had to change most of their names.

The Lowest of the Low, or: 'Doing the Outlaw Thing'

I don't think it's possible to achieve serious changes without somehow joining everyone else in the dirt. I have a terrible suspicion of any 'outside' action that risks being nothing but chatter.

Odile Simon, 'Diary of a Factory Worker'

I (Ali) am trying to get a job in the Jurid factory in Glinde near Hamburg: asbestos processing, brake linings. Turkish friends tell me that most of the health-endangering jobs are done by Turks. The strict safety regulations for asbestos processing don't apply here, they tell me. If there's a gust of wind, lethal, carcinogenic fibrous dust is swirled up in the air. Dust masks often aren't worn. I meet a few former workers who have come away with severe pulmonary and bronchial damage after working there for between six months and two years, and who are now – unsuccessfully so far – fighting for recognition of the damage to their health.

The only problem is that they're not taking anyone on at the moment. Some people have managed to get jobs time and again in spite of this: by giving certain foremen bribes, or 'presents', authentic carpets from Turkey or a valuable gold coin. I've already rustled up a suitable family treasure in the form of a gold coin from the old Ottoman Empire, which I bought from a dealer in coins, when I happen upon an easier way. I learn that the August-Thyssen-Hütte (ATH) in Duisburg has been laying off its regular workforce for some time, and, through subcontracted companies, taking on temporary workers who are cheaper and more willing, and quicker to hire and fire. Since 1974, around 17,000 regular workers have been dismissed. Many of their former jobs are now being done by men sent in by subcontractors. Thyssen has 400 such companies under contract in Duisburg alone.

Get up at 3 a.m., to be at the Remmert company's pitch, the Oberhausen–Buschhausen motorway exit. Remmert is an expanding business. The modern-looking green company logo bears the word 'services'. Remmert gets rid of all kinds of dirt.

Fine dust and coarse dust, toxic rubble and slurry, stinking and rotting oils, fats and filter-cleaning for Thyssen, Mannesmann, MAN and wherever. Integrated into Remmert, in turn, is Vogel's company. Vogel sells us to Remmert, and Remmert hires us on to Thyssen. The main sum paid by Thyssen – according to the job at hand, and special supplements of between 35 and 80 deutschmarks for dust, dirt or danger – is shared out among the business partners. Vogel pays the workers a pittance of five to ten DM.

A foreman is standing by the minibus – which is both ready to set off and ready for the scrapheap – ticking off a list of names. 'New?' he asks me (Ali) brusquely.

'Yes,' I reply.

'Worked here before?'

I can't quite work out whether the answer could be a help or a hindrance to my chances of employment, so I (Ali) shrug my shoulders just to be on the safe side. 'You not understand?' he replies.

'New,' I say, giving him the correct password.

'You join colleagues in car,' he says, pointing to the rickety Mercedes minibus. That was it. That's how easy it is to get a job in one of the most modern metallurgical plants in Europe. I'm not asked for any papers, or even for my name, and for the time being my nationality doesn't seem to concern anyone in this world-class international company. That's fine by me.

Nine foreigners and two Germans are squashed into the bus. The two Germans have made themselves comfortable on the only fixed seat. Their foreign colleagues are sitting on the cold, oil-smeared metal floor of the vehicle. I join them, and they make room for me.

Crammed to the brim, rattling and lurching, the bus sets off. A bench has been pulled from its fittings, and on bends it swings against the foreign workers, knocking some of them over. The heating doesn't work, and the rear door doesn't close, it's wrapped round with wire.

If the driver were to brake suddenly and one of the men were thrown against it, the door could give and he would fall into the road. Shaken and chilled to the bone, the nail-biting drive takes us, after fifteen minutes, to gate number 20 at the Thyssen plant. A supervisor issues me with a time card, and a Thyssen security man hands me a day pass. He is appalled by my name: 'That's not a name, that's an illness. No one can write that down.' I have to spell it out for him several times: S-i-n-i-r-l-i-o-g-l-u. Despite this, he puts down 'Sinnlokus', and as my first name. My middle name, Levent, becomes my surname. 'How can anyone have a name like that!' he says, horrified by my name, although his own, 'Symanowski' or whatever it is, would cause problems of its own to a Turk – and it also suggests Polish ancestry. The Polish emigrant workers who were introduced to the Ruhrgebiet in the nineteenth century were despised and initially ghettoised much as the Turks are today. There were towns in the Ruhr where over 50 per cent of the population were Poles who retained their own language and culture.

As I am having some difficulties with my time card, a German worker who has been held up because of me for a few seconds, remarks: 'I expect in Africa you lot get your heads stamped!'

My Turkish colleague Mehmet helps me and shows me how to stick the card in the right way round. I sense, from the shame and resignation on their faces, that the other foreign workers feel that the German's remark applies to them. Time and again I find that they seem to ignore and choke down even the most terrible insults.

There are several flights of stairs leading down, the light filters through more faintly, it becomes gloomier and dustier. You think there's already such an incredible amount of dust that you can hardly bear it. But this is only the start. You're handed a pressurised blower, with which you have to swirl up the finger-thick layers of dust on the machines and in the gaps between them. Within seconds there's such a concentration of dust that you can't see your hand in front of your face. You don't just inhale the dust, you swallow and eat it. It chokes you. Every breath you draw is torture. From time to time you try to hold your breath, but there's no escape, because you've got to do the work. Like the guard in charge of a punishment unit, the foreman stands on the landing, where there's still a bit of fresh air coming in. He says, 'Get a move on! Then you'll be finished in two or three hours and you'll be able to get back to the fresh air.'

But three hours means taking three thousand breaths, and that means pumping your lungs full of coke-dust. It also smells of coal-gas, and you soon feel dazed.

While we stand in the dust-cloud shovelling dust from the floor into plastic bags, Thyssen mechanics, working a few metres below us, dash past us and up into the open. 'You're round the bend, you can't work in filth like that!' one of them calls out as he runs by. And half an hour later a safety inspector from the Thyssen works honours us with a visit. As he hurries past us, holding his nose shut, he tells us, 'The other workers have been complaining that they can't work in the filth you're making. Hurry up and finish.' And with that he's gone. The work lasts until the end of the shift. For the final hour we're to carry the heavy bags of dust up the stairs on our backs to the open air and chuck them into a container. Despite the back-breaking work, it comes as a relief to be able to get a moment's 'fresh air' upstairs.

We pick out our work gloves from dustbins or waste containers. They're mostly oily or torn gloves that the Thyssen workers have thrown away after the plant gave them new ones.

We have to buy our own protective helmets, unless we're lucky enough to have found a battered one that somebody's thrown away. The heads of the German workers are considered to be more precious and worthy of protection than those of the foreigners. On two occasions the foreman tore my (Ali's) helmet from my head to give it to German workers who had forgotten their own.

The first time I (Ali) protested, 'Excuse me, bought, belong to me,' the foreman put me firmly in my place: 'Nothing here belongs to you except a bit of wet slurry. You can have your helmet back at the end of the shift.' So you're expropriated on the spot without being asked. The second time I was partnered up with a new German who had got his helmet free from Thyssen, but who was still working without it. Once again Ali was supposed to sacrifice his own head. This time I refused: 'Is private, belong to me.' To which the foreman replied, 'You give him helmet. Otherwise I fire you, on the spot!'

One German colleague takes it as read that he should be protected at my expense. When I (Ali) accost him about it, he only says, 'Nothing I can do about it. I just do what I'm told. You'll have to register your complaint elsewhere, I'm the wrong address.' But later on he also lets Ali feel his contempt. 'You Vogel people are absolutely worthless. No one could possibly take you seriously. For the few marks you get I wouldn't pick up a shovel.' That means, more or less, 'You have no rights. Officially you don't exist here. You don't have papers or a work contract or anything at all.'

Some of my colleagues work for months at a time without a day off. They no longer have a private life. They are dropped off at home because it's cheaper for the company if they pay for their own accommodation. Otherwise it would be more practical for them to spend the night at the plant. They're generally the younger men. After a few years at the very most in Thyssen's filth, they're worn out and run down, drained and ill – often for the rest of their lives. As far as the company's concerned, they're disposable people, throwaway workers, and there are enough of those who are queuing up for work and grateful for any, really any kind of work. That exhaustion also explains why it is that hardly anyone can stand this work for more than one or two years. One or two months are often enough to do you lifelong damage. Particularly when you're required to do double and triple shifts. One workmate of about twenty regularly works between 300 and 350 hours a month. The big guys at Thyssen know it, the plant profits from it, and the proof is stamped and stored on Thyssen time cards.

Thyssen often calls in the troops at very short notice. When that happens, workers will sometimes have been freighted back from Duisburg to Oberhausen after their strenuous work, and they're already in the shower when the foreman drags them out and sends them back into the dirt for another shift. Or men are hauled out of bed by phone and ordered to work just when they've finally managed to get to sleep after their total exhaustion. Most of the workmen you ask, even the relatively young and fit ones, say you can't bear more than twelve shifts a week. And then if you have a weekend free you sleep through, like a corpse.

Whenever any of them complain about the work, F. replies, 'We can be glad that we've got jobs at all,' and, 'I'll do anything.' Once when one of the Thyssen controllers discovered us taking a break, he's the only one still grafting away, and for that reason he gets a glowing report from the supervisor.

He tells me that his shift-working record consists of forty hours, with five to six hours' break in between. A few weeks ago, he says, he worked twenty-four hours straight through. He's constantly looking in wastepaper baskets and containers and collecting dirty work gloves thrown away by Thyssen workers. He's even interested in single gloves. At some point he'll find a matching one. He collects and he collects, and soon he has a whole pile of about twenty. I (Ali) ask him, 'What you do with them? You can't wear so much glove.' He says, 'You never know. We don't get any gloves. You can be glad they are there. You have no idea what I collect. You always need several protective helmet in case something falls on your head.' I feel sorry for him. He's always beaming.

A few weeks later I hear F., who is supposed to be assigned to another double shift at the weekend, begging the foreman, 'I can't do any more! I can't do it, I won't make it.' 'What's that? You've always stayed the course!' 'Please, not today. Please, please.' The foreman: 'I'll make a note. You've always been reliable before.' I (Ali) congratulate him afterwards: 'I think it's good that you say "no" today, you're exhausted.'

He simply couldn't go on. He could barely walk or stand upright. His face was ashen, and his hands were trembling.

One of our workmates says that the previous year they had to work for thirty-six hours without sleep in the Easter holidays.

The German worker T., about thirty-five years old, is among those keenest on putting in the most hours at the Thyssen plant. You can tell by looking at him. Greyish-white in the face. Completely drained and thin as a rake. He was unemployed for a while, and he's one of the few who are grateful for the chance to work until they drop. Since he started in February 1985, he has worked month after month like a man possessed, and in April, by his own account, he will have got up to 350 hours a month. T.: 'Over the past week I worked four shifts back to back from Friday to Saturday. On Friday morning I drove in to Thyssen with you at 6.00 in the morning, and on Saturday morning I clocked in at the gate at 2.15.'

I (Ali) am there when the foreman actually forces us – in legal terms it would count as compulsion – to work a double shift. We are being driven to the collection point in the bus. We're completely shattered. Some of the men have fallen asleep in their seats when the foreman stops our bus and says as though in passing: 'More work to be done! Double shift!'

Some of the men protest, they want to get home, they have to get home, they're utterly exhausted.

It's made quite clear to them that Thyssen demands that they go on working.

My Algerian workmate T., who desperately needs to get home, is fired on the spot. He is pulled out of the bus and dumped in the road. From now on he can fend for himself.

That had been preceded by the following authentic piece of dialogue:

Foreman: 'You've got to go on working, until ten in the evening.'

Algerian colleague: 'Without me, I'm not a robot.'

Foreman: 'You've *all* got to go on working.'

Algerian colleague: 'I've urgently got to get home.'

Foreman: 'Then there's no point in your coming in again. It's absolutely necessary now.'

Algerian colleague: 'But I've got to get home.'

Foreman: 'Then don't bother coming in tomorrow. Then out you get. It's all over for you. For ever.'

Foreman (to the others, sitting in terrified silence): 'I need forty men, and I need them tomorrow as well! Thyssen demands it of us! I'd like to knock off now too, but I've got to do it, no one asks me. I've got an appointment to have my teeth capped this afternoon. That's not going to happen either. There's an end to it. What do you expect? Things are even worse in wartime!'

While we are taking a break in one of the kilometre-long, dark, empty corridors in Sintering Plant III, a Thyssen boss comes over to us with one of the foremen. They're checking how much slurry and sinter-dust we've cleared away, because it's chiefly our work that decides when the plant can get going again. The younger boss feels prompted by Yussuf's oriental appearance to wallow in memories of his holidays: 'Are you from Tunisia?' Yussuf says he is. Boss: 'Wonderful country. We're going there again this year – my wife and I – on holiday. It's incredibly relaxing. And everything's so much cheaper than it is here.'

Yussuf gives him a grateful, friendly smile. It isn't often that a German superior condescends to talk to a foreigner about anything but work, and it's completely unheard-of for him to speak in such a positive way about his homeland. Yussuf explains that his parents have a house near the sea, mentions the address and invites the boss 'to visit them next time he's in Tunisia'. The boss immediately accepts: 'You can depend on it, I'll be there. You'll just have to get hold of a few addresses for me. You know what I mean. You've got some great women in your country. How much would that cost at the moment?' Yussuf replies, 'I don't know.' 'But you can get anything you like there for 20 marks!'

Yussuf's pride is clearly injured, and he answers, 'Have no idea.'

The boss is still in his element, and won't let go: 'Listen, you've got some gorgeous women down there. Real wild-cats. Once you get their veils off they're really hot. Haven't you got a sister? Or is she still too young? In your country you've got to get married straight away, after all.'

Yussuf tries to hide his humiliation from the rest of us, and says, 'But you're going there with wife!' Boss: 'Doesn't matter. She'll be lying on the beach all day and won't have a clue. Great hotel. Just like the "Interconti" here. Costs only 2,000 for two weeks. With all the trimmings. We took a trip into that other country, what's it called?' Yussuf can't bear it any longer. He turns away, and says, 'Got to go to toilet.'

The foreman takes this as his cue to sit down and join us, and get into the enthusiastic holiday spirit himself. He stretches out. 'Ah, to be in the south right now. No work. Always sun. And women, women.' Turning to me (Ali). 'Am I right? In your country, in Anatolia, you can buy a woman for the price of a goat.' When I (Ali) look indifferently in the other direction, he challenges me: 'Isn't that so? How did you get hold of your old woman?' 'German always think, money buy everything,' Ali replies. 'But finest things in world don't get for money. That's why German so poor, in spite of much money.' The foreman feels under attack, and pays Ali back in kind: 'I wouldn't take your Anatolian harem ladies if they were handed to me on a plate. They're dirty, they stink. You've really got to scrub them down. And by the time you've undressed them, got all that junk off them, you're too tired anyway.'

Then Yussuf takes me (Ali) aside and says, 'It's not good that we learn and understand German. Always many problems. Better act as though don't understand.' He talks about younger Arab colleagues who deliberately stop learning the German language because of similar experiences and humiliations and, 'whatever boss says, always say "yes boss", that way no nonsense'.

Many of the toilets in the Thyssen factory are scrawled with anti-foreigner slogans and fantasies. Xenophobic graffiti is often sprayed on the factory walls as well, and no one has seen any reason to get rid of it.

The Promotion

I feel so exhausted and wretched that I don't think I can keep up my work at Thyssen any longer, although Ali knows enough colleagues who are going on labouring for Vogel despite illness and injuries. Those who held out for sixteen hours despite flu and fever for fear that someone new would be hired in their place.

I can afford to stake everything on a single card. I've learned that Vogel is having trouble with his driver and general handyman, and try to use trickery to get hold of the driver's job. I (Ali) have shown up at Vogel's office to demand my money. As always he is very annoyed and asks what on earth I was thinking of, being absent for several days, but when I (Ali) apologise and say that I (Ali) have quite recovered and that it's never going to happen again, he shows mercy and says that in that case I (Ali) should come the following day. 'But right on time, please, 2 o'clock on the dot.' As you would expect: the one who's not there the following day is Vogel. Three hours later, at about 5 o'clock, I finally find him at home. He immediately keeps his distance: 'We can't have this. You've got to come earlier. I'm in the bath at the moment.' He isn't in the bath at all, as you can see that he's fully dressed.

Me (Ali): 'Can wait a while and sit on step. Wait three hours at the door already. Must help you, because otherwise something happen to you.'

Vogel: 'To me? Why? Who?'

Me (Ali): 'I'll come back, if you in bath.'

Vogel: 'No, wait, come right in.'

Ali hesitantly follows him into his office and tells him that one of the workmen to whom Vogel owes money wants to teach him a lesson, but Ali won't let him.

In what follows, Ali acts out the role of an over-eager simpleton, who is prepared to sacrifice himself for his master, to die for him if necessary. 'I have learn karat, special Turkish karat, is called sisu.' It's utter nonsense, of course, I can't do karate, and 'sisu' is a Finnish word meaning 'endurance, staying power, fortitude'. But he doesn't know that. 'I help you if someone do something to you. I do one blow, he's gone.' To underline my savage determination, Ali smashes his fist down on Vogel's desk with all his might. Vogel studies Ali, impressed and irritated at the same time. 'Who would want to hurt me?' he asks. 'This is all fine, I'm glad you want to defend me, but what sort of bastard would want to do anything to me?' 'I don't know name now,' says Ali, 'but I tell him anyone want to kill Vogel must first kill Ali, I Vogel's man.' He doesn't notice that in his enthusiasm Ali has, unusually, mastered the genitive in the German language.

Vogel has bitten. For about five minutes he reads from lists of names of Turkish and Arab, current and former employees to whom he clearly owes money, and who are now, in his eyes, all potential murderers. When certain names are mentioned Ali pricks up his ears, asks him to repeat them, but then energetically shakes his head, the name of the avenger isn't among them. Lest he actually place any of his workmates under suspicion, Ali invents a phantom avenger, an 'Arab, member of a Turkish wrestling club', who has these massive hands – Ali demonstrates in the air – and who recently took a German who had 'insulted and cheated him' and 'smashed half his face off with a single blow'.

Vogel looks very concerned, and Ali mentions his other merits: the fact that he can 'not only do karat, but was for a long time a taxi-driver', and had previously been 'driver for other boss' who 'had big factory'. 'What sort of factory?' Vogel wants to know. 'Make sort of speaking-machine,' Ali explains. 'You mean walkie-talkies,' Vogel deduces correctly, and Ali proudly agrees. If need be he could even get a reference from the factory, because the head of the company is a good friend of mine (G.W.) 'I still have uniform in cupboard,' Ali boasts, 'nice cap and good material.'

'Oh, yes, that is interesting,' says Vogel. 'So are you a good driver?' 'Yes, no problem,' says Ali, 'boss could always sleep when Ali drive, and could also fix everything when car break down.' A complete lie, but I (Ali) can be pretty sure that Vogel's Mercedes 280 SE, with special equipment and all kinds of frills, is hardly going to be in need of repair. 'We can talk about that,' says Vogel. 'I always have some driving to do, and you'll keep this troublemaker off my back. You just need to give me the names. I have a hotline to the immigration police. Then they'll be out of the country before they notice what's happening to them.' 'Let me do it,' I (Ali) say, trying to distract him. 'You no need be afraid if they know I am Vogel's agent, one blow from Ali and they're dead, one blow and he's gone. You don't need police, I do it better.' 'All right, then,' says Vogel. 'Show up at 10.30 a.m. on Monday, and let's see how it goes.'

And so it was that Ali was 'promoted', from hard labourer, swallowing dust all day, to chauffeur and bodyguard. There are still some undreamed-of opportunities for self-advancement in our society. Even for the lowliest foreign worker.

Vogel also immediately tries – as is his way – to follow up this new act of job creation with a fresh deception. 'You're still sick,' he says. 'Listen, we'll immediately report you to the health insurance company, you go to the doctor and get a sick note, then I don't need to pay you any money, the health insurance people have to pay you, and you'll be driving for me.'

Driving Vogel around over the next few weeks was going to be a terrible act of self-denial. He finds something to carp about every time I turn the wheel. 'Drive sensibly.' 'That's enough dangerous driving, thank you very much.' 'How many times must I tell you, these are valuable objects that you're driving around the place.'

At one point he almost threatens to unmask me (Ali). He has noticed me gesturing to the photographer who has just missed us setting off on the other side of the road. 'Who were you waving at?' Vogel asks, extremely suspiciously. 'No wave,' I say to distract him, 'was just quick reflex for karat training. If sit for long time, must always practise quick reaction and make arm, leg and hand jerk very quick.' And to confirm my explanation, I (Ali) start making rapid, twitching movements with my arms and hands as I drive. He observes them with thoughtful astonishment. I (Ali) tell him, to bear out the story of the hard training I have undergone (and also to keep him at a bit of a distance in case of my being unmasked) that my lightning reactions are particularly feared in the karate club: one fellow member, who had rashly tried a simulated blow at me, had spent 'four days in a coma'. The fact that I could smash my way through bricks, 'two together, but old stone, not new', with one blow from the side of my hand, had already won me (Ali) some respect from him on another occasion. 'One blow from Ali, you be dead,' I say, jerking my hand in his direction. But lest I alarm him further, I (Ali) add: 'But must sign paper that we only do this when serious attack against us, never attack first.' If only he knew that I refused to fight or use weapons on principle, and my only strength in such situations lies in running away!

'Stop contorting yourself in my car like that, you're pulling the whole seat apart! You can do whatever it is you're doing once you're outside,' he shouts all of a sudden, for no reason; because the seats are so stable that my harmless movements couldn't do them the slightest damage. To emphasise the seriousness of my karate training, and thus to dispel his initial suspicions once and for all, I practise shadow-boxing by the side of his car when I have to spend a long time waiting for him outside the Ruhrkohle Heating Technology plant in Essen. This draws a big audience of secretaries from the Association of Health Insurance Companies, whose building is on the other side of the road. The secretaries come to the windows of the multi-storey block to wave at the crazed bodyguard standing beside the luxury limousine, some of them yelling encouragement. Ali waves back, and manages to interrupt work in the Association for at least a quarter of an hour. When Vogel comes back and sees Ali leaping about, and spots the crowd at the windows, he loses his temper: 'Stop that imme-diately, you idiot, you'll have people talking about me. You can do that in your monkey house on Dieselstrasse, or in your Turkish club.' Ali says, 'OK,' opens the car door for his boss and sits down at the wheel again with a deferential manner.

While Vogel may have built his whole fortune on filth, dust and dirt, he keeps himself meticulously clean. He has an almost hyster-ical fear of contact with the dirt of the world. As far as he's concerned, his slave-labourers are the caste of the untouchables, they disgust him, he'd like to keep as far away from them as he possibly can. And when they descend upon his home to demand payment, his fury isn't only to do with the loss to his pocket. He is also horrified at his direct confrontation with sweat, dirt and misery, even if the petitioners in question always turn up clean and respectably dressed.

By now Ali has adapted his clothing to his Mercedes. Neatly ironed creases in his trousers, freshly washed white or grey shirt, tie, not clumping, dripping great work-boots, but shiny leather shoes. Nonetheless, as far as Vogel is concerned, Ali remains a subhuman member of the proletarian underworld. Even his address on Dieselstrasse is like a stigma. That's where, in his eyes, the lowest of the low live in dirt, and work, right next door, in filth.

When I (Ali), his chauffeur, have to spend more than half an hour waiting outside his house at 7.30 in the morning, Ali feels the urgent need to go to the toilet. He rings the bell and asks Vogel if he can use the toilet.

Vogel: 'Number one or number two?'

Me (Ali): 'Everything.'

Vogel (irritated): 'So do it outside.'

Me (Ali): 'Where outside?'

Vogel: 'Do it round the corner, anywhere, just go.'

Me (Ali): 'Where in corner?'

Vogel: 'It doesn't matter a damn.'

He sends Ali into the street like a dog. There's no chance of shitting in his front garden, it's visible from the street. I feel like depositing a dump on the bonnet of his Mercedes, right on the star. Ten minutes later, when Vogel comes down, I (Ali) ask him, 'Your toilet broken, or what?'

Vogel: 'No, it's not broken. We don't do that at other people's houses and so on and so on . . .'

Me (Ali): 'And if you have guest, they must always go out?'

Vogel (embarrassed, hesitant): 'As I've said before, I hardly ever have guests, but my workers and mechanics don't get to go on my toilet, and they all know that. No one asks to. As far as that's concerned I'm very, very careful.'

Vogel reflects further: 'I hardly ever shake anyone's hand or anything like that. And if I have to shake someone's hand, then I wash my hands immediately afterwards.'

Me (Ali): 'If everyone thought way you do, nothing happen any more?'

Vogel: 'There'd be no more sickness, sure. But not everyone does think that way. Some people are real pigs in that respect. It can really turn your stomach if you think about it.'

On one of his location inspections, Vogel should be taken to the two toilets at our disposal: covered with filth. The company doesn't supply toilet paper, and they're hardly ever cleaned. One of the toilets has no door. As there's always a considerable queue, you just squat on it. On this toilet a German has written, in felt-tip pen: 'Wogs only'.

Postscript

On 20 October 1986, Hans Vogel's trial begins in the financial criminal court in Duisburg. He is accused of deception, tax evasion and violations of the Temporary Personnel Assignment Act, and escapes with a relatively lenient punishment: he is given a fifteen-month suspended sentence, and fined 3,600 DM. (Thyssen is obliged to pay a fine of 1 million DM.)

BRIAN TOOHEY AND MARIAN WILKINSON

The Timor Papers

1987

Brian Toohey was editor of the *National Times*, for more than a decade Australia's investigative newspaper that specialised in revealing the secret agendas of governments and crime in high places. Marian Wilkinson was one of the paper's outstanding reporters. In their 1987 *Book of Leaks*, they devote a chapter to 'The Timor Papers', a series of classified official American documents, which disclose that the US and Australian Governments knew about, and condoned, Indonesia's plans for the invasion of East Timor in 1975. The invasion was the prelude to a genocide that saw the population of the Portuguese colony fall by 200,000, or a third: proportionally, a greater slaughter than the Holocaust.

In the following pages, Toohey and Wilkinson introduce the documents. How they acquired them they do not say, of course. Arranged in diary form, 'The Timor Papers' give a rare blow-by-blow account of an unfolding crime against humanity and the collaboration of the West. It is precisely the same account that was delivered to President Gerald Ford in his top-secret briefing every morning.

They also dip into the secret cables of Richard Woolcott, the Australian ambassador to Indonesia during the invasion, who urged the government of Gough Whitlam to take advantage of Suharto's bloody aggression and contemplate the rewards for backing him, such as the oil and gas reserves in the Timor Sea. As if speaking for a time-less colonialism, Woolcott cabled: 'I know I am recommending a prag-matic rather than a principled stand but that is what national interest and foreign policy is all about . . .'

In contrast, Toohey and Wilkinson describe the importance of revealing the truth and the true motives of governments. 'The Timor Papers', they write, contain 'information that provides members of the public with a better appreciation of the underlying attitudes, motivations and activities of politicians and government officials who supposedly act on their behalf. Accountability is enhanced by the transfer of this information from covert agendas to the public domain where it belongs . . . Reputations may be harmed and embarrassment caused, but no more than is deserved if there is to be discipline imposed upon those who wish to wield power in secret.'

THE TIMOR PAPERS

The Timor Papers were leaked at the same time that the Argentine invasion of the Falklands provoked a full-scale military counter-attack from the British. Many words were being spoken and written about the need to demonstrate the principle that aggression must never be allowed to pay. The reaction to the Falklands War was in strong contrast with the international apathy towards the 1975 Indonesian invasion of Portuguese Timor. That invasion was allowed to succeed. Tens of thousands of Timorese died in the process with scarcely an international voice raised in protest. In compiling this report, the authors gained access to a large range of classified US documents that provided a wealth of new information on one of the least publicised wars in modern history. The material was drawn primarily from the Central Intelligence Agency, its military counterpart the Defense Intelligence Agency, the super-secret National Security Agency, and the State Department.

Unless otherwise stated the documentary extracts published in this section came from the *National Intelligence Daily*. This news sheet, published by the Director of the CIA for an élite, specially cleared audience in Washington, was on the President's desk early each morning in 1975. The leaks showed that the US knew that Indonesia had been conducting a covert paramilitary campaign against East Timor for over a year before the full-scale invasion in late 1975. Under intelligence-sharing arrangements with Australia, a large part of this information was passed on to Canberra. Additionally, much of the intercepted communications that formed the core of the US

intelligence came from radio antennae at the base run by the Australian
DSD (Defence Signals Directorate) at Coonawarra, near Darwin.
Neither government attempted to dissuade Indonesia from its aggression. Indeed, they quietly condoned it. The intelligence data showed
for the first time the full dimensions of the Indonesian determination
to take over its small neighbour and its subsequent efforts to cover
up the behaviour of its occupation forces. These measures even extended
to serious planning to sink a ship bringing in a United Nations envoy.

What is presented in the first section is the secret history of the
Indonesian campaign against Timor – chiefly the *National Intelligence
Daily*'s account, blow by blow, as written for the then US President,
Gerald Ford. This account is presented in the form of a diary.

By way of contrast what follows the diary is an analysis of the
dispatches sent by the Australian ambassador to Indonesia at the time
of the Indonesian takeover of Timor, R. A. Woolcott.

The National Intelligence Daily, 1975–76

11 August: A false calm. 'Representatives from the Portuguese
Government and Timorese political parties will meet in Macao later
this week to talk about a decolonisation plan for Portuguese Timor.
Indonesian intelligence officials plan to monitor the Macao talks to
safeguard the interests of the pro-Indonesia party, which is largely a
product of Jakarta's clandestine activities in Timor. General Ali
Murtopo, who has been charged with overseeing the decolonisation
procedure for the Indonesians, believes the Portuguese will arrange
matters so that Timor is eventually incorporated into Indonesia. These
same considerations still apply, and Suharto's inclination will probably be to await developments in Timor before committing himself.'
(On the same day another CIA secret publication, the *National
Intelligence Bulletin*, elaborated on Indonesia's covert operations: 'Over
the past year, Indonesia has organised a large clandestine and propaganda operation designed to assure the peaceful absorption of Timor
into Indonesia. As part of this effort, Indonesian intelligence officials
have actively courted the leaders of the pro-independence groups,
seeking to convince them that Timor cannot be viable as an independent state and that they should join forces with Jakarta.')

12 August: Now the alarm bells ring. 'Indonesian military officials have advised President Suharto that parties hostile to Indonesia were responsible for the show of force in Portuguese Timor this weekend. They have recommended immediate Indonesian military action against the colony . . . Last fall [September], Suharto's top military advisers advocated a military move against Timor, but the President preferred to rely on a clandestine political and propaganda campaign. He was concerned about Indonesia's international reputation and particularly about the reaction in the US and Australia.'

15 August: 'Indonesian President Suharto reportedly has decided to authorise direct military intervention in Portuguese Timor if he is convinced that Communist elements were involved in the recent seizure of power or if the lives of pro-Indonesia Apodeti Party members are threatened. The situation in Timor is apparently deteriorating. Violent clashes are said to have taken place between rival factions both in Dili and in the interior.'

18 August: The US attitude is a definite factor in Indonesian behaviour. 'Suharto continues to worry about an adverse reaction from the US, particularly since a move against Timor at this time would come only a few weeks after his visit to Washington. Top military commanders, however, still favour swift action because they fear that the situation will soon turn irrevocably against pro-Jakarta elements in Timor and result in a threat to Indonesian security. Intelligence officials in charge of the clandestine operation inside Timor have stepped up their activities. On Saturday fifty Indonesian-trained Timorese guerrillas reportedly crossed the border into the Portuguese territory. Their immediate mission is not known, but they are probably assigned to assist pro-Indonesia Timorese who have reportedly been violently attacked in recent days. Indonesia's clandestine activities in Timor may lead to a more serious breakdown in law and order, forcing a military decision upon Suharto.'

20 August: There is no doubt that the supposed limits on the use of US military equipment are clear to the Indonesians. 'Indonesian military contingency preparations are continuing, as are clandestine operations inside Portuguese Timor. According to an intercepted message, a local Timorese leader is ready to call publicly for integration with Indonesia. Jakarta may well be planning to stage a series of such declarations in the near future. President Suharto evidently is still delaying on a decision to authorise military action. Apparently, a major consideration on his part is that an invasion of Timor, if it comes, must be justified as an act in defence of Indonesian security. He is acutely aware that conditions of US military assistance to Indonesia specifically limit the use of this equipment to defensive purposes.'

28 August: Suharto is said to draw support from Gough Whitlam's attitude. 'Indonesia's preparations for intervention have probably advanced too far for Jakarta to turn back now, even though Portuguese President Costa Gomes has reportedly decided against endorsing unilateral Indonesian military action to restore order. Indonesian President Suharto believes Jakarta must move carefully to avoid being accused of aggression against Timor. He undoubtedly hoped that a special Portuguese envoy scheduled to arrive in Jakarta last night would bring word that Lisbon was prepared to support publicly an Indonesian move. Costa Gomes has apparently decided that, for domestic political reasons, he cannot do so. Suharto will probably give the go-ahead for intervention anyway and may well announce his decision in such a way as to leave the impression that he is acting on behalf of Lisbon. Recent worldwide publicity about the deteriorating situation in Timor and the Portuguese admission that they have lost control will work to Jakarta's advantage. Unilateral Indonesian action undertaken now in the name of ending bloodshed and with the appropriate disclaimers about territorial ambitions will probably not draw sharp international criticism.' (On the same day the State Department reported on what it called Suharto's 'mystical' confidence, reinforced by Whitlam's attitude . . . 'Embassy contacts agree that Suharto is "mystically" sure Timor will eventually become Indonesian. Thus, drawing support from [Prime Minister] Whitlam's declaration of Australian non-intervention, he awaits a specific Portuguese request for him to take action.')

29 August: 'Indonesia's preparations for an invasion, originally discussed by Suharto and his military commanders on 8 August, now are expected to be complete by 31 August. The plan calls for a three-pronged attack on the north coast of the island. Two battalions are to launch a combined assault against Dili. The largest force of some 6,000 infantry will land at Atapupu in Indonesian Timor and then drive north into the Portuguese half of the island. One battalion will also land to secure the coastal strip extending eastward from Dili to

Tutuala, on the eastern tip of the island. The forces then are to link up and secure control of the complete northern coast from Atapupu to Tutuala. The Indonesians expect some stiff resistance, but are confident they will be successful. Once the north coast of the island is secured, the Indonesians plan to withdraw most of their regular forces. They also plan to leave commando units and units of ethnic Timorese to establish control over the central part of the island to contend with any guerrilla units that may be operating there.'

4 September: The State Department reported: 'Communications intelligence indicates that two Indonesian special forces groups, consisting of about 100 men each, may have entered Portuguese Timor on the evening of 3–4 September.'

8 September: Suharto is worried (unnecessarily) that an invasion might cause Australia to cut its military aid. 'Indonesian President Suharto's vacillation in recent weeks on how to handle Portuguese Timor reflects the disagreement among his advisers on how to deal with the situation. Suharto would prefer to avoid unilateral military action in Timor, but if he cannot show that Indonesia's interests will be protected by other means the pressure from his military commanders for armed intervention will be difficult to resist. Minister of Defence General Panggabean and Indonesia's top military commanders favoured unilateral intervention in Portuguese Timor long before the coup attempt in Dili last month plunged the territory into civil war. They have argued that Indonesia cannot afford to take the chance that an unstable or Communist regime may emerge in Timor. General Ali Murtopo, Suharto's long-time confidant and adviser, has been in charge of the diplomatic effort in Timor. For him, military action would be tantamount to a vote of no confidence in his ability. Murtopo and the special operations staff of the national intelligence agency have also been operating a major clandestine effort inside Portuguese Timor. Murtopo's group has organised and provided funds for the pro-Indonesia Apodeti Party and has provided training and weapons for Timorese guerrillas. The chaotic situation in Timor, in which ideological considerations have taken a back seat to clan and tribal rivalries, is tailor-made for such clandestine operations. Foreign Minister Adam Malik and his colleagues in the diplomatic corps are worried about the international consequences of whatever action Indonesia takes in Timor. Malik has been working hard to repair Jakarta's frayed

non-aligned image and fears that a move against Timor now when
the leftists are in control would reopen Indonesia to charges of being
anti-Communist and pro-West. President Suharto himself is ambivalent. Personally he would probably prefer military action because he
has an overwhelming fear of Communist subversion in Indonesia. He
is also concerned about his international image, however, and does
not want to revive the ghost of adventurist foreign policies practised
under former President Sukarno. Suharto is also concerned about the
impact on Indonesia's bilateral relations with Australia and the US.
In both cases he is worried about the loss of military assistance, which
he badly wants to improve Indonesia's outdated equipment. Suharto
has apparently relied heavily on this argument in counselling caution
to his military commanders and is now showing some concern that
if substantial aid is not forthcoming there will be severe political reper-
cussions for himself. In trying to balance off his various advisers,
Suharto has appeared to blow hot and cold on Timor. When meeting
with military advisers he has emphasised his willingness to authorise
an invasion should Indonesian security require it. In meetings with
his political and diplomatic advisers he has stressed the need to get
a new agreement with Lisbon that will settle the Timor problem.
Suharto's political position ultimately depends on support from his
military commanders. Indonesian military preparations for invading
Timor have taken on a life of their own, and it will be harder and
harder to reverse gears. The diplomatic and clandestine political
options, although showing some promise of success, will take time
and there is little certainty of the final result. Suharto professes to
have mystical assurance that Timor will eventually become part of
Indonesia regardless of what Jakarta does and therefore patience is
all that is needed. Unless either Malik or Murtopo can soon show
some clear proof that their methods will succeed, however, Suharto
will probably find that for political reasons he can no longer keep
saying no to his military commanders.'

18 September: Indonesian special forces are engaging in heavy fighting.
'Indonesia continues to follow a two-track approach towards the
Timor problem. Publicly, Jakarta denies any intention of unilateral
intervention and calls on Lisbon to move faster in arranging talks
between the Timorese parties. Privately, Jakarta has stepped up covert
military operations inside Timor, including use of Indonesian special
forces units to support pro-Indonesian Timorese. Indonesian special

forces units operating covertly in Portuguese Timor are meeting unexpected resistance in several areas, according to intercepted communications . . . President Suharto continues to look for a legal justification for an Indonesian military invasion. Last week, he instructed his Minister of Justice to come up with a plan to integrate Timor by military means but still avoid an accusation that Indonesia is expansionist.'

26 September: The *National Intelligence Bulletin* reported that Indonesian soldiers had been captured, but with little international reaction: 'Indonesian special forces have taken casualties in recent fighting in Portuguese Timor where they are assisting pro-Indonesian Timorese against the radical Fretilin forces that now control most important towns. Some Indonesian soldiers have been captured, but Fretilin efforts to stir up an international outcry by publicising Jakarta's involvement have evoked little response.'

10 October: The *Weekly Review* reported: 'According to a clandestine source, Malaysia provided Indonesia in early October with a small quantity of arms and ammunition that cannot be traced to any foreign military assistance given to Indonesia.'

11 October: Indonesian forces are to attack a Timor town wearing uniforms without insignia. 'President Suharto continues to hold out against pressure from his armed forces commanders for a military invasion of Portuguese Timor. He has, however, approved a plan of action that will increase military pressure on Fretilin forces operating near the border. The plan calls for the setting up of small military bases just inside Portuguese Timor. Indonesia's strategy is to nibble away at the Fretilin from these enclaves. The first of the enclaves is to be established on 14 October, when Indonesian units are to attack the town of Maliana. The troops participating in the operation will wear uniforms without insignia and are to carry older, Soviet-made weapons so as not to be identified as Indonesian regulars.'

31 October: The DIA *Weekly Summary* left no doubt that Indonesia was committing military aggression, even if it was largely ignored by the Western media: 'Some 2,000 Indonesian regular infantry troops, special forces, marines, and Timorese partisans, launched coordinated attacks along the border and captured at least six border towns in Portuguese Timor on 16 October. Fretilin defences quickly stiffened.

Indonesian units came under strong counter-attacks, and a company was apparently forced back across the border at Lebos. Despite increasingly visible military activities, Jakarta continues to deny its involvement and attributes all fighting to anti-Fretilin Timorese. President Suharto remains concerned about international reaction and continues to make an effort to deny any territorial ambitions.'

7 November: The *Weekly Review* under the heading *Timor Going Through The Motions* reported: 'Recently, Portugal compounded Jakarta's image problem by announcing that it had asked Jakarta to withdraw its forces from the Timor border area and nearby waters. The Australian Government last week also added to Jakarta's problems by publicly criticising for the first time Indonesia's military intervention in Timor. Indonesian forces now control most of the border area and at least five towns inside Portuguese Timor, and they are attempting to consolidate their positions.'

29 November: 'The declaration of independence for Portuguese Timor issued yesterday by the left-wing Fretilin group appears to be a desperate Fretilin effort to protect itself from Indonesian military operations. Fretilin probably hopes to deter an Indonesian advance towards the capital city of Dili by focusing greater international attention on the Timor problem. The group may hope that the publicity shortly before President Ford's visit to Indonesia on 5 December will inhibit the Indonesians.'

1 December: The State Department reported that President Ford's visit played a part in the timing of a full-scale invasion: 'According to a reliable source, Indonesia will not initiate large-scale military action against Portuguese Timor until after President Ford completes his visit on 7 December, despite Fretilin's unilateral declaration of independence. No judgement has yet been reached on the use of force after 7 December, but the matter is under consideration and the decision will be influenced greatly by Jakarta's determination of whether Portugal colluded with Fretilin over the independence announcement. Should an invasion be decided upon, the Indonesians estimate that Fretilin can be forced to capitulate in three to four weeks.'

5 December: The invasion is approved. 'President Suharto has reportedly approved a plan to begin overt Indonesian intervention in

Portuguese Timor soon after President Ford leaves Jakarta. The first step will be an appeal for support from the pro-Indonesian faction in Timor, followed by an official announcement that Jakarta is sending military forces to stabilise the situation. Both moves are scheduled for today, the day President Ford arrives. The Indonesians issued a statement yesterday on their "moral obligation to protect the people of Timor", a move that could presage the actions outlined in Suharto's reported plan. A date for the overt intervention has not been set. It could take place as early as tomorrow, but it is more likely to come a few days later . . . Suharto undoubtedly calculates that the pro-Indonesian forces now control enough territory to give credibility to their appeal for Jakarta's support to undercut expected international criticism of Indonesian intervention. Suharto is undoubtedly still concerned about the effects of an Indonesian invasion on his relations with the US, particularly the continuation of US military aid, and he will try hard to present a plausible justification. His military commanders may have worked out a battle plan that will not require the use of US-grant equipment in the final operation. Suharto is certain to try to elicit a sympathetic attitude from President Ford during their meetings.'

6 December: 'The Indonesians will launch their invasion of Portuguese Timor on Sunday.'

7 December: The State Department listed US interests in the wake of the invasion. The lives of the Timorese people were at no stage mentioned: 'As yet unconfirmed press reports from Portuguese Timor indicate Indonesian forces launched an attack early 7 December and have captured the colony's capital at Dili. The reports are consistent with previous intelligence estimates as well as Embassy Jakarta predictions. The invasion, following President Ford's visit, is likely to raise questions about the degree of US foreknowledge. Indonesia's intervention was probably designed to be surgical, but may prove more costly and difficult than Jakarta anticipates. An analysis of US interests sent to the Secretary [Kissinger] notes that US interests in Timor relate solely to our broader interests with respect to the principal parties involved – Portugal, Indonesia, Australia and Indonesia's ASEAN[1] neighbours; that the longer military intervention drags on

[1] Association of South-East Asian Nations.

and the less decisive it is, the more divisive the action will be in the international arena. The current cooperative stance of Portugal, Indonesia and Australia in co-sponsoring the UN resolution calling for a peaceful solution will be difficult to maintain; that Portugal could well condemn Indonesia's action and may take the matter to the Security Council; that Australia, only a week away from elections, is likely to be far more cautious but is unlikely to openly support Indonesia's move; and that other countries in the area will be embarrassed by the move but will not wish to stand up and be counted. US interests at this time would appear to be best served by following Indonesia's lead on the issue while remaining responsive and receptive to Australian and Portuguese views if pressed on us. Our efforts should be devoted to getting the three together to work out what is essentially their problem.'

8 December: Dili falls. 'Indonesian troops have captured Dili, the capital of Portuguese Timor.'

10 December: US equipment used. The State Department reported: 'Analysing the weekend action, Embassy Jakarta points out that "there is no doubt US Military Assistance Program equipment was used, and we could be in for part of the blame if the operation is not a quick success". The ambassador comments, "The Foreign Minister has already indicated to others the US understands and does not oppose Indonesia's action. I believe our best course is to take at face value Indonesia's professed desire for orderly self-determination. Indonesia probably would not resent a US vote at the UN for a ceasefire and an observed process of self-determination, but it certainly would resent US support for a return to the status quo ante."')

2 January: Australian Foreign Minister Andrew Peacock's attitude is resented. 'International reaction to Indonesia's military actions in Portuguese Timor continues to be troublesome for Jakarta, but the Government of President Suharto is confident Timor is a manageable problem. For Indonesia, the Security Council resolution of 22 December was little more than a slap on the wrist, and the Indonesian ambassador at the UN indicated in advance that Jakarta could live with its wording. Indonesia subsequently made a pro-forma statement regretting the UN action, but welcoming UN participation in settling the Timor problem. Jakarta is still taking a cooperative public position, while working behind the scenes to postpone the arrival of a fact-finding mission as called for in the resolution. Jakarta insists that all outside parties, including the UN, must work through the new provisional Timorese Government set up in Dili on 19 December. That government has said publicly that UN representatives should not come to Timor until their physical safety can be guaranteed. Once Indonesian forces have full control over the handful of towns in eastern Timor, a UN team could be allowed to go through the motions of a fact-finding visit . . . Indonesia was willing to overlook Australia's unfavourable General Assembly vote, believing it was directed at a domestic audience during an election campaign. This Indonesian forbearance could change, however, as Jakarta is certain to resent Foreign Minister Peacock's continuing strong statements against Indonesian actions on Timor. Australian public opinion is pushing the government towards a stronger public stance, but the new Fraser Government doubtless will work privately to minimise strains with Indonesia.'

13 January: Stage-managing the UN visit. 'Jakarta is preparing carefully for the arrival of a UN fact-finding mission to Timor early next week. The Indonesians want to ensure that Secretary-General Waldheim's representative submits a favourable report. Efforts are reportedly under way to conceal the presence of Indonesian troops and heavy equipment and to repair war damage to Dili. Reports say that the UN mission will be allowed to visit only Dili and other towns securely under Indonesian control, and formal contact will be allowed only with the carefully coached pro-Indonesian regime in Dili . . . Even if the UN mission were to make a report critical of Indonesia, there would be little sentiment at the UN to renew debate on the Timor issue.'

1 February: The State Department reported that the Indonesians actually considered sinking the ship carrying the UN envoy: 'UN envoy Guicciardi's attempts to arrange transportation to East Timor have aroused considerable concern among Indonesian leaders, according to a senior Indonesian intelligence official. Guicciardi, presently in Jakarta, is negotiating with Australia for permission to fly to Darwin to meet a Portuguese frigate which will take him to East Timor. The Indonesians are worried that, if the envoy reaches East Timor, he will find confirmation of the presence of a large Indonesian military force, and evidence that the Fretilin is stronger than is admitted. The degree

of importance which the Indonesians assign to blocking Guicciardi's
visit to East Timor is manifested by their plan to sink the Portuguese
frigate with the envoy on board. Having rejected this option due to
its ramifications, they are still considering whether to sink the vessel
before it reaches Darwin; to request the Australians to deny permission for Guicciardi to visit Darwin; or failing that, to ask the
Australians to refuse the Portuguese ship entry into Darwin.'

4 February: Blocking the UN continues. 'Jakarta had managed, during
the UN representative's visit to Indonesian-controlled areas in late
January, to conceal all signs of Indonesian military forces. The
Timorese had assured the mission that they did not want a refer-
endum because they had already decided to integrate with Indonesia.
The representative professed to be impressed that the Timorese had
a functioning civil administration, which included some former
members of Fretilin. On 1 February, however, the representative flew
to Darwin where, according to press reports, he accepted a Portuguese
offer to carry him to Fretilin-held areas of Timor aboard a Portuguese
frigate. Moving quickly to deny the frigate a place to land, the
Indonesians have captured the main Fretilin port on the south coast,
and the Jakarta-backed Timorese are threatening to turn back the
ship by force.'

10 February: The UN gives in. 'Indonesia has managed to thwart
efforts of a UN representative to visit Fretilin-held areas of Timor.
The representative left Australia for Geneva on Sunday after failing
to arrange safe passage to Eastern Timor to consult Fretilin leaders
there. UN Secretary-General Waldheim, who is visiting Australia, said
he did not consider the representative's mission terminated, but set
no timetable for his return. The Indonesians paid lip service to the
need to support the UN mission but put obstacles in its way, and
accelerated the occupation of populated places and airfields in Timor.
The Indonesians said they were unable to guarantee the mission's safe
passage because of the unsettled situation and left Waldheim's representative with no alternative but to meet with Fretilin exiles in
Australia. Jakarta will now attempt to delay the raising of the Timor
issue at the UN, at least until it can argue that Timor's integration
into Indonesia is an accomplished fact, and that the UN no longer
has a role to play.'

The Woolcott Cables

Early in March 1975, R. A. Woolcott replaced R. W. Furlonger as Australian ambassador to Indonesia. The series of leaked dispatches which follows discloses the substance of Australian–Indonesian dealings over Timor in the months before the Indonesian armed takeover. The series begins with a dispatch which canvasses the complaisant United Kingdom attitude to the East Timor 'problem child'. It was sent before the attempted seizure of power in Dili by the UDT[2] grouping and the subsequent ascendancy of Fretilin. The cable traffic became particularly heavy in August 1975, after the UDT failure, and only a part of it is reproduced here.

21 July 1975: British policy on Portuguese Timor. British ambassador Ford [Sir John Archibald Ford] has given me a personal basis copy of report of his Head of Chancery (Gordon Duggan) on his visit to Portuguese Timor earlier this month. We are sending copy by safe-hand bag today as non-Australian report could be of interest in complementing our own reporting. Meanwhile, you might be interested in following comment by Ford in covering letter to FCO [Foreign and Commonwealth Office]. Begins: 'One conclusion does seem to stand out from Gordon's report: the people of Portuguese Timor are in no condition to exercise the right of self-determination; their politicians are likely to continue their squabbling and dissension and, in the absence of a strong lead from Lisbon or a military coup, political confusion will grow worse and the territory's soil become even more fertile for trouble-making. Duggan saw no evidence that either the Russians or the Chinese were yet stirring the pot; but any increase in Soviet influence in Lisbon might increase the chances that the former will seek to exploit the situation, and we shall keep as close an eye out as possible for signs that they are doing so. Even without Soviet or Chinese intervention the territory seems likely to become steadily more of a problem child, and the arguments in favour of its integration into Indonesia are all the stronger. Though it still remains in our interest to steer clear of becoming involved in its future, developments in Lisbon

---

[2] Timorese Democratic Union, independence movement led by members of the colonial élite.

seem now to argue in favour of greater sympathy towards
Indonesia should the Indonesian Government feel forced to take
strong action by the deteriorating situation in Portuguese Timor.
Certainly as seen from here it is in Britain's interest that Indonesia
should absorb the territory as soon as and as unobtrusively as
possible; and that if it comes to the crunch and there is a row
in the United Nations we should keep our heads down and avoid
siding against the Indonesian Government.'

When told that the Australian Prime Minister might communicate to
President Suharto Australia's opposition to the use of force by
Indonesia, Woolcott argued strongly against such a move. Woolcott
pleaded that it would be easier to negotiate with Indonesia than with
Portugal or East Timor about the seabed border, where oil explo-
ration might take place. (In the event, Indonesia took a hard line on
the seabed question.) Woolcott also notes that the US could restrain
Indonesia because of its need for American military equipment, but
Henry Kissinger regarded other issues as more important and wanted
the cable traffic on Timor cut back.

17 August 1975: For Secretary [Alan Renouf] from Woolcott.
. . . As I stressed in Canberra last month we are dealing with a
settled Indonesian policy to incorporate Timor, as even Malik
[Adam Malik, Indonesian Foreign Minister] admitted to me on
Friday . . . I believe the Indonesians are well aware of our attitudes to Timor at all levels. Indonesia is simply not prepared to
accept the risks they see to them in an independent Timor and
I do not believe that we will be able to change their minds on
this. We have in fact tried to do so. What Indonesia now looks
to from Australia in the present situation is some understanding
of their attitude and possible action to assist public understanding
in Australia rather than action on our part which could contribute
to criticism of Indonesia. They believe they will get this understanding elsewhere in the region, including from Japan and New
Zealand . . . In considering whether or not there should be
another message from the Prime Minister [Gough Whitlam] to
the President [Suharto] we should also bear in mind that the
President has not formally answered the Prime Minister's March
letter although it could be argued that he did so orally in

Townsville [2–3 April]. I am sure that the President would not welcome another letter on this subject at this stage, especially after what he said publicly in Parliament only yesterday ... Suharto will be looking to Australia for understanding of what he, after very careful consideration, decides to do rather than what he might regard as a lecture or even a friendly caution. The Minister [Senator Willesee] and Prime Minister may feel that domestic pressure puts Australia under an obligation to act. One answer to this would be that Australia has already made more representations to the Indonesian Government, and been more active in making its serious concern known to the Indonesians, than any other country. The upshot of this is that Australia has been singled out by the Indonesians in their planning discussions as the country (along with China) that will be the most vocal in the event of Indonesian intervention in Portuguese Timor. They know that reaction in Australia – unlike other ASEAN countries and New Zealand – will probably be their main problem. I doubt whether we can expect a better result than that. Other alternatives to a message – although I would also not recommend them – would be an answer to a question in the House or a statement, possibly at a press conference. These could assert that Australia cannot condone the use of force in Timor, nor could we accept the principle that a country can intervene in a neighbouring territory because of concern, however well based that concern might be, over the situation there. At the same time such an answer to a question in Parliament or from the press could concede that Indonesia has had a prolonged struggle for national unity and could not be expected to take lightly a breakdown in law and order in Portuguese Timor, especially when the colony is surrounded by and geographically very much part of the Indonesian Archipelago.

While the situation in Portuguese Timor is not likely to get as bad as that in Angola, it is going to be a mess for some time. From here I would suggest that our policies should be based on disengaging ourselves as far as possible from the Timor question; getting Australians presently there out of Timor; leave events to take their course; and if and when Indonesia does intervene act in a way which would be designed to minimise the public impact in Australia and show privately understanding to Indonesia of their problems. Perhaps we should also make an effort to secure through Parliament and the media a greater understanding of our policy, and Indonesia's, although we do not want to become apologists for Indonesia. The United States might have some influence on Indonesia at present as Indonesia really wants and needs United States assistance in its military re-equipment programme. But Ambassador Newsom told me last night that he is under instructions from Kissinger personally not to involve himself in discussions on Timor with the Indonesians on the grounds that the United States is involved in enough problems of greater importance overseas at present. The State Department has, we understand, instructed the embassy to cut down its reporting on Timor. I will be seeing Newsom on Monday but his present attitude is that United States should keep out of the Portuguese Timor situation and allow events to take their course. His somewhat cynical comment to me was that if Indonesia were to intervene the United States would hope they would do so 'effectively, quickly and not use our equipment'. We are all aware of the Australian defence interest in the Portuguese Timor situation but I wonder whether the Department has ascertained the interest of the Minister or the Department of Minerals and Energy in the Timor situation. It would seem to me that this Department might well have an interest in closing the present gap in the agreed sea border and this could be much more readily negotiated with Indonesia by closing the present gap than with Portugal or independent Portuguese Timor. I know I am recommending a pragmatic rather than a principled stand but that is what national interest and foreign policy is all about . . .

MAX DU PREEZ AND JACQUES PAUW
Exposing Apartheid's Death Squads
1988–94

When I returned to South Africa in 1997, after having been banned for thirty years for my reporting of the apartheid regime, I turned on the television in my hotel room and watched an extraordinary programme called *Weekly Report*. The presenter was a fluent, blunt journalist with an apparent arsenal of facts. He had the kind of moral authority that distinguishes those who have resisted a totalitarian state. This was Max du Preez, a journalist whose career belies the stereotype of the Afrikaner.

Broadcast every Sunday night for more than two years, *Weekly Report* provided a glimpse of the blood, sweat and tears of South Africa. Max du Preez would analyse and sum up that week's hearing of the Truth and Reconciliation Commission, whose filmed evidence was often difficult to watch, yet at other times inspiring. Without Max's weekly appearance, most South Africans would have known little about the hearings and the crimes of the apartheid regimes. Max, whose native tongue had produced the word 'apartheid', would never let the whites in his national audience escape the sense of their own complicity; he pointedly referred to them as 'you'. When he himself gave evidence to the Commission, he was unsparing of his colleagues in the press. 'If the mainstream media had reflected and followed up these [death] squad confessions and revelations,' he said, 'the government would have been forced to stop the torture, the assassinations. It would have saved many, many lives.'

Max du Preez is best known in South Africa for a newspaper that he, Jacques Pauw and three other courageous journalists founded in 1988. This was *Vrye Weekblad*, the only Afrikaans-language paper to oppose apartheid. For four years, they published a stream of exposés, disclosing how the white supremacist government used death squads and assassins to silence its enemies and anyone else who got in the way.

Vrye Weekblad became one of the most read and most persecuted and prosecuted newspapers anywhere. Its offices were bombed, its staff received daily death threats and the regime showered it with criminal and civil prosecutions. The end came when the Assistant Police Commissioner, Lothar Neethling, sued for defamation and won on appeal. Ordered to pay damages and burdened with huge legal bills, the paper was forced to close in January 1994, a few months before South Africa's first democratic elections.

In revealing the atrocities of the apartheid state and those responsible, *Vrye Weekblad* played a significant part in forcing the Pretoria regime to negotiate a settlement with the freedom movements. The following essay, 'Exposing Apartheid's Death Squads', tells how *Vrye Weekblad* exposed 'Section C1', also known as the Vlakplaas, home of the death squads, a secret Gestapo-style unit of the South African police that specialised in kidnapping, torture, bombing and the murder of apartheid's opponents. The investigation was conducted by Max du Preez and Jacques Pauw over three years and eventually led to the smashing of 'C1'. Eugene de Kock, the death squads commander, was sentenced to 212 years' imprisonment. He is the most senior member of the apartheid gang to be successfully prosecuted and punished.

Reflecting their close collaboration, Max du Preez and Jacques Pauw jointly wrote this series of first-person accounts of years of 'danger and achievement on the part of those we must never forget', as Nelson Mandela said of South Africa's liberation movement.

EXPOSING APARTHEID'S DEATH SQUADS

It was a spring afternoon in September 1988, and on a farm 20 kilometres west of Pretoria, a group of burly South African policemen stood around a fire. They were sipping on the first of many glasses of 'police coffee', rum or brandy topped up with a little Coke. Hanging over the fire was a huge cast-iron pot with *potjiekos*, a traditional stew of mutton and vegetables.

All the men had nicknames, playful ones like *Chappies*, *Brood* (Bread), *Snorre* (Moustaches) and *Balletjies* (Little Balls), but there was also a man called *Duiwel* (Devil).

The commander of the group was stocky and bespectacled. If it were not for his ice-cold eyes, one could easily mistake him for a church elder or a school teacher. His nickname was *Brille* (Goggles), although behind his back his men referred to him as *Prime Evil*.

Colonel Eugene Alexander de Kock was a man who demanded fear and respect, for he could ultimately decide who would live and who would die. He was a highly decorated counter-insurgent who boasted that he based his battle strategies on the Mongolian warrior Attila the Hun, who invaded Europe in AD 350. Attila was renowned for his cruelty because he spared no one. Attila said he was driven by a 'lust for brutality' and would select only the most 'vicious and ferocious-looking warriors' to accompany him on his bloody campaigns.

If *Prime Evil* saw himself as Attila, the men around the fire were his Huns, a brotherhood of brutes who were apartheid's ultimate and most secret weapon. When all else had failed – detention without trial, torture, harassment, dirty tricks, state-of-emergency regulations and criminal prosecution – Eugene de Kock and his apartheid gladiators were sent out to 'finally solve the problem'.

This was Section C1, the most secret and élite unit in the South African Police. When C1 designed a unit emblem, they chose the honey badger, an animal legendary for its tenacity and ferocity. The animal was set against a red background of the African continent, which represented all the policemen who had spilled blood in their 'fight against Communism'.

Killing, bombing, kidnapping and torture were C1's business. And in the South African spring of 1988, business was good.

De Kock and his men were called together on this day to entertain very important people: the Minister of Law and Order and top generals in the South African Police. Earlier that day one of the men had to go and buy Chivas Regal whisky, the minister's favourite drink.

Minister Adriaan Vlok came to Vlakplaas – a picturesque farm in the Skurweberg mountain range which served as C1's headquarters – to bring tribute to Eugene de Kock and his men. For only a few days earlier, a building in downtown Johannesburg had gone up in smoke.

The Security Branch had believed that the headquarters of the South African Council of Churches in Khotso House was a stronghold of the banned liberation movement, the African National Congress. State President P. W. Botha ordered its destruction. The task was given to C1. The mission was so secret that de Kock was instructed that should other policemen come upon them, they should be shot.

On the night of 31 August, de Kock and his men entered the building and placed between eighty and ninety kilograms of explosives in the cellar of the building. Fifteen minutes later, the explosion shook the whole of central Johannesburg, injuring twenty-three and destroying the building.

This was not nearly de Kock's or C1's biggest operation, but it did bring the minister to Vlakplaas. After they had tucked into the *potjie* and refilled their glasses, Adriaan Vlok addressed the men and said: 'We will never surrender to the ANC, not in a thousand years.' The men raised their glasses – this was how they liked their politicians.

The minister, otherwise known as a man of sober habits, got slightly emotional and started congratulating C1 for 'that excellent operation the other day'. De Kock was angry at the minister's loose tongue, because not all the generals present knew of the Khotso House operation. He gesticulated to Vlok and the minister shut up.

Celebrations continued late into the night. To the government politicians, the bombing of Khotso House was proof that C1 was a precious arrow in the apartheid quiver. The minister had assured them that they were winning the war. De Kock and his men were revered and untouchable.

Or so they thought.

Because, unbeknown to Eugene de Kock, the unthinkable was happening. An insider, a man who once went out with them to kill, and kill again, was talking too much.

And barely a month after this celebration, in an old bank building in downtown Johannesburg, a new, independent newspaper was born. Its exposés over the next four years would lead to the closing down of C1 – and the jailing of Eugene de Kock.

Max du Preez:

Jacques and I are both Afrikaners. Pauw is a Dutch surname, du Preez is French. Our tribe is made up of descendants of the Dutch who came to the Cape of Good Hope in 1652, of the small group of French Huguenots who arrived in 1688, and a succession of German,

Scottish, Scandinavian and other European immigrants. But our blood is far from pure white European: especially during the first two centuries after colonial settlement there were quite a lot of interracial marriages and we all carry the genes of the aboriginal Khoi people, of slaves from Indonesia, Madagascar and Mozambique, and of the Bantu-speaking groups of southern Africa.

British colonialists later took over control of the Cape Colony from the Dutch, and a large chunk of our ancestors, by now calling themselves Boers, speaking a simplified dialect of Dutch heavily influenced by Malay and the Khoi languages, trekked to the interior of what is today South Africa. After a number of bloody battles with the African chiefdoms of these areas, they formed two independent Boer republics. The republics were defeated during the Anglo–Boer War of 1899–1902, and were then incorporated in the Union of South Africa in 1910 with the colonies of the Cape and Natal. Forty years later, after a fierce revival of Afrikaner nationalism, their main political party, the National Party, won the elections (for whites only) and started formalising the separation of racial groups, practised by the Dutch and the British since the early years of colonialisation, into a rigid ideology called apartheid.

By the 1980s South Africa was a deeply divided society traumatised by severe repression and the violent resistance to it by the liberation movements. State President P. W. Botha had militarised the government and declared that there was a 'Total Onslaught' on the country and all its institutions, which needed a 'Total Strategy' to counter it. This simply meant severe restrictions on the media, successive states of emergency and giving the security establishment a free hand to disrupt and destroy opponents without worrying too much about the law. Death squads, dirty tricks, torture, bannings, detention without trial and disinformation campaigns became the order of the day.

By 1987 the country was in a state of near civil war. Yet Botha and his ruling National Party continued to enjoy majority support from the white electorate. I was one of a small group of Afrikaners and other white South Africans who were appalled at what was being done in our name. In July that year I was part of a delegation of mostly Afrikaner opinion-formers who met with the exiled leadership of the banned African National Congress in Dakar, Senegal, in an effort to bridge the big divide and start loosening the deadlock. The Dakar Safari, as it became known, was condemned hysterically by Botha, his securocrats and virtually all white-run newspapers. It was

during this visit and conversations with many of the internal and
exiled leaders that I decided that something drastic had to be done
to shake white Afrikaners by telling them what their government was
really doing, and that the alternative, an open democracy, was actually in their interest. I decided to launch a newspaper in the Afrikaans
language, because Afrikaners dominated the government and the security forces – and it was my tribe. The paper's mission would be to
expose the evils of apartheid and the violent nature of the government's policies and to let white South Africans hear the voice of their
black countrymen and their leaders.

I sold everything I owned, cashed in my insurance policies and
launched *Vrye Weekblad* (free or independent weekly) on 4 November
1988. With me were four trusted and like-minded Afrikaans-speaking
journalists and a promising young reporter I had never met before,
Jacques Pauw. This was the closest you could ever get to an editorial collective and a democratic newsroom. It was every journalist's
dream: to own your own newspaper and to write what you like as
you like it. We set up shop in a vacant building in Johannesburg's
derelict Newtown district and did a primitive version of early desktop
publishing using cheap Taiwanese personal computers. Staff members,
their families and volunteers helped with the distribution. It was a
crazy idea.

Trouble with the government started on Day 1. The Minister of
Justice, Kobie Coetsee, declared that the publication would likely pose
a threat to the state and support its enemies, and raised the registration fee for the newspaper from the normal R10 to R30,000. We
collected the money from readers in a few days. But the first few
editions also brought the first of many dozens of criminal and civil
court cases against the newspaper: for quoting banned persons; for
contravening the state of emergency; for exposing a secret agent of
the state; breaking the Internal Security Act, the Public Safety Act
and the Terrorism Act. My criminal record grew by the month, but
we made sure that we did not blatantly break the same law twice,
so on every offence I was a first-time offender and got heavy fines
and long suspended jail sentences. But an even more effective strategy
was to sue us for defamation, because legal costs were extremely high
and the state knew we had no money. Among those who declared
we had defamed them were the President himself, the Attorney General
in Johannesburg, one military and two police generals. Only one was
successful. There were periods when I spent more time in court than

in the newsroom. Fortunately, we received financial support from Europe and anti-apartheid movements abroad to pay our legal bills.

But while all this legal and physical harassment was going on, we had to get down to the real business of exposing the corrupt and violent nature of the government and letting other voices be heard. To the horror of the government and most Afrikaners, our first front-page lead story was about the inevitability of the release from jail of 'that Communist terrorist' Nelson Mandela and the positive effects that could have on South African politics and the economy.

During the 1980s, a number of anti-apartheid activists disappeared or were murdered. There were even a few assassinations of high-profile people. The government and its security establishment not only denied responsibility, they even promised to investigate. We knew, as did every politician from at least the ruling party, that the murderers and kidnappers were policemen or soldiers. Ordinary white South Africans, I believed, subconsciously knew that too but preferred not to deal with it. Month after month activists brought before court would state that they were tortured, but the police would vehemently deny it, and the government told the public that it was standard Communist revolutionary tactics to discredit the legitimate government.

We were desperately looking for a smoking gun. We knew if we could prove that the government was using death squads and assassins, it would embarrass them deeply in the eyes of the international community. More importantly, we believed that a large number of ordinary white South Africans who preferred to believe that apartheid was actually a sensible form of 'separate development' of races, had to be confronted with the reality of the violent nature of that ideology. The National Party, like most white South Africans, regularly declared to the world that they were Christians. We wanted to prove that these 'Christians' were often murderers and torturers.

Our first big break came when we received irrefutable proof of the existence and nature of C1, the police death squad at Vlakplaas outside Pretoria. That opened the floodgates. More and more soldiers and policemen were prepared to give us information, and for about four years we carried an exposé virtually every week of some police or army atrocities or the existence of yet another secret unit. The exposés had extra impact because we were not black or English-speaking and therefore the 'natural enemies' of Afrikanerdom – we were ordinary Afrikaners and the stories were published in Afrikaans.

This is the story of one of those exposés: the Vlakplaas death squad.

Jacques Pauw:

It was easy to dismiss Captain Dirk Coetzee as a crazy man. When I met him the first time, he struck me as an open-faced Afrikaner, no different from many thousands with whom I would rub shoulders on a daily basis in my home town of Pretoria.

But the former security policeman was talking excitedly in a high-pitched voice. The police were waging a vendetta against him, he said. They were tapping his telephone, tried to kill him and broke into his house.

'I want to show you something,' he said. He picked up his telephone and started swearing. 'The police commissioner is a stupid motherfucker of a cunt that can't keep his dick for himself and has his dirty pig claws in the secret fund . . .'

He explained that as soon as he lifted the handset, the tape recorder at Security Branch Headquarters would start running and the policemen monitoring his calls would then have to listen to his vulgar diatribe.

I stared at Coetzee in disbelief as he spewed his filth in merriment for about five minutes, telling his former colleagues about a general who was having an affair with a judge's wife and a Cabinet minister who was beating up his wife. Then he slammed the phone down, smiled and said: 'I am going to sink them. I know too much.'

He took me to a storeroom in the back yard of his garden where he kept police documents. Before we entered, he warned me that a puff-adder (a deadly snake) was guarding his documents. I stood in the middle of the room while he pulled a file from a box. He showed me a document.

It was dated 1981 and contained a list of names. There was a headline: 'Section C1 (Security Branch)'. He pointed to his name: 'Captain Dirk Coetzee – Unit Commander'.

'What's C1?'

'Vlakplaas.'

'What's Vlakplaas?'

'Special Unit.'

'Doing what?'

'I'll tell you one day.'

Dirk Coetzee was an angry man. He felt betrayed, abandoned and discarded by the men to whom he had demonstrated the ultimate allegiance. By killing for them.

But this I would only find out a few weeks later when, one summer's night in early 1985, he told me: 'I was the commander of the police death squad at Vlakplaas. I was in the heart of the whore.' He told me how he and his team had murdered Griffiths Mxenge, a popular black lawyer famous for his defence of political activists.

On the morning of 20 November 1981, the bloodied body of Griffiths Mxenge was found on a soccer field near Durban. The police released a statement that rival ANC factions had killed him.

Coetzee also told the story of the young activist Sipiwo Mtimkulu, who was detained and poisoned by the security police. When he did not die, but instead sued the government, Coetzee kidnapped him, killed him and then burned his body.

Why was Coetzee gushing forth this tale of depravity and perversion, implicating himself in a host of capital crimes? He who was once the best police student of the year, the blue-eyed boy of the commissioner, founder of Vlakplaas in 1980 and entrusted with the assassination of enemies of the state? He committed at least twenty-three serious crimes in a bloodcurdling tale that spanned three countries and included murder, arson, bombing, kidnapping, torture, assault, house breaking and car theft.

He was at the peak of his career in August 1980 to set up Vlakplaas with seventeen 'rehabilitated and turned' black terrorists, called *askaris*, and a handful of white policemen. Of the seventeen *askaris*, three were killed by Coetzee and his men because they became 'security risks', another by Eugene de Kock, three deserted to the ANC and two landed up in prison for murder.

By the end of 1981, however, Coetzee had fallen out of favour with the Security Branch generals. He caused a diplomatic incident when he botched up a kidnapping attempt in Swaziland, became embroiled in a pornography scandal and his *askaris* 'accidentally' killed a Lesotho diamond dealer.

He was transferred from the Security Branch, and for the next four years found himself behind a desk in the uniform branch, attending car accidents, preparing reports and inspecting patrol cars and police stations. Before long, the man who once 'solved problems' for the Security Branch was a security risk himself. He befriended a state official who was blackmailing a Cabinet minister and, as a result, his telephone was tapped.

Coetzee was intent on revenge against his former masters. He went a step further. He had a meeting with the editor of an Afrikaans daily newspaper and told him about the police death squad at Vlakplaas. He had similar meetings with two Members of Parliament: one from the ruling National Party (NP) and another from the opposition Progressive Federal Party (PFP). Nobody did anything.

I was then a young reporter at an Afrikaans Sunday newspaper. I accompanied a colleague in search of Coetzee. We found him, and to our surprise, he was eager to talk.

Over the next weeks, Coetzee unravelled his story, piece by piece and event by event. There were bombing raids into Swaziland, a police general who manufactured poison to kill activists, and captured ANC guerrillas who were executed point-blank.

We knew we had a bombshell of a story, but who was going to be bold enough to publish it? The newspaper I had been working for supported the government of the day. The editor, although a man of great integrity, was the brother of F. W. de Klerk, then a Cabinet minister, later State President. I simply had to keep the information to myself.

I could do nothing more than stay in touch with Coetzee, who had then been put on early medical retirement by the police. We would go for dinner, drink two or more bottles of wine, and talk murder and torture. He stood steadfastly by his stories and never wavered on a single incident or fact. By then, I believed him absolutely.

When we started *Vrye Weekblad*, I told Max about Dirk Coetzee and we decided that this was a story we simply had to publish. But for the first few months we fought too hard just to survive financial and legal crises and could not get to the Vlakplaas story. It was only when death came knocking on our door that we were spurred into action.

On the night of 1 September 1989 Anton Lubowski, anti-apartheid lawyer and leading figure of the Namibian liberation movement, Swapo, was gunned down in front of his home in Windhoek, capital of Namibia. The country was then still under South African administration, but on the brink of independence.

When we received news of his assassination the next morning, I had no doubt in my mind about who had done it: C1, Vlakplaas, Eugene de Kock. Lubowski was a close friend of Max. As Max wrote a tribute to Lubowski, we decided that it was time for action. (It was later established that Lubowski had been killed by a Defence Force death squad, but at the time we didn't know about its existence.)

I took Dirk Coetzee to a Portuguese restaurant in Pretoria that night, and over a bottle of *Vinho Verde* asked him under what circumstances he would allow us to publish his story. His own position had changed from the desperation of a few years earlier. He had rebuilt his life and had a job. He also told me that he had destroyed the documents that were once guarded by a puff-adder.

'Get me out of the country and find me a safe place where my family and I can live in peace. Then I will tell the whole world what I did and what I know.'

Max and I discussed Coetzee's ultimatum the next morning. Our dilemma was simple: what to do with a self-confessed apartheid assassin? Even if we had the money to send him abroad (which we didn't), where to? No country would be willing to accept him, and furthermore, how would we protect him?

It was then that Max came up with an idea that was, for the moment, as crazy as starting an anti-apartheid voice in Afrikaans.

'The ANC,' he said, 'let's take him to the ANC.'

'You're mad.'

'If we can get him to the ANC and they are willing to protect him and look after him, we can publish.'

'Why would they?'

'It would be a political coup for them, and they should know what is really going on.'

The ANC was an outlawed and banned organisation. Handing Coetzee over to 'the enemy' constituted a very serious criminal offence and, according to the law, furthering the aims of the ANC warranted a lengthy jail sentence.

We had no qualms about allowing an apartheid assassin to escape justice. Allegations of shadowy death squads had been around for years, but for the first time we had evidence that could corroborate and substantiate the suspicions. We had our smoking gun. The story was at the heart of apartheid's most evil face and struck at the core of government ethics and morality. The murder of Anton Lubowski had proven to us that, despite the coming to power of F. W. de Klerk, people opposed to National Party policies were still dying.

We discussed the story with no one else, except with a friend who worked for a non-governmental organisation and was an underground operative for ANC intelligence. He frequently travelled to the Zambian capital of Lusaka to brief the Political-Military Council of the ANC on developments back home.

A few days later, he briefed ANC chief of intelligence Jacob Zuma

(today South Africa's Deputy President) about Coetzee, and he undertook to help us to get the former security policeman out of the country
and look after him and his family.

But before Zuma and the ANC could make any final decision, an
extraordinary event catapulted our plans into a whole new direction.

Early morning, 20 October 1989, and Max and I stared with shock
and bewilderment at the front page of the anti-apartheid English
newspaper *Weekly Mail*. The headline read: 'Death-row policeman
tells of Special Branch hit squad.'

The night before, thirty-two-year-old former security policeman
Butana Almond Nofemela had made a last-minute appeal for clemency
to the Minister of Justice to escape the hangman's noose awaiting
him the next morning. In his affidavit, Nofemela said he was a
member of a police death squad that was based at Vlakplaas.

'I wish to hereby reveal facts about my past which, I respectfully
contend, might very well have had a bearing on my conviction and
sentence of death had they been known to the trial court, Appeal
Court and Minister of Justice.

'During the period of my service in the Security Branch . . . I was
appointed as a member of the assassination squad, and I served under
Captain Dirk Coetzee, who was my commanding officer in the field.
I was involved in approximately eight assassinations.'

Sentenced in September 1987 for the cold-blooded murder of a
white farmer, Nofemela had hoped that his colleagues in the Security
Branch would save him from the gallows. Senior policemen had sent
messages to him in his death cell asking him not to talk about his
role in the death squads. They had promised to save his life in return
for his silence, but three days before he was due to hang, he was
visited by a security policeman who told him that he would 'have to
take the pain'. Nofemela realised he had been betrayed, called his
lawyer and made his affidavit.

Coetzee had already told me years ago that Nofemela was a
Vlakplaas operative and one of Griffiths Mxenge's killers. He visited
Nofemela from time to time, but always thought that he was going
to be saved from the gallows and would therefore not speak.
Nofemela's confession provided much-needed corroboration, as their
accounts of C1 murders and assassinations converged in nearly all
aspects.

But when I saw the ashen-faced Coetzee a few hours later, he was
deeply distressed. His biggest fear was that he would be isolated with

Nofemela and that his superiors would finger him as a rogue cop who committed these murders without their consent.

'Go to the ANC.'

'Go where?'

'The ANC. They will help you and look after you.'

'They'll kill me.'

'No, they won't. We've already spoken to them.'

That same night, after a wild car chase trying to dodge what we believed were police agents, we met with our ANC contact on a small-holding between Johannesburg and Pretoria. The thatched cottage was isolated from other homesteads, with a breathtaking view of the Johannesburg skyline. Coetzee went over his story again, piece by piece.

A day or so later, Coetzee arrived with a short, stocky fellow on the smallholding. His name was David Tshikalanga, and he was Coetzee's former gardener and driver at Vlakplaas. He wasn't a trained operative, Coetzee explained, but when the men went out that night to kill Mxenge, Tshikalanga went with them because he wanted to earn extra money.

The lights were burning low (the ANC man said it was for security reasons) when Tshikalanga told us how he had lodged a hunting knife in Mxenge's chest.

It was an eerie night. Max and I spoke until early morning to avoid going to bed. We had spent many days with Coetzee, grilling and cross-examining him, and we scrutinised all available records and newspaper clippings to check the facts as best we could. We decided Coetzee was telling the truth. But we also knew that publishing these stories would probably jeopardise our lives and our newspaper's very existence. There is an Afrikaans saying that the most dangerous thing one can do is to tickle the testicles of a sleeping lion. That was exactly what we were about to do.

Coetzee said he strolled the streets of Pretoria contemplating his life-changing decision. On the smallholding, Tshikalanga's words continued to linger in the air. Our ANC man went to sleep in the bath.

A few days later, we received a message from the ANC. They had agreed to take Coetzee, and Jacob Zuma would personally be in charge of the operation. The organisation undertook to ensure his safety in so far as it was humanly possible and to give him sanctuary, on condition that he was telling the truth.

We decided that Coetzee and I would fly to the Indian Ocean island of Mauritius, where we would stay for a week and do all the interviews. He would then fly on to London, where Jacob Zuma and the ANC would wait for him.

On the eve of his departure, Coetzee had second thoughts. He felt he couldn't leave his family behind. The enormity of leaving the country and entrusting his life to the ANC had finally caught up with him.

He said he had to go and speak to his eldest brother, Ben, whom he had always entrusted with the important decisions of his life and who knew about his death-squad operations. Later that evening, I received a call: 'I am ready to go. See you tomorrow.'

At six the next morning, Coetzee waited for me outside his house next to two suitcases. His wife, Karin, embraced him, and he picked up his two poodles and gave them a kiss. 'I am going to miss the dogs, I am so fond of them,' he said as he got into the car. On our way to the airport, he said Karin did not know what was happening or where he was going. The previous night, he had taken his two sons, Dirkie and Kalla, to stay with friends because he couldn't face saying goodbye to them.

On Sunday morning, 5 November 1989, we boarded a South African Airways flight to Durban. En route to Mauritius, while Coetzee was speaking non-stop in his maniacal fashion and slugging away on the complimentary liquor, I had mixed feelings about what we were trying to achieve. In a country so desperately in need of justice, we were helping an apartheid assassin to escape just that.

Just less than two weeks later, on 17 November, we published Dirk Coetzee's story. The front page shouted it out: 'Bloody trail of the SA Police', with a full-face photograph of Coetzee. For the next six pages we recounted his story in detail, implicating the highest command of the state in torture, assassinations and disappearances. He confessed to his own role in the murder of seven ANC activists; gave us the command structures and inside workings of C1; and told about other assassinations, such as the parcel bomb that killed the ANC-aligned academic Ruth First, wife of ANC military leader Joe Slovo, in Maputo.

I had returned from Mauritius four days earlier with fifteen hours of tape-recorded interviews, an affidavit and a series of photographs. Coetzee was safely in the hands of Jacob Zuma in London. In the meantime, David Tshikalanga had also left the country and was travelling through Zimbabwe to ANC Headquarters in Lusaka.

Before publication, we confided in only a handful of people: the layout artist at *Vrye Weekblad*, our lawyers and three foreign correspondents. We gave the correspondents translated copies of the stories to simultaneously publish in Europe and the United States. We were afraid that the state might stop publication under state-of-emergency regulations and we wanted the story to get out.

Our lawyer warned us that the assistant commissioner of police, Lothar Neethling, whom we implicated in the murders, would sue for defamation. Nonchalantly Max took out a coin and said: 'Heads he's in, tails he's out.' The lawyer stormed out of the office, shouting: 'You are irresponsible!' But Max had decided beforehand that Neethling's name had to stay in the story. He was a very respected figure in Afrikaner society, and naming no names in a sensational revelation like that would only undermine its credibility.

As *Vrye Weekblad* hit the streets and the story reverberated around the world, the police started with a massive discrediting campaign. Police public relations admitted that Vlakplaas did exist, but said it was merely a farm where 'rehabilitated' terrorists were accommodated. A week after publication, Lothar Neethling sued us for defamation and demanded one million rand.

Every inch of dirt against Coetzee was paraded in public. He was branded a liar, perjurer, traitor, gangster and psychopath. The police said he suffered from diabetes and was therefore delusional.

The mainstream media merrily played along. Transcripts of his telephone frenzies were given to newspapers to publish. A Sunday newspaper published an unsourced article saying that Coetzee had never left South Africa and was hiding somewhere on a farm outside Pretoria.

The biggest Afrikaans daily newspaper said one had to be mad to believe Coetzee. An English daily said that shortly before Coetzee left the country, he visited Nofemela in prison, where they 'cooked up' the story. Another claimed that *Vrye Weekblad* had paid Coetzee a substantial amount of money for his story.

A section of the white public probably believed the state's propaganda that Coetzee was a lunatic, but members of the South African Police knew he spoke the truth. To some of them, disillusioned with what they were doing or themselves angry with their superiors, the publication of his story had offered a glimpse of opportunity. The floodgates opened.

One day, a young policeman came knocking on our doors. He

claimed to have been a witness to a Vlakplaas death-squad operation in 1988 when Eugene de Kock and his men assassinated eight ANC infiltrators. As we published his story, he started making his way to the ANC in Lusaka.

Another young cop came to confess about torture in the force. He left the country for Israel, where he was detained by Israeli intelligence at the airport. He ended up in Holland. A senior security policeman who had a top job in the State Security Council, Colonel John Horak, told us about a large number of dirty-tricks operations and gave us documentation to prove it. Few of these policemen had a change of heart and had suddenly become non-racial democrats. Most had an axe to grind with their superiors. We knew that, and did not really care: as long as we were sure they were speaking the truth. Sometimes, that wasn't all that easy to establish. We often worked eighteen hours a day to find corroborating evidence, checking and re-checking, interviewing and re-interviewing to look for discrepancies. If we were not 100 per cent sure, we did not publish, always wary of the 'plant' that would discredit us.

Max du Preez and Jacques Pauw:

By late 1989, State President F. W. de Klerk, who had just taken over from P. W. Botha, who had had a stroke, could no longer ignore the evidence that his security forces were complicit in murder and blatant flouting of the law.

In January 1990, he was faced with revelations of another death squad in his midst: a covert unit within the Defence Force that was cynically called the Civil Co-operation Bureau (CCB). It was a network of reconnaissance soldiers, criminals and former policemen who operated all over southern Africa. Their actions ranged from shootings, bombings and poisonings to intimidation, breaking windows and hanging a monkey foetus in a tree at the residence of Nobel Peace Prize Laureate Desmond Tutu. They had also killed Anton Lubowski.

The CCB was exposed when police investigators, desperate to distract attention from their own evil, arrested two of its operatives for the murder of anti-apartheid activist Dr David Webster in May 1989.

'I will cut to the bone,' de Klerk promised when he appointed a judicial commission of inquiry to investigate death-squad allegations.

It was an exercise that was from its outset fatally flawed, designed to cover up. De Klerk prevented the commission from investigating operations conducted and atrocities committed outside South Africa's borders. Time and time again, as accounts were given to the commission of the death squads poised at South Africa's borders, the stories of their raids were cut short.

Security Branch policemen who were implicated in death-squad activities were appointed as commission investigators. Before the commission even started, police documentation was destroyed and crucial witnesses disappeared. Many death-squad operatives were allowed to appear before the commission in false beards and wigs.

A veil of secrecy was drawn across the activities of Vlakplaas and the CCB. The judge was faced with blank and bare denials. De Kock and his men were whitewashed and presented as knights in shining armour.

Judge Louis Harms introduced his final report with the Latin phrase *Felix qui potuit verum cognoscere caucus* (blessed is he who can recognise the truth). He found that no death squad had existed at Vlakplaas and that Dirk Coetzee was a liar.

At *Vrye Weekblad* we knew otherwise. Political activists continued to disappear and were mysteriously killed. Despite all the false testimony given to the Harms Commission, F. W. de Klerk had opened the floodgates of confession when he released Nelson Mandela and unbanned the ANC in February 1990.

The security forces were thrown into disarray. Many operatives felt unsure and unsafe about the future. It was for many the final act of betrayal when the government entered into negotiations with the ANC. They either wanted to take revenge or safeguard their future.

Many confided in *Vrye Weekblad*. Although they hated what we stood for, they knew that we could be trusted and that we were not afraid to publish. Furthermore, we were also Afrikaners; we could speak to them in their mother tongue and we understood what they meant by the religious doctrine of the Afrikaans churches and that their crusade was a *stryd vir Volk en Vaderland* (a battle for people and country).

Tracing down the cut-throats of apartheid took us from the drinking taverns of Pretoria to pubs in London, from Pretoria Central Prison to the Weskoppies Psychiatric Hospital, and from the smelly city of Beira in Mozambique to the opulence of the Hotel National in Lucerne in Switzerland. In the process, we had to consume enormous quantities of liquor and listen to bloody bravado and gleeful torture talk.

And be paranoid – about our physical safety, about staying out of jail and about plots to discredit us.

A security police agent once dumped an arsenal of weapons on us: an R-1 assault rifle with a bag of bullets and extra magazines, an assassination pistol with a telescope and a throwing knife. We drove around for weeks with the weapons in the boots of our cars before passing them on to our ANC contact.

The offices of *Vrye Weekblad* were bombed, right-wing fanatics threatened us at gunpoint and we received death threats on a daily basis. A flood of criminal and civil prosecutions was released on *Vrye Weekblad*. Years later, after the 1994 elections that brought the ANC to power, a senior military officer confessed to us over a bloody steak and litres of beer that he once tried to assassinate Max on his farm after recruiting his neighbour as an informer.

Jacques Pauw:

'I made mincemeat out of Albie's arm.'

Sitting in front of me was Pieter Botes, until just before our meeting a senior operative of the secret South African Defence Force unit, the Civil Co-operation Bureau. There was a broad grin on his cherubic face, something out of a Tarantino movie.

Botes was boasting about a day in April 1988 when he blew up ANC activist and law professor Albie Sachs in the Mozambican capital of Maputo.

On that day, one of Botes' men had attached a five-litre tin, filled with plastic explosives and connected to a tilt switch, beneath Sachs' car. The bomb, powerful enough to blow up a small house, was supposed to detonate as soon as somebody started the car.

As Sachs opened the door of the car, the Avenido Julio Vinti Quatro was engulfed in an inferno. For many seconds after the blast, the only sound audible was that of burning metal. Then people started screaming. All that remained of the car was a heap of crumpled metal. Sachs, his right arm dangling from his shoulder, tried to push himself up from the scorched tarmac.

Sachs did not die. Apart from his mutilated right arm, which had to be amputated, he had four broken ribs, a fractured right heel, a severed nerve in his left leg, a lacerated liver, scores of shrapnel wounds and ruptured eardrums. He is today a Constitutional Court judge.

Botes had assassinated six people, but Sachs was his pride and joy. 'I shook him,' he would say. Gleeful. Triumphant. Smug.

Botes had a score to settle with the CCB commander, who he claimed had blown up his shop after they had a fall-out about money. He came to *Vrye Weekblad*.

Botes remains the most senior member of the CCB to have spoken openly about the organisation. He had files, diagrams and photographs. He allowed me to look at some of them.

In 'fighting the enemy', Botes and his men had killed, maimed, blown up telephone installations, sabotaged railway lines, bribed officials and infected drinking water with cholera.

The day before *Vrye Weekblad* was due to publish Botes' revelations, he phoned and said he wanted to see Max and me as he was uncertain whether we should go ahead with publication. In order to persuade Botes of the importance of his story, we initiated a night of heavy drinking. After many double brandies and Coke, he lifted his glass and announced: 'Publish. I want to shake them.'

Late that night Botes took us to his house because he had a bottle of pear *mampoer* (a homebrew, about 80 per cent pure alcohol) that he wanted us to taste. By that time, Max and I were extremely drunk. Botes, on the other hand, showed few signs of intoxication. We sat around his dinner table gulping down the burning liquid. After two or three tots, we told him that we could not possibly swallow another one.

'I will show you what I do to people who refuse to drink my *mampoer*,' he said. He left the room and came back with a grain bag, from which he drew a Russian-manufactured RPG rocket launcher. He put the launcher against the wall and said: 'Now you will drink my *mampoer*.' When anyone hesitated between gulps, he pointed the rocket launcher in your face. On the way back to Johannesburg, Max temporarily lost his eyesight due to mild alcohol poisoning.

We published the story two days later.

It was a winter's day in 1990 when I received a message from a patient at the Weskoppies Psychiatric Hospital in Pretoria to come and see him. Vlakplaas stuff, he said.

Ronald Desmond Bezuidenhout was in maximum security, under psychiatric observation for assaulting his wife and threatening to kill her and blow up their house.

He was a small, nervous man with frantic and fierce blue eyes.

After he had stared at me for a while, he lifted his shirt and showed me his scars.

He had a remarkable story, for he was one of the only white *askaris* (turned and 'rehabilitated terrorists') in the history of Vlakplaas.

He joined the Defence Force in 1973 and was elected as a member of the élite reconnaissance unit. He left the army after a few years and became a mercenary before joining the ANC in 1985 and undergoing military training in Angola. The security police arrested him in 1989. Under interrogation, he agreed to cooperate with his captors. He was sent to Vlakplaas.

Bezuidenhout was an outcast at Vlakplaas. He accidentally shot somebody, drank heavily and smoked marijuana. The white policemen thought he was a 'Communist'. He was at Vlakplaas when Dirk Coetzee's revelations were published in *Vrye Weekblad*. 'God, we hated that duckfucker of a Coetzee.'

De Kock decided that Coetzee had to die. An explosives expert at Vlakplaas was ordered to build a letter bomb. Coetzee was then with the ANC in Lusaka. One day, Bezuidenhout said, he had to go with the expert to a butchery in Pretoria to buy a pig's head. The bomb was to be tested on the head. 'There was hardly anything left. Mincemeat. Another bomb was built and sent away.'

I remember sitting in Weskoppies staring at Bezuidenhout. Just a raving lunatic, or was there an element of truth? ANC intelligence confirmed that Bezuidenhout had been one of their guerrillas; we established that Bezuidenhout was on the farm when Coetzee spoke, and we discovered that Vlakplaas had indeed acquired the services of an explosives expert.

In fact, not long before I had met Bezuidenhout, a Johannesburg lawyer with the name of Bheki Mlangeni received a mysterious parcel. The parcel was addressed to Dirk Coetzee in Zambia, but had Mlangeni's name as the sender. Coetzee refused to accept the parcel, and as a result it was sent back to Mlangeni.

Mlangeni was Coetzee's lawyer and, as a result, I had also become friends with him. It was a mystery why Mlangeni opened the parcel. Inside was a Walkman cassette player with a cassette on which was written: 'Evidence: Hit Squads.'

Mlangeni took the earphones, put them on his ears and switched the Walkman on. He died instantly when the explosives, hidden inside the earphones of the Walkman, exploded and punched two holes in the base of his skull.

Bezuidenhout signed an affidavit and we published it in *Vrye Weekblad*. As expected, police reaction was swift, and this time they had plenty of ammunition to discredit the messenger. The man was after all in a psychiatric institution.

The day after the story was published, two security policemen, themselves implicated in the death squads, were appointed to investigate Bezuidenhout's allegations. It was later discovered that one was part of the conspiracy to kill Coetzee.

The two policemen visited Max and me, and as they were leaving, the one put his arm around Max and said to him: 'Old Maxie, we are in actual fact on the same side. We both serve the truth.'

We didn't know whether to laugh or cry. We knew nothing would come of the investigation, even though the authorities declared Bezuidenhout of sound mind a short time later.

As it turned out, this story was also true.

Max du Preez:

Vrye Weekblad eventually paid a much higher price for its investigative journalism than blown-up offices and harassment. In the initial stories on Vlakplaas, Coetzee implicated General Lothar Neethling, assistant commissioner of police, in the kidnapping and killing of anti-apartheid activists.

Neethling sued *Vrye Weekblad* for defamation. First he wanted R1 million, and when we refused to retract and published further evidence, he upped it to R1.5 million. A year later the case started in the Johannesburg Supreme Court. The general's legal costs were completely covered by the state. *Vrye Weekblad* had to rely on its own, scarce resources to fight the largest defamation case in this country's legal history.

As the case started, F. W. de Klerk released the report of his judicial commission of inquiry into death squads. The commission not only found that there wasn't a death squad in the police, but that Coetzee was an illusionist with psychopathic tendencies. The dice was loaded against *Vrye Weekblad*.

Neethling flatly denied ever having met Coetzee, and lined up witnesses to testify to his international scientific standing and his upstanding, Christian character – among them the former Commissioner of Police. Coetzee was still in hiding in London, and the whole court, bar the judge himself, had to move there to hear his evidence.

After many very expensive months, Mr Justice Kriegler dismissed Neethling's claim. He found that Neethling had not always spoken the truth, and that *Vrye Weekblad* had proved, on a balance of probabilities, that its reports were true. But more importantly, Kriegler said, to the delight of all journalists in South Africa who valued press freedom, that the public interest in this case was so high that it superseded the individual's rights. It was a devastating blow to Neethling, the police and the government. *Vrye Weekblad's* victory party lasted about seventy-two hours, also because Neethling was ordered to pay all costs.

But Neethling, sponsored fully by taxpayer money, hired new counsel and took the judgement on appeal. In December 1993 five ageing white judges of the Appellate Division decided it was 'one of those rare cases where the probabilities are evenly balanced', and that it was 'not possible to say with any degree of confidence who was telling the truth'. They rejected Judge Kriegler's finding of overwhelming public interest, stating that newspapers had to 'substantially' prove all facts before publication. Neethling had won. *Vrye Weekblad* not only had to pay him damages, it also had to pay the staggering legal bills. In January 1994, a few months before South Africa held its first national, democratic elections and elected Nelson Mandela its president, *Vrye Weekblad* closed down.

Max du Preez and Jacques Pauw:

In May 1994, a few days after the ANC won the elections, Eugene de Kock was arrested and charged with murder, conspiracy to commit murder, attempted murder, kidnapping, assault, manslaughter, defeating the ends of justice, the illegal possession of arms and ammunition, and fraud. Two-and-a-half years later he was convicted on all charges and sentenced to two life sentences and 212 years' imprisonment.

In his own testimony in court, Eugene de Kock implicated the South African State President, members of his Cabinet and top generals in his campaign of assassination, murder, bombing and torture.

The South African Truth and Reconciliation Commission (TRC), set up in 1996 to investigate violence and provide amnesty to members of the security forces and the liberation organisations who had committed violence with a political motive, refused amnesty to de Kock. He will spend the rest of his life behind bars.

In May 1997, Dirk Coetzee was found guilty of the murder of Griffiths Mxenge. Before sentencing, however, the TRC granted amnesty to Coetzee. He is now a senior official in the National Intelligence Service.

In June 1998, the TRC heard extensive evidence of the apartheid government's chemical and biological warfare programme. It was led by Dr Wouter Basson, who worked in the police force when General Lothar Neethling was assistant commissioner. It was much worse and much more extensive than *Vrye Weekblad* had reported: Basson had spent millions on concocting substances to paralyse people, make them talk, kill them without a trace of the cause. He devised rings with a hollow chamber to store the poison in and umbrellas with retractable, poisoned tips.

The Truth Commission found that the state had a deliberate policy to murder political opponents of its apartheid policies. It held the State President, his ministers and the heads of the armed forces ultimately responsible for these killings.

Eugene de Kock, however, remains the most senior member of the security forces to serve a prison sentence for apartheid's atrocities. His superiors have either never been charged or have received amnesty.

PAUL FOOT

The Great Lockerbie Whitewash
1989–2001

Paul Foot died as this book was going to the printer. He combined, for me, friend, unerring ally and inspiration. He was both a great journalist and a proud socialist, who understood, indeed lived, the natural partnership between a dedication to the betterment of his fellow human beings and the care for and defence of his readers, especially those with no one to speak for them. Indeed, Paul's triumphs are proof that investigative journalism, driven by a commitment to justice and humanity, and patience, can succeed. Typical of his many campaigns against miscarriages of justice was the 'Bridgewater Case'. When Paul was a colleague of mine at the *Daily Mirror,* in 1980, he received a letter from Ann Whelan, the mother of one of four men accused of murdering a thirteen-year-old London newspaper boy, Carl Bridgewater. It was one of those especially shocking murders that provoke public anger and bring pressure on the police. 'No one has looked into this case,' wrote Ann Whelan, 'because everyone assumes they are guilty. I can assure you they're not.' Paul believed her and went on to amass critical evidence that the confession of one of the four was beaten out of him and was false, and that the others were also innocent. In 1997, thanks largely to his *Mirror* investigation and to Jim Nichol, a young solicitor, the men were set free.

It is his investigation of the cover-up of the biggest mass murder in British criminal history that will, I believe, distinguish Paul Foot as one of Britain's greatest journalists. On 21 December 1988, Pan Am flight 103 exploded in mid-air over the Scottish town of Lockerbie, killing 270 people. A bomb had been planted on the aircraft. As Paul's many articles, mostly in *Private Eye,* have disclosed, the official investigation and the conviction by three Scottish judges of a Libyan citizen in 2001 amount to an Anglo-American government conspiracy.

At first, in the official investigation, Syria and Iran were implicated, along with a Palestinian group apparently paid by the Iranian Government to avenge the shooting-down of an Iranian airliner by an American warship the previous year. A Thatcher government minister promised 'early arrests', but these never materialised, and in December 1989, Thatcher herself turned down demands from the families of the British victims for a public inquiry. The reason, according to the *Washington Post* in 1990, was that Thatcher and President Bush Senior had agreed on a 'low-key' approach. During that year, when the United States was preparing to attack Iraq, it was negotiating secretly for the support of former enemies Iran and Syria; and the Lockerbie evidence that pointed to the two countries was quietly abandoned.

Libya now became the prime suspect. An unreliable identification by a Maltese shopkeeper and a Libyan CIA informer led to two Libyans, Abdel Baset Megrahi and Al Amin Khalifa Fimah. They were said to have planted the Pan Am bomb in a suitcase on a flight from Malta to Frankfurt, which went on to London and exploded as it flew over Lockerbie. Libya was made a pariah, with a United Nations embargo imposed for almost a decade. In 1998, Libyan President Gaddafi allowed the two men to give themselves up for a special trial before Scottish judges sitting in 'neutral' Holland.

When the trial opened in May 2000, most journalists complained about the long and tedious proceedings, and few stayed the course – unlike Paul Foot, whose reporting exposed the trial and its evidence as a cacophony of blunders, deceptions and lies: a whitewash almost certainly for sinister geo-political reasons.

Megrahi was convicted largely on the hearsay of discredited witnesses and was sentenced to life imprisonment. The Scottish judges' verdict was followed by an 'opinion' of ninety pages, which Paul describes as 'a remarkable document that claims an honoured place in the history of British miscarriages of justice'. The UN sanctions against Libya were duly lifted and Gaddafi has agreed to pay £1.7 billion in compensation. Many of the British relatives are convinced that this deal was brokered to allow oil-rich Libya to re-open its markets to the West. The final verdict, and justice, are still to come. When it does, much of the credit will be Paul Foot's legacy.

THE GREAT LOCKERBIE WHITEWASH

Why Weren't We Told?

On the eve of the anniversary of the Lockerbie disaster, bereaved friends and relations have had astonishing and shocking news.

Eighty per cent of the staff of the American embassy in Moscow who had reserved seats on Pan Am flights from Frankfurt cancelled their bookings before the ill-fated flight 103 crashed over Lockerbie, killing 270 passengers and crew.

Unlike the passengers, the embassy staff at Moscow were told of the intelligence warning that a terrorist attack was planned on a Pan Am flight out of Frankfurt.

The warning was put up on a noticeboard in the embassy soon after 5 December, when it was first issued.

The bereaved families have been trying to find out why they never heard about it, and why the Moscow embassy staff did.

Mr Martin Cadman, whose thirty-two-year-old son Bill, a brilliant sound engineer, was killed at Lockerbie, told me about a delegation of bereaved relatives to the Department of Transport in June.

'We were seen by Chris Harris, who was the head of aviation security,' he said.

'Harris told us the warning had been a hoax. We asked when it was dismissed as a hoax, and he said we couldn't know that.

'He then told us the posting of the warning in the Moscow embassy had been a mistake.

'We asked him: "Are you really telling us that there may be some Americans alive today because someone in the embassy in Moscow made a mistake in issuing a warning? Are you saying that 259 passengers are dead because the British Government did not make the same mistake?"

'He said something about being wise after the event.'

At no time have the British or US Governments said a word about the effect of the warning on the staff at the embassy.

Last Thursday, Mr and Mrs Cadman received through the post a document from top American lawyers fighting for compensation for the victims of Lockerbie.

It told them: 'Despite the Helsinki and Toshiba warnings and the knowledge that 80 per cent of the embassy staffers in Moscow had cancelled their reservations from Pan Am out of Frankfurt, Pan Am HQ chose not to go to levels of alert that would have required 100 per cent baggage search.'

I asked the lawyer who wrote the document exactly how many embassy staff had cancelled.

He replied: 'The information you have is highly confidential. You should not have it. I cannot possibly comment further.'

On the fatal Pan Am flight, on which all 259 passengers and 11 crew died, there were 159 empty seats.

Pan Am will not say how this compares with other transatlantic flights over Christmas last year.

The number of people on their flights are, they say, a commercial secret.

Mr Cadman says:

'We had a letter from Mrs Thatcher in August asking us to accept her assurances that the government was doing everything they could "to find those responsible for the outrage".

'But for us responsibility doesn't just rest with some unnamed terrorist.

'The British Government is responsible for aviation security in Britain. They have failed us all down the line, and are busy covering up their failure.'

Daily Mirror, 21 December 1989

The announcement of new year honours for citizens of Lockerbie who helped in the rescue effort after the Pan Am jumbo jet crashed into the town a year ago is another example of the Government's double standards over the disaster. While weeping and dishing out decorations, the real aim over Lockerbie is to cover it all up.

Every time a new set of questions is asked about Lockerbie, the government press gibbers speculation about which Arab terrorist planted the bomb, how and where. The impression is given that the bold men in blue from Dumfries and Galloway are about to pluck the guilty man from his desert hideout and prove how British detectives are the best in the world. Then, just as suddenly, as the interest in the disaster (or the anniversary) passes, everything subsides again into doubt and despair.

This was the position last spring when families of those who died had whipped up press interest in the various warnings issued by American intelligence over a likely attack on a Pan Am jumbo before the flight. Transport minister Channon swiftly 'revealed' to journalists at a Garrick Club lunch that the brilliant detectives from Galloway were about to clinch the case. Everyone fastened on to this grand (but entirely false) news, and forgot about the warnings.

The most interesting recent development has been the government's refusal to have a public judicial inquiry into the disaster, such as the Sheen inquiry over Zeebrugge or the Fennel inquiry into the King's Cross fire disaster.

More people died at Lockerbie than at Zeebrugge and King's Cross put together and the British Government (the Department of Transport, needless to say) was just as responsible for any breach of security at Heathrow as it was for rules about ferries or underground stations.

So why no judicial inquiry? The question is all the more vital when it is known (as it has not been known, up to now) that the idea for such an inquiry came originally from the present Transport Secretary, Mr Cecil Parkinson.

At a meeting with relatives of Lockerbie victims in September, Parkinson said an independent inquiry was needed under a high court judge. It could sit in public but in the event of there being any 'sensitive' intelligence information, it would be allowed to take evidence in secret. This, Parkinson urged the families, would be the fairest and most thorough way to answer the central question: namely how was it that warnings were given which frightened a lot of US Government officials off Pan Am flights, but which were completely unknown to the people who flew to their deaths?

The relatives agreed at once and promised they would not pass on the idea to the press or television. For his part Parkinson pledged to argue most passionately for the inquiry.

The relatives kept their side of the bargain but were horrified when Parkinson told them in December that, to his consternation and sorrow, the government had decided not to hold an independent inquiry under a judge, and was adamant about it. Parkinson was reminded that the judicial inquiry had been *his idea*. He said he was very sorry but he had not been able to convince his colleagues.

Which colleagues? If after a major tragedy a Secretary of State recommends a judicial inquiry into something which is his departmental responsibility, he is almost certain to get it. The exception would be if the colleague who resisted it was the Prime Minister.

But why would she block an inquiry? The only possible answer is that she was advised against it by MI5. Can it be that senior officers there, like their counterparts in the US and West Germany, are anxious to draw a veil over the Lockerbie incident? None of them wants anyone to know how a bomb, of a type which the security services already knew about, came to be placed in a suitcase which, if the current theory is to be believed, travelled from Malta to Frankfurt, where it changed planes, and then from Frankfurt to Heathrow, *where it changed planes again*, without being identified.

Unlike Zeebrugge, Piper Alpha and King's Cross, where the disasters were caused by bungling, inefficiency and greed, there is about Lockerbie an extra dimension which dates back to that curious allegation almost a year ago from a news editor at Radio Forth in Scotland that fragments of explosives were found in a case carried by a CIA agent. The darkest dungeon faced the news editor unless he revealed his source. But then, strangely, there were no charges and no further comment.

Private Eye, 5 January 1990

One of the many curious omissions in the American Presidential Commission's report on aviation security is its failure to report its meeting on 16 February with the British families of victims of the disaster. After the meeting, one of the Commission members took to one side a bereaved parent who had spoken with some passion about the way the families had been treated by both British and US Governments.

After pressing the parent to 'keep up the fight', the Commission member said two things:

1) That the British and American Governments knew perfectly well what happened at Lockerbie, and who was responsible, but that neither would say a word about it;
2) That much of the 'wilder speculation' in the press about the bombing was perfectly true.

The wildest (and most convincing) of the conspiracy theories about Lockerbie which had circulated up to that time was that certain luggage from Frankfurt airport had been designated 'no go' by the CIA, which

was organising a drugs run to the United States to finance the freeing
of hostages from Iran. This theory explains why the luggage at Frankfurt
was not properly screened before it went off to London and why it
was not checked at all when it arrived in London and was transferred
to the Pan Am flight which was destroyed over Lockerbie.

The drugs conspiracy theory also explains why nothing special was
ordered at either Frankfurt or London to meet the challenge of the
telephone warning which was put through to the American embassy
in Finland to the effect that a Pan Am airliner from Frankfurt was
the target for a bomb. So serious was this warning that it was posted
in the American embassy in Moscow; a posting which resulted, not
surprisingly, in a flood of cancellations on Pan Am flights from
Frankfurt that Christmas.

One recommendation of the report will annoy the British Prime
Minister. It suggests that in 'certain circumstances' (unspecified),
warnings of likely terrorist attacks like the prophetic one to Helsinki
should be published. Thatcher said last year that she thought it 'irresponsible' to publish warnings.

Thatcher's record on the Lockerbie disaster is quite appalling. She
has been the chief architect of the monumental cover-up of what
happened. When her new Transport Secretary, Cecil Parkinson, came
whining to her last September asking for a judicial inquiry with Privy
Councillors attached (an idea which Parkinson himself had put to the
bereaved families), she sent him away with a flea in his ear. She was
determined there should be no inquiry (except a Scottish 'fatal accident
inquiry' which can't find out how or why the bomb got on the plane
and how or why British airport security was so lax as not to trace it).

A report in the *Washington Post* on 11 January by Jack Anderson
and Dale Van Atta revealed that Thatcher and Bush had spoken about
Lockerbie in mid-March last year. Anderson suggested that the two
leaders had agreed to 'low-key' the disaster because neither could do
anything about it and did not want to appear impotent. Their intelligence services had reported 'beyond doubt' that the Lockerbie bomb
had been placed by a terrorist group led by Ahmed Jibril. The group,
the report went on, had been paid by the Iranian Government, which
wanted a reprisal for the shooting down of an Iranian airliner by an
American warship the previous year. Although they knew the terrorists responsible, however (Anderson's report concluded), Bush and
Thatcher agreed to keep it quiet.

There is no doubt that the phone call was made by Thatcher that March, but the reasons given by Anderson are unconvincing. Impotence in the face of terrorism has never been a reason for cutting down press 'shock, horror' stories after it, nor for covering up the names of those responsible. There has been a hysterical press campaign exposing Jibril, culminating in a flood of articles over Christmas last year, all of which predicted imminent arrests (which never happened). The real reason for the cover-up must have been far more serious. For want of a better explanation, the drugs-for-hostages claim seems the most plausible.

Private Eye, 8 June 1990

One unhappy side-effect of the Middle East crisis is that there is, for the foreseeable future, no chance of those responsible for bombing the Pan Am jet which crashed at Lockerbie in 1988 being brought to justice.

As newspapers reported in a series of huge features a year after the disaster (the *Sunday Times*, as ever with this sort of 'official news', took the lead) and as the then Transport Secretary Paul Channon was silly enough to blurt out at a lobby lunch, the governments and police of Britain and the United States know exactly who planted the bomb. It was a gang of Middle Eastern terrorists based in Syria.

As the *Eye* reported, both governments were reluctant to name the gang or to seek to bring them to justice.

Various reasons, all of them credible, have been given for this strange silence. One, reported by the *Eye*, is that the Syrian gang was either being used by Western intelligence or was running drugs via civil airlines or (most probably) both. Now, however, a new dimension is added to the need for silence.

The Syrian gang named repeatedly by the newspapers is known to be close to the Syrian Government. The strategy of the British and American Governments in the Gulf is to isolate Iraq's Saddam Hussein from other Arab leaders and in this matter, President Assad of Syria is crucial and equivocal.

He is less easy to 'bend' than, say, the Saudi monarchy or Mubarak of Egypt and diplomatic relations with him (abruptly cut off only recently) must be restored and fostered. One result will be that as a fatal accident inquiry starts in Scotland, the families of the Lockerbie victims will be kept even more bleakly in the dark.

Private Eye, 17 August 1990

One casualty of the Gulf crisis appears to be Mrs Thatcher's policy of No Dealing With Terrorists – particularly Syria.

It is not long since Britain and the United States cut off diplomatic relations with the country because of its connections with terrorism; but all is now forgotten and once more sweetness and light.

Thatcher and Bush have already agreed that they will not pursue any further the terrorists who bombed the plane over Lockerbie, since they are known to be close to the Syrian Government. This new policy extends to Iran and the Lebanon, and reached its climax on 11 September when the British ambassador in Beirut met the spiritual leader of the terrorist organisation Hizbollah, Sheikh Faddalah.

Private Eye, 28 September 1990

Lockerbie Special Report

'Does George Bush take us for fools?' The question was asked on 14 November by Bonnie O'Connor of Long Island, USA, whose brother died on the doomed Pan Am jumbo that exploded and crashed over Lockerbie two years ago.

Bonnie O'Connor was responding to the news, carefully synchronised by the US Justice Department and the Lord Advocate of Scotland, that two Libyan intelligence agents were responsible for the bomb.

There was no answer from the White House to Bonnie O'Connor's pertinent question, but in Britain the reaction to the naming of the two Libyans shows that President Bush certainly takes the Scottish police, the Lord Advocate, the Foreign Secretary, and, with one or two exceptions, the entire British press for blithering idiots – and that he is absolutely correct in that assessment.

Flashback to a small private dining-room in the Garrick Club in March 1989, three months after the Lockerbie disaster, and a prestigious lunch hosted by a bunch of top political correspondents:

Ian Aitken (*Guardian*), Julia Langdon (*Mirror*), Chris Buckland (*Today*), Robin Oakley (*The Times*) and Geoffrey Parkhouse (*Glasgow Herald*). Their guest was mega-rich old Etonian Transport Minister Paul Channon. Channon told them off the record that Scottish police investigating the Lockerbie disaster had tracked down the terrorists responsible and that there would be arrests in a matter of days.

Channon went out of his way to praise the brilliant detective work of the Galloway police and the forensic wizards from British police laboratories. All this praise and good news duly appeared on the front pages of the newspapers who had been lucky enough to win such a scoop from a Garrick Club lunch.

To their chagrin, however, there were no immediate arrests. Instead, there were tactful denials that the terrorists had been tracked down. Then it was leaked that Channon himself had been the source of the apparently false information. Channon denied it, was exposed as a liar and, after a decent interval, sacked.

Working closely with MI5, MI6 and the Scottish police, over the next few months the newspapers continued to 'expose' the terrorists responsible for the Lockerbie disaster. Leading the pack was the *Sunday Times* which, as its performance over the Gibraltar shootings the previous year had demonstrated, had replaced its previous commitment to investigative journalism with a new policy of printing without question any information supplied by the Ministry of Defence, MI5, MI6 or all three.

In a series of interminable articles starting in October 1989 and running up to the first anniversary of the disaster – 21 December – the *Sunday Times* set out the 'full facts' about the bombing.

It had been devised, it said, by the Iranian Government in revenge for the shooting down of an Iranian passenger airliner during the Iran–Iraq war by an American warship. The Iranians had hired a gang of extremist Palestinians, who had the protection of the Syrian Government. The gang had made a bomb looking like a Toshiba cassette recorder and had planted it in a suitcase in Malta on a plane which went through Frankfurt. The gang had been very active in Germany and had carefully studied the security system at Frankfurt airport, where the ill-fated Pan Am flight began.

All this was set out in the most meticulous detail. The leader of the Palestinian sect was named as Jibril. The leader of the Syrian-backed terrorist outfit was Nidal. Even the man who had been 'identified' as travelling to Malta to buy the clothes to put in the bomb suitcase was named as Talb – a Palestinian terrorist then (and still) in prison in Sweden.

No journalist could have put together this story without the assistance of official investigators from the Scottish police, MI5, the CIA or the Ministry of Defence. This was the detail of the story which Paul Channon had so ineffectually leaked to the country's top political reporters the previous March. But still there was no action. How was it possible for so much to be known by the authorities, with so little sign of an arrest?

An answer came in the *Washington Post* of 11 January 1990 when Jack Anderson and Dale Van Atta revealed that Margaret Thatcher and George Bush had spoken on the telephone in mid-March 1989, at almost the same time as Channon was blabbing to journalists in the Garrick Club. They agreed, the report revealed, to 'low-key' the disaster, even though their intelligence networks had established that Jibril/Nidal/Talb were responsible for it.

The reason for this 'low-key' approach (which was not passed on in time to the wretched Channon) was not clear. One plausible theory at the time was that the CIA was masterminding a drugs run through Frankfurt airport in exchange for promises by the Iranians to free hostages – an extension of the Irangate arms-for-hostages deal.

But the real reason may have had more to do with the generally shifting political scene in the Middle East.

During the Gulf War, both American and British authorities were delighted by the support they got against the bestial and inhuman government of Saddam Hussein from the bestial and inhuman government of Syria. Assad became the dictator everyone (except the Syrian people) loved to praise. Ever since VI[1] day, both American and British Governments have founded the New World Order on the rock of cooperation with Assad, the moderate wing of the Palestinians and even the ayatollahs in Iran. This was the basis of the recent summit in Madrid and of the steady flow of released hostages in Beirut.

In recent weeks, Bush and Major have been under some pressure from the families of people who died at Lockerbie. One US group of families recently visited Britain and started to agitate for action. The statement about the two Libyans was the two governments' answer. The wretched Lord Fraser, the Lord Advocate of Scotland, was ordered

[1] Victory in Iraq.

to read out 'results' of his police inquiry which were completely different from those already read out to newspapers all over the world, especially the *Sunday Times*.

In the House of Commons Douglas Hurd went out of his way to exculpate the 'other governments' (Syria and Iran) which his colleague Paul Channon had denounced in March 1989. Like lazy and overfed fish, the British media jumped to the bait. In almost unanimous chorus, they engaged in furious vilification and open warmongering against Libya, drooling praise for the 'plodding policeman' of Galloway, and almost total forgetfulness about those terrorists whom they themselves had exposed again and again for plotting the bombing. The *Sunday Times* (17 Nov) stated: 'The position of Iran and Syria remains obscure.' Obscurity, however, was the exact opposite of the five-week exposé of 'what really happened at Lockerbie' in the *Sunday Times* October–December 1989.

Press hysteria has had very little echo among the families of the Lockerbie dead. They remain incensed by the way they have been treated by the government.

The position of the government now is that it refuses to take the steps which an independent inquiry says are necessary to ensure the safety of airline passengers in future; it pins the responsibility for the disaster on two men never before named in the endless leaks and exposés about what happened at Lockerbie; and it exculpates other governments because they happen at the moment to be politically friendly. This has whipped up a fury against Libya which could develop into more air raids, more bloodshed, and, in revenge, more terrorist attacks on passenger aircraft.

Private Eye, 22 November 1991

Lockerbie Special

While consternation reigns in the office of Lord Fraser of Carmyle, the Lord Advocate, following the visit to Libya of Dr Jim Swire, who lost a daughter in the Pan Am flight which crashed at Lockerbie three years ago, the *Eye* can reveal that the fatal accident inquiry into the disaster was deliberately fed false information by the authorities.

Lord Fraser, the government's legal officer in Scotland, has been unsettled ever since he was bounced by the US State Department into making the unlikely announcement that two Libyan intelligence agents were responsible for the bombing. He has been bleating that the case against the Libyans is incontrovertible, and that the failure of the Libyan President Gaddafi to deliver them for trial in Scotland is an insult to international law and justice.

Dr Swire took this point up with Gaddafi, who apparently indicated that there was little or no sign of the two men's guilt, but said that if the Scottish authorities would present his government with the gist of the prosecution case, he would reconsider the possibility of their extradition.

Whether or not Gaddafi is to be believed, and he is not the world's most trustworthy political leader, the reply has put Fraser on the spot. Normal extradition proceedings are accompanied by at least some of the evidence that the wanted men are guilty. Up to now, no such evidence has been presented. The pressure on the Lord Advocate to release any evidence at all might prove either that he has none or that he has some against the Libyans though rather more against other terrorists patronised by that stout ally of the West and usher-in of the New World Order, the dictator of Syria, Assad.

Either alternative would do some damage to Lord Fraser's constant assertion that the inquiry into the bombing by the smallest police force in the country, Dumfries and Galloway, was a model of efficiency and self-discipline.

For a probable answer to many remaining questions turn to pages 67–77 of *Lockerbie – The Real Story* by the Scottish radio reporter David Johnston. Johnston describes the near-hysterical search in the hours following the crash by agents of the Central Intelligence Agency who rushed to the scene from Edinburgh. They were after the luggage of top CIA agents who had boarded the flight at Frankfurt. They were specially interested in the suitcase of Major Charles McKee, a top CIA agent who had been involved in sensitive negotiations for the freeing of hostages in Beirut (another CIA man who died at Lockerbie, Matthew Gannon, was deputy CIA station chief in Beirut). They were also interested in a suitcase full of heroin.

David Johnston suggested on radio at the time that the investigation on the ground at Lockerbie had been held up for at least two days while the CIA and the military hunted for these two cases. McKee's case, he said, had to be officially 'returned' to the fields round Lockerbie and 'found' after its sensitive contents had been removed by the CIA. When he said these things on radio, Johnston was approached by very senior police officers and told that if he wanted to disclose the source of his information, anyone in the country, even the Prime Minister, would be prepared to receive the information in confidence. He refused, and nothing further happened.

Private Eye, 20 December 1991

Bushwhacking

All sorts of things can happen when election year in Britain and the United States coincides – and the most heavily-backed plan for a stunt for 1992 by both the British Foreign Office and the US State Department is another 'revenge strike' on Libya.

The excuse for such a strike has already been carefully prepared. It will be 'a blow for justice' in retaliation for those killed on Pan Am flight 103 which crashed over Lockerbie just before Christmas, 1988. In March 1989, for reasons set out by the CIA (and, therefore, promptly by MI5) President George Bush and Margaret Thatcher agreed in a special telephone call to leave Lockerbie alone. Now Bush and Major are rediscovering their outrage at the atrocity, and are determined to bring to justice the two Libyans whom they have named as the planters of the bomb in the plane.

Tam Dalyell, who has upset so many similar plans in the past, told the House of Commons that on 29 March, the Dumfries and Galloway police issued a report entitled *Bombing of Pan Am 103. Interview of Marwan Abdel Razzaq Mufit Khreesat as a suspect.*

Khreesat is not a Libyan. He was held by the German police after an explosive device in a cassette recorder – similar to the one which is said to have blown up the plane over Lockerbie – was found in his car. The Scottish police's report concluded, not surprisingly: 'There can be little doubt that Khreesat is the bomb-maker for the PFLP-GC (a Palestinian terrorist group) and there is a possibility that he prepared the explosive device which destroyed PA-103. As such he should not be at liberty . . .'

This was the information which had prompted the then Transport Secretary Paul Channon on 17 March 1989 (only twelve days before the police report) to announce triumphantly to selected lobby journalists that the Scottish police had tracked down the man who bombed the plane and would be arresting him shortly. Alas, Channon did not know that while he was talking to lobby journalists in the Garrick Club, Thatcher and Bush were agreeing that they should 'play down' Lockerbie for fear that their beloved intelligence services would be embarrassed by any prolonged inquiry.

Khreesat therefore remained at liberty, despite increasingly hysterical press reports that he was the bomb-maker. Then suddenly last year the whole emphasis changed. The bombing was played up. The Palestinian and Syrian connections were played down. The entire blame was shifted on to the Libyans.

The Home Office minister Douglas Hogg, who answered Dalyell in the debate on 20 January, had a simple explanation. After eighteen months of suspecting Khreesat, the Palestinians and the Syrians, he explained, 'the facts of the investigation shifted'. Why and how? Hogg replied: 'As a result of forensic scientific evidence.'

All the forensic evidence was available to the police long before the suspects changed last year. The 'shifting facts' story does not stand up for a moment. The 'facts' of the police inquiry have remained very much the same since March 1989. They have been passed on again and again to journalists interested in the story. The *Sunday Times*, in an enormous series in December 1989, repeated the whole Khreesat, Syrian, Palestinian, Iranian saga *ad nauseam*. David Leppard's book *On the Trail of Terror* repeated it too.

There was no 'shift' of facts – the facts remained the same throughout, so what happened to shift the suspects?

The answer has its roots in Malta. The official line put out by the *Sunday Times*, Leppard and Woodhead (among countless others) was that the suitcase bomb was originally planted on a plane in Malta and that the suitcase was transferred to a jet at Frankfurt and then again on to flight 103 at Heathrow. The plot was hatched, so the story went, in a Maltese bakery.

At some time last year, the official story was further embellished. The people who planted the bomb in Malta, it was said, were agents of the Libyan Government who were posing as airline officials. This story was, incidentally (without any publicity in the British or US press), immediately and comprehensively denounced by the Maltese Government, whose deputy Prime Minister said police inquiries in Malta had found no link whatsoever between Malta and the bomb.

What, then, is the evidence which leads the US Government, and, in pathetic chorus, the Scottish Lord Advocate and his government in Whitehall to the certainty that the two Libyans are responsible? The answer is that they have a 'witness'.

In response to the US Government's offer of an enormous reward for information about the bombing, an airline official in Malta came forward with a story that the two Libyans planted the bomb. He was whisked off to the United States, given a false identity and paid a rumoured $4 million. This – not forensic evidence or anything so substantial – is the reason for the US and British Governments' sudden concern to clear up the Lockerbie bombing, and for their sudden lack of interest in all the suspects it has been pursuing up to now.

The new 'evidence', bought at such a fantastic price, convinces lawyers on both sides of the Atlantic that they can convict the Libya Two in a court of law, provided that court is in the US or Britain (the offer by the Maltese Government to hold the case in Valetta has been turned down contemptuously).

No one in the US Justice Department or the Lord Advocate's office expects the Libyans to be released for trial, and their star witness will therefore be spared the embarrassment of cross-examination about his huge pay-off and whether or not it affected his memory. Meanwhile, the consciences of both governments are clear. Though they know that someone else made the Lockerbie bomb, someone connected with their new allies in Syria and Iran, they can with a clear conscience go for others who are connected to a country which is not their ally.

Private Eye, 31 January 1992

One of the many irritations in the offices of George Bush and his admirer, John Major, is that plans to teach a 'short, sharp lesson' to Libya to boost their dreadful showing in the polls may be foiled.

President Bush's plan was to bomb Tripoli and other Libyan targets in reprisal for Colonel Gaddafi's refusal to extradite the two Libyan officials named by the US Justice Department and the Scottish Lord Advocate's department as suspects for the Lockerbie bombing.

The case against the two men is not strong: its essential weakness being the previous insistence of both US and British Governments that the bombing was carried out by a Palestinian group, funded and inspired by the Iranians. However, Bush and his advisers were certain Gaddafi would never release the two men.

Colonel Gaddafi may be mad – but he's not stupid. Major promised a resolution at the UN Security Council by the end of February at the latest, but Libyan manoeuvres have pushed the deadline further back, threatening to deprive at least Major of an electorally inspired anti-terrorist move.

By simultaneously sending the case to the International Court of Justice – and telling the UN that he would be prepared to consider handing over the two accused to the Americans in return for better diplomatic relations, Gaddafi has made it very difficult for the West to win a majority in the Security Council.

Calling for a trial in a neutral court in a neutral country makes things even more difficult. The British courts' record on terrorist trials probably rules them out, and the US courts are even having trouble pinning anything on General Noriega. So Gaddafi's offer looks reasonable enough for all the Third World delegates on the Security Council to get cold feet about any 'UN reprisals'.

Perhaps the West will have to think about another dictator who is a rather harder target. Remember Saddam Hussein?

Private Eye, 13 March 1992

Despite Libya referring the case of the two intelligence agents accused of the Lockerbie bombing to the International Court of Justice, it seems John Major and George Bush still want to inject the 'Falklands Factor' into their respective election campaigns.

Most members of the United Nations' Security Council seem inclined to a verdict of 'innocent but insane' on Colonel Gaddafi; but they also seem inclined to pipe any tune that Washington suggests. It is thus likely that air-travel sanctions will be imposed on Libya very shortly.

Not, it should be noted, oil sanctions. They would upset too many Europeans who get much of their crude from Libya, and could cause oil prices to rise. Since the Saudis are already over-pumping to keep prices down for Bush's election year, that would never do.

Cynicism is such that it has been suggested that the main purpose of the air blockade is to make it *impossible* for the Libyans to extradite the wanted intelligence agents and so speed the day when the vote-catching planes can swoop on Tripoli.

Private Eye, 27 March 1992

Lockerbie: How the Leppard Changed His Spots

Astonishing new information about the bombing of the Pan Am airliner at Lockerbie in 1988, which killed 270 people, was first presented to the British public by that most prestigious newspaper, the *Sunday Times*, and the deputy editor of its renowned Insight team, David Leppard.

On 17 December, almost exactly five years after the disaster, Leppard disclosed that a Swiss-made timing mechanism, which was alleged to have been sold exclusively in Libya, had also been sold in Germany. This undermined the only hard forensic evidence for the claim by the United States and British Governments that the Lockerbie bombers were Libyan.

This information came from BBC Radio's *File on Four*. Leppard was the obvious *Sunday Times* journalist to take on the scoop. Assisted throughout by generous sources in the Dumfries and Galloway police, he has written extensively about Lockerbie for four-and-a-half years. His reports and his book on the subject provide an interesting example of how a good story can change with the political wind.

Private Eye, 14 January 1994

Hemar Enterprises, a TV production company which has recently made a film about the Lockerbie air disaster in 1988, put out a press release shortly before Christmas about a break-in at their north London offices.

'Nothing of value was taken,' said the release, 'but archive tapes were strewn around the floor and at least one tape, containing off-the-record comments by a former government minister, appeared to be missing.'

The *Eye* understands that the missing tape features former Transport Secretary Cecil Parkinson, who appeared in a recent Channel 4 *Dispatches* programme about the *Marchioness* disaster in the Thames in 1989. During the programme, Parkinson admitted that the decision not to hold a public judicial inquiry into the Lockerbie disaster had been taken 'at Number Ten Downing Street' (occupied at that time by Margaret Thatcher).

Encouraged to expand on this after the programme, after insisting he was 'off the record', Parkinson revealed that the real problem with a public inquiry into Lockerbie was the role of the security services in the Lockerbie inquiry. This surprising revelation was duly taped as the cameras kept whirring. Copies were made and freely distributed. If the MI5 buggers really were looking for this tape, they should be reassured. The *Eye* understands there are at least twenty copies of it at different addresses (not the *Eye*'s, of course).

Private Eye, 30 December 1994

Lockerbie: Play It Again, Tam

A new stage has been reached in the great Lockerbie cover-up. Until now, important questions about the bombing have not been answered. Now they cannot even be asked.

On 9 May Labour MP Tam Dalyell, who is sceptical about the official version of what happened at Lockerbie, put down six questions to the Scottish Secretary Ian Lang. All were refused by the Table Office, which made it clear that any detailed questions about likely evidence in any forthcoming court case would be banned.

Dalyell sent his questions for publication in the *Eye*. Four of them are about the central piece of forensic evidence which, it is claimed, points to Libya as the source of the bomb which knocked out the airliner over Lockerbie. This is a tiny chip from a timing device allegedly found in a forest near Lockerbie. The timing device, it is claimed, was manufactured by a Swiss firm and sold to Libya.

This 'evidence' was slightly tainted when the head of the Swiss firm, Edwin Bollier, said that a lot of his timers had gone not to Libya but to East Germany; and that anyway he has never been shown the fragment itself, only a picture of it. Until he sees the fragment itself, he says, he can't possibly say whether or not it is part of one of his timers. Dalyell asked why Bollier was not shown the device and what was its colour. These questions go to the root of the Lockerbie mystery, but they are not even allowed on the Commons order paper.

Dalyell's two other questions were about Marwan Khreesat, who for nearly three years after the bombing was named by all the authorities as the bomb-maker. Khreesat was arrested by German police but was suddenly and mysteriously released after a court hearing. The FBI interviewed him, but Scottish police were not allowed to do so. Dalyell asked what information the Scottish police were given about the FBI interrogation of Khreesat and what the Secretary of State was told about Khreesat's mysterious release. All vital questions. All banned.

Private Eye, 19 May 1995

Lockerbie News

More bad news for the crown office in Scotland, which still insists that the mass-murder bombing of a Pan Am airliner over Lockerbie in 1988 was the work of two Libyans.

On 13 September ABC television broadcast a long programme in the United States about the forensic department of the FBI. At the centre of the programme was a memorandum from the former head explosives scientist at the FBI, Dr Frederic Whitehurst.

Whitehurst drew up a devastating indictment against a former colleague, Thomas Thurman, in a terrorist case in which a judge was killed by pipe bombs. According to Whitehurst: 'Thurman circumvented established procedures and protocols in the assignment of evidence to examiners . . . testified to areas of expertise that he had no qualifications in, therefore fabricating evidence . . .'

Thomas Thurman was the FBI forensic investigator on the Lockerbie case who appeared on television on 15 November 1991, the day after indictments were issued against the two Libyan suspects, bragging that he was the man who had fitted a tiny piece of circuit board to a timing device which might have been sold to Libyans. This is the only hard evidence linking the Libyans to the crime. If it is false or fabricated, the whole case collapses and the government has been leading the bereaved Lockerbie families up the garden path for four years.

Private Eye, 22 September 1995

Lockerbie: Another Warning, Another Denial

The great cover-up of the biggest mass murder in British history, the 1988 bombing of Pan Am 103 at Lockerbie, has been given a new boost by the Prime Minister.

On 29 July the *Guardian* published further evidence that the US Government was warned well before Lockerbie that Pan Am was a target for Palestinian terrorists.

The authorities were expecting a revenge bombing for the shooting down of an Iranian airliner by a US warship the previous summer. The danger to Pan Am was spelled out in an intelligence report from the US State Department on 2 December 1988, nineteen days before the Lockerbie bombing. The report warned: 'Team of Palestinians not associated with the PLO plans to attack American targets in Europe. Targets specified are Pan Am and US military bases.'

The report was met with great indignation by the families of the British Lockerbie victims, who have been assured that there was no relevant warning to Pan Am aircraft. Diligent previous inquiries by the families had established the following timetable:

26 October 1988: German police arrest a gang from the PFLP-GC, a Palestinian terrorist organisation opposed to the PLO and closely linked to Iran. In one of the gang's cars was a bomb built into a Toshiba radio-cassette player which was specifically designed to blow up aircraft.

5 December: A man with a Middle Eastern accent rings the US embassy in Helsinki warning that a woman would unwittingly carry a bomb on board a Pan Am flight from Frankfurt to the US in the next fortnight.

9 December: Pan Am security official Jim Berwick goes to Helsinki and is told by a US intelligence agent the warning is a hoax.

13 December: The alleged hoax Helsinki warning is posted on the noticeboard of the US embassy in Moscow. At least one diplomat cancels a Pan Am flight booking.

21 December: Pan Am flight 103 from Frankfurt to New York explodes, killing 270 people. The bomb in the plane was fitted into a Toshiba radio-cassette player.

The new evidence of an intelligence warning for Pan Am on 2 December 1988 fitted grimly into this timetable. On 31 July, UK Families Flight 103, which represents most of the British relatives of the Lockerbie dead, wrote to John Major with a series of urgent questions about the new warning. A reply from Edward Oakden, Major's private secretary, arrived eight weeks later on 22 September. It dealt with the questions as follows:

Q: Was this warning passed to the British intelligence services at the time? NO REPLY.

Q: If so, was this information passed to government departments, civil servants and/or ministers? NO REPLY.

Q: Was the warning given to the US Federal Aviation Authority and/or Pan Am by US or British intelligence? NO REPLY.

Q: What, if any, steps were taken by the intelligence services or government departments as a result of the warning? NO REPLY.

Q: Finally, in the light of the release of this information, do you still stand by your comment in a letter earlier this year to John Mosey [whose daughter Helga died on Pan Am 103] that 'no specific warnings were received before the Lockerbie disaster'?

REPLY: *'The analyst [of the report] assessed the threat as circular reporting, possibly versions of two earlier Counter Intelligence Daily Summaries. These earlier summaries remain classified, but the US authorities have assured us that neither made mention of Pan Am, nor of any other specific suspected target, but rather referred to a threat to US suspected targets generally. It appears that some with whom the original non-specific intelligence reports were shared jumped to conclusions about possible specific targets based on their own conjecture and that the December 2 report recycled this feedback. The US document was thus not the specific warning that it might first appear. I'm afraid that it adds nothing new of substance.'*

Translated from gobbledegook into English, Mr Oakden claims that an intelligence officer, reading previous reports that US targets generally were in danger from terrorist bombing, took it on himself, without any information or intelligence, to make a random guess that a target might be a specific airline – Pan Am – a guess which he coolly passed on in an official intelligence report. The 'guess' miraculously turned out to be completely (and hideously) accurate.

If Mr Major believes that, he will believe anything. The plain truth is that the 2 December warning, which after a four-year delay has been wrenched from the US Government under the Freedom of Information Act (and was certainly *not* passed on to Pan Am at the time), is the plainest proof that in the weeks before Lockerbie the authorities were issuing warnings that Pan Am was a terrorist target. Those warnings were effectively ignored; and now there is no limit to the cover-up by the authorities on both sides of the Atlantic.

Private Eye, 6 October 1995

Lockerbie Latest: FCO ... 1 FBI ... 0

In yet another adjournment debate launched by Tam Dalyell MP into the scandal of the 270 unsolved murders at Lockerbie, Foreign Office minister Jeremy Hanley surprised the Commons by revealing a piece of hard information.

The crucial piece of evidence which, according to British and US Governments, links the Lockerbie bombing to two Libyan airline officials is a fragment of circuit board which has allegedly been traced to a timing device sold to Libya.

Mr Hanley can't tell the House where this vital piece of evidence was found or where it is now. But he did reveal that the forensic work on the fragment was done at the MoD's Royal Armaments Research and Development Establishment (RARDE) in Kent.

That refutes the consistent claims of the American FBI that its expert Thomas Thurman was the forensic genius who linked the circuit board to the timer. Hanley's claim comes hard on the heels of the news, first published in the *Eye*, that Thurman is under investigation by the US department of justice for fabricating forensic evidence in another bombing case.

PS: The man in charge of the RARDE investigation was Dr Thomas Hayes, a prominent witness in the conviction of the Maguire family for having explosives in their house. No explosives were ever found there and the family, bitterly protesting their innocence, were solely convicted on the evidence of Hayes and his RARDE colleagues. The Maguires have since been cleared and RARDE scientists, including Hayes, trenchantly criticised in a special report on the case by Sir John May.

Private Eye, 15 December 1995

Lockerbie: Another Fit-up

Juval Aviv is an inquiry agent who was hired by Pan Am to investigate the 1988 bombing of its airliner over Lockerbie.

In his report Aviv suggested that the bomb had got on to the plane in a bag which avoided inspection because it was thought by officials to be part of a CIA-inspired drugs run from Lebanon to the United States. Aviv was interviewed for the 1995 Channel 4 film on Lockerbie which strongly contested the US authorities' view that the bombers were two Libyan airline officials.

Shortly before the film was shown, Aviv was arrested on charges of defrauding the General Electric Capital Corporation. The charges were used by the US Government to discredit Aviv and the Channel 4 programme. In a letter to editors all over Britain in the days before the film was broadcast in May 1995, Michael O'Brien, a senior official at the US embassy in London, wrote: 'Aviv was recently arrested in the US for defrauding an American company.'

On 7 May David 'Lockerbie' Leppard wrote an article in the *Sunday Times* under the challenging heading: FBI EXPOSES DOCUMENTARY ON LOCKERBIE AS A SHAM. The article asserted that Juval Aviv had been 'discredited' and that 'two months ago he was arrested on federal fraud charges'.

On 8 December Juval Aviv appeared before a federal judge and jury in New York accused of deceiving the General Electric company for whom he had carried out an investigation into security on a Caribbean island. It emerged at once that no complaint had ever been made by the company, which was quite satisfied with Aviv's work. He was charged only after special FBI agents had seized company documents.

Aviv's lawyers submitted that the entire case was trumped up to discredit Aviv over Lockerbie. The judge seemed to agree. 'The chronology of the investigation,' he said, 'and the fact that it results from no external complaint whatever, but simply internally within the FBI, leads to an inference that it was generated from some other source, and the only source on the record so far for which any such purposes could be ascribed is Mr Aviv's report in the other case, the Lockerbie case.'

The jury seemed to agree too. On 16 December they acquitted Juval Aviv on all charges.

Private Eye, 10 January 1997

Continuing proof that the government does not know its arse from its elbow emerged at the Commonwealth conference discussions on the great Lockerbie cock-up (*Eyes passim*).

Nelson Mandela started the panic with a speech in open conference denouncing the British Government's obstinate refusal to consider holding a trial of the so-called 'Libyan suspects' for the 1988 Lockerbie bombing in a neutral country.

Mandela's devastating attack caused consternation among spin doctors who had arranged glamorous photo calls starring Tony Blair and Mandela, New Labour and New South Africa in happy harmony.

The contradiction seemed too much for Robin Cook, Foreign Secretary. He started the day saying there could be no compromise on the imperative need to hold the trial in Scotland. He even hinted that the American Government might not cooperate with a trial held anywhere else, and that the Americans' agreement was crucial since they 'hold' most of the evidence.

Whoops! The argument that the trial must be held in Scotland has depended up to now on the assertion that the Lord Advocate, Lord Hardie, 'holds' all the evidence. Was Cook suggesting the US Government would hold back evidence unless it approves of the place the trial is held?

When such points were put forcefully to Cook in Edinburgh by Jim Swire, whose daughter died in the bombing, Cook seemed to soften a little, announcing that the government had not completely ruled out a trial out of Scotland. This was slapped down at once by Tony Blair, who said such a trial was out of the question.

Enter, stage left, the government's environment and transport supremo John Prescott, who was quoted as saying that an independent public inquiry into Lockerbie had not been ruled out. Whoops! Yes, it had – unequivocally, and twice on the same day (8 August) – in letters to bereaved families from Tony Lloyd MP, Minister of State at the Foreign Office, and Glenda Jackson MP, an Under-Secretary in Prescott's own department.

The contradictions might be further exposed if some discontented bereaved relative in England tried to get an inquest into his/her relative's death at Lockerbie – by an English coroner.

Private Eye, 31 October 1997

Lockerbie: Pik 'n' Miss

Looming over the prospect of the trial of two Libyan suspects for the Lockerbie bombing are two dreadful questions which haunt the intelligence communities on both sides of the Atlantic.

1 Why has Nelson Mandela, President of South Africa, shown such a lasting and dedicated interest in Lockerbie? True, he was for some of the time head of the Organisation of African Unity. True, he feels he owes the Libyans a debt for their long opposition to apartheid. But on their own these explanations can't explain the enormous amount of time and travelling Mandela has devoted to talks with the Libyan leader Colonel Gaddafi.

2 Why has Gaddafi conceded, and released the suspects in what seems like a climbdown? True, he was irritated by UN sanctions; but these hardly explain his uncharacteristic bowing the knee to the hated Americans.

Could the answer to both questions have anything to do with the most enduring mystery about Lockerbie: the warnings received *before* the bombing of a likely attack on a US airliner in revenge for the shooting down by the US Navy of an Iranian airliner in the Gulf, with the loss of many lives, a few months before Lockerbie?

The most persistent of all the 'warning' stories comes from South Africa. On 21 December 1988, the day of the bombing, the South African Foreign Minister Pik Botha was in London with a large entourage. The rumour was that they had planned to go to the US on Pan Am 103. But at the last moment had switched to a later flight. Had they been warned off?

Could it be that President Mandela has more information about this last-minute switch and that he has passed on the information to Colonel Gaddafi?

Private Eye, 2 April 1999

Lockerbie: Maltese Double Cross

For nearly all the twelve years since a bomb blew to pieces a Pan Am airliner above Lockerbie in Scotland, killing 270 people, the *Eye* has been asking the following questions:

1 Why did the initial suspects for the bombing – a Palestinian terrorist group hired by Iran to arrange a revenge for the shooting down by the American Navy in the summer of 1988 of an Iranian airliner in the Gulf – suddenly vanish from the scene in 1991?

2 How and why were they replaced as chief suspects by an apparently unrelated plot originating in Libya?

3 Could the switch in suspects have been inspired by political prior-ities in Washington and the CIA?

4 Were these priorities set by the 1991 Gulf War, in which Syria, previously regarded as a hostile state with terrorist inclinations, suddenly became a crucial ally of the US in the war against Saddam Hussein's Iraq?

5 Did the US and British Governments shelter behind the refusal of the Libyan Government to release the two suspects named in the US indictment in 1991, claiming for eight years that this refusal pointed to the two men's guilt?

6 In summary, has US intelligence, supported by its British equiv-alents, consistently hoodwinked the relatives of the Lockerbie dead with a cock-and-bull story manufactured by the CIA in the exclusive interests of US foreign policy?

Some answers to these questions have now begun to emerge at the trial in Holland of the two Libyan suspects.

The whole idea of a trial on neutral territory was originally and vociferously opposed by the US and British authorities, who agreed to the idea only under pressure from Third World countries, espe-cially from Nelson Mandela, the former President of South Africa.

The US Government refused to agree to the trial unless two offi-cials from the US justice department attended the trial, sat with pros-ecution lawyers and daily briefed the relatives of the US citizens who died at Lockerbie. So far, despite prodigious efforts, the prosecution has failed to establish that any bomb went on a feeder flight for Pan Am flight 103 from Malta, or that timers for the bomb were sold to Libya, or that in either case either of the two suspects was involved.

Looming over the whole prolonged and expensive proceedings has been the promised appearance of the prosecution's star witness – the man on whom the indictment was based. This witness, doubters were assured, would clear up the matter once and for all. He had worked for Libyan intelligence at Malta's airport and would be able to provide clear evidence linking the suspects to the planting of a bomb on a Maltese feeder flight to Frankfurt.

This witness has now been identified as Abdul Majid Razkaz Salam Giaka, who has not been interviewed by the Dumfries and Galloway police – theoretically the prosecution's investigators into the biggest mass murder in British criminal history. Under Scottish law, however, the witness had to be made available for interview by the defence. Before they were allowed to see Giaka, defence lawyers were blindfolded. To make doubly sure, Giaka insisted on wearing an extravagant disguise, including make-up and a female wig.

The lawyers have found out that Giaka had defected to the CIA in 1989, but at the time of his defection said nothing about the Lockerbie bombing a few months previously. It was not until early 1991, as the Desert Storm bombers started their attack on Baghdad, and Syrian involvement in the United Nations effort against Iraq became crucial, that Giaka, now safe under a witness protection scheme in the US, disclosed his evidence against his two former colleagues.

The important fact is that at the moment of the switch of Lockerbie suspects, the CIA had at its disposal a man who claimed to have defected from Libyan intelligence (though at the time of his defection he forgot to mention his alleged evidence about Lockerbie). Giaka is paid $1,000 a month and stands to make another $4m as a reward if the defendants are convicted.

The trial has now been postponed until 21 September pending legal arguments about the disclosure of CIA cables relating to Giaka. The cables released to the defence have been heavily edited and censored. The prosecution argue that this censorship is crucial to the security of the United States – an argument which has not gone down well with the presiding judge, Lord Sutherland.

It may well be that the CIA will refuse to release the edited versions, in which case the prosecution will be obliged not to call its star witness, and the charges will have to be dropped. This could be the best possible alternative for the prosecution and for both British and US Governments who are not looking forward to a full exposition of the defence case. Defence lawyers have amassed a large quantity of highly damaging information about the role of the CIA and British intelligence in the switching of suspects for the bombing.

Private Eye, 22 September 2000

Lockerbie Update

The amazing developments at Camp Zeist in Holland where two former Libyan intelligence agents are on trial for the murder twelve years ago of 270 people in a Pan Am airliner over Lockerbie have for the most part been glossed over in the British press.

The *New York Times*, however, has been more forthright. In a telling piece on 28 September it concluded: 'The most important witness in the Lockerbie trial . . . was systematically torn to pieces.'

The US Government has put it around that it has a 'star witness' whose evidence will nail the Libyan defendants once and for all. This man, Abdul Majid Giaka, a garage mechanic who once claimed to be related to King Idris of Libya, has now at last been hauled into the public gaze.

Defence lawyers claimed Majid was lying chiefly because he has been paid huge sums of money by the CIA. In a series of devastating questions which Majid could not credibly answer, they demonstrated that every time the CIA threatened to cut off his payments, Majid produced yet another piece of evidence against the accused.

His apparently relevant disclosures that he had seen one of the defendants with a brown Samsonite suitcase of the type on which the bomb was loaded on the doomed airliner and that he discussed with one of the defendants how to put an unaccompanied suitcase on a plane at Malta were all made in these highly suspicious circumstances.

Private Eye, 6 October 2000

Lockerbie: Campbell's Soup

How goes the trial in Holland of the two Libyan intelligence agents accused of bombing Pan Am airliner 103 over Lockerbie in December 1988? The short answer is that until 8 January it is not 'going' at all.

For the second time in six months the trial has been adjourned while the defence waits for more detailed evidence from Syria about a possible bomber who is not Libyan and is not one of the accused. For the moment, the most dramatic moment in the trial was the motion from Richard Keen QC for the defence that his client, Al Amin Khalifa Fimah, has no case to answer.

The three judges listened in near silence as Mr Keen set out his formidable case. They were not so silent when Mr Alistair Campbell (no relation to the Prime Minister's press secretary, but the Scottish Lord Advocate Depute and therefore a government minister) argued that the case against Fimah should continue.

The central points, he declared, were a) that 'an unaccompanied bag was carried on Air Malta flight KM 180 between Luga airport, Malta and Frankfurt'; b) that the bag was the brown Samsonite one containing the explosive which, after changing planes at Frankfurt and Heathrow, eventually blew the Pan Am flight and all its passengers to bits over Lockerbie; and c) that the man who played a crucial part in getting the bomb on the plane at Malta was Mr Fimah. Mr Campbell's difficulty was that there was hardly any evidence for any of these assertions.

First, did the bomb go on the Malta flight at all? Mr Campbell argued that there had been chaos at Luqa airport that morning (21 December 1988), and that an unaccompanied suitcase had defied the baggage checking system and had been slipped on to the plane.

His first problem was pointed out to him rather sharply by Lord Maclean, one of the judges. The 'chaos' at Luqa airport had involved a Libyan airlines flight, not the Maltese flight to Frankfurt. The exchange went like this:

Lord Maclean: *You've mentioned Libyan airlines?*

Campbell: *Yes. I am coming on in a moment to describe the situation on the morning of the 21st December where a number of flights were checking in, one of which was a Libyan airlines flight.*

Maclean: *But the crown case is that the bag would have to be got on to the Air Malta flight.*

Campbell: *Indeed, my Lords, it would have to be tagged with an Air Malta tag for an Air Malta flight, but that's not to say it couldn't be introduced at the check-in where Libyan Arab Airlines were checking in, if the system was to be subverted.*

Maclean: *Remind me, is there evidence that you could check in an Air Malta bag, or a bag with an Air Malta tag, on to a flight for Malta at Libyan Arab Airlines?*

Mr Campbell couldn't remind the judge of anything of the sort. All he could do was take a break and consult with his advisers. He then announced:

My Lords, what I am endeavouring to do is simply to identify possible routes into the system. I am not suggesting that the bag was introduced under a normal procedure. I am suggesting that Mr Fimah must have taken advantage of his being known at the airport to introduce a bag into the system rather than formally check it in.

Maclean: *It is accepted, though, that there is no evidence that Fimah was seen at the airport on the 21st of December.*

Campbell: *I accept that. It's a matter of inference.*

Almost at once, Mr Campbell was interrupted again on the same subject, this time by the presiding judge Lord Sutherland.

Sutherland: *I'm sorry to interrupt you, Advocate Depute. You are departing from your possible route, are you?*

Campbell: *Yes, I am illustrating the possibilities of the system being accessed either at the check-in or at some point airside.*

Sutherland: *Yes. But either of the two routes you've postulated would still have to go through the reconciliation process which appears from the evidence at Luqa to have been fairly good.*

Mr Campbell had to take another break, and get more advice. Then he said:

Yes, my Lords, I am just confirming that my recollection of the evidence was that the reconciliation between passenger and bags was only applied on the route to Cairo and not to Air Malta flights to Frankfurt.

Sutherland: *Well, there was at least a reconciliation between the number of bags checked in and the number of bags loaded on to the aircraft. The loadmaster did his actual count, checked that his figure agreed with the check-in figure, and both arrived at the number fifty-five, as I recall it.*

All Mr Campbell could say was that these 'figures could not be relied upon'. Then Lord Sutherland raised the further difficulty of the danger to any conspirator that the count of luggage on the plane might expose the fact that there was a bag not accounted for; that the bag might be taken out of the system, and inspected, to the frustration of the entire bombing conspiracy not to say the prompt arrest of the conspirators.

Mr Campbell replied:

Campbell: *I take your Lordship's point. That of course confirms the need for somebody with access beyond the public area, and that if the system was to be subverted it would require somebody with the sort of access and experience that Mr Fimah had to subvert the system.*

This was too much for the third judge. Lord Coulsfield, who interrupted the wretched Campbell for the third time:

Coulsfield: *But since we don't know how the system was subverted, what is the basis for inferring that it was Mr Fimah, rather than somebody else, like a loader who had been bribed, who actually subverted it?*

Campbell: *I take from the evidence of this whole chapter of days, taken as a whole, that Mr Fimah has been recruited by Mr Megrahi, his friend, to assist him.*

Coulsfield: *But I think this is open to the objection I was putting to your argument earlier, that you are tending to assume that Mr*

Fimah is involved, when that is the very thing that has to be inferred from the evidence: that he was involved knowingly.

Campbell: *What I am endeavouring to do is to outline the facts as to what he did along with Mr Megrahi. And from these facts taken as a whole, my submission is, the inference is that he (Fimah) assisted with this bag and must have known what the purpose of the exercise was.*

Coulsfield: *But there is no evidence to indicate that the defeating of the system at Malta airport was something that Mr Fimah even was in a position to do because the furthest that the evidence goes, as I understand it, is to indicate that on previous occasions he may have been able to put a bag on to the computer, on to the conveyor belt.*

There was no intelligible answer to that. There was indeed no evidence that the baggage system was subverted at Luqa airport. All the bags were counted as they went on to the plane. They corresponded with the bags that were checked in. The only evidence that an unaccompanied bag went on the flight from Malta was a computer print-out at Frankfurt which showed that an unaccompanied bag went on the Pan Am flight to London at Frankfurt; and that the timing of the arrival of this bag meant that it could conceivably have come from the Malta flight. All this evidence was entirely hypothetical. It did not even start to prove that the bomb went on at Malta, and certainly not that Mr Fimah put it there.

'What your Lordships are being asked to do at this stage,' said Mr Keen as he summed up, 'is to infer that a man who wasn't there did, by a means they did not know, smuggle a bomb on to a plane at Luqa airport.' Mr Campbell and his associates had, he argued, conspicuously failed to make out even the semblance of a case against Mr Fimah.

On 29 November, the judges decided nevertheless to allow the case against Fimah to continue. Lord Sutherland was careful to clarify that in rejecting the 'no case to answer' submission the judges had to take the crown case 'at its highest'. He added: 'And such matters as assessment of credibility and reliability of witnesses and assessment of what inferences should be drawn from such evidence as survives the test of credibility and reliability play no part whatever.' The judges, in other words, were not assessing the credibility or reliability of the evidence. Their test was simply: does the untested evidence add up to a case to answer? Yes, it did – just.

Private Eye, 29 December 2000

Lockerbie: The Khreesat Connection

As reported in the last *Eye*, the trial in Holland of two Libyans for the bombing of Pan Am airliner 103 over Lockerbie twelve years ago has been delayed for several weeks. The reason? An attempt by defence lawyers to get more information from the Syrian Government about a terrorist formerly with the Palestinian group PFLP-GC.

The terrorist, who has since died, is usually known by the name of Mobdi Goben. He was named, incidentally, during one of the most remarkable episodes in the trial so far: the evidence of a former FBI agent called Edward Marshman.

In November 1989, nearly a year after the bombing, Mr Marshman was sent by the FBI to Jordan where he interviewed an undercover Jordanian intelligence agent called Marwan Khreesat. The interview was possible only because of the close contacts over many years between Jordanian intelligence and the American CIA.

The Dumfries and Galloway police, officially in charge of the Lockerbie murder inquiry, were most upset when they discovered that the FBI had got to Khreesat before them. Khreesat has been named many times in Western media as the man who may have made the 'improvised explosive device' (bomb) which went off in the airliner on 21 December 1988, killing all passengers and crew.

Few if any of the Western commentators who named Khreesat realised that he was so closely connected to Jordanian intelligence. But when the FBI started to investigate the theory that Palestinian terrorists had blown up the airliner on the orders of the Iranian and Syrian Governments, Mr Marshman was sent to Amman to interview Khreesat. When Jordanian intelligence chiefs adamantly refused to release Khreesat for the Lockerbie trial last year, Mr Marshman was summoned to disclose what Khreesat told him all those years ago. Under questioning on 5 December, Mr Marshman told the following story.

On 13 October 1988, two months before the Lockerbie bombing, Khreesat, who had infiltrated the PFLP and was respected in the organisation as an expert with high explosives, travelled from Jordan to Germany with his wife. The couple were met by a PFLP terrorist called Dalkamoni, who told Khreesat he was expecting another PFLP contact, whom he named as Abu Elias. When Khreesat asked what role Elias would play in the PFLP's terrorist plot, he was told that Elias was an expert in airport security, while Khreesat was an expert in making bombs. The plan was for Khreesat to make bombs and for Elias to smuggle them on to an aircraft.

On 22 October Khreesat saw his wife off on a plane back to Jordan – from Frankfurt airport, where he spent some time researching plane schedules. That evening, in a house owned by another PFLP member, Khreesat started making five bombs and disguising them so that they could be put on an aircraft. Khreesat told Marshman that he did 'not know any of the details as to exactly how the devices were going to be put on board aircraft . . . Elias had all the details.'

On 24 October, Khreesat's story went on, he stopped work for a break. While he was in the shower, Dalkamoni knocked on the door and said he was leaving to go to Frankfurt. When Khreesat got back to his work, he noticed that one of the five bombs had disappeared. The next day, 25 October, he phoned his controlling officer in Jordanian intelligence with the news that he had made the bombs and that one of them had been passed on to Elias. Later that day, Khreesat and Dalkamoni went to Düsseldorf airport where they wandered round picking up timetables and discussing airline schedules. The next day still, 26 October, Khreesat and Dalkamoni left their home to go to meet Elias. Their car, with a bomb inside, was stopped by German police and the two men were arrested. As soon as the German police verified that Khreesat was an intelligence agent from Jordan he was released.

Neither Marshman nor Khreesat nor anyone else could say what happened to the bomb that went missing while Khreesat was in the shower except that it was disguised as a Toshiba cassette recorder (as was the Lockerbie bomb). Marshman's official note of the interview concluded: 'Khreesat advised that he does not think he built the device responsible for Pan Am 103, as he only built the four devices in Germany which are described herein.' But this is nonsense. 'Described herein' were not four, but five devices, and the missing one was disguised as a Toshiba.

Mr Marshman's evidence was heard out of sequence. He was a witness for the defence and was questioned first by William Taylor QC for Ali Megrahi, the first defendant. Mr Turnbull for the prosecution followed with a line of questions designed to prove that Khreesat did not make the bomb that brought down Pan Am 103. But his questions did not even start to shape the main point: that a few weeks before the Lockerbie bombing a gang working ostensibly for Palestinian terrorists, but mostly for various intelligence services, were busily building bombs disguised as cassettes and intended for planting on aircraft at Frankfurt airport from which the doomed flight 103 took off. Perhaps the most remarkable aspect of Mr Marshman's evidence was that neither he nor Mr Khreesat ever once mentioned the Libyan Government or Malta airport or anyone employed by either.

Private Eye, 12 January 2001

Lockerbie: Heathrow Connection

A disturbing theme emerged from the closing submission of Bill Taylor QC, counsel for one of the Libyans accused of murdering 270 people in the 1988 Lockerbie bombing.

Mr Taylor has already made much of the failure of the prosecution to establish the central point of its case: that the suitcase with the bomb was put on a plane in Malta. In his final speech, however, he argued that the bomb was put on the doomed flight at London's Heathrow.

He argued this case systematically, making twenty separate points and pointing out that a terrorist who wanted to destroy the plane was more likely to put it on a plane before it set off on its final flight for New York rather than on feeder flights from Frankfurt or Malta.

He could prove easily that security at Heathrow in December 1988 was abysmal. There were at least three places from where a suitcase could be smuggled on to the Pan Am flight without being picked up by airline staff. The container with baggage for the flight was left completely unattended for three-quarters of an hour.

Mr Taylor's most powerful point was his third: namely that 'a brown Samsonite suitcase was introduced into that part of the container at the interline area at Heathrow airport'. This was highly relevant since everyone agreed that the bomb that destroyed the plane had been packed in a brown Samsonite case. Mr Taylor's main evidence came from John Bedford, a baggage loader at Heathrow airport who was interviewed soon after the bombing. He then gave evidence at the initial fatal accident inquiry in 1991, which was referred to extensively by Mr Taylor. He was asked:

Q: Can you recall whether on 21 December 1988 any of the luggage that you dealt with or saw at the interline shed destined for Pan Am 103 was a bronze Samsonite case?

A: Yes, sir.

Q: Did you see a bronze Samsonite case?

A: A maroony-brown Samsonite case, yes.

Who put the case into the container? John Bedford was certain he did not. What of the other baggage handler of cases for the fatal flight – Sulkash Kamboj? He told the fatal accident inquiry: 'I did not place any luggage in the PA 103 tin that day.' Though Bedford suggested without any evidence that the Samsonite case might have been put into the container by Kamboj, Kamboj consistently denied any such thing.

Mr Taylor went on to deal in detail with the complicated evidence about the position of the loaded bags in the plane. He concluded that the Samsonite case had been loaded into the plane in almost exactly the position occupied by the suitcase from which the bomb eventually exploded. Mr Taylor also established that there was no other Samsonite bag in the plane. Mr Bedford was called by the crown as a reliable witness. There seemed no reason why he should invent the story of the mysterious Samsonite case which appeared as though by magic in the container of luggage for flight 103.

If the case with the bomb did go on the plane at Heathrow, the consequences for those in charge of the airport at the time are very severe. But what is beyond dispute is that if anyone did put a bag with a bomb on the plane at Heathrow it could not have been either of the two defendants.

Private Eye, 26 January 2001

Lockerbie: Three Lords A-leaping to Conclusions

NOW WE KNOW THAT THIS MAN PLANTED A BOMB ON FLIGHT 103, KILLING 270 PEOPLE AT LOCKERBIE. Thus, with a picture of Abdel Baset Ali Mohmed Ali Megrahi, the Libyan intelligence agent convicted of the Pan Am bombing, ran the headline in the *Independent* on 1 February – and thus, in varying degrees of hysteria and sensationalism, pretty well the entire British media.

The problem, however, is that after reading the ninety paragraphs of judgement produced by the three judges presiding over the interminable Lockerbie trial at Camp Zeist in Holland, no one knows any such thing. The judgement does not prove the guilt of Megrahi or anyone else. Instead it slips again and again into the same sort of

reckless assumptions which led to the great British injustices south of
the border of the last thirty years – the Birmingham Six, the Guildford
Four, Judy Ward, the Bridgewater Four and countless others.

So what was the 'case' against Megrahi? The judges summed it up
under three headings.

The Maltese Connection

The essence of the prosecution case was that the bomb that brought
down Pan Am flight 103 over Lockerbie twelve years ago was first
planted on an aircraft at Luqa airport, Malta, whence it travelled to
Frankfurt. There, it apparently changed planes to London, where it
changed planes again on to the doomed flight bound for the US.

What was the evidence from Luqa that the bomb went on a plane
there? None whatsoever. The fifty-five bags that went on the suspect
plane were all counted into the plane and checked against the passenger
list. All fifty-five arrived safely at Frankfurt. No one saw anything in
Malta to suggest that any unaccompanied bag had got into the plane.

Mr Megrahi was at the airport that morning. He left on a quite
different flight. He didn't have any baggage and nobody saw him do
anything remotely to indicate that he had smuggled a bag on to the
plane to Frankfurt.

The judges were obliged to admit (paragraph 39): 'If therefore the
unaccompanied bag was launched from Luqa, the method by which
it was done is not established, and the crown accepted that they could
not point to any specific route by which the primary suitcase [with
the bomb in it] could have been loaded . . . The absence of any explanation of the method by which the suitcase might have been placed
on board KM 180 [the flight from Malta to Frankfurt] is a major
difficulty for the crown case . . .'

That difficulty arose from the awkward fact that the guilt of the
accused depended entirely on the unproved theory that the bomb
went on the plane at Malta. If the crown could not prove that it went
on there, it could not prove the guilt of the accused.

Unable to prove anything in Malta, the crown case shifted to
Frankfurt airport where a single computer print-out appeared to show
that an unaccompanied bag went on the flight to Heathrow, from
where the doomed flight eventually took off. The timing of the mysterious appearance at the airport of this bag, according to the computer
print-out, made it possible in time that the bag could have come on

the flight from Malta. Possible, but not certain, and certainly not proved.

There was a further problem for this theory. The suspect bag at Frankfurt, if it ever existed, would have been part of a consignment of baggage taken for X-ray. The X-ray would almost certainly have revealed the explosive device, especially as Frankfurt staff had been warned only two months previously to keep a special watch out for explosive devices.

The judges were able to dispose of this objection on the grounds that the training given to the workers in charge of the X-ray at Frankfurt was 'poor', and the bomb might not have been noticed (par 34).

But might the bomb have been put on Pan Am 103 at Heathrow, shortly before it went off? There was evidence here from two Heathrow workers, reported in the last *Eye*. John Bedford said that a container with luggage bound for Pan Am 103 was left unattended for three-quarters of an hour before take-off. He said that when he returned to the container, there were two extra suitcases in it, including a 'maroony-brown' Samsonite case of the kind in which the bomb exploded over Lockerbie. Mr Bedford said that another worker, a Mr Sulkash Kamboj, had told him he put the two cases there. Mr Kamboj denied he'd said that. The judges believed Mr Bedford, not Mr Kamboj.

The Timer in the Shirt

A fragment of a circuit board found at Lockerbie after the crash came from a set of timers sold to Libya by a firm in Zurich. This fragment took up a lot of lawyers' time throughout the trial. It was discovered, miraculously, three weeks after the bombing and caught up in a charred shirt from the wreckage of the plane. When local policeman DC Gilchrist found the item he labelled it 'cloth (charred)'.

Some time later (no one knew how long) this was 'overwritten by the word debris'. 'There was,' say the judges (par 13), 'no satisfactory explanation as to why this was done, and DC Gilchrist's attempts to explain it were at worst evasive and at best confusing.' On the other hand, the judges concluded, 'there does not appear to be any particular reason for the alteration of the label.'

One reason they did not even consider was that an item labelled 'cloth' could not normally be expected to contain anything significant, while anything might be found in an item labelled 'debris'. The judges went on to explain how the item was examined closely by government scientists without revealing that one of those scientists, a Dr Thomas Hayes, was a prominent witness in the case which resulted in the monstrously false convictions of the Maguire family in the 1980s, and another, a Mr Allen Fereday OBE, was criticised in another case in which he had said that a timer 'could only have been used and manufactured for a terrorist operation' (11 March 1994). Nor did the judges comment on the fact that the FBI agent to whom the suspect timer was delivered for investigation, Tom Thurman, had been denounced by one of his own colleagues for 'fabricating evidence' and was subsequently 'removed'.

What did the judges have to say about Edwin Bollier, the Swiss businessman who made the timers and sold some to intelligence agents in Libya, including Megrahi to whom Bollier rented offices in Zurich? Mr Bollier and his two company colleagues were, said the judges, 'unreliable witnesses'. They explained: 'Earlier statements they made to the police and judicial authorities were at times in conflict with each another and the evidence they gave in court.' One fancy tale told by Mr Bollier, said the judges, 'belongs in our view to the realm of fiction'. Mr Bollier did indeed supply timers to Libya. He also supplied them to the Stasi, the secret police in East Germany.

Tony Gauci

What of the man who seems to have had more influence over the judges than anyone else – Tony Gauci, the owner of a clothes shop in Sliema, Malta, from which some clothes in the bomb suitcase were bought? His identification of Megrahi ten years after he says he saw him in his shop is described by the judges as 'a highly important element in the case'. But the pitiful story of Mr Gauci's identifications could grace any of the illustrious miscarriages of justice that have polluted British criminal history.

When Scottish police officers went to see him in 1989, less than a year after the bombing, they were not hunting Libyans. They were hunting a Palestinian terrorist gang, and therefore were hoping that the shopkeeper would identify one of their suspects. Again and again in the ensuing months police showed Mr Gauci photographs of suspects. He could not identify any of them, but he did say from the outset that the man who bought the clothes was a big man, some six feet tall, aged about fifty. (Megrahi is five foot eight inches and in 1988 was thirty-seven.)

When did the man visit the shop? That date too became a mystery. Mr Gauci said he'd been alone because his brother was watching a football match. The police narrowed the possible dates of the match to two: 23 November and 7 December 1988. Mr Gauci had said that it was raining when the man came, and he'd bought an umbrella. The defence called a Major Mifsud, a senior meteorologist from Luqa, five miles away. He said it was raining on 23 November, but not on 7 December. The judges concluded that the visit had taken place on 7 December, grasping at a straw offered by Mifsud who said there was a slender chance (about 10 per cent) that there had been a slight shower on the evening of 7 December. Rather more important, probably, was the fact that Mr Megrahi was in Malta on 7 December but not on 23 November.

The judges decided that Mr Gauci's identification was 'reliable' (par 67), adding the rather bizarre rider: 'There are situations where a careful witness who will not commit himself beyond saying that there is a close resemblance can be regarded as more reliable and convincing in his identification than a witness who maintains that his identification is 100 per cent.' The vaguer the better, in other words.

On the basis of not being able to prove that the bomb went on a plane at Malta, on the fact that Bollier's company sold some timers to Libya and rented offices to Megrahi in Zurich, and on the slightly strained identification by Tony Gauci, the judges convicted Ali Megrahi of the biggest murder in British criminal history.

At the same time they acquitted the man who was named throughout the trial as Megrahi's accomplice, Al Amin Khalifa Fimah. They rejected in the strongest possible language the evidence of Abdul Majid, the chief witness against Fimah (par 42).

Majid was a junior Libyan intelligence agent and vehicle maintenance man in the pay of the CIA who only remembered his 'evidence' against either defendant several months after the bombing when the CIA threatened to cut off his money. The judges did not even ask why this exotic liar and informer was produced to give evidence. The answer seems obvious. The CIA was using its paid hack to frame one of the defendants.

Had the judges come to that conclusion, they were in danger of moving on to a rather more serious analysis: that the entire expensive trial of the Libyans was an intelligence frame-up; and that among those most comprehensively hoodwinked were Lord Sutherland, Lord Coulsfield and Lord Maclean.

'We are also aware,' said the judges in their peroration (par 89), 'that there is a danger that by selecting parts of the evidence that seem to fit together and ignoring parts which might not fit, it is possible to read into a mass of conflicting evidence a conclusion which is not entirely justified.' So aware were they of the dangers of that course of action indeed that they proceeded faithfully to follow it.

Private Eye, 9 February 2001

Lockerbie: The Flight from Justice – A Special Report from Private Eye

The judgement and the verdict against Megrahi were perverse. The judges brought shame and disgrace, it is fair to say, to all those who believed in Scottish justice, and have added to Scottish law an injustice of the type which has often defaced the law in England. Their verdict was a triumph for the CIA, but it did nothing at all to satisfy the demands of the families of those who died at Lockerbie – who still want to know how and why their loved ones were murdered.

In February 1990, a group of British relatives went to the American embassy in London for a meeting with the seven members of the President's commission on aviation security and terrorism. Martin Cadman remembers: 'After we'd had our say, the meeting broke up and we moved towards the door. As we got there, I found myself talking to two members of the Commission – I think they were senators. One of them said: "Your government and our government know exactly what happened at Lockerbie. But they are not going to tell you."'

Eleven years later, after a prolific waste of many millions of pounds and words, that is still the position.

May 2001

ROBERT FISK

Terrorists

1990/2001

Robert Fisk confirmed his reputation as Britain's greatest modern war correspondent during the Israeli invasion of Lebanon in June 1982. This was a terrible, murderous episode which forced many Western journalists to recognise the terror of Israel, although none was prepared to make moral and historical sense of the facts they had witnessed, except the indefatigable Fisk.

In a plan conceived by Defence Minister Ariel Sharon, the Israeli military attacked Lebanon, intent on wiping out the Palestinian guerrilla movement and finishing off the Palestine Liberation Organisation. The PLO's fighters retreated to Beirut, which swelled with refugees who had fled the Palestinian camps in the south of the country. With so many civilians exposed to such violence, all the elements were in place for the execution of a great crime.

Laying siege to Muslim west Beirut, the Israelis cut off water, electricity and food supplies and began bombing the city, using phosphorous shells and American-supplied cluster bombs in the warren of streets. During the first two weeks of the invasion, an estimated 14,000 Palestinians and Lebanese were killed and 20,000 wounded, the vast majority of them civilians.

Sharon demanded the evacuation of all Palestinian guerrillas and Syrian forces from the city and, overseen by an international force, thousands of PLO men boarded ships that would take them to other Arab countries, while their women and children remained behind. With the evacuation over, Israeli forces invaded west Beirut, claiming that 2,000 'terrorists' were still there. Summoning their erstwhile allies, the Christian Phalangist militias, the Israeli high command sent them into the Palestinian camps of Sabra and Chatila, where they system-atically murdered hundreds of the elderly and women and children. In 1983, an Israeli Commission of Inquiry concluded that Sharon bore 'personal responsibility' for the massacre. The commission heard evidence of how the Israeli forces had allowed the Phalangists to take away prisoners, who 'disappeared'.

Robert Fisk, who was then Middle East correspondent of *The Times,* was one of the first to enter the Chatila camp after the militias had left. His book, *Pity the Nation,* draws together his reporting of the carnage and is both deeply moving and a critical examination of who was responsible. It is all the more powerful and disturbing for Fisk's dogged attempts to give the Israelis every chance to answer the charge sheet of their crime – a crime which other journalists were prepared to gloss over, or excuse in some semantic contortion, even debating among themselves whether a massacre had actually taken place. Almost single-handedly, Fisk ended the moral immunity that Israel had exploited in Europe, if not in the United States.

Since then, a great many people have come to depend on his dispatches – from Lebanon, where he lives, and Israel, and Iraq, and Afghanistan, and the Balkans, and elsewhere – in order to make sense of events in a way that governments of all stripes rightly fear.

He and I occasionally bump into each other, or talk on the phone from Beirut, or Islamabad, or somewhere. I was delighted to present him with the 2003 Martha Gellhorn Award for Journalism, for which the citation demands that the winner pursue 'a reporter's truth' while regarding with contempt that which Martha Gellhorn called 'official drivel'. To some, he is the brilliant eccentric, fond of quoting the clas-sics, collecting frequent flyer points and boasting that he has never sent an email, although the accuracy of the latter requires further sourcing. The following passages are from *Pity the Nation.*

TERRORISTS

Pregnant women will give birth to terrorists; the children when they grow up will be terrorists.

Phalangist involved in the Sabra and Chatila massacre, when
questioned by an Israeli tank crew, west Beirut
17 September 1982

We know, it's not to our liking, and don't interfere.

Message from an Israeli army battalion commander to his men,
on learning that Palestinians were being massacred
17 September 1982

It was the flies that told us. There were millions of them, their hum almost as eloquent as the smell. Big as bluebottles, they covered us, unaware at first of the difference between the living and the dead. If we stood still, writing in our notebooks, they would settle like an army – legions of them – on the white surface of our notebooks, hands, arms, faces, always congregating around our eyes and mouths, moving from body to body, from the many dead to the few living, from corpse to reporter, their small green bodies panting with excitement as they found new flesh upon which to settle and feast.

If we did not move quickly enough, they bit us. Mostly they stayed around our heads in a grey cloud, waiting for us to assume the generous stillness of the dead. They were obliging, these flies, forming our only physical link with the victims who lay around us, reminding us that there is life in death. Someone benefits. The flies were impartial. It mattered not the slightest that the bodies here had been the victims of mass murder. The flies would have performed in just this way for the unburied dead of any community. Doubtless it was like this on hot afternoons during the Great Plague.

At first, we did not use the word massacre. We said very little because the flies would move unerringly for our mouths. We held handkerchiefs over our mouths for this reason, then we clasped the material to our noses as well because the flies moved over our faces. If the smell of the dead in Sidon was nauseating, the stench in

Chatila made us retch. Through the thickest of handkerchiefs, we smelled them. After some minutes, *we* began to smell of the dead.

They were everywhere, in the road, in laneways, in back yards and broken rooms, beneath crumpled masonry and across the top of garbage tips. The murderers – the Christian militiamen whom Israel had let into the camps to 'flush out terrorists' – had only just left. In some cases, the blood was still wet on the ground. When we had seen a hundred bodies, we stopped counting. Down every alleyway, there were corpses – women, young men, babies and grandparents – lying together in lazy and terrible profusion where they had been knifed or machine-gunned to death. Each corridor through the rubble produced more bodies. The patients at a Palestinian hospital had disappeared after gunmen ordered the doctors to leave. Everywhere, we found signs of hastily dug mass graves. Perhaps 1,000 people were butchered; probably half that number again.

Even while we were there, amid the evidence of such savagery, we could see the Israelis watching us. From the top of the tower block to the west – the second building on the Avenue Camille Chamoun – we could see them staring at us through field-glasses, scanning back and forth across the streets of corpses, the lenses of the binoculars some-times flashing in the sun as their gaze ranged through the camp. Loren Jenkins[1] cursed a lot. I thought it was probably his way of controlling his feelings of nausea amid this terrible smell. All of us wanted to vomit. We were *breathing* death, inhaling the very putrescence of the bloated corpses around us. Jenkins immediately realised that the Israeli defence minister would have to bear some responsibility for this horror. '*Sharon!*' he shouted. 'That fucker Sharon! This is Deir Yassin[2] all over again.'

What we found inside the Palestinian Chatila camp at ten o'clock on the morning of 18 September 1982 did not quite beggar descrip-tion, although it would have been easier to retell in the cold prose of a medical examination. There had been massacres before in Lebanon, but rarely on this scale and never overlooked by a regular, suppos-edly disciplined army. In the panic and hatred of battle, tens of thou-sands had been killed in this country. But these people, hundreds of them, had been shot down unarmed. This was a mass killing, an inci-dent – how easily we used the word 'incident' in Lebanon – that was

[1] Correspondent for the *Washington Post*.
[2] Village in Palestine where members of the Jewish paramilitary organisation Irgun massacred 250 Arabs, half of them women and children, in April 1948.

also an atrocity. It went beyond even what the Israelis would have in other circumstances called a *terrorist* atrocity. It was a war crime.

Jenkins and Tveit[3] and I were so overwhelmed by what we found in Chatila that at first we were unable to register our own shock. Bill Foley of AP had come with us. All he could say as he walked round was 'Jesus Christ!' over and over again. We might have accepted evidence of a few murders; even dozens of bodies, killed in the heat of combat. But there were women lying in houses with their skirts torn up to their waists and their legs wide apart, children with their throats cut, rows of young men shot in the back after being lined up at an execution wall. There were babies – blackened babies because they had been slaughtered more than twenty-four hours earlier and their small bodies were already in a state of decomposition – tossed into rubbish heaps alongside discarded US Army ration tins, Israeli Army medical equipment and empty bottles of whisky.

Where were the murderers? Or, to use the Israelis' vocabulary, where were the 'terrorists'? When we drove down to Chatila, we had seen the Israelis on the top of the apartments in the Avenue Camille Chamoun but they made no attempt to stop us. In fact, we had first driven to the Bourj al-Barajneh camp because someone told us that there was a massacre there. All we saw was a Lebanese soldier chasing a car thief down a street. It was only when we were driving back past the entrance to Chatila that Jenkins decided to stop the car. 'I don't like this,' he said. 'Where is everyone? What the fuck is that smell?'

Just inside the southern entrance to the camp, there used to be a number of single-storey concrete-walled houses. I had conducted many interviews inside these hovels in the late 1970s. When we walked across the muddy entrance of Chatila, we found that these buildings had all been dynamited to the ground. There were cartridge cases across the main road. I saw several Israeli flare canisters, still attached to their tiny parachutes. Clouds of flies moved across the rubble, raiding parties with a nose for victory.

Down a laneway to our right, no more than fifty yards from the entrance, there lay a pile of corpses. There were more than a dozen of them, young men whose arms and legs had been wrapped around each other in the agony of death. All had been shot at point-blank range through the cheek, the bullet tearing away a line of flesh up to the ear and entering the brain. Some had vivid crimson or black scars

---

[3] Karsten Tveit of Norwegian radio.

down the left side of their throats. One had been castrated, his trousers torn open and a settlement of flies throbbing over his torn intestines.

The eyes of these young men were all open. The youngest was only twelve or thirteen years old. They were dressed in jeans and coloured shirts, the material absurdly tight over their flesh now that their bodies had begun to bloat in the heat. They had not been robbed. On one blackened wrist, a Swiss watch recorded the correct time, the second hand still ticking round uselessly, expending the last energies of its dead owner.

On the other side of the main road, up a track through the debris, we found the bodies of five women and several children. The women were middle-aged and their corpses lay draped over a pile of rubble. One lay on her back, her dress torn open and the head of a little girl emerging from behind her. The girl had short, dark curly hair, her eyes were staring at us and there was a frown on her face. She was dead.

Another child lay on the roadway like a discarded doll, her white dress stained with mud and dust. She could have been no more than three years old. The back of her head had been blown away by a bullet fired into her brain. One of the women also held a tiny baby to her body. The bullet that had passed through her breast had killed the baby too. Someone had slit open the woman's stomach, cutting sideways and then upwards, perhaps trying to kill her unborn child. Her eyes were wide open, her dark face frozen in horror.

Tveit tried to record all this on tape, speaking slowly and unemotionally in Norwegian. 'I have come to another body, that of a woman and her baby. They are dead. There are three other women. They are dead . . .' From time to time, he would snap the 'pause' button and lean over to be sick, retching over the muck on the road. Foley and Jenkins and I explored one narrow avenue and heard the sound of a tracked vehicle. 'They're still here,' Jenkins said and looked hard at me. They were still there. The murderers were still there, in the camp. Foley's first concern was that the Christian militiamen might take his film, the only evidence – so far as he knew – of what had happened. He ran off down the laneway.

Jenkins and I had darker fears. If the murderers were still in the camp, it was the witnesses rather than the photographic evidence that they would wish to destroy. We saw a brown metal gate ajar; we pushed it open and ran into the yard, closing it quickly behind us. We heard the vehicle approaching down a neighbouring road, its tracks clanking against pieces of concrete. Jenkins and I looked at each other in fear and then knew that we were not alone. We *felt* the presence of another human. She lay just beside us, a young, pretty woman lying on her back.

She lay there as if she was sunbathing in the heat, and the blood running from her back was still wet. The murderers had just left. She just lay there, feet together, arms outspread, as if she had seen her saviour. Her face was peaceful, eyes closed, a beautiful woman whose head was now granted a strange halo. For a clothes line hung above her and there were children's trousers and some socks pegged to the line. Other clothes lay scattered on the ground. She must have been hanging out her family's clothes when the murderers came. As she fell, the clothes pegs in her hand sprayed over the yard and formed a small wooden circle round her head.

Only the insignificant hole in her breast and the growing stain across the yard told of her death. Even the flies had not yet found her. I thought Jenkins was praying but he was just cursing again and muttering 'Dear God' in between the curses. I felt so sorry for this woman. Perhaps it was easier to feel pity for someone so young, so innocent, someone whose body had not yet begun to rot. I kept looking at her face, the neat way she lay beneath the clothes line, almost expecting her to open her eyes.

She must have hidden in her home when she heard the shooting in the camp. She must have escaped the attention of the Israeli-backed gunmen until that very morning. She had walked into her yard, heard no shooting, assumed the trouble was over and gone about her daily chores. She could not have known what had happened. Then the yard door must have opened, as quickly as we had just opened it, and the murderers would have walked in and killed her. Just like that. They had left and we had arrived, perhaps only a minute or two later.

We stayed in the yard for several more minutes. Jenkins and I were very frightened. Like Tveit, who had temporarily disappeared, he was a survivor. I felt safe with Jenkins. The militiamen – the murderers of this girl – had raped and knifed the women in Chatila and shot the men but I rather suspected they would hesitate to kill Jenkins, an American who would try to talk them down. 'Let's get out of here,' he said, and we left. He peered into the street first, I followed, closing the door very slowly because I did not want to disturb the sleeping, dead woman with her halo of clothes pegs.

Foley was back in the street near the entrance to the camp. The tracked vehicle had gone, although I could still hear it moving on the main road outside, moving up towards the Israelis who were still watching us. Jenkins heard Tveit calling from behind a pile of bodies and I lost sight of him. We kept losing sight of each other behind piles of corpses. At one moment I would be talking to Jenkins, at the next I would turn to find that I was addressing a young man, bent backwards over the pillar of a house, his arms hanging behind his head.

I could hear Jenkins and Tveit perhaps a hundred yards away, on the other side of a high barricade covered with earth and sand that had been newly erected by a bulldozer. It was perhaps twelve feet high and I climbed with difficulty up one side of it, my feet slipping in the muck. Near the top, I lost my balance and for support grabbed a hunk of dark red stone that protruded from the earth. But it was no stone. It was clammy and hot and it stuck to my hand and when I looked down I saw that I was holding a human elbow that protruded, a triangle of flesh and bone, from the earth.

I let go of it in horror, wiping the dead flesh on my trousers, and staggered the last few feet to the top of the barricade. But the smell was appalling and at my feet a face was looking at me with half its mouth missing. A bullet or a knife had torn it away and what was left of the mouth was a nest of flies. I tried not to look at it. I could see, in the distance, Jenkins and Tveit standing by some more corpses in front of a wall but I could not shout to them for help because I knew I would be sick if I opened my mouth.

I walked on the top of the barricade, looking desperately for a place from which to jump all the way to the ground on the other side. But each time I took a step, the earth moved up towards me. The whole embankment of muck shifted and vibrated with my weight in a dreadful, springy way and, when I looked down again, I saw that the sand was only a light covering over more limbs and faces. A large stone turned out to be a stomach. I could see a man's head, a woman's naked breast, the feet of a child. I was walking on dozens of corpses which were moving beneath my feet.

The bodies had been buried by someone in panic. They had been bulldozed to the side of the laneway. Indeed, when I looked up, I could see a bulldozer – its driver's seat empty – standing guiltily just down the road.

I tried hard but vainly not to tread on the faces beneath me. We all of us felt a traditional respect for the dead, even here, now. I kept telling myself that these monstrous cadavers were not enemies, that these dead people would approve of my being here, would want Tveit and Jenkins and me to see all this and that therefore I should not be frightened. But I had never seen so many corpses before.

I jumped to the ground and ran towards Jenkins and Tveit. I think I was whimpering in a silly way because Jenkins looked around, surprised. But the moment I opened my mouth to speak, flies entered it. I spat them out. Tveit was being sick. He had been staring at what might have been sacks in front of a low stone wall. They formed a line, young men and boys, lying prostrate. They had been executed, shot in the back against the wall and they lay, at once pathetic and terrible, where they had fallen.

This wall and its huddle of corpses were reminiscent of something we had all seen before. Only afterwards did we realise how similar it was to those old photographs of executions in occupied Europe during the Second World War. There may have been twelve or twenty bodies there. Some lay beneath others. When I leaned down to look at them closely, I noticed the same dark scar on the left side of their throats. The murderers must have marked their prisoners for execution in this way. Cut a throat with a knife and it meant the man was doomed, a 'terrorist' to be executed at once.

As we stood there, we heard a shout in Arabic from across the ruins. 'They are coming back,' a man was screaming. So we ran in fear towards the road. I think, in retrospect, that it was probably anger that stopped us leaving, for we now waited near the entrance to the camp to glimpse the faces of the men who were responsible for all this. They must have been sent in here with Israeli permission. They must have been armed by the Israelis. Their handiwork had clearly been watched – closely observed – by the Israelis, by those same Israelis who were still watching us through their field-glasses.

Another armoured vehicle could be heard moving behind a wall to the west – perhaps it was Phalangist,[4] perhaps Israeli – but no one appeared. So we walked on. It was always the same. Inside the ruins of the Chatila hovels, families had retreated to their bedrooms when the militiamen came through the front door and there they lay, slumped

[4] Modelled on the German and Italian Fascist parties, the right-wing Phalange Party was formed by Pierre Gemayel in the 1930s to represent Lebanon's Maronite Christian community. As part of the Christian Lebanese Front, the Phalange militia fought the Muslim Lebanese National Movement in the civil war that erupted in 1975.

over the beds, pushed beneath chairs, hurled over cooking pots. Many
of the women here had been raped, their clothes lying across the floor,
their naked bodies thrown on top of their husbands or brothers, all
now dark with death.

There was another laneway deeper inside the camp where another
bulldozer had left its tracks in the mud. We followed these tracks
until we came to a hundred square yards of newly ploughed earth.
Flies carpeted the ground and there again was that familiar, fine, sweet
terrible smell. We looked at this place, all of us suspecting what was
indeed the truth, that this was a hastily dug mass grave. We noticed
that our shoes began to sink into the soft earth, that it had a liquid,
almost watery quality to it, and we stepped back in terror towards
the track.

A Norwegian diplomat had driven down the road outside a few
hours earlier and had seen a bulldozer with a dozen corpses in its scoop,
arms and legs swaying from the vehicle's iron bucket. Who had dug
this earth over with such efficiency? Who drove the bulldozer? There
was only one certainty: that the Israelis knew the answer, that they had
watched it happen, that their allies – Phalangists or Haddad militiamen[5]
– had been sent into Chatila and had committed this act of mass murder.
Here was the gravest act of terrorism – the largest in scale and time
carried out by individuals who could see and touch the innocent people
they were murdering – in the recent history of the Middle East.

There were, remarkably, survivors. Three small children called to
us from a roof to say they had hidden while the massacre took place.
Some weeping women shouted at us that their men had been killed.
All said Haddad's men and the Phalange were responsible and gave
accurate descriptions of the different cedar tree badges of the two
militias.

There were more bodies on the main road. 'That was my neighbour,
Mr Nouri,' a woman shouted at me. 'He was ninety.' And there in
a pile of garbage on the pavement beside her lay a very old man with
a thin grey beard, a small woollen hat still on his head. Another old
man lay by his front door in his pyjamas, slaughtered as he ran for
safety a few hours earlier. Incredibly, there were dead horses, three
of them, big white stallions which had been machine-gunned to death
beside a hovel, one of them with its hoof on a wall, trying to leap
to safety as the militiamen shot it.

---

[5] Major Saad Haddad, leader of the pro-Israeli 'South Lebanon Army' militia.

There had been fighting inside the camp. The road near the Sabra mosque was slippery with cartridge cases and ammunition clips and some of the equipment was of the Soviet type used by the Palestinians. The few men here who still possessed weapons had tried to defend their families. Their stories would never be known. When did they realise that their people were being massacred? How could they fight with so few weapons? In the middle of the road outside the mosque, there lay a perfectly carved scale-model toy wooden Kalashnikov rifle, its barrel snapped in two.

We walked back and forth in the camp, on each journey finding more bodies, stuffed into ditches, thrown over walls, lined up and shot. We began to recognise the corpses that we had seen before. Up there is the woman with the little girl looking over her shoulder, there is Mr Nouri again, lying in the rubbish beside the road. On one occasion, I intentionally glanced at the woman with the child because I had half expected her to have moved, to have assumed a different position. The dead were becoming real to us.

Further north, in the Sabra section of the camp, women came up to us, crying with fear and appealing for help. Their men – sons, husbands, fathers – had been taken from their homes at the time of the massacre. A few had already been found at the execution walls but others were still missing. A Reuters correspondent had seen men being held under guard by Israeli troops in the ruins of the sports stadium. There were more journalists now, Lebanese newspaper photographers and diplomats. We found two Swiss delegates from the International Red Cross and told them where we had found mass graves. Swedish radio's correspondent was in the camp.

We found hundreds of the missing men in the stadium, just as the Reuters man had said. They were Lebanese for the most part – Lebanese as well as Palestinians lived in Sabra – and they were being taken away for 'interrogation' by militiamen. The whole western side of the ruined sports stadium was guarded by uniformed Israeli troops together with plain-clothes Shin Bet intelligence operatives, big, heavy-set men wearing Ray-Bans with Uzi machine-guns in their hands. There were also militiamen there, three of whom I saw leading a frightened man away from the stadium. The Israelis let them do this. They had agreed to this procedure. The Israelis themselves explained to us that this was a search for 'terrorists'. Terrorists.

The very word 'terrorists' now sounded obscene. It had become a murderous word, a word that had helped to bring about this atrocity.

Jenkins and I saw hundreds of prisoners, squatting on their heels or lying in the dust beneath the stadium wall. I walked across to them, ignoring the Israelis who obviously thought that Jenkins and I were Shin Bet. I walked right into one of the underground stadium rooms which was being used as a cell. 'Help us,' one man said. An Israeli soldier appeared. Press, I said. 'Get out of here, these men are terrorists.'

But they were not. A few yards away, the Reuters correspondent found his own telex operator – a Lebanese man whose home was on Corniche Mazraa – sitting in one of the cells. We found an Israeli officer. He was a *Tat Aluf*, a colonel. We told him we had found the Reuters telex operator. He had to be released. After much pleading, the man was given to us. The British Reuters reporter led him away, an arm around his shoulders.

I walked into another of the 'cells'. 'They take us away, one by one, for interrogation,' one of the prisoners said. 'They are Haddad men. Usually they bring the people back after interrogation but not always. Sometimes the people do not return.' Another Israeli colonel appeared, pointed at me and ordered me to leave. I wanted to go on talking. The prisoners were silent. Why could they not talk? 'They can talk if they want,' the Israeli colonel said. 'But they have nothing to say.'

The nearest bodies lay only 500 yards away. The stench of the corpses filled the air where these Israeli soldiers and Shin Bet men were standing. But they were still talking about 'terrorists'. It was surreal, grotesque. Jenkins found an officer whom he recognised. 'These people are being held here for questioning – they are terrorist suspects,' the Israeli was saying. It was irrelevant. Excuse me, excuse me for one moment, I asked, but what has been happening here? There are bodies everywhere, just over there – I pointed to the side of the stadium – there are piles of them. 'I don't know about that.' But you can *smell* them. 'I'm sorry, I have no information.'

I turned to the soldier. He was a tall man with short dark hair and a tanned complexion, well-built, slightly plump. Look, I said, forgive me for saying it like this, but there are scenes in there that look like something out of Treblinka. It was the first comparison I could think of to what I had just witnessed. I had not said 'Treblinka' because Jews were murdered there. Treblinka was an extermination camp. The Israeli looked at me without emotion.

I was trying to make him understand the enormity of what had happened, that this was not just a small excess but a massacre perpetrated by Israel's allies under Israel's eyes. I was trying to make him

understand. Could he not *smell* the air? I asked him that. The Israeli
should have argued with me. He could at least have pointed out –
correctly – that there was no comparison in scale between what had
happened in Chatila and what happened in Treblinka. But he did not.
He had to pretend that he did not know what was in Chatila.

Jenkins was angry. 'Why don't you tell us what happened? There's
been mass murder here. What happened? Tell us. Did you let the
Christian militia in here yesterday?'

'I wasn't here yesterday. I only arrived this morning.'

Jenkins' eyes narrowed and he stepped back in fury. 'You're lying,'
he said. 'You *were* here yesterday. I saw you. You stopped my fucking
car when I wanted to go to Chatila. I spoke to you yesterday. You *were*
here. You're lying.' The Israeli obviously remembered Jenkins. He held
up his hand. 'I thought you were asking me something different. I don't
remember. I have no idea what's been happening here.'

Along the main road, there was a line of Merkava tanks, their crews
sitting on the turrets, smoking, watching the men being led from the
stadium in ones and twos, some being set free, others being led away
by Shin Bet men or by Lebanese men in drab khaki overalls.

We walked back towards the camp. A Palestinian woman walked
up to me, smiling in a harsh, cruel way. 'Got some good pictures, have
you?' she asked. 'Got some good things to write? Is everything all
right for you? It's a nice day, isn't it?' I thought she was going to curse
me but she just kept up her controlled sarcasm. 'You press people take
good pictures. I hope everything is fine for you. Have a nice day here.'

Jenkins left to telex his office. Tveit drove to the Commodore Hotel
to use the telephone. I walked back through the camp with my handkerchief over my face, past Mr Nouri and the other old man, to the
left of the execution wall, below the barricade of corpses, the empty
bulldozer, the dead horses, the woman with the child looking over her
shoulder. Only when I was approaching the exit to Chatila, the track
that led onto the main road between the Kuwaiti embassy and Fakhani,
did I realise that I was the only living soul in this part of the camp.

There was a roaring of engines from the road and above the breeze-
block wall, beyond the trees, I could see an Israeli tank column. The
disembodied voice of an Israeli officer came floating through the trees
from a tannoy on an armoured personnel carrier. 'Stay off the streets,'
he ordered. 'We are only looking for terrorists. Stay off the streets.
We will shoot.'

This was more than grotesque. The Israelis were instructing the dead to stay off the streets. It was farcical, absurd, monstrous. I walked to the gate, my handkerchief still across my mouth and nose. The tank column was followed by two lines of Israeli infantry. They walked behind the camp wall and then, when they reached the entrance to Chatila, they sprinted across the opening, rifles at the ready, taking position at the other side, covering each other from the ghostly 'terrorists' inside.

I walked out into the street. 'Hey, you – get out of here.' A junior Israeli officer walked up to me. Press, I said. 'You are not permitted here. Get out of here.' I refused. I had simply seen too much. 'I'm ordering you to leave at once.' I just shook my head. I felt sick. My clothes stank. I smelled of dead people. But after what I had just seen, I was beyond obeying such instructions. And I was mesmerised by these soldiers. They were still running across the entrance to the camp to avoid the phantom 'terrorists'.

The officer walked up to me and glared in my face. There's no one there, I said. 'I've given you an order to leave here. Do as you're told,' the soldier shouted. You don't understand, I said. Everyone here is dead. They're all dead in there. There's no one there – only dead people. Three Israeli soldiers stood beside the officer, looking at me as if I was mad. I looked at the officer because I suspected he might himself be a little insane. No, I won't leave.

One of the three soldiers put his hand on my arm. 'There are terrorists in the camp and you will be killed.' That's not true, I said. Everyone there is dead. Can't you *smell* them? The soldier looked at me in disbelief. Really, I said, women and children have been murdered in there. There are dead babies. The officer waved his hand at me dismissively. 'You'll be killed,' he said, and walked away.

I began to feel like one of those characters in a mystery film who call the police to report a murder only to be accused of fabricating the story. Perhaps if I walked back into Chatila now, the bodies would be gone, the streets cleaned up, the hovels reconstructed, their dead owners cooking lunch or sleeping off the hot early afternoon in those back bedrooms. I went across to one of the lines of infantry that were approaching the entrance to the camp and walked along beside a tall, friendly-looking soldier.

What is going on? 'I don't know. I'm not allowed to talk to you.' No, seriously, what is going on? The man smiled. I could tell he wanted to be friendly. His uniform was dirty and he held his Galil assault rifle in his hands with ease, a professional soldier who was tired and needed friends. Everyone was dead in the camp, I said.

Women, children, all murdered. 'Why?' he asked. I was wondering if he knew. 'The Christians were there,' he said. Why? 'I don't know. It was nothing to do with me. I wasn't there.' We had come to the camp gate. He crouched down.

Even this likeable, friendly man was now ready to go into action against the ghosts. I walked into the entrance of Chatila, standing upright in the centre of the road. How obsessed were these young men? To my astonishment, they too began to crouch at one side of the entrance and then to run to the other side, a distance of perhaps thirty feet, bent double, scuttling past my feet with their rifles pointed into the camp. I thought they were mad. They, of course, thought I was mad. They believed – they were possessed of an absolute certainty and conviction – that 'terrorists' were in Chatila.

How could I explain to them that the terrorists had left, that the terrorists had worn Israeli uniforms, that the terrorists had been sent into Chatila by Israeli officers, that the victims of the terrorists were not Israelis but Palestinians and Lebanese? I tried. I walked alongside these soldiers and told them I was a journalist and asked their names. After some minutes, they grew used to my presence. So I met Moshe, Raphael, Benny, all carrying their heavy rifles down the road past Chatila, all fearful of terrorists. Terrorists, terrorists, terrorists. The word came up in every sentence, like a punctuation mark. It was as if no statement, no belief could be expressed without the presence of terrorists.

The AP computer line began functioning again at midday on Sunday. I filed a long dispatch to *The Times* on everything I had seen in Sabra and Chatila, on the Christian militias which were allied to Israel, on the ignominious withdrawal of Israeli troops from the perimeter of the camps, the collapse of Israel's 'law and order' mission to west Beirut. The Israelis now started blaming the Americans.

For once, just briefly, Palestinians and Israelis could share a common policy. Both blamed the United States. The Palestinians could at least do so with some justice. The PLO had been told by Philip Habib[6] that the Israelis would not enter west Beirut if the guerrillas left. The US Marines had left early – after only seventeen days in Beirut – and America's promise had been broken when the Israelis invaded west Beirut. So much for the guarantees.

Arafat was in Damascus when he was shown the video-tape of the

[6] US President Reagan's special envoy to Lebanon.

bodies. He said that Philip Habib had personally signed a piece of paper guaranteeing protection to the Palestinians who remained in west Beirut. He was right.

In the autumn of 1987, Habib admitted that Arafat was correct. 'What Arafat said is absolutely true,' he said. 'He was absolutely telling the truth. I signed this paper which guaranteed that these people [the Palestinians] in west Beirut would not be harmed. I got specific guarantees on this from Bashir and from the Israelis – from Sharon. I was sitting on my *terrasse* overlooking San Francisco Bay when I heard what happened. I was phoned about it. I called the president. I don't remember what I said or what the president said. What happened has never been a source of comfort to me. No, I didn't communicate with Arafat afterwards. I didn't need to. The Palestianians knew what I thought.'

The Palestinians principally blamed the Israelis, and not without reason. It was Israel which sent the murderers into the camps. But the Israeli authorities immediately blamed America. No less a figure than General Rafael Eitan, the Israeli chief of staff, held a hurried news conference near the sports stadium where he accused Morris Draper, the American deputy assistant secretary of state for Near Eastern Affairs, of refusing to establish contact between the Israeli and Lebanese armies. Because the Americans would not facilitate talks between the Israelis and the Lebanese, the Israelis had been unable to ask the Lebanese army to enter west Beirut after Bashir Gemayel's death[7] and thus had to get the Christian militias to do the job.

Even if anyone had taken this argument seriously, they could scarcely have overlooked the fact that the Israelis had commandeered numerous Lebanese army barracks over the previous three weeks and were therefore in rather intimate contact with the Lebanese military authorities without any help from the Americans. Indeed, Lebanese troops almost always saluted Israeli soldiers when the Israelis passed through their checkpoints.

Yes, the Israelis *knew*. By now some of the Israeli soldiers who were around Chatila – decent, honest men who could not accept the things

[7] Bashir Gemayel, leader of the Phalange militia, was elected as Lebanon's next president after the Israeli invasion in August 1982, but was assassinated two weeks later.

which they had heard about or even witnessed – had been telling journalists, in confidence, that yes, they knew what was going on. In some cases, they admitted, they *saw* the killings. But they did nothing. It transpired that at 7.30 on the morning of Friday, 17 September, Ze'ev Schiff, the military correspondent of the Israeli newspaper *Ha'aretz*, heard a report from a source in the Israeli army general staff in Tel Aviv that there was 'a slaughter' going on in the camps. He reported this to Mordechai Zippori, the Israeli minister of communications, who was an old friend of Schiff's. Zippori called Yitzhak Shamir, the Israeli foreign minister. Shamir did not act upon the call and never asked his staff to check the report of a massacre. But why did not Schiff at least call his colleagues in Beirut? If the international press corps in west Beirut could have been alerted to the massacre on the *Friday* morning – instead of discovering it for themselves on Saturday morning – then perhaps the killings could have been stopped. But Schiff chose instead to go to his friend, the Israeli minister. So even the Israeli press failed in their responsibilities at this critical moment.

But Schiff did not actually *see* the massacres taking place. He could not be certain that the report was true. Other Israelis were *watching* the slaughter take place, some of them from beside the sports stadium, from the very positions which the Israelis used to watch us as we walked among the corpses on the Saturday morning.

One such man was Lieutenant Avi Grabowski, the deputy commander of the Israeli army tank company who subsequently testified to the Israeli commission of inquiry into the massacre that he had witnessed the murder of five women and children. Between eight and nine o'clock on the Friday morning, according to the commission's final report, he saw two Phalangists hitting two young men in Chatila camp. 'The soldiers [*sic*] led the men back into the camp, after a short time he [Grabowski] heard a few shots and saw the two Phalangist soldiers coming out. At a later hour he . . . saw that Phalangist soldiers had killed a group of five women and children.' The commission report went on to relate how:

Lieutenant Grabowski wanted to report the event by communications sent to his superiors, but the tank crew told him that they had already heard a communications report to the battalion commander that civilians were being killed, [and] the battalion commander had replied, 'We know, it's not to our liking, and

272 *TELL ME NO LIES*

don't interfere.' Lieutenant Grabowski saw another case in which
a Phalangist killed a civilian.

In his evidence to the commission, Grabowski related how at noon
on the Friday, his tank crew had asked a Phalangist why they were
killing civilians. The Phalangist had replied: 'Pregnant women will give
birth to terrorists; the children when they grow up will be terrorists.'
Amid the protestations of moral decency that had become part of
the Israeli Army's propaganda defences, something had come adrift,
something that was both dangerous and obsessive. What was it that
Israeli lieutenant had told me on the hills above Beirut on 16 June? 'I
would like to see them all dead . . . I would like to see all the Palestinians
dead because they are a sickness wherever they go . . . Personally, I
don't think our government would take the responsibility of massacring
a lot of Palestinians.' He was right. Journalists who pointed out, with
factual accuracy, that as an occupier, Israel was responsible for what
went on inside the camps, were accused by Begin's government in
Jerusalem of committing a 'blood libel' against Jews. 'No one will
preach to us moral values or respect for human life, on whose basis
we were educated and will continue to educate generations of fighters
in Israel,' the Israeli Government portentously announced.
But Israeli moral values *were* at issue in this mass murder. The
Israelis had watched their allies massacre innocents and had done
nothing to prevent the atrocity. The Israelis would not have acted in
so disgraceful a manner had the victims been Israeli civilians rather
than Palestinians. Israel's 'respect' for human life evidently differen-
tiated between the human life of Israelis and Palestinians. The former
was sacrosanct. The latter expendable. The Palestinians whom that
Israeli lieutenant had wished to see 'all dead' had indeed been
murdered; the Israelis watched the cull through field-glasses – and
did nothing. To them, the Palestinians were 'terrorists'.
Even the Kahan commission's 1983 report[8] was a victim of Israel's
savage obsession with 'terrorism'. The Israelis portrayed the document as powerful evidence that their democracy still shone like a
beacon over the dictatorships of other Middle Eastern states. What

[8] *The Commission of Inquiry into the Events at the Refugee Camps in Beirut*,
1983, final report by Yitzhak Kahan, President of the Israeli Supreme Court,
Aharon Barak, Justice of the Supreme Court, and Yona Efrat, Reserve Major-
General, Israeli Defence Force. [Author's footnote.]

Arab nation had ever published a report of this kind, a condemnation of both its army and its leaders? Where was the PLO's report into intimidation in southern Lebanon? Where was President Assad's report on the massacres at Hama in 1982?

But the Kahan commission report was a flawed document. The title of the inquiry – into 'the events at the refugee camps ...' – managed to avoid the fatal, politically embarrassing word 'Palestinian'. Was this not in fact an inquiry into 'the events at the *Palestinian* refugee camps'? But that is not what it said. And why did the commission use the word 'events' when it meant 'massacre'?

There were repeated references in the commission's final report to Palestinian 'terrorists' in the camps – presumably the 2,000 strangely elusive and undiscovered 'terrorists' of whom Sharon had spoken in early September 1982 – but the judges provided not a single piece of evidence to substantiate the allegation that these 'terrorists' existed. Indeed, the only real terrorists in the camps – the Christian militiamen who were sent there by the Israelis – were respectfully described by the judges as Phalangists, or 'soldiers'. *Soldiers.*

Three foreign doctors, one of them Jewish, who had Palestinian sympathies and witnessed the start of the massacre, were rightly described by the commission as having no 'special sympathy for Israel'. Yet the evidence of Israelis – who could have had no 'special sympathy' for the Palestinians – was largely accepted at face value. Even the evidence of Haddad, whose cruel militia had taken dozens of innocent lives in southern Lebanon – including the murder of UN soldiers – was treated with respect. While the commission could not rule out 'the possibility ... that one [*sic*] of the men from Major Haddad's forces infiltrated into the camps', the judges nonetheless decided that 'no responsibility, either direct or indirect, is to be imputed to the commanders of Major Haddad's forces.' The commission did not point out that the 'commanders' of Haddad's militia were Israelis.

Begin, Sharon, Eitan, Drori and other Israeli officers were condemned with varying degrees of harshness. The commission wisely decided that it was 'unable to accept the position of the Prime Minister that no one imagined that what happened was liable to happen'; the judges could not accept that Begin was 'absolutely unaware' of the danger of a massacre if the Phalangists were sent into the camps.

Indeed not. Was this not, after all, the same Begin who had lectured the Irish ambassador to Israel on the principles of the Lebanese blood feud after the murder of the two Irish UN soldiers, Smallhorn and

Barrett, in 1978? This was not something the judges chose to recall.

The Kahan commission concluded that Sharon bore 'personal responsibility' for what happened in the camps and suggested that Begin remove him from office. It recommended that Major-General Yehoshua Saguy, the director of military intelligence, be fired, and it fixed considerable blame upon Drori 'without recourse to any further recommendation'.

Yet the Kahan report failed to address two intrinsically important factors in the massacre: the obsession with 'terrorism' and the extraordinary influence of the Second World War upon Begin and the actions of the Israelis during the Lebanon war. Even after the horror of Chatila, in the immediate aftermath of the massacre, it was clear that the Israelis had not learned their lesson. Until they left west Beirut, they would fire flares over the city every evening at seven o'clock. A cold yellow glow would bathe the buildings, the slums, ruins and Palestinian camps. A Hebrew voice over a crackling radio in a blacked-out street would issue orders to lonely, frightened soldiers. The Israelis were hunting for 'terrorists' again.

The real terrorists turned out to be Israel's Christian allies. Israel had armed them, paid them, uniformed them, in some cases fed them. They were Israel's creatures. Referring to Jewish suffering abroad, the Kahan commission had itself stated that 'the Jewish public's stand has always been that the responsibility for such deeds falls not only on those who . . . committed atrocities, but also on those who were responsible for safety and public order, who could have prevented the disturbances and did not fulfil their obligations in this respect.' The Israeli units around Chatila had not understood this. They were blind to it. They had forgotten the basic rule which all foreign armies invading Lebanon are forced to learn: that by making friends with one group of terrorists, you become a terrorist yourself.

Yet this still did not account for what happened at Chatila. The nature of Bashir Gemayel's militia leadership was there for all to see. His ascension to the presidency, so brutally cut short in September, was ominous. As early as June, Professor Yussef Ibish had compared Gemayel's putative rule with that of General Franco – 'With malice to all and charity to none, he will rule this place,' Ibish had said – and had predicted that the Israelis would use 'lists of names' which they would use in mass arrests and killings. 'They are going to shoot them – it is going to be a huge Tel al-Za'atar,' he said, referring to the Phalangist massacre of Palestinians in 1976. The man who did lead the Phalange into Chatila – Elie Hobeika – had once lived in Damour. His family were among those murdered there by the Palestinians. His fiancée was among the women butchered by the Palestinians in the town.

But the Israelis reserved the word 'terrorism' exclusively for their enemies, not their Phalangist friends, as the Kahan report demonstrated all too revealingly. Uri Avneri, the liberal Israeli journalist who interviewed Arafat during the siege of west Beirut – Israeli Cabinet ministers later demanded that he should as a result be tried for treason – described the use of the term 'terrorists' as 'a media crime, an excuse for murder'. It was, he told me in Tel Aviv in 1986, 'a Nazi kind of method' to influence minds, 'a process of dehumanising people that was essential to prepare for war'.

For the Israelis – for Sharon and Begin and their soldiers – 'terrorist' did not have the same connotation as it does elsewhere. In Europe and America, in many Asian countries, even in the Soviet Union, the word 'terrorism' evokes images of hijackings, bombs planted in restaurants or schools or airports, the murder of civilians on planes, buses, trains or ships. But in Israel, 'terrorist' means all Palestinian Arabs – and very often, all *Arabs* – who oppose Israel in word or deed. Loren Jenkins used to refer to 'the careless depreciation of meaning' that the Israelis imposed on the word, claiming that this distorted the reality of terrorism. But it was not 'careless'. It was deliberate. Like the Syrians, the Soviets, the Americans and the British, the Israelis drew a careful distinction between good terrorists and bad terrorists. In Israel's case, the former were sympathetic to Israel and were graced with various, less harmful epithets – 'militiamen', 'fighters', 'soldiers' – while the latter opposed Israel and were therefore terrorists pure and simple, guilty of the most heinous crimes, blood-soaked and mindless, the sort of people who should be 'cleansed' from society.

By labelling Palestinians as terrorists, the Israelis were describing their enemies as evil rather than hostile. If the Palestinians could be portrayed as mindless barbarians, surely no sane individual would dare regard their political claims as serious. Anyone who expressed sympathy for the Palestinians was evidently anti-Semitic – and therefore not just anti-Israeli or anti-Jewish, but pro-Nazi – which no right-thinking individual would wish to be. Anyone who even suggested that the Israelis might be wrong in their war against the Palestinians could be castigated in the same way. Do you think Hitler was right?

Do you agree with what happened at Auschwitz? No, of course not. If Israel called the PLO its enemy, then the Middle East dispute involved two hostile parties. But if the world believed that the Palestinians were *evil* – that they represented sin in its crudest form – then the dispute did not exist. The battle was between right and wrong, David and Goliath, Israel and the 'terrorists'. The tragedy of the Israelis was that they came to believe this myth.

The Israelis left west Beirut without warning or fanfare on 26 September 1982, driving their tanks out of town at speed, like an army that had done wrong and knew it. Even the Lebanese troops who had taken up position around the wreckage of Chatila had been unprepared for so hurried a departure. Many of the Israelis had moved out before dawn, driving their armour along the Corniche towards the port in the half-light. By nightfall, on the eve of Yom Kippur – a name that was once synonymous with Israeli military achievement – the Israelis had nearly all gone.

On the streets in their place stood the diminutive armoured vehicles of the Lebanese Army and a few truckloads of French paratroopers. For the multinational force had returned to the city, sent back by nations with a guilty conscience. The Americans, French and Italians understood that responsibility for the massacre touched them too. The French soldiers could even be seen, briefly, in Chatila, walking around the rubble, searching for mines, surgical masks over their faces to shield them from the stench of decomposition.

Tveit and I continued our inquiries. We questioned the survivors again. We heard strange stories. Foley was told that an Israeli photographer believed one of the massacre victims had been a Jewish Holocaust survivor from Auschwitz. Could it be true? The woman had travelled to Palestine with other Jewish immigrants in 1946, the tale went, but had married an Arab, travelling into exile with him in 1948 and eventually settling in the slums of Chatila. Someone, so the story had it, had seen her Auschwitz number tattooed on her wrist. The Phalangists had taken her away on 17 September, shot her and thrown her in a mass grave. Foley did not see the photographer again. We could never confirm the story.

In the years after the massacre, we would return to the camp at each anniversary to talk to the survivors. Some would tell us that the

Israelis were in the camp with the Phalange during the killing. Many elderly Palestinians can understand and speak Hebrew and claim that they talked in Hebrew to Israelis during the massacre. So were the Israelis in the camp?

As the years passed, there was more killing and destruction at Chatila. Shells would fall on the final mass grave of the hundreds of 1982 victims.

Scheherezade Faramarzi, AP's Iranian reporter, had formed a friendship with several Palestinian women and she would talk to them for hours about their memories, forcing them to repeat their experiences over and over to see if there was some detail, some minute fact that we had overlooked.

September 1984. Sawssan, aged fourteen: 'My wish is for a Phalange to come here so I could kill him with a knife and take my revenge. The *Kata'ib* [Phalange] killed my three brothers, my grandfather, my two uncles.' Amneh Shehadeh, aged forty, born at Khasayer near Haifa: 'I wish I had seen the body of my son. I wish I had seen him dead and I wish I knew who killed him so I could commit this crime against his murderer. There were Jews here too. They had more mercy than the *Kata'ib*. If it hadn't been for the Jews who came in here, all the women, girls and children would have been killed. One Jew was here, yes, at the massacre, and he said: "Come on, come on *madame, madame*, baby this way." There was a *Kata'ib* man there with a mask and holes in it showing his eyes.'

The women spoke in a wail that turned to shrieks when they approached the moment of personal catastrophe. Um Hussein, aged thirty-six. Her husband Hamid Mustafa Khalifeh, aged thirty-nine, was killed in the massacre. So were two of her sons. She has eight surviving children to care for. She has fine features and smiles at us when she speaks, as if to protect us from her own story.

Some people have pity for me and help me but it is difficult to accustom myself to this new life where I have nothing left. I am used to being treated like a lady, to be taken here and there, to have the door opened for me. Now my wings have been broken, shattered. My husband and the two boys were my columns, my support. You might say my house has collapsed. When I see people happy, I am sad. My son Mohamed keeps on calling for his father. He waits for him at the gate or at the window and stretches out his hands . . . I am worn out, my hands tremble.

I cannot work at home, can't clean up or sweep the house. I feel ever so lonely . . . I try to avoid passing the spot where they were killed. I remember how Hussein's head, his body were thrown here and there. I have even moved my house to avoid the place. Every Monday and Thursday, I go to the graveyard to pray over their souls. I go whenever their faces come into my mind. It happened on the Thursday afternoon, at six o'clock, the black day. They took them and killed them. I pray when I go to the graveyard. I take a tape-recording of the Koran and play it to them. I cry. I take flowers with me and throw them when I enter the graveyard. I don't know where my husband and my boys are lying. I wish I knew where they are buried so I could put up their pictures and build a marble stone for them and wash the marble every now and then. But I know they are there. So when I go to the graveyard, I just throw the flowers and hope they land on the right places.

1990

Another war on terror. Another proxy army. Another mysterious massacre. And now, after nineteen years, perhaps the truth at last . . .

Sana Sersawi speaks carefully, loudly but slowly, as she recalls the chaotic, dangerous, desperately tragic events that overwhelmed her just over nineteen years ago, on 18 September 1982. As one of the survivors prepared to testify against the Israeli prime minister Ariel Sharon – who was then Israel's defence minister – she stops to search her memory when she confronts the most terrible moments of her life. 'The Lebanese Forces militia [Phalangists] had taken us from our homes and marched us up to the entrance to the camp where a large hole had been dug in the earth. The men were told to get into it. Then the militiamen shot a Palestinian. The women and children had climbed over bodies to reach this spot, but we were truly shocked by seeing this man killed in front of us and there was a roar of shouting and screams from the women. That's when we heard the Israelis on loudspeakers shouting, "Give us the men, give us the men." We thought, "Thank God, they will save us."' It was to prove a cruelly false hope.

Mrs Sersawi, three months pregnant, saw her husband Hassan, thirty, and her Egyptian brother-in-law Faraj el-Sayed Ahmed standing in the crowd of men. 'We were told to walk up the road towards the Kuwaiti embassy, the women and children in front, the men behind. We had been separated. There were Phalangist militiamen and Israeli soldiers walking alongside us. I could still see Hassan and Faraj. It was like a parade. There were several hundred of us. When we got to the Cité Sportif, the Israelis put us women in a big concrete room and the men were taken to another side of the stadium. There were a lot of men from the camp and I could no longer see my husband. The Israelis went round saying "Sit, sit." It was 11 a.m. An hour later, we were told to leave. But we stood around outside amid the Israeli soldiers, waiting for our men.'

Sana Sersawi waited in the bright sweltering sun for Hassan and Faraj to emerge. 'Some men came out, none of them younger than forty, and they told us to be patient, that hundreds of men were still inside. Then about 4 p.m., an Israeli officer came out. He was wearing dark glasses and said in Arabic: "What are you all waiting for?" He said there was nobody left, that everyone had gone. There were Israeli trucks moving out with tarpaulin over them. We couldn't see inside. And there were jeeps and tanks and a bulldozer making a lot of noise. We stayed there as it got dark and the Israelis appeared to be leaving and we were very nervous. But then when the Israelis had moved away, we went inside. And there was no one there. Nobody. I had been only three years married. I never saw my husband again.'

Today, a Belgian appeals court will begin a hearing to decide if Prime Minister Sharon should be prosecuted for the massacre of Palestinian civilians at the Sabra and Chatila refugee camps in Beirut in 1982. (Belgian laws allow courts to try foreigners for war crimes committed on foreign soil.) In working on this case, the prosecution believes that it has discovered shocking new evidence of Israel's involvement.

The evidence centres on the Camille Chamoun Sports Stadium – the 'Cité Sportif'. Only two miles from Beirut airport, the damaged stadium was a natural holding centre for prisoners. It had been an ammunition dump for Yassir Arafat's PLO and repeatedly bombed by Israeli jets during the 1982 siege of Beirut so that its giant, smashed exterior looked like a nightmare denture. The Palestinians had earlier mined its cavernous interior, but its vast, underground storage space and athletics changing-rooms remained intact. It was a familiar landmark to all of us who lived in Beirut. At mid-morning on 18 September 1982 – about the time Sana Sersawi says she was brought to the stadium – I saw hundreds of Palestinian and Lebanese prisoners, probably well over 1,000, sitting in its gloomy, dark interior, squatting in the dust, watched over by Israeli soldiers and plain-clothes Shin Bet (Israeli secret service) agents and men who I suspected were Lebanese collaborators. The men sat in silence, obviously in fear. From time to time, I noted, a few were taken away. They were put into Israeli Army trucks or jeeps or Phalangist vehicles – for further 'interrogation'.

Nor did I doubt this. A few hundred metres away, inside the Sabra and Chatila Palestinian refugee camps, up to 600 massacre victims rotted in the sun, the stench of decomposition drifting over the prisoners and their captors alike. It was suffocatingly hot. Loren Jenkins of the *Washington Post*, Paul Eedle of Reuters and I had only got into the cells because the Israelis assumed – given our Western appearance – that we must have been members of Shin Bet. Many of the prisoners had their heads bowed. But Israel's Phalangist militamen – still raging at the murder of their leader and president-elect Bashir Gemayel – had been withdrawn from the camps, their slaughter over, and at least the Israeli Army was now in charge. So what did these men have to fear?

Looking back – and listening to Sana Sersawi today – I shudder now at our innocence. My notes of the time, subsequently written into a book about Israel's 1982 invasion and its war with the PLO, contain some ominous clues. We found a Lebanese employee of Reuters, Abdullah Mattar, among the prisoners and obtained his release, Paul leading him away with his arm around the man's shoulders. 'They take us away, one by one, for interrogation,' one of the prisoners muttered to me. 'They are Haddad [Christian militia] men. Usually they bring the people back after interrogation but not always. Sometimes the people do not return.' Then an Israeli officer ordered me to leave. Why couldn't the prisoners talk to me, I asked? 'They can talk if they want,' he replied. 'But they have nothing to say.'

All the Israelis knew what had happened inside the camps. The smell of the corpses was now overpowering. Outside, a Phalangist jeep with the words 'Military Police' painted on it – if so exotic an institution could be associated with this gang of murderers – drove by. A few television crews had turned up. One filmed the Lebanese Christian militiamen outside the Cité Sportif. He also filmed a woman pleading with an Israeli Army colonel called 'Yahya' for the release of her husband. (The colonel has now been positively identified by the *Independent*. Today, he is a general in the Israeli Army.)

Along the main road opposite the stadium there was a line of Israeli Merkava tanks, their crews sitting on the turrets, smoking, watching the men being led from the stadium in ones or twos, some being set free, others being led away by Shin Bet men or by Lebanese men in drab khaki overalls. All these soldiers knew what had happened inside the camps. One of the members of the tank crews, Lieutenant Avi Grabowski – he was later to testify to the Israeli Kahan commission – had even witnessed the murder of several civilians the previous day and had been told not to 'interfere'.

And in the days that followed, strange reports reached us. A girl had been dragged from a car in Damour by Phalangist militiamen and taken away, despite her appeals to a nearby Israeli soldier. Then the cleaning lady of a Lebanese woman who worked for a US television chain complained bitterly that Israelis had arrested her husband. He was never seen again. There were other vague rumours of 'disappeared' people.

I wrote in my notes at the time that 'even after Chatila, Israel's "terrorist" enemies were being liquidated in west Beirut'. But I had not directly associated this dark conviction with the Cité Sportif. I had not even reflected on the fearful precedents of a sports stadium in time of war. Hadn't there been a sports stadium in Santiago a few years before, packed with prisoners after Pinochet's *coup d'état*, a stadium from which many prisoners never returned?

Among the testimonies gathered by lawyers seeking to indict Ariel Sharon for war crimes is that of Wadha al-Sabeq. On Friday, 17 September 1982, she said, while the massacre was still (unknown to her) under way inside Sabra and Chatila, she was in her home with her family in Bir Hassan, just opposite the camps. 'Neighbours came and said the Israelis wanted to stamp our ID cards, so we went downstairs and we saw both Israelis and Lebanese Forces [Phalangists] on the road. The men were separated from the women.' This separation – with its awful shadow of similar separations at Srebrenica during the Bosnian war – was a common feature of these mass arrests. 'We were told to go to the Cité Sportif. The men stayed put.' Among the men were Wadha's two sons, nineteen-year-old Mohamed and sixteen-year-old Ali, and her brother Mohamed. 'We went to the Cité Sportif, as the Israelis told us,' she says. 'I never saw my sons or brother again.'

The survivors tell distressingly similar stories. Bahija Zrein says she was ordered by an Israeli patrol to go to the Cité Sportif and the men with her, including her twenty-two-year-old brother, were taken away. Some militiamen – watched by the Israelis – loaded him into a car, blindfolded, she claims. 'That's how he disappeared,' she says in her official testimony, 'and I have never seen him again since.'

It was only a few days afterwards that we journalists began to notice a discrepancy in the figures of dead. While up to 600 bodies had been found inside Sabra and Chatila, 1,800 civilians had been reported as 'missing'. We assumed – how easy assumptions are in war – that they had been killed in the three days between 16 September 1982 and the withdrawal of the Phalangist killers on the 18th, that their corpses had been secretly buried outside the camp. Beneath the golf course, we suspected. The idea that many of these young people had been murdered outside the camps or *after* the 18th, that the killings were still going on while we walked through the camps, never occurred to us.

Why did we not think of this at the time? The following year, the Israeli Kahan commission published its report, condemning Sharon but ending its own inquiry of the atrocity on 18 September with just a one-line hint – unexplained – that several hundred people may have 'disappeared' at about the same time. The commission interviewed no Palestinian survivors but it was allowed to become the narrative of history. The idea that the Israelis went on handing over prisoners to their bloodthirsty militia allies never occurred to us. The Palestinians of Sabra and Chatila are now giving evidence that this is exactly what happened. One man, Abdel Nasser Alameh, believes his brother Ali was handed to the Phalange on the morning of the 18th. A Palestinian Christian woman called Milaneh Boutros has recorded how, in a truckload of women and children, she was taken from the camps to the Christian town of Bikfaya, the home of the newly assassinated Christian president-elect Bashir Gemayel, where a grief-stricken Christian woman ordered the execution of a thirteen-year-old boy in the truck. He was shot. The truck must have passed at least four Israeli checkpoints on its way to Bikfaya. And heaven spare me, I realise now that I had even met the woman who ordered the boy's execution.

Even before the slaughter inside the camps had ended, Shahira Abu Rudeina says she was taken to the Cité Sportif where, in one of the underground 'holding centres', she saw a retarded man, watched by Israeli soldiers, burying bodies in a pit. Her evidence might be rejected were it not for the fact that she also expressed her gratitude for an Israeli soldier – inside the Chatila camp, against all the evidence given by the Israelis – who prevented the murder of her daughters by the Phalange.

Long after the war, the ruins of the Cité Sportif were torn down and a brand-new marble stadium was built in its place, partly by the British. Pavarotti has sung there. But the testimony of what may lie beneath its foundations – and its frightful implications – might give Ariel Sharon further reason to fear an indictment.

Independent, 28 November 2001

SEUMAS MILNE

The Secret War against the Miners

1994

In March 1990, the *Daily Mirror*, then owned by Robert Maxwell, and the *Cook Report*, a Central Television series, launched a campaign of corruption allegations against Arthur Scargill, the president of Britain's National Union of Mineworkers. The scandal attracted media coverage for almost a year, led to a dozen legal actions and official investigations and immobilised the miners' leadership just as the Conservative government was planning to run down and sell off the British coal industry. Every one of the original allegations (principally that the miners' leaders had used union funds, donated by Libya, to pay off mortgages during the 1984–85 coal strike) and 'fall-back' stories (that Scargill had diverted Soviet strike support cash from the union to serve his own political purposes) proved to be untrue.

What emerges from Seumas Milne's masterly investigation is the anatomy of a smear campaign like none other in modern Britain, involving phoney bank deposits, undercover spying by the state, telephone-tapping, forged documents and *agents provocateurs*. In assassinating the character of Scargill, a charismatic and 'ferociously principled' man, the conspirators hoped to destroy the miners' union, the only cohesive political force that had stood in the way of Thatcherism's 'revolution'. As Milne points out, the smear against Scargill was the work of an alliance based on a 'coincidence of purpose'. To the media empire of Robert Maxwell, the 'modernising' Labour Party leadership, the Conservative government and the British security and intelligence agencies, Arthur Scargill and 'Scargillism' were the 'the enemy within': an expression Thatcher had used to compare the miners with the Argentinian junta that invaded the Falklands two years earlier. The smear also served to distract public attention from Scargill's oft-repeated warning that the government was bent on wrecking the coal industry for ideological ends. Not only was he proven right, but the true source of crookedness was found among his accusers.

In 1991, in announcing Robert Maxwell's death by drowning, the *Daily Mirror* front page described him as 'THE MAN WHO SAVED THE MIRROR'. Two weeks later, in the same large typeface, a shamefaced *Mirror* revealed its former proprietor to be 'THE MAN WHO ROBBED THE MIRROR'. While he was orchestrating the damnation of Scargill, Maxwell was busy stealing millions of pounds from the *Mirror* pension fund, distinguishing him, writes Milne, as 'one of the greatest thieves and embezzlers of the twentieth century'.

Seumas Milne's investigation is as much about the state of journalism as a political conspiracy. 'Without the monopoly ownership grip by multinational companies on great swathes of the media,' he writes, 'the Scargill Affair would never have taken off.' Among many journalists, the charges against Scargill and Peter Heathfield, the miners' general secretary, were known to be fake, just as the involvement of the security services was widely accepted. Others merely went along with the media herd or with Maxwell's campaign. With the exception of the *Guardian*, Milne's paper, critical facts were suppressed or misrepresented and a malevolence or 'savagery', as Milne describes it, was directed against Scargill by tabloid and broadsheet commentators and editorial writers alike. Roy Greenslade was the *Daily Mirror* editor who ran the anti-Scargill campaign. He called it 'a genuine piece of investigative journalism' which he published 'more in sorrow than in anger'. When Maxwell bragged on television about his paper's 'story of the decade', Greenslade was at his side. It was almost ten years before Greenslade apologised to Scargill. He is now, remarkably, the *Guardian*'s commentator on the tabloid press and a professor of journalism at City University.

The following is extracted from *The Enemy Within*, Seumas Milne's 1994 book. It is the longest essay in this collection, because it was almost impossible to cut. In my view, it is one of the finest political exposés in our time and, as such, almost rescues the honour of our craft.

THE SECRET WAR AGAINST THE MINERS

In the spring of 1990, Arthur Scargill received an unexpected phone call at his Sheffield headquarters. Miles Copeland, a retired senior CIA officer and latter-day intelligence pundit, was anxious to speak to the embattled miners' leader. It was only a couple of days since the launch of one of the most savage media and legal campaigns against a public figure in Britain in recent times. The National Union of Mineworkers' (NUM) president, the country's best-known trade unionist and unrepentant class warrior, stood accused of flagrant embezzlement and corruption. The man described even by opponents as 'ferociously principled' was said to have lined his pockets with hardship funds intended for striking miners, and salted away millions of pounds secretly procured from the Soviet Union and Libya. Peter Heathfield, the union's general secretary, faced similar charges. The allegations were becoming daily more outlandish. Scargill had demanded not only cash from Colonel Gaddafi, it was claimed, but guns. With Robert Maxwell's *Daily Mirror* as cheerleader, Scargill's enemies crowed for his head. Some predicted he would be in jail by Christmas. What had erupted in the tabloid press and on prime-time television was being enthusiastically seized on by hostile trade-union leaders and politicians from both Tory and Labour parties, with calls for criminal prosecutions and public inquiries. Sir Geoffrey Howe, the Deputy Prime Minister, announced in the House of Commons that the police stood ready to act.

Scargill was on nodding terms with Copeland – better known to some as father of the drummer in the rock band The Police. The two men had met informally on a couple of occasions in television chat-show studios. But this time, the American dispensed with hospitality-room small talk and came brutally to the point. 'I don't like your views, Mr Scargill, and I never have,' he said, 'but I don't agree with the way you're being treated. You are being set up.' Copeland had made repeated attempts to track down the miners' leader, even calling the NUM's barrister, John Hendy, QC, at his Lincoln's Inn chambers in London, to leave an urgent message. Now he explained why. The former CIA man warned Scargill and Heathfield – who listened in to the discussion on a conference phone – that he had reliable information that both the domestic security service, MI5, and the

CIA had been closely involved in kick-starting the media campaign. They had, Copeland said, in different ways helped to frame the corruption allegations against the miners' leadership. However, he refused to expand on his remarks and promptly disappeared into the ether. Copeland was well known to have maintained close connections with the CIA's powerful London station after his retirement. Whether the crusty old spy was genuinely drawing on inside knowledge or instead relying on informed guesswork – or whether he simply wanted to fuel the NUM president's growing paranoia – must remain a matter for speculation. Copeland died shortly afterwards. Nonetheless, as the scandal-mongering onslaught against Scargill and Heathfield unfolded over subsequent months, and as each allegation was knocked down only to be replaced by another, evidence of the deep involvement of the intelligence services – among others – in the web of intrigue around what the *Daily Mirror* christened the 'Scargill Affair' relentlessly built up.

The story that Robert Maxwell called the 'Scoop of the Decade' was launched with all the razzmatazz and hype of a major national event. The first signal of what would turn into an unrestrained media, legal and political barrage against the leaders of the most important industrial dispute since the 1920s came at 6 p.m. on Friday, 2 March 1990, almost exactly five years to the day after the end of the strike. One of the most popular television programmes in the country, the travel show *Wish You Were Here . . ?*, was to be ditched the following Monday, Central Television announced. In its place there would be a special edition of the investigative *Cook Report*. It was to be entitled: 'The Miners' Strike – Where Did the Money Go?'

The programme was primed to run as a joint exposé with Robert Maxwell's *Daily Mirror*, and ITV's last-minute scheduling switch followed intense haggling by Central's director of broadcasting, Andy Allan, to secure a peak-viewing-time slot. It had been common knowledge for months in Fleet Street that the *Mirror* was sharpening its knives for a major hatchet-job on Arthur Scargill. Several disgruntled former NUM employees had been touting their wares around the media, and it was well known that Roger Windsor, the NUM's former chief executive, and Jim Parker, Scargill's ex-driver, had signed up with Maxwell. But Windsor was holed up in south-west France and Parker was under the *Mirror*'s 'protection'. Reporters working for Maxwell's competitors chased around the country trying to inveigle the *Mirror*'s witnesses. At the NUM's grandiose new head-quarters opposite Sheffield City Hall, tension was close to breaking point. Scargill cancelled a planned trip to Australia while his inner circle attempted to second-guess the direction of the coming media offensive.

Slavering to beat its arch-rival to the kill, the *Sun* – with the *Daily Star* in hot pursuit – launched an immediate front-page 'spoiler' in response to Central's rescheduling announcement. 'SCARGILL UNION IN £1M SCANDAL', the Murdoch tabloid screamed, correctly predicting that the *Cook Report* would claim that up to £1 million had been sent by Soviet miners to NUM strike funds, and at least £150,000 from Libya. 'The programme is dynamite. The allegations are sensational', the *Sun* enthused. The 'harlot of Fleet Street', as the *Mirror* liked to refer to the country's biggest-selling daily, also latched on to police investigations into 'Scargill's former right-hand man', Roger Windsor. An unfortunate *Star* reporter managed to button-hole Windsor at his new home in Cognac, but was sent packing in short order. 'The only guidance I will give you', Windsor told him, 'is how to get back to the airport.' A former NUM employee, the *Sun* predicted, would make 'very serious allegations' about the use of the Libyan money. But, for all its inventiveness, the rottweiler of daily journalism was unable to establish exactly what these allegations might be.

Nevertheless, the fear that the prize revelations his minions had been toiling over for the previous eight months, at a cost of hundreds of thousands of pounds, were being lost to his enemies sent the *Mirror*'s proprietor into a tailspin. His most recent acquisition as *Daily Mirror* editor, Roy Greenslade, was summoned and ordered to arrange for the Mirror Group's Sunday title to run a 'taster' of the following week's poison fare, trailed as the 'full and shocking truth'. That would turn out to be a remorseless seven days of bewildering allegations against the NUM leadership in the daily paper most widely read by British miners and Labour-supporting trade union-ists. In the week between 4 and 10 March 1990, the *Sunday* and *Daily Mirror* – each with a circulation of getting on for four million copies – would between them publish twenty-five pages of reports and commentary about Scargill and the 'dishonour' he had brought on the miners' union.

The taster chosen for the *Sunday Mirror* was a suitably titillating morsel about missing 'Moscow Gold'. In December 1984, at Mikhail Gorbachev's first meeting with Margaret Thatcher at Chequers, the paper revealed, the British Prime Minister had taken the future Soviet leader aside after lunch to express her 'great displeasure' about Soviet 'meddling' in the miners' strike, then in its ninth month. 'We believe that people in the Soviet Union . . . are helping to prolong the strike,' Thatcher told him. Gorbachev insisted that the strike was an internal British affair, and that as far as he was aware 'no money has been transferred from the Soviet Union'. The Prime Minister 'did not push the matter further' and later that day declared: 'This is a man we can do business with.'

But, the *Sunday Mirror* declared triumphantly, the NUM '*did* receive Soviet cash' and the paper produced what it called 'documentary proof': a copy of a letter written in November 1984 by Peter Heathfield to the Soviet president, Konstantin Chernenko, and subsequently 'removed' from NUM files. Heathfield was quoted expressing grati-tude for the solidarity of the Soviet trade unions, including 'financial assistance to relieve the hardship of our members'. The article quoted the Soviet miners' leader Mikhail Srebny as saying that 2.3 million roubles – equivalent to £2 million – had been collected for the NUM, including £1 million of hard currency in 'golden roubles'. Soviet miners had given up two days' pay for their British comrades, so it was said. 'The figures', the *Sunday Mirror* explained triumphantly, 'show a discrepancy of around £1 million. No one is saying what happened to the missing money.' The story was written by Alastair Campbell – then Neil Kinnock's closest friend and ally in Fleet Street, later Tony Blair's press secretary – while the main source for the British end of the tale was transparently Margaret Thatcher's devoted spin-doctor, Bernard Ingham. But, like John the Baptist, this was only a harbinger of greater things to come. The next day, the Sunday paper promised its readers, Maxwell's daily would treat them to the 'authentic inside story' of how Scargill also took Libyan money – and 'how he used some of it for personal transactions'.

On Monday, 5 March, the campaign began in earnest. 'SCARGILL AND THE LIBYAN MONEY: THE FACTS', the legend on the *Daily Mirror*'s front page proclaimed. The *Mirror*'s 'splash' headline – in two-inch-high letters – would later come to attract much ridicule and notoriety, but it was treated with the utmost seriousness at the time.

Across the top of the page, next to the mandatory 'exclusive' tag, the principal charge was set out: 'Miners' leaders paid personal debts with Gaddafi cash.' The following five pages were given over to the first set of 'authentic' revelations, under the joint byline of Terry Pattinson, the paper's industrial editor, Frank Thorne and Ted Oliver. The most dramatic and damaging claim – and the one that Scargill later remembered 'caused me real pain, real distress' – was that the NUM president had used £25,000 of Libyan money donated for striking miners to pay off his own mortgage. As it turned out, the long-awaited Libyan connection merely added spice to the central 'revelation': the entirely unexpected accusation of embezzlement.

Leaning heavily on the testimony of Roger Windsor, NUM chief executive officer from 1983 to 1989, the paper alleged:

> Miners' leader Arthur Scargill got £163,000 in strike support from Libya – and used a large chunk of it to pay personal debts. While miners were losing their homes at the height of the bitter 1984–5 strike, Scargill counted out more than £70,000 from a huge pile of cash strewn over an office table. He ordered that it should be used to pay back to the NUM his mortgage and the home loans of his two top officials.

These were Peter Heathfield, the union's elected general secretary, and Windsor himself. The *Mirror* traced the story back to the controversy during the strike over Windsor's dramatically publicised trip to Libya for the NUM, when he was filmed meeting Colonel Gaddafi. Scargill had always denied taking money from the Libyan regime, but here was Roger Windsor himself now revealing the 'incredible cloak-and-dagger operation to bring a secret hoard of Libyan money into Britain'. The cash had been ferried over from Tripoli in suitcases, it was said, on three separate trips by the man first revealed as a Libyan go-between in 1984. This was Altaf Abbasi, a 'mysterious Pakistani businessman . . . [who] had been jailed for terrorism in Pakistan'. Windsor was then supposed to have collected the money from Abbasi on three separate occasions in Sheffield and Rotherham in November 1984. Finally, Windsor had – according to the *Mirror* – brought the total of £163,000 into Scargill's office on 4 December 1984 on the NUM leader's instructions. Scargill explained he was anxious to see the union's accounts 'cleaned' in readiness for the imminent takeover by a court-appointed receiver. He was worried in case the 'receiver

Martha Gellhorn with Allied troops, Italy, 1944.

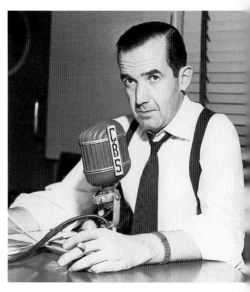

(*Above*) Edward R. Murrow,
New York, 1954.

(*Left*) James Cameron
during the Korean War, 1950.

(*Below*) Anna Politkovskaya,
Moscow, 2001.

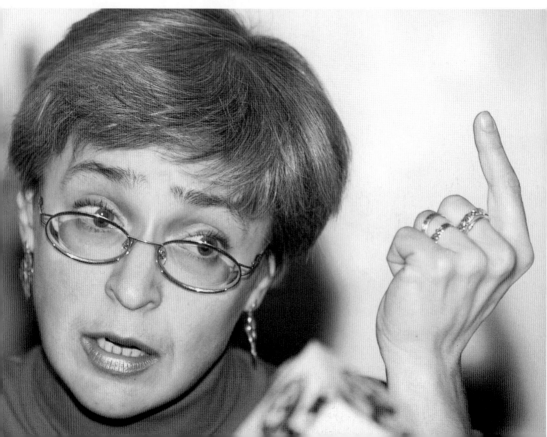

(*Above*) Max du Preez, in the offices of his anti-apartheid newspaper,
Vrye Weekblad, Johannesburg, 1989.
(*Below*) Felicity Arbuthnot, Baghdad, 1999.

(*Left*) Jessica Mitford, author of
The American Way of Death,
in the Sunset View mausoleum
and cemetery, California, 1963.

(*Below*) Paul Foot,
London, 2000.

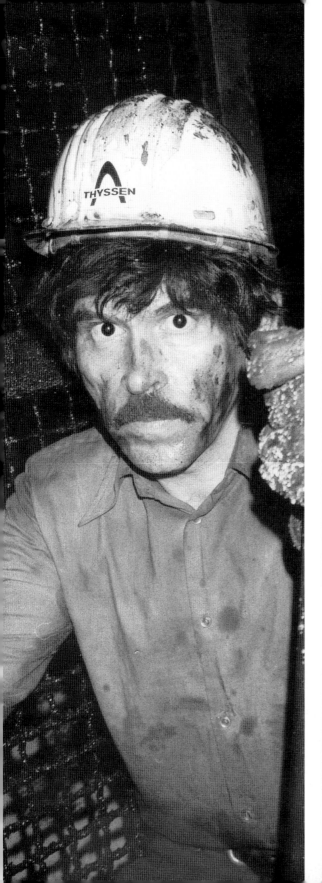

(*Left*) Undercover reporter Günter Wallraff, disguised as a Turkish worker, Germany, 1985.

(*Below*) Amira Hass on the West Bank, occupied Palestine, 2002.

Wilfred Burchett, occupied Japan, 1945.

(*Above*) Seymour Hersh, Washington, 1972.
(*Below left*) Robert Fisk, London, 1983, and (*right*) Edward Said, Paris, 1996.

John Pilger (*standing*, *left*) at Angkor Wat, Cambodia, 1979,
with ATV film crew David Munro, Gerry Pinches and Steve Phillips.

or sequestrator would find them to be . . . "not entirely one hundred per cent"'. The NUM president had then counted out three heaps of bank-notes, the former chief executive alleged, to settle the three officials' outstanding 'home loans': £25,000 to clear his own mortgage, 'around £17,000' for Heathfield's 'home improvements', and £29,500 to clear Windsor's own bridging loan advanced earlier in the year. A further £10,000 was also set aside to pay off legal expenses run up by the union's Nottinghamshire area.

It was a devastating series of allegations, which seemed to be thoroughly corroborated by other witnesses: Steve Hudson, the NUM's finance officer during the 1984–5 strike, who remembered being called to Scargill's office to pick up the cash for the repayments and provide receipts; Jim Parker, Scargill's estranged driver and minder, who confirmed taking Windsor to meet the Pakistani middleman for at least two of the cash 'pick-ups'; Abbasi himself, who described three trips to Libya to collect the money from 'Mr Bashir', head of the Libyan trade unions, and his subsequent deliveries to the NUM chief executive; Windsor's wife Angie, who remembered the Libyan cash being stored in the family house; and Abdul Ghani, who said he had acted as a witness at two of the cash handovers for his friend Abbasi.

The story could scarcely have looked more damning. The problem was not so much the confirmation that the NUM had secretly taken donations from the Soviet Union and Libya. For all the huffing and puffing, such funding had been widely assumed, despite the NUM leadership's denials. And in the case of the Soviet Union, the 'troika' of strike leaders – Scargill, Heathfield and McGahey – had all openly pressed for cash support in 1984. But the revelation that two of the miners' strike troika had apparently had their hands in the till was something else entirely. This was a real scoop. However much his critics disliked his politics and his leadership style, nobody imagined Scargill was personally corrupt. The same was true of the widely respected Heathfield. But now it seemed that the Robespierre of the British labour movement, the sea-green incorruptible, the trade-union leader that 'doesn't sell out', had been exposed as a grubby, silver-fingered union boss lining his pockets at his members' expense.

On 'Day One' of the *Mirror* campaign, the flagship of the Maxwell empire carried a special editorial, personally signed by 'Robert Maxwell, Publisher'. With the imprimatur of the great man himself and headlined 'Scargill's Waterloo', the *Mirror* conceded that the paper had never in fact supported the 1984–5 miners' strike. 'But there is no gloating on our part in exposing how hollow it was . . . the hypocrisy of the NUM's disastrous leadership' was only now revealed. 'Some shady manoeuvres', the man once described by government inspectors as unfit to run a public company went on, 'were probably inevitable'. But unions had to be 'open and honest, both with their members and with the public'. The *Mirror*'s revelations about the NUM 'show that it was neither'.

That night, the miners' leaders' pain was piled on in spadefuls as the *Cook Report* went into action before an even bigger audience. The saga of the Libyan money, home loans and Altaf Abbasi's international courier service was rehearsed in loving detail. As Roger Cook – the man who had unmasked a thousand small-time swindlers and petty crooks – described the scene in the programme's voice-over: 'It's December 1984, halfway through the strike, and the three men who run the NUM are counting out the cash to pay off their personal loans when many striking miners were losing their houses.' But the *Cook Report* took things a stage further, wildly upping the ante on the size of the supposed Libyan slush fund. The Libyans had not only donated £163,000, the programme declared. According to Altaf Abbasi, they had also come up with an extra $9 million – something he had apparently not thought fit to mention to the *Daily Mirror*. This huge sum had been made available, he said, for 'hardship purposes only'. Most of the money had then been returned during the previous three months after an unexplained 'official inquiry'.

There was more. At a secret meeting with Abbasi in Roger Windsor's house, it was said, Scargill had asked the Libyans to provide guns for his personal use. The former chief executive recalled: 'He wanted . . . a revolver for himself, a little ladies' revolver that he could keep in the car, and a pump action shotgun.' The viewer was then informed by Cook that 'Mr Scargill apparently asked other people for guns too' – we were not told who – 'but in Altaf Abbasi's case settled for the money instead.' The programme also made hay in passing with a Soviet strike donation of one million dollars – or pounds, it was not entirely clear which – that Windsor claimed had been paid into a Warsaw bank account with Scargill and Heathfield as sole signatories. Cook explained that the money had earlier appeared in an NUM account in Switzerland but been returned on Scargill's instructions, 'officially to keep it out of the hands of the sequestrators'. The clear implication was that the cash was diverted to finance Scargill's own private pet projects.

Stories were recounted of the sinister rewriting of NUM executive minutes, 'strange transactions', dodgy bank accounts, and the misuse of the International Miners' Organisation[1] for Scargill's 'Machiavellian machinations'. Jim Parker, lifelong Communist, Scargill bodyguard, driver and buddy, appeared on screen to insist that the widely reported police assault on Scargill at Orgreave in the summer of 1984 had been a propaganda fraud. 'If the truth were known . . . he actually slipped down a bank.' When he had been told about Scargill's mortgage scam, Parker declared, it was the last straw. 'That's something I shall never forgive him for.'

The *Mirror*, it has to be said, did at least print edited highlights of the NUM's denials, if only to insist that the paper was able to 'expose the big lie'. Roger Cook relied instead on the 'doorstepping' technique which made the heavyweight New Zealander's name. 'Did you or did you not', he demanded of the miners' president as Scargill drove off from his bungalow outside Worsbrough Dale near Barnsley, count out 'bundles of cash for you, for Peter Heathfield and for Roger Windsor on your office desk?' In the view of Roy Greenslade, the *Mirror's* editor, the scene of Scargill repeating mechanically through his car window 'If you've got any questions . . . put them in writing, send them to me and I'll make inquiries' was more incriminating for the viewer than any number of detailed allegations. The phrase had in fact been insisted on by the NUM's lawyers. But it was a gift to the *Cook Report*. The programme was, in the words of the following morning's *Daily Express* banner headline, truly a 'TV trial'.

The rest of the week was a true grotesquerie of the British media. The *Mirror* revelled in the melodrama of its daily claims of Scargillite skulduggery. Windsor had, it alleged ever more feverishly, adopted codewords to arrange the handover of the Libyan cash: Scargill was the 'patient', Abbasi the 'doctor', and the money referred to as 'X-rays'. Gaddafi's cash had been stored in biscuit tins in the Windsors' larder. Abbasi claimed to have flounced through customs at Heathrow airport after showing officers £50,000 in cash in his briefcase. 'Windsor the Whistleblower' was reported to be living in fear of a Gaddafi hit-squad in his French mansion because of his failure to repay the funds used to settle his bridging loan. The elderly left-wing barrister John

[1] International Miners' Organisation (IMO), an alliance of mining unions created on the initiative of the NUM and the French CGT.

Platts-Mills had admitted asking Gaddafi for a 'substantial sum' for the miners. Faithful Jim Parker, Scargill's pal 'for 34 years', described ferrying around hundreds of thousands of pounds in cardboard boxes during the strike – and how Scargill used lacquer to hide his baldness.

Maxwell was in his element, repeatedly appearing on television with Greenslade to promote himself and his 'classic piece of investigative journalism'. Complaining that Scargill's denial was 'convoluted', he insisted: 'We stand by the *Daily Mirror* story totally.' And in a refrain which would eventually become the *Mirror*'s only defence, Maxwell went on: 'If we are wrong, we challenge him to sue us.' Privacy was one thing for an ordinary, straightforward person. 'But if like Mr Scargill you have tried to bring down an elected constitutional government of the country and if, like Mr Scargill, you have led the Guards division of the trade-union movement to defeat, your conduct is . . . of the greatest importance.' The rest of the media enthusiastically leaped aboard the bandwagon, reporting every twist and turn of the revelations – and, with varying degrees of fastidiousness, the miners' leaders' denials. The *Sun* found itself in a particularly tricky position, alternately throwing its weight behind the Maxwell exposé with headlines such as 'SINISTER SECRET OF RED CASH', and then rubbishing its main competitor with the legend, 'IT'S ALL LIES', backed up by reports that Windsor was wanted for questioning by British police. Finally, it settled for turning its fire on Heathfield, who, it wrongly claimed, had moved into a house once owned by the village squire of North Anston.

For most of the press, at both ends of the market, the truth or otherwise of the allegations proved to be of less interest than the opportunity once again to thunder against the union which had launched, as the *Express* put it, a 'futile and misguided attempt to bring down a democratically-elected government'. The *Independent* denounced as 'shameful' the disclosure that large sums of money had been 'shuffled' about in suitcases and cardboard boxes to escape the long arm of the law. *Today* declared that 'everything Mr Scargill stands for is fit for history's dustbin'. *The Times* took the view that 'donkey' was 'altogether too benign a word to apply to the miners' leaders'. Even the left-of-centre *New Statesman* managed to compare the NUM president to the 'oppressive regimes' then falling like dominoes in Eastern Europe.

While Scargill and Heathfield denied the charges and called an emergency NUM executive for the Friday, their opponents inside and outside the union stoked up the political pressure. The former NUM receiver Michael Arnold weighed in to declare the NUM leaders' actions at least a breach of trust, at worst 'a criminal act'. The Labour leader, Neil Kinnock, was joined by Norman Willis, the TUC general secretary, in demanding a full public inquiry into the 'extremely serious' allegations. Kinnock's two closest parliamentary lieutenants with mining connections – Labour coal spokesman Kevin Barron and unofficial speech-writer and adviser Kim Howells – had both appeared on the *Cook Report*, and energetically took up the leader's cue. 'There are tears in the valleys of Wales,' Howells told Maxwell's daily, 'but the *Mirror* has done the union a great service.' Tory MPs pressed for the NUM leaders to be prosecuted, and Sir Geoffrey Howe – then Leader of the Commons – said that all the evidence should be turned over to the police, who were 'very ready' to act. Ministers were reported to be anxious to use the affair to divert attention from their own difficulties. *The Times* speculated that both NUM leaders could expect a ten-year jail sentence.

The central allegation made by the *Daily Mirror* and Central Television's *Cook Report* against the miners' leader – that he used Libyan hardship donations to pay off his mortgage during the 1984–85 miners' strike – was in fact entirely false and demonstrated to be so within a few months. Not only did Scargill have no mortgage to pay off, but – as new evidence now shows for the first time – the money identified as having been used for the phantasmic mortgage transaction never came from Libya at all. Indeed, the question of who did in fact advance that cash provides a key to explaining what lay behind the whole canard. The second main accusation, which the *Mirror* and the *Cook Report* fell back on once the first had disintegrated on the most cursory examination, was that Scargill had diverted a sum amounting to between one million dollars and ten million pounds, donated by Soviet miners, to a secret trust fund to further his personal political ambitions. That claim, too, was eventually shown to be wrong in almost all its details. The story ran on regardless. Facts were never allowed to get seriously in the way of a campaign that commanded such powerful support and offered the chance to destroy once and for all the symbol of militant class trade unionism that Scargill obstinately remained.

But it was not until disaffected employees at the government's GCHQ[2] electronic spying headquarters began to leak information about intelligence and secret-service dirty-tricks operations against the NUM to the *Guardian* in the winter of 1990–91 that the full extent of the secret war against Britain's miners started to become clear. Margaret Thatcher personally authorised a 'Get Scargill' campaign both during and after the 1984–85 strike, the GCHQ whistleblowers alleged, which was coordinated and run by MI5. She had also, they said, bent her government's own rules and ordered an unprecedented mobilisation of British and American electronic surveillance networks to underpin the anti-NUM operations. Our informants provided details of the large-scale misuse of GCHQ and its outstations in Britain, co-sponsored and co-financed by the US National Security Agency, to track the activities of NUM officials and the movement of the miners' funds around the European banking system. Action by the security service to discredit Scargill had, they said, led to abortive attempts to implicate him in the theft of phoney cash deposits of hundreds of thousands of pounds. The GCHQ moles also confirmed Copeland's claim that there had been a direct intelligence input into the 1990 Maxwell-funded media campaign against the miners' leadership.

Nothing like this had ever before emerged about security-service operations against domestic 'subversives' – the catch-all term still used by the British Government to target those active in campaigns for radical social or political change. Gradually, one part of the GCHQ eavesdroppers' story after another was corroborated, and the pieces of a remarkable jigsaw started to fit together. There was, however, plenty more to come. In December 1991, almost exactly a year after the original GCHQ material was passed to the *Guardian*, Stella Rimington became the first director-general of MI5 whose appointment would be publicly disclosed by the most secretive government bureaucracy in the Western world. But within twenty-four hours of the announcement, as the government preened itself over its unaccustomed glasnost and equal-opportunities policies for eminent spies, less palatable aspects of the new chief state-security mandarin's career emerged.

Stella Rimington was not, it transpired, quite the 'new face of the service' portrayed in official briefings. Climbing her way up MI5's greasy promotion pole, she had headed the department in charge of

[2] British Government Communications Headquarters.

'monitoring' the trade-union movement at the time of its greatest industrial conflict with the Thatcher government. In that job, she had played the central role in MI5 operations against the 1984–85 miners' strike – which, it was already becoming clear, had been the dirtiest outside the Northern Ireland conflict since the war. A House of Commons motion calling for a statement on her activities – and linking her with David Hart, the right-wing adviser to Margaret Thatcher who helped organise the 'back-to-work movement' during the strike – was tabled by the well-connected dissenting Labour MP, Tam Dalyell. His demand was given added credibility by public support from the former Labour Home Secretary, Merlyn Rees, himself the Cabinet minister technically in charge of MI5 in the late 1970s, and the ex-Solicitor General, Peter Archer. The motion needled bureaucratic wounds, already inflamed by MI5's predatory encroachments on police territory. A few weeks later, on the basis of briefings from two separate high-level Whitehall sources, Dalyell returned to Parliament with an even more startling claim. Roger Windsor – the NUM's chief executive during and after the miners' strike, and the main source for the allegations made by the *Daily Mirror* and the *Cook Report* against Scargill in 1990 – had also been 'involved' with Stella Rimington and MI5, the MP alleged on the floor of the House. Dalyell's Whitehall 'deep throats' continued to drip-feed him with further details and by the summer of 1993, Dalyell, George Galloway and a group of other Labour MPs were prepared to abandon the earlier euphemisms. Windsor was named in a Commons motion as an MI5 agent sent into the NUM by Stella Rimington to 'destabilise and sabotage' the union.[3] The new secret-service boss had 'subverted democratic liberties,' the MPs charged, and should be brought to account.

Taken together with an accumulation of other evidence, allegations and persistent leaks, it has now become apparent that the 1990 attack against the miners' leaders – and Scargill in particular – was the product of the single most ambitious 'counter-subversion' operation ever mounted in Britain. This was a covert campaign which reached its apogee during the 1984–85 strike, but continued long afterwards. In its breach of what had long been seen as the established rules of the political game, it went beyond even the propaganda, policing and industrial effort

[3] In 2000, Windsor brought a libel action against the *Sunday Express* over an article stating categorically that Windsor had worked as an MI5 agent for Rimington and wrongly claiming that this had been confirmed by the MI5 whistleblower David Shayler. Two years later, the paper reached an out of court settlement and published a retraction.

openly deployed by the government to destroy the country's most powerful trade union. As far as the Thatcherite faction in the Cabinet and their supporters in the security services were concerned, the NUM under Scargill's stewardship was the most serious domestic threat to state security in modern times. And they showed themselves prepared to encourage any and every method available – from the secret financing of strikebreakers to mass electronic surveillance, from the manipulation of *agents provocateurs* to attempts to 'fit up' miners' officals – in order to undermine or discredit the union and its leaders. It is a record of the abuse of unaccountable power which is only now returning to haunt both those who pulled the strings and those who carried out the orders.

The secret war against the miners has been the hidden counterpart to the open struggle by successive Tory governments against the NUM, a struggle which helped shape the course of British politics over two decades. The extraordinary nature of the covert operations against the miners' leaders only makes sense when seen in the context of the long-run determination of the Tory Party – and of Margaret Thatcher above all – to avenge absolutely and unequivocally their double humiliation at the hands of the miners in the historic strikes of 1972 and 1974. The problem of how to 'deal' with the miners and their recalcitrant leadership became one of the great obsessions of Conservative political life.

Confrontations between Tory administrations and the miners, for many years the most politicised and strategically important section of the country's workforce, have punctuated British twentieth-century history at its moments of greatest domestic political and industrial stress: 1926, 1972–74 and 1984–85. And just as the betrayal and defeat of the miners in 1926 remained a festering wound in mining communities for a generation or more, so in recent times it was the shattering experience for the Tory Party of the two pit strikes of the early 1970s which laid the ground for what became a twenty-year vendetta against the miners: a single-minded and ruthless drive to destroy the NUM and, if necessary, the bulk of the British coal industry in the process.

As one labour-movement observer commented in the early stages of the 1984–85 strike, Britain's ruling class 'has its folk memories, too, and miners emerging from the bowels of the earth to demand their rights touch a raw nerve'. The visceral Tory fear of the 'black avenging host', as Émile Zola described insurgent miners in *Germinal*, proved perfectly rational. After years of suffering heavy pit closures and declining relative pay under a right-wing corporatist leadership, the miners became in the early 1970s the cutting edge of a new working-class assertiveness. The decisive battle of the 1972 strike – when miners' flying pickets led by Scargill and others, with the support of 10,000 striking engineering workers, closed the Saltley coke depot in Birmingham, and clinched the strike victory – sent panic waves throughout the political and administrative establishment. The dispute of 1974, which led to a three-day week, precipitated a general election and brought about the defeat of the Heath government, was if anything even more devastating for the Conservative Party.

The Tories returned to power in 1979 determined to break the back of the entire trade-union movement. The NUM's unique industrial position, its unmatched radicalisation, and the Conservative Party's spectacular humbling at the miners' hands left little question as to which union would become the new government's most important target. There was none more single-minded in the pursuit of political revenge against the miners than Margaret Thatcher, one of only two Cabinet ministers during the coal dispute of 1974 to oppose Heath's decision to call a general election. As her biographer, Hugo Young, puts it:

> No name was scarred more deeply on the Conservative soul than that of the NUM. For Margaret Thatcher the miners were where she came in. If they hadn't humiliated the Heath government into fighting an election which it lost, she would not now be party leader and prime minister. But this mattered less than the memory of that bloody defeat itself, and the apprehension that it might always be capable of happening again.

In 1981, a few months before Scargill was elected NUM president with a majority of more than 100,000 votes, Thatcher had herself been compelled to back down in the face of spontaneous strikes which erupted across the coalfields against the threat of large-scale pit closures. Peter Walker, Energy Secretary during the 1984–85 strike, remembered the 1981 climbdown as being 'scorched' on Thatcher's mind. But as Mick McGahey, the NUM's vice-president, predicted at the time, it was 'not so much a U-turn, more a body swerve'.

Serious thinking about how to settle the coal question for good had begun during the 1973 oil crisis, at a time when the pre-1974-strike overtime ban was already in force. Wilfred Miron, a National

Coal Board (NCB) member, prepared a secret report for Derek Ezra, then NCB chairman, arguing that the rise of the Communist and Marxist left in the NUM would have to be broken by 'reinforcing union moderates', reintroducing pit and area incentive payments, which had been phased out after 1966, and promoting membership of non-NUM unions. All this was attempted or carried out in the 1970s and 1980s. 'The aims should be', Miron concluded, 'to limit the future manning of the industry, to restrict, to neutralise, alien or subversive political influences' and to 'ensure that of those employed in the mining industry the maximum number should be outwith the NUM'.

Five years later, while the Tories were still in opposition, Nicholas Ridley, the right-wing MP and Thatcher ally, drew up the necessary contingency plans to take the miners on. Even in such a vulnerable industry, with the likelihood of the 'full force of Communist dis-rupters', Ridley assured his future Prime Minister that a strike could be defeated. What was needed was a build-up of coal stocks and imports, the encouragement of non-union road hauliers to move coal, the rapid introduction of dual coal–oil firing at all power stations, the withdrawal of social-security benefits from strikers' families, and the creation of a large, mobile squad of police. All these steps were in the event taken during, or in the run-up to, the 1984–85 coal strike, when Ridley was a member of the Cabinet committee in charge of the government's strike tactics. A decade on, Nigel (now Lord) Lawson, who had been intimately involved in planning for a confrontation with the miners as Energy Secretary, recalled that government preparation for the strike was 'just like re-arming to face the threat of Hitler in the late 1930s'.

But the Tory commitment to solving Britain's coal problem once and for all went far beyond the tactical preparations for, and all-out resistance to, a major national strike. As one set of ministerial memoirs from the Thatcher era after another has made indisputably clear, the overriding aim of the British Government's entire energy policy from 1979 onwards was to destroy for ever the power-base of the National Union of Mineworkers and exorcise the Tory nightmares of the early 1970s. The miners' industrial muscle was based on their grip on elec-tricity supply. Throughout the 1970s and 1980s, around 80 per cent of Britain's electricity was generated from domestic coal. For the Tories, that dependence on coal had to be broken, at almost any cost. This was the principal motivation behind the government's systematic promotion of nuclear power at enormous public expense, the break-up and privatisation of electricity supply, the 'dash for gas', and the long-delayed sale of the coal industry itself.

The strategy began with nuclear power. The fact that the Thatcher government's enthusiastic support for a pressurised-water-reactor (PWR) programme was mainly aimed at undercutting the NUM was first revealed in leaked Cabinet minutes during her first administration. Nigel Lawson, Energy Secretary in the early 1980s and later Chancellor, explained much later: 'The need for "diversification" of energy sources, the argument I used to justify the PWR programme, was code for freedom from NUM blackmail.' Lawson regarded Scargill as one of the two 'energy tsars' of the industrialised world – the other being Sheikh Yamani, the Saudi oil minister. Money was therefore no object. But despite the billions of pounds of subsidy poured into the nuclear industry – the nuclear-featherbedding 'fossil fuel levy' was still running at over £1.2 billion a year in 1994 – nuclear power never proved enough by itself to knock 'King Coal' off its throne.

To hold the line, there was a determined bid to drive up coal imports by encouraging the building of new ports and terminals. When that proved insufficient, the Tories turned to denationalisation and industrial break-up to achieve their perennial ambition. At the 1988 Tory Party conference in Brighton, Cecil Parkinson, then Thatcher's Energy Secretary, announced that the coal industry – the jewel in the crown of the 1945 Attlee government's public-ownership programme – would be sold off. This, he declared, would be the 'ultimate privatisation'. Parkinson later explained in the privacy of his own memoirs: 'What was ultimate about the proposed privatisation of coal was that it would mark the end of the political power of the National Union of Mineworkers.'

Despite the bravado, the denationalisation of coal would have to be repeatedly postponed. Instead, it was the privatisation of electricity supply, combined with a market rigged in favour of the nuclear and gas industries, that would finally destroy coal's historic pre-eminence and create the conditions for its replacement as the country's industrial lifeblood in the 1990s. The ministers responsible for this Alice-in-Wonderland industrial architecture were at least frank in retrospect about what had been their intention. As Parkinson described the planned impact of electricity privatisation: 'It was obvious that the reorganisation of the electricity industry, and the weakening of British Coal's monopoly as a coal supplier, would fundamentally change the shape of the [coal] industry.' Breaking the monopoly of either electricity or coal would, he argued, 'curtail the power of the miners'. Privatising both would 'destroy' the 'political and economic power' of the NUM for good.

The rigging of the market against coal was as ruthless as it was neat. By splitting the old state-owned monopoly Central Electricity Generating Board into a private duopoly of National Power and PowerGen, the government gave the newly privatised regional electricity-distribution companies a compelling interest in building their own new gas-fired power stations as a way of buying commercial independence from the two big generators. It was of little consequence to the new privateers if power generated from gas turned out to be more expensive than electricity from coal-fired stations – let alone exorbitantly subsidised nuclear power – so long as the government kept handing out gas-station licences and the industry regulator allowed costs to be passed on to consumers. Thus was the 'dash for gas' born and the NUM's grip on electricity generation finally brought to an end.

When the Major government's pit-closure plans ran into an unforeseen wall of popular protest in the autumn of 1992, much public comment focused on the supposed irrationality of the relentless promotion of coal imports and expensive nuclear power and gas. But it was only irrational if judged primarily in terms of cost. Market forces, competition and costs were never the Conservative government's primary concerns when it came to dealing with the mining industry. In the words of two widely respected energy economists, Mike Parker and John Surrey: 'Throughout the period [1979–92], the underlying policy objective for coal was primarily to break the power of the NUM and the perceived stranglehold of coal on the electricity supply industry.' Privatisation and the devastating 1992–94 closure programme was the endgame of that strategy.

But it was a process which took many years to bear fruit. As late as 1990, the year of the Scargill Affair and of Margaret Thatcher's fall from office, almost four-fifths of Britain's power supply was still being generated from domestic coal. And around the same proportion of that coal was still produced by NUM members. For all the dramatic fall in the size of the mining workforce – achieved at a cost of £8 billion in redundancy payments – Thatcher failed while in office to achieve her strategic goal of destroying the source of the NUM's strength. The massive cuts in the mining workforce in the aftermath of the 1984–85 strike were to a large extent the result of large-scale productivity gains, both from longer hours and the effects of long-term investment in new machinery. Between 1983 and 1990, output from BC[4] pits fell from 90 to 76 million tonnes. At 16 per cent, that was a significant cut, but nothing like the dramatic 64 per cent reduction in the number of miners which slashed the corporation's industrial workforce from 181,000 to 65,000 over the same period. The number of working BC pits was cut from 170 to 73, as production was concentrated in the most productive 'big hitter' collieries.

In other words, by the end of the 1980s a far smaller group of miners potentially exercised even more concentrated industrial power than before. The NUM was very far from being the busted flush of received media and labour-movement wisdom. To keep the Tories' wolf from the door, the Thatcher government was forced to rely on gigantic coal stockpiles and the careful encouragement of divisions within and between the mining and other energy unions. What ultimately held the miners back from flexing their industrial muscle were internal splits, fostered both from within and from without, and the continuing presence of the government-promoted breakaway Union of Democratic Mineworkers in the Nottinghamshire coalfield.

Michael Heseltine's politically disastrous decision in October 1992 to close thirty-one of the surviving fifty British Coal collieries at a stroke and to sack 30,000 miners was not only an inevitable result of the long-term Tory strategy to destroy the NUM. It was also clear confirmation that the government's enthusiasm for its war on the miners had by no means evaporated with Thatcher's political demise. Of course, mining jobs had been lost throughout the world, mostly as a result of higher productivity and changing energy costs. But the destruction of the British market for coal and the closure of collieries producing far below the cost of imports and other fuels was a deliberate act of policy. Even as late as the spring of 1993, domestic coal still accounted for 60 per cent of electricity generation, but that proportion would fall dramatically as British Coal's guaranteed sales to the privatised generators were cut by more than half. By that point, the torrent of redundancies had become the straightforward outcome of the calculated rundown of the industry and the ruthless displacement of coal in the newly privatised electricity market. Despite the political cost,

[4] British Coal (formerly National Coal Board, NCB).

Major's government made sure the job was finished. By the tenth anniversary of the 1984–85 strike, Heseltine's much-vaunted 'agonising' over pit closures had miraculously subsided. The 'political power of the extremist-led union' had, he now explained, been to blame for the most drastic industrial rundown in Britain's history.

For the Tories and the British establishment as a whole, Arthur Scargill came to embody all that they most feared and hated about trade-union power in general and the miners in particular. Originally one of a group of charismatic militant rank-and-file union leaders thrown up by the industrial upheavals of the early 1970s, Scargill in time became 'a man apart' for the Conservatives, the living 'embodiment of the enemy within'. There was cause enough for the obsession – which was also well represented in the labour-movement hierarchy. It was Scargill who in 1972 had masterminded the single most successful mass-picketing operation of the post-war period. In 1974, he and other left-wing NUM area leaders pushed through a strike which helped bring down the government of the day. And in 1984–85, he led the longest national strike in the country's history and was the central actor in the decisive confrontation of the Thatcher decade. It can be argued that a mythology around Scargill was encouraged on both sides of Britain's 'coal wars' – and that the origins of the Tory vendetta against the miners pre-date his national leadership of the NUM. But there is also no doubt that Scargill became the focus of everything it was designed to root out.

Unlike the strikes of 1972 and 1974, the cataclysmic battle of 1984–85 – the 'most important industrial dispute since the General Strike of 1926' and 'one of the most significant events in Britain's post-war history', as the Thatcherite editor of the *Sunday Times* described it shortly afterwards – was essentially defensive.

It was a last-ditch fight to defend jobs, mining communities and the NUM itself against a government prepared to bring into play unlimited resources and its entire panoply of coercive powers as and where necessary to break the union and its backbone of support. It was also a challenge to the 'logic of capital', to the savage, job-devouring 'restructuring' of industry on the basis of narrow profit-and-loss criteria, rather than social costs and benefits. The strike was, of course, a gamble: but not, as is often implied, in the sense of throwing away the opportunity of a gentle and humane decline in exchange for the chance of all-out political and industrial victory. Rather, it gambled the certainty of accelerated rundown and Thatcherisation of the coal industry against the chance of stopping that assault in its tracks. The only two periods when pit closures were temporarily suspended were the years of resistance: 1984–85 and 1992–93. Otherwise, the rate of closures ran at about the same level – between ten and twenty collieries a year – both before and after the strike.

For the miners, the die had been cast before Scargill became NUM president. But what he, Heathfield and McGahey – the troika who led the 1984–85 strike – ensured was that the national union was mobilised without reserve behind miners who were prepared to resist the closure programme. None of the three was prepared to hide behind a phoney compromise deal which might briefly postpone the day of reckoning to even less propitious circumstances. On the government side, Thatcher and her shadowy acolytes made certain that nothing else was available.

The 1984–85 miners' strike is an episode which demands a 'revisionist' reassessment. For the government, most of the media and for the Labour and TUC leaders who left the NUM to fight alone, the strike was – and remains – a regrettable saga of picket-line violence, undemocratic manoeuvring, ranting obscurantist dogmatism and inevitable defeat: the tragic product of one man's overweening political and personal ambitions. For those who actively took part, along with millions of their supporters in Britain and abroad, it was a principled – even heroic – stand, which directly confronted the Thatcher administration and its battery of anti-democratic trade-union legislation in a way that no other force in the country was prepared or able to do. Peter Heathfield was speaking for many beyond the shrinking mining communities when at his retirement he described the strike as 'the most courageous and principled struggle in British trade-union history'. It was also a campaign which transformed people's lives and view of the world, drew hundreds of thousands from outside the mining communities into active solidarity, and threw up new forms of organisation – notably the Women Against Pit Closures support groups – utterly at odds with the textbook caricature of the dispute.

As one highly critical account of the strike concedes of the miners who took part: 'Many said they would do it all again and many had clearly enjoyed the experience: they had lived at a pitch, physically, intellectually, morally even, which they could not expect to again, and which most who have not undergone war would never emulate.'

As Scargill's Cassandra-like warnings of what lay in store for the miners were eerily borne out by the flood of job losses and pit closures after 1985, the wider popular perception of the strike in retrospect began to change. The image of striking miners as the protagonists of picket-line violence was also dented by later revelations and events. There was, for example, the decision by South Yorkshire police in 1991 to pay half a million pounds in damages to thirty-nine miners arrested on 18 June 1984 at Orgreave coking plant, the single most dramatic and violent physical confrontation of post-war industrial relations. The miners had sued the police for assault, wrongful arrest, malicious prosecution and false imprisonment after their original trial for riot had collapsed ignominiously in 1985. As the civil-rights organisation Liberty remarked of the battle of Orgreave – where 8,000 riot police mounted medieval-style mounted charges of unprecedented ferocity: 'There *was* a riot. But it was a police riot.'

The virulence of the denunciations of Scargill and the miners during and long after the 1984–85 strike went far beyond the established boundaries of modern-day mainstream British politics. It reached a peak in the summer of 1984, when the Prime Minister compared the struggle with the miners to the war against the Argentine junta over the Falklands/Malvinas islands two years earlier. 'We had to fight an enemy without in the Falklands,' she declared at a gathering of Conservative backbench MPs. Now the war had to be taken to 'the enemy within, which is much more difficult to fight and more dangerous to liberty'. A few months later, Margaret Thatcher would return to her theme in the Carlton Club, the clubland temple of High Toryism:

> At one end of the spectrum are the terrorist gangs within our borders and the terrorist states which finance and arm them. At the other are the hard left, operating inside our system, conspiring to use union power . . . to break, defy and subvert the laws.

Her senior ministers were no less extreme. Thus Leon Brittan, the

Home Secretary responsible during the strike for overseeing Britain's largest and longest-running police mobilisation ever, fulminated:

> Mr Scargill does not just hate our free and democratic system and seek to do everything he can to discredit and damage it; he also feels equal hatred and contempt for those miners whose servant he is meant to be but whose tyrant he has become.

The message conveyed by these remarks by Thatcher and Brittan was unmistakable, down to the use of the words 'conspiring' and 'subvert': this false prophet and his bands of untamed red guards and coalfield sans-culottes should be treated as outlaws. They were enemies of the state. By branding the miners 'the enemy within', the Prime Minister was giving a calculated signal of unambiguous clarity to all government agencies that the gloves should come off in the war with the NUM.

The private instructions were inevitably more explicit. One police chief constable recalls being formally warned by a senior Home Office official early on in the dispute of the Prime Minister's frustrations at what she saw as official pussyfooting in the coalfields. She was, he was told, 'convinced that a secret Communist cell around Scargill was orchestrating the strike in order to bring down the country', and that infiltration and intelligence-gathering needed to be sharply stepped up to prove the conspiracy. The NUM found itself facing the concentrated power of the state in an unprecedented form. And the much-reported nationwide police deployment, the 11,000 arrests, the road blocks and large-scale use of force by the police were only the public face of the covert campaign – which increasingly came to guide and dominate the tactics used to try to break the miners' resistance.

The end of the strike did not end the war. As far as the Tories were concerned, there would continue to be unfinished business until Scargill and the miners' union – and indeed the coal industry in any recognisable form – were consigned to the recesses of history. But, gallingly for the government, the NUM did not accept defeat. The union had been stampeded into returning to work, divided and without a settlement, but it had not been broken. Despite being severely weakened and permanently tied up in legal action and internal battles; despite the remorseless attrition of the Coal Board, the Nottinghamshire-based breakaway outfit, the rundown of the coalfields and the dismal aftermath of the country's most intense industrial confrontation since 1926, the NUM leaders did not accept the role allotted to them. Scargill did not go the way of his hero, Arthur Cook, the syndicalist miners' leader at the time of the 1926 General Strike, who would eventually lose heart, move to the right and die a broken man. Barely four months after the miners returned to work, Scargill was telling NUM conference delegates that the union had 'challenged the very heart of the capitalist system . . . we are involved in a class war . . . you have written history. The only way is to fight again with the same determination, the same pride.'

It was against this background that Margaret Thatcher authorised 'special measures' by the security services against Scargill, Heathfield and their core supporters towards the end of the 1980s, and that the media and legal barrage was launched in March 1990. There was much speculation in the early stages of the Scargill Affair as to why so much attention was being focused on a broken union, whose leader was a 'dead duck politically', a man who had 'slid to the very periphery of events'. In reality, there was more than a little wishful thinking in such triumphalist claims. Not only was the miners' underlying industrial clout far less affected by their decline in numbers than generally understood. But, for the Tory Prime Minister in particular, the survival of 'King Arthur' – albeit scarred, bloodied and presiding over a much-diminished kingdom – was a permanent affront and a constant reminder of a job uncompleted.

Thatcher's worries over the continuing dangers posed by the miners and their president were later richly borne out at her successor's expense during the October 1992 pit-closures crisis. To the astonishment of most miners themselves, Middle England rose momentarily as one against the vandalisation of the country's coal industry. In the *Guardian*'s formulation at the time: 'The most astonishing thing is that the forward march of Thatcherism should be halted in the coalfields, of all places . . . The unique moral status of the miners in British life has reasserted itself.' The NUM president was transmogrified overnight from 'most hated man in Britain' into vindicated folk hero. Remarkably, in view of his media portrayal as a political dinosaur living in a class-war time-warp, Scargill was singled out by teenagers and young people as one of their foremost heroes in a 1993 poll because of what they saw as his principled stand against the government. In an exhaustive survey of the attitudes of eleven- to twenty-four-year-olds, the NUM president was ranked alongside Martin Luther King and John Kennedy. Even Chief Superintendent John Nesbit, who had arrested Scargill at Orgreave in 1984, was forced to change his tune: 'Arthur was right . . . I hope he wins this time.' And the *Daily Mirror*, admittedly under new management, ran a full front-page colour picture of the three men it had most savagely vilified two years earlier – Scargill, Heathfield and the International Miners' Organisation official Alain Simon – clutching bouquets of flowers and grinning happily under the benign gaze of a police super-intendent as they led the biggest demonstration in London for a decade. 'Cor!', the banner legend ran, 'Look What Major's Done for Old Arthur . . . Yesterday, Arthur Scargill was a hero to both rich and poor.'

Needless to say, the new-found media love affair was not to last. And the government had no intention of allowing its quarry to get away. The Cabinet minister given the job of negotiating the govern-ment's way around the public outcry against pit closures – the appro-priately unelected Lord Wakeham – made sure there would be no tampering with the privatised structure he had himself put in place as Energy Secretary. The war on the miners and their union would be seen through to the finish. The squeeze on coal would continue. And in the process, the world's most advanced mining industry, billions of pounds of investment, and one of the country's most skilled and adaptable workforces would be sacrificed in the service of the Tory vendetta. By the autumn of 1994 only 8,000 British Coal miners remained on the books at sixteen deep-mine collieries, in an industry which had employed well over a million men at the time of the 1926 General Strike. As another former Energy Secretary, Tony Benn, described the frantic forced closure of twenty-one publicly owned collieries in a couple of months during the early summer of 1993: 'This is a search-and-destroy mission against the National Union of Mineworkers.'

Yet, for all its determined role in the cauterisation of the nationalised coal industry, the Conservative government was not the only power in the land anxious to see the back of the miners' union and its

leadership. And likewise, the secret services were only one element of
the tacit coalition that turned the 1990 Maxwell-funded campaign of
corruption allegations against Scargill and Peter Heathfield into a
sustained political and legal attack – an onslaught that would have
destroyed almost any other public figure and could well have put the
miners' leaders behind bars. The Scargill Affair depended on a coincidence of purpose between an exotic array of interests, foremost
among which were the Thatcher administration and the Labour leadership. The government was determined to privatise the coal industry
and continued to regard Scargill – acknowledged in the City of
London to be a significant turn-off for potential buyers – as a malign
influence from the past. Neil Kinnock, who later described how he
had felt impotent and humiliated during the 1984–85 strike, saw the
miners' leader and all he represented as a deeply unwelcome presence
in the new-model Labour Party he was trying to create. Robert
Maxwell, the slippery-fingered media baron, was, as ever, happy to
do favours for both of them.

The hares set off by Maxwell's *Daily Mirror* and the *Cook Report*
in 1990 were subsequently chased with great relish by the rest of the
media, Tory and Labour MPs, Scargill's opponents inside the NUM,
the Fraud Squad, the courts, the government-appointed Certification
Officer and Commissioner for Trade Union Rights, the UDM and
the maverick right-wing electricians' union, Cabinet ministers, the
TUC, an eccentric alliance of Soviet trade-union bureaucrats and
dissident union breakaway outfits, the Inland Revenue, even Colonel
Gaddafi, as well as a vast array of accountants and lawyers – who,
needless to say, made a fortune out of the affair. All had their own
special axe to grind and took every opportunity of the open season
on the NUM and its leaders. For six months, while the threat of
accelerated closures and privatisation hung over the miners, the
Scargill Affair circus moved from Sheffield to London to Paris to
Budapest and Moscow. Teams of NUM officials, solicitors and financial advisers searched across Europe for the miners' 'lost treasure',
and official investigations and legal actions were launched with wild
abandon.

The campaign was a bizarre, almost surreal, episode which revealed
much about the way British public life works: its double standards
and workaday corruption; the myriad ties and connections which
allow different parts of the establishment to move in tandem as soon
as the need arises; the comfortable relationship between sections of

the Labour hierarchy and the government and security apparatus; the way politicians, government and its various agencies, newspapers, broadcasters and professionals feed off the same political menu as if to order. It also served to highlight, in exemplary fashion, the political venality and pliability of the bulk of the British media.

When the *Guardian* first published details of large-scale counter-subversion operations against the NUM and an account of some of the political undercurrents behind the Scargill Affair, the *Daily Mirror*'s immediate response was to cry: 'conspiracy theory!' In two full-page tirades, the *Guardian* was accused of stringing together 'an unlikely chain of people who, it implies, took part in a great conspiracy: the KGB, CIA, Margaret Thatcher, MI6, Mikhail Gorbachev, and the *Mirror* – and all of them out to get poor old Arthur'. The *Guardian*'s purpose, it was said, was to prove the NUM president to be a 'maliciously maligned hero of the working class'. In fact, the stringing together was done by the *Mirror* itself.

In a resolutely empiricist culture like Britain's – where 'practical men' prefer to shun the bigger picture and eminent historians can take delight in claiming that world wars break out because of the requirements of railway timetables – it is hardly surprising perhaps that many people feel unhappy with any suggestion of behind-the-scenes collusion and manipulation of events. To suggest anything else is regarded as somehow naïve and insufficiently worldly. Among journalists in particular, it is an article of faith to insist on the 'cock-up theory' rather than the 'conspiracy theory' of history. Real life is, of course, a mixture of the two. One side-effect of this dogmatic insistence that events are largely the product of an arbitrary and contingent muddle has been a chronic refusal by the mainstream media in Britain – and most opposition politicians – to probe or question the hidden agendas and unaccountable, secret power structures at the heart of government. This is in striking contrast to North American journalism, which, for all its failings, does at least maintain some tradition of investigation and scepticism about the activities of its country's rulers. As Stephen Dorril and Robin Ramsay, two authors who have attempted to unearth some of Whitehall's dirtier secrets, have commented: 'For the most part the areas which the British state does not want examined are still left alone by our serious papers.'

The result is that an entire dimension of politics and the exercise of power in Britain is habitually left out of standard reporting and analysis. And by refusing to acknowledge that dimension, it is often impossible to make proper sense of what is actually going on. Worse, it lets off the hook those whose abuse of state authority is most flagrant. The security services in Britain, as elsewhere, exercise unaccountable power through the control and manipulation of privileged information. It is a world of what one American writer describes as 'parapolitics': of 'the conduct of public affairs not by rational debate and responsible decision-making but by indirection, collusion and deceit . . . the political exploitation of irresponsible agencies or para-structures, such as intelligence agencies'. With the special exception of Britain's corrosive 'security' role in the north of Ireland, there have been no clearer cases of such covert action, of such comprehensive mobilisation of the normally submerged power centres of the Whitehall empire, than in the history of the secret war against the miners.

There is no question in retrospect, if it was not self-evident at the time, that the 1984–85 strike was the most important industrial dispute since 1926 and a defining moment of post-war British history. Indeed, there has been nothing quite like it – in its size, its duration and its national and international impact – anywhere else in the world. It is scarcely surprising, therefore, that the return to work without a settlement in March 1985 was not going to prove enough for the British Government. Not only would the Coal Board be licensed to use every form of industrial and financial intimidation to change the balance of power in the country's most industrially strategic sector. It was also necessary to discredit the strike itself, to rubbish its leadership, to paint it as the work of a clique of violent, unrepresentative and undemocratic extremists. This the bulk of the media toiled loyally to do in the years after 1985, assisted by those in the labour movement who were desperate, for their own reasons, to draw a line under the dispute and fix it in the collective memory as an insurrectionary throwback which had demonstrated once and for all that militancy doesn't pay.

But however assiduously the story of the strike and its outcome was rewritten, the strikers and their leaders continued to be regarded by large sections of the population as people of principle who had dared to resist when others had bent the knee. How better to seal the image of this epic confrontation and close an entire chapter of working-class history than to reveal its leaders to be men of straw, grubbing around with the rest for the perks of office, shuffling vast sums of money between foreign bank accounts for personal advancement and pocketing strike funds to pay off their home loans? It is small wonder that the tales peddled by the *Mirror, Cook Report* and later Gavin Lightman, QC, were devoured with such an insatiable political appetite. But as time passed, the Scargill Affair turned out to be the very opposite of the drama that was originally played out through the British media in the spring and summer of 1990. And the inversions of fact and fantasy it entailed became a cruelly illuminating commentary on our public life and times.

What was billed as the ultimate exposé of the last dinosaurs of militant trade unionism ended up exposing those who led the chorus of denunciation. Robert Maxwell, the newspaper baron who falsely accused Arthur Scargill and Peter Heathfield of theft and embezzlement, was revealed eighteen months later to be one of the greatest thieves and embezzlers of the twentieth century. Gavin Lightman, the eminent QC and judge-to-be who savaged Scargill in 1990 for assorted breaches of duty and misapplications of funds – later shown to be unfounded – was four years later facing, with his publisher, a six-figure bill in costs and damages after the NUM sued him for breach of confidence and fiduciary duty.[5] Roger Windsor, the former NUM chief executive who charged the two miners' leaders with having used strike funds to pay off their home loans, had, it transpired, been the only one of the three who was guilty of the allegation. This same hired witness is now shown to have been wrong in every detail about the 'Libyan money' he claimed had been used for the repayments. Of

[5] Gavin Lightman, QC, was appointed by the NUM executive to head an inquiry into the *Mirror* and *Cook Report* allegations. His report, released on 3 July 1990, cleared Scargill and Heathfield of personal corruption but accused Scargill of impropriety, breaches of duty and the misapplication of funds, and recommended that the NUM take legal action. That action was abandoned and the case brought by the government-appointed Certification Officer over the miners' leaders' handling of strike funds (also on the basis of Lightman's report) was dismissed by the magistrate, after only three days in court, in June 1991. But the Lightman Report had also triggered an investigation by the tax authorities. On 14 May 1992, however, the Inland Revenue, after a twenty-month-long investigation, cleared Scargill and Heathfield of all charges of breaches of duty and the misapplication of funds.

the other whistleblowers, one had been imprisoned in Pakistan for allegedly plotting to blow up a mosque, another jailed in Britain for fraud. Two of the dissident Russian miners' 'representatives' flown over to accuse Scargill of misappropriating Soviet cash donations were soon afterwards expelled from their own Western-funded organisation for taking equipment.

In the event, every single one of the original claims proved to be untrue, unfounded, wildly misrepresented or so partial as to be virtually unrecognisable from any factual foundation. Neither Scargill nor Heathfield paid off – or ever could have paid off – mortgages with Libyan or any other strike funds, as the *Daily Mirror* and the *Cook Report* insisted to fifteen-million-odd readers and viewers, because neither *had* a mortgage. Absurdly, the claim was never put in any recognisable way to either man in advance. It was just 'too sensitive', the *Cook Report* producer explained at the time. Nor, as the evidence now makes clear, could what in fact were simply 'paper refinancings' have ever been made with Libyan cash – because the fabled 'Gaddafi money' never even arrived in Britain until long after the transactions were carried out. The central allegation was a paper-thin lie, the by-product of a deliberate set-up, but also the vital hook on which the whole campaign depended.

The fall-back stories fared little better. As original Soviet documentation has now confirmed, it was Mikhail Gorbachev and Yegor Ligachev – not Arthur Scargill and Alain Simon,[6] as alleged by the *Daily Mirror*, the *Cook Report* and Gavin Lightman – who took the decision to 'divert' Soviet strike support cash to the Miners' Trade Union International (MTUI), from where it was transferred – again on Soviet instructions – to a specially created MTUI solidarity fund in Dublin. Once the money arrived late, almost all of it after the strike was over, the operation of the Dublin trust account – including the donation of hundreds of thousands of pounds to the British miners' hardship fund long before the *Mirror* and *Cook Report* ran their stories – was incontestably known of and approved by the Soviet miners' union leadership. Then there was the matter of the 'secret accounts' used to beat sequestration and receivership. The Inland Revenue's acceptance that they were either valid independent trusts or 'constructive trusts' for the donors – in other words, that they were legally independent and that none of the cash that passed through

[6] General Secretary of the International Miners' Organisation.

them belonged to the NUM – demolished the entire basis of the Lightman Report's repeated claims that the union leadership was guilty of financial impropriety, breaches of duty and misapplications of union funds.

At every stage and in every aspect of the affair, the fingerprints of the intelligence services could be found like an unmistakable calling card. From the openly advertised intelligence contacts used in the original *Sunday Times* scoop on Roger Windsor's 1984 Libyan trip, to the CIA's tame Russian miners who helpfully called in the Fraud Squad, to the explicit intelligence sources of the lawyers' surveillance report on Alain Simon, through Robert Maxwell's own longstanding links with the security services, to the CIA's funding of Windsor's former employers at PSI,[7] to the GCHQ leaks on secret-service manipulation of the *Mirror–Cook Report* stories, to Miles Copeland's warning to Scargill and Heathfield about an intelligence set-up, to Tam Dalyell's Whitehall and police tip-offs about Windsor and Stella Rimington, to the Libyan leadership's pained recognition of Altaf Abbasi as a double agent: the intelligence connection ran like a poisoned thread throughout the 1990 campaign, the last great propaganda thrash against the NUM and its recalcitrant leadership.

The attempt to 'stitch up' the NUM leadership exemplified the cynicism and corruption that spread so deeply into political and public life in the 1980s and 1990s: the tacit complicity between government and opposition; the breathtaking double standards of the courts and the press; the pliancy of supposedly independent public-office-holders; the hounding of anyone who demonstrated political independence by the political establishment and its cheerleaders, busily lining their pockets at the public expense. As the 1980s wore on, financial scandals multiplied among the Conservative government's closest allies and supporters in the City of London. Tory corporate financiers were routinely discovered up to their necks in fraud and misappropriation on a gargantuan scale. While the media pursued the mirage of embezzlement and misappropriation in the miners' union throughout 1990, real financial scandals were erupting on an almost weekly basis in City and corporate boardrooms: at Polly Peck,

[7] Public Services International, a global umbrella organisation for public sector unions.

Rover, Lloyd's, Ferranti, Barlow Clowes, House of Fraser, Guinness, British & Commonwealth, Dunsdale Securities. Such standards, set by Thatcher's administration, became the norm under her successor.

The late 1980s and the early 1990s were the years of high sleaze. The four Conservative election victories between 1979 and 1992 were underwritten with millions of pounds donated by five foreign businessmen implicated in criminal tax evasion, insider dealing and fraud. At least two of the party's largest donors – Asil Nadir, the Turkish Cypriot tycoon, and Octav Botnar, the ex-chairman of Nissan UK, who between them gave £1.5 million – fled the country to avoid criminal prosecution. Another couple of Hong Kong businessmen who gave the Tory Party several hundred thousand pounds hedged their bets as part-time advisers to the Chinese Government. The largest single Conservative Party donor was an alleged Nazi collaborator and enthusiastic supporter of the Greek colonels' dictatorship in the early 1970s, John Latsis. He paid over £2 million to John Major's party in 1991. The system of Tory funding was underpinned for many years by a network of secret companies to secure covert donations. Latterly, Conservative Party treasurers set up a special offshore account in Jersey for donors who preferred to avoid the attentions of the tax authorities. Quite independently of its Maxwell connection, the Labour Party was also found to have taken money – though on a far more modest scale than the governing party – from a fraudulent runaway businessman in the early 1990s.

At the same time, these masters of political corruption were the very people who excoriated the miners' leadership and bayed for the Fraud Squad over the use of foreign bank accounts and Communist-bloc cash donations to protect the NUM. But the financing of the 1984–85 coal strike and the maintenance of an independent miners' union in the face of the most far-reaching judicial action against organised labour for more than a century was the very opposite of corruption. Those who had money gave to those who did not and the City of London and the courts were for the most part simply bypassed. The strikers and their families, the picketing operations, the national and area organisations were all funded by individual supporters and sympathetic unions, in Britain and abroad, on the basis of trust, without reference to the official legal and financial system. As the legal vice tightened, almost the entire operation came to be carried out in cash. The realisation that militant trade unionists were handling millions of pounds, mostly in plastic bags and cardboard boxes, without reference to the high priests of finance came as a great shock to the powers-that-be. The control of such large sums of money was, after all, their preserve. The interlopers had to be brought to heel.

The web of legislation and litigation woven around the trade unions in the 1980s achieved its greatest effect in the case of the miners. While the government made enormous efforts to ensure that contract and common law – rather than its own anti-trade-union statutes – were used against the NUM during the year-long strike, it encouraged David Hart's Gulliver strategy to tie up the union leadership in unending, energy-sapping legal battles. Throughout the post-strike period, the ability of Scargill and other NUM leaders to concentrate on the indus-trial and political war being waged by the Coal Board and the govern-ment was hampered by the litigious aftermath of sequestration, receivership, the receiver's breach-of-trust action and other legal disputes. Time and again – most notably in the case of receivership – the jud-iciary jettisoned received legal wisdom and precedent with cheerful abandon in its enthusiasm to deliver the Enemy Within bound and gagged. Trust and injunction law was rewritten on the hoof by the judges during the strike, and a whole raft of decisions had to be over-turned by the Appeal Court after receivership was lifted in 1986 to clear up the damage to the legal system. The avalanche of cases unleashed in 1990 was, in effect, an extension of the Gulliver tactic. By dragging the miners' leaders into another legal maze, the opportunity to rebuild NUM members' confidence and resist the oncoming threat of privat-isation and sweeping pit closures was drastically undermined.

At crucial stages of the 1990 campaign, lawyers formally employed by the NUM played decisive roles in driving this process forward. Gavin Lightman's decision to demand an extension of his terms of reference led directly to the legal action for 'recovery' of the Soviet money and to the prosecution of the national officials by the Certification Office. Even as the central arguments in his report began to look increasingly shaky, Lightman took the manuscript to Penguin to rush it out as an instant paperback book – a decision he would regret at his leisure. And it was Lightman's friend Bruce Brodie who took the NUM's four-man team in hand after the executive had been 'advised' to sue its own leadership, who commissioned a private secu-rity firm to spy on Alain Simon and who proved so strikingly reluc-tant to hand over vital case papers to his own client, the NUM, once the action had been abandoned.

For the new-model Labour Party and the 'me-too', 'one of us' philosophy that flourished within its leadership during the Thatcher years, the *Mirror*–Cook campaign was manna from heaven. From the point of view of the labour-movement hierarchy, this was an ideal opportunity to bury the spectre of class politics and trade-union militancy which haunted its efforts to construct a post-social-democratic electoral machine. As Hugo Young puts it in his biography of Thatcher:

> In the miners' strike . . . the Conservatives could have been said to be doing Kinnock's work for him. By eliminating Scargill from the board, they removed not only an enemy of the state but a major embarrassment for the middle-of-the-road brand of Socialism which Kinnock was seeking to advance. But that is not the way the public saw it, or the way Kinnock was able to exploit it. He was left with . . . a party in which significant numbers continued to see Scargill as he saw himself: the only one in all that multitude who dared to stand and fight against the evil of Thatcherism.

Neil Kinnock's courtiers lost no opportunity to tighten Scargill's rack in the service of their much-vaunted – but little-availing – 'new realism'. The speed and enthusiasm with which Kevin Barron and Kim Howells, the Labour leader's two closest allies in and around the miners' union, seized on the *Mirror*–*Cook Report* allegations was an unmistakable signal that this was an operation which had the unstinting blessing of the Labour Party *apparat*. Even after the central allegations in the campaign had been comprehensively discredited, Kinnock was there personally to hand out the 'reporter of the year' prizes to the *Mirror* journalists responsible for peddling them.[8] And in case anyone missed the point, the ill-fated Labour leader had himself photographed with the three reporters in an extravagant showbusiness pose.

The multimedia onslaught unleashed by Maxwell's *Mirror* and Central Television on the miners' leaders was in reality a classic smear campaign. Indeed, the treatment of the whole farrago of allegations

[8] In June 1991 Neil Kinnock presented the British Press Awards' 'Reporter of the Year' prize to Frank Thorne, Ted Oliver and Terry Pattinson, the *Mirror* team responsible for the anti-Scargill campaign.

and legal cases was a particularly revealing example of how the British media – and particularly the press – routinely operates against designated enemies. Facts were not checked, inconvenient angles not investigated. They didn't need to be. For the most part, even the broadsheet press and television news programmes simply repeated the sensational claims, without any serious attempt to investigate allegations or sources. The story casually changed from one day to the next. As each allegation was shown to be false or misleading, another took its place. Against all the supposed rules of journalism, the story continued to run regardless of the accumulating mass of counter-evidence. It is inconceivable that such serious accusations – fraud, falsification, theft and corruption – would ever have been made in a national newspaper against almost any other public figure without a watertight case of compendious detail.

At the height of the 1990 campaign, Paul Foot, then the *Daily Mirror*'s top columnist, suggested an analogy. Imagine, he said, that he had run a story on the front page of the *Mirror* about two Tory MPs who had paid off their mortgages out of funds they had raised for charity. 'I'm sure you'd agree that's a very good story,' he said. Suppose, he went on, that an official inquiry had then found that one of the MPs had never had a mortgage at all and the other MP had paid his mortgage off long before the charity money had even been raised. And say it was also revealed that the paper's main source – and this was, he said, the 'most extraordinary thing about a source that I have ever come across in a lifetime of investigative journalism' – had been shown to be the 'only person on earth' who was guilty of the allegation he had made against the two MPs in the *Mirror* and was still paid handsomely for his testimony. And imagine that his other main source was a man convicted of plotting to blow up mosques in Pakistan. 'First of all,' he said, 'I would never have been able to get such a story published. But if I had had such a story published and all these facts had then come out, my feet wouldn't have touched the ground. I'd have been fired and nobody would ever have believed a word I'd have written ever again about Tory MPs or anything else.' But in the case of the Scargill story, instead of the journalists being called to account or the Press Council protesting at such an abuse, the allegations were repeated again and again even though they had been proved to be false. And each time one allegation was discredited, another took its place, like the multi-headed Hydra of ancient Greek legend. 'Since these allegations have nothing to do with

facts or investigative journalism,' Foot queried, 'how and why is it
that the story continues to run?' It ran, he concluded, because the
most powerful vested interests in society wanted it to run.

The author was passed information supporting the miners' leaders'
case by another national newspaper journalist during the 1990 media
campaign because the reporter's own 'quality' paper was not interested in publishing stories that contradicted the general line of attack.
Such things are utterly unexceptional in the media. They are the
mostly unspoken daily norm. In a highly concentrated communications industry, where 93 per cent of the daily and Sunday newspaper
market is 'serviced' by five media conglomerates and their multimil-
lionaire proprietors, the control and manipulation of information
constitutes a permanent negation of free debate. Without the monopoly
ownership grip by multinational companies on great swathes of the
media, the Scargill Affair could never have taken off. It would have
been quickly exposed as a malevolent and fraudulent set-up. While
those promoting the smears constantly pointed to Scargill's failure to
sue Maxwell as evidence of guilt, his inability in practice to do so
when the accusations against him were so demonstrably false constituted an indictment of the libel laws rather than the miners' leader.
As a rule, libel action is a practical and effective option only for the
very wealthy or for those on whom they bestow their favours.

The 1990 media attacks were in any case only the most extreme
of a string of propaganda campaigns over the previous decade against
the NUM leadership. As the journalist Hunter Davies remarked of
Scargill in the wake of the pit-closures controversy of 1992–93: 'No
living person in the land has had a worse press.' Only the treatment
meted out to Tony Benn has come near to the anti-Scargill savagery,
and even Benn arguably never quite matched the sustained level of
vilification that Scargill was subjected to from the early 1980s. Both
have been 'abused by the media to the point of harassment and
beyond', in the words of the BBC Television and *Financial Times*
industrial editors who covered the 1984–85 miners' strike. In the case
of the NUM president, a pitch was reached during the dispute which
only really subsided with the public outcry over colliery closures in
1992. Nicholas Jones, the BBC political correspondent who covered
the 1984–85 strike, believes journalists were 'caught up in an anti-
Scargill feeding frenzy'. Simon Jenkins, the former *Times* editor,
described press coverage of the miners' strike while the dispute was
still raging as 'ludicrously biased . . . Fleet Street's loathing for [Scargill]

is almost palpable . . . a public kept in ignorance of the nature of his support, and told merely of his idiocy, grows ever more mystified at his survival. It is the tale of duff propaganda down the ages.'

To leaf through newspaper cuttings from the strike period a decade later is to be transported back to an Alice-in-Wonderland world of long-suffering policemen and saintly strikebreakers fighting the good fight against swaggering picket-line thugs with money to blow, of impossible return-to-work figures and fantastic power-supply projections. Take, more or less at random, the banner front-page headline run by the *Sunday Express* on 25 November 1984: 'SUITCASES OF CASH PAY FOR TERROR'. The story was about the cash loans and donations then keeping the NUM afloat at a time when its own funds had been frozen by the sequestrators. 'Suitcases packed with thousands of pounds in £1 and £5 notes are being ferried to NUM leaders in Yorkshire', the piece began, accurately enough. But by the second paragraph, the reporter was already away with the fairies. 'Moderates in the NUM are convinced the cash is being used to finance terror squads of militant youths', he fantasised, 'and a group of intimidators selected to "persuade" working pitmen to rejoin the strike . . . free-spending intimidators leading the campaign to stop the flood of miners returning to work have been nicknamed "Fat Cats" in Yorkshire.'

A report more remote from reality would be hard to imagine. Or at least it would have been hard had it not been for the multiplicity of other, similar episodes during the dispute, such as the *Sun*'s attempt to publish a front-page picture of Scargill appearing to give a Nazi salute – which Fleet Street printworkers refused to typeset – under the legend: 'MINE FUHRER'. Then there was the case of the BBC coverage of the most violent confrontation of the strike, at Orgreave on 18 June 1984, when footage broadcast on television was reversed to show the mounted police charge as a response to missile-throwing from pickets. The real, diametrically opposite, sequence of events was only later demonstrated when the police's own video was produced at the insistence of the defence in the subsequent riot trial.

But press and, to a lesser extent, broadcasting coverage of the strike and its protracted aftermath was not simply distinguished by bias and vitriol. It was also marked by a level of government, police and secret-service manipulation unmatched in the reporting of any other running domestic story. Security-service media guidance was insistently offered, at all levels. Sir John Jones, then MI5 director-general, for example, called in editors and senior broadcasting executives in the autumn of

1984 to 'reveal' Soviet backing for Scargill and the danger the intelligence services believed this posed to the state. Press, radio and television should, he told them, reflect an appreciation of this in its coverage of the strike. Lower down the media hierarchy, the intervention was far cruder. As Nicholas Jones puts it:

> [Thatcher] was using agencies at the side which we'd not actually come across before – people who were capable of manipulating the newspapers in a way that we hadn't seen before. And we know that sections of the news media were closely involved, the security services were involved, a lot of information was being passed about. We saw the conduct of journalists changing, because a closer relationship developed between journalists and some police officers handling the dispute. The flow of information . . . from the police and the security forces . . . to the news media was, I think, quite a significant factor in that dispute.

This cosy trade continued long after the end of the strike. 'Offside' steers and leaks abounded. At the beginning of June 1985, for example, with the NUM in the hands of the court-appointed receiver, Scargill was in Paris discussing with Alain Simon and other French CGT[9] officials the union's plight and the forthcoming foundation of the new International Miners' Organisation. With no prior warning, Simon asked him to travel the same day to Czechoslovakia to meet the leadership of the Communist-led World Federation of Trade Unions (WFTU) in Prague. Scargill joined a Czechoslovak airline flight in Paris that night at the last minute, after all the other passengers were already on board. Throughout the flight he sat alone at the back of the aircraft. At Prague airport, he waited until the plane was empty before crossing to the terminal building, where visa formalities were waived and he was whisked, apparently unseen, behind the sliding-door entrance reserved for VIP guests. There he was greeted by the Sudanese WFTU general secretary, Ibrahim Zakaria, and other WFTU and Czechoslovak trade-union officials. After two days in Prague, he flew back to Britain, via Paris. At the NUM, only Roger Windsor and Nell Myers[10] were told about Scargill's trip.

[9] Confederation générale du travail, French trade union.
[10] Scargill's personal assistant and NUM press officer.

But four days later, a well-briefed front-page story in, once again, the *Sunday Express* regaled readers with details of the WFTU visit. 'Arthur Scargill has sparked off a new wave of alarm in the NUM', the piece began, 'over his links with the Communist bloc with a hush-hush trip behind the Iron Curtain . . . When the Executive meets on Thursday Mr Scargill will be asked why he goes to Communist countries in secret, who pays for the trips and what he discusses. And he will be asked in particular to explain reports that on arrival in Prague he was met by four "Afghan-looking types" waiting for the Prague–Kabul connection.' Clearly, someone had been monitoring Scargill's travelling arrangements very closely, even if they did have trouble distinguishing Afghans – a connection which would have been politically more suggestive at a time when there were 100,000 Soviet troops in Afghanistan – from Sudanese. When the *Sunday Express* reporter rang Nell Myers at the NUM to check the details, he apologised in advance for running such a story.

The incestuous relationship between the intelligence services and sections of the media is, of course, nothing new. The connection is notoriously close in the case of some foreign correspondents. Kim Philby was, after all, offered a job as Middle East correspondent for both *The Economist* and the *Observer* – at a time when the security services had yet to uncover his real allegiances – after a couple of discreet telephone calls from the Foreign Office. More recently, Sandy Gall, the ITN reporter and newsreader, boasted of his work for MI6 in Afghanistan during the 1980s and his liaison meetings with MI6 officers at Stone's Chop House in Piccadilly. 'Soon after I returned to London', Gall wrote in his memoirs, 'I received an invitation to have lunch with the head of MI6 . . . I was flattered, of course, and . . . resolved to be completely frank and as informative as possible, and not try to prise any information out of him in return. This is not normally how a journalist's mind works.' Indeed not.

But Gall was far from being alone. David Cornwell, the former intelligence officer turned best-selling spywriter John le Carré, has remarked that in his time 'the British secret service controlled large sections of the press, just as they may do today'. After US Senate hearings in 1975 revealed the extent of CIA recruitment of both American and British journalists, 'sources' let it be known that half the foreign staff of a British daily were on the MI6 payroll. There are several recent cases known to the author of well-known reporters in both television and print journalism – and these are doubtless a

handful among many – who became entangled with MI6, sometimes
to their cost as well as benefit. Needless to say, those journalists who
double up as part-time spies do no favours for their colleagues, who
can come under dangerous and unjustified suspicion as a result. But
far less appreciated is the extent of MI5 manipulation of the press
at home, which intensified in the years of industrial unrest in the
1970s and 1980s and reached a peak during the miners' strike and
its pulverising aftermath. This was the period when the security services are said to have recruited three-quarters of national labour and
industrial correspondents, along with a small army of agents and
informers inside the trade unions themselves.

The 1990 smear campaign against the NUM was, it is now clear,
in part the poisoned fruit of this corrosive relationship. The accumulation of evidence now uncovered about the events surrounding
Roger Windsor's disastrous visit to Tripoli in the autumn of 1984
shows that there was unquestionably a deliberate and meticulously
constructed attempt to 'set up' the miners' leadership during the most
finely balanced weeks of the dispute. The broadcast meeting with
Gaddafi, the convict middleman, the staged banknote drops, the officials' home 'repayments' carried out on advice, the timely cash advance
on the real Libyan money, the phoney laundering of funds through
the CGT: all were primed to cause maximum propaganda damage if
and when required. The first phase of the sting was activated with
the detailed revelations of Windsor's Libyan connection and the 'scoop
of the year' in the *Sunday Times*. The second – and far more damaging
– phase was held in reserve, as the looming threat of defeat for the
government receded in the final weeks of 1984. Just over five years
later, it would be brought into play with devastating effect in the
Daily Mirror and *Cook Report*.

Behind this operation stood the most secretive and unaccountable
arms of a secretive state. Britain's intelligence and security services
remain a profoundly anti-democratic force. As the account by Peter
Wright and others of the conspiracy against the Wilson government
has shown, it is the security services – rather than the left and the
trade unions – who have been the real subversives, operating through
fear and an effective veto on political and public appointments, under-
mining democratic government and accountability. When Michael
Hanley, then director-general of MI5, confirmed to Harold Wilson in
August 1975 that 'only a small number' of 'disaffected right-wing'
security-service officers had been plotting against him, the intimidated

Labour Prime Minister was reduced to swearing at his chief spycatcher, rather than sacking him. When Jim Callaghan succeeded Wilson, he politely asked the intelligence services to confirm that they had done nothing wrong and they duly obliged.

Ten years later, at the height of the publicity about the *Spycatcher* allegations, Callaghan accepted that he had been misled, while his successor Margaret Thatcher repeated the whole charade of allowing MI5 to investigate its own treachery and give itself a clean bill of health. If no action was taken over an attempt to destabilise an elected government, it can hardly be surprising that the Tory beneficiary of that destabilisation should be prepared to countenance comprehensive covert operations – infiltration, provocation, fraud, forgery, bugging and frame-ups – against a trade union which had faced down two Conservative governments three times in a decade.

Clive Ponting, the former Ministry of Defence official, remembered senior MI5 officers he dealt with as 'utterly reactionary'. Edward Heath, the former Prime Minister, described the secret force supposedly under his control as follows:

I met people in the security services who talked the most ridiculous nonsense and whose whole philosophy was ridiculous nonsense. If one of them were on a tube and saw someone reading the *Daily Mirror* they would say: 'Get after him, that is dangerous. We must find out where he bought it.'

The whole apparatus would simply be the butt of ridicule and contempt if it were not also a powerful and poisonous influence in political and industrial life. At the same time, there is not the slightest reason to suppose that if the extent of the covert action taken against the NUM had become known during or after the miners' strike it would have commanded public support. The security services thrive in secrecy not least because they would not survive the glare of accountability.

And thrive they continue to do. Despite the end of the Cold War, the disappearance of large sections of the left and the manifest weakness of the trade unions, MI5 carried on expanding its apparatus, power and influence – a process highlighted by its widely publicised turf-war victory against police Special Branch in 1992 over control of 'mainland' intelligence operations against the IRA. At the time of writing, the IRA ceasefire has intensified speculation that MI5 is bound to launch other hostile takeover bids for police work – such as drug trafficking and organised crime – to keep itself in business. There were even some signs that – despite, or perhaps because of, its supposed overriding allegiance to the crown – the security service had taken to intervening in the affairs of the royal family, apparently with the aim of protecting the House of Windsor from itself. Naturally, Stella Rimington dismissed the allegations out of hand. But, then – as she obliquely admitted – who was ever to know, when under the 1989 Official Secrets Act MI5 officers commit a criminal offence if they disclose any evidence of MI5 activity, illegal or otherwise, even to their MP? Meanwhile, the threat of smear and whispering campaigns continued to hang over anyone in public life – or indeed outside it – who failed to play the part allotted to them. Britain's secret state remains a dangerous political and bureaucratic cesspit, uniquely undisturbed by any meaningful form of political accountability.

In a sense, the smear campaign against the NUM leadership was successful. The planned merger with the TGWU[11] – concern about which in both government and the Labour hierarchy was one reason for the virulence of the onslaught – failed to come off, partly because of the time and confidence that were lost while Scargill and Heathfield fought to clear their names. The position of the IMO, under heavy attack in the wake of the collapse of the Communist regimes in the East, was significantly weakened. Scargill's reputation among his own membership, the left and labour movement, and the British public at large, was damaged. Despite the collapse of the main charges – itself largely unreported in the press and broadcast media – there continued to be a widespread sense that something dodgy had been going on at the heart of the miners' union. Some of the mud had stuck. And the NUM national officials were tied up in litigation and internal argument for well over a year, when the union was already demoralised and needed a determined mobilisation to fight privatisation and pit closures. The revival of Scargill's popularity in 1992 owed more to the government's incompetence and a widespread public sense that he had been dramatically vindicated than to his dogged success in fighting off the earlier media and legal attacks.

No doubt those who lent their support, tacitly or overtly, to the

[11] Transport and General Workers' Union.

orchestrated scandal felt it had all been worthwhile, even if the ulti-mate prize of the NUM president's head on a platter finally eluded them. But the Scargill Affair also had less welcome spin-offs for its sponsors. For one thing, it revealed for the first time the NUM leaders' remarkable success in short-circuiting the attempt to outlaw their organisation. It laid bare the extraordinary lengths the strike leader-ship went to during, but more especially after, the 1984–85 dispute to evade the judicial takeover of the union and maintain its resist-ance to the Thatcher government. In doing so, the campaign exposed to other trade unionists options its sponsors would have preferred to remain hidden. The secret funding of the NUM after the autumn of 1984, in defiance of the courts, using both millions of pounds in cash and a hidden and parallel system of trust-fund accounts, was an oper-ation unprecedented in the history of the British labour movement. Most alarmingly for the government – as Tory ministers admitted in private when Scargill disclosed details of the arrangements in 1990 to clear his name of the corruption charges – it worked.

And unlike the ill-fated transfer of NUM funds overseas in 1984, the system of independent accounts and funds Scargill and Heathfield used to keep the NUM afloat was never cracked by the sequestrators and the receiver – nor, indeed, by the security services. Significantly, although Scargill's friend Jean McCrindle and his secretary Yvonne Fenn were involved in part of the funding arrangements, the system was known in its entirety only to Scargill, Heathfield and Nell Myers. The NUM president was strongly criticised, when the details of the secret accounts were finally revealed, for having failed to 'come clean' with his executive before. Running such an operation until receiver-ship was lifted in 1986 – or even until the receiver dropped his breach-of-trust action against the union leadership in 1988 – was one thing, the argument went. But continuing to keep the details secret once the legal threat had gone was intolerable, it was said, even if the unions which had lent money to the various trusts and accounts wanted their involvement kept confidential.

But the criticism missed the essential point. Only if all the funds and accounts were kept scrupulously independent and had no formal link with the union whatever could they be protected from seizure or, later on, from other forms of retrospective action. To have declared them to the executive at any time would have been to accept that they were in reality NUM accounts. The proof of the pudding was in the eating. As soon as the seventeen accounts were in fact disclosed, in 1990, a string of investigations and legal actions was sparked off. They hinged crucially on Gavin Lightman's claim that all the trusts and accounts were shams, and that all the money which had passed through them in fact belonged to the union. The claim was put to the test in law and found wanting. As a result of the Inland Revenue investigation, which ruled in 1992 that the money used to maintain the NUM had either belonged to the donors or to genuine trusts, three of the unions that gave or lent money during the NUM's receivership found themselves facing tax bills for tens of thousands of pounds. Clearly, anything that had undermined the independent status of the accounts at any stage would have attracted a still greater flood of claims and litigation against Scargill and the NUM.

The secret funding operation showed a willingness to take the fight for independent trade unionism to its logical conclusion. It incidentally put into practice the Trades Union Congress's own 1982 decision to defy the government's legal attack on the labour movement. Most importantly, it demonstrated that unions can face down such anti-democratic legislation and continue to function. The experience of the NUM and other unions that came up against the Tory anti-union laws – such as the print and seafarers' unions – convinced many British trade unionists that defiance and non-cooperation were a dead end. It fuelled the so-called 'new realism' that came to dominate trade-union thinking in the late 1980s and early 1990s. If you embark on an unlawful strike, workers were told, your union will be subject to crippling fines and may be destroyed altogether. Given that nine pieces of anti-union legislation had made almost any kind of effective industrial action potentially illegal, the threat of union fines and sequestration – let alone receivership – combined, along with mass unemployment and job insecurity, to bring organised labour to its knees.

But the NUM's experience showed that it was possible both to defy anti-union laws and for the official full-time union organisation to survive. In August 1990, Scargill declared: 'With hindsight I now know exactly how to beat sequestration without getting into a breach of trust action or a receiver being appointed.' And he teasingly offered a foolproof package to any union prepared to fight the Tory legislation. In the political conditions of the early 1990s, there were few takers for such an approach. Full-time officials were especially threatened by the government's legal battery, which was quite deliberately aimed at formal union structures and assets and designed to drive a wedge between union full-timers and ordinary members. The legislation was intended to force union officials to police their own membership. The NUM's independent funding system revealed how to short-circuit that divide-and-rule tactic. The full existing panoply of anti-trade-union laws – and most crucially, the statutes outlawing solidarity or 'secondary' action – will ultimately only be repealed if trade unionists are prepared to fight it. No Labour government would have the political will to go beyond some modest loosening of the legal straitjacket without relentless pressure on the ground to assert trade-union independence. As workers inevitably come into conflict with the legislation once again, the NUM's little-understood success in defeating sequestration and receivership in the 1980s has the potential to become a powerful industrial and political weapon.

From 1972, the NUM posed the single most powerful challenge to the increasingly determined attempts to reorder British capitalism and shift the balance of power sharply in favour of the employers and the freedom of capital. The 1984–85 coal dispute was the most serious frontal assault on organised labour and the sharpest political and industrial confrontation with the state in Britain since the General Strike of 1926. The war against the miners was not a political aberration, but the inevitable response to a political and industrial force that could not be accommodated within the existing order. As David Lloyd George, Prime Minister of the day, told a delegation from the Triple Alliance of miners, railway and transport workers on the point of a united strike in 1919: 'If a force arises in the state which is stronger than the state itself, then it must be ready to take on the functions of the state, or it must withdraw and accept the authority of the state.'

From the mid-1970s, the Conservative Party and its allies in the security services and the wider governmental machine set themselves the strategic objective of breaking the NUM. That overriding goal refashioned the country's energy sector, underlay the privatisation of electricity and coal, and brought about fundamental changes in both the law and methods of policing. Arthur Scargill and his supporters became the focus and core of resistance to that process, as the disintegration of the Communist Party corroded the traditional centres of left-wing miners' leadership in South Wales and Scotland. Quarantined by the labour-movement hierarchy throughout the late 1980s and early 1990s, Scargill and his uncompromising syndicalist-influenced politics endured, a symbol of a militant class and trade-union tradition that stubbornly refused to give way to the politics of the self-proclaimed 'new realists'. The conventional wisdom that Scargill's intransigence and refusal to play by the established rules of the trade-union game hastened – or even brought about – the destruction of the mining industry is an inversion of what actually took place. There is no evidence that a more pliant and flexible leadership during the 1980s – such as that offered by the government-sponsored breakaway Union of Democratic Mineworkers – would have saved the miners or their collieries.

The lead given by Scargill and the NUM in 1984 offered the miners and the trade-union movement as a whole the chance to stop the Tory government's offensive in its tracks against the alternative of certain further retreat and defeat. In a different context, the same could be said about the opportunity handed to the labour movement in 1992, when the Major government's ill-prepared attempt to force through the closure of more than half the surviving coal industry led to a national political crisis. By then, Scargill and his dramatically diminished union were ripe for rehabilitation. It became customary, even in the press, to marvel at how the NUM president's predictions about Conservative intentions towards the miners and their industry – derided as scare-mongering a decade earlier – had been proved right after all. Memories of the months of smear and character assassination in 1990 and the years of hatred and ridicule momentarily melted away.

But once the government had temporarily backed down, the political momentum to halt the destruction of the coal industry became bogged down in court cases, reviews, consultants' reports and select-committee inquiries. While the Industry Secretary Michael Heseltine regained his political balance and his minions traded pits for parliamentary votes with Conservative MPs, the deep longstanding distrust of the NUM and its leaders resurfaced in the Labour and TUC hierarchies. There was little appetite for harnessing the overwhelming public support for the miners to a mass campaign to defeat the government. As the reality of the Cabinet's manoeuvring became apparent, Norman Willis, the TUC general secretary, wrote to John Major to complain that his efforts to persuade the NUM to 'pursue legal means of redress' were going unrewarded.

By the time the miners' leaders began to agitate for industrial action as the only weapon left to them in defence of mining jobs and communities, the eleventh-hour reconciliation was well and truly over. With massive coal stocks, increasing imports and a rapidly shrinking market, the NUM's capacity to make an industrial impact by itself was severely limited. But the miners voted for a campaign of national strikes – the first such ballot result for twenty years. And throughout the early months of 1993, Scargill coaxed and cajoled the reluctant railway workers' leaders to back a joint campaign of industrial action against job losses and the threat of privatisation in both industries. The outcome was a successful rail ballot and two days of synchronised strikes which simultaneously closed down the NUM-controlled mines and the entire rail network, keeping millions of employees from work throughout the country. Bloodied and massively weakened though his organisation was, the NUM president demonstrated he was not quite the 'broken man' his opponents claimed. The assault on the miners and their union would continue unabated.

The NUM and its leadership were the object of attack not for their weaknesses, but for their strengths. In the wake of the last wave of pre-privatisation pit closures, that came to be more widely understood. The NUM was seen to have stuck by its principles and paid for them. No other union could have inspired the sort of direct-action campaigns run by Women Against Pit Closures. No other group of workers could bring a quarter of a million people out onto the streets of London twice in one week to defend their industry. Few other trade unionists had been prepared to make the sacrifices the miners had made in the fight to defend their industry. Isolated and shrunken, the wreckage of its industry up for sale to the new coal owners of the 1990s, the miners' union remained the conscience of the labour movement.

AMIRA HASS

Under Siege

1996

The most courageous reporter of occupied Palestine is an Israeli correspondent, Amira Hass. Her book, *Drinking the Sea at Gaza: Days and
Nights in a Land under Siege*, inspired me to return to Palestine and
make a documentary film based on her exposé. I phoned her in
Ramallah, where she was covering Israel's siege of the West Bank
towns in 2002 for her newspaper *Ha'aretz*. We conducted our conversation as she crouched on the floor of a house with gunfire in the
background.

'If I go out, the army will kill me,' she said.

'But you're an Israeli.'

'Makes no difference. Everybody here is a target.'

In 1993, Amira did what no Israeli journalist had ever done: she
went to live and report from among the people of the Gaza Strip, the
147-square-mile 'open prison' where more than a million Palestinians
are forced to live in almost destitute conditions. To most Israelis, Gaza
is *terra incognita*, a breeding ground for terrorism and fundamentalism. To Amira, it was where she wanted to understand, 'down to
the last detail, a world that is, to the best of my political and historical comprehension, a profoundly Israeli creation. To me, Gaza
embodies the whole saga of the Israeli–Palestinian conflict; it represents the central contradiction of the State of Israel – democracy for
some, dispossession for others; it is our exposed nerve.'

For three years, she lived among Gaza's taxi drivers and farmers,
doctors and housewives, activists and Islamic leaders. She charted the
initial euphoria of the Oslo Accords, which in 1994 established a
form of Palestinian self-rule in Gaza and elsewhere in the occupied

territories, and which quickly gave way to despair and hardship as Israel imposed 'closure' – a new policy of arbitrarily sealing off the Strip and preventing a semblance of normal life. In her daily dispatch to Ha'aretz, Amira illuminated a world in which ordinary people were denied basic personal and economic freedoms, and a recurring cycle of state killing, Palestinian rebellion and collective punishment deferred peace and justice indefinitely.

Today, the situation is worse. In 2002, when I was on the West Bank and in Gaza, Palestinians were suffering malnutrition comparable with the Congo; the Israeli siege was the cause. The people of Gaza, trapped behind barbed wire and facing Israeli guns, were desperate; the UN estimated their food warehouses would be empty within weeks.

How evocative of the Jewish past all this is, and Amira Hass is ever anxious to ensure that you understand the importance of the Holocaust in her life and her reasons for reporting from 'the other side'. 'My desire to live in Gaza stemmed from the dread of being a bystander,' she says, recalling the moment her mother, Hannah, was being marched from a cattle train to the concentration camp of Bergen-Belsen on a summer day in 1944. 'She and the other women had been ten days in the train from Yugoslavia. They were sick and some were dying. Then my mother saw these German women looking at the prisoners, just looking. This image became very formative in my upbringing, this despicable "looking from the side". It's as if I was there, and saw it myself.'

Amira's parents were secular Jews. Her mother joined Tito's partisans and was forced to surrender to the Nazis when they threatened to kill every woman in the Montenegrin town of Cetinje; her father, Avraham, was trapped in the Transnistria ghetto and survived a plague of typhus. Both came to Israel, 'naïvely', she says. 'They were offered a house in Jerusalem. But they refused it. They said, "We cannot take the house of other refugees." They meant Palestinians so you see, it's not such a big deal I write what I do – it's not a big deal that I live among Palestinians.'

For some of her compatriots, it is a big deal. 'I get messages saying I must have been a kapo [a Jewish camp overseer for the Nazis] in my first incarnation.' But many urge her to keep writing, regarding her as Israel's conscience. When I last saw her, a big red scarf protecting her against the wind, she was skilfully cajoling Israeli soldiers into allowing waiting Palestinian families to pass a checkpoint. Never the bystander, she does this almost every day.

The following extract from *Drinking the Sea at Gaza* is the chapter 'Yesterday's Permit', in which she reveals the effects of Israeli policy on Palestinians dependent on medical treatment outside the Gaza Strip, and reflects on her own role as a journalist. To this, I have added her fine epilogue.

UNDER SIEGE

'The only thing that's missing here in Gaza is the morning roll call,' said Abu Majed. We were sitting on thin mattresses – the sole furniture in the room – drinking tea and nibbling cookies, a special treat for the Id al-Fitr holiday, which marks the end of the month-long Ramadan fast. Abu Majed's past reads like the saga of a Fatah everyman: occasional menial jobs in Israel, arrests and interrogations as a teenager, ten years in Israeli jails, eventual work as a Palestinian police officer. I can see him, a skinny boy mixing cement in Beersheba or hauling crates in Tel Aviv's Carmel market, making the most of his few Hebrew sentences, awed at first by the tall buildings and wide city streets, stealing glances at the women, then chiding himself for his weakness. I imagine him coming home to Gaza in the evenings with some cash for his family and a small present for his sister. And then the *intifada* and joining a UNL cell,[1] arrests and more arrests, trial and prison.

It was Abu Majed who made the connection between Gaza, prison and peppers, the hot little red and green variety that, chopped up fine with garlic and tomatoes, gives Gazan salad its fierce reputation. 'We missed those peppers in prison,' he said, 'the way they'd bring tears to your eyes. We could have pretended it was the sting that was making us cry and not our longing for home.' Abu Majed went on to tell a story he had heard from some Israeli – a guard or one of his bosses, he couldn't remember which. Investigating a series of attacks on northern Israeli farms on the Lebanese border in the 1970s, the IDF[2] concluded the infiltrators originated from Gaza, even though they had come by way of Lebanon. They had broken water pipes,

[1] United National Leadership, a revolutionary group in Gaza that prepared the ground for the *intifada* in 1987.
[2] Israeli Defence Forces.

smashed greenhouses, and ruined the fields, but one crop, though somewhat plundered, had escaped serious harm – the bushes of little green and red peppers. At least now, Abu Majed concluded ruefully, Gazans have plenty of peppers. 'It's just the roll call that's missing.' That and the constant presence of Israelis. 'It's been so long since I've spoken Hebrew,' Abu Majed said. 'You're the first Israeli I've met in two years, since I got out of prison. You're a real museum piece.'

After our meeting, I repeated Abu Majed's quip about the morning roll call at every opportunity. Gazans – ex-prisoners and others – reacted with peals of laughter. 'Why didn't we think of that?' I heard more than once. Israelis, however, usually needed an explanation and even then I am not sure they thought the joke was funny. For the most part, Israelis continue to believe that the closures, sealing off the Strip – in effect locking up Gaza's entire population – are simply a response to terror and a means to prevent it, that they are in fact the only way to avoid having buses blown up. For many, the Oslo Accords evoke only the horrifying, bloody spectacles that Israel has experienced with such frightening regularity. But what is seen as a remedy by Israelis has become collective punishment in Palestinian eyes. For Gazans, the siege of the Strip serves only to provoke the anger that produced the suicide bombings and perpetuate the circumstances that, to some extent, explain them. In Gaza, 'Oslo' and the 'peace process' are now synonymous with mass internment and suffocating constriction. It is impossible to understand developments in Gaza since the beginning of Palestinian self-rule in 1994 without considering the grinding daily ramifications of keeping the Strip closed.

On and off since 1991 – but for increasingly longer periods since 1994 – some one million people have been confined to the 147-square-mile Strip. Twenty per cent of that land is restricted to Jewish settlements and barred to Palestinians. For most Gazans, most of the time, there is no exit, not to Israel, not to Egypt and not to the West Bank.

'You can get an exit permit if you're about to die,' Gazans observe wryly. According to the Israeli Coordination and Liaison Office (CLO) – the post-Oslo incarnation of the civil administration, responsible for issuing exit permits – there are several categories of people who may ask to enter Israel, at least when the checkpoints are open: workers with steady jobs in Israel, truck owners importing or exporting goods (but only with an Israeli military escort), businessmen, sick people, those with special permits for 'personal reasons' (to visit a sick relative or to catch a flight abroad, for example), and high-ranking Palestinian officials and police. In June 1996, 17,000 workers were allowed to leave the Strip; 300 of Gaza's 2,000 trucks, some twenty to forty taxis daily of a fleet of 1,200, twenty-eight businessmen, and between ten and twenty sick people each day. (Before 1991, there were no figures because no records were kept – Gazans needed no permits and moved freely between the Strip, Israel and the West Bank. However, even conservative estimates would put the pre-1991 number of Gazans working in Israel at 80,000.)

'Once I used to dream of a state,' a Palestinian cameraman told me. 'Now I dream of getting to the other side of the Erez checkpoint.' Article 4 of the Declaration of Principles states clearly: 'Both sides regard the West Bank and the Gaza Strip as one territorial unit whose geographical integrity will be preserved during the interim period.' Yet the Strip has been cut off from the West Bank since the agreements were signed. To implement the principle of territorial integrity, the Cairo agreement, signed in May 1994, confirms that a 'safe passage' will connect the Strip with the territory under Palestinian autonomous rule in the West Bank. To date, negotiations over the safe passage – who will control it and who will be entitled to use it – have come to nothing. Palestinians who must reach the West Bank have, in some cases, travelled via Egypt to Jordan, where they crossed the Allenby Bridge, all because they could not get a permit to make a two-hour journey across Israel.

One cannot leave Gaza on a sudden impulse to visit friends in Ramallah, take care of some bit of business that can be done only in East Jerusalem (Palestinians' religious, commercial and cultural capital) or see one's family in Israel. Even in the rare instance when permission is granted, it never includes an overnight stay. There is little point in travelling several hours to one's destination, only to turn right around and come back home – and few Gazans can afford the cost, anyway. These restrictions on movement are not imposed only after a terrorist attack; they are in force all the time.

Sometimes it is impossible to leave even for an officially sanctioned 'objective' reason. One Gazan doctor, for example, could not get permission to accompany his terminally ill mother to the hospital in Tel Aviv; she died alone. The doctor's brother, a well-known

Palestinian writer, was not allowed to leave the West Bank to attend his mother's funeral in Gaza. A Palestinian journalist invited to teach part of a course in the United States was refused permission to pick up her visa at the American embassy in Tel Aviv. A young man from the Meghazi refugee camp got engaged to a woman from the Jelazun camp in the West Bank and was unable to visit her for five months. Another young man, whose fiancée was in Jordan, was denied a travel permit for security reasons. When I wrote about his case he received a permit, but he was turned down two months later when he needed to travel again. One woman was unable to fly to England to defend her doctoral thesis, even though her husband was director-general of a Palestinian ministry. A group of physicians employed by the Palestinian health ministry were not allowed to attend a ministry conference in Ramallah. A couple undergoing fertility treat-ment in Israel received one permit for the day of their appointment – for the wife only.

Whole categories of people are unable to leave the Strip. Men under forty, for example, are rarely granted exit permits; unmarried men, even those over forty, are also not allowed to leave. Many Gazan students enrolled in West Bank colleges and universities have now lost at least three years of their education. Even when students have been granted exit permits, they have been forbidden to stay in the West Bank. Sometimes students who have ignored the prohibition and stayed in the West Bank anyway have returned home for holidays and been refused new permits.

The all-important exit permit, the restrictions and refusals and contradictory, unfathomable logic behind its issue, has come to domi-nate life in the Strip. In most cases security reasons are cited. In most cases – including all those above – this excuse makes no sense.

'What do you want? We're actually making progress,' one Fatah activist told a gathering of bitter Gazans. The man had been impris-oned in Ketziot, the mass-detention camp in the Negev desert, also known as Ansar. 'There were seven blocks of tents in Ketziot and we weren't allowed to move between one block and another. Now we're down to three blocks – Gaza, the north West Bank, and the south West Bank. In Ketziot there were just us men. Here at least we've got our children and wives and parents. In Ketziot we weren't allowed to go anywhere. Here we can drive around Gaza.' He went on: 'And it's a good thing the roads are in such bad shape – it takes a whole hour to get from one end of the Strip to the other and you don't notice how small it all is. If you drive really slowly, say fifteen miles an hour, you can pretend that you're actually going a very long way.'

Since 1994 and the beginning of Palestinian self-rule, leaving Gaza has entailed the following:

First, a person must submit a written request to the appropriate Palestinian ministry: someone seeking medical treatment to the health ministry, a worker to the labour ministry, a businessperson to the ministry of commerce and industry, a driver to the transportation ministry, a student to the ministry of education. (In 1996 responsibility for students was transferred to the Palestinian Civilian Liaison Committee, the body that represents Palestinian interests directly to the Israeli CLO.) One may request a one-day exit permit to Israel or the West Bank, a permit of several days' or weeks' duration, or a permit to enter Egypt via the Rafah border or Jordan via the Allenby Bridge in the West Bank.

Second, Palestinian officials transfer the exit requests to the CLO headquarters located near the Erez checkpoint, in the northern part of the Strip. The CLO is staffed by Israelis, both military officials and civilians; most worked in the old civil administration and many rank high in the Israeli military bureaucratic hierarchy. Some have been at their jobs – governing the Palestinian population – for five, ten or even twenty years; since 1994 only their titles have changed. The former staff officer, for example, is now called the 'coordinator'. Anyone who needs to leave the Strip on a regular basis, like workers, has to carry a magnetic card,[3] an additional form of identification introduced early in the *intifada* to increase control over the population. The magnetic card is the only document Palestinians must procure directly from the CLO, without the mediation of Palestinian representatives; the Israelis who issue magnetic cards are either Shabak[4] officers or soldiers subject to their oversight.

Next, the CLO officials examine and evaluate the Palestinian applications, reviewing, among other data, Shabak records. Exit permits are usually granted to sick people within a day. In especially urgent cases, permission may be granted by telephone or fax. But many

[3] Computer-readable ID, introduced by the Israeli authorities in Gaza in 1989 and distributed to 'clean' Palestinians.
[4] Israeli secret service.

requests are turned down; some are answered too late and the applicant simply misses his or her course or flight or meeting. Over the
last few years, most Gazans have simply got used to the idea that
they cannot leave the Strip. They curb needs and desires that the rest
of the world takes for granted. They do not even try to test the system
and demand the basic human right of freedom of movement.

When Israel imposes its most extreme measure, sealing Gaza
'hermetically', all exit permits are automatically cancelled. A permit
holder may well have been waiting six months for an appointment
with a specialist in Jerusalem; indeed, she may be scheduled for an
operation. Another person may be booked on a flight abroad.
Nevertheless, no one can leave or enter the Strip. The word 'hermetic'
is applied literally: no one comes in and no one goes out. As the
closure gradually begins to ease, those same permit holders must
submit their applications all over again.

The rumour quickly spread through Gaza that I, an Israeli, could
help. In fact, my ability to intervene was limited, and I did not believe
that I should get involved in individual cases. Still, people placed
their hopes in me, overwhelmed as they were by the jumble of prohibitions and procedures and criteria, by the hidden workings of an
arbitrary system that could, they believed, yield the elusive piece of
paper if only handled correctly. People clutched at any possibility
and told their stories to any receptive ear. Most Gazans have the
mistaken idea, gained during the years of direct contact with the
occupation and all its capricious rulings, that any Israeli can 'work
something out' with the authorities. 'Can't you speak to someone
there?' they would ask me. Wasn't there something I could do at the
CLO or the Shabak or the IDF? Usually I rejected the entreaties –
which presumed I had links with the military authorities – and I
soon earned a reputation for being short-tempered. 'Okay, okay, now
you're upset,' Gazans would say. 'Don't worry, we'll just forget the
whole thing.'

Nevertheless, a fairly typical day would bring a string of appeals.
At 8 a.m. the phone would ring (when the phone was working): the
anonymous worker who called faithfully once a week, wanting to
understand why he was not allowed to stay overnight in Jericho, in
the West Bank. He worked in Jerusalem and was obliged to return
each night to Gaza, a three-hour journey. There is no direct bus and
he spent half his wages on transportation. 'It would make so much
more sense for me to sleep with friends in the West Bank and come

home to Gaza once a week, with more money,' he says (as he did before the Israeli redeployment in 1994). He hopes I can perform a miracle. Once again, he politely expresses his disappointment.

At 11.00 my friend Abu Basel might call: some workers had been turned back at the Erez checkpoint, forbidden to leave the Strip. All the men had been employed in Israel for at least fifteen years; only the day before, they had gone to work as usual. Now they were considered a security risk. Why? Who had made the decision? Was there anything they could do?

An hour later, Abu Naji, who owns a sewing workshop, would be on the phone. He had twenty-five truckloads of clothing ready to send to Tel Aviv and had scheduled an Israeli military escort to accompany the shipment, but the trucks had stood idle at the Erez checkpoint for eight hours. No one knew why. On their return trip, the trucks were going to bring back cloth for Abu Naji's next order. Now he was stuck with his merchandise and he had neither cloth nor buttons to give his workers. What should he do?

In the afternoon I might hear from Dr P., who had been attending a course at a Palestinian hospital in East Jerusalem when Israel sealed the Strip hermetically. He had stayed in Jerusalem to help at the hospital, which the closure had deprived of most of its medical and nursing staff. Now it was time for him to return to Gaza but his exit permit had expired. He knew he would be detained at the Erez checkpoint for having stayed in Jerusalem illegally. 'I heard you could help,' he says.

Sometimes people called just to pour out their hearts; also, they knew that as a journalist I needed information. So I collected stories, about a truck filled with flowers that was kept waiting at the checkpoint for a full day in the searing heat, about an ambulance that was held up for two hours, about a Palestinian policeman coming back from the West Bank who violated the terms of his exit permit and found himself in detention in Israel. Without these stories, one cannot understand the Gaza Strip.

Sometimes I was actually able to advise people. When the permit was health-related, I sent them to the Association of Israeli and Palestinian Physicians for Human Rights (PHR), located in Tel Aviv; in other civil matters I referred people to Tamar Peleg, a human rights lawyer, who handled, among many other similar cases, those of West Bank residents stranded in the Strip for two months when the checkpoints were sealed. Only very rarely, though, was I able to alter the current by writing an article or requesting an official response to some arbitrary ruling. In a few instances I appealed directly to Israelis with political clout to intervene in situations that were glaringly unreasonable, especially where health was concerned; usually I turned to Knesset members Yossi Sarid, Naomi Hazan or Yael Dayan. In time, I began to get a bad name at the CLO and even with some low-level negotiators. 'She helps people and that's not right,' they complained to my fellow journalists. 'It's a conflict of interest.' I even heard that I had opened an office in Gaza City to dispense advice – a far cry from accepting telephone calls in my rented apartment.

I departed from my self-imposed rule only once, when a friend's mother was dying of heart disease in a Tel Aviv hospital. On and off, hermetic closures had been imposed for several weeks, most recently following a suicide bombing in Jerusalem that had killed four people. Only those deemed 'humanitarian cases' by the IDF and the CLO could leave. Three days after the bombing it turned out that the perpetrator had come from Dahariya in the West Bank, but Gaza stayed sealed off.

It was during this time that my friend A. called, asking me to take some X-rays, medical reports and two sets of pajamas to her mother in a Tel Aviv hospital. In the urgent rush of moving her from Gaza, these items had been forgotten. The doctors in Gaza had decided some two days earlier that A.'s mother needed immediate treatment in Tel Aviv, but it had taken a day to procure exit permits for the woman and one daughter, R. The following day at 6 a.m., mother and daughter had left for the Erez checkpoint in an ambulance, only to be held up there for almost three hours while soldiers insisted that no one could cross. Eventually R. lost her temper, the Palestinian officer who liaised at the border was called, and, after a security check, the ambulance was allowed to leave. R.'s permit did not include permission to spend the night in Israel, and violating the restriction could mean arrest or even being barred from receiving future permits. So R. had decided to return to Gaza the same night, reassured that her mother's condition was stable.

The next day, a Thursday, R. applied for a new permit, which ended up being granted three days later. A., her sister, who works in Israel, had a one-month permit but that day a new regulation was announced: people with long-term permits were now required to register with the Palestinian Civilian Liaison Committee each night prior to their departure from the Strip; the list would then be transferred to the Israeli

CLO. (The regulation was quickly revoked; people were simply unable to comply.) In the meantime, A.'s father and a third sister had applied for their own permits and were awaiting approval. The family's only son was under thirty, below the minimum age for men to leave the Strip at that time, so there seemed little point in trying to obtain a permit for him at this stage.

That same Thursday evening I visited the mother, bringing the documents, the pajamas and a kiss from her daughter. I was shocked to see her looking so frail and thin, while her legs were badly swollen. 'When will my children come?' she whispered. 'What about my son? I want to see my children.' I brought her a little water and plumped up her pillows. Two days later, on Saturday, I returned at the request of the daughters. The mother had been moved to a different room and I found her connected to various tubes. A team of doctors surrounded her bed. 'Where's the family?' one doctor asked me. 'This woman won't live through the day.'

I called the daughters, telling them to run to the Civilian Liaison Committee office and demand permits immediately, even though the Israeli CLO was closed on Saturdays. Next, I contacted the regional IDF spokesperson and was put through to a CLO representative, who took the family's particulars and promised that the permits would be delivered to the Erez checkpoint right away. So the father and daughters were allowed to leave but not to stay overnight. Still, the father spent several hours with his wife and hurried back to Gaza before his permit expired (all this by taxi, since cars bearing Gaza licence plates are not allowed out of the Strip). A. decided to risk staying the night; the eldest daughter, M., who lives in the West Bank, had no exit permit but found a way to 'steal across the border'. I offered these illegals my apartment in Tel Aviv to sleep, or at least rest for a few hours during the day. That evening the mother showed signs of improvement; there is no doubt her family's visit gave her strength.

Over the next few days, the family fought for permits and ferried back and forth between Gaza and Tel Aviv. The eldest daughter stayed at her mother's bedside, an enemy infiltrator breaking the law. One week after entering the hospital, the mother slipped into a coma and the whole family – save the son, G. – simply ignored regulations and spent the night at her side. A relative with connections and influence – in Palestinian intelligence, I believe – managed to arrange retroactive permits, including permission to stay in Israel overnight. Then G. began his odyssey to leave the Strip; surprisingly he was able to receive a magnetic card, a prerequisite for a single man of his age, without trouble. He submitted a request to enter Israel, attaching a letter from the hospital describing his mother's condition, but was told he already had a permit – the CLO had confused his name with his father's. When the mistake was cleared up, he was promised a permit for the following day. But before G. could reach the hospital, his mother died.

Bringing her body directly back to Gaza for burial meant securing a driver's permit and supplying the registration number of the Gaza municipal vehicle that transports the dead and is allowed to enter Israel for that purpose. A driver was located, but he was denied permission to cross into Israel. Until a second driver was found several hours had passed and the family decided to wait no longer. The body was brought back to Gaza in an Israeli ambulance for transfer to a local Palestinian vehicle, a procedure people preferred to avoid if they could. When the ambulance reached the Erez checkpoint, a Palestinian policeman approached the IDF soldier on duty and explained the circumstances. Special permission was required for the two ambulances to meet on one side of the checkpoint. The soldier called his superiors at the CLO and asked for the green light, using a common Erez phrase to describe shifting goods from an Israeli truck to a Palestinian one. 'I need to transfer a body back to back,' he said. Mercifully, permission was granted, but yet more prohibitions prevented the family from being together at the funeral and during the mourning period. M., the eldest daughter, was allowed to cross from the West Bank into Gaza; her husband, also a native of Gaza, wanted to attend the burial and stay with his wife's family during the mourning period but his request was turned down. He was denied permission to leave the West Bank for 'security reasons', but no one knew what those were. The man had never been arrested and was still living in an area directly controlled by the Israeli Army, which could long since have detained him had he truly posed a security threat.

Within a few months of Palestinian autonomy, it was clear that this family's trial was not an exception. Many people fared worse. Of the numerous cases that came to my attention, however, I wrote about only a fraction; these stories quickly became old news and readers grew tired of them unless there was some newly shocking element.

Nor did anyone want to read a meticulous breakdown of the heartless
bureaucratic procedures that were becoming increasingly entrenched.
So I found myself caught in a contradiction: I had hoped that my
reports would wake Israelis up to what was happening in the Strip,
but while readers have a right to know they do not have an obligation, nor are they required to translate knowledge into action. In time,
this contradiction began to influence the style and frequency with
which I wrote about the closures, which were so central to life in
Gaza but so remote from Israeli concerns. I was caught in the journalist's dilemma: should I write about the things that interest readers
or about what is actually happening? While I carried on writing about
what I saw, my reports did not seem to convey a coherent picture of
what was taking place at the Erez checkpoint, nor did they force the
necessary conclusions, published as they were in a scattershot and
fragmentary way. The occasional human interest story, one journalistic device, would only reinforce the sense that such incidents were
regrettable isolated instances, and not – as I hoped to show – a
constant occurrence. Rather than sounding a warning bell, each new
report seemed to dissolve into the last, received with indifference and
denial even by those most poised to care – the peace advocates and
human rights organisations such as Peace Now, the Association for
Civil Rights in Israel (which warily attempted legal action in a few
select cases), the International Centre for Peace, and the Israeli human
rights organisation B'tselem (which procrastinated for a long time
before beginning to deal with the issue of closure in a comprehensive
manner). Supposedly, peace had come, and the sound of congratula-
tory backslapping drowned out the evidence that the spirit of occupation was alive and well and basic human rights were being violated
even more than before. Erstwhile militant peace activists now made
regular pilgrimages to Palestinian and Fatah leaders, paying homage
to the Oslo process and ignoring the lessons of the past: that the
human distress of a million people is a sea of nitrogylcerin.

I would be lying, of course, if I said my concern with the closures
was just that of a journalist. Unlike my Palestinian friends, I was free
to leave Gaza at will. Who better than I could testify to the need to
get out of the Strip? One's soul and one's sanity cry out for the open
horizons beyond the Erez checkpoint, for conversation about something other than exit permits and magnetic cards, for the freedom to
drive for miles without barbed wire and concrete roadblocks. I more
than anyone knew the urge to escape and the destructive consequences

of the inability to do so. Day by day, I saw my friends lose their spontaneity and the impulse, even the desire, to do something, go somewhere, for no good reason except the fun of it.

I began to learn something about us Israelis too, something not quite obvious in the cafés and parks of Tel Aviv. Large numbers of my compatriots, I came to realise, were hard at work devising ways to stop people from leaving the Strip and spinning sophisticated security arguments to justify their actions. And many more – those who paid daily lip service to the transformations of peace – preferred not to disturb the status quo by challenging the siege of Gaza. It was hard not to think of a remark I once heard from Ihab al-Ashqar. 'The trouble with you Israelis,' he said, 'is that you think we just weren't made the same way you were.'

And then, too, I was a student of history given that rare chance to watch a process taking place that would one day be summed up in a few paragraphs. I was able to track the evolving relationship between those who give the orders and those ordinary individuals who either carry them out or have to live with their consequences. I wanted to understand whether Israeli soldiers and officials were executing explicit instructions or interpreting unstated policy. Moving between Tel Aviv and Gaza, between the Israeli and Palestinian perceptions of what was taking place, I needed to know whether security concerns were an adequate explanation for imposing closures or whether some other political motive was at work.

Thus every request for an exit permit also served as raw historical material, providing clues to the real cause for this Palestinian experience. For one thing, I came to learn just how limited Palestinian power is, and how one issue like health care, for example, reflected the larger scheme of things. The Israeli occupation's harsh legacy included a stunted, underfunded health care system that trailed far behind the general standard of medical care in Israel. Although the Palestinian health ministry drew up a greatly increased budget, no one expected an immediate leap in the level of services. Thus many sick Gazans continued to seek treatment in Israel or in Palestinian hospitals in East Jerusalem even after the Authority ostensibly took over responsibility. Gazan patients clearly benefited from the high level of care received in Israel, but the practice also served to perpetuate the local system's inferiority, keeping Gaza's doctors from expanding their skills and knowledge, from developing long-term commitments to their patients, and from gaining the confidence of those patients. The situation would best be remedied by sending local doctors on professional courses at superior facilities like al-Maqassed Hospital in East Jerusalem or those elsewhere in Israel or abroad, but the closures crippled that effort.

The Israeli soldiers and civil administration officials in the occupied territories were accountable only to the IDF and the government, not to the people under their control. By its very nature, a non-elected administration acts on arbitrary regulations; without doubt, a cumulative cause of the *intifada* was Israel's changeable, whimsical decisions, which were never open to review and which Palestinians encountered daily in one form or another, from the soldier at the roadblock to the civil administration clerk who inexplicably denied a business licence or a trip abroad or permission to add a second storey to one's house. When civil and policing responsibilities were transferred to the Palestinians, there was hope that people's everyday lives would finally be free of the control of an alienated power acting in the interests of a foreign occupation. Such a change would not only improve the quality of people's lives, but reinforce their support for the negotiating process leading to a peaceful settlement with Israel.

The post-Oslo reality, however, proved terribly disappointing; in many ways, the accords made life even more difficult. The Palestinian economy and institutions were still dependent on Israel, which continued to hold ultimate sovereignty over the occupied territories. The interim agreements state that various responsibilities and documents – among them population registries, tax rolls, maps and records of commercial agreements with Israeli firms, regulations governing import and export procedures, payments from the Palestinian Authority to Israeli institutions, and tax transfers – would devolve to the Authority through an ongoing process of negotiation and Israeli oversight even as economic and legal committees ('coordination and liaison committees') were hammering out permanent new arrangements. As it turned out, Palestinian reliance on Israel in just about every sphere of activity, including passage between Gaza and the West Bank, meant that these committees devoted most of their time to issuing exit permits.

Whereas the two sides' intelligence branches have shared information and the two police forces have joined in patrols, there has been no common effort to decide, through cooperation and with established criteria, who will be prevented from leaving Gaza. Logic would dictate that in a new system of coordination between equals, the act of denying an individual's freedom of movement would be subject to review and control by both sides. Rationally, setting exit quotas for workers, merchants and medical personnel should involve consideration both of Israel's security needs and of the Palestinians' economic and civil requirements. In reality, though, the Palestinian Authority's representatives were little more than what they themselves called mailmen, merely delivering responses from the CLO, which, in turn, took its lead from the Israeli Government.

In addition to the usual administrative roles, the Authority became responsible for mediating between the Israeli authorities and individual Palestinians. A test of the Authority's power has been its ability not only to improve people's lives but also to demand that Israel change its behaviour towards civilians. The Israeli establishment was not unaware of the demands of the new age; the army and the former civil administration even gave courses to their staffs aimed at instilling new standards of conduct. 'Changing the disk' was the military jargon for the switch: now, the message was, Palestinians had to be treated with respect.

But the series of hideous suicide bombings that began after the Baruch Goldstein massacre in Hebron in February 1994 overshadowed all other considerations.[5] A number of Gazans were directly involved in attacks in October 1994 and January 1995 and in a later attempt using explosives smuggled out of the Strip in a truck filled with chickens; indeed, Israeli sources believe that a significant share of the explosives used in the various bombings were smuggled out of the Strip and that some of the masterminds were based there too. Two suicide bombers reportedly crossed the Erez checkpoint disguised as blind men, and the CLO claimed that some forged medical referrals had also been used by militants to gain entry into Israel. Even the most vigilant systems, it seemed, had not succeeded in completely preventing people without permits from leaving Gaza.

Nevertheless, security measures were tightened considerably in the spring of 1995, in direct response to the possibility of terrorist infiltration: the Strip was circled by an electrified fence; Palestinians were denied access to Jewish settlements in Gaza; only 300 trucks were allowed out daily, and only to collect or deliver goods. These trucks now required Israeli military escorts and were thoroughly examined over inspection pits for explosives. Ambulances were also inspected,

---

[5] A Jewish settler, Baruch Goldstein, had massacred twenty-nine Muslims at prayer.

and only patients in critical condition were exempted from a body search. No longer permitted to leave in Gazan vehicles, workers were ferried by Israeli buses. Only a very few merchants, and even those extremely rarely, were allowed to travel in their own cars.

Every Gazan, regardless of religion, sex or age, became suspect, a person capable of committing an act of terror. But like every occupation force before it, Israel – despite having controlled the territories since 1967 – had still not learned that resistance and terror are responses to occupation itself and to the form of terror embodied by the foreign ruler. Nor had it learned to distinguish between such acts of resistance as throwing stones or shooting at soldiers within the occupied territories and killing citizens inside Israel's international borders. Both sets of manifestations were seen as one virus that could infect the Palestinian population indiscriminately. Although the PLO had pledged in 1994 to renounce violence and only a small segment of Palestinians continued to carry out random acts, Israel persisted in ignoring the distinction.

Clearly, though, a policy of wholesale siege – in violation of the spirit of the Oslo process – could only strengthen the virus rather than isolate it. Nevertheless, as in the past, the Israeli political establishment closed its eyes and plugged its ears. Moreover, the decision has been translated into practice not by high-ranking officials but by those lowest in the chain of command, the soldier at the checkpoint and the CLO clerk, who will inevitably give the policy its harshest interpretation: they will view each individual who crosses or submits a request to cross the border as a potential terrorist, so as not to risk responsibility for a possible attack.

There is no better backdrop than the Erez checkpoint for the Orwellian drama being played out in the Gaza Strip since the advent of Palestinian self-rule. At a quick glance it looks like a perfectly ordinary border crossing with a clean, bright, international terminal, bold signs welcoming visitors, policemen at their posts checking passports and other documents, and an efficient freight area off to one side. The throng of traffic carries foreign delegations on their way to call on Yassir Arafat, Israeli officials, overseas diplomats, Palestinian ministers, Fatah leaders, and police off to meet with colleagues in Israel or the West Bank.

A high embankment, raised with cinder blocks, spares these dignitaries the sight of the narrow, fenced-in pen where, on ordinary days of standard closure, 20,000 lucky men with exit permits stir up the dust on their way to work inside Israel. What they do see, though, is a long line of trucks inching over the inspection pits, waiting for the signal to head into Israel and collect food and raw materials or deliver Palestinian produce. There is, it seems, a brisk, non-stop flow of goods and people back and forth.

Visitors aware of the bustle may well not realise that the legions of trucks and hordes of workers represent twenty-seven years of direct military rule and economic standstill, during which Israel and its products have become the Strip's lifeline. They may not understand that, even now, Israel controls down to the very last detail the kinds of cargo the trucks may carry, the amounts, the destinations and the frequency – who will leave and how often, and how many hours they will waste waiting to do so. The economists, diplomats and army brass, all of whom are charged with shepherding the fledgling Palestinian Authority towards some goal unspecified in the Oslo Accords, draw on a lexicon of military and commercial jargon to obscure the misery of one million individuals trapped behind Gaza's electrified fence. Easing of restrictions. Upping the quota of workers. Job creation. Growth. Positive GNP.

We know that the jargon conceals the truth: by 1996 Gaza's per capita GNP had fallen by 37 per cent since 1992; the total GNP had declined by 18.5 per cent. In six months, unemployment had risen by 8.2 per cent to reach 39.2 per cent. Gazans fortunate enough to hold jobs in the Strip saw a 9.6 per cent drop in real wages in 1995. Those who worked in Israel lost 16 per cent of their salaries. Beyond a doubt, Israel's policy of closure bears responsibility for the appalling figures. One can hardly imagine that Israel's decision-makers did not realise the inevitable consequences of imposing what is, in effect, a siege of years' duration. As we have seen, Israel explains the closures solely as an inevitable response to terrorism and as the only way to prevent more attacks. But careful analysis of the policy and its consequences – along with other Israeli steps taken in the context of the Oslo Accords, such as blocking the safe passage route between Gaza and the West Bank – suggests a different understanding of closures.

To grasp their significance, we need only consider that the Oslo Accords do not define the last step in the process. The ultimate goal was meant to emerge through negotiations. During the discussions, however, Israel's Labour-led coalition never declared its ultimate intention, while the Palestinians have always stated their aim clearly:

an independent state in the West Bank and the Gaza Strip. The
Palestinians' bargaining chips are primarily the various UN resolutions concerning their refugee status and their right to the land
(including the 'right of return' and the designation of the Jewish settlements as illegal), as well as the universal principles of self-determination and independence. An additional source of Palestinian leverage
is the Israeli promise that all fundamental issues will be resolved in
the final-status negotiations – the refugee question, the Jewish settlements, the borders, Jerusalem and access to water sources. One way
or another, Palestinians, or at least those who support the process
and their leaders, understand the accords to mean that the Israeli
occupation will gradually fade away. In exchange, Yassir Arafat and
Palestinian negotiators agreed to give up a key bargaining chip of
their own: armed opposition or any other act of resistance that the
occupation regards as 'violence', historically the one form of leverage
available to people in occupied territory.

As stated, Israel did not disclose its intentions although it did hold
on to its prerogative, as the ruling power, to shape the future. And
it has shaped it with a vengeance: between the peak years of the Oslo
negotiations and implementation of the agreements, 1992 to 1996,
the Labour-led government allowed a 50 per cent increase in the
number of Jewish settlers in Gaza and the West Bank, from 100,000
to 150,000 (which does not include the settlements in East Jerusalem).
Furthermore, with Arafat's consent, the government began to carry
out an old plan to link the West Bank settlements to Israel through
a network of expressways. In the new parlance of Oslo, these have
become 'bypass roads' – broad, high-speed slashes of asphalt that
will, Israel argues, ensure safety and freedom of movement for the
Jewish settlers. This massive construction project has involved confis-
cating and destroying thousands of acres of cultivated Palestinian land
and has forever altered the natural weave connecting West Bank towns
and villages. Palestinian consent was easily obtained – ostensibly, the
bypass roads were designed to boost the success of the interim stage
by protecting the Jewish settlers and thereby enabling all parties to
reach the final-status negotiations without too much acrimony.

Built at a cost of billions of shekels, solely for the needs of the tiny
Jewish minority, the network of bypass roads will play no small part
in Israel's negotiations over retaining territory. Anyone who invests a
fortune in roads does not intend to dismantle the communities that
use them. Moreover, this network, which guarantees Jewish settlers

in the West Bank and Gaza Strip a safe and speedy lifeline to Israel, was put in place at exactly the same time as even greater constraints were imposed on Palestinian freedom of movement. It is true that since 1994, more land has come under the jurisdiction of the Authority, but the blocs of Jewish settlements and the patchwork of new roads are in effect the nail in the coffin of a contiguous Palestinian state, whatever form it might take. The new geography means that Palestinian society will be splintered, fragmented into isolated enclaves; the size and proximity of these enclaves are yet to be fixed and will be determined by the strength of the Palestinians' bargaining position, but movement between the enclaves will always involve passing roadblocks and checkpoints manned by Israeli soldiers. In the West Bank, social, cultural and economic life have already been harmed by the region's fragmentation, and especially by the separation of north and south into two distinct areas. But for the real model of the future, one need only look to the 147-square-mile enclave of the Gaza Strip.

Israel has been able to shape the outcome of negotiations in another way as well: its bargaining position has been immeasurably improved by being able to exert economic pressure on its Palestinian partner, creating a sense of material urgency and managing to postpone crucial decisions in order to wrestle over immediate practical needs. A few more work permits, another convoy of trucks – these are presented as Palestinian achievements and evidence of Israeli good will. In this way, the occupation's balance of power between ruler and petitioner has been redoubled, leaving the Palestinians even more dependent. And it is the policy of closure that has proved to be the most effective means of control and leverage.

The decaying economy has also undermined the Palestinian Authority's standing among its people. The Authority has proved weak at the negotiating table yet hungry to maintain its power – a combination that guarantees submission and compromise. Under other circumstances a more resolute Authority might have rejected the concessions it has made. Furthermore, the economic decline has narrowed many Palestinians' expectations and demands. The same people who hoped and struggled at the beginning of the *intifada*, who fought to push back the limits of their freedom, are now more weighed down by everyday material concerns than ever before. Workers' rights for Palestinians – in Gaza as in Israel – are considered luxuries that no one even bothers to protect. The growing economic despair has brought Palestinians to the point where they are willing to accept a new arrangement: closed industrial zones along the borders, à la Mexico.

Palestinians suspect that the real purpose behind the closures, the bypass roads, and the separation of the West Bank, Gaza and Jerusalem – ostensibly for security reasons – is to carve up the occupied territories permanently, keep them under different political systems, and complete the destruction of the Palestinian social structure that began in 1948. In mid-1993 Shimon Peres unveiled his notion of separation in a closed meeting with Jews from America and Europe. He floated the idea of an 'independent' mini-state in Gaza and an autonomous West Bank linked to Jordan, where a local parliament would resolve matters jointly with the Jewish settlers. Palestinian leaders rejected a similar proposal in the spring of 1995, but practical measures subsequently implemented by the Rabin–Peres government indicate that the idea had not been abandoned.

That such separation contravenes the Declaration of Principles is not in dispute, but Palestinians cite several restrictions that, they believe, prove that separation has little to do with security concerns either: relatives are not allowed to move freely between the two territories to visit immediate family members; Gazans who are allowed into the West Bank are always forbidden to spend the night there; people who enter Egypt via the Rafah border are not permitted to return to Gaza via Jordan and the Allenby Bridge; trucks from the Strip and the West Bank are not allowed to transport goods between the two areas. Crucial negotiations over a 'safe passage' corridor between Gaza and the West Bank have been dragging on since 1994. For many long months, the Israelis refused to include in any safe-passage agreement a specific citation of the Declaration of Principles' confirmation that the two territories form one integral unit. Precious time was squandered on this point. Although both sides finally agreed to simply cite the relevant article number without the explicit words, Israel's resistance speaks volumes.

The most painful and symbolic example of the separation is provided by the 1,300 Gazan students enrolled in West Bank universities who are not allowed to attend classes. The continuous interruption of their studies began in 1991, when Israel revoked the general exit permit enabling Palestinian residents to move about freely. After the 1994 transfer of authorities, Israel withheld the students' travel permits until long after the semester began and sometimes indefinitely. Some West Bank academic institutions no longer accept students from Gaza because of their erratic attendance. The uncertainty and difficulties have discouraged the many students who would prefer to study at West Bank universities, which are known to be superior. The students represent a small group compared with the millions who suffer the effects of Gaza's separation from the West Bank, but their treatment is significant for the future of Palestinian society and emblematic of the post-Oslo reality: the students' freedom of choice, so vital for the whole community's intellectual and professional development, has been narrowed to an unprecedented degree.

By 1990, the Israeli goal of demographic separation – that is, keeping Israelis and Palestinians apart – had been quite clearly articulated. Mass participation in the *intifada* had fallen off; the uprising continued, however, more as a series of armed activities by discrete groups, and still with the support of the majority despite the growing oppression and collective punishment meted out by Israel. For its part, Israel was caught at an impasse: while unwilling to address the core demand of the *intifada* – independence – there were limits to the instruments of suppression at its disposal. Bombing refugee camps (as in Lebanon) or mass deportations were out of the question. The physical proximity of the two peoples, Israelis and Palestinians, and the inevitable condemnation by an international community that had just ended the Cold War ruled out such overt and brutal action. Instead, Israel devised an administrative policy as a way out of the impasse, carried out under the guise of 'security measures'.

In 1970, opening up the Israeli labour market to the occupied territories was intended to weaken Palestinian nationalism and preclude territorial separation; in the 1990s, shutting off the source of labour became a means of quashing the drive to independence. For Israelis, the immediate consequence of demographic separation was that Palestinians disappeared from their streets, thereby quelling their increasing fears of Palestinians 'just roaming around', in the words of a CLO official. (Their fear contained an intuitive understanding of the frustration building in Gaza and the West Bank, and Israelis seemed to know that such frustration would inevitably lead to a reaction, one that might not pose a strategic threat to the State of Israel but would instead endanger individual civilians.) For the Palestinian political élite and the Israeli peace camp, segregation was seen as a harbinger of political and territorial separation. With hindsight, this was clearly wishful thinking.

The expansion of Jewish settlement in the occupied territories during the Oslo years revealed that Israel continued to consider the land as a resource for Jews alone: a Palestinian presence is tolerated but Palestinian needs have no claim. Israel continues to deprive Palestinians of access to most of the undeveloped land in the occupied territories even as it designates those areas for future Jewish development. Effectively, Israel has declared that Palestinian prospects will always be subjugated to Jewish needs, desires and strength. And it has done so under the watchful eye of the Oslo Accords, which explicity upheld Israel's position as the sovereign power.

But ultimately, land remains negotiable – a resource that isn't going away. Time, on the other hand, is another matter. Palestinians have lost precious years shut up in their enclaves, unable even to travel to other Palestinian cities. The ability to visit friends, look for work or attend university is no less a human right than freedom of speech or religion. For Palestinians, though, freedom of movement is no longer a right but a privilege, alloted to an entitled few. Israel awards the privilege incrementally, by means of a pass system that has carved up Palestinian society in much the same way as the new geography has carved up the land. Each segment is defined by its access to move-ment: there are workers allowed into Israel with sleeping permits and workers restricted to one-day permits only; some businessmen may enter with their cars, others may not; one class of manufacturers is permitted to enter the West Bank, another allowed only into Israel; VIP 1 status is awarded to the most senior Authority officials, VIP 3 status to lesser functionaries. The quota of those who are privileged is fluid; the principle is not: it is Israel that sets the criteria and controls the benefits.

Most people's livelihoods depend on this system. Protesting the injustice of it may mean losing one's meagre portion of the benefits. And for the Palestinian leadership, which enjoys the lion's share even as it continues to negotiate with Israel, freedom of movement has translated into power, business opportunities and great material comfort. By creating such divisions and dependency, Israel has ensured Palestinian complicity with separation, an extremely sophisticated method of restraint reminiscent of apartheid. To sum up: the Oslo Accords have ensured Palestinian segregation from the Jewish-Israeli population, which elects the sovereign power, enjoys geographic and economic domination, commands all natural resources and controls a pass system limiting the Palestinians' movements.

In the meantime, Palestinians in the Strip find ways to go on – or to escape. Students have been prevented from returning to the universities for some three years, yet an unknown number have developed complicated ways of leaving Gaza and going 'underground' in the West Bank. They cannot see their families for months at a time and live in constant danger of being caught at one of the many IDF roadblocks. A Western consul reports that his country's embassy has seen a drastic increase in Palestinians applying to emigrate. Others migrate inwards, closing their eyes and ears, stifling their fury and sense of indignity, trying not to dwell on the shortfall between the words in an agreement and the absence of an exit permit. Most people live in a narrowly proscribed space: friends, weddings, courses, books, although some cannot endure the claustrophobia – police statistics show a persistent increase in suicides.

In September 1996, the pressure exploded in violence. For several days, masses of demonstrators poured out their wrath on settlers and soldiers after the Israeli Government opened an entrance to an ancient Jewish tunnel that happened to face the holy Islamic sites in Jerusalem's Old City. The demonstrations – organised, according to rumours, primarily by Fatah on Arafat's instructions – spilled over into the Strip, where young men hurled rocks at a Jewish settlement, an IDF outpost and the Rafah border. (They also set out for the Erez checkpoint but were stopped by the Palestinian police.) Thirty-one Gazans and three Israelis were killed in the Strip alone, and some 500 Palestinians were wounded. Israel blamed Arafat for orchestrating the demonstrations but to people in the occupied territories, and in Gaza in particular, the outbreak seemed inevitable. People responded to the call out of a need to communicate their frustration to the world.

At the time, my friend Abu Basel was on his way to Gaza City. When he saw the clusters of men outside Kfar Darom, the Jewish settlement, he stopped his taxi and walked towards the clash. As Israeli soldiers opened fire, Abu Basel, a thirty-five-year-old father, a man who saw little point in throwing stones, found himself running towards the guns. Like others at that moment, he felt the urge to die.

One could have predicted that the demonstrators would find their way to the settlements and checkpoints, sites of friction with Israeli power and emblems of the intractable view that the country's Jews are more deserving than its Palestinians. Even more, these are the sites that expose the Orwellian language of what is applauded as a peace process. When, in the heat of their rage, the young Palestinians shook the fences at Kfar Darom and Rafah, they were pounding on the walls that are closing in on their people and their future, that deny their freedom as if they were animals in a cage.

In their hearts Palestinians will persist in seeing all the land as theirs; they will not renounce their longing for the fields that now bear Hebrew names; they will not forget the pain of expulsion, the very first link in a chain of loss that goes on. But from living in Gaza I learned that its people have the ability and an honest desire to separate their heartfelt wishes from the need for a peaceful political solution. 'We are, after all, the mother of the child,' they say, alluding to King Solomon's judgement to explain their readiness to share the country. On condition, of course, that any solution treats the Palestinians with dignity, as a people with elemental rights and a claim equal to that of the others who live in this land and call it home.

PHILLIP KNIGHTLEY

The Thalidomide Scandal:
Where We Went Wrong

1997

At the beginning of their book, *Suffer the Children: The Story of Thalidomide*, the journalists of the *Sunday Times* Insight team describe a meeting between the parents of thalidomide children and Enoch Powell, the Minister of Health (remembered for his racist attacks on Britain's ethnic minorities). Having ignored the plight of the children until one of the mothers had written in frustration to her local newspaper in Bristol, Powell finally agreed to see a delegation. One by one, he dismissed out of hand their pleas for justice, calling a suggestion that the government alert the nation to the dangers of the drug a 'scaremonger stunt'. According to one parent, the minister 'expressed not one word of compassion or understanding. He astounded us by his coldness.'

It is understandable they were astounded, though their innocence was short-lived. Powell's 'coldness' was but an authentic glimpse of the ruthlessness of established forces when ranged against ordinary people seeking justice for scandalous negligence and cover-up at the top. Every twist and turn of the *Sunday Times*'s decade-long investigation and campaign on behalf of the victims of thalidomide demonstrates this. Compassion and real justice were never a consideration for the politicians, judges, barristers, solicitors and assorted 'experts' who effectively fought to deny the children the right to proper compensation and decent lives. Reading again the *Sunday Times* reports, the disgrace belongs, above all, to the stalling, incompetence and amoral caprice of much of the British legal profession.

Discovered in 1954, thalidomide was marketed throughout the world as an 'ideal' sedative, especially as an anti-morning-sickness remedy for pregnant women. In 1961, an Australian obstetrician, William McBride, discovered that the drug was responsible for abnormalities in foetuses and caused children to be born without arms or legs. By the time the drug was withdrawn, some 8,000 deformed children had been born throughout the world.

No public inquiry was held in Britain, and the parents were forced to take legal action against the multinational liquor company, Distillers, which had produced the drug under licence from a German company. Instead of opening the scandal to public scrutiny, the parents' writs, lamented the *Sunday Times,* meant that 'the whole affair was sealed by the laws of contempt of court into a legal cocoon from which it did not emerge until 1977 – too late for the law to help the children'.

The same could be said for the most damning disclosures of the newspaper's campaign. In 1968, Phillip Knightley began drafting the definitive article about how thalidomide had been 'sold' to doctors and patients. It was not published until 1977. In the meantime, the paper struggled to maintain its campaign and avoid contempt of court with a series of articles that simply described the children's suffering and called for a settlement on moral grounds. This had little effect, it seemed, until a major Distillers shareholder, Legal & General Assurance, announced it was in favour of a more generous settlement than the relative pittance offered by Distillers. The threat of an American boycott of Distillers' products – which include Johnnie Walker and other famous liquor brands – led to a settlement of £37 million. But that proved inadequate; in the 1990s, the children's trust fund soon ran out of money, and the Guinness group, which had taken over Distillers, agreed to top it up.

The *Sunday Times* Insight team comprised Phillip Knightley, Elaine Potter and Marjorie Wallace, and was led by Bruce Page, an outstanding investigative and analytical journalist. The following extract is from Phillip Knightley's autobiography, *A Hack's Progress.* Knightley, an Australian, was twice winner of Britain's Journalist of the Year award. The chapter, entitled 'The Thalidomide Scandal: Where We Went Wrong', is painfully honest and self-critical about the effectiveness of a press campaign in the face of such an opposing legal 'campaign', and Knightley questions whether the *Sunday Times* deserved to claim a victory for investigative journalism. He quotes Bruce Page that a newspaper editor can have some influence on, for example, British

Government policy in Northern Ireland, the success of a new West End play, the outcome of an industrial dispute 'or, for that matter, the behaviour of a big corporation like Distillers. But he could not have *decisive* influence on anything; the power to report or not to report could not be compared with the power of judges, ministers, civil servants, corporate directors or trade union leaders.'

That said, why did the *Sunday Times* editor, Harold Evans, having recognised that the law had consistently failed the children, not 'publish and be damned', even if that would have meant accepting the consequences: prosecution for contempt of court? Other editors had gone to prison for as much. As Knightley recounts, the *Sunday Times* editor-in-chief, Denis Hamilton, who came from deep within the British establishment, had refused to countenance it.

This means, surely, that the power of investigative journalism, if it is not to be overrated, requires both journalistic excellence and a moral and *political* will. As the European Court's judgement on the case put it: 'Not only do the media have the task of imparting such information and ideas: the public also has a right to receive them.'

That right came vividly to mind when we sought permission to include an extract from *Suffer the Children: The Story of Thalidomide*, a book by the original *Sunday Times* team. Permission was refused by the present-day *Sunday Times*, now owned by Rupert Murdoch.

THE THALIDOMIDE SCANDAL:
WHERE WE WENT WRONG

In journalism schools and media courses they use the thalidomide scandal as an example of campaigning journalism at its finest – fearless journalists take on a huge corporation which is behaving badly towards child victims of the corporation's horror drug and after a long, bitter battle win for them decent compensation. But, in truth, that is too simple and the reality much more ambivalent. It has taken me twenty years to face up to the fact that the *Sunday Times* thalidomide campaign was not the great success it was made out to be and that the full story is as much about the failures of journalism as its triumphs. It is hard for me to write this because the thalidomide campaign was one of the high points of my career and that of many others – there has been nothing to equal it since and it is still with us. We remain involved with the thalidomide victims, their parents and the professionals who were caught up in the tragedy. But when some of us get together and look back at the fight on behalf of the children, we end up discussing two crucial questions: Did we do it right? Would it have been better to have kept out of the whole affair?

Thalidomide had been discovered by accident in 1954 by a small German company called Chemie Grunenthal and appeared to be a dream sedative. It had none of the drawbacks of barbiturates, then the fashionable drug, and best of all, it was impossible to take an overdose – an important marketing point in those suicide-by-overdose Fifties. Anxious to capitalise on their discovery, Grunenthal had sold the drug all over the world, aggressively promoting it as an anti-morning-sickness pill for pregnant women and emphasising its absolute safety – it would harm neither the mother nor the child in the womb.

The latter guarantee turned out to be wrong. Thalidomide crossed the placental barrier and with devilish precision sabotaged the developing limb buds of the foetus, so that children were born with hands emerging direct from their shoulders, and feet emerging direct from their hips and, in a few horrific cases, with both abnormalities. It was eventually withdrawn in 1961 after an Australian obstetrician, Dr William McBride, made the link. But it was too late to prevent a major disaster and some 8,000 babies around the world were born with thalidomide deformities. No one was prepared and few could cope. In Britain, where the drug was marketed by the giant liquor company Distillers, some hospitals kept the baby from its parents, then sent it home swaddled in baby clothes for the mother to discover there what her child looked like; some fathers took one look at their offspring and walked out of the hospital and out of the marriage. Freddie Astbury's father remembers the doctors telling him – but not his wife – that Freddie had no head and would not live more than a couple of days. Then a little later they gave him the good and the bad news: we've found your son's head, but he has no legs. Then came the final version: Freddie has a head but no arms and no legs.

Even the specialists found this type of deformity hard to handle. Dr Gerard Vaughan, in charge of the Children's Unit at Guy's Hospital, London, remembers, 'I have never seen such a reaction among my staff as when they were faced with the thalidomide children. They were horrified. I had great difficulty in getting them to carry out a psychological test or examination. They were repelled in a way I have only witnessed on the faces of people going into a major burns unit for the first time. And these were doctors and nurses.' But they felt under pressure from some community conscience to put the tragedy right and many of the thalidomide children underwent operation after operation to try to make them look as normal as possible. Vaughan says, 'It was a kind of collusion between doctors and parents to expiate their guilt.' Other children needed surgery just to survive. Patrick Pope, who had major internal abnormalities, was operated on forty-two times. 'My son keeps asking me, "Mummy, please don't let me have any more operations,"' his mother, Julia Pope, wrote in a letter to the *Sunday Times* in 1973.

This was a terrible tragedy, but governments declared that since the testing and marketing of the drug had met all the legal requirements of the time, what had happened was not their responsibility. Road deaths, air crashes, major fires and other disasters are all customarily followed by searching public inquiries, but the biggest drug disaster of its kind was left to the law. Civil legal actions were instituted by the parents of the damaged children and vigorously contested by Chemie Grunenthal and Distillers. But far from opening up the whole matter to public scrutiny, these legal actions – except in the United States – closed everything down. No newspaper felt it could examine the thalidomide tragedy without prejudging the outcome of any eventual trial and in most countries this was a serious legal offence: contempt of court, punishable by imprisonment. So, in a terrible failure of journalism, newspapers carried stories on the lines of 'Look how well these plucky children are getting on', while the truth was that the thalidomide children and their desperate parents were suffering agonies in a silence imposed upon them by the system.

So what was going on behind the scenes? The lawyers acting for the British families who had sued Distillers, believing that they had a weak case, reached a settlement with the company in 1968/69 – the company would pay 40 per cent of what it would have paid if the children had been able to win a negligence action in court. When it came to a test case to decide how much would represent the 100 per cent, the judge rejected evidence from John Prevett, an actuary with the London firm of Bacon and Woodrow, and even refused to allow for inflation . . . because the government had promised to control it! This so outraged Prevett that he wrote two articles in the *Modern Law Review* attacking the court's decision and pointing out that even the full 100 per cent award for the armless and legless boy in the test case would not have been enough because the money would run out when he was twenty-seven – and he was receiving only 40 per cent of that. All this emerged in open court and routine court reporting should have been sufficient to expose the disaster. But Fleet Street treated the awards like a pools win. True, the *Sunday Times* ran a leader page article under the headline 'WHAT PRICE A POUND OF FLESH?' but as the editor, Harry Evans, later admitted, 'It was inadequate in the light of the Prevett memorandum: the thalidomide story concerns some shortcomings in journalism as well as a legal débâcle.'

When the *Sunday Times* campaign on behalf of the thalidomide children eventually got under way in 1972 it had two main themes – that the level of damages settled in 1968/69 was immorally low irrespective of whether Distillers was 100 per cent liable, and since the children would get only 40 per cent then the damages were laughably inadequate. And secondly, that the claim by Distillers that they had followed the best practices of the time because no one then tested drugs on pregnant animals was simply untrue – other drug companies did. But we could have discovered all this four years earlier in 1968. Prevett's articles in the *Modern Law Review* were basically what he had said in the witness box and the reason he had written them was that no journalist would listen to him. All the scientific material to rebut Distillers' defence was available to anyone who had the inclination and time to find it. How could the thalidomide children's case have gone steadily down the drain during those years without our noticing it? When the *Sunday Times* team looked back after the campaign was over, the team leader, Bruce Page, warned that we had no right to feel triumphant. He asked, 'What excuses can we offer for having totally missed the whole bloody thing till it was practically too late? I'm not too happy with my own: they go along the lines of saying that I was in America in 1968, largely concerned with Robert Maxwell in 1969, Bernie Cornfeld and the IOS scandal in 1970, and Ulster in 1971. I hope this will do, but it's nothing to brag about. We were, after all, demanding very high standards for other kinds of human organisations. Why should ours be any lower?' Then, half in jest, he said any book we wrote on the campaign should be called,

'How the *Sunday Times* Gradually Recovered From Its Own Mistakes and Did Something about the Thalidomide Scandal – Just in Time'. It wasn't, of course – it was called *Suffer the Children*. But Page, as always, had a point.

I suppose that at the back of all our minds was the inconvenient fact that we had come to the thalidomide scandal via what critics of the press call 'cheque book journalism', the buying of information. Critics argue that buying stories encourages the informant to say anything in order to get the money. But some information can only be had for cash – you have to approach each case on its merits. Evans rightly considered the thalidomide scandal so important that to get the information we needed he wrote out not just one cheque but two. One was for Henning Sjöström, a leading Stockholm lawyer who had approached the paper in 1967 with an offer we could not refuse. Sjöström was representing the 105 Swedish thalidomide children in their case against the drug's distributors in Sweden, Astra. A criminal prosecution had been launched in Germany against executives of Chemie Grunenthal on charges that included the German equivalent of manslaughter, causing grievous bodily harm, and selling drugs by misleading statements. Sjöström had gained access to the documents that the German authorities had seized from Chemie Grunenthal when mounting this case. No German newspaper could publish what Sjöström had gleaned from these papers because of the contempt of court rule. But a German court's jurisdiction did not extend abroad, so there was nothing to stop a foreign newspaper from doing so. To make any impact, it would need to be a big newspaper and preferably one in a country that had a large number of thalidomide children itself. The answer, Sjöström decided, was the *Sunday Times* of London.

Sjöström's proposition was not as simple as it looked because he wanted to be paid for the documents – his agent proposed £2,500. The *Sunday Times* had to weigh the propriety of paying for information it would use to break the laws of a friendly country against the public interest in knowing the truth about a major medical, commercial and legal scandal. The difficulty of the decision was reflected in the fact that although Harold Evans eventually decided to pay, he was defensive about it. But first he had to have an idea of what he would be getting for his money, so I went off to Stockholm to join up with the *Sunday Times* German correspondent, Antony Terry. We would size up Sjöström, Terry would translate a selection of the German documents, and we would plan an article which Evans would run either on the eve of the German trial, or immediately if the trial were to be abandoned.

We learned enough in Stockholm for Evans to decide to go ahead with the Sjöström deal and Terry brought the Grunenthal documents to London in three suitcases. The next step was daunting – to translate them all. The paper set up a little unit in one of the many spare rooms in the old part of Thomson House, moved the Grunenthal files into it, engaged a German translator, and arranged for a researcher and a floating staff of two or three journalists to process the material. The translator did a literal translation of each Grunenthal document and passed it to a journalist who made a decision on its relevance and then summed it up in a sentence or two. The journalists handed their summaries to the researcher who filed them along with the original document and the translation, and then cross-indexed them with a card system she had started. You could follow the development of thalidomide at Chemie Grunenthal week by week in the chronological index, or, say, through the eyes of the managing director or the chief chemist under their names. It took nearly a year of painstaking, time-consuming work. But that, rather than the dramatic, television-style confrontation, is the real basis of investigative journalism.

The journalists were dragged off for other, more urgent assignments; there were periods when only the translator and the researcher were in the 'thalidomide room'; there were doubts about the value of such expensive, long-term projects. Yet by the end of it everyone working on the story had mastered the history of this dreadful drug and probably knew more about its development than individual Grunenthal executives – Page could more than hold his own with experienced pharmacologists when discussing thalidomide's scientific aspects.

In January 1968 I took the boxes of cards that made up the Grunenthal index out of the thalidomide room and transferred them to my house. There, away from the distractions and gossip of the office, I began to write the narrative. The problem was the plethora of material. Newspaper readers sometimes wonder why some facet of a story has been ignored, why the journalist has not considered all the alternative explanations for what has occurred. The answer is that journalists write to length. A book ends when the author has said all he wants to say. An academic paper ends when the point has been made. Except in rare circumstances, the length of an article written by a journalist is determined by the amount of white space left on a particular page or pages after the advertisements have been allocated. If that space will hold, say, 2,000 words, then that's it, that's what the journalist has to write and this inevitably means leaving things out.

Harold Evans had said that he was prepared to devote four pages to the thalidomide story – an exceptional amount of space. But four pages with display (headlines, photographs, diagrams) is still only about 10,000 words, the equivalent of a long chapter in a book. This is why it took me nearly three months to write a draft of the story, paring down the details without distorting events, discarding sections that, although interesting, drifted away from the mainstream. Then, because Insight was a team operation, its then editor, Godfrey Hodgson, took over and ran the draft through his typewriter, adding the drive and drama to the story that, because I had now been so close to the project for so long, I had underplayed.

The *Sunday Times* published it on 19 May 1968, a week before the German trial. 'There has been nothing remotely comparable in Germany, in scale or emotional intensity, since Nuremberg,' the article said. Well, that might have been so in Germany, but in Britain the trial passed almost unnoticed. British newspapers consulted their lawyers and were warned that since the issues being decided in the German court impinged on those concerning the British thalidomide cases, it would be dangerous to publish anything except reports of what went on in the German courtroom. Even these were brief, and eventually the British press once again lost interest.

But four months earlier the *Sunday Times* had written out another cheque, this time to Dr Montagu Phillips, a consulting pharmacologist and chemical engineer. Phillips had been engaged by solicitors representing the British thalidomide families to act as their professional adviser, to look at the case and if necessary be the expert witness for them. As part of the British legal process called 'discovery', the children's solicitors had been able to obtain from Distillers all their files relating to thalidomide and had passed them to Phillips for evaluation. Outraged by what he read, Phillips had simmered away, waiting for his moment in court. But the years had passed and it began to look as if the case would never be heard and the issues never

366

TELL ME NO LIES

debated. So Phillips had gone to an acquaintance, John Fielding, a business reporter on the *Sunday Times*. He said he would let the *Sunday Times* see the 10,000 documents Distillers had been obliged to disclose and the newspaper could assess for itself what had caused the disaster. Phillips's genuine anger was one reason he had decided to do this, but money was another. He argued that he was a professional witness, we would need his help to interpret the files, and he wanted to be paid for it.

Harold Evans hesitated, again weighing the inevitable accusations of 'cheque book journalism' against the public interest in the telling of the story. Evans eventually offered Phillips £8,000 for sight of the Distillers documents and technical advice, a logical and defensible decision. Phillips accepted and the team that had handled the German documents now began much the same process with the British ones. Again I took time off from the office and wrote a narrative of how thalidomide came to be marketed in Britain, some 120 pages that became known in legal circles as 'the draft article'.

I worked on the article only intermittently because the continuing legal restraints offered little chance of early publication and it is hard to get excited about a story which might never appear. It was not until April 1971 that I could report to Page and Evans that I had a 12,000-word draft ready and had identified a number of people as candidates for interviews. The article sat in the *Sunday Times* office while the British legal processes ground slowly on. Then a West End art dealer, David Mason, the father of a thalidomide daughter, Louise, angered by the paltry compensation sums Distillers were continuing to offer and by their condition that, if even only one parent objected, then the offer would be withdrawn from all, became the touch-paper that ignited the *Sunday Times* campaign. He decided to go public. At first he did not know how to begin, but a friend of his was an acquaintance of the editor of the *Daily Mail*, David English, so Mason went there with his story.

The *Mail* printed three articles on Mason's theme that he was being legally blackmailed into accepting compensation he thought inadequate: 'MY FIGHT FOR JUSTICE, BY THE FATHER OF HEART-BREAK GIRL, LOUISE', said the headline on the first article. Then, abruptly, the articles stopped. Distillers' lawyers had complained to the attorney-general that the articles constituted contempt of court. He agreed and warned the *Daily Mail*, and – to English's lasting regret

– the paper ceased publication of the story. The rest of the media, which had interviewed Mason and confirmed his account, took fright and carried nothing. Even the BBC backed off. The television programme *Twenty-Four Hours* thought it could get round the contempt problem by doing just a series of interviews with thalidomide parents. Distillers threatened action and the BBC cancelled the programme. When Mason went to court and won the right to refuse the proposed settlement, there was a brief flurry of headlines about that aspect alone, and then silence once more. I became convinced that my draft article would suffer a similar fate, and, not quite knowing what to do about it, I went to see Mason to lure him away from the *Mail* and get him on our side.

In the background all this time, but about to play a major part, was the *Sunday Times* legal manager, James Evans. A handsome man with high rosy cheeks and a most unlawyer-like friendly manner, he was not only deeply interested in journalism and its problems but was constantly seeking new legal stratagems that would help journalists get their stories into their paper. He was there to be consulted as the story developed, to advise on what extra work might be needed to make it legally watertight and then to work through the writing with the journalist, fine-tuning phrases and sentences to lessen the libel risk, testing the journalist's sources and his proof, until finally he would say, 'We can't get rid of the risk altogether and he may sue but I don't think he'll go into the witness box.' He was right nine times out of ten. We had consulted him all along the way with the thalidomide story and he knew the legal minefield we were trying to cross but he could see no safe way through it.

I brought Mason into the *Sunday Times* and he met Page and Harold Evans. Then, just briefly, the project lost its momentum. We were still going to do the story, but it was not top of the news list. I thought Mason understood this, but as seen through his eyes, the *Sunday Times* was either slipping into the same state of procrastination that had marked the parents' legal case against Distillers or, like the *Daily Mail*, was being frightened off by Distillers and the attorney-general. Mason is a shrewd man, with an art dealer's skill in reading people. He had learned enough in his relationships with newspapers to know how to galvanise us back into action. He rang me at the *Sunday Times*. 'I've just heard that the *News of the World* is looking at the story,' he said. 'Apparently Rupert Murdoch is very interested in it.' He let me simmer on that for a few days and then rang me again. 'The *News of the World* is going to run a series,' he said. 'Rupert doesn't give a damn about the attorney-general. It's due to start the Sunday after next. They want to interview me. What do you think?'

I knew Murdoch well enough to decide that Mason's story was believable. And indeed, later Murdoch was behind the thousands of posters that appeared around the country overnight – including on the doors, windows and railings of Distillers' elegant London head-quarters in St James's Square – savagely attacking the company. The national press got copies of these posters with a press release saying that they were a private campaign aimed at hitting Distillers where it hurt – in its pockets. The release was not signed, gave no address or telephone number, and the posters did not give any indication of the printer, who could be prosecuted. Police ripped them down and began a search for the originator. They never found him, because Murdoch had gone to elaborate lengths to keep the operation secret. A senior *News of the World* executive, Graham King, organised it. He first resigned from the *News of the World* so that he would be acting as a private individual, and a few days after the posters appeared, stuck up at night by small groups of volunteers, he left for a convenient appointment in Australia. (He later returned to the *News of the World*.)

I told Mason to stall the *News of the World* and I went to see Harold Evans. I caught him outside his office talking to Denis Hamilton, so I brought them both up to date with what Mason said was happening. Evans was determined not to lose the story. 'I'm tempted to publish anyway,' he said. 'I'll go to jail. That's what I'll do. I'll go to jail. Bloody hell, it'd be worth it.' Hamilton shook his head. 'We can't have the editor of a serious newspaper breaking the law,' he said. 'If the law's bad, campaign to change it. But we can't break it.' He turned to me, 'Are you sure the *News of the World* is going to run the story?' I said I was not. I knew only what Mason had told me and it was possible that he was simply putting pressure on us to act, but if he were to be right, how would we feel after so much effort and money when the *News of the World* scooped us?

Evans decided that he would get James Evans to look again at the legal problems and if necessary take an outside opinion on what could be done. If Mason's information was correct, we had ten days. James Evans needed only three. The law of contempt prevented us from campaigning in the newspaper for a better settlement for the thalidomide children because we would have to discuss the merits of their case and this was the prerogative of the courts. It did not matter that there had been no substantive hearings and that nothing had happened for years. A writ had been issued, the case had not been settled, and as far as the law was concerned, it was an ongoing matter.

But Evans the lawyer had been struck by a remark made by Lady Hoare, who ran a charitable trust for thalidomide children. She said that the parents resented being made to feel that they were going cap in hand for charity 'rather than moral justice from the wealthy Distillers'. The words 'moral justice' gave James Evans an idea. Suppose the *Sunday Times* were to campaign for a better settlement for the children on purely *moral* grounds. We would not discuss the issues in the case, make no attempt to apportion blame, but simply say that these desperately disabled children *deserved* better compensation than Distillers had so far offered. 'Without in any way surrendering on negligence,' James Evans wrote in a draft leader for the editor, 'Distillers could and should think again.' With this as the basis of the campaign, we could go on endlessly about the wretched lives that the children were being forced to lead. True, this might be seen to be putting pressure on one party in a case to settle but it would be moral pressure and nothing to do with the merits of the matter. 'If the attorney-general moves against us,' James Evans said, 'we'd have an arguable defence.'

James Evans's plan appealed to everyone. To sustain the campaign we would need as many human interest stories about thalidomide children as we could get, so reporters were sent up and down Britain to interview all the most desperate cases that we could find. Most of these reporters were women, the prevailing view in journalism then still being that a tragic human interest story needed a woman's touch. Marjorie Wallace, the leading human interest writer, quartered the United Kingdom, doggedly and courageously working her way through the alphabetical list of victims, staying where possible with the families, learning first-hand about their problems. She had reached the 'Ws' and reported to Bruce Page that she had found a child who could well be the worst afflicted in the country, Terry Wiles. Page asked me to accompany Wallace to write about Wiles. Since she was quite capable of doing it on her own, I suspect that he wanted me to meet a thalidomide child, perhaps to add fire to the draft article, to remind us all that at the end of the formula and the marketing ploys, a human being takes the drug and its consequences.

If so, he could not have chosen a better case. Few human beings could have been given a worse start in life than Terry. His mother had taken Distaval (the name under which thalidomide was marketed in Britain) when she was pregnant. Terry was born without any limbs at all, just a trunk and a head. One eye hung halfway down his cheek and had to be surgically removed. Then as if to torment him, Nature gave him a high IQ and an inquiring mind. Yet – and we came across other examples of this – Terry's tragedy had drawn from others a courage and compassion that make one proud of the human species. Terry's mother, thinking he would not survive, abandoned him at the East Anglian hospital where he had been confined. His father had long since gone, so Terry spent his first five years in an institution for severely handicapped children. There, one day, he was visited by Leonard Wiles, a sixty-year-old van driver, who had been asked by one of Terry's ageing relatives to be the boy's guardian. He began taking Terry to his home for visits and four years later Wiles and his wife, Hazel, a large, volatile woman eighteen years his junior, the sister of Terry's mother, legally adopted this armless, legless, half-blind little boy whose only obvious attraction was his bubbling good spirits and sense of humour.

Terry's affliction now revived in Leonard a long neglected engineering skill that not only enabled him to devise and build mechanical devices to make life easier for his adopted son, but helped him find a satisfaction in his own life that he had previously missed. 'Just looking at a child like Terry turns you into a kind of visionary,' he said. He designed many gadgets, but the most remarkable was his Supercar – a chair that, working on the principle of a fork-lift truck, could raise Terry from ground level until he stood six feet high and could talk to people face-to-face, transforming him from the fairytale frog into the prince.

I have to admit that I had deliberately avoided meeting a thalidomide child as, I suspected, had other reporters and even the editor. I had three young children of my own and I was not anxious to be reminded how lucky my wife and I had been. So my first encounter with the nine-year-old Terry was traumatic. Leonard Wiles drove Marjorie Wallace and me to the local village school where Terry was a pupil. We waited by the car while Leonard went into the classroom to collect him. Wallace and I were chatting when suddenly Leonard appeared carrying Terry in his hands like a damaged doll. He fumbled to open the car door, found he could not manage it, and simply thrust

Terry at me saying, 'Hold him a minute.' I did my best. There were no armpits, so was around the chest the best place? But this meant that Terry's face was only inches from mine. Should I look at him? Should we talk? What should I say? I took the coward's way out and passed him to Wallace for whom, by now, thalidomide deformities were no surprise, and the two were quickly immersed in conversation.

By the end of the afternoon, after watching Terry eat his own supper with a mechanical spoon he manipulated to his mouth with his shoulder, and hearing his account of the detective stories he enjoyed writing, I was more at ease. But the idea of signing up for day-to-day life with him for an indeterminate number of years left me with two powerful emotions – admiration for the Wiles, and a conviction that anything the *Sunday Times* needed to do in order to bring the real face of thalidomide before the world and obtain for people like the Wiles the only thing that could ease their burden, money, was absolutely justified – so I bear my share of responsibility for the fact that it was money that later created so many problems for the thalidomide children.

When the paper published the opening shot in its campaign, the skill of the two Evans in their respective fields – Harold in journalism and James in law – was immediately apparent. The headline: 'OUR THALIDOMIDE CHILDREN: A CAUSE FOR NATIONAL SHAME' grew out of James Evans's draft leader, polished by Harold Evans. Harold wrote the 'our' – to try to make readers feel personally responsible for the state and fate of the children; the '*national* shame' was to make them blame the government. At the end of the article was a tactical smart-bomb aimed and primed by James. It read, 'In a future article the *Sunday Times* will trace how the tragedy occurred.' This put Distillers on notice that we had learned enough to reconstruct the history of thalidomide and were going to publish it. If they kept quiet this might go against them if they then moved after the event. If they tried to stop us before publication – prior restraint – the public would wonder what they were trying to suppress. And with these few little words James Evans had lifted any risk of Evans the editor going to jail – the paper had not *published* anything, only announced that at some future date it *intended* to do so – and had shifted the onus for testing the law of contempt on this issue from the *Sunday Times* to Distillers, or as it turned out, the attorney-general.

At the urging of Distillers, the attorney-general applied for an injunction to restrain the *Sunday Times* from publishing the draft article. He got it, we appealed, he appealed, we appealed again – and the lawyers loved us. The story of this mammoth legal battle through the British courts all the way to the House of Lords – where we lost – and then on to Europe has been told in detail elsewhere. Suffice to say here that it might have all ended with the House of Lords decision had Marjorie Wallace not gone to Ireland to look for thalidomide children there. Officially there were two victims in Ireland but Wallace suspected that there would be more, probably labelled an Act of God, hidden away and cared for in convents. She found more than ninety. During the search she met the renowned jurist Sean McBride, then a European Commissioner. McBride told Wallace that even if the *Sunday Times* had reached the end of the legal road in Britain, there was still Europe. She told Evans of McBride's view and five years later Evans, Wallace, Elaine Potter and I found ourselves in Strasbourg listening to the European Commission rule that when the British Government banned the draft article it had violated our right of free speech protected under the European Convention of Human Rights. We presented this as a triumph, but it was a flawed one. We had fought valiantly for the right to publish an article that we knew all along we could never publish anyway.

During the early stages of our legal struggle with Distillers and the British Government, the attorney-general said he wanted Distillers to see the draft article. The *Sunday Times* sent it to the chairman of Distillers, Sir Alexander McDonald, emphasising that it was only a draft, and asked for his comments. Distillers complained to the attorney-general that publication would be contempt, and this was the beginning of the legal battle that got all the publicity. But, in a completely separate action, Distillers moved to gag us another way. When the company's lawyers read the draft article they immediately realised that we had seen their internal documents. It did not take them long to work out that the documents had reached us via Dr Phillips and that we had probably paid for them. So they began an action both for their return and for a permanent injunction to prevent us from using any information the documents contained.

They had a winning case. The practice of discovery is an integral part of the British legal system designed to save the court's time: if each side has read the other's documentation before the hearing begins, surprises and delays are less likely in the courtroom. But the system depends on each side knowing that its documentation will remain confidential within the court process and each set of lawyers pledges such confidentiality. Distillers argued that the lawyers for the thalidomide children were bound to respect the confidentiality of their disclosure of the company documents and that when the children's lawyers engaged the services of a professional adviser, Dr Phillips, then the obligation of confidentiality automatically passed to him. He had no right, Distillers argued, to pass copies of the documents to the *Sunday Times* and, since we were planning to publish them, the courts had a duty to restrain us so as to protect the whole discovery process.

We had only one defence. An exception to the confidentiality rule might be made if disclosure documents reveal acts of such iniquity that publication would be justified in the public interest. I prepared for James Evans a paper arguing that a company (Distillers) had marketed a drug (thalidomide) with advertising that stressed that it was safe for pregnant women, and that drug then caused those women to give birth to grossly deformed children; that the company, in its greed for sales, had ignored early warnings that the drug might cause such deformed births. If this was not iniquitous behaviour, what was?

It was no use. In August 1974, Mr Justice Talbot ruled that even if it could be proved that Distillers had been negligent in marketing thalidomide in Britain, such negligence would not constitute an exception to the need to protect confidentiality. 'The protection of discovery documents is paramount to the public interest for the proper administration of justice,' the judge said. The fact that we had paid Dr Phillips for the documents did not help our case. A decision that would have appeared to approve – for whatever reason – a professional witness's decision to sell to a newspaper documents revealed under discovery would have set too dangerous a precedent. We considered an appeal but all advice was that it would be a waste of time and money.

So when we went to Strasbourg it was with the knowledge that no matter what the European Court decided we would still not be able to publish the draft article. Our win therefore appeared a hollow victory – the British attorney-general had infringed our right to freedom of expression by stopping us from publishing the draft article because it was in contempt of court. We were now free to publish the draft article – except that a permanent injunction for breach of confidentiality prevented us from doing so. In the history of newspaper publishing, had a single article ever run into such a wall of complex legal blocks? But the European Commission, perhaps unfamiliar with British court procedure, perhaps accidentally, perhaps out of mischief (I like to think the latter), attached the whole draft article as an appendix to its decision. It thus became a court privileged document – we could publish as long as we did not change it, and on 31 July 1977 we celebrated by printing the Commission's ruling and, along with it, the draft article. It was exactly as I had written it six years earlier even though by now it was outdated and wrong in parts because of further research and new facts that had emerged during our legal battle. Anyway, by then the campaign was long over, and journalism pure and simple had won a proper settlement for Britain's thalidomide children. Or had it?

Well into the *Sunday Times* campaign there was evidence that far from convincing Distillers that they should pay up, we had only made them more determined to stick to their guns. In fact, Sir Alexander McDonald suggested that the *Sunday Times* might make things *worse* for the children. He said that if our campaign caused negotiations with the parents to break down, Distillers might decide to withdraw its compensation offer entirely and instead stand on the legal issues. McDonald was not impressed by our argument that Distillers had a moral obligation to pay more. Writing to an unhappy shareholder, Tony Lynes, then one of the leaders of the Child Poverty Action Group, who had urged Distillers to pay more, McDonald said, 'Even if the directors had agreed with you (which they do not) that there were overwhelming moral reasons for giving away £20 million as you suggest, you must realise that directors of a public company which acted in such a way and on such a scale might at once become subject to legal proceedings at the hands of those shareholders who disagreed.' Sir Alexander said that it was all very well for a shareholder to take a moral stand that involved him in little responsibility towards others – 'and I would observe in passing that it is even easier for a newspaper editor.' There was, however, a great difference between individual shareholders giving away funds to a charity and the directors of a company giving away funds for moral reasons which did not have the unanimous approval of shareholders, and when legal reasons did not justify it – a view which had more support at the time than we realised.

If this attitude was shared by a majority of the shareholders then the campaign would probably collapse, so Lynes began testing it.

He was soon joined in this task by Roger and Sarah Broad, neighbours of mine, who had read the first article in the *Sunday Times* and then came to me and asked how they could help. The Rowntree Trust provided them with the £8,000 they needed to buy a list of shareholders from Distillers (thirty-two volumes) and the cost of postage to circularise them. Among them were big insurance companies and a number of city and town authorities. The Broads gave the names to the *Guardian*, which asked these local authorities for their views on the stance adopted by Distillers. Most said that they would support a move for an emergency general meeting to discuss the issue. But it was the stance taken by Legal & General Assurance Society that proved decisive. It had no fewer than 3.5 million shares in Distillers, worth £6 million, and it told the *Guardian* that it would support a more generous settlement. The *Guardian* led the paper with this scoop, creating a stir in the City – never before had an institutional investor taken a public line on such a controversial matter.

Harsh commercial pressure was also building up. The Wrenson chain of shops and supermarkets announced a total boycott of Distillers products and in Washington, Ralph Nader, the consumers' campaigner, met David Mason and together they laid down an anti-Distillers barrage at a press conference. Nader said he would consult consumer and union organisations and within a month expected to be able to announce a boycott of Distillers products throughout the United States. This made headlines in Britain and in the next nine days nervous dealers in the City knocked £35 million off the value of Distillers' shares. Distillers surrendered. It might well have weathered the *Sunday Times* journalism campaign but the hostility of its own shareholders and the damage that a commercial boycott would have caused were more than it could bear.

It appeared that, one way or another, our newspaper campaign in Britain had achieved all its aims. The children got a decent financial settlement; the process for licensing drugs for sale in Britain was tightened, the law on contempt was reformed and – although we did not boast about it – we had stood up to Distillers' attempt to use the power of its advertising budget. (The *Sunday Times* advertising manager, Donald Barrett, had warned Harold Evans that Distillers was the paper's largest single advertiser, spending £600,000 a year. Then he added, 'I know that won't stop you and it shouldn't.'

Immediately the *Sunday Times* began its campaign, Distillers cancelled all its advertising.) But as the years passed some of us became painfully aware that the power of this dreadful drug to blight the lives of all who came in contact with it had not ended with the *Sunday Times*'s campaign.

To start with, some of the parents found the exposure in the press a painful experience. 'We have not sought the publicity which has been thrust upon us, although we are naturally grateful for the support which has followed,' wrote Alec Purkis in a letter to the paper. 'The glaring limelight has undoubtedly caused further distress to the affected parents and the children – most of the latter now read newspapers extensively.'

Next, there was discontent over the way the compensation was paid. Individual payments were made directly to the victims according to the severity of their deformities, but £32 million (£27 million from Distillers and £5 million from the British Government) was paid in instalments into the specially created Thalidomide Trust. The trustees decided from the start that most of this money should be allocated to individual accounts, the sum being decided according to the severity of the deformity. But, because of British tax laws relating to charit- able trusts, the money could not be paid directly to the victims. They had to apply to the Trust for amounts to cover specific needs. If their account was in credit, then the Trust would buy the item requested. No one was *entitled* to any sum of money – only help for needs *as judged by the trustees*. There were inevitable resentments. Parents who had fought for ten years for the compensation and thought that the *Sunday Times* had won it for them were disillusioned to discover that the money did not come directly to the children. They accused the Trust of encouraging a 'begging bowl' regime and of being high- handed and autocratic in dispensing the money. The Trust adminis- trators admitted that there was some truth in this. One, Allan White, said, 'It's an awful business playing God. But, as I tell them, unless they can convince me that what they need is genuine, how can I convince the trustees?'

Then in 1995 it became apparent that the Trust was going to run out of money, probably by 2009. We had been dazzled by the fact that our campaign had played a part in forcing Distillers to increase its original offer from £3.25 million to £32.5 million. It had occurred to no one that many of the victims would understandably be so deter- mined to live as much like normal people as possible – no matter what the cost – that even £32.5 million would not be enough. Fortunately, the Guinness group, which had taken over the Distillers company and had inherited the tragedy – but certainly not any legal or financial responsibility – promptly topped up the Trust in 1996 with another £37.5 million and the government added a further £7 million.

But there was already evidence that although the money brought physical comfort to the thalidomide children it did not always bring happiness. One victim, Graham Tindale, complained, 'People look on us as though we're football-pool winners.' Disturbing stories of greed and envy began to emerge. One limbless thalidomide victim was attending a special school along with seven other thalidomide victims who were less severely handicapped. When the seven learned how much the limbless boy was to receive in compensation from Distillers, they attacked him, kicking him with their artificial legs as he rolled helplessly across the playground.

Allan White told Marjorie Wallace that the compensation money attracted gold-diggers. 'The girls in particular are vulnerable. Some collect the most dreadful types and if we know that 90 per cent of what we are giving out is going on these leeches, we have to refuse. We get a lot of stick for doing so, but, in the end, the girls are often grateful. When the money dries up, the chap disappears.'

The most hurtful situations arose when a young thalidomide man or woman wanted to marry or live alone away from his or her parents. If they had put some of their compensation money into a house with their parents and then they wanted to realise the cash, the parents risked becoming homeless. In 1979 Freddie Astbury took his mother to court to remove her as a trustee of his £30,000 private trust and to evict her from the specially adapted house he had bought. He claimed that his mother was drinking heavily, had tried to sabotage his marriage, and had even punished him by removing the batteries from his electrically powered wheelchair. His mother, Ruby, then forty-nine, had to go to a hostel for the homeless. She was very bitter. 'I looked after Freddie for twenty years,' she said at the time. 'But now I am rejected and abandoned.'

Freddie Astbury was not the only one to become estranged from his parents. Terry Wiles met and married a divorcee, renounced Leonard and Hazel Wiles on television, and went to live in New Zealand, cutting off all contact. Leonard Wiles died of diabetes in 1996. Just before his death he learned that Terry had met his natural mother. According to Hazel, Leonard's last words were, 'How did Terry get on with his Mum?'

Once we knew about the thalidomide scandal, we had to write about it, imperfect though the *Sunday Times* campaign was. But we cannot claim all the credit for the outcome. The truth is that the power of the press is greatly overrated – a proposition we had occasionally discussed in the Blue Lion pub on a Saturday night when the *Sunday Times* had gone to bed. Page's view prevailed – that a newspaper editor could have *some* influence on policy in Ulster, the success of a play, the outcome of an industrial dispute or, for that matter, the behaviour of a big corporation like Distillers. But he could not have *decisive* influence on anything; the power to report or not to report could not be compared with the power of judges, ministers, civil servants, corporate directors or trade union leaders.

The other lesson from the thalidomide campaign is that editors and newspapers move on and the pages that made up their successful campaigns become faded library clippings. But for the reporters in the field, the victims they met and the stories they wrote remain part of their lives, not easily put aside. Not a week passes for Marjorie Wallace, now director of the mental health charity SANE, without one of the thalidomide victims ringing, writing or calling on her.

The thalidomide children have grown up, some have married, and some have children of their own. Most of these are normal, healthy human beings. But at least twelve have thalidomide-type deformities, raising the spectre that the drug's effects could be passed down the generations – that the thalidomide children could have thalidomide children. Dr William McBride, who has always said that the thalidomide tragedy is greater than anyone has realised, believes this to be so and in 1995 offered evidence to the annual conference of the European Teratology Society that thalidomide binds to the DNA in the cells. Other experts reply that some children were accepted as thalidomide-damaged who in fact had alternative explanations for their deformities and some of these may have been genetic. But if McBride turns out to be right, we will have to face the fact that the curse of thalidomide will be with us for ever.

AFTERWORD:
'THE FINAL CHAPTER'

John Pilger, 1985

In August 1978, a press conference was held in the Fish Room at Admiralty House in London to announce what Jack Ashley, the Labour MP, described as 'the final chapter of a harrowing struggle for justice'. He was referring to the thalidomide drug scandal, then in its twenty-first year. At the top table were Alfred Morris, Minister for the Disabled in the Callaghan government, Dr Gerard Vaughan, Conservative MP and chairman of the thalidomide assessment panel, Jack Ashley and Sir Alan Marre, a former parliamentary ombudsman.

Glasses of sweet white wine were sipped in an atmosphere of mutual congratulation as each man rose to tell of the great and good the others had done. On hand were copies of a letter from the chairman of the Distillers Company, John Cater, in which he not only gave his assent to 'the final chapter' but added his own effusive end-of-term congratulations; and for this he, too, was congratulated.

The occasion was the publication of a report by Sir Alan Marre on what to do with seventy-four youngsters known as the thalidomide 'Y list', who were still awaiting compensation from the Distillers Company, manufacturers of thalidomide, and whose childhoods had slipped away, mostly in poverty, without aids or special comforts or holidays. Their parents had signed a settlement in 1973 with Distillers and, in so doing, had signed away the right to sue the company for negligence, although many of them were unaware at the time that two lists of children had been drawn up, labelled 'X' and 'Y', and that only children on the X list would be compensated.

The 324 children on the X list were the subject of the Sunday Times's tenacious campaign to force the makers of Johnnie Walker whisky to establish a decent trust fund. Theirs was the lucky list, for the selection between X and Y was done by lawyers and was often arbitrary. Being on the Y list meant that these families still had somehow to prove to Distillers that the mother had taken thalidomide during the critical period of pregnancy all those years ago: in some cases, more than twenty years ago.

These mothers lacked written proof; either they had not retrieved the original prescription or their doctor's files had been lost, or their doctor had moved away or had died or did not want to cooperate for fear of implicating himself; or they had been given thalidomide tablets without a prescription. It is not uncommon for doctors simply to pass on a manufacturer's 'sample'.

This stringent condition of proof was applied unerringly to the Y group, even though many on the X list had been accepted into the 1973 settlement without it. What the X children had in their favour was the approval of one man, Professor Richard Smithells of Leeds University, who 'passed' and 'failed' a number of the children without seeing them and, in some cases, after viewing only a few snapshots. Professor Smithells later protested to me that he had been completely unaware that Distillers was using his judgement to determine the future of each child, and said he was deeply upset by the apparent consequences of any misunderstanding.

By the time the Y list parents knew about the two lists, it was too late; their signatures had indemnified Distillers.

At the time of the 1973 settlement, there were ninety-eight Y list children. In the rejoicing they were forgotten. The legal struggle had been bitter, complex, divisive and expensive; to continue and perhaps to jeopardise that which had been won for the majority of the children, the 'proven' cases, was unthinkable; and most of the Y list families obliged by remaining silent and slipping back into a world of hardship.

Many of them lived in the North of England, in Scotland and in remote rural areas and they could not afford to travel to London; and they were exhausted, having had their hopes raised, then unceremoniously dashed. They were also deeply and justifiably aggrieved. One Y list parent had overheard lawyers saying that they had been instructed to keep the list down to 'no more than 300 kids' which was the figure 'Distillers will agree to'.

It therefore was hardly a coincidence that the lucky and unlucky lists divided in favour of those able to stand up to the outrage of arbitrary and secretive decision-making: those articulate and literate and with access to London lawyers and bank managers and overdrafts, or merely with time and a telephone.

There was a vocal list and a muted list: a list of the strong and a list of the weak. No one dared to say it publicly at the time, but the lists of thalidomide-damaged children divided, with exceptions, just as the nation divided. One who did say it was Olwen Jones, a case worker for the Lady Hoare Thalidomide Trust. 'It's the old story,' she told me. 'The X list families included a strong body of middle-class parents who could get the best legal advice, who knew how to follow the twists and turns and to stay ahead . . . *who knew how to fight.* The Y list families are mostly working-class people, who often find it difficult to deal with a local authority, let alone endless legal matters and who feel betrayed and even ashamed.'

They were not completely forgotten. Olwen Jones had known all the families, X and Y, and had kept case histories on many from the time of birth. Olwen is a woman whose compassion is matched only by her unshakeable determination, and she was incensed at the 'cowardly abandonment', as she put it, 'of those who most needed our help'. She persuaded Jack Ashley, the campaigner for the disabled (he is himself deaf), to convene a meeting at the House of Commons in November 1973. At this meeting Dr Gerard Vaughan, who had chaired the assessment panel, said that sixty of the Y list children 'appear to be thalidomide victims' and he promised that his panel would examine them.

Six months later nothing had happened. With Olwen Jones, I began a campaign in the *Daily Mirror* which ran for four years and ended in the Fish Room at Admiralty House.

Following a highly unusual front page in the *Daily Mirror*, which showed two seriously handicapped children side by side,[1] one from the X list and the other from the Y list, and with almost identical deformities, Dr Vaughan again committed himself to reconvene the medical panel to see all the Y list children. My own argument for the Y list children to be included in the original settlement was based largely on a long interview I conducted in May 1974 with Dr David Poswillo, a world authority on birth deformities who had just completed five years' research into thalidomide. He told me that, given two suspected cases, it was impossible to say beyond reasonable doubt that one child was thalidomide-damaged and the other was not. 'Beyond reasonable doubt' was a premise of British justice. Distillers were now beyond reach of the law, but the issue surely was wider.

Here was a multinational company which, although it denied negligence, had continued to market thalidomide after tests in Germany and Britain had shown that the drug could kill laboratory animals and was therefore dangerous. Given this, and Dr Poswillo's statement, it

[1] This was considered something of a 'first' in 1974 as disabled people were seldom seen in mass circulation newspapers and never on the front page.

seemed to me that a clear responsibility rested with the company either to prove that the Y list children were *not* damaged by thalidomide or simply to 'top up' the 1973 settlement so that *all* the Y list children could be included. One thalidomide parent, Alec Purkis, who had struggled to get his daughter Catherine on to the X list and was chairman of the Thalidomide Society, had written a report estimating that this topping-up would cost Distillers less than £3 million after corporation tax. 'It's peanuts,' he said.

But it was the evidence of the children themselves and the suffering of their families which underlined the company's responsibility and also revealed something of the role of sections of the medical profession in the affair. For example, in 1964 Brian Huckstepp, an east London boy, who was then three, was examined by a leading surgeon, Michael Harmer of St Mary's Hospital, London. Harmer wrote in case notes that he believed this must have been a thalidomide baby. Ten years later Harmer reaffirmed this diagnosis in reply to solicitors acting for Brian's parents. He wrote that he had 'no doubt whatsoever' that Brian Huckstepp's deformities had been caused by thalidomide.

But shortly afterwards Harmer wrote again to say that he had been in touch with Professor Richard Smithells – whose opinion was adopted by Distillers as a verdict – and that Professor Smithells had denied Brian was a thalidomide child. In view of Professor Smithells's opinion, wrote Dr Harmer, he would not be willing to go into the box. The family's confusion was complete.

Brian's father, Harry Huckstepp, told me, 'We knew nothing about thalidomide until the word Distaval leapt at me out of the paper one day. We had kept a bottle of Distaval until we moved house, when it was lost. I went straight to my doctor who was our GP at the time of the birth, but he denied he had prescribed thalidomide . . . but what puzzled me was that he wouldn't say Brian was not thalidomide.'

When I first met Brian he was sixteen and attempting to play football in artificial legs which were old and heavy and caused him much pain. The family had spent everything they had on legal fees and could not afford lighter, specially made legs. Brian's current GP, Dr John Clougherty, said, 'There appears to be no doubt regarding the presence of thalidomide in young Huckstepp. I cannot for one minute understand the hesitancy of including this unfortunate child in the division of compensation.'

Sandra Allen, whose case was fairly typical, was seventeen. Her mother, Betty Allen, said, 'We hadn't heard of thalidomide until we heard a surgeon say to some students, "This girl is a classic example of the damage done by thalidomide."' When Sandra was eight she was seen by Professor Smithells, who, declared her not to be a thalido-mide child. Betty Allen subsequently discovered the remainder of the Distaval tablets she had taken and sent these to Professor Smithells; but by that time Distillers had had his previous opinion and their deci-sion appeared to be final.

By December 1977, more than three years after Dr Vaughan had given his second commitment, few of the children had been exam-ined by the panel and only thirteen of the ninety-eight on the Y list had been transferred to the X list and compensated. Dr Vaughan told me he had passed several cases to Distillers and had asked them to exercise 'a little bit of humanity'. During the winter of 1977–78, Olwen Jones and I travelled up and down the country interviewing the families, trying to assist them to recollect details such as which neighbour had given them thalidomide tablets 'for depression' or where they might have stored away old papers and perhaps a prescription.

As the years had passed, so the toll of breakdowns and family disunity and divorce had increased. One teenage girl suffered jeers such as: 'We know you're getting a fortune.' She still had received nothing. Both Alfred Morris, the then Minister for the Disabled, and Jack Ashley wrote to the Distillers chairman, John Cater, expressing disquiet that many of the children had not been examined. Cater replied that Distillers had given all the families 'the benefit of the doubt' and that the company 'cannot possibly compensate the thou-sands of handicapped children born every year'. But nothing of the kind had been suggested. Only the children of those parents who signed the 1973 settlement were eligible for compensation.

However, the company proposed that the families not only submit their cases all over again, but travel to Germany to get the opinion of another specialist. So here were desperate and confused people, burdened by a manifest injustice, yet again being force-marched through a Kafkaesque maze. There was no suggestion by Distillers of a final gesture, no act of magnanimity. The profits on the sale of Johnnie Walker, Haig, Vat 69, White Horse and Dewar whiskies, Booth's and Gordon's gins and Cossack vodka had just trebled to £127 million.

I phoned Ralph Nader in Washington. Nader, who had taken General Motors to court over faulty cars and had won, was supreme at consumer litigation and boycott. It was his intervention on behalf of the X list chil-dren that had helped secure their settlement. 'I thought thalidomide was all wrapped up,' he said. I explained that it was not, and I asked him if he would again consider arranging a boycott of Distillers' products in the United States, where the bulk of its profits were made. He agreed in principle and I sent him files on all the children.

When the *Mirror* published news of this impending boycott, I received an anxious call from Distillers, asking for details. A few days later, on 16 January 1978, I wrote in the *Mirror* an open letter to John Cater, whose picture was prominently displayed above a 1960 advertisement for Distaval. The advertisement showed a small child taking bottles from a bathroom cabinet. It read:

> This child's life may depend
> on the safety of Distaval . . .

> Consider the possible outcome in a case such as this – had the bottle contained a conventional barbiturate. Year by year the barbiturates claim a mounting toll of childhood victims. Yet it is simple enough to prescribe a sedative and hypnotic which is both highly effective . . . and outstandingly safe. 'Distaval' [thalidomide] has been prescribed for nearly three years in this country . . . but there is no case on record in which even gross overdosage with 'Distaval' has had harmful results. Put your mind at rest. Depend on the safety of 'DISTAVAL'.

The open letter asked the Distillers chairman to read again his own advertisement. To consider the salesmanship aimed directly at human vulnerability and fears and the reassuring boast which turned out to be false. It also asked him to consider his recent statement that all the children had been given 'the benefit of the doubt' by Distillers.

> Mr Cater, what benefit of the doubt has ever been given to Brian Huckstepp? Brian was twice declared a thalidomide child by a surgeon who wrote he had 'no doubt whatsoever' that Brian's mother had taken the drug. What benefit of the doubt was given to Andrew Lowe? Andrew's parents fought for sixteen years for justice until their son died last year. Right up until Andrew's death, your lawyers were suggesting that Andrew saw yet another specialist, get yet another 'opinion'. Andrew died a few days before his parents could give him his first real holiday – the first they could afford.

Shortly afterwards, Distillers agreed to abide by the recommendations of the inquiry conducted by Sir Alan Marre. This was the way out for Distillers, not for the children. When Sir Alan called me to the inquiry to give evidence, he listened with apparent sympathy, then said he did not wish to be seen 'punishing' Distillers. In his report, Sir Alan wrote:

> My inquiry has satisfied me that, in general, Distillers has tried to apply fairly the test of the balance of probabilities in deciding whether a Y list child should be accepted as thalidomide damaged . . .

The families regarded this statement as unbelievable. What 'fairness' had been applied to any of them? Sir Alan had consulted none of the experts, like Dr David Poswillo, who held that the onus of proof ought to be on Distillers. Incredibly, he produced two more lists: this time the unlucky list was called 'A category' and the lucky list 'B category'. Forty-nine youngsters were offered a derisory £10,000, only twenty were included in the 1973 settlement and five were told they must 'await further reports'. It was not surprising that Distillers all but sent a sprinter with their congratulations.

What was it about the thalidomide affair in all its stages that brought out in so many of those involved a bias against these families? It was a bias which at times bordered on institutional spite. Was it that the Y list families, however self-effacing, were living reminders of twenty years' manoeuvre and duplicity, collusion and ineptitude by public men, corporate men, lawyers and assorted licensed do-gooders?

Was it that the Y list families posed questions which were all too revealing and embarrassing? Questions such as: what *were* the deals that lawyers did with Distillers? Why *did* so few doctors speak out for the children, particularly doctors who had known them as patients? Why *did* Dr Gerard Vaughan (who went on to become a junior health minister) let four years elapse before honouring the public commitment he made that the panel, for which he was responsible, would examine all the children? These were years during which, for most of the children, their adolescence was spent in dire poverty. And why did no government order an open public inquiry into what surely was one of the most unremitting scandals of the post-war period?

The established order is masonic; when it is challenged, it closes ranks and sends emissaries to smile weakly. The genteel celebration in the Fish Room at the Admiralty was such an occasion.

EDUARDO GALEANO

The Upside-Down World

1998

Born in Uruguay, Eduardo Galeano is one of Latin America's most daring journalists, writers, historians and poets. He defies any single category. He says: 'I am a writer obsessed with remembering, with remembering the past of America above all, and above all that, of Latin America, intimate and condemned to amnesia.' For me, he is also a brilliant investigator of ideas.

At the age of fourteen, he sold his first political cartoon to *El Sol*, a Socialist Party weekly. In the 1960s, he became a journalist and rose to editor-in-chief of *Marcha*, an influential weekly journal, whose contributors included Mario Vargas Llosa and Mario Benedetti. While he was editing the daily newspaper *Epocha*, a military junta took power in Uruguay, and he was imprisoned, then forced into exile. In Argentina, he founded the cultural magazine *Crisis*. A military coup in that country saw his name added to a list of those condemned by death squads, and he moved to Spain.

It was at the beginning of this turbulent time, the 1970s, that he wrote *The Open Veins of Latin America*, his best-selling book in which he described the systematic exploitation of the continent by foreign capital. 'In difficult times,' he wrote, 'democracy becomes a crime against national security – that is, against the security of internal privilege and foreign investment.'

Like all of Galeano's work, *Open Veins* makes the connection between First World abundance and Third World poverty and emphasises that poverty is neither a natural state nor the collective responsibility of the ordinary people of Latin America, but the result of pillage: first by the European colonial powers, then by the United

States and the élites that are its local agents. The continent's 'veins' are gold and silver, cacao and cotton, rubber and coffee, fruit and forests. 'Everything,' he writes, ' . . . has always been transmuted into European – and later United States – capital, and as such has accumulated in distant centres of power. Everything: the soil, its fruits and its mineral-rich depths, the people and their capacity to work and to consume, natural resources and human resources . . . For those who see history as a competition, Latin America's backwardness and poverty are merely the result of its failure. We lost; others won . . .'

Asked to elaborate on his argument, he said, 'When under-developed countries are called "developing" countries, it's a way of saying they are like children – growing, developing. And it's a lie. They are underdeveloped because more powerful countries are growing at their expense. Third World underdevelopment is a *conse-quence* of First World development, and not a stage towards it.'

In his *Memories of Fire* trilogy (1982–86), he blends literary styles as few authors can. Anecdotes and essays, poetry and news items become a 'secret history' of Latin America, from the 'conquest' to the present day. His characters are real historical figures: generals, artists, revolutionaries, workers, conquerors and the conquered, beginning with pre-Columbian creation myths and ending in the unresolved struggles of the 1980s.

His latest book, *Upside Down*, is also a mixture of reportage and satire, history and social critique. It deconstructs systems of power and presents a series of mock 'lesson plans' with titles such as 'Injustice 101' and 'The Sacred Car'. Global consumerism, he writes, has created an 'upside-down world that rewards in reverse . . . The worst viola-tors of nature and human rights never go to jail. They hold the keys . . . the countries that guard the peace also make and sell most weapons. The most prestigious banks launder the most drug money and harbour the most stolen cash . . .'

In the following extract from *Upside Down*, Galeano describes twin illusions that grow divisions in humanity. The first is advertising, which 'enjoins everyone to consume, while the economy prohibits the vast majority of humanity from doing so . . .' The second is the illusion of 'world peace in the hands of the powerful': how imperial America has created 'the chimera of an international conspiracy against its freedom-loving self' while spawning the demon enemies – Osama bin Laden, Saddam Hussein – that justify this paranoia and, most impor-tant, the vast profits to be made from its 'defence'.

THE UPSIDE-DOWN WORLD

Models of Success

The upside-down world rewards in reverse: it scorns honesty, punishes work, prizes lack of scruples and feeds cannibalism. Its professors slander nature: injustice, they say, is a law of nature. Milton Friedman teaches us about the 'natural rate of unemployment'. Studying Richard Herrnstein and Charles Murray, we learn that blacks remain on the lowest rungs of the social ladder by 'natural' law. From John D. Rockefeller's lectures, we know his success was due to the fact that 'nature' rewards the fittest and punishes the useless: more than a century later, the owners of the world continue to believe Charles Darwin wrote his books in their honour.

Survival of the fittest? The 'killer instinct' is an essential ingredient for getting ahead, a human virtue when it helps large companies digest small and strong countries devour weak, but proof of bestiality when some jobless guy goes around with a knife in his fist. Those stricken with 'antisocial pathology', the dangerous insanity afflicting all poor people, find inspiration in the models of good health exhibited by those who succeed. Lowlifes learn their skills by setting their sights on the summits. They study the examples of the winners and, for better or worse, do their best to live up to them. But 'the damned will always be damned', as Don Emilio Azcárraga, once lord and master of Mexican television, liked to say. The chances that a banker who loots a bank can enjoy the fruits of his labour in peace are directly proportional to the chances that a crook who robs a bank will land in jail or the cemetery.

When a criminal kills someone for an unpaid debt, the execution is called a 'settling of accounts'. When the international technocracy settles accounts with an indebted country, the execution is called an 'adjustment plan'. Financial capos kidnap countries and suck them dry even when they pay the ransom: in comparison, most thugs are about as dangerous as Dracula in broad daylight. The world economy is the most efficient expression of organised crime. The international bodies that control currency, trade and credit practise international terrorism against poor countries, and against the poor of all countries, with a cold-blooded professionalism that would make the best of the bomb throwers blush.

The arts of trickery, which con men practise by stalking the gullible on the street, become sublime when certain politicians put their talents to work. In the shantytown nations of the world, heads of state sell off the remnants of their countries at fire-sale prices, just as in the shantytowns of cities criminals unload their booty for peanuts.

Hired guns do much the same work, albeit at retail, as the generals whose wholesale crimes get billed as acts of glory. Pickpockets lurking on street corners practise a low-tech version of the art of speculators who fleece the multitudes by computer. The worst violators of nature and human rights never go to jail. They hold the keys. In the world as it is, the looking-glass world, the countries that guard the peace also make and sell the most weapons. The most prestigious banks launder the most drug money and harbour the most stolen cash. The most successful industries are the most poisonous for the planet. And saving the environment is the brilliant endeavour of the very companies that profit from annihilating it. Those who kill the most people in the shortest time win immunity and praise, as do those who destroy the most nature at the lowest cost.

Walking is risky and breathing a challenge in the great cities of the looking-glass world. Whoever is not a prisoner of necessity is a prisoner of fear, deprived of sleep by anxiety over the things he lacks or by terror of losing the things he has. The looking-glass world trains us to view our neighbour as a threat, not a promise. It condemns us to solitude and consoles us with chemical drugs and cybernetic friends. We are sentenced to die of hunger, fear or boredom – that is, if a stray bullet doesn't do the job first.

Is the freedom to choose among these unfortunate ends the only freedom left to us? The looking-glass school teaches us to suffer reality, not change it; to forget the past, not learn from it; to accept the future, not invent it. In its halls of criminal learning, impotence, amnesia and resignation are required courses. Yet perhaps – who can say – there can be no disgrace without grace, no sign without a countersign, and no school that does not beget its counterschool.

Equalisation and Inequality

Advertising enjoins everyone to consume, while the economy prohibits the vast majority of humanity from doing so. The command that everybody do what so many cannot becomes an invitation to crime.

In the papers, crime stories have more to say about the contradictions of our times than all the articles about politics and economics.

This world, which puts on a banquet for all, then slams the door in the noses of so many, is simultaneously equalising and unequal: *equalising* in the ideas and habits it imposes and *unequal* in the opportunities it offers.

Twin totalitarianisms plague the world: the dictatorships of consumer society and obligatory injustice.

The machinery of compulsory equalisation works against the finest trait of the human species, the fact that we recognise ourselves in our differences and build links based on them. The best of the world lies in the many worlds the world contains, the different melodies of life, their pains and strains: the 1,001 ways of living and speaking, thinking and creating, eating, working, dancing, playing, loving, suffering and celebrating that we have discovered over so many thousands of years.

Equalisation, which makes us all goofy and all the same, can't be measured. No computer could count the crimes that the pop culture business commits each day against the human rainbow and the human right to identity. But its devastating progress is mind-boggling. Time is emptied of history, and space no longer acknowledges the astonishing diversity of its parts. Through the mass media the owners of the world inform us all of our obligation to look at ourselves in a single mirror.

Whoever doesn't have, isn't. He who has no car or doesn't wear designer shoes or imported perfume is only pretending to exist. Importer economy, impostor culture: we are all obliged to take the consumer's cruise across the swirling waters of the market. Most of the passengers are swept overboard, but thanks to foreign debt the fares of those who make it are billed to us all. Loans allow the consuming minority to load themselves up with useless new things, and before everyone's eyes the media transform into genuine needs the artificial demands the North of the world ceaselessly invents and successfully projects onto the South. ('North' and 'South', by the way, are terms used here to designate the carving up of the global pie and do not always coincide with geography.)

Cultural equalisation, the process of casting all in the single mould of consumer society, can't be reduced to statistics, but inequality can.

The World Bank, which does so much to encourage inequality, freely admits – and several agencies of the United Nations confirm – that never has the world economy been less democratic, never has the world been so scandalously unjust. In 1960, the richest 20 per cent of humanity had thirty times as much as the poorest 20 per cent. By 1990, that figure had increased to seventy times. And the scissors continue to open: in the year 2000 the gap will be ninety times.

Between the richest of the rich, who appear on the porno-financial pages of *Forbes* and *Fortune,* and the poorest of the poor, who appear on the streets and in the fields, the chasm is even greater. A pregnant woman in Africa is 100 times more likely to die than a pregnant woman in Europe. The value of pet products sold annually in the United States is four times the GNP of Ethiopia. The sales of just the two giants General Motors and Ford easily surpass the value of all black Africa's economies. According to the United Nations Development Programme, 'Ten people, the ten richest men on the planet, own wealth equivalent to the value of the total production of fifty countries, and 447 multimillionaires own a greater fortune than the annual income of half of humanity.' The head of this UN agency, James Gustave Speth, declared in 1997 that over the past half century the number of rich people doubled while the number of poor tripled and that 1.6 billion people were worse off than they had been only fifteen years earlier.

Not long before that, the president of the World Bank, James Wolfensohn, threw cold water on the annual meeting of the bank and the International Monetary Fund. He warned those celebrating the achievements of the world government run by those two bodies that if things continue as they are, in thirty years there will be five billion poor people in the world, and inequality will explode in the face of future generations. Meanwhile, an anonymous hand wrote on a Buenos Aires wall, 'Fight hunger and poverty! Eat poor people!'

As if to confirm our optimism, as Mexican writer Carlos Monsiváis suggests, the world carries on: the injustice that rules between countries is reproduced within each country, and year after year the gap between those who have everything and those who have nothing widens. We know it well in the Americas. In the United States half a century ago, the rich earned 20 per cent of national income; now they get 40 per cent. And in the South? Latin America is the most unjust region in the world. Nowhere else are bread and fish distributed as unfairly; nowhere else does such an immense distance separate

the few who have the right to rule from the many who have the duty
to obey.

Latin America is a slave economy masquerading as postmodern: it
pays African wages, it charges European prices, and the merchandise
it produces most efficiently is injustice and violence. Official statistics for Mexico City from 1997: 80 per cent poor, 3 per cent rich,
the rest in the middle. The same Mexico City is the capital of the
country that in the 1990s spawned more instant multimillionaires
than anywhere else on earth: according to UN figures, one Mexican
has as much wealth as seventeen million of his poor countrymen.

There is no country in the world as unequal as Brazil. Some analysts
even speak of the 'Brazilianisation' of the planet in sketching a portrait
of the world to come. By 'Brazilianisation' they certainly don't mean
the spread of irrepressible soccer, spectacular carnivals or music that
awakens the dead, marvels that make Brazil shine brightest; rather
they're describing the imposition of a model of progress based on
social injustice and racial discrimination, where economic growth
only increases poverty and exclusion. 'Belindia' is another name for
Brazil, coined by economist Edmar Bacha: a country where a minority
lives like the rich in Belgium while the majority lives like the poor
of India.

In this era of privatisation and free markets, money governs without
intermediaries. A state that is judge and police and not much else
keeps cheap labour in line and represses the dangerous legions of
those without work. In many countries, social justice has been reduced
to criminal justice. The state takes charge of public security; everything else is left to the market. And where the police can't handle it,
poverty – poor people, poor regions – is left to God. Even when
government tries to dress up like some kindly mother, it has only the
strength to exercise vigilance and mete out punishment. In these
neo-liberal times, public rights are reduced to public charity and
handed out only on the eve of elections.

Every year poverty kills more people than the entire Second World
War, which killed quite a few. But from the vantage point of the
powerful, extermination is not a bad idea if it helps regulate a population that is growing too fast. Experts decry 'surplus population' in
the South, where ignorant masses violate the Sixth Commandment
day and night: 'surplus population' in Brazil, where there are seventeen inhabitants per square kilometre, or in Colombia, where there
are twenty-nine. Holland has 400 inhabitants per square kilometre

and no Dutchman dies of hunger, but Brazil and Colombia belong
to a handful of gluttons. Haiti and El Salvador are the most over-
populated countries in the Americas – just as over-populated as
Germany.

Power, which practises and lives by injustice, sweats violence
through every pore. The damned of dark skin, guilty of their poverty
and their hereditary criminal traits, exist in shantytown hells.
Advertising makes their mouths water and the police chase them
from the table. The system denies what it offers: magic lamps that
make dreams come true, neon lights announcing paradise in the city
night, the splendours of virtual wealth. As the owners of real wealth
know, there is no Valium to calm so much anxiety, no Prozac to
snuff out so much torment. Jails and bullets are the proper therapy
for the poor.

Twenty or thirty years ago, poverty was the fruit of injustice. The
left decried it, the centre admitted it, the right rarely denied it. How
quickly times have changed: now poverty is fair reward for inefficiency. Poverty may arouse pity, but it no longer causes indignation.
People are poor by the law of chance or the hand of fate. The dominant language – mass-produced images and words – nearly always
serves a carrot-and-stick system that conceives of life as a pitiless race
between a few winners and many losers, who were born to lose
anyway. Violence is generally portrayed not as the child of injustice
but as the fruit of bad behaviour by poor sports, the numerous socially
inept who fill poor neighbourhoods and poor countries. Violence is
their nature. It corresponds, like poverty, to the natural order of
things, to the biological or perhaps zoological order. That's how things
are, that's how they've been and that's how they will be.

The moral code of the end of the millennium condemns not injustice but failure. Robert McNamara, one of those responsible for the
war in Vietnam, wrote a book in which he admitted it was a mistake.
That war, which killed more than three million Vietnamese and 58,000
Americans, was a mistake not because it was unjust but because the
United States carried on in full knowledge that it could not win. By
1965, according to McNamara, there was already overwhelming
evidence that the invading force could not prevail; nonetheless, the
US Government continued as if victory were possible. The fact that
the United States spent fifteen years visiting international terrorism
on Vietnam in order to impose a government the Vietnamese did not
want does not even enter into the discussion. That the world's premier

military power dropped more bombs on a small country than all the bombs dropped during the Second World War is utterly irrelevant.

After all, during that long butchery the United States was exercising the right of big powers to invade whomever they wish and impose whatever they choose. Officers, businessmen, bankers and makers of opinions and emotions in ruling countries have the right to create military dictatorships or docile governments. They can dictate economic or any other kind of policy, give the orders to accept ruinous trade deals and usurious loans, demand servitude to their lifestyles and enforce consumer trends. This right is a 'natural one', consecrated by the impunity with which it is exercised and the rapidity with which its exercise is forgotten.

Power recalls the past not to remember but to sanctify, to justify the perpetuation of privilege by right of inheritance, absolving those who rule of their crimes and supplying their speeches with alibis. What schools and the media teach as the only possible way of remembering the past simply passes on the voices that repeat the boring litany of power's self-sacralisation. Exoneration requires unremembering. There are successful countries and people and there are failed countries and people because the efficient deserve rewards and the useless deserve punishment. To turn infamies into feats, the memory of the North is divorced from the memory of the South, accumulation is detached from despoliation, opulence has nothing to do with plunder. Broken memory leads us to believe that wealth is innocent of poverty. Wealth and poverty emerge from eternity and towards eternity they march, and that's the way things are because God or custom prefers it that way.

The Eighth Wonder of the World, Beethoven's Tenth, the Eleventh Commandment of the Lord: on all sides one hears hymns of praise to the free market, source of prosperity and guarantor of democracy. Free trade is sold as something new, as if born from a cabbage or the ear of a goat, despite its long history reaching back to the origins of the unjust system that reigns today:

- three or four centuries ago, England, Holland and France practised piracy in the name of free trade, through the good offices of Sir Francis Drake, Henry Morgan, Piet Heyn, François Lolonois and other neo-liberals of the day
- free trade was the alibi all Europe used while enriching itself selling human flesh in the slave trade

- later on, the United States brandished free trade to oblige many Latin American countries to accept its exports, loans and military dictatorships
- wrapped in the folds of that same flag, British soldiers imposed opium smoking on China, while by fire and in the name of freedom, the filibuster William Walker re-established slavery in Central America
- paying homage to free trade, British industry reduced India to the worst penury and British banks helped finance the extermination of Paraguay, which until 1870 had been the only truly independent country in Latin America
- time passed, and in 1954 it occurred to Guatemala to practise free trade by buying oil from the Soviet Union, and the United States promptly organised a devastating invasion to set things straight
- shortly thereafter, Cuba, also failing to see that free trade consisted of accepting prices as imposed, purchased outlawed Russian oil; the terrible fuss that ensued led to the Bay of Pigs invasion and the interminable blockade.

These historical antecedents teach us that free trade and other such monetary freedoms are to free peoples what Jack the Ripper was to St Francis of Assisi. The free market has transformed the countries of the South into bazaars filled with imported trinkets that most people can see but not touch. Nothing has changed since the far-off days when merchants and landowners usurped the independence won by barefoot soldiers and put it up for sale. That's when the workshops that might have incubated national industries were annihilated, when ports and big cities razed the hinterlands, choosing the delights of consumption over the challenges of creation. Years have passed and in Venezuela's supermarkets I have seen little plastic bags of water from Scotland to drink with your whisky. In Central America's cities, where even rocks sweat buckets, I have seen fur stoles on fancy ladies. In Peru, I've seen German electric floor waxers for homes with dirt floors and no electricity; in Brazil, plastic palm trees bought in Miami.

Another path, the inverse one, was taken by developed countries. They never had Herod to their childhood birthday parties. The free market is the only commodity they produce without any subsidies, but it's only for export. They sell it, the South buys it. Their governments generously aid national agricultural production so that they can flood the South with food at ridiculously low prices despite ridiculously high costs, and so condemn the farmers of the South to ruin. The average rural producer in the United States receives state subsidies 100 times greater than the income of a farmer in the Philippines, according to UN figures. And don't forget the ferocious protectionism practised by developed countries when it's a matter of what they want most: a monopoly on state-of-the-art technologies, biotechnology and the knowledge and communications industries. These privileges are defended at all costs so that the North will continue to know and the South will continue to repeat, and thus may it be for centuries upon centuries.

Many economic barriers remain high, and human barriers higher yet. No need to look further than Europe's new immigration laws or the steel wall being erected by the United States along its border with Mexico. This is no homage to the Berlin Wall but one more door slammed in the face of Mexican workers who refuse to acknowledge that the freedom to change countries is money's privilege. (To make the wall less unpleasant, the plan is to paint it a salmon colour, display tiles of children's artwork on it and leave little holes to peek through.)

Every time they get together, and they get together with pointless frequency, the presidents of the Americas issue resolutions insisting that 'the free market will contribute to prosperity'. Whose prosperity, they don't say. Reality – which exists even if sometimes barely noted and which is not mute even if sometimes it keeps its mouth shut – tells us that the free flow of capital only fattens drug traffickers and the bankers who offer refuge to their narco-dollars. The collapse of public financial and economic controls provides good cover, allowing for the more efficient organisation of drug distribution and money-laundering networks. Reality also tells us that the green light of the free market helps the North express its generosity, by offering the South and East as gifts its most polluting industries, its nuclear waste and other garbage.

Enemy Wanted

Never have so many economic resources and so much scientific and technological knowledge been brought to bear on the production of death. The countries that sell the world the most weapons are the same ones in charge of world peace. Fortunately for them, the threat of world peace is receding. The war market is on the rebound and the outlook for profits from butchery is promising. The weapons factories are as busy as those producing enemies to fit their needs.

Good news for the military economy, which is to say, good news for the economy: the weapons industry, selling death, exporting violence, is flourishing. Demand is steady, the market is growing, and good harvests continue to be reaped from the cultivation of injustice across the globe. Crime and drug addiction, social unrest, and national, regional, local and personal hatred are all on the rise.

After a few years of decline at the end of the Cold War, arms sales have turned around. The world market in weaponry, with total sales of $40 billion, grew 8 per cent in 1996. Leading the list of buyers was Saudi Arabia at $9 billion. For several years that country has also led the list of countries that violate human rights. In 1996, says Amnesty International, 'reports of torture and ill-treatment of detainees continued, and the judicial punishment of flogging was frequently imposed. At least twenty-seven individuals were sentenced to flogging, ranging from 120 to 200 lashes. They included twenty-four Philippine nationals who were reportedly sentenced for homosexual behaviour. At least sixty-nine people were executed.' And also: 'The government of King Fahd bin 'Abdul 'Aziz maintained its ban on political parties and trade unions. Press censorship continued to be strictly enforced.'

For many years that oil-rich monarchy has been the top client for US weapons and British war planes. Arms and oil, two key factors in national prosperity: the healthy trade of oil for weapons allows the Saudi dictatorship to drown domestic protest in blood, while feeding the US and British war economies and protecting their sources of energy from threat. A sceptic might conclude that those billion-dollar purchase orders bought King Fahd impunity. For reasons that only Allah knows, we never see, hear or read anything about Saudi Arabia's atrocities in the media, the same media that tend to get quite worked up about human rights abuses in other Arab countries. Best friends are those who buy the most weapons. The US arms industry wages a struggle against terrorism by selling weapons to terrorist governments whose only relation to human rights is to do all they can to trample them.

In the Era of Peace, the name applied to the historical period that began in 1946, wars have slaughtered no fewer than twenty-two

million people and have displaced from their lands, homes or countries over forty million more. Consumers of TV news never lack a
war or at least a brushfire to munch on. But never do the reporters
report, or the commentators comment, on anything that might help
explain what's going on. To do that they would have to start by
answering some very basic questions: Who benefits from all that
human pain? Who profits from this tragedy? 'And the executioner's
face is always well hidden,' Bob Dylan once sang.

In 1968, two months before a bullet killed him, the Reverend Dr
Martin Luther King Jr declared that his country was 'the world's
greatest purveyor of violence'. Thirty years later the figures bear him
out: of every ten dollars spent on arms in the world, four and a half
end up in the United States. Statistics compiled by the International
Institute of Strategic Studies show the largest weapons dealers to be
the United States, the United Kingdom, France and Russia. China
figures on the list as well, a few places back. And these five countries, by some odd coincidence, are the very ones that can exercise
vetoes in the UN Security Council. The right to a veto really means
the power to decide. The General Assembly of the highest international institution, in which all countries take part, makes recommendations, but it's the Security Council that makes decisions. The
Assembly speaks or remains silent; the Council does or undoes. In
other words, world peace lies in the hands of the five powers that
profit most from the big business of war.

So it's no surprise that the permanent members of the Security
Council enjoy the right to do whatever they like. In recent years, for
example, the United States freely bombed the poorest neighbourhood
in Panama City and later flattened Iraq. Russia punished Chechnya's
cries for independence with blood and fire. France raped the South
Pacific with its nuclear tests. And every year China legally executes
ten times as many people by firing squad as died in Tiananmen Square.
As in the Falklands war the previous decade, the invasion of Panama
gave the air force an opportunity to test its new toys, and television
turned the invasion of Iraq into a global display case for the latest
weapons on the market: Come and see the new trinkets of death at
the great fair of Baghdad.

Neither should anyone be surprised by the unhappy global imbal-
ance between war and peace. For every dollar spent by the United
Nations on peace-keeping, the world spends $2,000 on war-keeping.
In the ensuing sacrificial rites, hunter and prey are of the same species

and the winner is he who kills more of his brothers. Theodore Roosevelt put it well: 'No triumph of peace is quite so great as the supreme triumphs of war.' In 1906, he was awarded the Nobel Peace Prize.

There are 35,000 nuclear weapons in the world. The United States has half of them; Russia and, to a lesser degree, other powers the rest. The owners of the nuclear monopoly scream to the high heavens when India or Pakistan or anyone else achieves the dream of having its own bomb. That's when they decry the deadly threat of such weapons to the world: each weapon could kill several million people, and it would take only a few to end the human adventure on this planet and the planet itself. But the great powers never bother to say when God decided to award them a monopoly or why they continue building such weapons. During the Cold War, nuclear arms were an extremely dangerous instrument of reciprocal intimidation. But now that the United States and Russia walk arm in arm, what are those immense arsenals for? Whom are these countries trying to scare? All of humanity?

Every war has the drawback of requiring an enemy – if possible, more than one. Without threat or aggression – spontaneous or provoked, real or fabricated – the possibility of war is hardly convincing and the demand for weaponry might face a dramatic decline. In 1989, a new Barbie doll dressed in military fatigues and giving a smart salute was launched onto the world market. Barbie picked a bad time to start her military career. At the end of that year the Berlin Wall fell; everything else collapsed soon after. The Evil Empire came tumbling down and suddenly God was orphaned of the Devil. The Pentagon and the arms trade found themselves in a rather tight spot.

Enemy wanted. The Germans and the Japanese had gone from Bad to Good years earlier, and now, from one day to the next, the Russians lost their fangs and their sulphurous odour. Fortunately, lack-of-villain syndrome found a quick fix in Hollywood. Ronald Reagan, lucid prophet that he was, had already announced that the Cold War had to be won in outer space. Hollywood's vast talent and money were put to work to fabricate enemies in the galaxies. Extraterrestrial invasion had been the subject of films before, but it was never depicted with much sorrow or glory. Now the studios rushed to portray ferocious Martians and other reptilian or cockroachlike foreigners with the knack of adopting human form to fool the gullible or reduce production costs. And they met with tremendous box-office success.

Meanwhile, here on earth, the panorama improved. True, the supply of evils had fallen off, but in the South there were longstanding villains who could still be called on. The Pentagon should put up a monument to Fidel Castro for his forty long years of generous service. Muammar al-Gaddafi, once a villain in great demand, barely works any more, but Saddam Hussein, who was a good guy in the Eighties, became in the Nineties the worst of the worst. He remains so useful that, at the beginning of 1998, the United States threatened to invade Iraq a second time so people would stop talking about the sexual habits of President Bill Clinton.

At the beginning of 1991, another president, George Bush, saw there was no need to look to outer space for enemies. After invading Panama, and while he was in the process of invading Iraq, Bush declared: 'The world is a dangerous place.' This pearl of wisdom has remained over the years the most irrefutable justification for the highest war budget on the planet, mysteriously called the 'defence budget'. The name constitutes an enigma. The United States hasn't been invaded by anybody since the English burned Washington in 1812. Except for Pancho Villa's fleeting excursion during the Mexican Revolution, no enemy has crossed its borders. The United States, in contrast, has always had the unpleasant habit of invading others.

A good part of the US public, astonishingly ignorant about everything beyond its shores, fears and disdains all that it does not understand. The country that has done more than any other to develop information technology produces television news that barely touches on world events except to confirm that foreigners tend to be terrorists and ingrates. Every act of rebellion or explosion of violence, wherever it occurs, becomes new proof that the international conspiracy continues its inexorable march, egged on by hatred and envy. Little does it matter that the Cold War is over, because the Devil has a large wardrobe and doesn't dress just in red. Polls indicate that Russia now sits at the bottom of any enemy list, but people fear a nuclear attack from some terrorist group or other. No one knows what terrorist group has nuclear weapons, but as the noted sociologist Woody Allen points out, 'Nobody can bite into a hamburger any more without being afraid it's going to explode.' In reality, the worst terrorist attack in US history took place in 1995 in Oklahoma City,[1] and the attacker wasn't a foreigner bearing nuclear arms but a white US citizen with a fertiliser bomb who had been decorated in the war against Iraq.

[1] This text was published prior to the events of 11 September 2001.

Among the ghosts of international terrorism, 'narco-terrorism' is the one that's most frightening. To say 'drugs' is like saying 'the plague' in another epoch: it evokes the same terror, the same sense of impotence, of a mysterious curse from the Devil incarnate, who tempts his victims and carries them off. Like all misfortune, it comes from outside. Not much is said any more about marijuana, once the 'killer weed', and perhaps that has something to do with the way it has become a successful part of local agriculture in eleven states of the Union. In contrast, heroin and cocaine, produced in foreign countries, have been elevated to the category of enemies that erode the very foundations of the nation.

Official sources estimate that US citizens spend $110 billion a year on drugs, the equivalent of one-tenth the value of the country's entire industrial production. Authorities have never caught a single US trafficker of any real importance, but the war against drugs has certainly increased the number of consumers. As happened with alcohol during Prohibition, outlawing only stimulates demand and boosts profits. According to Joe McNamara, former chief of the San Jose police force in California, profits can be as high as 17,000 per cent.

Drugs are as 'American' as apple pie – a US tragedy, a US business, but they're the fault of Colombia, Bolivia, Peru, Mexico and other ingrate nations. In a scene straight out of the Vietnam war, helicopters and planes bomb guilty-looking Latin American fields with poisons made by American chemical companies. Devastating to the earth and to human health, the sprayings are next to useless because the drug plantations simply relocate. The peasants who cultivate coca or poppies, the moving targets in these military campaigns, are the smallest fish in the drug ocean. The cost of the raw materials has little effect on the final price. From the fields where coca is harvested to the streets of New York where cocaine is sold, the price multiplies 100–500 times, depending on the ups and downs of the underground market for white powder.

Is there a better ally than drug trafficking for banks, weapons manufacturers or the military hierarchy? Drugs make fortunes for the bankers and offer useful pretexts for the machinery of war. An illegal industry of death thus serves the legal industry of death: vocabulary and reality become militarised. According to a spokesman for the military dictatorship that razed Brazil from 1964 on, drugs and free love were 'tactics of revolutionary war' against Christian civilisation. In 1985, the US delegate to a conference on narcotic and psychotropic drugs in Santiago, Chile, announced that the fight against drugs had become 'a world war'. In 1990, Los Angeles police chief Daryl Gates suggested that drug users be riddled with bullets 'because we are at war'. Shortly before that, President George Bush had exhorted the nation to 'win the war' against drugs, explaining that it was 'an international war' because the drugs came from overseas and constituted the gravest threat to the nation. This war is the one subject never absent from presidential speeches, whether it's the president of a neighbourhood club inaugurating a swimming pool or the president of the United States, who never misses a chance to exercise his right to grant or deny other countries certification for their good conduct in it.

A problem of public health has been turned into a problem of public security that respects no borders. It's the Pentagon's duty to intervene on any battlefield where the war against 'narco-subversion' and 'narco-terrorism' (two new words that put rebellion and crime in the same bag) is being waged. After all, the National Anti-Drug Strategy is directed not by a doctor but by a military officer.

Frank Hall, former head of the New York police narcotics squad, once said, 'If imported cocaine were to disappear, in two months it would be replaced by synthetic drugs.' Commonsensical as that might seem, the fight against the Latin American sources of evil continues because it offers the best cover for maintaining military and, to a large degree, political control over the region. The Pentagon wants to set up a Multilateral Anti-Drug Centre in Panama to run the drug war waged by the armies of the Americas. For the entire twentieth century, Panama was a major US military base. The treaty that imposed that humiliation on the country expired on the final day of the century, but the drug war could well require that the country be rented out for another eternity.

For some time now, drugs have been the major justification for military intervention in the countries south of the Rio Grande. Panama was the first to fall victim. In 1989, 26,000 soldiers burst into Panama, guns blazing, and imposed as president the unpresentable Guillermo Endara, who proceeded to step up drug trafficking under the pretext of fighting it. In the name of the war on drugs, the Pentagon is making itself at home in Colombia, Peru and Bolivia. This sacred crusade – Get thee hence, Satan! – also gives Latin America's armies another reason for existing, hastens their return to the public stage, and provides them with the resources they need to deal with frequent explosions of social protest.

General Jesús Gutiérrez Rebollo, who headed up the war on drugs in Mexico, no longer sleeps at home. Since February 1997, he's been in jail for trafficking cocaine. But the helicopters and sophisticated weaponry the United States sent him to fight drugs with have proved quite useful against upstart peasants in Chiapas and elsewhere. A large portion of US anti-drug aid to Colombia is used to kill peasants in areas that have nothing to do with drugs. The armed forces that most systematically violate human rights, like Colombia's, are those that receive the most US aid in weapons and technical assistance. For years, they have been making war on the poor, enemies of the established order, while defending the established order, enemy of the poor.

After all, that's what it's about: the war on drugs is a cover for social war. Just like the poor who steal, drug addicts, especially poor ones, are demonised in order to absolve the society that produces them. Against whom is the law enforced? In Argentina, a quarter of the people behind bars who have not been sentenced are there for possession of less than five grams of marijuana or cocaine. In the United States, the anti-drug crusade is focused on crack, that devastating poor cousin of cocaine consumed by blacks, Latins and other prison fodder. US Public Health Service statistics show that eight out of ten drug users are white, but of those in jail for drugs only one in ten is white. Several uprisings in federal prisons labelled 'racial riots' by the media have been protests against unjust sentencing policies. Crack addicts are punished a hundred times more severely than cocaine users. Literally 100 times: according to federal law, a gram of crack is equivalent to 100 grams of cocaine. Practically everyone imprisoned for crack is black.

In Latin America, where poor criminals are the new 'internal enemy', the war on drugs takes aim at a target described by Nilo Batista in Brazil: 'black teenagers from the slums who sell drugs to well-off white teenagers'. Is this a question of drugs or of social and racial power? In Brazil and everywhere else, those who die in the war on drugs far outnumber those who die from an overdose.

The End of the Millennium as Promise and Betrayal

Faith in the powers of science and technology fed expectations of progress throughout the twentieth century. When the century was halfway through its journey, several international organisations were promoting the development of the under-developed by handing out powdered milk for babies and spraying fields with DDT. Later we learned that when powdered milk replaces breast milk it helps babies die young and that DDT causes cancer. At the turn of the century, it's the same story: in the name of science, technicians write prescriptions for curing under-development that tend to be worse than the disease, and in the process they humiliate people and annihilate nature.

Perhaps the best symbol of the epoch is the neutron bomb, the one that burns people to a crisp and leaves objects untouched. A sad fate for the human condition, this time of empty plates and emptier words. Science and technology, placed at the service of war and the market, put us at their service: we have become the instruments of our instruments. Sorcerer's apprentices have unleashed forces they can neither comprehend nor contain. The world, that centreless labyrinth, is breaking apart, and even the sky is cracking. Over the course of the century, means have been divorced from ends by the same system of power that divorces the human hand from the fruit of its labour, that enforces the perpetual separation of words and deeds, that drains reality of memory and that turns everyone into the opponent of everyone else.

Stripped of roots and links, reality becomes a kingdom of count and discount, where price determines the value of things, of people and of countries. The ones who count arouse desire and envy among those of us the market discounts, in a world where respect is measured by the number of credit cards you carry. The ideologues of fog, the pontificators of the obscurantism now in fashion, tell us reality can't be deciphered, which really means reality can't be changed. Globalisation reduces international relations to a series of humiliations, while model citizens live reality as fatality: if that's how it is, it's because that's how it was; if that's how it was, it's because that's how it will be. The twentieth century was born under a sign of hope for change and soon was shaken by the hurricanes of social revolution. Discouragement and resignation marked its final days.

Injustice, engine of all the rebellions that ever were, is not only undiminished but has reached extremes that would seem incredible if we weren't so accustomed to accepting them as normal and deferring to them as destiny. The powerful are not unaware that injustice is becoming more and more unjust, and danger more and more dangerous. When the Berlin Wall fell and the so-called Communist regimes collapsed or changed beyond recognition, capitalism lost its pretext. During the Cold War, each half of the world could find in the other an alibi for its crimes and a justification for its horrors. Each claimed to be better because the other was worse. Orphaned of its enemy, capitalism can celebrate its unhampered hegemony to use and abuse, but certain signs betray a rising fear of what it has wrought. As if wishing to exorcise the demons of people's anger, capitalism, calling itself 'the market economy', now suddenly discovers its 'social' dimension and travels to poor countries on a passport that features its new full name, 'the social market economy'.

A McDonald's ad shows a boy eating a hamburger. 'I don't share,' he says. This dummy hasn't learned that now we're supposed to give away our leftovers instead of tossing them in the garbage. Solidarity is still considered a useless waste of energy and critical consciousness is but a passing phase of stupidity in human life, but the powers that be have decided to alternate the carrot with the stick. Now they preach social assistance, which is the only form of social justice allowed. Argentine philosopher Tato Bores, who worked as a comedian, knew all about this doctrine years before ideologues started promoting it, technocrats started implementing it and governments started adopting it in what some call the Third World. 'You ought to give crumbs to the elderly,' Don Tato counselled, 'instead of to the pigeons.'

The most mourned saint of the end of the century, Princess Diana, having been abandoned by her mother, tormented by her mother-in-law, cheated on by her husband and betrayed by her lovers, found her vocation in charity. When she died, Diana was the head of eighty-one public charities. If she were still alive, she would make a great minister of the economy in any government of the South. After all, charity consoles but does not question. 'When I give food to the poor, they call me a saint,' said Brazilian bishop Helder Cámara. 'And when I ask why they have no food, they call me a Communist.'

Unlike solidarity, which is horizontal and takes place between equals, charity is top-down, humiliating those who receive it and never challenging the implicit power relations. In the best of cases, there will be justice some day, high in heaven. Here on earth, charity doesn't worry injustice, it just tries to hide it.

The twentieth century was born under the sign of revolution, but the adventurous attempts to build societies based on solidarity were shipwrecked, leaving us to suffer a universal crisis of faith in the human capacity to change history. Stop the world, I want to get off.

In these days of collapse, the number of penitents – repenters of political passion or of all passion – multiplies. More than a few fighting
cocks have become hens a-laying, while dogmatists, who thought they
were safe from doubt and discouragement, either take refuge in
nostalgia for nostalgia that evokes more nostalgia or simply lie frozen
in a stupor. 'When we had all the answers, they changed the questions,' wrote an anonymous hand on a wall in the city of Quito.

With a speed and efficiency that would arouse Michael Jackson's
envy, many revolutionary activists and parties of the red or pink left
are undergoing an ideological colour change. I once heard it said that
the stomach shames the face, but contemporary chameleons prefer to
explain it another way: democracy must be consolidated, we have to
modernise the economy, there is no alternative but to adapt to reality.

Reality, however, says that peace without justice, the peace we enjoy
today in Latin America, is a field sown with violence. In Colombia,
the country that suffers the most violence, 85 per cent of the dead
are victims of 'common violence', and only 15 per cent die from 'political violence'. Could it be that common violence somehow expresses
the political impotence of societies that have been unable to establish a peace worthy of the name?

History is unambiguous: the US veto has blocked or closed off to
the point of strangulation most of the political experiments that have
sought to get at the roots of violence. Justice and solidarity have been
condemned as foreign aggression against the foundations of Western
civilisation, leaving it plain as can be that democracy has limits and
you'd better not test them. The story is a long one, but it's worth
recalling at least the recent examples of Chile, Nicaragua and Cuba.

End of the century, end of the millennium, end of the world? How
much unpoisoned air do we have left? How much unscorched earth?
How much water not yet befouled? How many souls not yet sick?
The Hebrew word for 'sick' originally meant 'with no prospect', and
that condition is indeed the gravest illness among today's many plagues.
But someone – who knows who it was? – stopped beside a wall in
the city of Bogotá to write, 'Let's save pessimism for better times.'

In the language of Castile, when we want to say we have hope,
we say we shelter hope. A lovely expression, a challenge: to shelter
her so she won't die of the cold in the bitter climate of these times.
According to a recent poll conducted in seventeen Latin American
countries, three out of every four people say their situation is

unchanged or getting worse. Must we accept misfortune the way we accept winter or death? It's high time we in Latin America asked ourselves if we are to be nothing more than a caricature of the North. Are we to be only a warped mirror that magnifies the deformities of the original image: 'Get out if you can' downgraded to 'Die if you can't'? Crowds of losers in a race where most people get pushed off the track? Crime turned into slaughter, urban hysteria elevated to utter insanity? Don't we have something else to say and to live?

At least now we hardly ever hear the old refrain about history being infallible. After all we've seen, we know for sure that history makes mistakes: she gets distracted, she falls asleep, she gets lost. We make her and she looks like us. But she's also, like us, unpredictable. Human history is like soccer: her finest trait is her capacity for surprise. Against all predictions, against all evidence, the little guys can sometimes knock the invincible giants for a loop.

On the woof and warp of reality, tangled though it be, new cloth is being woven from threads of many radically different colours. Alternative social movements don't just express themselves through parties and unions. They do that, but not only that. The process is anything but spectacular and it mostly happens at the local level, where across the world 1,001 new forces are emerging. They emerge from the bottom up and the inside out. Without making a fuss, they shoulder the task of reconceiving democracy, nourishing it with popular participation and reviving the battered traditions of tolerance, mutual assistance and communion with nature. One of their spokesmen, ecologist Manfred Max-Neef, describes these movements as mosquitoes on the attack, stinging a system that repels the hug and compels the shrug: 'More powerful than a rhinoceros,' he says, 'is a cloud of mosquitoes. It grows and grows, buzzes and buzzes.'

In Latin America, they are a species at risk of expansion: organisations of the landless, the homeless, the jobless, the whateverless; groups that work for human rights; mothers and grandmothers who defy the impunity of power; community organisations in poor neighbourhoods; citizens' coalitions that fight for fair prices and healthful produce; those that struggle against racial and sexual discrimination, against machismo and against the exploitation of children; ecologists, pacifists, health promoters and popular educators; those who unleash collective creativity and those who rescue collective memory; organic agriculture cooperatives, community radio and television stations, and myriad other voices of popular participation that are neither auxiliary wings of political parties nor priests taking orders from any Vatican. These unarmed forces of civil society face frequent harassment from the powerful, at times with bullets. Some activists get shot dead. May the gods and the devils hold them in glory: only trees that bear fruit suffer stonings.

With the odd exception, like the Zapatistas in Chiapas or the landless in Brazil, these movements rarely garner much public attention – not because they don't deserve it. To name just one, Mexico's El Barzón emerged spontaneously in recent years when debtors sought to defend themselves from the usury of the banks. At first it attracted only a few, a contagious few; now they are a multitude. Latin America's presidents would do well to learn from that experience, so that our countries could come together, the way in Mexico people came together to form a united front against a financial despotism that gets its way by negotiating with countries one at a time. But the ears of those presidents are filled with the sonorous clichés exchanged every time they meet and pose with the president of the mother country, the United States, always front and centre in the family photos.

It's happening all across the map of Latin America: against the paralysing nerve gas of fear, people reach out to one another, and together they learn to not bow down. As Old Antonio, Subcommandante Marcos's alter ego, says, 'We are as small as the fear we feel, and as big as the enemy we choose.'

ANNA POLITKOVSKAYA

Chechnya: A Dirty War
1999–2002

Unlike the wars in the former Yugoslavia, the war in Chechnya has been all but ignored by the West. Although Russia's behaviour in Chechnya has been condemned by human rights organisations, the Putin government continues to enjoy membership of the Council of Europe, is a signatory to the European Convention for the Protection of Human Rights and is answerable to the European Court of Human Rights.

The dissolution of the Soviet Union was relatively non-violent – except in Chechnya, where calls for autonomy led to a war with Russia in December 1994. Fierce Chechen resistance, mounting casualties and a small but articulate opposition in the Russian parliament and media forced President Yeltsin to reach an agreement with Chechnya's leaders in August 1996.

Three years later, the war resumed when two Chechen warlords, Shamil Basayev and Khattab, staged an armed rebellion in neighbouring Daghestan. The new Russian prime minister, Vladimir Putin, once head of the counterintelligence service FSB, successor of the KGB, ordered an uncompromising response and Russian troops attacked two Islamic villages in Daghestan. In response, bombs tore apart a Russian Army compound in Daghestan, then killed more than 200 people in Moscow and southern Russia. On 1 October 1999, Russian forces attacked Chechnya.

This time, following a wave of anger at the explosions inside Russia, military intervention in Chechnya appeared to have broad popular support. Russian propaganda linked the attacks to 'international terrorism' and to Osama bin Laden, who at that time was wanted by the United States for attacks on American embassies in East Africa. Doubts remain, however, that the bombings were the work of Chechens; there is the strong possibility that Islamic militants from Daghestan and Russian provocateurs played a part. Certainly, the main beneficiary of these events was Vladimir Putin, who now emerged as Russia's new autocrat.

Putin's 'anti-terrorist campaign' destroyed the Chechen capital, Grozny. The civilian population fled to the neighbouring republics of Daghestan and Ingushetia, where they live today under appalling conditions in refugee camps. Although the war has been declared officially over, Russian soldiers continue to shoot civilians for no discernible reason. Torture is commonplace, 2,000 civilians have 'disappeared' and there seems to be no accountability for Russia's 'excesses'. Moreover, the maltreatment of the civilian population has bred a culture of revenge: the rebels are replenishing their ranks with new recruits from decimated families. More than 4,000 Russian soldiers and many more Chechens have been killed.

Russia has refused Western mediation, pointing to NATO's compromising attack on Serbia. Although the Council of Europe had temporarily suspended the voting rights of the Russian delegation, Tony Blair invited Putin to London at the height of the fighting, with his spokesman claiming that Russia was facing a 'terrorist insurrection' in Chechnya. Having demonstrated his ability to keep post-Soviet Russia under control, Putin was Washington's and London's man, and in return received *carte blanche* in troublesome Chechnya.

Most Russian journalists reported the war from the point of view of Moscow. The most honourable exception was Anna Politkovskaya, writing for the independent *Novaya gazeta*. Politkovskaya visited Chechnya thirty-nine times, doggedly uncovering atrocities and human rights abuses. In her dispatches from July 1999 to January 2001, she concentrated on the civilian victims of war caught between the Chechen fighters and the Russian Army. 'Both sides support the same ideology,' she wrote. 'Neither one or the other has any pity for the civilian population.' Reporting from the refugee camps in Daghestan and Ingushetia as well as from the front line in Chechnya, she has shown that, through the use of indiscriminately applied firepower, the civilian population has become the main target of the Russian 'anti-terrorist operation'. Still, she treats both the victims and the victimisers with compassion and describes the plight of the rank-and-file Russian soldiers as hungry, abandoned cannon-fodder.

Politkovskaya is outraged that the suffering in Chechnya has been ignored in Russia and the West. She likens the refugee camps in Daghestan and Ingushetia to the Nazi concentration camps and compares the branding of the Chechens as a 'nation of criminals' to the Nazi treatment of the Jews. The destroyed Chechen capital of Grozny is an 'appalling contemporary Stalingrad'. Not surprisingly, she has made powerful enemies. When, in February 2001, she investigated a Russian Army torture centre, she was detained overnight and repeatedly threatened with rape by senior Russian officers. She has received numerous death threats, including an attempted poisoning in 2004. She lives and works in Moscow.

The following dispatches are followed by her remarkable reporting from a Moscow theatre captured by Chechen guerrillas in July 2002.

CHECHNYA: A DIRTY WAR

You probably think I'm writing all this to stir your pity. My fellow citizens have indeed proved a hard-hearted lot. You sit enjoying your breakfast, listening to stirring reports about the war in the North Caucasus, in which the most terrible and disturbing facts are sanitised so that the voters don't choke on their food.

But my notes have a quite different purpose, they are written for the future. They are the testimony of the innocent victims of the new Chechen war, which is why I record all the detail I can.

4 November 1999

We know of instances when air-force pilots jettisoned their bombs into the river on the outskirts of villages so as not to commit the sin of bombing their peaceful inhabitants.

We know cases of quite the opposite kind. The pilots deliberately fired on the Rostov–Baku Highway when refugees were fleeing along it from the war zone, and then flew past a second, third and even a fourth time when they saw that someone below was still moving. The war is rapidly acquiring two faces and each potential victim hopes and prays that they will be lucky and meet the 'kind' face of this war.

Asya Astamirova, a young twenty-eight-year-old inhabitant of the Katyr-Yurt village in the Achkhoi-Martan district, has looked at both the one and the other. She survived physically because some soldiers saved her. But she is now dead to the world because other soldiers carried out a dreadful and cynical atrocity before her very eyes.

On 16 November Asya was bringing the body of her husband Aslan back to be buried in Katyr-Yurt. He had died in the Sunzhensk district hospital from the wounds he received when he came under fire. With her in the car were her children, six-year-old Aslanbek and two-year-old Salambek. In another car were Aslan's older sister Oeva, a mother of two, and their two uncles who were no longer young men. At the checkpoint between Achkhoi-Martan and Katyr-Yurt they were stopped and, without a word, the soldiers opened fire on both vehicles. When the first burst into flames Asya and the little boys leapt out. 'For Allah's sake, save us!' they cried. The contract soldiers in their bandannas, who were not raw youths, continued shooting and told her: 'There's no Allah, you Chechen bitch! You're dead.'

They fired directly at her and the children. Aslanbek fell unconscious, Salambek screamed and Asya saw the car and her husband's body burn. Young conscripts observed the whole scene from a distance. When the contract soldiers had finished and went off to rest, the conscripts loaded the wounded Asya into an armoured vehicle and took her away. After several hours driving across the fields, avoiding the military posts, the soldiers unloaded the wounded family outside Sunzhensk hospital and without a word to anyone they left.

Asya is still in a state of shock. She gazes blankly round ward No. 1 where she and the children were placed. Her mother Esita Islamova asks each new visitor, 'How can I tell anyone after this that we belong together, that we're citizens of Russia? I can't!'

I try to stroke tiny Salambek's hair – his right leg is encased in plaster where fragments hit him – but the boy begins to scream and cry. He turns away and hides in the pillow.

'He's afraid,' Esita explains. 'You're a Slav, like the contract soldiers.'

'But what about the conscripts, they're also Slavs?'

'He's only a child . . . It's what he remembers and that's what he's reacting to.'

Our losses are immeasurable as we let the army get out of hand and degenerate into anarchy. By allowing such a war to be fought in our own country, without any rules, not against terrorists but against those who hate their own bandits perhaps even more strongly than we do, we are the losers and the loss is irreversible.

28 November 1999

She was lying on her back, arms by her side, shoulders square, like a soldier on parade, unaware of anything in the world around her apart from her pain. Some people came up, threw back the sheet, and looked at the eleven bullet holes scattered across her slight, girlish body and sewn together by the doctors. But even then Mubarik Avkhadova did not react. Her enormous dry eyes were fixed on the ceiling. Her arms lay helplessly by her side. Her only link with the world was the drip running into her vein.

For the third week twenty-two-year-old Mubarik has hovered between life and death. No one will give any guarantees. No one who visits her in Ward 8 of the Nazran republican hospital talks about the future. And everyone looks away when, worn by her struggle to keep alive, this once cheerful and carefree fourth-year student at the languages faculty in Grozny university suddenly shifts her gaze from the ceiling and stares at them as they repeat their meaningless phrases.

What happened? By current standards it was a very ordinary case. The Russian Army were advancing on the village of Alkhan-Yurt, only a kilometre from Grozny. Mubarik, the younger daughter, had stayed there on Suvorov Street with her elderly parents, her mother Tumish and father Ali, convinced until the last that the soldiers would not open fire on peaceful civilians and residential areas. On 1 December Ali decided that they could wait no longer and, stopping a passing *Zhiguli*,[1] which already contained six people, he persuaded them to also take his wife and daughter. He stayed behind.

Round midday the vehicle with a white flag tied to its radio aerial was moving towards Goity. The village is now overflowing with refugees and it was there, a few days earlier, that Mubarik's elder sister, Aiza, had gone with her four small children. Two kilometres down the Goity road, off the main Rostov–Baku Highway, a plane began to pursue the unfortunate *Zhiguli* and finally opened fire.

[1] Name given to Lada cars in Russia.

An old woman and her grown-up daughter died immediately. To this day their names are not known. Mubarik and a thirteen-year-old girl, the old woman's granddaughter, were wounded. While the plane prepared for a second swoop, Tumish dragged the girl and her own daughter out of the car and shielded their bodies with her own, already bleeding from a number of wounds. She feverishly tucked their arms and legs under her and when the plane returned and again fired it only killed Tumish. On the evening of 1 December it was announced on TV that the air force had destroyed a *Zhiguli* full of Chechen fighters who were trying to flee. Only on 11 December, on a Saturday, was Aiza able to get her wounded sister to hospital in Ingushetia, after bribing each and every post now set up on the Rostov–Baku Highway. (At Goity the village elders had collected 3,000 roubles to help her.)

And what about Mubarik's village? On 9 December the federal forces arrived at Alkhan-Yurt. What did they gain there at the cost of such torment to this pretty young woman?

The same day that Mubarik was brought to Ingushetia, 11 December, the area around the village was swarming with soldiers and their officers, tanks and armoured vehicles. At first sight it looked exactly the way the books describe the front line in a war or the fictional versions of the present Chechen campaign that they show, hour after hour, on every TV channel. Machine-guns, bullet-proof jackets, mud, and helicopters boastfully zooming overhead.

The closer you look, however, the stranger the sights you see. The officers, for instance, are standing with their backs to the front line. Whoever heard of such a thing? The soldiers follow their example. They sprawl over their armoured vehicles in such a way that they cannot possibly observe the territory of their opponent because it is located directly behind them.

'Where's the front then?'

'Over there.'

All cheerfully pointed to a pile of tree trunks that have been chopped down and laid straight on the road to Grozny. This means that from where we're talking to the front line, beyond which there was fierce fighting, is at most fifty metres. You could hit the trees with a slingshot, let alone a machine-gun or a sniper's rifle.

'And the fighters are over there, in that belt of trees,' the officers continue, with no concern for the absurdities they themselves are offering me.

'But we're no distance from them, and you're not even wearing bullet-proof jackets? Why aren't the fighters firing? Where are those snipers that everyone is so scared of? We're sitting ducks here.'

The ordinary soldiers are even more open targets on this strange front. Contemptuous of the dangers concealed in the surrounding area (if, that is, one believes this talk of a front outside Grozny), they stand on the roofs of the ugly concrete bus-shelters and seem in no fear for their lives.

So where are the Chechen fighters? Are there any here at all, and were they ever here? It all feels like some show put on by the military and not really the front line in an uncompromising struggle with international terrorism. What physical evidence can we see here of the fierce war that Russia's forces already, in their tens of thousands, have been waging in the North Caucasus since mid-December?

The refugees are unanimous. They talk today of a slaughter only of the civilian population, and the death of children, pregnant women and old men, instead of Basayev[2] and Khattab.[3] That is why I am here to record such testimony from those around Alkhan-Yurt. This is the area the military call the front. We know that here, one kilometre from Grozny, there were particularly fierce battles and pitiless operations to 'cleanse' the territory. I want to understand the reason why the nameless passengers of that *Zhiguli* on the Goity road lost their lives, and Mubarik was shot.

I want to know why twenty-three people died here in Alkhan-Yurt between 1–8 December: farmers, their wives and children. Only three died as the result of bombing, the rest perished during a check on 'ID documents and residence permits' (information from Human Rights Watch):

1 Alkhanpasha Dudayev
2 Humid Khazuyev
3 Isa Muradov
4 Musa Geikhayev
5 Arbi Karnukayev

[2] Shamil Basayev, most famous Chechen field commander, leader of the defence of Grozny in 1994–95.
[3] Alias of Saudi-born citizen, fighting in Chechnya since 1995.

    6   Nebist Karnukayeva
    7   Enist Sulimova
    8   Turka Sulipova
    9   Musa Yakubov
   10   Sharani Arsanov
   11   Marvan Karnukayev
   12   Aset Karnukayeva
   13   Kantash Saidullayev
   14   Sovdat Saidullayeva
   15   their child
   16   Isa Omarkhadjiev
   17   Doka Omarkhadjieva
   18   Zara Omarkhadjieva
   19   Matag Abdulgazhiev
   20   Belkiz Madagova
   21   Birlant Yakhayeva
   22   Alimpasha Asuyev
   23   Amat Asieva

How are we to go on living after this? Who is our friend or enemy now?

On the eve of Constitution Day the 'liberated' Chechen settlement of Alkhan-Yurt was as empty as a film-set in the middle of the night. There was not a single human being anywhere, not a cow, a chicken or a goose. Not a single living thing, nor any sound that might distantly suggest a mooing or clucking. If someone had been weeping, shouting or lamenting it would have been less frightening.

Silence. On the hill a churned-up graveyard. The officers tell me that Chechen fighters had dug themselves in there, so they had to fire straight at the graves. But where then are the dead fighters' bodies or the prisoners?

'Where they should be,' the officers reply.

Perhaps it would be better to show them to everyone. To put the survivors on trial. Then that would really be the triumph of the legitimate authorities over international terrorism.

The silence that greets these elementary proposals is the most telltale sign of this war. We continue gazing in silence at Alkhan-Yurt. The cupola of the mosque has been turned into a sieve. A few jagged rafters are all that remain, at best, of the roofs of hundreds of houses. The walls are like some worn and discarded garment, with gaping holes of all sizes (depending on the calibre of weapon the officer chose to shoot with). Alkhan-Yurt lies quiet and deathly still, in the tight grip of the encircling armoured vehicles. If people can be wounded, so can the villages they leave behind them.

So this is the 'fierce struggle with the Chechen fighters'. The army tells us, 'We are not shooting at people's homes', and the result is a devastated village and not one piece of evidence that the fighters have been there. And the front? There are no fighters there either.

But where are all the people? There must be someone on the front line in Alkhan-Yurt. Where is Mubarik's father, Ali, who couldn't get into the *Zhiguli* on 1 December and stayed behind at their house on Suvorov Street?

The commanding officer issued a very straightforward order. The civilian population has the right to leave their cellars and basements only between 11 a.m. and 1 p.m., carrying a white flag. If there is no white flag, they will be shot and also if they come out after 1 p.m. But why, I ask? The village has already been 'liberated'. And why only at those times, why not from 9 a.m. to 9 p.m.? The military here prefer to answer every question with a brief and clear 'Because'. That's how General Shamanov,[4] our newly decorated Hero of Russia, has taught his subordinates to reply when asked about his imposition of this twenty-two-hour curfew, an unfathomable addition to the theory of military strategy at the close of the twentieth century.

That is why they do not allow journalists here who have not first been thoroughly tested and processed by the press service of the combined forces in Mozdok. Without such ideological preparation the picture is all too clear. They call it the front, but it's nothing of the kind. And there can be no justification for the sufferings of Alkhan-Yurt. Who then are they fighting against? When the remaining inhabitants are allowed back, to walk again through their village and fields as they wish, they will know the soul-wrenching answer. Well, what would you say if you found yourself in the position of these hunted and tormented villagers who have been deprived of every human right?

The answer is obvious. But let me offer one more picture, this time from the 'liberated' northern areas of Chechnya, a region opposed to

[4] Major-General Anatoly Shamanov commanded troops in both Chechen wars.

Maskhadov,[5] Dudayev,[6] Basayev and all of their kind. The snapshot comes from Goragorsk on 10 December. This large and once unbelievably beautiful village, spread out like Moscow over 'seven hills', lies roughly eighty kilometres north-west of Grozny. There were also fierce battles here and people died on both sides. A great deal of destruction is evident, as are the fresh graves. A rough-hewn cross commemorates Private Alexei Mitrofanov, who died fighting for Goragorsk, and stands next to the vast and gaping holes left in the oil tanks by heavy artillery shells. This speaks more eloquently than any briefing: Mitrofanov died for someone else's oil.

You can't help noticing that they took particular and malicious delight in targeting the mosque in Goragorsk. It has been reduced to its foundations. The villagers give a welcoming smile to all visiting 'persons of Slav nationality', but their silent response came during the night. The statue of the Unknown Soviet Soldier, which stands as always in the central square, was neatly decapitated. No one can find the head. There are those here who fought the Germans in the Great Patriotic War,[7] but even that did not halt the villagers who have driven inwards their feelings of hate and desire for revenge.

The memorial itself suffered from the fighting nearby. The words NO ONE IS FORGOTTEN, have fallen off; the words NOT ONE DEED IS FORGOTTEN remain.

16 December 1999

The Independent Expert Legal Council in Moscow, at the request of the Memorial Human Rights Centre, has recently provided its analysis of certain aspects of events in Chechnya. This voluntary group of lawyers, headed by Mara Polyakova, has spoken out firmly and clearly, as international law and Article 2 of our own Constitution ('the rights of the individual take priority over all other values') demand.

---

[5] Aslan Maskhadov, elected president of Chechnya in 1997.
[6] Jokher Dudayev, first president of Chechnya (1991–96).
[7] In 1945, at the end of the war, the male Chechens who had fought the Germans did not take part in victory parades (even the 132 among them who as Heroes of the Soviet Union had won the ultimate accolade for their bravery) but were sent off to join the old men, women and children deported to Kazakhstan in their absence the year before. [Author's footnote.]

There can be no talk of a guilty nation that must answer for the actions of certain of its members. The Criminal Code and Russia's law 'On the Struggle against Terrorism' both define a terrorist action as a specific event. An anti-terrorist operation is therefore an action taken against specific individual criminals. Any restrictions on the rights and liberties of the population as a whole can only be imposed by the law 'On the State of Emergency'. In this case, that law has not been invoked. Additional Protocol No. 2 of the Geneva Conventions (to all of which Russia is a signatory) is expressed in even more uncompromising terms: 'collective punishment for a specific crime is categorically prohibited'.

Are we witnessing an anti-constitutional putsch? Without a doubt. When you carelessly congratulate yourself that we have just had democratic elections to the Duma, stop and think for a moment. We are living under a Constitution that has in part been revoked and now functions only in those parts that continue to receive the approval of the Kremlin. If they then take a dislike to other articles they will toss them aside, just as they will quickly deal with any of us. Yet what will Chechnya look like in the year 2000? We are moving towards the creation of some anti-constitutional territory, a reservation jointly controlled by the harsh military rule of the federal authorities and the so-called police force of the Gantamirov band.[8] This reservation has been set aside for people of an inferior status, Russia's Red Indians of the late twentieth century, who are guilty of having been born in the Chechen Republic. Russia, it seems, cannot live without a Pale of Settlement.[9] At the end of the last century the Jews were thus confined and, as a consequence, they provided many of the young revolutionaries and terrorists of Bolshevism. By creating a reservation for the Chechens we are preparing an inevitable rebellion, led by the hot-headed youths who will grow up there.

27 December 1999

---

[8] A Dudayev ally until 1993, Beslan Gantamirov then aligned himself with the federal authorities and returned with them in October 1999. [Author's footnote.]
[9] The nineteenth-century Pale of Settlement restricted Jewish residence to the western provinces of Tsarist Russia (modern-day Ukraine, Belarus and Lithuania). [Author's footnote.]

Picture a classroom. Children sit on their small chairs. One is scratching her leg, another picks his nose, while over there a boy in ragged sports trousers examines a gaping hole in his shoe as if no one else exists.

What can you expect? They've only been going to school for three years and are still little children by ordinary standards. They have just written a composition on the most universal school subject of all: 'My Homeland'. Which of us has not done the same, and committed the minor offence of filching wise words from some book or other?

But as I read through this pile of papers I was horrified. This hackneyed subject produced a series of burning revelations. It proved so wounding and painful a subject for those gathered in that classroom that I could hardly bring myself to call them children, let alone small children. Outwardly eight- or nine-year-olds, tragic circumstances had filled them with an adult and fully formed view of the world. Moreover, there were no exceptions, it affected each and every one.

But before you read about 'My Homeland' I should set the scene. We are in Ingushetia on the outskirts of the village of Yandara, not far from the Chechen border, at a refugee camp called 'Goskhoz' (State Enterprise). Tents, sheds and dugouts. Nothing to eat, nowhere to sleep, no clothes to wear and nowhere to wash, not even once a month. Nothing to provide any cheer. Yet the school is working and, an unbelievable luxury by local standards, it has been given several tents.

Officially we are in 'Tent School No. 8'. Almost 500 children are taught by twenty-one volunteer teachers. Of course they are not being paid, though there have been a great many promises. The admirable young director, Minkail Ezhiev, is devoted to his profession and, until September, was Head of School 21 in Grozny. Today that school is nothing but ashes.

Class 3C. Russian Language. Composition. Jamila Djamilkhanova, the young teacher from Grozny, speaks a faultless literary Russian; she does not conceal her surprise and pride at the patriotism of her pupils.

There's nothing else to add. I did not select the best compositions. There were only twelve altogether because the classes in the school are small. The tents are not large and many children cannot attend regularly; they have nothing to wear. As a rule, one member of a family attends school today, and tomorrow a different child goes. No one complains if they miss their studies; no one calls in the parents for an explanation.

There is something else distinctive about these compositions. The girls are usually more lyrical, but the boys are severe, single-minded and uncompromising. It's frightening, isn't it?

The first important discovery: not one of the children said that the Russian Federation was their homeland. That's all finished! They have cut themselves off from us.

Second, and equally important: these texts are the work of small children and so they have made quite a few mistakes. Their teacher Jamila has given them all full marks, however, no matter what errors they made in spelling or grammar.

'In our situation could you possibly say to one of them: "I'm giving you top marks for love of your homeland," and tell another, "You're only getting three out of five?"' she asks. 'I thought I could also learn some patriotism from them, and so could many other adults. Full marks are a very small reward for the suffering through which these children have learned to love Chechnya. Not one other child in Russia has had a comparable experience.'

She handed me the flimsy scraps of paper. Condensed emotion. Undeniable proof and material expression of their love. It does not get any more truthful than this.

And in the short interval before her next lesson we talked: you can still do something about hatred (for instance, by using superior force to overcome it) but, we agreed, there is nothing you can do about love. The only reaction is one of resignation and acceptance.

'I'm giving you these compositions,' concluded Jamila, 'with one purpose in mind: so that people in Moscow will finally understand.'

And their authors seem to be talking to us; even in the pages of our newspaper you can feel how much they want to make us listen.

Abdelazim Makhauri:

I have only one homeland. Grozny. It was the most beautiful city in all the world. But my beautiful city was destroyed by Russia and together with it, all Chechnya and the people living there. The people that Russia had not yet managed to destroy went to Ingushetia, as I did. But I miss my home. I so terribly want to go home although I know already that my house has been bombed to pieces. All the same, I want to go . . . Why do I want to live at home? So I can have the right to do what I want, and no one would tell me off.

LEAVE US ALONE, RUSSIA. WE'RE ALREADY FED UP WITH YOU. There were only a few Chechens before you started. GO HOME and put things in order there, not in our country . . .

Ali Makaev:

I always wanted to see my country Chechnya free from terrorism. Now here I am studying in a cold tent while Russian children can work on computers in warm schools . . . I do not know if Putin has a heart. But if he did he would not have started such a war. Putin thinks that human life is worth fifty kopecks. He is deeply mistaken. He is stealing these lives from people. I'd like Putin to know that we are also human beings. Until war came Chechnya was more beautiful than Moscow. I would like to go home and live there to the end of my life.

Islam Mintsaev:

I very much miss my school, my friends and all that I know and love. We don't live badly here in Ingushetia. We go to school in a tent settlement. But Ingush children go to big schools, to a three-storey building like we had in Grozny.

At night I often wonder when this cursed war will come to an end and we can go home. Grown-ups say that the houses are no longer beautiful there: everything has been destroyed and each day young people and our furniture are carried away on APCs [armoured personnel carriers]. They take the young people to Mozdok and torture them there like in the worst films. When I hear the roar of aeroplanes I again feel terrified, just like when we were at home. Again they are bombing my homeland. How many of our relatives have died? And how many are left homeless?

[no name]:

I love my homeland, the village of Urus-Martan because it is the most beautiful village in the world. Now I miss it very much. At night I dream that I am running with my satchel in my hands and my girl friends to our own school.

Here in Ingushetia planes and helicopters often fly past and I get scared, as though I am at home again. During the last war the soldiers from Russia killed my father. Mum searched for him everywhere. Finally she found a dead, mutilated body buried in the ground. I was six then, my brother was eight and my younger sister was eleven months old. After everything that happened I thought, the war has ended for good. But in a short time it all started again.

Now every day I hear the grown-ups weeping and telling of their murdered relatives. I would like to live under a peaceful sky! But will there be such a thing?

Marina Magomedkhadjieva:

My city Grozny always radiated beauty and goodness. But now all that is gone like a beautiful dream and only memories remain. The war is blind, it doesn't see the city, the school or the children. All this is the work of the armadas from Russia, and therefore not only our eyes are weeping but also our tiny hearts.

Now we have nowhere to go to school, to play and enjoy ourselves. Now we run back and forth and don't know what to do. But if they asked us we would say: 'That's enough bloodshed. If you do not stop this senseless war we shall never forgive you.' Soldiers! Think of your children, of your own childhood! Remember the things you wanted in childhood and what your children want, and you'll understand how sad and difficult it is for us. Leave us alone! We want to go home.

March 2000

A real war has its own bitter and proud symbols. Like May 1945. Like the words of the songs that little grandsons know today. This war has nothing. We don't even know if it's a real war or not. We already know that there will never be a victory. It's like some crazy, broken merry-go-round dangling little zinc coffins instead of horses.

In December 1999 I went with Galina Matafonova to Paveletsky Station in Moscow to meet her son Lyonya. All that remained of this young man over six feet tall were some ashes in a little box no bigger than the palm of my hand. We met an empty wooden crate, in other words. Perhaps I should have written about it then. But at the time I was writing about another boy who died in Mozdok: he had been shot by one of our lieutenants and then they lied to his mother that the Chechen fighters had killed him. Six months later a letter from Galina arrived at *Novaya gazeta*. We had both wept at the station, but I doubt if she remembered where I worked. Evidently, she had written to the newspaper because every mother needs to preserve such memories. 'My name is Galina Nikolayevna Matafonova, I'm the mother of three children.

'My eldest son Alexei was taken into the army on 15 May 1998. He went out of a sense of duty and served for a year and a half. Every fortnight he wrote home. Suddenly there was silence for two months and I began to fret. I was afraid he was in Daghestan, but I reassured myself with the words of [Prime Minister] Putin: our boys would not be sent off to fight, he said, without their voluntary agreement.

'After two months a letter nevertheless arrived. He wrote to me as they were on their way to Mozdok. He told us he had been shown how to drive a military reconnaissance vehicle (MRV) four hours before they set out. He wrote:

> I don't know what will happen next. There was neither the time nor a good reason to get out of it. We only learned where we were going when we'd been travelling for twenty-four hours. You know, Mum, I've only now realised that there's nothing worth doing in the army. It's just shameful. There's a young lad who's only served two months and he's travelling with me. He doesn't even know how to shoot, so how's he going to fight anyone? They're proud and fearless, though: 'We'll show 'em,' that kind of thing . . . the number of my death warrant is F-926411, MRV No. 110, Convoy No. 10115. Love to everyone.

The letter arrived in September. He had just over a week left to live.

'I went up to Moscow. There they told me that two women would soon fly to Daghestan to demand the return of their sons. I was to call them on 15 October. But the day before, I received a telegram that my son had died. The coffin and body did not come back for a long time. The boys from Alexei's unit told us how they were forced to sign a formal declaration of their agreement to fight. They were brought to the banks of the Terek River and told: "If you don't agree, hand back your weapons. You're free to go. You can make your own way back. You're Russian soldiers, wearing uniform, and you won't get back alive . . . It's that or sign up." The coffin turned up in Rostov-on-Don at Forensic Laboratory No. 124. I then first learned of this terrible place.

'In Rostov I met with the parents of Andrei Pyrlikov from the Altai Region. He and my son died together, when their MRV went up in flames. Our boys were tall six-footers, but all that remained of them could fit into a small plastic bag. They wrapped camouflage shirts around these little bags, and added trousers and shoes, then sealed the lot in a zinc coffin.

'I left without waiting for the representatives from Alexei's unit, who, according to army regulations, should have been at his funeral. On the baggage slip that accompanied Lenka's body (that's what we called him at home) to Moscow was written: NATURE OF CONSIGN-MENT: COFFIN WITH BODY OF MINISTRY OF DEFENCE SOLDIER. WEIGHT: 300 KG. DECLARED VALUE: 0.00 ROUBLES.

'Galina Matafonova, Tver Region'

24 July 2000

Klavdia Anufriyeva, seventy-three, is blind and lives in apartment 85 at house No. 46 on International Street. She has not washed for a long time, and her hair is uncombed. Today is a happy day for her, she tells me: there were two pieces of bread for lunch.

'But where do they take you to wash?'

The old woman does not want to say that she is not taken anywhere to wash. And the toilet is out among the anti-personnel mines. Going there several times a day is like playing Russian roulette.

'Why don't your relatives come and get you? Where are they?'

Klavdia tries from memory to repeat the Moscow telephone number of her one·and only son who, it turns out, is in charge of the fire brigade at Mytishchi near the capital: 'But you must say that every-thing is fine.'

'I'll tell him what I saw.'

'Not under any circumstances! He'll be upset. And he's a very important man, always at work and that's why he can't come to get me.'

Klavdia Anufriyeva's fate is typical of Grozny today. Tens of thou-sands remain here because no one has come to take them away or even invited them to leave. Our old woman is living on what is a most typical courtyard in contemporary Grozny. (Just round the corner is Minutka, the city's famous central square. These days it's like a firing range.) In the courtyard they let down a bucket on a rope through an inspection cover into a hole where everything liquid gathers in such a heatwave, and they use what they find there as water.

In the middle of their courtyard is an enormous pit. It appeared several days back when unknown people dug up a body there. Now the children swarm at the edge of the open grave. For them it's like a sandpit. They make pies there and their parents are not shocked.

Unexpectedly Klavdia turns harshly: 'O do shut up, Volodya! I'm fed up with your whining.'

Vladimir Smola, a tiny dried-out figure on stiff reedy legs, stands on top of a pile of rubble. Above him the sky and under him, his mother. Seven months ago that heap of bricks was apartment 24, his apartment. 'Don't shoot!' he yells. 'I'm fifty-one, I want to live!' He looks up into the sky above Grozny and just as we might wave away persistent flies from a pot of jam he tries to bat aside the military helicopters flying overhead. Back and forth energetically, left to right . . .

Mad? Yes, Vladimir no longer remembers that helicopters are not flies. He used to be an electrician. He gradually went out of his mind, beginning on 15 January 2000 when the third staircase on which he lived was directly hit. He survived, but his mother and two of her old women friends were buried in the rubble. Since then Volodya has lived on this common grave.

At first he searched everywhere for an excavator to dig them out. Then he went mad.

'Don't get the wrong idea, before this war our Volodya was quite normal.' Maryam Barzayeva, from 55 Lenin Street, is talking. 'Let's go and pay our respects to Auntie Amina, Auntie Katya and Auntie Rosa.'

We set off and behind us runs a crowd of the local children. They listen to this talk about graves and dead people and do not show any reaction at all, as if it were normal that the corpses of three old women lie only a short distance away and no one has dug them out; with the temperature around 50°C the smell is predictable. The children whisper to one another: 'Go and call Yura.'

Here he is. Yury Kozerodov. Swollen from hunger, his age is uncertain and if he did not carry his passport opened in front of him (as everyone who wants to stay alive here has learned to do) you could not tell his sex. In order not to go mad at the beginning of the siege of Grozny, Yura thought up the fairy tale that he was guarding the city's McDonald's.

'Where is it then,' I ask, 'the McDonald's?' It's hard to imagine that this ploughed-up corner of the earth has room for a fancy fast-food outlet.

'Over there,' Yury points at a door. He didn't even go down in the basement but remained guarding the door he had chosen. It is still intact, but leads nowhere. Yura, though, is now just another crazy person in the courtyard.

'Yura was quite normal before the war. He was a very good man. But it was hell here,' explains Zinaida Mingabiyeva. She was once an 'Honoured Stockbreeder' in the USSR and lives in the same court-yard. Zina is convinced that her mind, at least, has not been affected at all by the war, but three times she repeats exactly the same story: what records of milking production she achieved at the collective farm and how many times they sent her abroad to learn from the experi-ence of milkmaids in the GDR, Czechoslovakia and Hungary. 'I grew to hate eating meat then. Now I don't remember when I last ate some meat. How I want to eat, all the time.'

I turn to Yury Kozerodov. 'Yura, do you have any relations?'

'Near Tikhoretsk, but they call me a "Russian Chechen" and don't want to take me in.'

'And you, Volodya?'

'Near Smolensk, but they won't take me either.'

'What about you, Zina?'

'I'm even less welcome.'

That's just one courtyard in Grozny. I picked it at random, by chance. It was to ensure that this courtyard lived in peace that they began the 'anti-terrorist operation'.

Hospital No. 9 is the only accident and emergency hospital in Grozny. You come here to be saved or to die. All emergencies end up here, from appendicitis to a stab-wound in the chest. Most of its patients, though, are people wounded by mines. Not a day passes without an amputation, because the main scourge of the city are the anti-personnel mines that were scattered everywhere and today turn up in places where they were not to be found yesterday. During June there were forty-one amputations, not counting the patients who did not survive. Ilyas Talkhadov in Ward 3 was blown up on a route he had safely used the day before, driving to collect hay from the '60th October Revolution Anniversary' collective farm. The six neighbours travel-ling with him were torn apart. Both Ilyas' legs are broken and his hip joints were smashed to pieces. The only hope for him is Hospital No. 9. However, there is nothing here today apart from healing hands and souls. Nothing that could distinguish a hospital of the early twenty-first century from a rural dispensary of 100 years ago. The only modern equipment is an X-ray machine that works one day in two because the electric current is unreliable and the machine itself is old.

A diesel engine roars fiercely outside the office window. The military donated it so that the hospital could occasionally have some electric light. Abdul Ismailov, deputy chief surgeon of the hospital, explains why the engine has just started: the relatives of a patient have finally found some fuel and the doctors have begun to operate.

Another way of operating is described by Salman Yandarov, a middle-aged and highly qualified specialist. Today he is the chief traumatologist and orthopaedic surgeon of the Chechen Republic, having recently returned, after appeals from his colleagues, from St Petersburg where he had everything: a professorship, students, respect and a very good position in a famous clinic (not to mention a salary).

'This is my native country, so I gave up everything. But what can I offer people who are blown up by mines every day? The hospital is not functioning, it simply exists,' he says. 'For instance they often bring in someone who has lost both legs and needs urgent amputation if they're not to die. I carry in the battery from my car, connect it to the X-ray machine and take an X-ray. Only then do we operate. When the relatives don't have any money to buy diesel I again go and get my battery, rig it up to my car-lamp and operate. It's shameful . . .'

'But they've surely been bringing you some equipment from Moscow?'

'Yes,' replies the doctor, who has the hands of a pianist and the manners of a gentleman. 'They donated three operating tables. I can tell you, they are so out of date that no self-respecting hospital in Russia would accept them today.'

To begin with I thought how senseless everything happening here was. If you look at it from the state's point of view, why scatter a vast number of mines around the city and receive in return an astronomic growth in the number of disabled people, who require tons of medicine, artificial limbs and so on? And then scatter more mines. And again ferry in medicine, etc. Now it's clear what the state is up to. Its concern for the situation is purely virtual; the only reality is the scattering of mines. No matter how much we want to believe the reverse, or attribute everything to our chronic disorder or thieving, the reality is that the inhabitants of Grozny have been sentenced to this fate. Evidently, the ultimate aim is to ensure that as many people in the city as possible are either left without legs – or dead. Perhaps this is a new stage in the 'anti-terrorist operation', an unhurried punitive mission directed against one ethnic community, which now requires hardly any more ammunition, just the patience to wait for the inevitable outcome.

It all fits together. Why bother to rebuild if there is no fundamental need to rebuild? Why feed people if there is no fundamental reason for them to be fed . . . ?

27 July 2000

*

On 23 October 2002, Chechen guerrillas stormed a Moscow theatre and held 750 people hostage for four days. In the rescue operation staged by Russian special forces, at least sixty-seven hostages (the official figure is 128) and all fifty Chechens were killed. On the third day of the siege, Anna Politkovskaya returned to Moscow from exile and entered the theatre. Her aim was to save the hostages. This is her report.

I TRIED AND FAILED

'I am Politkovskaya, I am Politkovskaya,' I cried out at about 2 p.m. on 25 October, when I was entering the theatre at Dubrovka seized by terrorists. I had no expertise under my belt, absolutely no experience of negotiating with terrorists. If I did have something, it was my desire to help the people who were in trouble through no fault of their own. And also, as the terrorists had chosen me as a person they wanted to talk to, I couldn't refuse.

My soles squeaked on the floor of the theatre, and the sharp noise made by my feet on the broken glass will always reverberate painfully in my heart. I kicked spent cartridges as I walked, tossing them up. My legs felt like rubber from fear. 'Why have I, a woman, got myself into this hellish situation?' I thought. 'We have macho men at every crossroads, just whistle for them. Why did I have to come here?'

'I am Politkovskaya . . . Is there anybody here?' I cried. 'Hello, I am Politkovskaya . . . I have come to meet the commander. Reply!'

It was completely silent and calm around me. To my right, the theatre's cloakroom was filled with raincoats and jackets. Coats but no people, and no people sounds. It felt like walking into a school while all the children were sitting quietly in their classes.

I walked up the stairs to the second level, still crying out. I stepped into the half-lit area, without a soul in sight. Finally, a man wearing a black mask and carrying a sub-machine-gun appeared. 'I am Politkovskaya. I have come to meet with your commander,' I said.

'I will call him right away,' he replied. He looked me up and down and we exchanged a few words.

'Where are you from?' I asked him.

'From Tovzeni.' (A big village in the Chechen mountains.)

'I have been there.'

'You have? How was it? Did you like it there?'

I shrugged. We had already been waiting for fifteen or twenty minutes. What were they up to? I thought I heard a rustling noise coming from behind the green door just a couple of metres away, where I imagined hundreds of people were sitting trapped and frightened, the people whose plight I had come here for. Then the green door opened. Another masked person led out a frail teenage girl with a bluish-whitish face, wearing a yellow blouse. She was led past me, then they came back, and I plucked up my courage and asked, 'How are you doing?'

'What?' the girl replied.

And that was it; she was pushed away with a sub-machine-gun, back behind this damned dark-green door. With all my expertise and education, I was still totally unable to help the child. The helplessness was terrible.

Masked people were going to and fro, talking to each other and asking me, 'Are you Politkovskaya?' Curious heads bent down from the third-level balcony. I could see through the mouth slits that they were smiling behind their masks. In order to shake off the heavy weight of silence, I tried talking to them.

'Your mothers. Do your mothers know about this?'

'No, but we have gone past the point of return. Either the war stops, or we will blow up the hostages.'

'When will the commander come?' I asked.

'Wait. Are you in a hurry? Don't hurry. You'll have everything right away,' one of them replied. The words made me tremble again.

What's next? Will they kill me? Will they take me hostage?

Soon, someone entered from that door, behind which were the hostages, and told me to follow him. A minute later, we were talking in a dirty room with no windows, adjoining the hall. There was light in here, and for the first time I could see everything properly. The chief negotiator from their side turned out to be a twenty-nine-year-old man called Abubakar, who introduced himself as deputy commander of the subversion and intelligence battalion. At the beginning, the conversation was strained. Abubakar seemed nervous at first, but then calmed down. He became angry when he talked about his generation of Chechens, aged twenty to thirty, who had been through the two wars and knew nothing except fighting.

'You won't believe it, but for the first time in many years we feel calm here.'

'In the theatre?'

'Yes. We will die here for the freedom of our land.'

'You want to die?'

'You won't believe it but we want it very much. Our names will remain in the history of Chechnya.'

I am, of course, a very poor negotiator. I had no idea what to say. And he – who had lived for half a life without taking off his military uniform and with a sub-machine-gun in his hands – he didn't know how to do it either. That is why we kept slipping into conversations about the meaning of their life, for instance. Some of the other rebels came in to listen.

Abubakar became calm again, put aside the sub-machine-gun and said he wanted to clear his soul before death. I listened to him attentively but also tried to interject about the plight of the hostages.

'Let the teenagers out,' I suggested.

'No. We suffered at the hands of your people. Now let your people suffer. And the parents there, outside the theatre, let them feel what it was like for our parents.'

'At least let us feed the children.'

'No. Our children are hungry – let yours also go hungry.'

Abubakar said he did not expect mercy and that he dreamed of dying in the battlefield. I think he was being honest and frank with me because he was in the presence of a woman the age of his mother. And that is what I told him – that he was the same age as my son and that even in the worst nightmare, I would not see my son cornered by people.

'If he were a Chechen, he would be. And he would also wish to die like myself because of everything that you are doing to us in Chechnya.'

'And if you have to die tomorrow?'

'Praise be to the Almighty.'

Finally, we decide it is time for us to part. We have not agreed on much and I'm not convinced that the talks were in any way effective. But I am no negotiator. We had only agreed that in the coming hours I would carry water and juice into the theatre and I would try to bring them enough for almost 700 people.

I left the theatre in complete silence. Again, I had the feeling that there was no one around me. Lonely jackets and raincoats watched my steps. It was cold, very cold in this dreadful theatre – and there has never been a theatre in the entire world so stuffed with explosives. I just said to myself, 'Go and get the juice, look for it, do now only this and don't think.'

Had I done a lot or a little? A little, of course. But I could not do more. When the place was stormed, all the terrorists I had spoken to died. And with them died sixty-seven of the hostages who had drunk my juice before death. Let war be damned.

Guardian, 30 October 2002

LINDA MELVERN

A People Betrayed

2000

The British journalist Linda Melvern's investigation into the Rwanda genocide in 1994, and the complicit role of the 'international community', is a classic work. Its strength is the link she makes between those of eminent respectability in centres of power and the victims of their decisions taken at great remove in distance, culture and moral responsibility. The following pages are abridged from her book, *A People Betrayed: The Role of the West in Rwanda's Genocide*, in which she reveals that the tragedy of Rwanda, far from being an exclusively 'tribal conflict', as many in the West preferred, was also the sum of indifference and cynicism in Europe and the United States.

With the testimony of witnesses to the genocide and access to documents in Kigali, the Rwandan capital, as well as unpublished evidence submitted to the United Nations Security Council, Melvern reveals the true scale and intensity of the genocide that took up to a million lives, and why Western governments and the United Nations failed to intervene, why information was deliberately withheld from the UN commander in Rwanda and why the World Bank and the International Monetary Fund also stand indicted for having approved massive loans to the Rwandan Government, knowing that millions of dollars were being spent on weapons. In the following extract, the first massacres are discovered by the UN peace-keeping mission, whose commander asks for reinforcements and instead is told to leave: a shocking decision that was to prove fatal for countless people.

A PEOPLE BETRAYED

The first large massacre to be discovered by the peace-keepers was at Gikondo, a parish in the heart of Kigali and a CDR[1] stronghold. It was Saturday, 9 April 1994, and they were answering a desperate call from two Polish military observers living there.

The investigating peace-keepers were two Polish majors, Stefan Steck and Marec Pazik, who had served in the UN mission to Cambodia. With them went Major Brent Beardsley, Dallaire's[2] staff officer. They took the one working Russian-made armoured personnel carrier (APC) and a three-man Bangladeshi crew who warned that the APC could break down at any moment.

The APC slowly made its way through the streets. A group of people screamed at them to stop, but they drove on without speaking. The climb up the hill at Gikondo was laborious, for the road was steep and there were deep ruts made by the torrential downpours. At the top of the hill was a Catholic mission operated by Polish priests and nuns, set in terraced gardens surrounded by eucalyptus trees. It was a large mission, self-contained and dominated by a redbrick church.

They left the Bangladeshi crew with the APC, and walked into the church gardens. It was there they found the bodies. Whole families had been killed with their children, hacked by machetes. There were terrible wounds to the genitalia. Some people were not dead. There was a three-month-old baby, the mother raped and the baby killed with a terrible wound. There were children, some with their legs or feet cut off, and their throats cut. Most of the victims had bled to death. Steck returned to the APC. He wanted to get his camcorder to film it. There must be proof.

They found the two Polish UN observers huddled together in the church. The observers said that the Interahamwe[3] did the killing under the direction of the Presidential Guard. The priests were in the porch trying to stem the bleeding of the few survivors. The priests thought that the Rwandan Army had cordoned off the parish. They said their

---

[1] Coalition for the Defence of the Republic, extremist Hutu party.
[2] Brigadier-General Roméo A. Dallaire, Canadian commander of the UN mission in Rwanda.
[3] Hutu militia, formed as the youth wing of the ruling party, Mouvement Revolutionnaire National pour le Développement.

parishioners did the killing. When the president's plane went down, there had been shooting all night long. The next day Tutsi had fled to the church for safety and some people were so afraid that they hid beneath floors, in cupboards or in the rafters.

On Saturday, 9 April, at about 9 a.m., the priests had organised a mass and around 500 people, sheltering in the compound, turned up at the church. While they were holding the mass there was shooting outside and grenades went off. There was a commotion and two Presidential Guards and two gendarmes burst into the church followed by Interahamwe. The Interahamwe wore their distinctive clothing, the *Kitenge*, multi-coloured trousers and tunics. 'The militia began slashing away,' a witness remembered. 'They were hacking at the arms, legs, genitals, breasts, faces and necks.' There was total panic. Some people were dragged outside and beaten to death. The killing lasted about two hours and then the killers had walked slowly among the bodies, looting them and finishing off the wounded.

One of the Polish military observers, Jerzy Maczka, had watched the local police entering the buildings in the compound, followed by militia armed with machetes and clubs. One of the militia had what looked like a Kalashnikov. Maczka had seen militia climb over the fence and said he had tried to contact UNAMIR[4] headquarters but the radio channels were jammed. Maczka helped the wounded and had noticed how ears and mouths were slashed, clothes had been pulled off and the genitals of men and women mutilated. Maczka took photographs.

There was a pile of identification cards with the ethnic designation of Tutsi burned in an attempt to eradicate all evidence that these people had existed. The next day the Interahamwe came back. They discovered that the survivors were hiding in a small chapel. When they failed to break down the door, the militia poured petrol in through the windows of the chapel and threw in hand grenades.

Over the next three months, massacres like this became commonplace. But at Gikondo there was photographic proof. The Polish peace-keepers thought that Gikondo should alert the world, for they recognised what was happening as genocide.

Three times Dallaire was told to plan an evacuation of the peace-keepers. The first occasion was when Booh-Booh[5] ordered him to

[4] United Nations Assistance Mission for Rwanda.
[5] Jacques-Roger Booh-Booh, the UN Secretary-General's special representative.

begin a withdrawal. Dallaire replied that Booh-Booh could issue all the orders he liked but that UNAMIR was staying put. 'I will not withdraw,' Dallaire had said. There were about 15,000 people under UN care. What would happen to them? On Sunday, 10 April, Dallaire received a telephone call from the Secretary-General's special political adviser, an Indian official called Chinmaya Gharekhan. Gharekhan told Dallaire to plan a withdrawal. Dallaire again said it was out of the question; if UNAMIR pulled out, the situation would only get worse. Dallaire said that what he needed was a new mandate and that there should be a modest reinforcement of 5,000 soldiers to put an end to the massacres.

On 12 April, Dallaire received a call from Boutros-Ghali in Bonn. It was brief. The moment the Secretary-General came on the phone, Dallaire told him that a UN withdrawal could not be contemplated. Boutros-Ghali failed to persuade him otherwise. Later, Boutros-Ghali said that asking for a plan to be prepared did not necessarily mean that the plan would be carried out.

No one could have been left in any doubt about the danger to people in UN care, or about the nature of the killings. New York was told in a cable from Dallaire on 8 April that there was a well-planned, organised, deliberate and orchestrated campaign of terror, with indications of large-scale massacres, and with the Tutsi as targets. Dallaire started to formulate concrete proposals for the reinforcements needed to stop the killing. He believed that a show of force by the UN, with tanks and guns, would intimidate the gangs roaming the streets. Even taking into account the dangers of a renewed civil war between the RPF[6] and Rwandan Government soldiers, a modest expansion of UNAMIR of between 2,500 to 5,000 could knock out the radio station inciting the militia to kill. Protected sites could be set up for civilians. Dallaire wanted to make the most of what he called 'a balance of fear'.

Dallaire did not believe that his chapter VI mandate, dealing with the pacific resolution of disputes, prevented him from taking action. He had written his own rules of engagement in which it was quite clear that he could prevent crimes against humanity. Clause 17 specified:

There may also be ethnically or politically motivated criminal acts committed during this mandate. I will morally and legally

---

[6] Rwandan Patriotic Front, political movement opposed to Hutu nationalism.

require UNAMIR to use all available means to halt them. Examples are execution, attacks on displaced persons or refugees, ethnic riots, attacks on demobilised soldiers etc. During such occasions, UNAMIR military personnel will follow the ROE[7] outlined in this directive in support of UNCIVPOL[8] and local authorities or in their absence UNAMIR will take the necessary action to prevent any crime against humanity.

Only a lack of means prevented him from taking action.

Some people have argued the validity of Dallaire's judgement about reinforcements, and claimed that this estimate is problematic given the determination of the extremists. But three years after the genocide the Carnegie Commission on Preventing Deadly Conflict, the Institute for the Study of Diplomacy at Georgetown University, and the US Army undertook a project to assess it. An international panel of senior military leaders was convened. In a report to the Carnegie Commission based on the discussion at the conference, Colonel Scott Feil pointed to a consensus that a force with air support, logistics and communications would have prevented the slaughter of half a million people. The window of opportunity was between 7 and 21 April while the political leaders of the violence were still susceptible to international influence. This would have forestalled expansion of the genocide to the south; it was still relatively contained at this point. An intervention would have altered the political calculations of the extremists as to whether they could get away with it. A larger force was needed after 21 April because by then the genocide had spread. US forces, backed by air power, could have protected Rwandan civilians with little or no risk to US soldiers.

Marchal[9] is convinced that if the evacuation force which came to rescue the expats had not pulled out, then the killing could have been stopped. There were already 2,500 peace-keepers in Rwanda, 2,000 of whom would have taken part in an operation. There were 500 Belgian para-commandos, part of the evacuation operation, and 450 French and 80 Italians from parachute regiments. In Kenya there were 500 Belgian para-commandos, also a part of the evacuation operation. In Burundi there were 250 Rangers, élite US troops, who had

---

[7] Rules of engagement.
[8] United Nations Civil Police.
[9] Colonel Luc Marchal, commander of the Kigali sector of UNAMIR.

come to help to evacuate American nationals. There were 800 more French troops on stand-by in the region. Together with Rwandan soldiers who wanted peace there would have been ample troops to restore calm. In this case there would have been no valid reason for the RPF to mount an offensive.

For the peace-keepers of UNAMIR, the pull-out of the troops that came to rescue the expats was an affront to their mission. It was unbelievable that these troops could leave, knowing the dangers. Dallaire said that it was inexcusable by any human criteria. 'We were left to fend for ourselves,' he said, 'with neither mandate nor supplies – defensive stores, ammunition, medical supplies or water, with only survival rations that were rotten and inedible – which is a description of inexcusable apathy by the sovereign states that made up the UN, that is completely beyond comprehension and moral acceptability.'

The meetings held by the Security Council to discuss what to do about the peace-keeping mission in Rwanda took place behind closed doors. Twenty years ago, when most Council meetings were held in public, it would have been possible to hear the options discussed, but nowadays most debates take place in a side room where the deals are concluded which make up 'UN policy'. This means that the policies of each member government are hidden from public scrutiny.

Throughout the genocide the Security Council was in almost constant secret session, meeting sometimes twice daily and long into the night. There were multiple crises and, in April 1994, the Security Council was preoccupied with a worsening Bosnia, where a Serb bombardment on the safe area of Gorazde was grabbing the headlines. However, having established the mission for Rwanda, the Security Council was now responsible for its future.

The meetings held to discuss Rwanda would usually have remained secret for ever, were it not for the leak from within the Council of a remarkable 155-page document containing an account of them. This invaluable primary source gives a unique view of the Council's secret world and without it an account of the international failure over Rwanda would be incomplete. The document exposes some unpleasant truths – not least of which is the fact that the plans to try to prevent the organised killing of civilians using a modest reinforcement of troops were not discussed in the first few weeks of killing.

Those states which had advocated a tough line on compliance with Arusha a few weeks earlier – America and Britain – were now inclined to carry out their threat to withdraw the force, although the immediate reaction in the Council was to concentrate on whether or not it was possible to get a ceasefire in the renewed civil war. One of the ambassadors occupying a non-permanent seat, Karel Kovanda of the Czech Republic, recalled: 'No one was sure what, if anything, needed to be done. Into this absolutely bizarre situation came the big powers . . . who said they could do nothing.'

At each of these informal meetings there were briefings from secretariat officials. One of these officials, Iqbal Riza, assistant secretary-general in the DPKO[10] and a member of Boutros-Ghali's inner cabinet, who had overseen the UN's successful mission in El Salvador, has said that later in the first week there was confusion. All the assessments coming from the field, apart from one, concerned the resumption of the conflict. Riza claims that only in one cable in the first week, on 8 April, was there any mention of organised killing.

This was the cable in which Dallaire described to New York the deliberate campaign of terror initiated principally by the Presidential Guard since the morning after the death of the head of state. But in the same cable a report from the Secretary-General's special representative, Jacques-Roger Booh-Booh, attributed the worsening of the security situation to the fighting between the Presidential Guard and the RPF.

Riza said that for the first week they were under the impression that they were dealing with a breakdown in a ceasefire, except for one sentence, in one cable. Later, Dallaire would query this reaction. In his daily situation reports and more frequent telephone calls he had made it abundantly clear that genocide was looming. Of the briefings given to the Council, Riza said: 'Possibly we did not give all the details . . . And if we did not, I really can't tell you what happened then to prevent us from giving those details.'

At a meeting on Monday, 11 April, the Council was told about the thousands of people seeking safety wherever they could, in hospitals and in churches and wherever they saw the UN flag. The next day, 12 April, Riza told the Council of 'chaotic, ethnic, random killings' but most of his briefing concerned the activities of the interim

---

[10] UN Department of Peace-keeping Operations.

government. In the days to come there would be requests from the non-permanent members for the views of both the force commander and the Secretary-General. The views of the force commander were never forthcoming. Complaints began to surface that no options for action had been presented and that the Secretary-General was absent from New York.

At this point, and while American diplomats were expressing doubts about the viability of the force, it was the British ambassador, David Hannay, who came up with four options. The first was to re-inforce the troops and give the peace-keepers a stronger mandate to intervene to halt the bloodshed. But this, Hannay warned, would be a repetition of Somalia. Peace-keeping was not appropriate for civil war, for situations where there was no peace to keep and where fighting factions were unwilling to cooperate. Inadequate efforts were worse than no efforts at all.

Second, UNAMIR could pull out completely but the negative signal to public opinion would be damaging. Third, the troops could stay on, although he did query what they could effectively do, for there was no evidence that UNAMIR was in any position to protect civilians.

The fourth and last idea was to pull most of them out leaving behind 'some elements'. Although this might initially attract public criticism, it seemed to be the safest course. Hannay warned the Council that the decision could not be delayed.

The Americans agreed. No country should be expected to send soldiers into this chaotic environment. It was doubtful whether the peace-keepers could even be resupplied. If the UN failed to protect its own soldiers, then the Security Council would have serious diffi-culties obtaining any more troops for other UN operations. The USA did not want to be seen to be responsible for the gradual depletion of an isolated force, but the peace-keepers could be flown out and kept in a neighbouring country and then go back in at some later date. It was highly improbable that an outside force could halt the terror in Rwanda.

The Nigerian ambassador, Ibrahim Gambari, pointed out that tens of thousands of civilians were dying all the time.

The meeting adjourned. They decided to ask for the views first of the Secretary-General, and then of those states contributing troops to UNAMIR. The Council thought of one action: it urged a ceasefire. The African group at the UN was one step ahead. It urged the Security

Council to take urgent action to protect the lives of civilians and reinforce UNAMIR.

The RPF offensive had begun along an eighty-kilometre demilitarised zone in three main axes, putting into place a plan long in preparation. Its aim was to defeat an army three times its size and with far superior weaponry. In a radio address on the RPF station, Radio Muhabura, people had been told that there had been a 'bloodbath' in Rwanda undertaken by the Presidential Guard that had wiped out almost the entire government. A new government had been formed of people who were opposed to the Arusha peace agreement. A military communiqué announced that the RPF was to fight the 'murderous clique' which had taken over in Rwanda; the RPF was willing to work with Rwandan Government soldiers in order to bring the murderers to book.

The lead element of the RPF moved through the east along the border with Tanzania, a central axis of soldiers went through Byumba, and the western thrust advanced through Ruhengeri, where there was preparatory bombardment to draw out a large concentration of Rwandan Army forces. Some soldiers on the central thrust also moved towards Kigali. In this way, Major-General Paul Kagame held down the Rwandan Army on central and western fronts. Throughout the advance, the RPF used mortar fire to maximum advantage and, after a period of sustained fire, often succeeded in intimidating the government forces and cutting off supply lines.

The RPF advance on the east was amazing for its speed. The first battalion group from the brigade on the eastern front, some 1,500 soldiers, entered Kigali on 12 April, only four days after the start of the campaign and covering a distance of some seventy-five kilometres. The soldiers moved in small numbers during the night, infiltrating their heavy weapons and combat supplies and carrying out dawn attacks.

Kagame said he knew the genocide was under way in the first week because as his troops advanced they found evidence of it. There were similarities in the stories they were told, and soon people with machete wounds were searching out RPF bases.

In Kigali on 13 April, there was the sound of heavy machine-guns, multiple rockets and artillery fire. An attack on the city by the RPF came from the east and north-east with the main bombardment on the barracks of the Presidential Guard, the most fortified place in the city. The Guard held on, and for the next eight weeks, on this front line, there would be no more than 100 metres separating the RPF from the Presidential Guard. Once in Kigali, the RPF joined with their troops already in the city, and this battalion's barracks, the CND building,[11] would become their base. It was where RPF casualties were evacuated for prompt medical attention. But the RPF held only a portion of the city. The battle for Kigali lasted three months.

In the weeks to come, the Rwandan Army became expert in well-planned and executed withdrawals at night, and whole areas fought over were often found to be empty in the morning. The Rwandan Army lacked an established line of defence; if they had advanced on the RPF battalion in the CND building, they could have defeated that single battalion. Instead, the army held back and allowed the RPF to form a firm base, linking up with its battalions from the north.

The Rwandan forces, with a new commander, Major-General Augustin Bizimungu, previously commander of the northern Ruhengeri garrison, had low morale. There had been rapid recruitment in the previous three years. It was the militia which had the strong political indoctrination and an effective command structure, at times intimidating government soldiers at roadblocks.

While the RPF advanced, the images portrayed of them on RTLMC[12] became increasingly horrific. One announcer warned that the Tutsi soldiers were devils who killed their victims 'by extracting various organs ... for example, by taking the heart, the liver, the stomach ... the cruelty of the inyenzi [cockroach] is incurable, the cruelty of the inyenzi can only be cured by their total extermination'. The radio station described this as a final attack, using the Kinyarwanda word 'simusiga', the same word which would be used to describe the genocide. It was a war which must be waged without mercy, the announcers encouraged. The broadcasters advocated the killing of Tutsi by identifying them with the RPF, and the RPF was going to exterminate all the Hutu. People were encouraged to phone in and reveal where people were hiding. In one broadcast, Valérie Bemeriki read out the names and addresses of thirteen people along with their jobs and even their nicknames, and she urged her listeners to find them. The vehicle number-plates of those who were trying to escape were read on air. Requests from civil servants or militia leaders were broadcast calling for the resupply of weapons, ammunition or grenades to certain areas.

---

[11] Conseil National pour le Développement, the parliament building.
[12] The Hutu Power radio station.

Dallaire pleaded with New York for permission to neutralise the station: 'It was inciting people to kill, it was explaining how to kill, telling people who to kill, including whites, including me.' On 18 April, the RPF mounted a machine-gun attack on the studios of RTLMC and the broadcasting was stopped, but only temporarily, resuming within hours.

There were several frontlines in the RPF offensive, and Kigali was divided into RPF- and government-held zones. Where there were no soldiers, militia ruled the streets. Neighbourhood boundaries were defined by roadblocks, with their piles of bodies. Thousands of people now decided to leave Kigali and follow the interim government to Gitarama. On Wednesday, 13 April, a week after the genocide began, a column of people, about five kilometres long, moved slowly along the road out of the city. Some rich Rwandans travelled in Mercedes saloons with armed escorts in civilian clothes. A news reporter with Associated Press saw a bulldozer with dozens of people clinging to it and twenty people in the bucket at the front.

When the interim government arrived in Gitarama[13] it brought in its wake Presidential Guard and more than 1,000 Interahamwe. It might have been possible to have spared Gitarama from genocide because the prefect there, Fidèle Uwizeye, was opposed to the killing, and had organised the bourgmestres to defend the prefecture. Once the interim government arrived and arms were distributed, however, and with hate-propaganda from RTLMC, opposition was soon destroyed. The genocide spread.

Marcelline lived in the commune of Taba in Gitarama. The Interahamwe rounded up her family and killed all the men. The women were made to dig graves to bury the men, and then throw the children in the graves. 'I will never forget the sight of my son pleading with me not to bury him alive ... he kept trying to come out and was beaten back. And we had to keep covering the pit with earth until ... there was no movement left.'

The debate in the Security Council is often shaped by recommendations from the Secretary-General acting on advice from officials in

[13] The interim government had fled the fighting in Kigali on 12 April.

the secretariat who receive all the cables from UN commanders. When it came to Rwanda no such recommendations were forthcoming. Some of the non-permanent members speculated that either the secretariat had no options at all, in which case it was not up to the task of managing the conflict, or it was overwhelmed to the point of paralysis.

Colin Keating, president of the Security Council in April, complained that the Council needed more information from the force commander, particularly on the consequences for UNAMIR once the Belgian peace-keepers withdrew.

The letter to the president of the Security Council, written in Bonn by Boutros-Ghali and dated 13 April, confirmed the Belgian decision to pull out. It was greeted with consternation by the Council. The letter stated that unless the Belgian contingent was replaced by another 'equally well-equipped', then it would be extremely difficult for UNAMIR to carry out its tasks; in these circumstances, Boutros-Ghali had asked the special representative and the force commander to prepare plans for the withdrawal of UNAMIR. Some of the non-permanent members were surprised. Was this all the Secretary-General had to offer after a week?

The British permanent representative, David Hannay, found the letter far from adequate. The Secretary-General seemed to think, quite bizarrely, that if the Belgians were to stay on, then all would be well. It was not right to give the impression that two battalions could protect the civilian population of Rwanda. The peace-keepers, with their limited capacity, could not protect civilians. If a small military presence was left behind, then it could encourage the parties to move back to the peace deal.

The French delegation wanted to know why the Secretary-General had assumed that Belgian withdrawal would lead to an automatic pull-out for UNAMIR. There was every reason for the Belgians to leave Rwanda, for every Belgian national was a target, but if everyone left then the situation would deteriorate further.

An American representative said it was 'unfortunate' for the Secretary-General to appear to blame Belgium for a total withdrawal; while it was not possible to pull the plug completely on Rwanda, the ambassadors remembered Somalia. The best course was to leave a skeletal group of peace-keepers and pull out everyone else.

Some years later, Boutros-Ghali defended this letter. He explained that he was trying to put pressure on the Security Council to authorise a new force; he had requested the force commander to prepare plans for withdrawal, 'unless we received additional forces'. He said he wanted a strengthened mission and an enforcement operation and that his views were not well received.

The briefing at this meeting on 13 April was given by Iqbal Riza. He offered the ambassadors an update on the progress of the battle for Kigali, and told them that the RPF would not agree a ceasefire. The situation was deteriorating, Riza said. Dallaire was conducting some rescue missions and he continued to try for a ceasefire. There were an estimated 14,000 Rwandan refugees sheltering with the UN and the protection of these people required more resources. But there was a question over how prolonged this protection could be, and the Council must consider whether peace-keeping should involve such tasks. Gambari, for Nigeria, said that the protection of civilians must be of concern and wanted to know if Africa had fallen off the map of moral concern.

The remainder of the 13 April meeting was taken up with a discussion on a draft resolution from Nigeria suggesting that peace-keepers be allowed to 'enforce public order and the rule of law and create temporary state institutions'. The resolution pointed to the thousands of innocent civilians being killed but, although it was circulated among ambassadors, it was never tabled. It stood little chance. A US ambassador, Karl Inderfurth, told them of a strong feeling in Washington that peace-keeping was not appropriate for Rwanda. The Americans would not be pushing in the Council for total withdrawal, but the whole Council should give consideration to the future of the mission.

China disagreed. China was the only country not to have closed its embassy in Kigali, and a Chinese delegate pointed out that there was no immediate danger to the remaining UN peace-keepers. Only the untrained contingent from Bangladesh were in a panic. The others – the sixty Tunisians and the 800 Ghanaians – were doing useful work under the force commander. The Rwandan ambassador, Jean-Damascène Bizimana, a representative of the interim government, had sat impassively throughout all these exchanges. Rwanda had a non-permanent seat on the Council, the right to vote, the right to participate in procedural decisions, and the right to block the required consensus on presidential statements. Bizimana, well-dressed and fluent in French, became an essential element in the interim government's propaganda campaign. He was in a superb position to peddle the interim government line that the killings in Rwanda were part of the civil war. Bizimana circulated a letter on 13 April, written by the interim government's minister of foreign affairs, Jérôme Bicamumpaka, which claimed that the situation in Rwanda was improving and that the presence of UN peace-keepers was helping to stabilise the country. Because of the death of the president, the military and the people of Rwanda had 'reacted spontaneously', attacking those under suspicion, but a new government had been created and was giving great hope to the people.

The prime minister in this interim government, Jean Kambanda, was meanwhile broadcasting on RTLMC to tell the population to search out the enemy, those who 'do not share our opinion'. Kambanda ordered the construction of roadblocks. He distributed arms and ammunition. He ordered, incited and helped other ministers, prefects, bourgmestres and other local officials to exterminate the Tutsi and pro-democracy Hutu. There were seventeen Cabinet meetings held by the interim government during the genocide from which directives went to local bureaucrats to 'pacify' their areas – 'pacification' was the word the interim government used to describe the genocide. The very first decision of this interim government, on 8 April, had been to call to Kigali all Rwanda's prefects to ensure that, in the weeks to come, each would obey instructions. A minister was designated for each prefecture whose job was pacification. Prefects passed orders to bourgmestres who alerted councillors who held meetings to inform all residents of 'the work in hand' – clearing their areas of Tutsi. Sometimes the councillors went from house to house to sign up all the young males for 'the work'. Administrative officials in possession of birth and death records knew exactly how many Tutsi lived in each area; during the genocide, they kept track of the dead.

The massacres in Rwanda were the result of a chain of command, the result of a prepared strategy. The genocide was a conspiracy at national level, but without the complicity of the local and national civil and military authorities, the large-scale massacres would not have occurred.

On Thursday, 14 April, a Red Cross ambulance was stopped at a roadblock in Kigali and six wounded people were dragged from the back and shot. Earlier that day the same ambulance had passed the same roadblock with no problems, but it was raining then. When it rained, the roadblocks were not manned. But in the early afternoon the sun was shining and armed civilians and soldiers had returned; this time there was a man with a sub-machine-gun, and grenades had recently been distributed. The ambulance was in a convoy with two cars carrying wounded people and driven by a Rwandan who worked for the Red Cross. This stretch of road had one checkpoint every 100 metres. There had been a recent RTLMC broadcast that the Red Cross was transporting the RPF disguised as wounded.

Gaillard's[14] fury at the ambulance killings was volcanic and he immediately suspended the collection of wounded from the streets. He gave an interview to a journalist in which he asked what was the point of saving people, only to see them killed. He drove to the radio station. He shared a beer with some of the announcers, and asked them to counter-balance the broadcasts in order to guarantee respect for the Red Cross emblem. Gaillard later spoke with the ICRC Geneva headquarters and a press release was issued appealing for the Red Cross to be allowed to assist the wounded. There were articles in the Western press about the ambulance killings, and this was considered unwelcome attention by the interim government. A retraction was broadcast on RTLMC and in the days to come ambulances were allowed to circulate. Gaillard said: 'The assassination of these wounded allowed us to save thousands more.'

Gaillard went to Nyamirambo on 15 April, south of Kigali, where on 8 April dozens of people had been killed in a church. Several days later hundreds of people sheltering in a mosque were murdered, the massacre preceded by an announcement on RTLMC that Tutsi were hiding there. Nyamirambo had a large Tutsi population; in the months before the genocide started, Tutsi living in other communes had moved there for safety.

Nine days after the genocide started, the news that large-scale killing was taking place was made known to the outside world with a report of a massacre in the parish of Musha, twenty-five miles east of Kigali. The story appeared in a Belgian newspaper, *Het Volk*, with details later picked up by other Western media. Associated Press said that this was the biggest massacre reported so far. An attack had taken place on 13 April in a church in which hundreds were sheltering. The Presidential Guard had kicked in the door, opened fire

[14] Philippe Gaillard, chief delegate of the International Committee of the Red Cross (ICRC) in Rwanda.

448   *TELL ME NO LIES*

with semi-automatic weapons, and thrown in grenades. 'Afterwards they attacked defenceless people with knives, bats and spears. There were 1,180 bodies in my church including 650 children,' *Het Volk* quoted the pastor there, Danko Litrick.

At a further informal meeting of the Security Council on Thursday, 14 April, there was a spirited defence of the Secretary-General by another of his senior officials, Alvaro de Soto, Assistant Secretary-General in the Department of Political Affairs. De Soto told the Council that, although he was touring Europe, the Secretary-General was in constant contact with UN headquarters, the force commander and the special representative. It was not correct to say that Boutros-Ghali was in favour of total withdrawal, but the problem was that the peace-keepers were prevented from carrying out their mandate. The Secretary-General had formulated two options: UNAMIR could remain as it was without the Belgians or it could be reduced. Both options were predicated on a ceasefire.

The delegate for Oman called for written proposals from the Secretary-General. Spain wanted to know why no mention had been made of a possible change in mandate. France thought that any mission in Rwanda would have to serve some useful purpose. The UK thought that the Secretariat should be more precise about the minimum force level which could remain behind. The USA said that what the Security Council needed was a resolution to provide for the orderly evacuation of the mission.

The following day, Friday, 15 April, Willy Claes, the Belgian foreign minister, wrote to Boutros-Ghali to tell him officially that the Belgian peace-keepers were all leaving. He recommended that the whole of UNAMIR be withdrawn. Based on an intimate knowledge of events, the scale of the massacres which peace-keepers were witnessing, together with a deteriorating military situation, there was no alternative and no chance of a ceasefire. By waiting to make a decision, the Security Council was increasing the risks to the soldiers. Claes asked that Boutros-Ghali give the instruction to the force commander to release immediately the Belgian soldiers from UNAMIR. There followed a diplomatic blizzard from Belgium to persuade everyone that the entire mission must pull out at once.

Later that day a disagreement developed between the Belgian diplomats and the officials in the DPKO. Kofi Annan did not favour a complete pull-out, and he argued that this would only make the humanitarian situation worse. Dallaire had faxed a long and urgent wish-list of supplies, including water, fuel, medicine and flak-jackets. The list was so long because the UN's Field Operations Division had no cash and no method for crisis resupply. A Belgian saw the list and joked about Dallaire's optimism.

The next day another cable arrived from Kigali, this time from Major Marec Pazik, one of the Polish peace-keepers who had discovered the massacre at Gikondo and who was now employed as humanitarian plans officer. Pazik was faxing to headquarters details of the people sheltering in the Amahoro football stadium. There were 5,000 people, 2,402 of whom were children under the age of fifteen. The majority were orphans whose parents had been massacred. There was no food. There were two local doctors without equipment or medicine. Twenty people urgently needed limb amputations, 150 people were seriously injured, there were 150 cases of malaria, 115 with serious diarrhoea, 205 people with bronchitis, thirty-two with dysentery, and fifteen with chicken-pox. In the stadium, at a makeshift clinic under one of the spectator stands, they were handing out small sachets of apricot jam. 'It's all we have got,' said someone. 'We have to give them something.'

Just before an informal Security Council meeting, on Friday, 15 April, the Nigerian ambassador Ibrahim Gambari had a private meeting with Colin Keating. He advised Keating to pay particular attention to the views of the force commander and told him that Belgium's reaction was slightly hysterical, due in part to historic and domestic concerns. Keating then met with Belgium's UN ambassador, Paul Noterdaeme, who told him that when the Belgian peace-keepers left, there would be a bloodbath.

UN officials told Keating that peace-keeping was suitable only for the most benign environments and that the Council was reaping what it had sown by putting in a force with inadequate equipment, inadequate training and lack of firepower. Without the Belgians, UNAMIR was going to be in very deep trouble. Other troop-contributing governments would soon withdraw their troops and UNAMIR would disintegrate. It would be the UN's most ignominious failure.

At the informal meeting that day Gambari made a plea for reinforcements. However weighty the advice from Belgium, he said, the ambassadors must realise no other country had withdrawn its troops

– not Ghana, not Bangladesh. The peace-keepers had a vital role to play protecting the population and promoting a ceasefire. The USA objected. America would not accept any resolution except one which withdrew all the peace-keepers. The UK agreed but thought that a compromise could be reached, leaving a token force behind. The UN could hardly leave two battalions in Rwanda to be slaughtered. Gambari said that the troops on the ground were at least accomplishing something, but the USA was adamant. If a vote were to be taken, based on an 'independent assessment' of the situation in Rwanda, the USA would have no choice but to decide that there was no role for peace-keepers. The Council's primary obligation was to ensure that each UN mission was do-able and the priority was the safety of UN personnel. They adjourned for the weekend.

Details of the Council meeting were relayed to the 'interim government' by the Rwandan ambassador. The next day, 16 April, a Saturday, the 'interim government' held a meeting and, confident of no significant international opposition, it was decided to push ahead with 'pacification' in the south.

On 14 April a group of Western journalists was taken by UN peace-keepers from the Hôtel des Mille Collines to the airport to be evacuated. As they prepared to leave the hotel, there were dozens of Rwandans in the lobby, crowding around them and begging to go with them. On the road to the airport the journalists saw houses burned and shops looted and in one place corpses piled in a heap. The journalists flew to Nairobi with some forty Rwandan refugees. Five journalists remained in Kigali.

By now UN headquarters in Kigali had been given a written report from two UN military observers who had been present in Gisenyi, the north of the country, when the genocide began. They had witnessed a massacre in which an estimated 10,000 people had died. The news was relayed to New York.

The peace-keepers were now faced with the withdrawal of the Belgian contingent. When Marchal first heard this news he was incredulous. 'Under no circumstances could we leave,' he said. 'This was the point of view I expressed to my superiors until the moment when the political decision was made to leave UNAMIR. Our political leaders should have known that in leaving UNAMIR, we would condemn thousands of men, women and children to certain death.'

On Sunday, 17 April, Dallaire wrote a long and detailed cable to UN headquarters that started with his thoughts on the Belgian contingent: 'These men were our best trained, experienced, equipped and motivated . . . even though they suffered heavily with the loss of their comrades.' He then outlined his problems. 'A radical change of key staff at such a critical moment is most distressing and may cause us some serious degradation of control in the force.' Dallaire was pessimistic about a ceasefire. The RPF was adamant that the priority and the pre-condition of any ceasefire must be the stopping of massacres behind government lines by groups armed with machetes. He described to New York how the killing was the work of some soldiers, gendarmes and groups of militia who were increasingly organising themselves. In the ranks of the Rwandan Government army, Dallaire told New York, the hardliners had pushed aside the moderates: 'The stopping of the massacres may become more and more difficult as the local groups/militia are becoming seemingly bolder . . . The ethnic killings are continuing and in fact unconfirmed reports indicate it is even increasing in scale and scope in the areas just ahead of the RPF advance.'

In his long cable to UN headquarters on 17 April, Dallaire wrote:

> due to the militia and self-defence groups controlling important arteries and areas of the city . . . they are a very large, dangerous and totally irrational group of people . . . The force simply cannot continue to sit on the fence in the face of all these morally legitimate demands for assistance/protection, nor can it simply launch into chapter VII type of operations without the proper authority, personnel and equipment . . . maintaining the status quo on manpower under these severe and adverse conditions is wasteful, dangerously casualty-causing and demoralising to the troops . . . either UNAMIR gets changes . . . in order to get into the thick of things . . . or it starts to thin out.

A day after Dallaire sent the cable, Annan and Riza began to argue that since there was no prospect of a ceasefire then they must report to the Council that a total withdrawal of UNAMIR needed to be envisaged.

Dallaire need not have bothered to write this cable. In the first four weeks of genocide, the fact that a systematic and continuing slaughter was taking place in Rwanda was not once discussed at length in Council meetings. Everyone in the Secretariat in New York was preoccupied with the civil war, from the officials in the Department of Peace-keeping, those in the Secretary-General's suite of offices on the thirty-eighth floor, and the ambassadors during the secret discussions in the Security Council.

There was an assumption that only a massive and dramatic intervention would succeed in Rwanda, and that this was out of the question. The preoccupation with civil war meant that no attention was given to the contribution that the peace-keepers could continue to make, even without reinforcements. Dallaire continued to believe that reinforcements for UNAMIR were the only answer. Stopping the killings was far more important than bargaining for a ceasefire.

The Security Council finally addressed the question of genocide on 29 April, after Keating, whose presidency of the Security Council was over at the end of the month, proposed a presidential statement recognising the fact. Keating believed that if the Security Council were to admit that this was genocide, then under the terms of the 1948 Genocide Convention all but three member states – Djibouti, Nigeria and Oman, which had not signed the convention – were legally bound to act. Keating was supported by Argentina, Spain and the Czech Republic. The latter's ambassador, Karel Kovanda, had already confronted the Council with the fact of genocide at an informal meeting a day earlier, telling ambassadors that it was scandalous that so far 80 per cent of Council efforts had been spent discussing withdrawing the peace-keepers, and 20 per cent trying to get a ceasefire in the civil war. 'It was rather like wanting Hitler to reach a ceasefire with the Jews,' he told them. What was happening in Rwanda was genocide, conducted by the interim Hutu regime. Yet the Council avoided the question of mass killing. There were objections to Kovanda's outburst and afterwards, he says, British and American diplomats quietly told him that on no account was he to use such inflammatory language outside the Council. It was not helpful.

A draft of Keating's proposed presidential statement was submitted to the Council. It included the paragraph:

the horrors of Rwanda's killing fields have few precedents in the recent history of the world. The Security Council reaffirms that the systematic killing of any ethnic group, with intent to destroy it in whole or in part, constitutes an act of genocide as defined by relevant provisions of international law . . . the council further points out that an important body of international law exists that deals with perpetrators of genocide.

The draft warned the interim government of its responsibility for immediately reining in and disciplining those responsible for the brutality.

There were objections. The British ambassador, David Hannay, did not want the word genocide to be used, and argued that were the statement to be used in an official UN document, then the Council would become a 'laughing stock'. To name this a genocide and not to act on it would be ridiculous. Nor did America want the word used, and China argued against it. The Rwandan ambassador said that the civilian deaths were the result of civil war and he was ably supported in this by the French-influenced ally, Djibouti, whose ambassador said later that he was against the statement because it was 'sensationalist'.

The debate went round in circles. Keating, whose term as president would end the following day, tried the somewhat desperate measure of threatening a draft resolution, tabled in his national capacity. This would require a vote, and a vote was always taken in public. This would expose the positions of each country to public scrutiny. In the end, a compromise was reached. Thanks to the drafting ability of the British, known for framing resolutions with mind-numbing ambiguity, a watered-down statement was issued, and while the statement quoted directly from the Genocide Convention, it did not use the word genocide.

The Security Council condemns all the breaches of international humanitarian law in Rwanda, particularly those perpetrated against the civilian population, and recalls that persons who instigate or participate in such acts are individually responsible. The Security Council recalls that the killing of members of an ethnic group with the intention of destroying such a group in whole or in part constitutes a crime punishable by international law.

The statement recognised that the massacres were systematic, although it did not identify the targets, but it did describe how 'attacks on defenceless civilians have occurred throughout the country, especially in areas under the control of members of supporters of the armed forces of the interim government of Rwanda'. To satisfy French demands that massacres had also been conducted by the RPF, it went on: 'The Security Council demands that the interim government of Rwanda and the Rwandese Patriotic Front take effective measures to prevent any attacks on civilians in areas under their control.' The statement appealed to all states to refrain from providing arms or any military assistance to the two sides in Rwanda and reiterated the call for a ceasefire. It provided that the Secretary-General 'investigate serious violations of human rights law'.

The statement was finally voted at 1.15 a.m. on Saturday, 30 April. 'We ended April exhausted but hopeful that the first few weeks of May would bring action to reinforce UNAMIR with a real force capable of doing what Dallaire had been urging,' Keating said.

On the day of this debate, Boutros Boutros-Ghali recommended a reversal of the decision to withdraw. In a letter to the Council he suggested that they reconsider resolution 912, which had mandated a reduction in the force levels of UNAMIR. Boutros-Ghali told them that the force commander reported a further deterioration in Kigali. This was a humanitarian catastrophe. He urged them to consider what action, including forceful action, was necessary to restore law and order and to put an end to the massacres:

> Such action would require a commitment of human and material resources on a scale which the member states have so far proved reluctant to contemplate. But I am convinced that the scale of human suffering in Rwanda, and its implications for the stability of neighbouring countries, leave the Security Council with no alternative but to examine this possibility.

His letter was greeted with stunned silence. In the secretariat, staff were again surprised by his failure to suggest options to the Council. Options for action had been discussed at length by officials, and with the force commander. Why Boutros-Ghali failed at this stage to guide the Council has never been explained.

The last Hutu Power stronghold in Rwanda fell on 18 July, and Kagame declared the civil war was over. The next day in Kigali a broad-based government of national unity was sworn in comprising the representatives of all political parties apart from the MRNDD.[15] Twelve of the eighteen ministers were Hutu. The president was Pasteur Bizimungu, the oldest of the RPF Hutu. A new position was created for Paul Kagame as vice-president.

There was no triumphant victory. The country had been ransacked. There was not a penny in the public coffers. There were no offices intact, no chairs, no desks, no paper, no telephones, nothing at all.

The streets of Kigali were almost empty. From a previous population of 300,000, there were 50,000 people left and half of these were displaced. Their condition was disastrous, and they lacked adequate food and clean water. Outside the capital, whole families and communities had been destroyed. Livestock had been killed and crops laid to waste. Everywhere there were ditches filled with rotting bodies. The people had been terrorised and traumatised. The hospitals and schools were destroyed or ransacked. Rwanda's health centres, one in each commune, were ruined. The stocks of basic drugs and health supplies had been looted. Water supply lines were non-operational. Qualified staff had been killed or fled the country, including most of the teachers. An estimated 250,000 women had been widowed. In the whole country there were six judges and ten lawyers. There were no gendarmes.

At least 100,000 children had been separated from their families, orphaned, lost, abducted or abandoned. Most of Rwanda's children had witnessed extreme forms of brutality and 90 per cent of them had at some point thought they would die. Most children felt they had no future. They did not believe that they would live to become adults. More than 300 children, some less than ten years old, were accused of genocide or murder. An estimated 300,000 children were thought to have been killed.

Rwanda was divided, this time into victims, survivors, returnees and perpetrators. It was as though in 1945 the Jews and the Germans were to live together in Germany after the Holocaust, under a Jewish-dominated army, and with roughly one-third of all Germans outside the country.

We will never know the number of victims in the genocide. The million figure is agreed by Gaillard, based on information gathered while the genocide unfolded. This figure was also provided by Charles

[15] Mouvement Républicain National pour la Démocratie et le Développement, the ruling party of President Habyarimana.

Petrie, vice-coordinator of the UN Rwandan Emergency Office, who said on 24 August 1994 that he did not think the figure of one million dead was an exaggeration. For reasons which remain obscure, the figure now generally accepted is 800,000.

In a report for the Commission on Human Rights, special rapporteur René Dégni-Ségui estimated that between 200,000 and 500,000 people had died. He reached this conclusion at the end of two months of killing, and said that he thought it was far lower than the actual figure, adding that some observers thought the figure nearer one million. A commission of experts, established by the Security Council to investigate the genocide, reported on 9 December 1994 that 500,000 unarmed civilians had been murdered.

The failure of the international community to act while one million people in Rwanda were slaughtered was one of the greatest scandals of the twentieth century. But there was nothing secret about it. There were no sealed trains or secluded camps in Rwanda. The genocide was broadcast on the radio. Conclusive proof that a genocide was taking place was provided to the Security Council in May and June while it was happening. A report from the Commission on Human Rights concluded that the massacres were planned and systematic. There was a determination to destroy Tutsi. 'No one escapes . . . not even newborn babies . . . the victims are pursued to their very last refuge and killed there.'

For the first time in possession of overwhelming proof of genocide, the Council thought of one action: to create a committee of experts to 'evaluate the evidence'. That evidence was contained in an interim report in October 1994 which concluded that although both sides of the armed conflict had perpetrated serious breaches of international humanitarian law and crimes against humanity, there existed a mass of evidence that the extermination of the Tutsi and moderate Hutu had been planned months in advance. There had been a 'concerted, planned, systematic and methodical nature of . . . criminal acts' committed by government soldiers and the Hutu militia against the Tutsi. Racial propaganda had been disseminated on a widespread basis; posters, leaflets and radio broadcasts had dehumanised the Tutsi as snakes, cockroaches and animals. There had been training camps where men had been indoctrinated in hatred against the Tutsi minority and given information about methods of mass murder. There were ample grounds to prove that the genocide convention had been violated between 6 April and 15 July.

More evidence arrived. It was grim and detailed. There was a provisional list of massacre sites. There were more than six sites in the towns of Gitarama and Cyangugu. At Nyundo, three septic tanks had been used to try to get rid of 300 people. In Nyarubuye there was no burial and there the bodies were strewn about courtyards and alleys, piled upon each other in the classrooms of the parish school and in the church. Yet no real investigations had begun. As early as May the RPF in Rwanda had called for an international tribunal to punish the guilty. Only arrests could end the cycle of violence. Others lobbied the UN Secretary-General to create a tribunal. However, it took until 8 November 1994 before the Security Council voted to create the International Criminal Tribunal for Rwanda.

In view of the enormity of the genocide and the continuing questions surrounding what had happened, Kofi Annan, who was then Secretary-General, announced in March 1999 that an independent inquiry be set up to establish the facts. Nine months later the inquiry issued a report that blamed everyone: the Secretary-General, the Secretariat, the Security Council and the membership of the UN.

On the role of Secretary-General Boutros Boutros-Ghali, it concluded diplomatically that he 'should have done more' to argue the case for reinforcement. Under the UN Charter the Secretary-General had a responsibility and the opportunity to bring to the attention of the Council issues requiring action. He could have had a decisive influence on decision-making with the capacity to mobilise political will. Yet Boutros-Ghali was absent from New York during much of the key period. The UN's report says: 'the Secretary-General cannot be present at every meeting . . . and although Boutros-Ghali was kept informed of key developments . . . the role of the Secretary-General is limited if performed by proxy.' These statements sit uneasily together.

Boutros-Ghali lives in Paris now, and is secretary-general of Francophonie, the grouping of French-speaking countries. He also heads an international panel on democracy-building created by UNESCO (the UN Educational, Scientific and Cultural Organisation). In an interview shortly after the UN report on Rwanda was published,

Boutros-Ghali angrily blamed the Americans for what had happened. He revealed that during the genocide he had private meetings individually with the ambassadors of America and Britain, Madeleine Albright and David Hannay. To each ambassador he had urged action to stop the killing in Rwanda. Boutros-Ghali described their reaction: 'Come on, Boutros, relax ... Don't put us in a difficult position ... the mood is not for intervention, you will obtain nothing ... we will not move.'

The Americans, liable for the lion's share of the peace-keeping bill, were adamantly against UN intervention, but were happy for the French to take action since they were willing to pay for it themselves. The Council, Boutros-Ghali said, was adequately informed: 'Everybody knew that the people coming from Uganda were Tutsi and the people in power were Hutu and that it was a war between Hutu and Tutsi. We did not need to tell them that, it was evident. What was not evident was that there was a plan of genocide.' The Council had meekly followed the US lead, he said. Had the Council created the UN stand-by force which he had suggested two years earlier, then the genocide might never have taken place. His own failure was to convince member governments to act. 'But believe me,' he said, 'I tried.'

So why *did* the Security Council fail to act? Colin Keating, the permanent representative for New Zealand, and the president of the Security Council in April 1994, once described the Council as a bunch of diplomatic amateurs. 'The UN was not ready to deal with all this,' Keating said. The Security Council was not equipped at ambassadorial level to address professional military issues, and the situation in Rwanda cried out for military and technical advisers to sit together to discuss what the options were. No one had listened to Dallaire. The Council had a right and a duty to know the details in order to decide the issues. In the end, politicians had to be made accountable by their own publics.

Even before Rwanda, Keating had lobbied for a change in the system of secret and informal consultations held by the Security Council, for he did not believe that it was an appropriate way of working. Keating had suggested that the informal consultations be filmed on closed-circuit television so that at least other UN members could watch the secret proceedings, a proposal not well received by the permanent five. The argument persisted that 'proper discussions' could not take place in public. The fact that the Council was unaccountable was a recipe for disaster, said Keating. At one point, on

29 April, Keating had threatened to hold the debate about genocide in public in order to shame those ambassadors for their refusal to name it a genocide.

No one can know how humanitarian intervention will work out. If it ends in disaster, then those who take the decision to sacrifice soldiers to save citizens have to answer for it. In 1994 the politicians were determined to conduct casualty-free interventions and, with a lack of public awareness because of the inadequate press coverage, there were no choices given and no risks were taken. There was no moral outcry about genocide and this made it easier for politicians to claim that the hatred in Rwanda was impervious to military intervention and that public opinion was not prepared to pay the price of casualties. And so, like the Jews, the Tutsi were abandoned to their fate.

The Rwandan genocide should be the defining scandal of the presidency of Bill Clinton. Rwanda had been an issue requiring leadership and responsibility, as Senator Paul Simon had reminded Clinton in his letter of 13 May 1994. But the administration took the easy option and failed to push the moral boundaries; there were no votes to be gained advocating help for another collapsed African state. Africa was less important since the end of the Cold War. The recent example of Somalia had shown the risks of intervention.

For three months the Clinton administration played down the crisis and tried to impede effective intervention by UN forces. The secretary of state, Warren Christopher, avoided the issue altogether. Senior officials in the department put Rwanda low on the agenda for fear, according to the Washington director of Human Rights Watch, Holly J. Burkhalter, of another Somalia. Christopher continued to distort the reality of Rwanda as late as 24 July 1994, when he told a television programme that there had been a 'tremendous civil war' in Rwanda and that the USA had done all it could to try to support the UN, but that it was not a time for the USA to try to intervene.

There was even reluctance to take the slightest action, such as jamming the hate-radio, RTLMC, which could have saved lives. The question was raised several times in May during daily video conferences. The Defense Department's official response was always that jamming the broadcasts was technically and legally impossible, and it was properly the decision of the State Department or the National

Security Council. At the National Security Council, neither Don Steinberg, senior director for Africa, nor national security adviser Anthony Lake formulated a policy other than to do nothing.

According to James Woods, deputy assistant secretary of defence, the fact of genocide was known as early as the second week. Recalling the misery of that time, Woods said: 'I think it was sort of a formal spectacle of the US in disarray and retreat, leading the international community away from doing the right thing and I think that every-body was perfectly happy to follow our lead – in retreat.' Everyone knew the true nature of what was going on; no official in the American administration could claim not to have known. Yet in 1998 that is precisely what Clinton did when he visited Kigali and offered a *mea culpa* excuse:

> All over the world there were people like me sitting in offices, day after day after day, who did not fully appreciate the depth and speed with which you were being engulfed by this unimag-inable terror.
>
> The international community, together with nations in Africa, must bear its share of responsibility for this tragedy, as well. We did not act quickly enough after the killing began . . . we did not immediately call these crimes by their rightful name, geno-cide.
>
> Never again must we be shy in the face of the evidence.

The decision-making process within the government of Prime Minister John Major leading to British policy on Rwanda in 1994 will doubtless remain a mystery. There is secrecy in government and a lack of interest in the media.

The only glimpse into British Government thinking is afforded in a letter sent on 7 July 1995 by the Foreign and Commonwealth Office (FCO) to an international inquiry. In this letter, written a year after the genocide ended, the FCO said it did not accept the term geno-cide. The FCO was inclined to see a discussion of whether or not the massacres constituted genocide as 'sterile'. The Foreign Office approach was characterised from the outset by a determination to play the matter down and, for a body which once regarded Africa as its area of special interest, an almost deliberate ignorance. To begin with, it maintained that it did not know what was going on in Rwanda, which was not in the British sphere. This is an extraordinary claim from a permanent member of the Security Council, with responsibilities as a veto power, a country which had voted in the Council to create a mission for Rwanda.

David Hannay, the UK permanent representative at the UN, confirms that the British were 'extremely unsighted' over Rwanda. There was no British embassy there. There were no British interests. Rwanda was a long way down the list of priorities and the telegrams about Rwanda, received from British embassies in Brussels, Paris and Washington, were not treated as high-grade. At the time a large amount of time and resources was being channelled into the problems of Bosnia, and in trying to disarm Iraq. The staff at the British mission in New York were overstretched.

Hannay says the information coming from the Secretariat was insufficient; he complained about the inadequate briefings available to the Security Council. Boutros-Ghali controlled the flow of information to the council, Hannay said, allowing only those officials with his permission to brief ambassadors. In all the discussions held about Rwanda before the genocide began, the focus had been on how to implement the Arusha Accords. Hannay said: 'Events proved we were looking in the wrong direction, and that the Secretariat was telling us to look in that direction.' He had seen none of the force commander's cables from Rwanda because the Council was not meant to be involved in the day-to-day running of peace-keeping missions.

Even so, Hannay is convinced that there was nothing the UN could have done to prevent the genocide in Rwanda, not with a Hutu-led government intent upon it. Even had the Security Council recognised the killing as genocide, it would not have saved any lives. Hannay said that he was not a lawyer and was therefore not in a position to decide whether or not what was happening was genocide. 'We knew a lot of Tutsi were being killed by a lot of Hutu,' he said. The Council could not conjure up troops and although he believes that Dallaire did a fantastic job, Hannay remains deeply sceptical of Dallaire's belief that 5,500 troops could have prevented much of the slaughter. In any case, to have mounted an enforcement mission with so few troops was totally against American military doctrine.

Some years later, in December 1998, in a BBC Radio 4 interview, Hannay talked specifically about the Genocide Convention in relation to Rwanda: 'nobody ever started to say and who will actually do the intervening and how will it be done'.

In the House of Commons there was no attempt to address the

issue and the government was preoccupied with the civil war. After nearly five weeks of genocide and more than 500,000 victims, Mark Lennox-Boyd, the parliamentary under-secretary of state for foreign and Commonwealth affairs, told the House in a written answer on 9 May: 'There are estimates that more than 200,000 people may have perished in the recent fighting in Rwanda. It is a horrific and tragic civil war where we will probably never know the true figure of those killed and injured.'

A debate in the House on Rwanda did not take place until 24 May when Tony Worthington, MP (Labour, Clydebank and Milngavie), expressed shock that so little attention had been paid to Rwanda. 'It is inconceivable that an atrocity in which half a million white people had died would not have been extensively debated in the House,' Worthington said. The press in Britain had a terrible tendency to dismiss the events as tribalism. 'Genocide is certainly involved,' Worthington told the House. Britain was a signatory to the Genocide Convention. 'Has there ever been a clearer example of genocide?' he asked. Lennox-Boyd replied that Rwanda had had a tragic history of ethnic-political violence since independence. The UN had to operate with the consent of the opposing factions.

The Labour Party waited until May before putting pressure on the government to act, and then only because Oxfam telephoned the office of David Clark, shadow secretary of state for defence. Clark called for the UN and the OAU[16] to organise an immediate deployment of forces to try to end the mass killing of civilians and appealed to Malcolm Rifkind, the secretary of state for defence, that the 'advice and expertise that our armed forces possess could be made available to the UN'.

On 23 May Rifkind wrote back to say that troops for Rwanda would 'probably come from regional forces in Africa'. The UK, wrote Rifkind, 'has not been asked to provide any personnel for the operation'. It was an extraordinary sentence for Rifkind to write. Only a few days earlier, Britain had voted in the Security Council to authorise more troops for Rwanda and at the time officials in the Secretariat were making desperate efforts to find soldiers. Annan said that every UN member government, with spare military capacity, had received a fax with a list of urgently needed troops and equipment.

So was military intervention by Britain simply impracticable? The

[16] Organisation of African Unity.

British Army has two main units that can be rapidly mobilised for deployments overseas, each occupying a very different niche in low- to mid-intensity combat capabilities: the Fifth Airborne Brigade and the Special Air Service (SAS). The level of readiness of the Fifth Airborne Brigade, the only airborne and air-trained brigade in the British Army, is routinely set at five days and fewer in a crisis. The brigade consists of two battalions of parachutists plus a command structure – a total of about 5,000 men. (It was to be integrated into a NATO rapid deployment force.) The SAS, described as a precise cutting tool for political policy, is an élite force for covert military operations.

In July 1994 Britain's minister for overseas development, Baroness Lynda Chalker, visited Kigali. She met Dallaire and she asked him what he needed. Dallaire had shown Chalker his list of basic requirements, which by then had been faxed around the world. 'I gave her my shopping list,' he remembered. 'I was up to my knees in bodies by then.' Britain had previously promised Dallaire fifty four-ton, four-wheel-drive trucks but they had not materialised. On a BBC2 *Newsnight* programme about Rwanda, Baroness Chalker later blamed Dallaire's lack of resources on 'the UN' which, she explained, ought to 'get its procurement right'.

Only after the genocide was over, and in response to the massive flight of people from Rwanda, did Britain become more generous. Chalker called the refugee tragedy the most ghastly in living memory, a replay of the Middle Ages, and on 28 July Britain offered military assistance in the form of 600 personnel from the Royal Electrical and Mechanical Engineers (REME) to repair the large number of unroadworthy vehicles which belonged to Dallaire's mission, a field ambulance and a field squadron of Royal Engineers to repair roads and drill wells.

Dallaire's only offers during the genocide, as a matter of record, were fifty trucks from Britain, a promise from Italy of one C-130 aircraft plus crew, and six water trucks, a signals squadron plus aircraft from Canada, from the USA fifty armoured personnel carriers, leasehold, and from Japan, US$3 million towards the cost of equipment.

There was a time when the sight of a single blue helmet at a checkpoint flying the UN flag was a symbol of peace, security and a determination to impose standards of justice that were understood the world over. The peace-keeper's weapon was not the rifle slung over the shoulder but his credibility; the peace-keeper represented a world community of states and the Security Council's will for peace. After Rwanda that symbol may have been irreparably tarnished. Certainly it will take enormous effort for it ever to regain its potency. That is not to denigrate the individual soldiers of UNAMIR, although criticism was frequent throughout the genocide, and is common today.

This is to lose sight of the remarkable and heroic efforts made by some of the peace-keepers. Jean-Hervé Bradol, MSF,[17] has described how in Kigali, despite the danger to their own lives, peace-keepers had tried to bring help to threatened civilians. James Orbinksi, MSF, paid tribute to their courage and that of their commander. Gerry McCarthy, UNICEF,[18] thought that in the entire UN, Dallaire was the one shining beacon.

Not everyone betrayed the people of Rwanda. The steadfastness of the Ghanaian Government allowed its troops to stay, saving UNAMIR from certain collapse. Other countries allowed their soldiers – all volunteers – to stay in Rwanda. Without the Canadian Government providing a C-130 for logistics and medical evacuation, the small mission would have been forced to withdraw. There were individuals, including Philippe Gaillard, and others who worked for the ICRC, MSF and the joint UN–Agency cell, who took extraordinary risks to provide a drop of humanity. It remains incredible to Dallaire that people had been massacred in their thousands almost every day and yet the world remained impassive.

In Rwanda, the anger and bitterness against the UN will last for decades. Hundreds of thousands of victims of genocide had thought that with the UN in their country they would be safe. But in the end the barbarians were allowed to triumph. There is nothing the West can say now to the people of Rwanda to compensate for the failure to intervene in their hour of need. That this genocide should have happened in the dying years of a century already stained by genocide makes it even harder to comprehend.

Only by revealing the failures, both individual and organisational, that permitted it, can any good emerge from something so bleak and so terrible. Only by exposing how and why it happened can there ever be any hope that the new century will break with the dismal record of the last.

---

[17] Médecins Sans Frontières.
[18] United Nations Children's Fund.

GREG PALAST

How to Steal the Presidency and Get Away with It
2000–1

If a 'scoop' is the true measure of a reporter, then Greg Palast is one of the best. It was the indefatigable Palast who exposed the theft of voting rights from more than 50,000 people in Florida during the US election in 2000. This enabled George W. Bush to 'win' Florida by 537 votes and helped him 'defeat' Al Gore for the presidency. So close was the national vote that the Supreme Court, stacked with conservatives, handed the election to Bush.

How this happened is no less than amazing. 'In the months leading up to the November balloting,' wrote Palast,

> Florida Governor Jeb Bush and his Secretary of State Katherine Harris ordered local elections supervisors to purge 57,700 voters from registries on grounds they were felons not entitled to vote in Florida. As it turns out, these voters weren't felons, at most a handful. However, the voters on this 'scrub list' were notably African-American (about 54 per cent) and most of the others wrongly barred from voting were white and Hispanic Democrats.

Palast discovered that the Republicans had spent almost their entire budget for Florida conducting a computer hunt for black voters, so they could be de-registered. Letters were sent direct from the office of Governor Bush, instructing county supervisors not to register ex-felons if they had been given clemency by other states and were entitled to vote under Florida law.

Palast, who often works from London, broke the story in the *Observer*.

Written in the 'wise guy' style of earlier muckrakers like Walter Winchell, his scoop was published in the United States only in the small-circulation weekly *The Nation* the following February, *after* Bush had been declared the winner. It took the *Washington Post*, scourge of Watergate, seven months to report it. *The New York Times* finally reported it on 16 February 2004. It is this silence of the American media, and its fear of breaking from the 'pack', that Palast illuminates almost as vividly as his exposé of the scandal in Florida. The following is an extract from his subsequent book, *The Best Democracy Money Can Buy* (2003).

HOW TO STEAL THE PRESIDENCY
AND GET AWAY WITH IT

In the days following the 2000 presidential election, there were so many stories of African-Americans erased from voter rolls you might think they were targeted by some kind of racial computer program. They were.

I have a copy of it: two silvery CD-Rom disks right out of the office computers of Florida Secretary of State Katherine Harris. Once decoded and flowed into a database, they make for interesting, if chilling, reading. They tell us how our president was elected – and it wasn't by the voters.

Here's how it worked: mostly, the disks contain data on Florida citizens – 57,700 of them. In the months leading up to the November 2000 balloting, Florida Secretary of State Harris, in coordination with Governor Jeb Bush, ordered local elections supervisors to purge these 57,700 from voter registries. In Harris's computers, they are named as felons who have no right to vote in Florida.

Thomas Cooper is on the list: criminal scum, bad guy, felon, *attempted* voter. The Harris hit list says Cooper was convicted of a felony on 30 January 2007.

2007?

You may suspect *something's wrong* with the list. You'd be right. At least 90.2 per cent of those on this 'scrub list', targeted to lose their civil rights, are innocent. Notably, over half – about 54 per cent – are Black and Hispanic voters. Overwhelmingly, it is a list of Democrats.

Secretary of State Harris declared George W. Bush winner of Florida, and thereby president, by a plurality of 537 votes over Al Gore. Now do the arithmetic. Over 50,000 voters wrongly targeted by the purge, mostly blacks. My BBC researchers reported that Gore lost at least 22,000 votes as a result of this smart little black-box operation.

The first reports of this extraordinary discovery ran, as you'd expect, on page one of the country's leading paper. Unfortunately, it was in the wrong country: Britain. In the USA, it ran on page *zero* – the story was simply not covered in American newspapers. The theft of the presidential race in Florida also grabbed big television coverage. But again, it was in the wrong continent: on BBC Television, broad-casting from London worldwide – everywhere, that is, but the USA.

Was this some off-the-wall story that the British press misreported? Hardly. The chief lawyer for the US Civil Rights Commission called it the first hard evidence of a systematic attempt to disenfranchise Florida's black voters. So why was this story investigated, reported and broadcast only in *Europe*, for God's sake? I'd like to know the answer. That way I could understand why a Southern California ho'daddy like me has to commute to England with his wife and kiddies to tell this and other stories about my country.

I will take you along the path of the investigation, step by step, report by report, from false starts to unpretty conclusions. When I first broke the story, I had it wrong. Within weeks of the election, I said the Harris crew had tried to purge 8,000 voters. While that was enough to change the outcome of the election (and change history), I was way off. Now, after two years of peeling the Florida elections onion, we put the number of voters wrongly barred from voting at over 90,000, mostly blacks and Hispanics, and by a wide majority, Democrats.

That will take us to the Big Question: was it *deliberate*, this purge so fortunate for the Republicans? Or just an honest clerical error? Go back to the case of Thomas Cooper, Criminal of the Future. I counted 325 of these time-travelling bandits on one of Harris's scrub lists. Clerical error? I dug back into the computers, the email traffic in the Florida Department of Elections, part of the secretary of state's office. And sure enough, the office clerks were screaming: they'd found a boatload like Mr Cooper on the purge list, convicted in the future, in the next century, in the next *millennium*.

The jittery clerks wanted to know what to do. I thought I knew the answer. As a product of the Los Angeles school system, where I Pledged my Allegiance to the Flag every morning, I assumed that if someone was wrongly accused, the state would give them back their right to vote. But the Republican operatives had a better idea. They told the clerks to *blank out* the wacky conviction dates. That way, the county elections supervisors, already wary of the list, would be none the wiser. The Florida purge lists have over 4,000 blank conviction dates.

How did British newspapers smell the Florida story all the way across the Atlantic? At the time, I was digging into George Bush Senior's gold-mining business, when researcher Solomon Hughes spotted a note in an article by Sasha Abramsky on the *Mother Jones* internet bulletin board flagging a story in the *Palm Beach Post* printed months before the election. The *Post*'s back pages mentioned that 8,000 voters had been removed from the voter rolls by mistake. That's one heck of a mistake. Given the *Sturm und Drang* in Florida, you'd think that an American journalist would pick up the story. Don't hold your breath. There were a couple of curious reporters, but they were easily waylaid by Florida's assurances that the 'mistake' had been corrected, which the *Post* ran as truth.

But what if the Florida press puppies had been wrong? What if they had stood on their hind legs and swallowed a biscuit of bullshit from state officials – and the 'mistakes' had *not* been corrected?

It was worth a call.

From London, I contacted a statistician at the office of the county elections supervisor in Tampa. Such an expert technician would have no reason to lie to me. The question at the top of my list: '*How many of the voters on the scrub list are BLACK?*'

And the statistician said, 'You know, I've been waiting for someone to ask me that.' From his leads, I wrote:

BLACK-OUT IN FLORIDA
The Observer, London, 26 November 2000

Vice-President Al Gore would have strolled to victory in Florida if the state hadn't kicked up to 66,000 citizens off the voter registers five months ago as former felons. In fact, not all were ex-cons. Most were simply guilty of being African-American. A top-placed election official told me that the government had conducted a quiet review and found – surprise – that the listing included far more African-Americans than would statistically have been expected, even accounting for the grievous gap between the conviction rates of blacks and whites in the US.

One list of 8,000 supposed felons was supplied by Texas. But these criminals from the Lone Star State had committed nothing more serious than misdemeanours such as drunk driving (like their governor, George W. Bush).

The source of this poisonous blacklist: Database Technologies, acting under the direction of Governor Jeb Bush's frothingly partisan secretary of state, Katherine Harris. DBT, a division of ChoicePoint, is under fire for misuse of personal data in state computers in Pennsylvania. ChoicePoint's board is loaded with Republican sugar daddies, including Ken Langone, finance chief for Rudy Giuliani's aborted Senate run against Hillary Clinton.

When the *Observer* report hit the streets (of London), Gore was still in the race.

Reporter Joe Conason pushed *Salon.com* to pick up my story and take it further. But that would not be easy. The Texas list error – 8,000 names – was corrected, said the state. That left the tougher question: what about the 57,700 *other* people named on that list? The remaining names on the list were, in the majority, black – not unusual in a nation where half of all felony convictions are against African-Americans. But as half the names were black, and if this included even a tiny fraction of *innocents*, well, there was the election for Bush.

The question was, then, whether the 'corrected' list had in fact been corrected. Finding the answer would not be cheap for *Salon*. It meant big bucks; redirecting their entire political staff to the story and making hotshot reporters knuckle down to the drudgery of calling and visiting county elections offices all over Florida. But they agreed, and *Salon*'s Alicia Montgomery, Daryl Lindsey and Anthony York came back with a mother lode of evidence proving that, by the most conservative analysis, Florida had purged enough innocent black voters – several thousand – to snatch the presidency from Al Gore.

On 4 December, 2000, I sent this to *Salon*:

FLORIDA'S ETHNIC CLEANSING OF THE
VOTER ROLLS
From *Salon.com*

If Vice-President Al Gore is wondering where his Florida votes went, rather than sift through a pile of chads, he might want to look at a 'scrub list' of 57,700 names targeted to be knocked off the Florida voter registry by a division of the office of Florida Secretary of State Katherine Harris. A close examination suggests thousands of voters may have lost their right to vote based on a flaw-ridden list of purported 'felons' provided by a private firm with tight Republican ties.

Early in the year, the company ChoicePoint gave Florida officials the names of 8,000 ex-felons to 'scrub' from their list of voters.

But it turns out none on the list was guilty of felonies, only misdemeanours.

The company acknowledged the error, and blamed it on the original source of the list – the state of Texas.

Florida officials moved to put those falsely accused by Texas back on voter rolls before the election. Nevertheless, the large number of errors uncovered in individual counties suggests that thousands of other eligible voters have been turned away at the polls.

Florida is the only state that pays a private company that promises to provide lists for 'cleansing' voter rolls. The state signed in 1998 a $4 million contract with DBT Online, since merged into ChoicePoint, of Atlanta. The creation of the scrub list, called the central voter file, was mandated by a 1998 state voter fraud law, which followed a tumultuous year that saw Miami's mayor removed after voter fraud in the election, with dead people discovered to have cast ballots. The voter fraud law required all 67 counties to purge voter registries of duplicate registrations, deceased voters and felons, many of whom, but not all, are barred from voting in Florida. In the process, however, the list invariably targets a minority population in Florida, where 31 per cent of all Black men cannot vote because of a ban on felons.

If this unfairly singled out minorities, it unfairly handicapped

Gore: in Florida, 93 per cent of African-Americans voted for the vice-president.

In the ten counties contacted by *Salon*, use of the central voter file seemed to vary wildly. Some found the list too unreliable and didn't use it at all. But most counties appear to have used the file as a resource to purge names from their voter rolls, with some counties making little – or no – effort at all to alert the 'purged' voters. Counties that did their best to vet the file discovered a high level of errors, with as many as 15 per cent of names incorrectly identified as felons.

News coverage has focused on some maverick Florida counties that rejected the scrub lists, including Palm Beach and Duval. The *Miami Herald* blasted the counties for not using the lists; but local officials tell us they had good reason to reject the scrub sheets from Harris's office. Madison County's elections supervisor, Linda Howell, had a peculiarly personal reason for distrusting the central voter file. She had received a letter saying that since she had committed a felony, she would not be allowed to vote.

Howell, who said she has never committed a felony, said the letter she received in March 2000 shook her faith in the process. 'It really is a mess,' she said.

'I was very upset,' Howell said. 'I know I'm not a felon.' Though the one mistake did get corrected and law enforcement officials were quite apologetic, Howell decided not to use the state list because its 'information is so flawed'.

She's unsure of the number of warning letters that were sent out to county residents when she first received the list in 1999, but she recalls that there were many problems. 'One day we would send a letter to have someone taken off the rolls, and the next day, we would send one to put them back on again,' Howell said. 'It makes you look like you must be a dummy.'

Following the *Salon* investigation I was confident that at least 7,000 innocent voters had been removed from voter rolls, half of them black, and that swung the election. But my investigation was far from over – and I found yet another 2,834 eligible voters targeted for the purge, almost all Democrats.

It was 10 December 2000 – Gore was still hanging in there – when I wrote this for British readers:

A BLACKLIST BURNING FOR BUSH
The Observer, London, 10 December 2000

Hey, Al, take a look at this. Every time I cut open another alligator, I find the bones of more Gore voters. This week, I was hacking my way through the Florida swampland known as the office of Secretary of State Katherine Harris and found a couple of thousand more names of voters electronically 'disappeared' from the voter rolls. About half of those named are African-Americans.

They had the right to vote, but they never made it to the balloting booths.

On 26 November, we reported that the Florida Secretary of State's office had, before the election, ordered the elimination of 8,000 Florida voters on the grounds that they had committed felonies in Texas. None had.

For Florida Governor Jeb Bush and his brother, the Texas blacklist was a mistake made in heaven. Most of those targeted to have their names 'scrubbed' from the voter rolls were African-Americans, Hispanics and poor white folk, likely voters for Vice-President Gore. We don't know how many voters lost their citizenship rights before the error was discovered by a few sceptical county officials before ChoicePoint, which has gamely 'fessed-up to the Texas-sized error, produced a new list of 57,700 felons. In May, Harris sent on the new, improved scrub sheets to the county election boards.

Maybe it's my bad attitude, but I thought it worthwhile to check out the new list. Sleuthing around county offices with a team of researchers from internet newspaper *Salon*, we discovered that the 'correct' list wasn't so correct.

Our ten-county review suggests a minimum 15 per cent misidentification rate. That makes another 7,000 innocent people accused of crimes and stripped of their citizenship rights in the run-up to the presidential race, a majority of them black.

Now our team, diving deeper into the swamps, has discovered yet a third group whose voting rights were stripped. The state's private contractor, ChoicePoint, generated a list of about 2,000 names of people who, earlier in their lives, were convicted of felonies in Illinois and Ohio. Like most American states, these two restore citizenship rights to people who have served their time in prison and then remained on the good side of the law.

Florida strips those convicted in its own courts of voting rights for life. But Harris's office concedes, and county officials concur, that the state of Florida has no right to impose this penalty on people who have moved in from these other states. (Only thirteen states, most in the Old Confederacy, bar reformed criminals from voting.)

Going deeper into the Harris lists, we find hundreds more convicts from the thirty-seven other states that restored their rights at the end of sentences served. If they have the right to vote, why were these citizens barred from the polls? Harris didn't return my calls. But Alan Dershowitz did. The Harvard law professor, a renowned authority on legal process, said: 'What's emerging is a pattern of reducing the total number of voters in Florida, which they know will reduce the Democratic vote.'

How could Florida's Republican rulers know how these people would vote?

I put the question to David Bositis, America's top expert on voting demographics.

Once he stopped laughing, he said the way Florida used the lists from a private firm was 'a patently obvious technique to discriminate against black voters'. In a darker mood, Bositis, of Washington's Center for Political and Economic Studies, said the sad truth of American justice is that 46 per cent of those convicted of felony are African-American. In Florida, a record number of black folk, over 80 per cent of those registered to vote, packed the polling booths on 7 November. Behind the curtains, nine out of ten black people voted for Gore.

Mark Mauer of the Sentencing Project, Washington, pointed out that the white half of the purge list would be peopled over-whelmingly by the poor, also solid Democratic voters.

Add it up. The dead-wrong Texas list, the uncorrected 'corrected' list, plus the out-of-state ex-con list. By golly, it's enough to swing a presidential election. I bet the busy Harris, simultaneously in charge of both Florida's voter rolls and George Bush's presidential campaign, never thought of that.

Thursday, 7 December, 2 a.m. On the other end of the line, heavy breathing, then a torrent of words too fast for me to catch it all. 'Vile . . . lying . . . inaccurate . . . pack of nonsense . . . riddled with errors . . .' click! This was not a ChoicePoint whistleblower telling me about the company's notorious list. It was ChoicePoint's own media communications representative, Marty Fagan, communicating with me about my 'sleazy disgusting journalism' in reporting on it.

Truth is, Fagan was returning my calls. I was curious about this company that chose the president for America's voters.

They have quite a pedigree for this solemn task. The company's Florida subsidiary, Database Technologies (now DBT Online), was founded by one Hank Asher. When US law enforcement agencies alleged that he might have been associated with Bahamian drug dealers – although no charges were brought – the company lost its data management contract with the FBI. Hank and his friends left and so, in Florida's eyes, the past is forgiven.

Thursday, 3 a.m. A new, gentler voice gave me ChoicePoint's upbeat spin. 'You say we got over 15 per cent wrong – we like to look at that as up to 85 per cent right!' That's 7,000 votes-plus – the bulk Democrats, not to mention the thousands on the faulty Texas list. (Gore lost the White House by 537 votes.)

I contacted San Francisco-based expert Mark Swedlund. 'It's just fundamental industry practice that you don't roll out the list statewide until you have tested it and tested it again,' he said. 'Dershowitz is right: they had to know that this jeopardised thousands of people's registrations. And they would also know the [racial] profile of those voters.'

'They' is Florida State, not ChoicePoint. Let's not get confused about where the blame lies. Harris's crew lit this database fuse, then acted surprised when it blew up. Swedlund says ChoicePoint had a professional responsibility to tell the state to test the list; ChoicePoint says the state should not have used its 'raw' data.

Until Florida privatised its Big Brother powers, laws kept the process out in the open. This year, when one county asked to see ChoicePoint's formulas and back-up for blacklisting voters, they refused – these were commercial secrets.

So we'll never know how America's president was chosen.

Now it gets weird. *Salon* was showered with praise – by columnists in the *New York Times*, *LA Times*, *Washington Post* and *Cleveland*

Plain Dealer (almost to a one black or Jewish), who were horrified by, as Bob Kuttner of the *Boston Globe* put it, Florida's 'lynching by laptop'. And still no *news* editor from print or television called me (except a CBS *Evening News* producer, who ran away with tail tucked as soon as Governor Jeb denied the allegations).

My work was far from over. On a tip, I began to look into the rights of felons in Florida – those actually convicted.

Every paper in America reported that Florida bars ex-criminals from voting. As soon as every newspaper agrees, you can bet it probably isn't true. Someone *wants* the papers to believe this. It did not take long to discover that what everyone said was true was actually false: *some* ex-cons could vote, thousands in fact. I knew it . . . and so did Governor Jeb Bush. Was Jeb Bush involved?

So I telephoned a clerk in First Brother Jeb's office, who whispered, 'Call me tomorrow before official opening hours.' And when I did call the next morning, this heroic clerk spent two hours explaining to me, 'The courts tell us to do *this*, and we do *that*.'

She referred to court orders that I'd got wind of, which ordered Governor Bush to stop interfering in the civil rights of ex-cons who had the right to vote.

I asked Jeb's clerk four times, 'Are you telling me the Governor knowingly violated the law and court orders, excluding eligible voters?'

And four times I got, 'The courts tell us to do *this* [allow certain felons to vote] and we do *that* [block them].'

But *Salon*, despite a mountain of evidence, stalled – then stalled some more.

Resentment of the takeover of the political coverage by an 'alien' was getting on the team's nerves. I can't blame them. And it didn't help that *Salon* was facing bankruptcy, staff were frazzled and it was nearly Christmas.

The remains of the year were lost while I got hold of legal opinions from top lawyers saying Bush's office was wrong; and later the Civil Rights Commission would also say Bush was wrong. But the political clock was ticking and George W. was oozing toward the Oval Office.

E. J. Dionne of the *Washington Post* told me, 'You have to get this story out, Greg, right away!' Notably, instead of directing me to the *Post*'s newsroom, E. J. told me to call *The Nation*, a kind of refugee centre for storm-tossed news reports.

After double-checking and quintuple-checking the facts, *The Nation* held its breath and printed the story of the 'third group' of wrongly

purged ex-felon voters (numbering nearly 3,000), and a *fourth* group
of voters wrongly barred from registering in the first place – *yet
another 40,000 of them, almost all Democratic voters.*

It was now 5 February 2001 – so President Bush could read this
report from the White House:

FLORIDA'S DISAPPEARED VOTERS
The Nation, 5 February 2001

In Latin America they might have called them *votantes desa-
parecidos*, 'disappeared voters'. On 7 November 2000, tens of
thousands of eligible Florida voters were wrongly prevented
from casting their ballots – some purged from the voter registries
and others blocked from registering in the first instance.

Nearly all were Democrats, nearly half of them African-
American. The systematic programme that disfranchised these
legal voters, directed by the offices of Florida's Governor Jeb
Bush and Secretary of State Katherine Harris, was so quiet,
subtle and intricate that if not for George W. Bush's 500-vote
eyelash margin of victory, certified by Harris, the chance of the
purge's discovery would have been vanishingly small.

The group prevented from voting – felons – has few defenders
in either party.

It has been well reported that Florida denies its nearly half a
million former convicts the right to vote. However, the media
have completely missed the fact that Florida's own courts have
repeatedly told the governor he may not take away the civil rights
of Florida citizens who have committed crimes in other states,
served their time and had their rights restored by those states.

People from other states who have arrived in Florida with a
felony conviction in their past number 'clearly over 50,000 and
likely over 100,000', says criminal demographics expert Jeffrey
Manza of Northwestern University.

Manza estimates that 80 per cent arrive with voting rights
intact, which they do not forfeit by relocating to the Sunshine
State. In other words, there are no fewer than 40,000 reformed
felons eligible to vote in Florida.

Nevertheless, agencies controlled by Harris and Bush ordered
county officials to reject attempts by these eligible voters to
register, while, publicly, the governor's office states that it adheres

to court rulings not to obstruct these ex-offenders in the exercise of their civil rights. Further, with the aid of a Republican-tied database firm, Harris's office used sophisticated computer programs to hunt those felons eligible to vote and ordered them thrown off the voter registries.

David Bositis, the Washington expert on voter demographics, suggests that the block-and-purge program 'must have had a partisan motivation. Why else spend $4 million if they expected no difference in the ultimate vote count?'

White and Hispanic felons, mostly poor, vote almost as solidly Democratic as African-Americans. A recently released University of Minnesota study estimates that, for example, 93 per cent of felons of all races favoured Bill Clinton in 1996. Whatever Florida's motive for keeping these qualified voters out of the polling booths on 7 November, the fact is that they represented several times George W. Bush's margin of victory in the state. Key officials in Bush's and Harris's agencies declined our requests for comment.

Pastor Thomas Johnson of Gainesville is minister to House of Hope, a faith-based charity that guides ex-convicts from jail into working life, a programme that has won high praise from the pastor's friend, Governor Jeb Bush. Ten years ago, Johnson sold crack cocaine in the streets of New York, got caught, served his time, then discovered God and Florida – where, early last year, he attempted to register to vote. But local election officials refused to accept his registration after he admitted to the decade-old felony conviction from New York. 'It knocked me for a loop. It was horrendous,' said Johnson of his rejection.

Beverly Hill, the election supervisor of Alachua County, where Johnson attempted to register, said that she used to allow ex-felons like Johnson to vote.

Under Governor Bush, that changed. 'Recently, the [Governor's Office of Executive] Clemency people told us something different,' she said. 'They told us that they essentially can't vote.'

Both Alachua's refusal to allow Johnson to vote and the governor's directive underlying that refusal are notable for their timing – coming after two court rulings that ordered the secretary of state and governor to recognise the civil rights of felons arriving from other states. In the first of these decisions, *Schlenther v. Florida Department of State*, issued in June 1998, Florida's

Court of Appeal ruled unanimously that Florida could not require a man convicted in Connecticut twenty-five years earlier 'to ask [Florida] to restore his civil rights. They were never lost here.' Connecticut, like most states, automatically restores felons' civil rights at the end of their sentence, and therefore 'he arrived as any other citizen, with full rights of citizenship'.

The *Schlenther* decision was much of the talk at a summer 1998 meeting of county election officials in Orlando. So it was all the more surprising to Chuck Smith, a statistician with Hillsborough County, that Harris's elections division chief Clayton Roberts exhorted local officials at the Orlando meeting to purge all out-of-state felons identified by DBT. Hillsborough was so concerned about this order, which appeared to fly in the face of the court edict, that the county's elections office demanded that the state put that position in writing – a request duly granted.

The Nation has obtained the text of the response to Hillsborough. The letter, from the Governor's Office of Executive Clemency, dated 18 September 2000, arrived only seven weeks before the presidential election. It orders the county to tell ex-felons trying to register that even if they entered Florida with civil rights restored by another state's law, they will still be 'required to make application for restoration of civil rights in the state of Florida', that is, ask Governor Bush for clemency – the very requirement banned by the courts. The state's directive was all the more surprising in light of a second ruling, issued in December 1999 by another Florida court, in which a Florida district court judge expressed his ill-disguised exasperation with the governor's administration for ignoring the prior edict in *Schlenther*.

Voting rights attorneys who reviewed the cases for *The Nation* explained that the courts relied on both Florida statute and the 'full faith and credit' clause of the US Constitution, which requires every state to accept the legal rulings of other states. 'The court has been pretty clear on what the governor can't do,' says Bruce Gear, assistant general counsel for the NAACP.[1] And what Governor Bush can't do is demand that a citizen arriving in Florida ask him for clemency to restore a right to vote that the citizen already has.

Strangely enough, the governor's office does not disagree.

[1] National Association for the Advancement of Colored People.

While Harris, Bush and a half-dozen of their political appointees have not returned our calls, Tawanna Hayes, who processes the requests for clemency in the governor's office, states unequivocally that 'we do not have the right to suspend or restore rights where those rights have been restored in another state'. Hayes even keeps a copy of the two court decisions near her desk and quotes from them at length. So, why have the governor and secretary of state ordered these people purged from the rolls or barred from registering? Hayes directed us to Greg Munson, Governor Bush's assistant general counsel and clemency aide.

Munson has not responded to our detailed request for an explanation.

A letter dated 10 August 2000, from Harris's office to Bush's office, obtained under Florida's Freedom of Information Act, indicates that the chief of the Florida State Association of Supervisors of Elections also questioned Harris's office about the purge of ex-cons whose rights had been restored automatically by other states. The supervisors' group received the same response as Hillsborough: strike them from the voter rolls and, if they complain, make them ask Bush for clemency.

While almost all county supervisors buckled, Carol Griffin did not. Griffin, Washington County's elections chief, concluded that running legal voters through Jeb Bush's clemency maze would violate a 1993 federal law, the National Voter Registration Act (NVRA), which was designed to remove impediments to the exercise of civil rights. The law, known as 'motor voter', is credited with helping to register 7 million new voters. Griffin quotes from the Florida section of the new, NVRA-certified registration form, which says: 'I affirm I am not a convicted felon, or if I am, my rights relating to voting have been restored.' 'That's the law,' says the adamant Griffin, 'and I have no right stopping anyone registering who truthfully signs that statement. Once you check that box there's no discussion.' Griffin's county refused to implement the scrub, and the state appears reluctant to challenge its action.

But when Pastor Johnson attempted to register in Alachua County, clerks refused and instead handed him a fifteen-page clemency request form. The outraged minister found the offer a demeaning Catch-22. 'How can I ask the governor for a right I already have?' he says, echoing, albeit unknowingly, the words of the Florida courts.

Had Johnson relented and chosen to seek clemency, he would have faced a procedure that is, admits the clemency office's Hayes, 'sometimes worse than breaking a leg'. For New Yorkers like Johnson, she says, 'I'm telling you it's a bear.' She says officials in New York, which restores civil rights automatically, are perplexed by requests from Florida for non-existent papers declaring the individual's rights restored. Without the phantom clemency orders, the applicant must hunt up old court records and begin a complex process lasting from four months to two years, sometimes involving quasi-judicial hearings, the outcome of which depends on Jeb Bush's disposition.

Little wonder that out of tens of thousands of out-of-state felons, only a hardy couple of hundred attempted to run this bureaucratic obstacle course before the election. (Bush can be compassionate: he granted clemency to Charles Colson for his crimes as a Watergate conspirator, giving Florida resident Colson the right to vote in the presidential election.)

How did the governor's game play at the ballot box? Jeb Bush's operation denied over 50,000 citizens their right to vote. Given that 80 per cent of registered voters actually cast ballots in the presidential election, at least 40,000 votes were lost. By whom? As 90 per cent or more of this targeted group, out-of-state ex-cons, votes Democratic, we can confidently state that this little twist in the voter purge cost Al Gore a good 30,000 votes.

Was Florida's corrupted felon-voter hunt the work of cosy collusion between Jeb Bush and Harris, the president-elect's brother and state campaign chief, respectively? It is unlikely we will ever discover the motives driving the voter purge, but we can see the consequences. Three decades ago, Governor George Wallace stood in a schoolhouse door and thundered, 'Segregation now! Segregation tomorrow! Segregation for ever!' but failed to block entry to African-Americans. Governor Jeb Bush's resistance to court rulings, conducted at whisper level with hi-tech assistance, has been far more effective at blocking voters of colour from the polling station door. Deliberate or accidental, the error-ridden computer purge and illegal clemency obstacle course function, like the poll tax and literacy test of the Jim Crow era, to take the vote away from citizens who are black, poor and, not coincidentally, almost all Democrats. No guesswork there: Florida is one of the few states to include both party and race on registration files.

Pastor Johnson, an African-American wrongfully stripped of his vote, refuses to think ill of the governor or his motives. He prefers to see a dark comedy of bureaucratic errors: 'The buffoonery of this state has cost us a president.' If this is buffoonery, then Harris and the Bushes are wise fools indeed.

ERIC SCHLOSSER

Fast Food Nation

2001

Eric Schlosser exposed the global 'fast food' industry in his landmark book, *Fast Food Nation: What the All-American Meal Is Doing to the World*. In his investigation of famous names like McDonald's, Burger King and Kentucky Fried Chicken, Schlosser shows how industrial food production has transformed and endangered not only our diet, but our environment, economy and culture, even our basic human rights. The exploitation of the most vulnerable workers and of children, the ethos of a robotic assembly line, the relentless lobbying and pressure to standardise, monopolise, automate and, above all, dehumanise – Schlosser reveals this as the true face of the 'global economy' behind its seductive corporate mask.

Like a consumerist Pentagon, McDonald's calls its foreign conquests 'global realisation'. Nothing must get in its way. When the company opened a branch in Dachau, Germany, in 1997, it distributed flyers in the car park of the concentration camp museum: 'Welcome to Dachau and welcome to McDonald's.'

As a correspondent for *The Atlantic* magazine, Eric Schlosser previously exposed the conditions of immigrant workers in California's strawberry industry. His crisp angry prose is reminiscent of John Steinbeck's *Grapes of Wrath*. 'The workers I met in the meatpacking plants in Colorado and Nebraska,' he says, 'were the same kinds of people I met in the strawberry fields of California. They are peasants from rural villages in Mexico and Guatemala, many of them illiterate. When they get badly hurt, which happens all the time, they're unable to do manual labour the same way ever again . . . If we bring the minimum wage up to the level it was thirty years ago, in real terms, and we enforce the rules about overtime, and make it easier to organise service workers, the fast food chains will have to change. Or go out of business. In a way, the future of the fast food industry is tied to the future of America.' The following is a nightmarish glimpse of where 'fast food' begins: in a slaughterhouse.

FAST FOOD NATION

One night I visit a slaughterhouse somewhere in the High Plains. The slaughterhouse is one of the nation's largest. About 5,000 head of cattle enter it every day, single file, and leave in a different form. Someone who has access to the plant, who's upset by its working conditions, offers to give me a tour. The slaughterhouse is an immense building, grey and square, about three storeys high, with no windows on the front and no architectural clues to what's happening inside. My friend gives me a chain-mail apron and gloves, suggesting I try them on. Workers on the line wear about eight pounds of chain mail beneath their white coats, shiny steel armour that covers their hands, wrists, stomach and back. The chain mail's designed to protect workers from cutting themselves and from being cut by other workers. But knives somehow manage to get past it. My host hands me some wellingtons, the kind of knee-high rubber boots that English gentlemen wear in the countryside. 'Tuck your pants into the boots,' he says. 'We'll be walking through some blood.'

I put on a hardhat and climb a stairway. The sounds get louder, factory sounds, the noise of power tools and machinery, bursts of compressed air. We start at the end of the line, the fabricating room. Workers call it 'fab'. When we step inside, fab seems familiar: steel catwalks, pipes along the walls, a vast room, a maze of conveyor belts. This could be the Lamb Weston plant in Idaho, except hunks of red meat ride the belts instead of french fries. Some machines assemble cardboard boxes, others vacuum-seal subprimals of beef in clear plastic. The workers look extremely busy, but there's nothing unsettling about this part of the plant. You see meat like this all the time in the back of your local supermarket.

The fab room is cooled to about 40 degrees, and as you head up the line, the feel of the place starts to change. The pieces of meat get bigger. Workers – about half of them women, almost all of them young and Latino – slice meat with long slender knives. They stand at a table that's chest high, grab meat off a conveyor belt, trim away fat, throw meat back on the belt, toss the scraps on to a conveyor belt above them, and then grab more meat, all in a matter of seconds. I'm now struck by how many workers there are, hundreds of them, pressed close together, constantly moving, slicing. You see hardhats, white coats, flashes of steel. Nobody is smiling or chatting, they're too busy, anxiously trying not to fall behind. An old man walks past me, pushing a blue plastic barrel filled with scraps. A few workers carve the meat with Whizzards, small electric knives that have spinning round blades. The Whizzards look like the Norelco razors that Santa rides in the TV ads. I notice that a few of the women near me are sweating, even though the place is freezing cold.

Sides of beef suspended from an overhead trolley swing towards a group of men. Each worker has a large knife in one hand and a steel hook in the other. They grab the meat with their hooks and attack it fiercely with their knives. As they hack away, using all their strength, grunting, the place suddenly feels different, primordial. The machinery seems beside the point, and what's going on before me has been going on for thousands of years – the meat, the hook, the knife, men straining to cut more meat.

On the kill floor, what I see no longer unfolds in a logical manner. It's one strange image after another. A worker with a power saw slices cattle into halves as though they were two-by-fours, and then the halves swing by me into the cooler. It feels like a slaughterhouse now. Dozens of cattle, stripped of their skins, dangle on chains from their hind legs. My host stops and asks how I feel, if I want to go any further. This is where some people get sick. I feel fine, determined to see the whole process, the world that's been deliberately hidden. The kill floor is hot and humid. It stinks of manure. Cattle have a body temperature of about 101 degrees, and there are a lot of them in the room. Carcasses swing so fast along the rail that you have to keep an eye on them constantly, dodge them, watch your step, or one will slam you and throw you on to the bloody concrete floor. It happens to workers all the time.

I see: a man reach inside cattle and pull out their kidneys with his bare hands, then drop the kidneys down a metal chute, over and over again, as each animal passes by him; a stainless steel rack of tongues; Whizzards peeling meat off decapitated heads, picking them almost as clean as the white skulls painted by Georgia O'Keeffe. We wade through blood that's ankle deep and that pours down drains into huge vats below us. As we approach the start of the line, for the first time I hear the steady *pop, pop, pop* of live animals being stunned.

Now the cattle suspended above me look just like the cattle I've seen on ranches for years, but these ones are upside down swinging on hooks. For a moment, the sight seems unreal; there are so many of them, a herd of them, lifeless. And then I see a few hind legs still kicking, a final reflex action, and the reality comes hard and clear.

For eight and a half hours, a worker called a 'sticker' does nothing but stand in a river of blood, being drenched in blood, slitting the neck of a steer every ten seconds or so, severing its carotid artery. He uses a long knife and must hit exactly the right spot to kill the animal humanely. He hits that spot again and again. We walk up a slippery metal stairway and reach a small platform, where the production line begins. A man turns and smiles at me. He wears safety goggles and a hardhat. His face is splattered with grey matter and blood. He is the 'knocker', the man who welcomes cattle to the building. Cattle walk down a narrow chute and pause in front of him, blocked by a gate, and then he shoots them in the head with a captive bolt stunner – a compressed-air gun attached to the ceiling by a long hose – which fires a steel bolt that knocks the cattle unconscious. The animals keep strolling up, oblivious to what comes next, and he stands over them and shoots. For eight and a half hours, he just shoots. As I stand there, he misses a few times and shoots the same animal twice. As soon as the steer falls, a worker grabs one of its hind legs, shackles it to a chain, and the chain lifts the huge animal into the air.

I watch the knocker knock cattle for a couple of minutes. The animals are powerful and imposing one moment and then gone in an instant, suspended from a rail, ready for carving. A steer slips from its chain, falls to the ground, and gets its head caught in one end of a conveyor belt. The production line stops as workers struggle to free the steer, stunned but alive, from the machinery. I've seen enough.

I step out of the building into the cool night air and follow the path that leads cattle into the slaughterhouse. They pass me, driven towards the building by workers with long white sticks that seem to glow in the dark. One steer, perhaps sensing instinctively what the others don't, turns and tries to run. But workers drive him back to join the rest. The cattle lazily walk single-file towards the muffled sounds, *pop, pop, pop*, coming from the open door.

The path has hairpin turns that prevent cattle from seeing what's in store and keep them relaxed. As the ramp gently slopes upwards, the animals may think they're headed for another truck, another road trip – and they are, in unexpected ways. The ramp widens as it reaches ground level and then leads to a large cattle pen with wooden fences, a corral that belongs in a meadow, not here. As I walk along the fence, a group of cattle approach me, looking me straight in the eye, like dogs hoping for a treat, and follow me out of some mysterious impulse. I stop and try to absorb the whole scene: the cool breeze, the cattle and their gentle lowing, a cloudless sky, steam rising from the plant in the moonlight. And then I notice that the building does have one window, a small square of light on the second floor. It offers a glimpse of what's hidden behind this huge blank façade. Through the little window you can see bright red carcasses on hooks, going round and round.

Knocker, Sticker, Shackler, Rumper, First Legger, Knuckle Dropper, Navel Boner, Splitter Top/Bottom Butt, Feed Kill Chain – the names of job assignments at a modern slaughterhouse convey some of the brutality inherent in the work. Meatpacking is now the most dangerous job in the United States. The injury rate in a slaughterhouse is about three times higher than the rate in a typical American factory. Every year more than a quarter of the meatpacking workers in this country – roughly 40,000 men and women – suffer an injury or a work-related illness that requires medical attention beyond first aid. There is strong evidence that these numbers, compiled by the Bureau of Labor Statistics, understate the number of meatpacking injuries that occur. Thousands of additional injuries and illnesses most likely go unrecorded.

Despite the use of conveyor belts, forklifts, dehiding machines, and a variety of power tools, most of the work in the nation's slaughter-houses is still performed by hand. Poultry plants can be largely mech-anised, thanks to the breeding of chickens that are uniform in size. The birds in some Tyson factories are killed, plucked, gutted, beheaded, and sliced into cutlets by robots and machines. But cattle still come in all size and shapes, varying in weight by hundreds of pounds. The lack of a standardised steer has hindered the mechanisation of beef plants. In one crucial respect meatpacking work has changed little in the past hundred years. At the dawn of the twenty-first century, amid an era of extraordinary technological advance, the most important tool in a modern slaughterhouse is a sharp knife.

Lacerations are the most common injuries suffered by meatpackers, who often stab themselves or stab someone working nearby. Tendinitis and cumulative trauma disorders are also quite common. Meatpacking workers routinely develop back problems, shoulder problems, carpal tunnel syndrome, and 'trigger finger' (a syndrome in which a finger becomes frozen in a curled position). Indeed, the rate of these cumulative trauma injuries in the meatpacking industry is far higher than the rate in any other American industry. It is roughly thirty-three times higher than the national average in industry. Many slaughterhouse workers make a knife cut every two or three seconds, which adds up to about 10,000 cuts during an eight-hour shift. If the knife has become dull, additional pressure is placed on the worker's tendons, joints, and nerves. A dull knife can cause pain to extend from the cutting hand all the way down the spine.

Workers often bring their knives home and spend at least forty minutes a day keeping the edges smooth, sharp and sanded, with no pits. One Iowa Beef Packers (IBP) worker, a small Guatemalan woman with greying hair, spoke with me in the cramped kitchen of her mobile home. As a pot of beans cooked on the stove, she sat in a wooden chair, gently rocking, telling the story of her life, of her journey north in search of work, the whole time sharpening big knives in her lap as though she were knitting a sweater.

The 'IBP revolution' has been directly responsible for many of the hazards that meatpacking workers now face. One of the leading determinants of the injury rate at a slaughterhouse today is the speed of the disassembly line. The faster it runs, the more likely that workers will get hurt. The old meatpacking plants in Chicago slaughtered about 50 cattle an hour. Twenty years ago, new plants in the High Plains slaughtered about 175 cattle an hour. Today some plants slaughter up to 400 cattle an hour – about half a dozen animals every minute, sent down a single production line, carved by workers desperate not to fall behind. While trying to keep up with the flow of meat, workers often neglect to resharpen their knives and thereby place more stress on their bodies. As the pace increases, so does the risk of accidental cuts and stabbings. 'I could always tell the line speed,' a former Monfort nurse told me, 'by the number of people with lacerations coming into my office.' People usually cut themselves; nevertheless, everyone on the line tries to stay alert. Meatpackers often work within inches of each other, wielding large knives. A simple mistake can cause a serious injury. A former IBP worker told me about boning knives suddenly flying out of hands and ricocheting off machinery. 'They're very flexible,' she said, 'and they'll spring on you . . . zwing, and they're gone.'

Much like french fry factories, beef slaughterhouses often operate at profit margins as low as a few pennies a pound. The three meat-packing giants – ConAgra, IBP, and Excel – try to increase their earnings by maximising the volume of production at each plant. Once a slaughterhouse is up and running, fully staffed, the profits it will earn are directly related to the speed of the line. A faster pace means higher profits. Market pressures now exert a perverse influence on the management of beef plants: the same factors that make these slaughter-houses relatively inefficient (the lack of mechanisation, the reliance on human labour) encourage companies to make them even more dangerous (by speeding up the pace).

The unrelenting pressure of trying to keep up with the line has encouraged widespread methamphetamine use among meatpackers. Workers taking 'crank' feel charged and self-confident, ready for anything. Supervisors have been known to sell crank to their workers or to supply it free in return for certain favours, such as working a second shift. Workers who use methamphetamine may feel energised and invincible, but are actually putting themselves at much greater risk of having an accident. For obvious reasons, a modern slaughter-house is not a safe place to be high.

In the days when labour unions were strong, workers could complain about excessive line speeds and injury rates without fear of getting fired. Today only one-third of IBP's workers belong to a union. Most of the non-union workers are recent immigrants; many are illegals; and they are generally employed 'at will'. That means they can be fired without warning, for just about any reason. Such an arrange-ment does not encourage them to lodge complaints. Workers who have travelled a great distance for this job, who have families to support, who are earning ten times more an hour in a meatpacking plant than they could possibly earn back home, are wary about speaking out and losing everything. The line speeds and labour costs at IBP's non-union plants now set the standard for the rest of the industry. Every other company must try to produce beef as quickly and cheaply as IBP does; slowing the pace to protect workers can lead to a competitive disadvantage.

Again and again workers told me that they are under tremendous pressure not to report injuries. The annual bonuses of plant foremen and supervisors are often based in part on the injury rate of their workers. Instead of creating a safer workplace, these bonus schemes encourage slaughterhouse managers to make sure that accidents and injuries go unreported. Missing fingers, broken bones, deep lacerations, and amputated limbs are difficult to conceal from authorities. But the dramatic and catastrophic injuries in a slaughterhouse are greatly outnumbered by less visible, though no less debilitating, ailments: torn muscles, slipped discs, pinched nerves.

If a worker agrees not to report an injury, a supervisor will usually shift him or her to an easier job for a while, providing some time to heal. If the injury seems more serious, a Mexican worker is often given the opportunity to return home for a while, to recuperate there, then come back to his or her slaughterhouse job in the United States. Workers who abide by these unwritten rules are treated respectfully; those who disobey are likely to be punished and made an example. As one former IBP worker explained, 'They're trying to deter you, period, from going to the doctor.'

From a purely economic point of view, injured workers are a drag on profits. They are less productive. Getting rid of them makes a good deal of financial sense, especially when new workers are readily available and inexpensive to train. Injured workers are often given some of the most unpleasant tasks in the slaughterhouse. Their hourly wages are cut. And through a wide variety of unsubtle means they are encouraged to quit.

Not all supervisors in a slaughterhouse behave like Simon Legree, shouting at workers, cursing them, belittling their injuries, always pushing them to move faster. But enough supervisors act that way to warrant the comparison. Production supervisors tend to be men in their late twenties and early thirties. Most are Anglos and don't speak Spanish, although more and more Latinos are being promoted to the job. They earn about $30,000 a year, plus bonuses and benefits. In many rural communities, being a supervisor at a meatpacking plant is one of the best jobs in town. It comes with a fair amount of pressure: a supervisor must meet production goals, keep the number of recorded injuries low, and most importantly, keep the meat flowing down the line without interruption. The job also brings enormous power. Each supervisor is like a little dictator in his or her section of the plant, largely free to boss, fire, berate or reassign workers. That sort of power can lead to all sorts of abuses, especially when the hourly workers being supervised are women.

Many women told me stories about being fondled and grabbed on the production line, and the behaviour of supervisors sets the tone for the other male workers. In February 1999, a federal jury in Des Moines awarded $2.4 million to a female employee at an IBP slaughterhouse. According to the woman's testimony, co-workers had 'screamed obscenities and rubbed their bodies against hers while supervisors laughed'. Seven months later, Monfort agreed to settle a lawsuit filed by the US Equal Employment Opportunity Commission on behalf of fourteen female workers in Texas. As part of the settlement, the company paid the women $900,000 and vowed to establish formal procedures for handling sexual harassment complaints. In their lawsuit the women alleged that supervisors at a Monfort plant in Cactus, Texas, pressured them for dates and sex, and that male co-workers groped them, kissed them and used animal parts in a sexually explicit manner.

The sexual relationships between supervisors and 'hourlies' are for the most part consensual. Many female workers optimistically regard sex with their supervisor as a way to gain a secure place in American society, a green card, a husband – or at the very least a transfer to an easier job at the plant. Some supervisors become meatpacking Casanovas, engaging in multiple affairs. Sex, drugs and slaughterhouses may seem an unlikely combination, but as one former Monfort employee told me: 'Inside those walls is a different world that obeys different laws.' Late on the second shift, when it's dark outside, assignations take place in locker rooms, staff rooms and parked cars, even on the catwalk over the kill floor.

Some of the most dangerous jobs in meatpacking today are performed by the late-night cleaning crews. A large proportion of these workers are illegal immigrants. They are considered 'independent contractors', employed not by the meatpacking firms but by sanitation companies. They earn hourly wages that are about one-third lower than those of regular production employees. And their work is so hard and so horrendous that words seem inadequate to describe it. The men and women who now clean the nation's slaughterhouses may arguably have the worst job in the United States. 'It takes a really dedicated person,' a former member of a cleaning crew told me, 'or a really desperate person to get the job done.'

When a sanitation crew arrives at a meatpacking plant, usually around midnight, it faces a mess of monumental proportions.

3,000–4,000 cattle, each weighing about 1,000 pounds, have been slaughtered there that day. The place has to be clean by sunrise. Some of the workers wear water-resistant clothing; most don't. Their principal cleaning tool is a high-pressure hose that shoots a mixture of water and chlorine heated to about 180 degrees. As the water is sprayed, the plant fills with a thick, heavy fog. Visibility drops to as little as five feet. The conveyor belts and machinery are running. Workers stand on the belts, spraying them, riding them like moving sidewalks, as high as fifteen feet off the ground. Workers climb ladders with hoses and spray the catwalks. They get under tables and conveyor belts, climbing right into the bloody muck, cleaning out grease, fat, manure, leftover scraps of meat.

Glasses and safety goggles fog up. The inside of the plant heats up; temperatures soon exceed 100 degrees. 'It's hot, and it's foggy, and you can't see anything,' a former sanitation worker said. The crew members can't see or hear each other when the machinery's running. They routinely spray each other with burning hot, chemical-laden water. They are sickened by the fumes. Jesus, a soft-spoken employee of DCS Sanitation Management, Inc., the company that IBP uses in many of its plants, told me that every night on the job he gets terrible headaches. 'You feel it in your head,' he said. 'You feel it in your stomach, like you want to throw up.' A friend of his vomits whenever they clean the rendering area. Other workers tease the young man as he retches. Jesus says the stench in rendering is so powerful that it won't wash off; no matter how much soap you use after a shift, the smell comes home with you, seeps from your pores.

One night while Jesus was cleaning, a co-worker forgot to turn off a machine, lost two fingers, and went into shock. An ambulance came and took him away, as everyone else continued to clean. He was back at work the following week. 'If one hand is no good,' the supervisor told him, 'use the other.' Another sanitation worker lost an arm in a machine. Now he folds towels in the locker room. The scariest job, according to Jesus, is cleaning the vents on the roof of the slaughterhouse. The vents become clogged with grease and dried blood. In the winter, when everything gets icy and the winds pick up, Jesus worries that a sudden gust will blow him off the roof into the darkness.

Although official statistics are not kept, the death rate among slaughterhouse sanitation crews is extraordinarily high. They are the ultimate in disposable workers: illegal, illiterate, impoverished, untrained. The nation's worst job can end in just about the worst way. Sometimes these workers are literally ground up and reduced to nothing.

A brief description of some cleaning-crew accidents over the past decade says more about the work and the danger than any set of statistics. At the Monfort plant in Grand Island, Nebraska, Richard Skala was beheaded by a dehiding machine. Carlos Vincente – an employee of T and G Service Company, a twenty-eight-year-old Guatemalan who'd been in the United States for only a week – was pulled into the cogs of a conveyor belt at an Excel plant in Fort Morgan, Colorado, and torn apart. Lorenzo Marin Sr, an employee of DCS Sanitation, fell from the top of a skinning machine while cleaning it with a high-pressure hose, struck his head on the concrete floor of an IBP plant in Columbus Junction, Iowa, and died. Another employee of DCS Sanitation, Salvador Hernandez-Gonzalez, had his head crushed by a pork-loin processing machine at an IBP plant in Madison, Nebraska. The same machine had fatally crushed the head of another worker, Ben Barone, a few years earlier. At a National Beef plant in Liberal, Kansas, Homer Stull climbed into a blood-collection tank to clean it, a filthy tank thirty feet high. Stull was overcome by hydrogen sulphide fumes. Two co-workers climbed into the tank and tried to rescue him. All three men died. Eight years earlier, Henry Wolf had been overcome by hydrogen sulphide fumes while cleaning the very same tank; Gary Sanders had tried to rescue him; both men died; and the Occupational Safety and Health Administration (OSHA) later fined National Beef for its negligence. The fine was $480 for each man's death.

During the same years when the working conditions at America's meat-packing plants became more dangerous – when line speeds increased and illegal immigrants replaced skilled workers – the federal government greatly reduced the enforcement of health and safety laws. OSHA had long been despised by the nation's manufacturers, who considered the agency a source of meddlesome regulations and unnecessary red tape. When Ronald Reagan was elected president in 1980, OSHA was already underfunded and understaffed: its 1,300 inspectors were responsible for the safety of more than five million work-places across the country. A typical American employer could expect an OSHA inspection about once every eighty years. Nevertheless, the Reagan administration was determined to reduce OSHA's authority even further, as part of the push for deregulation. The number of OSHA inspectors was eventually cut by 20 per cent, and in 1981 the agency adopted a new policy of 'voluntary compliance'. Instead of arriving unannounced at a factory and performing an inspection, OSHA employees were required to look at a company's injury log before setting foot inside the plant. If the records showed an injury rate at the factory lower than the national average for all manufacturers, the OSHA inspector had to turn around and leave at once – without entering the plant, examining its equipment or talking to any of its workers. These injury logs were kept and maintained by company officials.

For most of the 1980s OSHA's relationship with the meatpacking industry was far from adversarial. While the number of serious injuries rose, the number of OSHA inspections fell. The death of a worker on the job was punished with a fine of just a few hundred dollars. At a gathering of meat company executives in October of 1987, OSHA's safety director, Barry White, promised to change federal safety standards that 'appear amazingly stupid to you or overburdening or just not useful'. According to an account of the meeting later published in the *Chicago Tribune*, the safety director at OSHA – the federal official most responsible for protecting the lives of meat-packing workers – acknowledged his own lack of qualifications for the job. 'I know very well that you know more about safety and health in the meat industry than I do,' White told the executives. 'And you know more about safety and health in the meat industry than any single employee at OSHA.'

OSHA's voluntary compliance policy did indeed reduce the number of recorded injuries in meatpacking plants. It did not, however, reduce the number of people getting hurt. It merely encouraged companies, in the words of a subsequent congressional investigation, 'to under-state injuries, to falsify records, and to cover up accidents'. At the IBP beef plant in Dakota City, Nebraska, for example, the company kept two sets of injury logs: one of them recording every injury and illness at the slaughterhouse, the other provided to visiting OSHA inspectors and researchers from the Bureau of Labor Statistics. During a three-month period in 1985, the first log recorded 1,800 injuries and illnesses at the plant. The OSHA log recorded only 160 – a discrepancy of more than 1,000 per cent.

At congressional hearings on meatpacking in 1987, Robert L. Peterson, the chief executive of IBP, denied under oath that two sets of logs were ever kept and called IBP's safety record 'the best of the best'. Congressional investigators later got hold of both logs – and found that the injury rate at its Dakota City plant was as much as one-third higher than the average rate in the meatpacking industry. Congressional investigators also discovered that IBP had altered injury records at its beef plant in Emporia, Kansas. Another leading meat-packing company, John Morrell, was caught lying about injuries at its plant in Sioux Falls, South Dakota. The congressional investig-ation concluded that these companies had failed to report 'serious injuries such as fractures, concussions, major cuts, hernias, some requiring hospitalisation, surgery, even amputation'.

Congressman Tom Lantos, whose sub-committee conducted the meatpacking inquiry, called IBP 'one of the most irresponsible and reckless corporations in America'. A Labor Department official called the company's behaviour 'the worst example of underreporting injuries and illnesses to workers ever encountered in OSHA's sixteen-year history'. Nevertheless, Robert L. Peterson was never charged with perjury for his misleading testimony before Congress. Investigators argued that it would be difficult to prove 'conclusively' that Peterson had 'wilfully' lied. In 1987 IBP was fined $2.6 million by OSHA for underreporting injuries and later fined an additional $3.1 million for the high rate of cumulative trauma injuries at the Dakota City plant. After the company introduced a new safety programme there, the fines were reduced to $975,000 – a sum that might have appeared large at the time, yet represented about one-hundredth of a per cent of IBP's annual revenues.

Three years after the OSHA fines, a worker named Kevin Wilson injured his back at an IBP slaughterhouse in Council Bluffs, Iowa. Wilson went to see Diane Arndt, a nurse at the plant, who sent him to a doctor selected by the company. Wilson's injury was not serious, the doctor said, later assigning him to light duty at the plant. Wilson sought a second opinion; the new doctor said that he had a disc injury that required a period of absence from work. When Wilson stopped reporting for light duty, IBP's corporate security department began to conduct surveillance of his house. Eleven days after Wilson's new doctor told IBP that back surgery might be required, Diane Arndt called the doctor and said that IBP had obtained a videotape of Wilson engaging in strenuous physical activities at home. The doctor felt deceived, met with Wilson, accused him of being a liar, refused to provide him with any more treatment, and told him to get back to work. Convinced that no such videotape existed and that IBP had fabricated the entire story in order to deny him medical treatment, Kevin Wilson sued the company for slander.

The lawsuit eventually reached the Iowa Supreme Court. In a decision that received little media attention, the Supreme Court upheld a lower court's award of $2 million to Wilson and described some of IBP's unethical practices. The court found that seriously injured workers were required to show up at the IBP plant briefly each day so that the company could avoid reporting 'lost workdays' to OSHA. Some workers were compelled to show up for work on the same day as a surgery or the day after an amputation. 'IBP's management was aware of, and participated in, this practice,' the Iowa Supreme Court noted. IBP nurses regularly entered false information into the plant's computer system, reclassifying injuries so that they didn't have to be reported to OSHA. Injured workers who proved uncooperative were assigned to jobs 'watching gauges in the rendering plant, where they were subjected to an atrocious smell while hog remains were boiled down into fertilisers and blood was drained into tanks'. According to evidence introduced in court, Diane Arndt had a low opinion of the workers whose injuries she was supposed to be treating. The IBP nurse called them 'idiots' and 'jerks', telling doctors that 'this guy's a cry-baby' and 'this guy's full of shit'. She later admitted that Wilson's back injury was legitimate. The Iowa Supreme Court concluded that the lies she told in this medical case, as well as in others, had been partly motivated by IBP's financial incentive programme, which gave staff members bonuses and prizes when the number of lost workdays was kept low. The programme, in the court's opinion, was 'somewhat disingenuously called "the safety award system"'.

IBP's attitude towards worker safety was hardly unique in the industry, according to Edward Murphy's testimony before Congress in 1992. Murphy had served as the safety director of the Monfort beef plant in Grand Island. After two workers were killed there in 1991, Monfort fired him. Murphy claimed that he had battled the company for years over safety issues and that Monfort had unfairly made him the scapegoat for its own illegal behaviour. The company later paid him an undisclosed sum of money to settle a civil lawsuit over wrongful termination.

Murphy told Congress that during his tenure at the Grand Island plant, Monfort maintained two sets of injury logs, routinely lied to

OSHA, and shredded documents requested by OSHA. He wanted Congress to know that the safety lapses at the plant were not accidental. They stemmed directly from Monfort's corporate philosophy, which Murphy described in these terms: 'The first commandment is that only production counts . . . The employee's duty is to follow orders. Period. As I was repeatedly told, "Do what I tell you, even if it is illegal . . . Don't get caught."'

A lawsuit filed in May 1998 suggests that little has changed since IBP was caught keeping two sets of injury logs more than a decade ago. Michael D. Ferrell, a former vice-president at IBP, contends that the real blame for the high injury rate at the company lies not with the workers, supervisors, nurses, safety directors or plant managers, but with IBP's top executives. Ferrell had ample opportunity to observe their decision-making process. Among other duties, he was in charge of the health and safety programmes at IBP.

When Ferrell accepted the job in 1991, after many years as an industrial engineer at other firms, he believed that IBP's desire to improve worker safety was sincere. According to his legal complaint, Ferrell later discovered that IBP's safety records were routinely falsified and that the company cared more about production than anything else. Ferrell was fired by IBP in 1997, not long after a series of safety problems at a slaughterhouse in Palestine, Texas. The circumstances surrounding his firing are at the heart of the lawsuit. On 4 December 1996, an OSHA inspection of the Palestine plant found a number of serious violations and imposed a fine of $35,125. Less than a week later, a worker named Clarence Dupree lost an arm in a bone-crushing machine. And two days after that, another worker, Willie Morris, was killed by an ammonia gas explosion. Morris's body lay on the floor for hours, just ten feet from the door, as toxic gas filled the building. Nobody at the plant had been trained to use hazardous-materials gas masks or protective suits; the equipment sat in a locked storage room. Ferrell flew to Texas and toured the plant after the accidents. He thought the facility was in terrible shape – with a cooling system that violated OSHA standards, faulty wiring that threatened to cause a mass electrocution, and safety mechanisms that had deliberately been disabled with magnets. He wanted the slaughterhouse to be shut down immediately, and it was. Two months later, Ferrell lost his job.

In his lawsuit seeking payment for wrongful termination, Ferrell contends that he was fired for giving the order to close the Palestine plant. He claims that IBP had never before shut down a slaughterhouse purely for safety reasons and that Robert L. Peterson was enraged by the decision. IBP disputes this version of events, contending that Ferrell had never fitted into IBP's corporate culture, that he delegated too much authority, and that he had not, in fact, made the decision to shut down the Palestine plant. According to IBP, the decision to shut it was made after a unanimous vote by its top executives.

IBP's Palestine slaughterhouse reopened in January 1997. It was shut down again a year later – this time by the US Department of Agriculture. Federal inspectors cited the plant for 'inhumane slaughter' and halted production there for one week, an extremely rare penalty imposed for the mistreatment of cattle. In 1999 IBP closed the plant. As of this writing, it sits empty, awaiting a buyer.

When I first visited Greeley in 1997, Javier Ramirez was president of the UFCW, Local 990, the union representing employees at the Monfort beef plant. The National Labor Relations Board had ruled that Monfort committed 'numerous, pervasive, and outrageous' violations of labour law after reopening the Greeley beef plant in 1982, discriminating against former union members at hiring time and intimidating new workers during a union election. Former employees who'd been treated unfairly ultimately received a $10.6 million settlement. After a long and arduous organising drive, workers at the Monfort beef plant voted to join the UFCW in 1992. Javier Ramirez is thirty-one and knows a fair amount about beef. His father is Ruben Ramirez, the Chicago union leader. Javier grew up around slaughterhouses and watched the meatpacking industry abandon his home town for the High Plains. Instead of finding another line of work, he followed the industry to Colorado, trying to gain better wages and working conditions for the mainly Latino workforce.

The UFCW has given workers in Greeley the ability to challenge unfair dismissals, file grievances against supervisors, and report safety lapses without fear of reprisal. But the union's power is limited by the plant's high turnover rate. Every year a new set of workers must be persuaded to support the UFCW. The plant's revolving door is not conducive to worker solidarity. At the moment some of the most pressing issues for the UFCW are related to the high injury rate at the slaughterhouse. It is a constant struggle not only to prevent workers from getting hurt, but also to gain them proper medical treatment and benefits once they've been hurt.

Colorado was one of the first states to pass a workers' compensation law. The idea behind the legislation, enacted in 1919, was to provide speedy medical care and a steady income to workers injured on the job. Workers' comp was meant to function much like no-fault insurance. In return for surrendering the right to sue employers for injuries, workers were supposed to receive immediate benefits. Similar workers' comp plans were adopted throughout the United States. In 1991, Colorado started another trend, becoming one of the first states to impose harsh restrictions on workers' comp payments. In addition to reducing the benefits afforded to injured employees, Colorado's new law granted employers the right to choose the physician who'd determine the severity of any work-related ailment. Enormous power over workers' comp claims was handed to company doctors.

Many other states subsequently followed Colorado's lead and cut back their workers' comp benefits. The Colorado bill, promoted as 'workers' comp reform', was first introduced in the legislature by Tom Norton, the president of the Colorado State Senate and a conservative Republican. Norton represented Greeley, where his wife, Kay, was the vice-president of legal and governmental affairs at ConAgra Red Meat.

In most businesses, a high injury rate would prompt insurance companies to demand changes in the workplace. But ConAgra, IBP and the other large meatpacking firms are self-insured. They are under no pressure from independent underwriters and have a strong incentive to keep workers' comp payments to a bare minimum. Every penny spent on workers' comp is one less penny of corporate revenue.

Javier Ramirez began to educate Monfort workers about their legal right to get workers' comp benefits after an injury at the plant. Many workers don't realise that such insurance even exists. The workers' comp claim forms look intimidating, especially to people who don't speak any English and can't read any language. Filing a claim, challenging a powerful meatpacking company and placing faith in the American legal system requires a good deal of courage, especially for a recent immigrant.

When a workers' comp claim involves an injury that is nearly impossible to refute (such as an on-the-job amputation), the meatpacking companies generally agree to pay. But when injuries are less visible (such as those stemming from cumulative trauma) the meatpackers often prolong the whole workers' comp process through litigation, insisting upon hearings and filing seemingly endless appeals. Some of the most painful and debilitating injuries are the hardest to prove.

Today it can take years for an injured worker to receive workers' comp benefits. During that time, he or she must pay medical bills and find a source of income. Many rely on public assistance. The ability of meatpacking firms to delay payment discourages many injured workers from ever filing workers' comp claims. It leads others to accept a reduced sum of money as part of a negotiated settlement in order to cover medical bills. The system now leaves countless unskilled and uneducated manual workers poorly compensated for injuries that will forever hamper their ability to earn a living. The few who win in court and receive full benefits are hardly set for life. Under Colorado's new law, the payment for losing an arm is $36,000. An amputated finger gets you anywhere from $2,200 to $4,500, depending on which one is lost. And 'serious permanent disfigurement about the head, face or parts of the body normally exposed to public view' entitles you to a maximum of $2,000.

As workers' comp benefits have become more difficult to obtain, the threat to workplace safety has grown more serious. During the first two years of the Clinton administration, OSHA seemed like a revitalised agency. It began to draw up the first ergonomics standards for the nation's manufacturers, aiming to reduce cumulative trauma disorders. The election of 1994, however, marked a turning point. The Republican majority in Congress that rose to power that year not only impeded the adoption of ergonomics standards but also raised questions about the future of OSHA. Working closely with the US Chamber of Commerce and the National Association of Manufacturers, House Republicans have worked hard to limit OSHA's authority. Congressman Cass Ballenger, a Republican from North Carolina, introduced legislation that would require OSHA to spend at least half of its budget on 'consultation' with businesses, instead of enforcement. This new budget requirement would further reduce the number of OSHA inspections, which by the late 1990s had already reached an all-time low. Ballenger has long opposed OSHA inspections, despite the fact that near his own district a fire at a poultry plant killed twenty-five workers in 1991. The plant had never been inspected by OSHA, its emergency exits had been chained shut, and the bodies of workers were found in piles near the locked doors. Congressman Joel Hefley, a Colorado Republican whose district includes Colorado Springs, has introduced a bill that makes Ballenger's seem moderate. Hefley's 'OSHA Reform Act' would essentially repeal the Occupational Safety and Health Act of 1970. It would forbid OSHA from conducting any workplace inspections or imposing any fines.

MARK CURTIS

Complicity in a Million Deaths

2003

In 1967, Richard Nixon said of Indonesia: 'With its 100 million people and its 300-mile arc of islands containing the world's richest hoard of natural resources, Indonesia is the greatest prize in South-East Asia.' Thirty years later, the World Bank described the dictatorship of General Suharto as 'a model pupil of globalisation'.

As you fly into Jakarta, the capital, you see a city ringed by vast, walled and guarded compounds. These are known as Export Processing Zones, or EPZs, and enclose hundreds of factories that make products for foreign corporations: the 'designer-look' clothes that people buy in a British high street or a shopping mall in America and Australia. Posing as a London fashion buyer, I was given a tour of one such factory, which made clothes for the Gap company, based in San Francisco. I found more than a thousand mostly young women working, battery-style, under the glare of strip lighting, in temperatures that reach 40 degrees centigrade. The only air-conditioning was upstairs where the Taiwanese bosses were. What struck me was the claustrophobia, the sheer frenzy of the production and a fatigue and sadness that were like a presence. The faces were silent, the eyes downcast; limbs moved robotically. The women had no choice about the hours they had to work for little more than a dollar a day, including a notorious 'long shift': thirty-six hours without going home. And these are the 'lucky ones'; in the 'model pupil of globalisation', 36 million people had no work.

Suharto's seizure of power in 1965–66 was critical to Indonesia's conversion to World Bank model pupil. His onslaught on the popular movements that supported the deposed president Sukarno led to what

the CIA called 'the greatest massacre of the second half of the twentieth century'. Up to a million people were slaughtered. Military equipment, logistics, intelligence and propaganda were secretly supplied by
the United States and Britain. Royal Navy warships escorted Suharto's
troop carriers. None of this was reported at the time.

Moreover, according to CIA operations officers I interviewed, the
Suharto terror provided another 'model' – for the American-backed overthrow of Salvador Allende in Chile seven years later, and for 'Operation
Phoenix' in Vietnam, whose American-run death squads assassinated
up to 50,000 people. At the time of writing, a similar campaign is
planned to combat the resistance in American-occupied Iraq.

Thus, Nixon's 'greatest prize' was won, and its booty handed out
in the most spectacular fashion. In 1967, the Time-Life Corporation
sponsored an extraordinary conference in Geneva which, in the course
of three days, designed the 'globalisation' – corporate takeover – of
the world's fifth largest nation. All the corporate giants of the West
were represented: the major oil companies and banks, General Motors,
Imperial Chemical Industries, British Leyland, British American
Tobacco, American Express, Siemens, Goodyear, the International Paper
Corporation, US Steel. They were led by arguably the most powerful
capitalist in the world, David Rockefeller. Across the table were
Suharto's men, known as the 'Berkeley Mafia', as several had enjoyed
US Government scholarships at the University of California in Berkeley.
They were eager to comply; the spoils would be divided with the new
dictatorship they represented.

On the second day of the conference, the entire Indonesian economy
was carved up, sector by sector. One room was allotted to mining,
another to services, others to light industry, forestry, banking and finance.
The Freeport Company got a mountain of copper in West Papua. An
American and European consortium got West Papua's nickel. The giant
Alcoa company got the biggest slice of Indonesia's bauxite. A group
of American, Japanese and French companies got the tropical forests
of Sumatra, West Papua and Kalimantan. A Foreign Investment Law,
hurried on to the statutes by Suharto, made this plunder tax free. Real,
and secret, control of the Indonesian economy passed to the Inter-
Governmental Group on Indonesia (IGGI), whose principal members
were the US, Canada, Europe and Australia, and the International
Monetary Fund and the World Bank. 'The profit potential,' celebrated
a Wall Street investors' report, 'fairly staggers the imagination.'

The then British Foreign Secretary, Michael Stewart, spoke of the 'great potential opportunities to British exporters'. A Foreign Office report lauded the 'potentially rich market' now that 'the economy has been brought under control'. Other euphemisms for mass slaughter abounded.

The dissenting historian Mark Curtis was among the first to document the little-known British role in the massacres of 1965–66. In articles and books, he produced astonishing evidence mined from formerly secret official files in the Public Record Office in London. Indeed, he did as no journalist had done, and his work is a brilliant object lesson in the true nature of power. 'There is no mention in any of the files,' he writes, 'of the morality of [the carve-up]. The slaughter was simply an irrelevance.'

The following passages are from his book *Web of Deceit: Britain's Real Role in the World*.

COMPLICITY IN A MILLION DEATHS

I have never concealed from you my belief that a little shooting in Indonesia would be an essential preliminary to effective change.
> Britain's ambassador to Indonesia,
> letter to the Foreign Office, 1965

In July 1996, I published an article in the *Observer* revealing British complicity in the slaughter of a million people in Indonesia in 1965. The article was based on the release of formerly secret files available at the Public Record Office. I only just managed to persuade the editors to publish it after the *Guardian* turned it down. Following the appearance of the article, I did a couple of minor radio interviews. The story then disappeared into oblivion, with only one or two subsequent mentions in the mainstream media.

I happened to be watching the ITV lunchtime news on 1 January 1997, which carried a report on just-released secret files from 1966. It mentioned two items: a row between prime minister Harold Wilson and the governor of the Bank of England over interest rates; and the world cup football match between England and Argentina. Yet the 1966 files reveal much about the British role in the 1965 slaughters – an everyday indication of media selection that keeps important issues from the public.

The history of British complicity in massive human rights abuses in Indonesia has been buried by the mainstream media and academia. When the Suharto regime fell in May 1998, barely any journalists mentioned that Britain had supported the brutally repressive regime for the past thirty years as well as its murderous accession to power after 1965. Britain supported Indonesia's invasion of East Timor in 1975 – killing 200,000 people, a third of the population – and proceeded to give effective support to Indonesia in its illegal occupation. This basic fact was not noticed by journalists in reporting East Timor's independence from Indonesia in May 2002. Neither did the mainstream media appear to notice Britain's culpability in the human rights abuses committed in East Timor around the historic election in 1999.

The case of Indonesia shows how repressive the political culture is of basic facts when they provide the wrong picture about the role of the state. Perhaps in a democracy the truth would have been reported about British complicity in the tragedies of the peasant families massacred in 1965, the Timorese villagers sliced up by Indonesian troops in 1975, and the families forced to flee Indonesian terror in 1999. Instead, the British role in these tragic plights has been met largely by silence.

'A Necessary Task'

The formerly secret British files, together with recently declassified US files, reveal an astonishing story. Although the Foreign Office is keeping many of the files secret until 2007, a clear picture still emerges of British and US support for one of the post-war world's worst bloodbaths – what US officials at the time called a 'reign of terror' and British officials 'ruthless terror'.

In his 600-page-long autobiography, Denis Healey, then Britain's Defence Minister, failed to mention at all Suharto's brutal seizure of power, let alone Britain's role. It is not hard to see why.

The killings in Indonesia started when a group of army officers loyal to President Sukarno assassinated several generals on 30 September 1965. They believed the generals were about to stage a coup to overthrow Sukarno. The instability, however, provided other anti-Sukarno generals, led by General Suharto, with an excuse for the army to move against a powerful and popular political faction with mass support, the Indonesian Communist Party (PKI). It did so brutally: in a few months hundreds of thousands of PKI members and ordinary people were killed and the PKI destroyed. Suharto emerged as leader and instituted a brutal regime that lasted until 1998.

Close relations between the US and British embassies in Jakarta are indicated in the declassified files and point to a somewhat coordinated joint operation in 1965. These files show five ways in which the Labour government under Harold Wilson together with the Democratic government under Lyndon Johnson were complicit in this slaughter.

First, the British wanted the army to act and encouraged it. 'I have never concealed from you my belief that a little shooting in Indonesia would be an essential preliminary to effective change', the ambassador in Jakarta, Sir Andrew Gilchrist, informed the Foreign Office on 5 October.

The following day the Foreign Office stated that 'the crucial question still remains whether the Generals will pluck up enough courage to take decisive action against the PKI'. Later it noted that 'we must surely prefer an Army to a Communist regime' and declared:

> It seems pretty clear that the Generals are going to need all the help they can get and accept without being tagged as hopelessly pro-Western, if they are going to be able to gain ascendancy over the Communists. In the short run, and while the present confusion continues, we can hardly go wrong by tacitly backing the Generals.

British policy was 'to encourage the emergence of a Generals' regime', one intelligence official later explained.

US officials similarly expressed their hope of 'army at long last to act effectively against Communists' [sic]. 'We are, as always, sympathetic to army's desire to eliminate communist influence' and 'it is important to assure the army of our full support of its efforts to crush the PKI'.

US and British officials had clear knowledge of the killings. US Ambassador Marshall Green noted three weeks after the attempted coup, and with the killings having begun, that: 'Army has . . . been working hard at destroying PKI and I, for one, have increasing respect for its determination and organisation in carrying out this crucial assignment.' Green noted in the same dispatch the 'execution of PKI cadres', putting the figure at 'several hundred of them' in 'Djakarta area alone' [sic].

On 1 November, Green informed the State Department of the army's

'moving relentlessly to exterminate the PKI as far as that is possible
to do'. Three days later he noted that 'Embassy and USG [US
Government] generally sympathetic with and admiring of what army
doing' [*sic*]. Four days after this the US embassy reported that the
army 'has continued systematic drive to destroy PKI in northern
Sumatra with wholesale killings reported'.

A British official reported on 25 November that 'PKI men and
women are being executed in very large numbers.' Some victims 'are
given a knife and invited to kill themselves. Most refuse and are told
to turn around and are shot in the back.' One executioner considered it 'his duty to exterminate what he called "less than animals"'.

A British official wrote to the ambassador on 16 December, saying:

> You – like me – may have been somewhat surprised to see esti-
> mates by the American embassy that well over 100,000 people
> have been killed in the troubles since 1 October. I am, however,
> readier to accept such figures after [receiving] some horrifying
> details of the purges that have been taking place . . . The local
> army commander . . . has a list of PKI members in five cate-
> gories. He has been given orders to kill those in the first three
> categories . . . A woman of 78 . . . was taken away one night
> by a village execution squad . . . Half a dozen heads were neatly
> arranged on the parapet of a small bridge.

The US Consulate in Medan was reporting that 'much indiscriminate killing is taking place':

> Something like a reign of terror against PKI is taking place. This
> terror is not discriminating very carefully between PKI leaders
> and ordinary PKI members with no ideological bond to the party.

By mid-December the State Department noted approvingly that
'Indonesian military leaders' campaign to destroy PKI is moving fairly
swiftly and smoothly.' By 14 February 1966 Ambassador Green could
note that 'the PKI has been destroyed as an effective political force
for some time to come' and that 'the Communists . . . have been decimated by wholesale massacre'.

The British files show that by February 1966 the British ambassador was estimating 400,000 dead – but even this was described by
the Swedish ambassador as a 'gross underestimate'. By March, one

British official wondered 'how much of it [the PKI] is left, after six months of killing' and believed that over 200,000 had been killed in Sumatra alone – in a report called 'The liquidation of the Indonesian Communist Party in Sumatra'. By April, the US embassy stated that 'we frankly do not know whether the real figure is closer to 100,000 or 1,000,000 but believe it wiser to err on the side of the lower estimates, especially when questioned by the press'.

Summarising the events of 1965 the British Consul in Medan said: 'Posing as saviours of the nation from a Communist terror, [the army] unleashed a ruthless terror of their own, the scars of which will take many years to heal.' Another British memo referred to 'an operation carried out on a very large scale and often with appalling savagery'. Another simply referred to the 'bloodbath'.

British and US officials totally supported these massacres, the files show. I could find no reference to any concern about the extent of killing at all – only constant encouragement for the army to continue. As the files above indicate, there is no question that British and US officials knew exactly what they were supporting.

One British official noted, referring to 10,005 people arrested by the army: 'I hope they do not throw the 10,005 into the sea . . . otherwise it will cause quite a shipping hazard.'

It was not only PKI activists who were the targets of this terror. As the British files show, many of the victims were the 'merest rank and file' of the PKI who were 'often no more than bewildered peasants who give the wrong answer on a dark night to bloodthirsty hooligans bent on violence', with the connivance of the army.

Britain connived even more closely with those conducting the slaughter. By 1965, Britain had deployed tens of thousands of troops in Borneo, to defend its former colony of Malaya against Indonesian encroachments following territorial claims by Jakarta – known as the 'confrontation'. British planners secretly noted that they 'did not want to distract the Indonesian Army by getting them engaged in fighting in Borneo and so discourage them from the attempts which they now seem to be making to deal with the PKI'.

The US was worried that Britain might take advantage of the instability in Indonesia to launch an offensive from Singapore 'to stab the good generals in the back', as Ambassador Gilchrist described the US fear.

So the British ambassador proposed reassuring those Indonesians who were ordering mass slaughter, saying that 'we should get word to the Generals that we shall not attack them whilst they are chasing the PKI'. The British intelligence officer in Singapore agreed, believing this 'might ensure that the army is not detracted [*sic*] from what we consider to be a necessary task'.

In October the British passed to the Generals, through a US contact, 'a carefully phrased oral message about not biting the Generals in the back for the present'.

The US files confirm that the message from the US, conveyed on 14 October, read:

> First, we wish to assure you that we have no intention of inter-fering [in] Indonesian internal affairs directly or indirectly. Second, we have good reason to believe that none of our allies intend to initiate any offensive action against Indonesia [*sic*].

The message was greatly welcomed by the Indonesian Army: an aide to the Defence Minister noted that 'this was just what was needed by way of assurances that we (the army) weren't going to be hit from all angles as we moved to straighten things out here'.

According to former BBC correspondent Roland Challis, the coun-sellor at the British embassy, (now Sir) James Murray, was authorised to tell Suharto that in the event of Indonesian troops being trans-ferred from the confrontation area to Java, British forces would not take military advantage. Indeed, in his book, Challis notes a report in an Indonesian newspaper in 1980 stating that Britain even helped an Indonesian colonel transport an infantry brigade on confrontation duty back to Jakarta. 'Flying the Panamanian flag, she sailed safely down the heavily patrolled Malacca Strait – escorted by two British warships', Challis notes.

The third means of support was propaganda operations, mainly involving the distribution of anti-Sukarno messages and stories through the media. This was organised from Britain's MI6 intelligence base in Singapore known as Phoenix Park. The head of these operations, Norman Reddaway, told Roland Challis to 'do anything you can think of to get rid of Sukarno'.

On 5 October Reddaway reported to the Foreign Office in London that:

> We should not miss the present opportunity to use the situation to our advantage . . . I recommend that we should have no

hesitation in doing what we can surreptitiously to blacken the
PKI in the eyes of the army and the people of Indonesia.

The Foreign Office replied:

We certainly do not exclude any unattributable propaganda or
psywar [psychological warfare] activities which would contribute
to weakening the PKI permanently. We therefore agree with the
[above] recommendation . . . Suitable propaganda themes might
be . . . Chinese interference in particular arms shipments; PKI
subverting Indonesia as agents of foreign communists.

It continued:

We want to act quickly while the Indonesians are still off balance
but treatment will need to be subtle . . . Please let us know of
any suggestions you may have on these lines where we could be
helpful at this end.

On 9 October the intelligence officer confirmed that 'we have made
arrangements for distribution of certain unattributable material based
on the general guidance' in the Foreign Office memo. This involved
'promoting and coordinating publicity' critical of the Sukarno government to 'news agencies, newspapers and radio'. 'The impact has been
considerable', one file notes. British propaganda covered in various
newspapers included fabrications of nest-eggs accumulated abroad by
Sukarno's ministers and PKI preparations for a coup by carving up
Jakarta into districts to engage in systematic slaughter (forerunners
of current modern propaganda on Iraq).

The fourth method of support was a 'hit list' of targets supplied
by the US to the Indonesian Army. As the journalist Kathy Kadane
has revealed, as many as 5,000 names of provincial, city and other
local PKI committee members and leaders of the mass organisations
of the PKI, such as the national labour federation, women's and youth
groups, were passed on to the Generals, many of whom were subsequently killed. 'It really was a big help to the army,' noted Robert
Martens, a former official in the US embassy. 'They probably killed
a lot of people and I probably have a lot of blood on my hands, but
that's not all bad. There's a time when you have to strike hard at a
decisive moment.'

The recently declassified US files do not provide many more details about this hit list, although they do further confirm it. One list of names, for example, was passed to the Indonesians in December 1965 and 'is apparently being used by Indonesian security authorities who seem to lack even the simplest overt information on PKI leadership at the time'. Also, 'lists of other officials in the PKI affiliates, Partindo and Baperki, were also provided to GOI [Government of Indonesia] officials at their request'.

The final means of support was provision of arms – although this remains the murkiest area to uncover. Past US support to the Indonesian military 'should have established clearly in minds Army leaders that US stands behind them if they should need help [*sic*]', the State Department noted. US strategy was to 'avoid overt involvement in the power struggle but . . . indicate, clearly but covertly, to key Army officers our desire to assist where we can.'

The first US supplies to the Indonesian Army were radios 'to help in internal security' and to aid the Generals 'in their task of overcoming the Communists', as British Ambassador Gilchrist pointed out. 'I see no reason to object or complain', he added.

The US historian Gabriel Kolko has shown that in early November 1965 the US received a request from the Generals to 'arm Moslem and nationalist youths . . . for use against the PKI'. The recently published files confirm this approach from the Indonesians. On 1 November Ambassador Green cabled Washington that:

As to the provision of small arms I would be leery about telling army we are in position to provide same, although we should act, not close our minds to this possibility . . . We could explore availability of small arms stocks, preferably of non-US origin, which could be obtained without any overt US government involvement. We might also examine channels through which we could, if necessary, provide covert assistance to army for purchase of weapons.

A CIA memo of 9 November stated that the US should avoid being 'too hesitant about the propriety of extending such assistance provided we can do so covertly, in a manner which will not embarrass them or embarrass our government'. It then noted that mechanisms exist or can be created to deliver 'any of the types of the materiel requested to date in reasonable quantities'. One line of text is then not declassified before the memo notes: 'The same can be said of purchasers and transfer agents for such items as small arms, medicine and other items requested.' The memo goes on to note that 'we do not propose that the Indonesian army be furnished such equipment at this time' [*sic*]. However, 'if the army leaders justify their needs in detail . . . it is likely that at least will help ensure their success and provide the basis for future collaboration with the US'. 'The means for covert implementation' of the delivery of arms 'are within our capabilities'.

In response to Indonesia's request for arms, Kolko has shown that the US promised to provide such covert aid, and dubbed the arms 'medicines'. They were approved in a meeting in Washington on 4 December. The declassified files state that 'the army really needed the medicines' and that the US was keen to indicate 'approval in a practical way of the actions of the Indonesian Army'. The extent of arms provided is not revealed in the files but the amount 'the medicines would cost was a mere pittance compared with the advantages that might accrue to the US as a result of "getting in on the ground floor"', one file reads.

The British knew of these arms supplies and it is likely they also approved them. Britain was initially reluctant to see US arms go to the Generals for fear that they might be used by Indonesia in the 'confrontation'. The British files show that the US State Department had 'undertaken to consult with us before they do anything to support the Generals'. It is possible that the US reneged on this commitment; however, in earlier discussions about this possibility, a British official at the embassy in Washington noted that 'I do not think that is very likely'.

The Threat of Independent Development

The struggle between the army and the PKI was 'a struggle basically for the commanding heights of the Indonesian economy', British officials noted. At stake was using the resources of Indonesia for the primary benefit of its people or for businesses, including Western companies.

British and US planners supported the slaughter to promote interests deemed more important than people's lives. London wanted to see a change in regime in Jakarta to bring an end to the 'confrontation'

with Malaya. But commercial interests were just as important. South-
East Asia was 'a major producer of some essential commodities' such
as rubber, copra and chromium ore; 'the defence of the sources of
these products and their denial to a possible enemy are major interests to the Western powers', the Foreign Office noted. This was a
fancy way of saying that the resources would continue to be exploited
by Western business. Indonesia was also strategically located at a
nexus of important trading routes.

British Foreign Secretary Michael Stewart wrote in the middle of
the slaughter:

> It is only the economic chaos of Indonesia which prevents that
> country from offering great potential opportunities to British
> exporters. If there is going to be a deal in Indonesia, as I hope
> one day there may be, I think we ought to take an active part
> and try to secure a slice of the cake ourselves.

Similarly, one Foreign Office memo noted that Indonesia was in a
'state of economic chaos but is potentially rich . . . American exporters,
like their British counterparts, presumably see in Indonesia a potentially rich market once the economy has been brought under control.'

For the US, Under Secretary of State George Ball had noted that
Indonesia 'may be more important to us than South V-N [Vietnam]',
against which the US was at the same time massively stepping up its
assault. 'At stake' in Indonesia, one US memo read, 'are 100 million
people, vast potential resources and a strategically important chain
of islands.'

US priorities were similar in Vietnam and Indonesia: to prevent the
consolidation of an independent nationalist regime that threatened
Western interests and that could be a successful development model
for others.

President Sukarno clearly had the wrong economic priorities. In
1964, British-owned commercial interests had been placed under
Indonesian management and control. However, under the Suharto
regime, the British Foreign Secretary told one Indonesian Army general
that 'we are . . . glad that your government has decided to hand back
the control of British estates to their original owners.'

The US ambassador in Malaysia cabled Washington a year before
the October 1965 events in Indonesia saying that 'our difficulties
with Indonesia stem basically from deliberate, positive GOI

[Government of Indonesia] strategy of seeking to push Britain and the US out of South-East Asia'. George Ball noted in March 1965 that 'our relations with Indonesia are on the verge of falling apart'. 'Not only has the management of the American rubber plants been taken over, but there are dangers of an imminent seizure of the American oil companies.'

According to a US report for President Johnson:

> The [Indonesian] government occupies a dominant position in basic industry, public utilities, internal transportation and communication . . . It is probable that private ownership will disappear and may be succeeded by some form of production-profit-sharing contract arrangements to be applied to all foreign investment.

Overall, 'the avowed Indonesian objective is "to stand on their own feet" in developing their economy, free from foreign, especially Western, influence.'

This was a serious danger that needed to be removed. As noted elsewhere, Third World countries are to develop under overall Western control, not by or for themselves, a truism about US and British foreign policy revealed time and again in the declassified files.

It is customary in the propaganda system to excuse past horrible British and US policies by referring to the Cold War. In Indonesia, the main threat was indigenous nationalism. The British feared 'the resurgence of Communist and radical nationalism'. One US memo says of future PKI policy: 'It is likely that PKI foreign policy decisions, like those of Sukarno, would stress Indonesian national interests above those of Peking, Moscow or international communism in general.'

The real danger was that Indonesia would be too successful, a constant US fear well documented by Kolko and Noam Chomsky in policy towards numerous other countries. A Special National Intelligence Estimate of 1 September 1965 referred to the PKI's moving 'to energise and unite the Indonesian nation' and stated that '*if these efforts succeeded, Indonesia would provide a powerful example for the underdeveloped world and hence a credit to communism and a setback for Western prestige*'. One critical area was the landlessness of the poor peasants – the source of the grinding poverty of most Indonesians – and land reform more generally, the key political issue in rural areas and the smaller cities. The PKI was recognised by British and US officials as the champion of the landless and poor in Indonesia.

Britain was keen to establish good relations with Suharto, which were to remain for thirty years. A year after the beginning of the slaughter, the Foreign Office noted that 'it was very necessary to demonstrate to the Indonesians that we regarded our relations with them as rapidly returning to normal'. Britain was keen to establish 'normal trade' and provide aid, and to express its 'goodwill and confidence' in the new regime. British officials spoke to the new Foreign Minister, Adam Malik, of the 'new relationship which we hope will develop between our two countries'. A Foreign Office brief for the Cabinet said that Britain 'shall do all we can to restore good relations with Indonesia and help her resume her rightful place in the world community'.

There is no mention in any of the files – that I could find – of the morality of engaging with the new regime. The slaughter was simply an irrelevance.

Michael Stewart recalled in his autobiography that he visited Indonesia a year after the killings and was able to 'reach a good understanding with the Foreign Minister, Adam Malik', a 'remarkable man' who was 'evidently resolved to keep his country at peace'. Suharto's regime is 'like Sukarno's, harsh and tyrannical; but it is not aggressive', Stewart stated. Malik later acted as a primary apologist for Indonesian atrocities in East Timor. In 1977, for example, he was reported as saying: '50,000 or 80,000 people might have been killed during the war in East Timor . . . It was war . . . Then what is the big fuss?'

A combination of Western advice, aid and investment helped transform the Indonesian economy into one that, although retaining some nationalist orientation, provided substantial opportunities and profits for Western investors. President Suharto's increasingly corrupt authoritarian regime kept economic order. Japan and the United States, working through consortia and the multilateral banks, used aid as a lever to rewrite Indonesia's basic economic legislation to favour foreign investors. Western businesses moved in. By the mid-1970s, a British CBI report noted that Indonesia presented 'enormous potential for the foreign investor'. The press reported that the country enjoyed a 'favourable political climate' and the 'encouragement of foreign investment by the country's authorities'. RTZ, BP, British Gas and Britoil were some of the companies that took advantage. One consequence was that landlessness increased as land ownership became more concentrated; the peasants were afraid to organise, and the prospects of fundamental economic changes to *primarily* benefit the poor were successfully eradicated even though poverty levels were reduced.

With Suharto gone after May 1998, one British minister at least was able to talk frankly of the regime Britain had supported. It could now be admitted that under Suharto there was 'severe political repression', the 'concentration of economic and political power in a few, extremely corrupt hands', and the 'involvement of the security forces in every tier of social and political life', for example. All these things had been miraculously discovered.

DAVID ARMSTRONG

Drafting a Plan for Global Dominance

2002

Since 11 September 2001, the Bush administration's 'pre-emptive strategy' of threatening and attacking countries is said to have the single aim of defeating terrorism. This is a grand illusion, says David Armstrong in the conclusion to his remarkable investigation into American global power. Drawing on four major planning and policy documents,* he reveals what he calls 'the Plan'. The aim of the Plan 'is for the United States to rule the world . . . It says not that the United States must be more powerful, or most powerful, but that it must be absolutely powerful.'

In a *Harper's Magazine* article entitled 'Dick Cheney's Song of America', Armstrong traces the Plan back to President George Bush Senior in 1990, whose proposal of a 'new world order' at the end of the Cold War was widely misinterpreted as a 'peace dividend'. It was the opposite. Using the language of multilateral diplomacy, Bush was outlining the vision of Dick Cheney, then secretary of defense, and Colin Powell, the newly appointed chairman of the Joint Chiefs of Staff. Their goals were anything but diplomatic. 'I want [the United States] to be the bully on the block,' said Powell, putting the lie to his cultivated image as a 'liberal'. At a point in history that millions believed offered hope, they chose war over peace.

* Defense Planning Guidance for the 1994–1999 Fiscal Years (Draft), Office of the Secretary of Defense, 1992; Defense Planning Guidance for the 1994–1999 Fiscal Years (Revised Draft), Office of the Secretary of Defense, 1992; Defense Strategy for the 1990s, Office of the Secretary of Defense, 1993; Defense Planning Guidance for the 2004–2009 Fiscal Years, Office of the Secretary of Defense, 2002.

The conquest of Iraq was to be the pivot. The 'neo-conservatives' – the jargon description of far-right Republicans, such as Cheney, Donald Rumsfeld and Paul Wolfowitz, who had served Ronald Reagan and the Bush family – wanted Iraq to be 'the message to the world'. Fighting terrorism had nothing to do with it; Saddam Hussein was the sworn foe of Islamic fundamentalism. However, incessant propaganda would 'link' Iraq with al-Qaida in the American public mind, which was the most notable achievement of the 'neo-cons'. Within hours of '9/11', Rumsfeld (who had gone to Baghdad in 1984 to reassure Saddam Hussein that his use of chemical and biological weapons made no difference to his close relationship with the Reagan administration) wrote a memorandum to his aides: 'Judge whether good enough to hit S.H. Go massive. Sweep it all up. Things related and not.'

Iran would be next, then Syria, North Korea, even China. The Plan was to ensure that nothing got in the way of America's dominance of the strategic world, its resources and politics. The Rubicon had been crossed; it was a 'message' as old as Imperial Rome. Days after David Armstrong's *Harper's* article appeared, the Bush administration unveiled its national security strategy, validating Armstrong's revelation that the United States was seeking overwhelming military superiority. Of course, the United States has been seeking military superiority in the world for a long time, and it is striking that David Armstrong, like other liberal American journalists, distinguishes the imperialism of Bush not as a more threatening expression of that which went before; he refers to Clinton's invasion of Haiti, in principle no different from the invasion of Iraq, as an 'ill-fated democracy-building effort'.

David Armstrong is the Washington bureau chief of the National Security News Service, a relatively small organisation specialising in investigation and long distinguished by its revelations from inside government. Among his many exposés is new, previously classified, information about America's secret intention to use 'tactical' nuclear weapons in Vietnam. He is best known for his disclosures of the Bush family's business and intelligence connections. The following analysis of the plans and actions of the very dangerous men around George W. Bush is in the finest tradition of investigative journalism.

DRAFTING A PLAN FOR GLOBAL DOMINANCE

Few writers are more ambitious than the writers of government policy papers, and few policy papers are more ambitious than Dick Cheney's masterwork. It has taken several forms over the last decade and is in fact the product of several ghostwriters (notably Paul Wolfowitz and Colin Powell), but Cheney has been consistent in his dedication to the ideas in the documents that bear his name, and he has maintained a close association with the ideologues behind them. Let us, therefore, call Cheney the author, and this series of documents the Plan.

The Plan was published in unclassified form most recently under the title of Defense Strategy for the 1990s, as Cheney ended his term as secretary of defense under the elder George Bush in early 1993, but it is, like *Leaves of Grass*, a perpetually evolving work. It was the controversial Defense Planning Guidance draft of 1992 – from which Cheney, unconvincingly, tried to distance himself – and it was the somewhat less aggressive revised draft of that same year. In June 2002 it was a presidential lecture in the form of a commencement address at West Point, and in July it was leaked to the press as yet another Defense Planning Guidance (this time under the pen name of Defense Secretary Donald Rumsfeld). It will take its ultimate form, though, as America's new national security strategy – and Cheney et al will experience what few writers have even dared dream: their words will become our reality.

The Plan is for the United States to rule the world. The overt theme is unilateralism, but it is ultimately a story of domination. It calls for the United States to maintain its overwhelming military superiority and prevent new rivals from rising up to challenge it on the world stage. It calls for dominion over friends and enemies alike. It says not that the United States must be more powerful, or most powerful, but that it must be absolutely powerful.

The Plan is disturbing in many ways, and ultimately unworkable. Yet it is being sold now as an answer to the 'new realities' of the post-September 11 world, even as it was sold previously as the answer to the new realities of the post-Cold War world. For Cheney, the Plan has always been the right answer, no matter how different the questions.

Cheney's unwavering adherence to the Plan would be amusing, and maybe a little sad, except that it is now our plan. In its pages are the ideas that we now act upon every day with the full might of the United States military. Strangely, few critics have noted that Cheney's work has a long history, or that it was once quite unpopular, or that it was created in reaction to circumstances that are far removed from the ones we now face. But Cheney is a well-known action man. One has to admire, in a way, the Babe Ruth-like sureness of his political work. He pointed to centre field ten years ago, and now the ball is sailing over the fence.

Before the Plan was about domination it was about money. It took shape in late 1989, when the Soviet threat was clearly on the decline, and, with it, public support for a large military establishment. Cheney seemed unable to come to terms with either new reality. He remained deeply suspicious of the Soviets and strongly resisted all efforts to reduce military spending. Democrats in Congress jeered his lack of strategic vision, and a few within the Bush administration were whispering that Cheney had become an irrelevant factor in structuring a response to the revolutionary changes taking place in the world.

More adaptable was the up-and-coming General Colin Powell, the newly appointed chairman of the Joint Chiefs of Staff. As Ronald Reagan's national security adviser, Powell had seen the changes taking place in the Soviet Union first hand and was convinced that the ongoing transformation was irreversible. Like Cheney, he wanted to avoid military cuts, but he knew they were inevitable. The best he could do was minimise them, and the best way to do that would be to offer a new security structure that would preserve American military capabilities despite reduced resources.

Powell and his staff believed that a weakened Soviet Union would result in shifting alliances and regional conflict. The United States was the only nation capable of managing the forces at play in the world; it would have to remain the pre-eminent military power in order to ensure the peace and shape the emerging order in accordance with American interests. US military strategy, therefore, would have to shift from global containment to managing less-well-defined regional struggles and unforeseen contingencies. To do this, the United States would have to project a military 'forward presence' around the world; there would be fewer troops but in more places. This plan still would not be cheap, but through careful restructuring and superior technology, the job could be done with 25 per cent fewer troops. Powell insisted that maintaining superpower status must be the first priority of the US military. 'We have to put a shingle outside our door saying,

"Superpower Lives Here", no matter what the Soviets do,' he said at the time. He also insisted that the troop levels he proposed were the bare minimum necessary to do so. This concept would come to be known as the 'Base Force'.

Powell's work on the subject proved timely. The Berlin Wall fell on 9 November 1989, and five days later Powell had his new strategy ready to present to Cheney. Even as decades of repression were ending in Eastern Europe, however, Cheney still could not abide even the force and budget reductions Powell proposed. Yet he knew that cuts were unavoidable. Having no alternative of his own to offer, there-fore, he reluctantly encouraged Powell to present his ideas to the pres-' ident. Powell did so the next day; Bush made no promises but encouraged him to keep at it.

Less encouraging was the reaction of Paul Wolfowitz, the under-secretary of defense for policy. A lifelong proponent of the unilater-alist, maximum-force approach, he shared Cheney's scepticism about the Eastern bloc and so put his own staff to work on a competing plan that would somehow accommodate the possibility of Soviet backsliding.

As Powell and Wolfowitz worked out their strategies, Congress was losing patience. New calls went up for large cuts in defence spending in light of the new global environment. The harshest critique of Pentagon planning came from a usually dependable ally of the military establishment, Georgia Democrat Sam Nunn, chairman of the Senate Armed Services Committee. Nunn told fellow senators in March 1990 that there was a 'threat blank' in the administra-tion's proposed $295 billion defence budget and that the Pentagon's 'basic assessment of the overall threat to our national security' was 'rooted in the past'. The world had changed and yet the 'develop-ment of a new military strategy that responds to the changes in the threat has not yet occurred'. Without that response, no dollars would be forthcoming.

Nunn's message was clear. Powell and Wolfowitz began filling in the blanks. Powell started promoting a Zen-like new rationale for his Base Force approach. With the Soviets rapidly becoming irrele-vant, Powell argued, the United States could no longer assess its mili-tary needs on the basis of known threats. Instead, the Pentagon should focus on maintaining the ability to address a wide variety of new and unknown challenges. This shift from a 'threat-based' assess-ment of military requirements to a 'capability-based' assessment would become a key theme of the Plan. The United States would move from countering Soviet attempts at dominance to ensuring its own dominance. Again, this project would not be cheap.

Powell's argument, circular though it may have been, proved sufficient to hold off Congress. Winning support among his own colleagues, however, proved more difficult. Cheney remained deeply sceptical about the Soviets, and Wolfowitz was only slowly coming around. To account for future uncertainties, Wolfowitz recommended drawing down US forces to roughly the levels proposed by Powell, but doing so at a much slower pace: seven years as opposed to the four Powell suggested. He also built in a 'crisis response/reconstitution' clause that would allow for reversing the process if events in the Soviet Union, or elsewhere, turned ugly.

With these new elements in place, Cheney saw something that might work. By combining Powell's concepts with those of Wolfowitz, he could counter congressional criticism that his proposed defence budget was out of line with the new strategic reality, while leaving the door open for future force increases. In late June, Wolfowitz, Powell and Cheney presented their plan to the president, and within a few weeks Bush was unveiling the new strategy.

Bush laid out the rationale for the Plan in a speech in Aspen, Colorado, on 2 August 1990. He explained that since the danger of global war had substantially receded, the principal threats to American security would emerge in unexpected quarters. To counter those threats, he said, the United States would increasingly base the size and structure of its forces on the need to respond to 'regional contingencies' and maintain a peacetime military presence overseas. Meeting that need would require maintaining the capability to quickly deliver American forces to any 'corner of the globe', and that would mean retaining many major weapons systems then under attack in Congress as overly costly and unnecessary, including the 'Star Wars' missile-defence programme. Despite those massive outlays, Bush insisted that the proposed restructuring would allow the United States to draw down its active forces by 25 per cent in the years ahead, the same figure Powell had projected ten months earlier.

The Plan's debut was well timed. By a remarkable coincidence, Bush revealed it the very day Saddam Hussein's Iraqi forces invaded Kuwait.

The Gulf War temporarily reduced the pressure to cut military spending. It also diverted attention from some of the Plan's less appealing aspects. In addition, it inspired what would become one of the Plan's key features: the use of 'overwhelming force' to quickly defeat enemies, a concept since dubbed the Powell Doctrine.

Once the Iraqi threat was 'contained', Wolfowitz returned to his obsession with the Soviets, planning various scenarios involving possible Soviet intervention in regional conflicts. The failure of the hard-liner coup against Gorbachev in August 1991, however, made it apparent that such planning might be unnecessary. Then, in late December, just as the Pentagon was preparing to put the Plan in place, the Soviet Union collapsed.

With the Soviet Union gone, the United States had a choice. It could capitalise on the euphoria of the moment by nurturing cooperative relations and developing multilateral structures to help guide the global realignment then taking place; or it could consolidate its power and pursue a strategy of unilateralism and global dominance. It chose the latter course.

In early 1992, as Powell and Cheney campaigned to win congressional support for their augmented Base Force plan, a new logic entered into their appeals. The United States, Powell told members of the House Armed Services Committee, required 'sufficient power' to 'deter any challenger from ever dreaming of challenging us on the world stage'. To emphasise the point, he cast the United States in the role of street thug. 'I want to be the bully on the block,' he said, implanting in the mind of potential opponents that 'there is no future in trying to challenge the armed forces of the United States'.

As Powell and Cheney were making this new argument in their congressional rounds, Wolfowitz was busy expanding the concept and working to have it incorporated into US policy. During the early months of 1992, Wolfowitz supervised the preparation of an internal Pentagon policy statement used to guide military officials in the preparation of their forces, budgets and strategies. The classified document, known as the Defense Planning Guidance (DPG), depicted a world dominated by the United States, which would maintain its superpower status through a combination of positive guidance and overwhelming military might. The image was one of a heavily armed City on a Hill.

The DPG stated that the 'first objective' of US defence strategy was 'to prevent the re-emergence of a new rival'. Achieving this objective required that the United States 'prevent any hostile power from dominating a region' of strategic significance. America's new mission would be to convince allies and enemies alike 'that they need not aspire to a greater role or pursue a more aggressive posture to protect their legitimate interests'.

Another new theme was the use of pre-emptive military force. The options, the DPG noted, ranged from taking pre-emptive military action to head off a nuclear, chemical or biological attack to 'punishing' or 'threatening punishment of' aggressors 'through a variety of means', including strikes against weapons-manufacturing facilities.

The DPG also envisioned maintaining a substantial US nuclear arsenal while discouraging the development of nuclear programmes in other countries. It depicted a 'US-led system of collective security' that implicitly precluded the need for rearmament of any kind by countries such as Germany and Japan. And it called for the 'early introduction' of a global missile-defence system that would presumably render all missile-launched weapons, including those of the United States, obsolete. (The United States would, of course, remain the world's dominant military power on the strength of its other weapons systems.)

The story, in short, was dominance by way of unilateral action and military superiority. While coalitions – such as the one formed during the Gulf War – held 'considerable promise for promoting collective action', the draft DPG stated, the United States should expect future alliances to be '*ad hoc* assemblies, often not lasting beyond the crisis being confronted, and in many cases carrying only general agreement over the objectives to be accomplished'. It was essential to create 'the sense that the world order is ultimately backed by the US' and essential that America position itself 'to act independently when collective action cannot be orchestrated' or in crisis situations requiring immediate action. 'While the US cannot become the world's "policeman",' the document said, 'we will retain the pre-eminent responsibility for addressing selectively those wrongs which threaten not only our interests, but those of our allies or friends.' Among the interests the draft indicated the United States would defend in this manner were 'access to vital raw materials, primarily Persian Gulf oil, proliferation of weapons of mass destruction and ballistic missiles, [and] threats to US citizens from terrorism'.

The DPG was leaked to the *New York Times* in March 1992. Critics on both the left and the right attacked it immediately. Then-presidential candidate Pat Buchanan portrayed it as giving a 'blank cheque' to America's allies by suggesting the United States would 'go to war to defend their interests'. Bill Clinton's deputy campaign manager, George Stephanopoulos, characterised it as an attempt by Pentagon officials to 'find an excuse for big defence budgets instead of down-sizing'. Delaware Senator Joseph Biden criticised the Plan's vision of a 'Pax Americana, a global security system where threats to stability are suppressed or destroyed by US military power'. Even those who found the document's stated goals commendable feared that its chau-vinistic tone could alienate many allies. Cheney responded by attempting to distance himself from the Plan. The Pentagon's spokesman dismissed the leaked document as a 'low-level draft' and claimed that Cheney had not seen it. Yet a fifteen-page section opened by proclaiming that it constituted 'definitive guidance from the secretary of defense'.

Powell took a more forthright approach to dealing with the flak: he publicly embraced the DPG's core concept. In a TV interview, he said he believed it was 'just fine' that the United States reign as the world's dominant military power. 'I don't think we should apologise for that,' he said. Despite bad reviews in the foreign press, Powell insisted that America's European allies were 'not afraid' of US military might because it was 'power that could be trusted' and 'will not be misused'.

Mindful that the draft DPG's overt expression of US dominance might not fly, Powell in the same interview also trotted out a new rationale for the original Base Force plan. He argued that in a post-Soviet world, filled with new dangers, the United States needed the ability to fight on more than one front at a time. 'One of the most destabilising things we could do,' he said, 'is to cut our forces so much that if we're tied up in one area of the world . . . and we are not seen to have the ability to influence another area of the world, we might invite just the sort of crisis we're trying to deter.' This two-war strategy provided a possible answer to Nunn's 'threat blank'. One unknown enemy wasn't enough to justify lavish defence budgets, but two unknown enemies might do the trick.

Within a few weeks the Pentagon had come up with a more compre-hensive response to the DPG furore. A revised version was leaked to the press that was significantly less strident in tone, though only slightly less strident in fact. While calling for the United States to prevent 'any hostile power from dominating a region critical to our interests', the new draft stressed that America would act in concert with its allies – when possible. It also suggested the United Nations might take an expanded role in future political, economic and secu-rity matters, a concept conspicuously absent from the original draft.

The controversy died down, and, with a presidential campaign under way, the Pentagon did nothing to stir it up again. Following

Bush's defeat, however, the Plan re-emerged. In January 1993, in his very last days in office, Cheney released a final version. The newly titled Defense Strategy for the 1990s retained the soft touch of the revised draft DPG as well as its darker themes. The goal remained to preclude 'hostile competitors from challenging our critical interests' and preventing the rise of a new superpower. Although it expressed a 'preference' for collective responses in meeting such challenges, it made clear that the United States would play the lead role in any alliance. Moreover, it noted that collective action would 'not always be timely'. Therefore, the United States needed to retain the ability to 'act independently, if necessary'. To do so would require that the United States maintain its massive military superiority. Others were not encouraged to follow suit. It was kinder, gentler dominance, but it was dominance all the same. And it was this thesis that Cheney and company nailed to the door on their way out.

The new administration tacitly rejected the heavy-handed, unilateral approach to US primacy favoured by Powell, Cheney and Wolfowitz. Taking office in the relative calm of the early post-Cold War era, Clinton sought to maximise America's existing position of strength and promote its interests through economic diplomacy, multilateral institutions (dominated by the United States), greater international free trade, and the development of allied coalitions, including American-led collective military action. American policy, in short, shifted from global dominance to globalism.

Clinton also failed to prosecute military campaigns with sufficient vigour to satisfy the defence strategists of the previous administration. Wolfowitz found Clinton's Iraq policy especially infuriating. During the Gulf War, Wolfowitz harshly criticised the decision – endorsed by Powell and Cheney – to end the war once the UN mandate of driving Saddam's forces from Kuwait had been fulfilled, leaving the Iraqi dictator in office. He called on the Clinton administration to finish the job by arming Iraqi opposition forces and sending US ground troops to defend a base of operation for them in the southern region of the country. In a 1996 editorial, Wolfowitz raised the prospect of launching a pre-emptive attack against Iraq. 'Should we sit idly by,' he wrote, 'with our passive containment policy and our inept covert operations, and wait until a tyrant possessing large quantities of weapons of mass destruction and sophisticated delivery systems strikes out at us?' Wolfowitz suggested it was 'necessary' to 'go beyond the containment strategy'.

Wolfowitz's objections to Clinton's military tactics were not limited to Iraq. Wolfowitz had endorsed President Bush's decision in late 1992 to intervene in Somalia on a limited humanitarian basis. Clinton later expanded the mission into a broader peace-keeping effort, a move that ended in disaster. With perfect twenty-twenty hindsight, Wolfowitz decried Clinton's decision to send US troops into combat 'where there is no significant US national interest'. He took a similar stance on Clinton's ill-fated democracy-building effort in Haiti, chastising the president for engaging 'American military prestige' on an issue 'of little or no importance' to US interests. Bosnia presented a more complicated mix of posturing and ideologies. While running for president, Clinton had scolded the Bush administration for failing to take action to stem the flow of blood in the Balkans. Once in office, however, and chastened by their early misadventures in Somalia and Haiti, Clinton and his advisers struggled to articulate a coherent Bosnia policy. Wolfowitz complained in 1994 of the administration's failure to 'develop an effective course of action'. He personally advocated arming the Bosnian Muslims in their fight against the Serbs. Powell, on the other hand, publicly cautioned against intervention. In 1995 a US-led NATO bombing campaign, combined with a Croat-Muslim ground offensive, forced the Serbs into negotiations, leading to the Dayton Peace Accords. In 1999, as Clinton rounded up support for joint US–NATO action in Kosovo, Wolfowitz hectored the president for failing to act quickly enough.

After eight years of what Cheney et al regarded as wrongheaded military adventures and pinprick retaliatory strikes, the Clinton administration – mercifully, in their view – came to an end. With the ascension of George W. Bush to the presidency, the authors of the Plan returned to government, ready to pick up where they had left off. Cheney, of course, became vice-president, Powell became secretary of state, and Wolfowitz moved into the number-two slot at the Pentagon, as Donald Rumsfeld's deputy. Other contributors also returned: two prominent members of the Wolfowitz team that crafted the original DPG took up posts on Cheney's staff. I. Lewis 'Scooter' Libby, who served as Wolfowitz's deputy during Bush I, became the vice-president's chief of staff and national security adviser. And Eric Edelman, an assistant deputy undersecretary of defense in the first Bush administration, became a top foreign policy adviser to Cheney.

Cheney and company had not changed their minds during the Clinton interlude about the correct course for US policy, but they did not initially appear bent on resurrecting the Plan. Rather than present a unified vision of foreign policy to the world, in the early going the administration focused on promoting a series of seemingly unrelated initiatives. Notable among these were missile defence and space-based weaponry, longstanding conservative causes. In addition, a distinct tone of unilateralism emerged as the new administration announced its intent to abandon the Anti-Ballistic Missile Treaty with Russia in order to pursue missile defence; its opposition to US ratification of an international nuclear-test-ban pact; and its refusal to become a party to an International Criminal Court. It also raised the prospect of ending the self-imposed US moratorium on nuclear testing initiated by the president's father during the 1992 presidential campaign. Moreover, the administration adopted a much tougher diplomatic posture, as evidenced, most notably, by a distinct hardening of relations with both China and North Korea. While none of this was inconsistent with the concept of US dominance, these early actions did not, at the time, seem to add up to a coherent strategy.

It was only after September 11 that the Plan emerged in full. Within days of the attacks, Wolfowitz and Libby began calling for unilateral military action against Iraq, on the shaky premise that Osama bin Laden's al-Qaida network could not have pulled off the assaults without Saddam Hussein's assistance. At the time, Bush rejected such appeals, but Wolfowitz kept pushing and the president soon came around. In his State of the Union address in January 2002, Bush labelled Iraq, Iran and North Korea an 'axis of evil', and warned that he would 'not wait on events' to prevent them from using weapons of mass destruction against the United States. He reiterated his commitment to preemption in his West Point speech in June. 'If we wait for threats to fully materialise we will have waited too long,' he said. 'We must take the battle to the enemy, disrupt his plans and confront the worst threats before they emerge.' Although it was less noted, Bush in that same speech also reintroduced the Plan's central theme. He declared that the United States would prevent the emergence of a rival power by maintaining 'military strengths beyond challenge'. With that, the president effectively adopted a strategy his father's administration had developed ten years earlier to ensure that the United States would remain the world's pre-eminent power. While the headlines screamed 'preemption', no one noticed the declaration of the dominance strategy.

In case there was any doubt about the administration's intentions, the Pentagon's new DPG lays them out. Signed by Wolfowitz's new boss, Donald Rumsfeld, in May 2002 and leaked to the *Los Angeles Times* in July, it contains all the key elements of the original Plan and adds several complementary features. The pre-emptive strikes envisioned in the original draft DPG are now 'unwarned attacks'. The old Powell–Cheney notion of military 'forward presence' is now 'forward deterrence'. The use of overwhelming force to defeat an enemy called for in the Powell Doctrine is now labelled an 'effects-based' approach.

Some of the names have stayed the same. Missile defence is back, stronger than ever, and the call goes up again for a shift from a 'threat-based' structure to a 'capabilities-based' approach. The new DPG also emphasises the need to replace the so-called Cold War strategy of preparing to fight two major conflicts simultaneously with what the *Los Angeles Times* refers to as 'a more complex approach aimed at dominating air and space on several fronts'. This, despite the fact that Powell had originally conceived – and the first Bush administration had adopted – the two-war strategy as a means of filling the 'threat blank' left by the end of the Cold War.

Rumsfeld's version adds a few new ideas, most impressively the concept of pre-emptive strikes with nuclear weapons. These would be earth-penetrating nuclear weapons used for attacking 'hardened and deeply buried targets', such as command-and-control bunkers, missile silos, and heavily fortified underground facilities used to build and store weapons of mass destruction. The concept emerged earlier this year when the administration's Nuclear Posture Review (NPR) leaked out. At the time, arms-control experts warned that adopting the NPR's recommendations would undercut existing arms-control treaties, do serious harm to non-proliferation efforts, set off new rounds of testing, and dramatically increase the prospects of nuclear weapons being used in combat. Despite these concerns, the administration appears intent on developing the weapons. In a final flourish, the DPG also directs the military to develop cyber-, laser- and electronic-warfare capabilities to ensure US dominion over the heavens.

Rumsfeld spelled out these strategies in *Foreign Affairs* earlier this year, and it is there that he articulated the remaining elements of the Plan: unilateralism and global dominance. Like the revised DPG of 1992, Rumsfeld feigns interest in collective action but ultimately rejects it as impractical. 'Wars can benefit from coalitions,' he writes, 'but they should not be fought by committee.' And coalitions, he adds, 'must not determine the mission'. The implication is the United States will determine the missions and lead the fights. Finally, Rumsfeld expresses the key concept of the Plan: preventing the emergence of rival powers. Like the original draft DPG of 1992, he states that America's goal is to develop and maintain the military strength necessary to 'dissuade' rivals or adversaries from 'competing'. With no challengers, and a proposed defence budget of $379 billion for next year, the United States would reign over all it surveys.

Reaction to the latest edition of the Plan has, thus far, focused on pre-emption. Commentators parrot the administration's line, portraying the concept of pre-emptory strikes as a 'new' strategy aimed at combating terrorism. In an op-ed piece for the *Washington Post* following Bush's West Point address, former Clinton adviser William Galston described pre-emption as part of a 'brand-new security doctrine', and warned of possible negative diplomatic consequences. Others found the concept more appealing. Loren Thompson of the conservative Lexington Institute hailed the 'Bush Doctrine' as 'a necessary response to the new dangers that America faces' and declared it 'the biggest shift in strategic thinking in two generations'. *Wall Street Journal* editor Robert Bartley echoed that sentiment, writing that 'no talk of this ilk has been heard from American leaders since John Foster Dulles talked of rolling back the Iron Curtain.'

Pre-emption, of course, is just part of the Plan, and the Plan is hardly new. It is a warmed-over version of the strategy Cheney and his co-authors rolled out in 1992 as the answer to the end of the Cold War. Then the goal was global dominance, and it met with bad reviews. Now it is the answer to terrorism. The emphasis is on pre-emption, and the reviews are generally enthusiastic. Through all of this, the dominance motif remains, though largely undetected.

This country once rejected 'unwarned' attacks such as Pearl Harbor as barbarous and unworthy of a civilised nation. Today many cheer the prospect of conducting sneak attacks – potentially with nuclear weapons – on piddling powers run by tin-pot despots.

We also once denounced those who tried to rule the world. Our primary objection (at least officially) to the Soviet Union was its quest for global domination. Through the successful employment of the tools of containment, deterrence, collective security, and diplomacy – the very methods we now reject – we rid ourselves and the world of the Evil Empire. Having done so, we now pursue the very thing for which we opposed it. And now that the Soviet Union is gone, there appears to be no one left to stop us.

Perhaps, however, there is. The Bush administration and its loyal opposition seem not to grasp that the quests for dominance generate backlash. Those threatened with pre-emption may themselves launch pre-emptory strikes. And even those who are successfully 'pre-empted' or dominated may object and find means to strike back. Pursuing such strategies may, paradoxically, result in greater factionalism and rivalry, precisely the things we seek to end.

Not all Americans share Colin Powell's desire to be 'the bully on the block'. In fact, some believe that by following a different path the United States has an opportunity to establish a more lasting security environment. As Dartmouth professors Stephen Brooks and William Wohlforth wrote recently in *Foreign Affairs*, 'Unipolarity makes it possible to be the global bully – but it also offers the United States the luxury of being able to look beyond its immediate needs to its own, and the world's, long-term interests . . . Magnanimity and restraint in the face of temptation are tenets of successful statecraft that have proved their worth.' Perhaps, in short, we can achieve our desired ends by means other than global domination.

REPORTING THE TRUTH ABOUT IRAQ

John Pilger introduces Felicity Arbuthnot, Joy Gordon, Richard Norton-Taylor, Robert Fisk and Jo Wilding

1998–2004

'Few of us,' wrote the playwright Arthur Miller, 'can easily surrender our belief that society must somehow make sense. The thought that the state has lost its mind and is punishing so many innocent people is intolerable. And so the evidence must be internally denied.'

In October 1999, I stood in a ward of dying children in Baghdad with Denis Halliday, who had recently resigned as Assistant Secretary-General of the United Nations. He said,

> The very provisions of the Charter of the United Nations and the Declaration of Human Rights are being set aside. We are waging a war, through the United Nations, on the children and people of Iraq, and with incredible results: results that you do not expect to see in a war under the Geneva Conventions. We're targeting civilians. Worse, we're targeting children . . . What is this all about? It's a monstrous situation, for the United Nations, for the Western world, for all of us who are part of some democratic system, who are in fact responsible for the policies of our governments and the implementation of sanctions on Iraq.

Halliday had been thirty-four years with the UN. As one of the most respected in his field of 'helping people, not harming them', as he put it, he had been sent to Iraq to take charge of humanitarian relief under the so-called Oil for Food Programme, which he subsequently denounced as a sham. 'I am resigning,' he wrote, 'because the policy of economic sanctions is . . . destroying an entire society. Five thousand children are dying every month . . . I don't want to administer a programme that satisfies the definition of genocide . . .'

Halliday's successor in Iraq, Hans von Sponeck, another Assistant Secretary-General with more than thirty years' service, also resigned in protest. Jutta Burghardt, the head of the World Food Programme in Iraq, followed them, saying she could no longer tolerate what was being done to the Iraqi people. Their collective action was unprecedented.

The Oil for Food Programme, administered by the UN Security Council in New York, allowed little more than $100 for each Iraqi to live on for a year. This had to pay for the entire society's infrastructure and essential services, such as power and water. Moreover, American and British officials knew that the economic and humanitarian siege of Iraq, which they had driven since its imposition in August 1990, would have a devastating impact on a nation almost entirely dependent on imports.

No modern society can survive without infrastructure and, as official documents show, Iraq's had been crippled deliberately by the American-led bombardment in 1991. On 22 January 1991, the US Defense Intelligence Agency reported that 'unless water treatment supplies are exempted from UN sanctions for humanitarian reasons, no adequate solution exists . . .' The report anticipated epidemics of cholera, hepatitis and typhoid, and predicted that 'full degradation of the water treatment system probably will take another six months'. In fact, it took about a month. Visiting Iraq in the wake of the war, UN Under Secretary-General Martti Ahtisaari reported that the effects of the bombing of infrastructure were 'near apocalyptic'. Twenty-eight hospitals had been hit, along with major water and sewage facilities, all eight of Iraq's hydropower dams and grain storage silos and irrigation systems. Unless Iraq was helped, wrote Ahtisaari, 'it is unmistakable that the Iraqi people may soon be facing a further imminent catastrophe . . .'

He was right, and the cost in lives was staggering. Between 1991 and 1998, reported the United Nations Children's Fund (UNICEF), 500,000 children under the age of five had died, unable to cope with chronic malnutrition, polluted water and the lack of medical care. 'If you include adults,' said Denis Halliday, 'the figure is now almost certainly well over a million.' In 1999, seventy members of the US Congress appealed to President Clinton to lift the embargo and end what they called 'infanticide masquerading as policy'. The Clinton administration had already given its reply. In 1996, in an interview on the American current affairs programme *60 Minutes*, Madeleine Albright, then US Ambassador to the United Nations, had been asked: 'We have heard that half a million children have died . . . is the price worth it?' Albright had replied, ' . . . We think the price is worth it.'

The American television company CBS has since refused to allow the videotape of that interview to be shown again and the reporter will not discuss it. Halliday and von Sponeck are *persona non grata* in most of the American and British media, whereas Albright's auto-biography, published in 2003, was reviewed widely and favourably in Britain, with not a single mention of Iraq and her dismissal of the deaths of half a million infants.

As of July 2002, more than $5 billion worth of humanitarian supplies, approved by the UN Sanctions Committee and paid for by Iraq, were blocked by the Bush administration, backed by the Blair government. They included items related to food, health, water and sanitation, agri-culture and education. Not a single reference to this is to be found in the American and British mainstream media. Instead, Saddam Hussein was blamed incessantly for 'diverting' and 'hoarding' UN supplies: a charge made by George W. Bush and Tony Blair as often as they made false claims about his weapons of mass destruction. Almost no journalist challenged them. Saddam was, after all, 'The Beast of Baghdad'. That records of the UN Sanctions Committee show no evidence to support allegations that UN supplies were 'diverted' by the regime or culpably withheld was never news. When Halliday and von Sponeck described the rigorous monitoring of supplies in Iraq, overseen by them and a hundred of their UN colleagues, they were abused as 'apologists for Saddam'.

Of course, there is little doubt that had the tyrant foretold political advantage in starving and otherwise denying his people, he would have done so. In truth, he was a beneficiary of the embargo, which actually reinforced his domestic position, ensuring direct state control over people's lives through their dependence on the apparatus of the state for survival.

The same suppression applied to the bombing of Iraq during the 1990s by the United States and Britain. On average, Iraq was hit with

bombs or missiles every three days since the ceasefire that purport-
edly ended the first Gulf War in 1991. The longest Anglo-American
bombing campaign in history, this received scant media attention,
even though, as UN documents show, farming communities, fishing
villages and other civilian targets were struck. In 1999, the United
States faced a 'genuine dilemma' in Iraq, reported the *Wall Street
Journal*. 'After eight years of enforcing a no fly zone in northern [and
southern] Iraq, few military targets remain. "We're down to the last
outhouse," one US official protested.'

At a time when Iraq continues to dominate the news, this section
of *Tell Me No Lies* will, it is hoped, serve to counter some of the
censorship of 'our' crimes in Iraq, which rival those of our former
client, Saddam Hussein. The suppression is not far removed from the
denial of the Jewish Holocaust and bears a striking likeness to the
'missing' phases in the reporting of the genocide in Cambodia, identified by Noam Chomsky and Edward Herman in their book *Manufacturing Consent: The Political Economy of the Mass Media* (1988).

The work of five people follows: Felicity Arbuthnot is an irrepressible
journalist who evokes the maverick spirit of Martha Gellhorn. Having
made the dangerous overland journey to Iraq many times, she has
often been a lone voice on Iraq in the British press. Two articles by
her are followed by Joy Gordon's 'Cool War: Economic Sanctions as
a Weapon of Mass Destruction', which originally appeared in *Harper's
Magazine* in the United States. That the author is an academic, not
a journalist, is significant; in the United States, I could find no equivalent journalistic inquiry into the effects of sanctions and, in that sense,
her work demonstrates the great negative power of the media. Richard
Norton-Taylor of the *Guardian* is another honourable exception, whose
contacts in the intelligence world have neither undermined his independence nor dimmed his anger at the deceit of politicians, as 'Under
a False Pretext', a selection of his reporting and analysis on Iraq,
demonstrates. Robert Fisk's investigation published in the *Independent*
in 2003, 'Another Day in the Bloody Death of Iraq', cuts like a stiff
breeze through the 'fog' of the occupation, as does Jo Wilding in
'Eyewitness in Falluja'.

In April 2004, American forces attacked the Iraqi city of Falluja
with seventy-ton main battle tanks, bombers and helicopter gunships.
Hospitals reported 600 dead and 1,700 wounded, at least half of them
women, children and the elderly. Compared with the recent terrorist
bombing of Madrid, the media expressed no discernible outrage at

the spectacle of a superpower's massacre of slum dwellers. Jo Wilding, a young British human rights observer, went where only a few free-lance correspondents dared to go. Her raw dispatch, 'Eyewitness in Falluja', published on the worldwide web, is the best and bravest eyewitness journalism.

FELICITY ARBUTHNOT
Iraq: The Unending War
1998–99

Jassim, the Little Poet – R.I.P.

In February, in a hospital in Baghdad, I met thirteen-year-old Jassim. Suffering from a virulent form of leukaemia, he was lying listlessly, watching his small world of the ward through huge dark eyes, made larger by the contrast with his beautiful, pale, almost translucent, skin. His thick, black, curly hair shone as if it had been polished, belying his precarious state of health.

Until he became ill, he had been selling cigarettes in the street, in his home town of Basra, in southern Iraq. Basra, Iraq's ancient second city, was bombarded mercilessly in the 1991 Gulf War, lying literally in the eye of Desert Storm. The sixfold increase in childhood cancers in Iraq has been linked to the use of missiles and bullets coated with depleted uranium (DU), waste from the nuclear industry, which on impact left a residue of radioactive dust throughout the country. Whilst there is an epidemic of cancer throughout Iraq, in Basra it is an explosion. 'If DU enters the body, it has the potential to generate significant medical consequences. The risks associated with DU in the body are both chemical and radiological,' states the US Army Environmental Policy Institute. The residual dust, travelling where the wind blows, remains radioactive for 4,500 million years.

As a result of the embargo, child labour is now another endemic tragedy in a country which had previously deemed good education so paramount that parents were fined for not sending their children to school. As I sat down to talk to Jassim, the doctor mentioned that I made my living by writing.

The transformation was instant: he sat up, his face lit with anima-tion and excitement, and produced an exercise book from under his pillow. Mickey Mouse decorated the cover, and inside, in beautiful Arabic, were the poems he spent his days writing. He was going to be a poet when he grew up. They were extraordinary in their craft, talent and insight far exceeding his years.

One, called 'The Identity Card', read:

> The name is love,
> The class is mindless,
> The school is suffering,
> The governorate is sadness,
> The city is sighing,
> The street is misery,
> The home number is one thousand sighs.

He had collected quotes special to him. 'Life does not take into consideration our passion' was one, and another: 'I asked death what is greater than you, separation of lovers is greater than death.' He watched my face intently for my reaction to the content of his little book. I was lost for words. Eventually I said, 'Jassim, you must fight as hard as you can and get well, because you are already the most astonishingly talented poet. If you can create art like this at thirteen, I cannot imagine what you will have achieved by the time you are twenty.' He was going to be part of Iraq's great, ancient literary tradition in this country that brought the world writing, I said. He glowed. Did he know, I asked, of the saying that 'books were written in Egypt, printed in Lebanon and read in Iraq'? And that it is only by reading and collecting the special phrases, facts, words, all the time, that one can write, just as he was doing. He didn't know, and so ill, but totally absorbed and enthused, carefully wrote it all down. I told him about poets and their lives and quoted lines special to me – and he wrote them down and glowed again that someone understood his passion and spoke the language of his thoughts.

I have written much about Jassim and his poem has been widely published. Jassim's life depended on a European aid agency returning within ten days with the chemotherapy he needed.

Three weeks ago, a friend went to Iraq and I sent with him the clippings of these articles, specially bound, and asked that he be sure to deliver them to Jassim to show him his first printed poem – and I thought of his face again lighting up.

Last night my friend returned and telephoned. 'How is Jassim?' The aid agency didn't make it, but Jassim had fought and fought, he had hung on, but he lost the battle just before my friend arrived. He never saw his poem in print – and is now just another statistic in the 'collateral damage' of sanctions.

I had told Jassim of poems living on and quoted to him James Elroy Flecker:

> Since I can never see your face
> And never take you by the hand
> I send my soul through time and space
> To greet you. You will understand.

Flecker sent his 'words as messengers, The way I shall not pass along.' He asked a 'friend, unseen, unborn, unknown' to 'read out my words, at night, alone: I was a poet, I was young.'

Just like you, Jassim. Rest in peace, little poet: 1985–1998.

August 1998

Letter from Basra

In beautiful, relentlessly battered Basra, Iraq's second city, founded in the mists of time, where the Tigris and Euphrates meet at Shat Al Arab, Iraq's plight under sanctions and recent history are encapsulated. Towering bronze figures line the water front, heroes of the Iran–Iraq war, each with his right arm extended towards Iran, forefinger pointing accusingly. Damage from the eight-year onslaught, from which losses have been compared to the First World War, is everywhere – and from the Gulf War, barely three years later, and the four-day bombardment last December by the United States and Britain. 'We have a saying that if there was a war between France and Germany, Basra would be bombed,' said a resident wryly.

Cancer, leukaemia and malignancies have risen by up to 70 per cent since the Gulf War, increases linked to the depleted uranium (DU) weapons used primarily by Britain and the United States, leaving a radioactive dust throughout the country, which according to experts has entered the food chain via the water table and soil. In Basra we witness a silent holocaust. Starvation, multiple congenital abnormalities, cancer, heart defects, leprosy, water-borne diseases – death stalks Basra's children from the moment of birth.

Iraq's child mortality will surely go down in history as one of the great crimes of the twentieth century alongside the Holocaust, the bombing of Dresden and the excesses of Pol Pot. 'Between 6,000 and 7,000 children under five a month are dying of embargo-related causes,' states Denis Halliday, a former Assistant Secretary-General of the UN, who resigned last July as UN Humanitarian Co-ordinator in Iraq, in protest at 'the destruction of an entire nation'.

The unimaginable can also be found in Basra. One doctor's thesis compares the abnormalities occurring since the Gulf War with Hiroshima. Dr Jenan Hussein has recorded them all. Photographs taken in 1998 show full-term babies undeveloped and the 'bunch of grapes' syndrome reminiscent of abnormalities in the Pacific islands after nuclear testing in the 1950s. Others have no face, no eyes, no limbs, no brain . . .

'If you are not prone to fainting, I will show you a baby born an hour ago,' said Dr Jenan. The tiny being made small bleating noises. It had no genitalia, no eyes, nose, tongue, oesophagus or hands. Twisted legs were joined by a thick 'web' of flesh from the knees. 'We see many similar,' said the doctor. Vegetation in the area shows up to eighty-four times background radiation.

The rise in cleft lip and palate is striking. 'We used to see cleft palate only rarely. I have two operating sessions a week and on average there are two in each. One family had three daughters all with both cleft lip and palate. The parents begged me to operate on them all in the same day – they had no money for fares to return,' remarked facio-maxillary surgeon Dr Mustafa Ali, who had worked in Edinburgh, Glasgow and Dundee but returned to Iraq as the Iran–Iraq war began, honing his skills on unimaginable injuries. But even that pales compared to life after nine years of sanctions. 'There are children whose parents have just the fare to come for surgery. When they arrive we have no oxygen, no anaesthetic – so they go away and never return.'

In a nearby village, where tiny children play in the sewage and poverty is endemic, we found two-year-old Widyan (his name translates as 'valley between two mountains'). His mother had fled, mindless, and he was being nurtured by his grandmother in a spotless house, without even one item of furniture. Paralysed, arms foreshortened, legs deformed, his breathing agonising. In the face of a frail pixie, just his eyes moved, watching, alert. Dr Faisal at Basra General Hospital felt he would not survive another year. There are common denominators amongst the deformities, wherever they are found, say experts. Either the families live in areas heavily bombarded during the Gulf War – or the fathers were in the army in bombarded areas.

Twenty-five per cent of all babies are now born prematurely or of premature weight, due to malnutrition and/or environmental factors. No incubators work at optimum capacity, there is no oxygen or gastro-nasal feeding, no rehydration or hygiene – even disinfectant is vetoed by the UN Sanctions Committee. In the premature unit were seventeen babies. 'We have not had one premature baby survive since 1994,' said the doctor. I noted each face on seventeen fledgling lives, all almost certainly by now another embargo-related statistic.

As we left, Dr Ali asked: 'What will we do if we are bombed again – how can we respond to the casualties?' Heading north on the Basra road, synonymous with the carnage of General Norman Schwartzkopf's 'turkey shoot', burned-out vehicles still remain – the lasting reminder of unimaginable horror. It was Sunday night. Basra was bombed at 9.30 the following morning.

Basra has a memorial to Iraqi Airways. It reads: 'Iraqi Airways, 1947–1990'. It could be a metaphor for Iraq, for the 'Rights of the Child' and the 7,000 children under five who die every month and who have not 'failed to comply with United Nations resolutions'.

February 1999

JOY GORDON

Cool War: Economic Sanctions as a Weapon of Mass Destruction

2002

In searching for evidence of the potential danger posed by Iraq, the Bush administration need have looked no further than the well-kept record of US manipulation of the sanctions programme since 1991. If any international act in the last decade is sure to generate enduring bitterness toward the United States, it is the epidemic suffering needlessly visited on Iraqis via US fiat inside the United Nations Security Council. Within that body, the United States has consistently thwarted Iraq from satisfying its most basic humanitarian needs, using sanctions as nothing less than a deadly weapon, and, despite recent reforms, continuing to do so. Invoking security concerns – including those not corroborated by UN weapons inspectors – US policy-makers have effectively turned a programme of international governance into a legitimised act of mass slaughter.

Since the UN adopted economic sanctions in 1945, in its charter, as a means of maintaining global order, it has used them fourteen times (twelve times since 1990). But only those sanctions imposed on Iraq have been comprehensive, meaning that virtually every aspect of the country's imports and exports is controlled, which is particularly damaging to a country recovering from war. Since the programme began, an estimated 500,000 Iraqi children under the age of five have died as a result of the sanctions – almost three times as many as the number of Japanese killed during the US atomic bomb attacks.

News of such Iraqi fatalities has been well documented (by the United Nations, among others), though underreported by the media. What has remained invisible, however, is any documentation of how and by whom such a death toll has been justified for so long. How was the danger of goods entering Iraq assessed, and how was it weighed, if at all, against the mounting collateral damage? As an academic who studies the ethics of international relations, I was curious. It was easy to discover that for the last ten years a vast number of lengthy holds had been placed on billions of dollars' worth of what seemed unobjectionable – and very much needed – imports to Iraq. But I soon learned that all UN records that could answer my questions were kept from public scrutiny. This is not to say that the UN is lacking in public documents related to the Iraq programme. What are unavailable are the documents that show how the US policy agenda has determined the outcome of humanitarian and security judgements.

The operation of Iraq sanctions involves numerous agencies within the United Nations. The Security Council's 661 Committee[1] is generally responsible for both enforcing the sanctions and granting humanitarian exemptions. The Office of Iraq Programme (OIP), within the UN Secretariat, operates the Oil for Food Programme. Humanitarian agencies such as UNICEF and the World Health Organisation work in Iraq to monitor and improve the population's welfare, periodically reporting their findings to the 661 Committee. These agencies have been careful not to publicly discuss their ongoing frustration with the manner in which the programme is operated.

Over the last three years, through research and interviews with diplomats, UN staff, scholars and journalists, I have acquired many of the key confidential UN documents concerning the administration of Iraq sanctions. I obtained these documents on the condition that my sources remain anonymous. What they show is that the United States has fought aggressively throughout the last decade to purposefully minimise the humanitarian goods that enter the country. And it has done so in the face of enormous human suffering, including massive increases in child mortality and widespread epidemics. It has sometimes given a reason for its refusal to approve humanitarian goods, sometimes given no reason at all, and sometimes changed its reason three or four times, in each instance causing a delay of months. Since August 1991 the United States has blocked most purchases of materials necessary for Iraq to generate electricity, as well as equipment for radio, telephone and other communications. Often restrictions

[1] The sanctions were imposed under UN Security Council Resolution 661.

have hinged on the withholding of a single essential element, rendering many approved items useless. For example, Iraq was allowed to purchase a sewage-treatment plant but was blocked from buying the generator necessary to run it; this in a country that has been pouring 300,000 tons of raw sewage daily into its rivers.

Saddam Hussein's government is well known for its human rights abuses against the Kurds and Shi'ites, and for its invasion of Kuwait. What is less well known is that this same government had also invested heavily in health, education and social programmes for two decades prior to the Persian Gulf War. While the treatment of ethnic minorities and political enemies has been abominable under Hussein, it is also the case that the well-being of the society at large improved dramatically. The social programmes and economic development continued, and expanded, even during Iraq's gruelling and costly war with Iran from 1980 to 1988, a war that Saddam Hussein might not have survived without substantial US backing. Before the Persian Gulf War, Iraq was a rapidly developing country, with free education, ample electricity, modernised agriculture, and a robust middle class. According to the World Health Organisation, 93 per cent of the population had access to health care.

The devastation of the Gulf War and the sanctions that preceded and sustained such devastation changed all that. Often forgotten is the fact that sanctions were imposed before the war – in August of 1990 – in direct response to Iraq's invasion of Kuwait. After the liberation of Kuwait, sanctions were maintained, their focus shifted to disarmament. In 1991, a few months after the end of the war, the UN secretary-general's envoy reported that Iraq was facing a crisis in the areas of food, water, sanitation and health, as well as elsewhere in its entire infrastructure, and predicted an 'imminent catastrophe, which could include epidemics and famine, if massive life-supporting needs are not rapidly met'. US intelligence assessments took the same view. A Defense Department evaluation noted that 'Degraded medical conditions in Iraq are primarily attributable to the breakdown of public services (water purification and distribution, preventive medicine, water disposal, health-care services, electricity, and transportation) . . . Hospital care is degraded by lack of running water and electricity.'

According to Pentagon officials, that was the intention. In a 23

June 1991 *Washington Post* article, Pentagon officials stated that Iraq's electrical grid had been targeted by bombing strikes in order to undermine the civilian economy. 'People say, "You didn't recognise that it was going to have an effect on water or sewage,"' said one planning officer at the Pentagon. 'Well, what were we trying to do with sanctions – help out the Iraqi people? No. What we were doing with the attacks on infrastructure was to accelerate the effect of the sanctions.'

Iraq cannot legally export or import any goods, including oil, outside the UN sanctions system. The Oil for Food Programme, intended as a limited and temporary emergency measure, was first offered to Iraq in 1991, and was rejected. It was finally put into place in 1996. Under the programme, Iraq was permitted to sell a limited amount of oil (until 1999, when the limits were removed), and is allowed to use almost 60 per cent of the proceeds to buy humanitarian goods. Since the programme began, Iraq has earned approximately $57 billion in oil revenues, of which it has spent about $23 billion on goods that actually arrived. This comes to about $170 per year per person, which is less than one half the annual per capita income of Haiti, the poorest country in the Western Hemisphere. Iraqi diplomats noted last year that this is well below what the UN spends on food for dogs used in Iraqi de-mining operations (about $400 per dog per year on imported food, according to the UN).

The severe limits on funds created a permanent humanitarian crisis, but the situation has been worsened considerably by chronic delays in approval for billions of dollars' worth of goods. As of last July more than $5 billion in goods was on hold.

The Office of Iraq Programme does not release information on which countries are blocking contracts, nor does any other body. Access to the minutes of the Security Council's 661 Committee is 'restricted'. The committee operates by consensus, effectively giving every member veto power. Although support for the sanctions has eroded considerably, the sanctions are maintained by 'reverse veto' in the Security Council. Because the sanctions did not have an expiration date built in, ending them would require another resolution by the council. The United States (and Britain) would be in a position to veto any such resolution even though the sanctions on Iraq have been openly opposed by three permanent members – France, Russia and China – for many years, and by many of the elected members as well. The sanctions, in effect, cannot be lifted until the United States agrees.

Nearly everything for Iraq's entire infrastructure – electricity, roads, telephones, water treatment – as well as much of the equipment and supplies related to food and medicine has been subject to Security Council review. In practice, this has meant that the United States and Britain subjected hundreds of contracts to elaborate scrutiny, without the involvement of any other country on the council; and after that scrutiny, the United States, only occasionally seconded by Britain, consistently blocked or delayed hundreds of humanitarian contracts.

In response to US demands, the UN worked with suppliers to provide the United States with detailed information about the goods and how they would be used, and repeatedly expanded its monitoring system, tracking each item from contracting through delivery and installation, ensuring that the imports are used for legitimate civilian purposes. Despite all these measures, US holds actually increased. In September 2001 nearly one third of water and sanitation and one quarter of electricity and educational supply contracts were on hold. Between the springs of 2000 and 2002, for example, holds on humanitarian goods tripled.

Among the goods that the United States blocked last winter: dialysis, dental and fire-fighting equipment, water tankers, milk and yogurt production equipment, printing equipment for schools. The United States even blocked a contract for agricultural bagging equipment, insisting that the UN first obtain documentation to 'confirm that the "manual" placement of bags around filling spouts is indeed a person placing the bag on the spout'.

Although most contracts for food in the last few years bypassed the Security Council altogether, political interference with related contracts still occurred. In a 20 March 2000 661 Committee meeting – after considerable debate and numerous US and UK objections – a UNICEF official, Anupama Rao Singh, made a presentation on the deplorable humanitarian situation in Iraq. Her report included the following: 25 per cent of children in south and central governorates suffered from chronic malnutrition, which was often irreversible, 9 per cent from acute malnutrition, and child-mortality rates had more than doubled since the imposition of sanctions.

A couple of months later, a Syrian company asked the committee to approve a contract to mill flour for Iraq. Whereas Iraq ordinarily purchased food directly, in this case it was growing wheat but did not have adequate facilities to produce flour. The Russian delegate argued that, in light of the report the committee had received from the UNICEF official, and the fact that flour was an essential element of the Iraqi diet, the committee had no choice but to approve the request on humanitarian grounds. The delegate from China agreed, as did those from France and Argentina. But the US representative, Eugene Young, argued that 'there should be no hurry' to move on this request: the flour requirement under Security Council Resolution 986 had been met, he said; the number of holds on contracts for milling equipment was 'relatively low'; and the committee should wait for the results of a study being conducted by the World Food Programme first. Ironically, he also argued against the flour-milling contract on the grounds that 'the focus should be on capacity-building within the country' – even though that represented a stark reversal of US policy, which consistently opposed any form of economic development within Iraq. The British delegate stalled as well, saying that he would need to see 'how the request would fit into the Iraqi food programme', and that there were still questions about transport and insurance. In the end, despite the extreme malnutrition of which the committee was aware, the US delegate insisted it would be 'premature' to grant the request for flour production, and the UK representative joined him, blocking the project from going forward.

Many members of the Security Council have been sharply critical of these practices. In a 20 April 2000 meeting of the 661 Committee, one member after another challenged the legitimacy of the US decisions to impede the humanitarian contracts. The problem had reached 'a critical point', said the Russian delegate; the number of holds was 'excessive', said the Canadian representative; the Tunisian delegate expressed concern over the scale of the holds. The British and American delegates justified their position on the grounds that the items on hold were dual-use goods that should be monitored, and that they could not approve them without getting detailed technical information. But the French delegate challenged this explanation: there was an elaborate monitoring mechanism for telecommunications equipment, he pointed out, and the International Telecommunication Union had been involved in assessing projects. Yet, he said, there were holds on almost 90 per cent of telecommunications contracts. Similarly, there was already an effective monitoring mechanism for oil equipment that had existed for some time; yet the holds on oil contracts remained high. Nor was it the case, he suggested, that providing prompt, detailed technical information was sufficient to get holds released: a French contract for the supply of ventilators for intensive-care units had been on hold for more than five months, despite his government's prompt and detailed response to a request for additional technical information and the obvious humanitarian character of the goods.

Dual-use goods, of course, are the ostensible target of sanctions, since they are capable of contributing to Iraq's military capabilities. But the problem remains that many of the tools necessary for a country simply to function could easily be considered dual use. Truck tyres, respirator masks, bulldozers and pipes have all been blocked or delayed at different times for this reason. Also under suspicion is much of the equipment needed to provide electricity, telephone services, transportation and clean water.

Yet goods presenting genuine security concerns have been safely imported into Iraq for years and used for legitimate purposes. Chlorine, for example – vital for water purification, and feared as a possible source of the chlorine gas used in chemical weapons – is aggressively monitored, and deliveries have been regular. Every single canister is tracked from the time of contracting through arrival, installation and disposal of the empty canister. With many other goods, however, US claims of concern over weapons of mass destruction are a good deal shakier.

Last year the United States blocked contracts for water tankers, on the grounds that they might be used to haul chemical weapons instead. Yet the arms experts at UNMOVIC[2] had no objection to them: water tankers with that particular type of lining, they maintained, were not on the '1051 list' – the list of goods that require notice to UN weapons inspectors. Still, the United States insisted on blocking the water tankers – this during a time when the major cause of child deaths was lack of access to clean drinking water, and when the country was in the midst of a drought. Thus, even though the United States justified blocking humanitarian goods out of concern over security and potential military use, it blocked contracts that the UN's own agency charged with weapons inspections did not object to. And the quantities were large. As of September 2001, '1051 disagreements' involved nearly 200 humanitarian contracts. As of

[2] UN Monitoring, Verification and Inspection Commission.

March 2002, there were $25 million worth of holds on contracts for hospital essentials – sterilisers, oxygen plants, spare parts for basic utilities – that, despite release by UNMOVIC, were still blocked by the United States on the claim of 'dual use'.

Beyond its consistent blocking of dual-use goods, the United States found many ways to slow approval of contracts. Although it insisted on reviewing every contract carefully, for years it didn't assign enough staff to do this without causing enormous delays. In April 2000 the United States informed the 661 Committee that it had just released $275 million in holds. This did not represent a policy change, the delegate said; rather, the United States had simply allocated more financial resources and personnel to the task of reviewing the contracts. Thus millions in humanitarian contracts had been delayed not because of security concerns but simply because of US disinterest in spending the money necessary to review them. In other cases, after all US objections to a delayed contract were addressed (a process that could take years), the United States simply changed its reason for the hold, and the review process began all over. After a half-million-dollar contract for medical equipment was blocked in February 2000, and the company spent two years responding to US requests for information, the United States changed its reason for the hold, and the contract remained blocked. A tremendous number of other medical-equipment contracts suffered the same fate. As of September 2001, nearly a billion dollars' worth of medical-equipment contracts – for which all the information sought had been provided – was still on hold.

Among the many deprivations Iraq has experienced, none is so closely correlated with deaths as its damaged water system. Prior to 1990, 95 per cent of urban households in Iraq had access to potable water, as did three-quarters of rural households. Soon after the Persian Gulf War, there were widespread outbreaks of cholera and typhoid – diseases that had been largely eradicated in Iraq – as well as massive increases in child and infant dysentery, and skyrocketing child and infant mortality rates. By 1996 all sewage-treatment plants had broken down. As the state's economy collapsed, salaries to state employees stopped, or were paid in Iraqi currency rendered nearly worthless by inflation. Between 1990 and 1996 more than half of the employees involved in water and sanitation left their jobs. By 2001, after five years of the Oil for Food Programme's operating at full capacity, the situation had actually worsened.

In the late 1980s the mortality rate for Iraqi children under five years old was about fifty per thousand. By 1994 it had nearly doubled, to just under ninety. By 1999 it had increased again, this time to nearly 130; that is, 13 per cent of all Iraqi children were dead before their fifth birthday. For the most part, they die as a direct or indirect result of contaminated water.

The United States anticipated the collapse of the Iraqi water system early on. In January 1991, shortly before the Persian Gulf War began and six months into the sanctions, the Pentagon's Defense Intelligence Agency projected that, under the embargo, Iraq's ability to provide clean drinking water would collapse within six months. Chemicals for water treatment, the agency noted, 'are depleted or nearing depletion', chlorine supplies were 'critically low', the main chlorine-production plants had been shut down, and industries such as pharmaceuticals and food processing were already becoming incapacitated. 'Unless the water is purified with chlorine,' the agency concluded, 'epidemics of such diseases as cholera, hepatitis, and typhoid could occur.'

All of this indeed came to pass. And got worse. Yet US policy on water-supply contracts remained as aggressive as ever. For every such contract unblocked in August 2001, for example, three new ones were put on hold. A 2001 UNICEF report to the Security Council found that access to potable water for the Iraqi population had not improved much under the Oil for Food Programme, and specifically cited the half a billion dollars of water- and sanitation-supply contracts then blocked – one third of all submitted. UNICEF reported that up to 40 per cent of the purified water run through pipes is contaminated or lost through leakage. Yet the United States blocked or delayed contracts for water pipes, and for the bulldozers and earth-moving equipment necessary to install them. And despite approving the dangerous dual-use chlorine, the United States blocked the safety equipment necessary to handle the substance – not only for Iraqis but for UN employees charged with chlorine monitoring there.

It is no accident that the operation of the 661 Committee is so obscured. Behind closed doors, ensconced in a UN bureaucracy few citizens could parse, American policymakers are in a good position to avoid criticism of their practices; but they are also, rightly, fearful of public scrutiny, as a fracas over a block on medical supplies last year illustrates.

In early 2001, the United States had placed holds on $280 million in medical supplies, including vaccines to treat infant hepatitis, tetanus and diphtheria, as well as incubators and cardiac equipment. The rationale was that the vaccines contained live cultures, albeit highly weakened ones. The Iraqi Government, it was argued, could conceivably extract these, and eventually grow a virulent fatal strain, then develop a missile or other delivery system that could effectively disseminate it. UNICEF and UN health agencies, along with other Security Council members, objected strenuously. European biological-weapons experts maintained that such a feat was in fact flatly impossible. At the same time, with massive epidemics ravaging the country, and skyrocketing child mortality, it was quite certain that preventing child vaccines from entering Iraq would result in large numbers of child and infant deaths. Despite pressure behind the scenes from the UN and from members of the Security Council, the United States refused to budge. But in March 2001, when the *Washington Post* and Reuters reported on the holds – and their impact – the United States abruptly announced it was lifting them.

A few months later, the United States began aggressively and publicly pushing a proposal for 'smart sanctions', sometimes known as 'targeted sanctions'. The idea behind smart sanctions is to 'contour' sanctions so that they affect the military and the political leadership instead of the citizenry. Basic civilian necessities, the State Department claimed, would be handled by the UN Secretariat, bypassing the Security Council. Critics pointed out that in fact the proposal would change very little since everything related to infrastructure was routinely classified as dual use, and so would be subject again to the same kinds of interference. What the 'smart sanctions' would accomplish was to mask the US role. Under the new proposal, all the categories of goods the United States ordinarily challenged would instead be placed in a category that was, in effect, automatically placed on hold. But this would now be in the name of the Security Council – even though there was little interest on the part of any of its other members (besides Britain) for maintaining sanctions, and even less interest in blocking humanitarian goods.

After the embarrassing media coverage of the child-vaccine débâcle, the State Department was eager to see the new system in place, and to see that none of the other permanent members of the Security

Council – Russia, Britain, China and France – vetoed the proposal. In the face of this new political agenda, US security concerns suddenly disappeared. In early June 2001, when the 'smart sanctions' proposal was under negotiation, the United States announced that it would lift holds on $800 million of contracts, of which $200 million involved business with key Security Council members. A few weeks later, the United States lifted holds on $80 million of Chinese contracts with Iraq, including some for radio equipment and other goods that had been blocked because of dual-use concerns.

In the end, China and France agreed to support the US proposal. But Russia did not, and immediately after Russia vetoed it, the United States placed holds on nearly every contract that Iraq had with Russian companies. Then in November 2001, the United States began lobbying again for a smart-sanctions proposal, now called the Goods Review List (GRL). The proposal passed the Security Council in May 2002, this time with Russia's support. In what one diplomat, anonymously quoted in the *Financial Times* of 3 April 2002, called 'the boldest move yet by the US to use the holds to buy political agreement', the Goods Review List had the effect of lifting $740 million of US holds on Russian contracts with Iraq, even though the State Department had earlier insisted that those same holds were necessary to prevent any military imports.

Under the new system, UNMOVIC and the International Atomic Energy Agency make the initial determination about whether an item appears on the GRL, which includes only those materials questionable enough to be passed on to the Security Council. The list is precise and public, but huge. Cobbled together from existing UN and other international lists and precedents, the GRL has been virtually customised to accommodate the imaginative breadth of US policymakers' security concerns. Yet when UN weapons experts began reviewing the $5 billion worth of existing holds in July 2002, they found that very few of them were for goods that ended up on the GRL or warranted the security concern that the United States had originally claimed. As a result, hundreds of holds have been lifted in the last few months.

This mass release of old holds – expected to have been completed in October 2002 – should have made a difference in Iraq. But US and British manoeuvres on the council last year make genuine relief unlikely. In December 2000, the Security Council passed a resolution allowing Iraq to spend 600 million euros (about $600 million) from its oil sales on maintenance of its oil-production capabilities. Without this, Iraq would still have to pay for these services, but with no legal avenue to raise the funds. The United States, unable in the end to agree with Iraq on how the funds would be managed, blocked the measure's implementation. In the spring of 2001, the United States accused Iraq of imposing illegal surcharges on the middlemen who sell to refiners. To counter this, the United States and Britain devised a system that had the effect of undermining Iraq's basic capacity to sell oil: 'retroactive pricing'. Taking advantage of the fact that the 661 Committee sets the price Iraq receives from each oil buyer, the United States and Britain began to systematically withhold their votes on each price until the relevant buying period had passed. The idea was that then the alleged surcharge could be subtracted from the price after the sale had occurred, and that price would then be imposed on the buyer. The effect of this practice has been to torpedo the entire Oil for Food Programme. Obviously, few buyers would want to commit themselves to a purchase whose price they do not know until after they agree to it. As a result of this system, Iraq's oil income has dropped 40 per cent since last year, and more than $2 billion in humanitarian contracts – all of them fully approved – are now stalled. Once again, invoking tenuous security claims, the United States has put in place a device that will systematically cause enormous human damage in Iraq.

Some would say that the lesson to be learned from September 11 is that we must be even more aggressive in protecting what we see as our security interests. But perhaps that's the wrong lesson altogether. It is worth remembering that the worst destruction done on US soil by foreign enemies was accomplished with little more than hatred, ingenuity, and box cutters. Perhaps what we should learn from our own reactions to September 11 is that the massive destruction of innocents is something that is unlikely to be either forgotten or forgiven. If this is so, then destroying Iraq, whether with sanctions or with bombs, is unlikely to bring the security we have gone to such lengths to preserve.

RICHARD NORTON-TAYLOR
Under a False Pretext
2002–3

For months, while their political masters have been increasingly obsessed by Saddam Hussein, Western intelligence agencies have warned of planned terrorist attacks by al-Qaida or, more likely, other Islamist extremist groups with similar objectives and outlook.

They have warned in particular about the likelihood of attacks on such American and British targets as bases and embassies – targets, in other words, which represent the governmental, military presence of major Western countries in the Muslim world. Commercial targets, equally symbolic, were also in their sight.

The awful message of the bombing of the Bali nightclub is that Islamist extremists appear to have changed their tactics with horrific implications. Bali may be a Hindu region dominated by Western tourists in the world's largest Muslim country, but the nightclub was the easiest and softest of targets.

US officials early this year said that five suspected members of the al-Qaida network had arrived in Indonesia from Yemen in July 2001 planning to blow up the American embassy in Jakarta. They said the men were allowed to get out of the country after they realised they had been discovered.

More recently, the US had expressed concern about the failure of President Megawati Sukarnoputri's government – caught between Washington, on whom Indonesia relies for aid, and opposition in the country to US policy, including the war in Afghanistan – to face up to the threat of Islamist extremism. The US has contrasted the attitude of the Indonesian Government with the Philippines, Malaysia and Singapore, which have taken a far more robust approach.

Western intelligence sources yesterday pointed the finger of responsibility for the Bali attack on Jamaah Islamiyah, an extreme group whose leaders are said to have met Ayman al-Zawahiri, a fifty-year-old Egyptian regarded as al-Qaida's deputy leader, in Indonesia two years ago.

Whoever was responsible for the attack, al-Qaida and its supporters have not been defeated. Just a week ago, a French oil tanker was attacked off the coast of Yemen, not far away from the October 2000 attack on the American destroyer, the USS *Cole,* in Aden.

Since 11 September last year, Pakistani-based extremist groups have attacked a Christian church frequented by Western diplomats, and a bus carrying French technicians working in Karachi's military port.

Intelligence sources have revealed a foiled plot this summer by al-Qaida agents to bomb US or British warships in the Straits of Gibraltar, and a possible attack on British military bases in Cyprus. And early this year, the Singapore authorities foiled an elaborate plot by al-Qaida-linked terrorists to blow up Western embassies, American warships, the offices of US companies and a bus carrying American soldiers.

But while Western intelligence agencies have been trying to track the movements of al-Qaida sympathisers and warned of the certainty of further terrorist attacks, their governments have been preoccupied by quite another matter – Saddam Hussein and his weapons of mass destruction. Al-Qaida – a word which in Arabic can mean a base but also a model or principle – has lost its base in Afghanistan, Osama bin Laden is either dead or in hiding, it doesn't matter. That has been the prevailing attitude in Washington, and also in many parts of Whitehall. The Taliban and al-Qaida have been quashed in Afghanistan, now let's take on the next target, Iraq.

For security and intelligence agencies with their ear closer to the ground, it is not so simple. Al-Qaida is not a traditional terrorist organisation with a disciplined hierarchy like the IRA. It is used, misleadingly, as shorthand for any Islamist extremist group. It is more like a movement, almost amoeba-like, with varying degrees of support and contacts with other groups throughout much of the Muslim world, including Algeria, Egypt, Yemen, Indonesia and elsewhere in the Gulf, including Saudi Arabia. But not among Palestinians, a generally secular people, and certainly not in Baghdad, home of the most secular country in the Middle East, Israel included.

Short-sighted politicians in Washington, notably Donald Rumsfeld, the US defense secretary, and his deputy, Paul Wolfowitz, are putting it about that there are links between al-Qaida and Saddam Hussein. They have been trying desperately to come up with evidence to prove it, a task which they have singularly failed to achieve. But in trying they have diverted the resources of their intelligence agencies, including the CIA, and worse, they are trying to manipulate intelligence-gathering for political ends.

No one in any competent position in Whitehall believes there is any link between al-Qaida and Saddam. They do not want this said publicly for fear, it seems, of upsetting the Bush administration. Bush, meanwhile, having dealt with Afghanistan, wants to get on with the task of toppling Saddam, claiming it is part of the war on terror.

To begin with, Afghanistan is not dealt with. It remains unstable. Asked the other day what the US approach was to rebuilding nationhood and to the struggle for hearts and minds – one of the key ingredients of the war against terror, according to British ministers – a senior Whitehall official replied: 'The Americans are on another planet.'

This frustration with the Bush administration is expressed publicly by former president Bill Clinton and his vice-president, Al Gore. Tony Blair and his ministers are now silent about the dangers of fighting a war on two fronts, against Saddam and against terrorism.

Yet before they were told by Bush, in his domestic political interest, that the time had come to concentrate on Saddam, British ministers, even Geoff Hoon, the defence secretary, made eminently sensible speeches about the need to confront terrorism inspired by Islamist extremism not only by good intelligence work but by tackling the causes. Terrorism may never end, but at least there are ways to limit it other than throwing around one's military might. It will now be even more difficult for Bush to justify an invasion and occupation of Iraq, which is only likely to encourage further recruits to the cause of Islamist extremism.

Jack Straw was right recently when he warned in a little-noticed speech of the twin dangers of terrorism and failing states. But these dangers were overlooked in Indonesia, as hundreds of innocent victims have now found to their cost.

Guardian, 10 October 2002

Telegrams from British embassies and missions around the world are urging Tony Blair to step up pressure on President Bush to pull back from a war against Iraq. In what amounts to a collective *cri de coeur*, our envoys – congregating in Whitehall today for an unprecedented Foreign Office brainstorming session – are warning of the potentially devastating consequences of such an adventure, including its impact on a greater threat than Saddam Hussein: al-Qaida-inspired terrorism.

The warnings are not just coming from our envoys and defence attachés in Arab capitals. They are also, I am told, coming from Washington. This, our diplomats suggest, could be one of Blair's – and Britain's – finest hours, a unique opportunity to make a constructive contribution to world affairs. They also know, not least from American opinion polls, that the Bush administration needs Britain onside. Our contribution would be a token one in military terms, but significant politically. That gives Britain leverage.

It is hard to find anyone in Whitehall who supports a war against Iraq and who is not deeply concerned about the influence of the hawks around Bush. They cannot say so in public, of course.

Whitehall gives Blair the credit for helping to persuade Bush to go down the UN route – a prime example of what Whitehall describes as Britain 'punching above its weight'. But this should be put into perspective. Richard Falk, Princeton's emeritus professor of international law, notes in the latest issue of *Le Monde Diplomatique*: 'This belated recourse to the UN does not fool many people outside the US, and is not very persuasive to Americans themselves. It is obvious that Bush is no friend of the UN, and only sought UN approval for US policy to defuse domestic opposition to blatant unilateralism.'

Falk addresses a key issue: 'For the US to insist, in voting for resolution 1441 on 8 November, that the UN act as an enforcement agency by reviving weapons inspection, and in so onerous a form that it almost ensures a breakdown, is to enlist the UN in the dirty work of war-making.'

It is a key issue because UN Security Council backing for military action will be seized on by ministers to convince those, including Labour MPs and bishops, who have grave doubts about a war against Iraq. The fact is that the Security Council has always considered itself above any tenet of international law.

In his biography, *The Politics of Diplomacy*, former US secretary of state James Baker shamelessly admits how, before the 1991 Gulf War, he met his Security Council counterparts 'in an intricate process of cajoling, extracting, threatening, and occasionally buying votes'. America's relative power, and its willingness to use it, has increased over the past twelve years. James Paul, head of Global Policy Forum, a non-governmental body that monitors the UN, says: 'The capacity of the US to bring to heel virtually any country in the world is unbelievable.'

The US is corrupting the Security Council by bribing its permanent members – Russia with dollars, China with trade concessions, France and Britain (if it needs any carrots) with the prospect of oil concessions. And Turkey will be amply rewarded if it allows the US to use its bases for an assault on Iraq. Is this how international relations are going to be conducted among the world's most powerful countries in future? Is it that difficult for Blair to go down in history as the leader who prevented a potentially disastrous war fought, as one Whitehall official puts it, simply to prevent Bush from having egg over his face?

What kind of country meekly succumbs to demands for war dictated by domestic party politics, even those of its closest ally? Where is the evidence that Iraq is lying about its weapons of mass destruction? Worried Whitehall officials ask: even if evidence is found, and Saddam Hussein is discovered to have lied, is it not better to keep the UN inspectors – the best deterrence against the use or development of such weapons – on the ground?

One lie ministers could nail is that put about by elements in Washington and Israel – that there are links between Saddam Hussein and al-Qaida. British and American intelligence insist there is no evidence of such a link, yet ministers are frightened to say so for fear of upsetting Washington.

Though there is no love lost between the Iraqi regime and Islamist fundamentalists, an Anglo-American attack on Iraq is likely to attract more recruits to al-Qaida, thereby increasing the risk of terrorist strikes against British and American interests, as well as the destabilisation of other secular Arab states and the West's Middle East allies.

So we come to double standards. While the US demands that Baghdad abide by UN resolutions, it ignores Israel's refusal to do so over the occupied territories. While the US pursues a diplomatic course towards North Korea – a country which has thrown out UN nuclear inspectors – it threatens military action against Iraq, where UN inspectors are busy on the ground. And while the US says international inspectors must investigate the rest of the world to ensure they are not producing chemical or biological weapons, Washington rejects such inspections in the US.

We know, too, that the campaign to topple Saddam Hussein has little to do with democracy. Despite public utterances in support of democratic change in Iraq, Richard Haas, former director of Middle East affairs in Washington's National Security Council, has admitted that US policy 'is to get rid of Saddam Hussein, not his regime'. There are those in the Israeli Government and Bush administration who argue that the fall of Saddam would encourage the populations of other Arab states to get rid of their undemocratic governments, make peace with Israel and embrace pro-Western policies.

Our diplomats and military commanders are clinging to the hope that pressure on Iraq from the build-up of American military force in the Gulf will lead to an 'implosion' of Saddam Hussein's regime without a war. They want the organs of the Iraqi state, including the Republican Guard, to remain in place, to maintain law and order with the help of American and British forces and prevent the oil-rich nation's disintegration.

But even if that scenario does come off, it will not address the fundamental questions – about the future conduct of relations between states, the role of the UN, international law, peace in the Middle East, disarmament, and the proliferation of weapons of mass destruction – being asked behind the scenes in Whitehall. Since officials can't talk openly, it is up to MPs to force ministers to give answers.

Guardian, 6 January 2003

Why now? The question is of course being asked by those opposed to a war against Iraq, and those who have not made up their minds. But it has also been asked by one of the most senior Whitehall officials at the centre of the fight against terrorism. The message was clear: the threat posed by Islamist extremists is much greater than that posed by Saddam Hussein. And it will get worse when the US and Britain attack Iraq.

Tony Blair may not want to admit it, but this is the common view throughout the higher reaches of government. As a leaked secret document from the defence intelligence staff puts it: 'Al-Qaida will take advantage of the situation for its own aims but it will not be acting as a proxy group on behalf of the Iraqi regime.' Osama bin Laden must be praying for a US assault on Iraq.

'Do we help or hinder the essential struggle against terrorism by attacking Iraq?' asks the former Conservative foreign minister, Lord Hurd. 'Would we thus turn the Middle East into a set of friendly democratic capitalist societies ready to make peace with Israel, or into a region of sullen humiliation, a fertile and almost inexhaustible recruiting ground for further terrorists for whom Britain is a main target?' He poses the rhetorical questions in the latest journal of the Royal United Services Institute.

Blair says 'now' because George Bush says so. Put it another way, had Washington decided to continue with a policy of containment, Blair would have followed suit. This, too, is the common view in Whitehall. It helps explain the government's problem in justifying a war.

Claims that the Iraqi regime is linked with al-Qaida were dropped when ministers failed to provide the evidence. Blair and his ministers follow the wind from Washington and then counter public opinion at home. First, the objective was to rid Iraq of weapons of mass destruction. When the UN inspectors reported progress and 'intelligence' dossiers were seen to be bogus, the emphasis shifted to regime change. When this was met with objections, notably of legality, Blair went for the moral high ground.

The objectives were muddied further when Blair defended the 'moral case' for war as follows: 'It is not the reason we act. That must be according to the UN mandate on weapons of mass destruction. But it is the reason, frankly, why if we do have to act, we should do so with a clear conscience.'

Then, as Blair added the humanitarian case for war to the moral one, his spokesman further confused the message. 'If Saddam cooperates,' he said, 'then he can stay in power.' A senior adviser to Blair remarked recently that the Bush administration's aim is the 'export of American democracy' throughout the Middle East and Blair shared this vision.

In his new book, *Paradise and Power*, the former US State Department official Robert Kagan argues: 'America did not change on September 11. It only became more itself. The myth of America's "isolationist" tradition is remarkably resilient. But it is a myth. Expansion of territory and influence has been the inescapable reality of American history.'

The latest issue of *Le Monde Diplomatique* reminds us that the US supported Marcos in the Philippines, Suharto in Indonesia, the Shah in Iran, Somoza in Nicaragua, Batista in Cuba, Pinochet in Chile, and Mobutu in Congo/Zaire. 'Some of the bloodiest tyrants are still supported by the US,' it adds, noting that Teodoro Obiang of Equatorial Guinea was received with full honours by Bush last September. Now the US is cuddling up to Uzbekistan, another country with an appalling human-rights record, because it is convenient for US bases.

Ah, says the government, but Saddam poses a unique threat, not only to his own citizens – ministers now claim they have intelligence that the Iraqi dictator is planning to poison all Iraqi Shi'as – but to the national security of Britain and the US.

The US, meanwhile, barters with Turkey for bases from which to attack Iraq. How much is a decision opposing the will of more than 90 per cent of Turks worth in dollars? What is the morality in bribing the UN Security Council to support a war waged, we are told, on moral grounds?

Every time Blair and his ministers repeat a truth – that Saddam used gas against the Kurds and Iranian troops in the 1980s – they remind us that Britain responded by secretly encouraging exports of even more nuclear and other arms-related equipment to Iraq while Washington supplied the regime with more crucial intelligence.

In his speech on the 'moral case' for war last Friday, Jack Straw referred to Saddam's 'ethnic cleansing' of the Marsh Arabs in the 1990s. That was after the US and Britain encouraged the south, and the Kurds in the north, to rise up following the 1991 Gulf War, only to betray them. The southern 'no fly' zone is said by Britain and the US to be a humanitarian initiative, yet it has not achieved any humanitarian purpose, any more than sanctions have. Its purpose is to disable potential threats to US and British forces rather than to protect the Iraqi people – US and British planes have bombed Iraqi missile, radar and communications systems forty times this year, the last occasion on Saturday.

While those responsible for protecting Britain's national security are concerned about the increased threat of terrorism from a military attack on Iraq, there is deep disquiet in Britain's military establishment about the confused objectives of a war and a pre-emptive strike against a country that poses no threat to the attackers. The latest dispute over the marginal excess range of Iraq's Samoud 2 missiles only highlights the weakness of the US–British argument.

Saddam may believe he has nothing to gain by cooperating fully with UN inspectors if the Bush administration has already decided to invade, whatever concessions he makes. But those advocating war have yet to make anything like a convincing case for military action.

Guardian, 24 February 2003

Members of Parliament returning to Westminster after their Easter break, and congressmen in America for that matter, may well be asking if they have been duped.

Saddam Hussein, they were repeatedly told, posed a threat not just to his own people, but to the national security of the US and Britain. But where is the evidence that he possessed stockpiles of chemical and biological material, and the ability to use them as weapons?

Ministers and intelligence agencies say they are confident that these will turn up and that they were dismantled and hidden well before Hans Blix and his team of UN inspectors started looking for them at the end of last year.

It will take weeks, perhaps months, to track them down, we are warned. Yet isn't this precisely what Blix told the UN Security Council, only to be met with the response that London and Washington could not wait?

What is now clear, and admitted by all sides, is that whatever weapons of mass destruction Iraq did possess, they were not a threat, not even to British and American forces, from the time the UN inspectors went in.

Iraq, say London and Washington, duped Blix. Only the US and Britain could be trusted to search for the putative weapons.

Yet these are the same governments that have been engaged in the most outrageous abuse of information supplied by their security and intelligence services. 'In my experience,' Robin Cook, the former foreign secretary, said last week, 'the intelligence services are scrupulous in spelling out the limitations of their knowledge. Frankly, I doubt whether there is a single senior figure in the intelligence services who is surprised at the difficulty in finding a weapon of mass destruction in working order. If the threat from Saddam does turn out to have been overstated, the responsibility must rest with those who made the public statements.'

Saddam's 'military planning', said Tony Blair in last September's government dossier on Iraq's 'weapons of mass destruction', 'allows for some of the WMD to be ready within forty-five minutes of an order to use them'.

Blair and his ministers made much of the discovery of Iraq importing aluminium tubes – evidence, they claimed, of Saddam's nuclear weapons programme. Further evidence, they insisted, was Iraq's attempt to procure uranium from Niger. Experts from the International Atomic Energy Agency exposed the documents on which the claims were made as forgeries.

Britain's intelligence services now admit they were forged. Have ministers come clean? No – and by failing to do so they have further undermined their credibility.

Ministers may be rubbing their hands with glee at journalists in Baghdad turning up documents allegedly implicating George Galloway, the anti-war Labour MP, in the use of funds from Saddam's regime, and suggesting there were links between the regime and al-Qaida, and that France told Baghdad about its private diplomatic conversations with the US.

All very convenient. There must be doubts about the documents' authenticity. [Moreover,] intelligence services are notorious for hoarding tittle-tattle, exaggerating and distorting, not least to stress the importance of their own role in their bids for more funds. Heaven knows what we would find if the archives of MI5 and MI6 – and the CIA and FBI – were plundered.

Yet, significantly, it is not ministers who are warning of the dangers of jumping to conclusions. It is the intelligence agencies themselves. 'They do not take things further forward,' said an intelligence source about the *Sunday Telegraph*'s publication of Iraqi documents appearing to show that Baghdad was keen to meet an 'al-Qaida envoy' in 1998.

Tony Blair, we learn, was constantly asking the intelligence services if Saddam would fall like Ceausescu, or if British and US forces would be mired in a new Vietnam. He wanted assurances. Yet intelligence is an imprecise art. Snippets are picked up from communications traffic, informants pass on information that cannot be verified. Saddam and his entourage were notoriously difficult to penetrate.

Of course, questions should be asked about the information Blair and his ministers were given by the intelligence agencies, including about what military commanders were told to expect when they invaded Iraq. (One said he anticipated the Republican Guard coming over to help British and US forces to keep law and order.)

But as important, perhaps more so, is what ministers did with the information. There is sufficient evidence that they and their political advisers doctored it for the consumption of MPs and the public to warrant a parliamentary investigation.

Guardian, 30 April 2003

We must not allow ourselves to be diverted by Downing Street, and in particular by Alastair Campbell, the prime minister's chief spin doctor, from extremely serious issues which go to the very heart of how we are being ruled. Ministers are desperate to reduce it all to a row about the BBC, its questioning of the reasons for going to war in general and a report by its defence correspondent, Andrew Gilligan, in particular.

On the face of it, they seem to be succeeding. Mr Campbell took on the BBC after giving evidence to the Commons foreign affairs committee on Thursday, knowing the media would lap it up. Yesterday Jack Straw continued the onslaught on the beleaguered Gilligan.

Mr Gilligan's crime was to report that an intelligence source had told him last September's dossier on Iraq's weapons of mass destruction was changed at the behest of Downing Street and the claim that such weapons were ready for use in forty-five minutes was inserted into it.

I have no idea who the source was. What is certain is that for months the intelligence and security services had been expressing deep concern about pressure placed on them by their political masters and the use to which their secret information would be put.

They never wanted an intelligence dossier published. They successfully kiboshed the idea early last year by telling Downing Street that there was nothing new to say. But pressure continued to grow. They argued that there was still nothing new to say, adding as an excuse that any new intelligence could not be published anyway since that would reveal sensitive sources.

The security and intelligence services knew full well that any dossier would be shamelessly used by the government to promote a war against Iraq. They were generally opposed to a war on the grounds that, far from making the world a safer place, it would make it more dangerous, because they saw the real enemy as extreme Islamist terrorism.

They asked why a war should be fought now. Iraq was being successfully contained. It was an argument which became even stronger when UN inspectors returned to Iraq at the end of last year only to be withdrawn for failing to find in a few weeks what tens of thousands of invading Americans and Britons have yet to discover.

Early in September, the intelligence community was still expressing confidence that Tony Blair and his Downing Street advisers had been persuaded to forget the whole idea of publishing a dossier. 'The dossier will no longer play a role, there's very little new to put in it,' I was told by a well-placed source. I don't know where MPs get their information, but certainly other journalists were getting the same message as I was.

When it finally became clear that Blair, on Campbell's advice, was adamant that a dossier which had been drawn up half-heartedly by the joint intelligence committee (JIC), would indeed be published, MI6, MI5, GCHQ and the Defence Intelligence Staff bowed to the inevitable. What John Scarlett, chairman of the JIC, described as a 'debate' with Mr Campbell then took place.

The result was a fifty-page document containing everything MI6 and others could possibly think of. It included the forty-five-minute claim – mentioned four times – and the claim that Saddam Hussein had tried to procure uranium from the west African state of Niger.

Only later did we learn through the UN's International Atomic Energy Agency that the claim was first made on the basis of forged documents. Subsequently, British intelligence sources insisted there was separate information pointing in the same direction. Blair said nothing about the forgeries.

As the controversy grew over the forty-five-minute claim, it was said first to come from an Iraqi source 'deemed to be reliable', then a 'senior Iraqi', and then an 'Iraqi general'. (Ministers admitted the claim came from a single uncorroborated source, the charge they are now making against Mr Gilligan for his story.)

Mr Campbell insists the claim was in the original draft of the dossier which, he told the Commons committee, had been put together 'over many months'. Yesterday, Mr Straw said the claim was not included until a matter of weeks before the dossier's publication on 24 September last year.

Mr Scarlett and his colleagues may not be politicians but they have astute political antennae. They know what their masters wanted. The dossier was cleverly worded, with enough conditional phrases to satisfy their professional consciences but also enough for ministers and their spin doctors to play with. With gritted teeth, Mr Scarlett took the view that what ministers chose to do with the dossier, once published, was up to them, though others in the intelligence world were not so sanguine. Thus Mr Campbell and ministers can argue that the contents of the dossier were fully approved by the JIC.

By early this year, Mr Campbell clearly wanted more. Without telling the JIC – though he says his relations with Mr Scarlett are excellent – he concocted the now famous 'dodgy dossier' which included material from a Californian PhD student.

Mr Campbell told MPs this week that it was intended only as a briefing note for 'six Sunday newspaper journalists'. However, it was placed in the Commons library, and described by Mr Blair to MPs in these terms and with no hint of irony: 'I hope that people have some sense of the integrity of our security services. They are not publishing this, or giving us this information, and making it up.' Colin Powell, the US secretary of state, described this dossier in his address to the UN Security Council as 'exquisite'. Mr Campbell has apologised for the dossier.

Mr Straw yesterday was still trying to scrape the bottom of the barrel, describing to MPs the discovery of mobile trailers in Iraq as 'significant evidence of the existence' of Iraq's banned weapons programme. There is no evidence for this, as a secret US State Department intelligence report confirms.

In evidence to the Scott arms-to-Iraq inquiry, ministers put intelligence reports into perspective. 'In my early days', said the former foreign secretary, Lord Howe, 'I was naïve enough to get excited about intelligence reports. Many look, at first sight, to be important and interesting and significant and then when we check them they are not even straws in the wind. They are cornflakes in the wind.'

His successor, Lord Hurd, remarked: 'There is nothing particularly truthful about a report simply because it is a secret one. People sometimes get excited because a report is secret and they think that therefore it has some particular validity. It is not always so in my experience.'

It seems that in his determination to go to war, Mr Blair believed his trump card would be the publication of 'secret intelligence', a kind of exotic substance that, he hoped, when released, would convince even the most sceptical. Yet intelligence of this kind is rarely, if ever, foolproof as any practitioner of the art will tell you. It certainly cannot be used to stifle suspicion that we were all taken to war under a false pretext.

Guardian, 28 June 2003

ROBERT FISK

Another Day in the Bloody Death of Iraq
2003

In the Baghdad suburb of Shu'ale: the piece of metal is only a foot high, but the numbers on it hold the clue to the latest atrocity in Baghdad.

At least sixty-two civilians had died by yesterday afternoon, and the coding on that hunk of metal contains the identity of the culprit. The Americans and British were doing their best yesterday to suggest that an Iraqi anti-aircraft missile destroyed those dozens of lives, adding that they were 'still investigating' the carnage. But the coding is in Western style, not in Arabic. And many of the survivors heard the plane.

In the Al-Noor hospital yesterday morning, there were appalling scenes of pain and suffering. A two-year-old girl, Saida Jaffar, swaddled in bandages, a tube into her nose, another into her stomach. All I could see of her was her forehead, two small eyes and a chin. Beside her, blood and flies covered a heap of old bandages and swabs. Not far away, lying on a dirty bed, was three-year-old Mohamed Amaid, his face, stomach, hands and feet all tied tightly in bandages. A great black mass of congealed blood lay at the bottom of his bed.

This is a hospital without computers, with only the most primitive of X-ray machines. But the missile was guided by computers and that vital shard of fuselage was computer-coded. It can be easily verified and checked by the Americans – if they choose to do so. It reads: 30003-704ASB 7492. The letter 'B' is scratched and could be an 'H'. This is believed to be the serial number. It is followed by a further code which arms manufacturers usually refer to as the weapon's 'Lot' number. It reads: MFR 96214 09.

The piece of metal bearing the codings was retrieved only minutes after the missile exploded on Friday evening, by an old man whose home is only 100 yards from the 6ft crater. Even the Iraqi authorities do not know that it exists. The missile sprayed hunks of metal through the crowds – mainly women and children – and through the cheap brick walls of local homes, amputating limbs and heads. Three brothers, the eldest twenty-one and the youngest twelve, for example, were cut down inside the living room of their brick hut on the main road opposite the market. Two doors away, two sisters were killed in an identical manner. 'We have never seen anything like these wounds before,' Dr Ahmed, an anaesthetist at the Al-Noor hospital told me later. 'These people have been punctured by dozens of bits of metal.' He was right. One old man I visited in a hospital ward had twenty-four holes in the back of his legs and buttocks, some as big as pound coins. An X-ray photograph handed to me by one of his doctors clearly showed at least thirty-five slivers of metal still embedded in his body.

Like the Sha'ab highway massacre on Thursday – when at least twenty-one Iraqi civilians were killed or burned to death by two missiles fired by an American jet – Shu'ale is a poor, Shia Muslim neighbourhood of single-storey corrugated iron and cement food stores and two-room brick homes. These are the very people whom Messrs Bush and Blair expected to rise in insurrection against Saddam. But the anger in the slums was directed at the Americans and British yesterday, by old women and bereaved fathers and brothers who spoke without hesitation – and without the presence of the otherwise ubiquitous government 'minders'.

'This is a crime,' a woman muttered at me angrily. 'Yes, I know they say they are targeting the military. But can you see soldiers here? Can you see missiles?' The answer has to be in the negative. A few journalists did report seeing a Scud missile on a transporter near the Sha'ab area on Thursday and there were anti-aircraft guns around Shu'ale. At one point yesterday morning, I heard an American jet race over the scene of the massacre and just caught sight of a ground-to-air missile that was vainly chasing it, its contrail soaring over the slum houses in the dark blue sky. An anti-aircraft battery – manufactured circa 1942 – also began firing into the air a few blocks away. But even if the Iraqis do position or move their munitions close to the suburbs, does that justify the Americans firing into those packed civilian neighbourhoods, into areas which they know contain crowded main roads and markets – and during the hours of daylight?

Last week's attack on the Sha'ab highway was carried out on a main road at midday during a sandstorm – when dozens of civilians are bound to be killed, whatever the pilot thought he was aiming at. 'I had five sons and now I have only two – and how do I know that even they will survive?' a bespectacled middle-aged man said in the bare concrete back room of his home yesterday. 'One of my boys was hit in the kidneys and heart. His chest was full of shrapnel; it came right through the windows. Now all I can say is that I am sad that I am alive.' A neighbour interrupted to say that he saw the plane with his own eyes. 'I saw the side of the aircraft and I noticed it changed course after it fired the missile.'

Plane-spotting has become an all-embracing part of life in Baghdad. And to the reader who thoughtfully asked last week if I could see with my own eyes the American aircraft over the city, I have to say that in at least sixty-five raids by aircraft, I have not – despite my tiger-like eyes – actually seen one plane. I hear them, especially at night, but they are flying at supersonic speed; during the day, they are usually above the clouds of black smoke that wash over the city. I have, just once, spotted a cruise missile – the cruise or Tomahawk rockets fly at only around 400 mph – and I saw it passing down a boulevard towards the Tigris river. But the grey smoke that shoots out of the city like the fingers of a dead hand is unmistakable, along with the concussion of sound. And – when they can be found – the computer codings on the bomb fragments reveal their own story. As the codes on the Shu'ale missile surely must.

All morning yesterday, the Americans were at it again, blasting away at targets on the perimeter of Baghdad – where the outer defences of the city are being dug by Iraqi troops – and in the centre. An air-fired rocket exploded on the roof of the Iraqi Ministry of Information, destroying a clutch of satellite dishes. One office building from which I was watching the bombardment literally swayed for several seconds during one long raid. Even in the Al-Noor hospital, the walls were shaking yesterday as the survivors of the market slaughter struggled for survival.

Hussein Mnati is fifty-two and just stared at me – his face pitted with metal fragments – as bombs blasted the city. A twenty-year-old man was sitting up in the next bed, the blood-soaked stump of his left arm plastered over with bandages. Only twelve hours ago, he had a left arm, a left hand, fingers. Now he blankly recorded his memories. 'I was in the market and I didn't feel anything,' he told me. 'The rocket came and I was to the right of it and then an ambulance took me to hospital.'

Whether or not his amputation was dulled by painkillers, he wanted to talk. When I asked him his name, he sat upright in bed and shouted at me: 'My name is Saddam Hussein Jassem.'

Independent, 30 March 2003

Ahmed Qasm Hamed was dumped in a black sack at the mortuary of the Yarmouk hospital last week. Taleb Neiemah Homtoush turned up at the city morgue with three bullets in his head. Amr Alwan Ibrahim's family brought him to the morgue five minutes later with a bullet through his heart. Amr was to have married his fiancée Naghem in a week's time.

There are flies around the mortuaries and the smell of death, and up at Yarmouk they had so many bodies the other day that I found them lying in the yard because the fridge was already filled with corpses. On stretchers with blankets thrown over them, on the hot concrete beneath the sun, the flies already moving to them in the 45-degree heat. At the city morgue, the morticians appear in dirty green overalls, scarcely glancing at the wailing relatives by the gate, slumped in tears beside a lake of sewage.

After a while – after hours, day after day at the mortuaries – you get to know the victims. Their fathers and wives and cousins tell you how they dressed, how they worked, how many children they have left behind.

Often the children are there beside the cheap wooden coffins, screaming and crying and numb with loss. The families weep and they say that no one cares about them and, after expressing our sorrow to them over and over again, I come to the conclusion they are right. No one cares. '*Al baqiya fi hayatek*,' we tell them in Arabic which, roughly translated, means 'May his lost life be yours in the future.' But it is lost for ever – his life, and, by even the most conservative estimates, those of 10,000 other Iraqi civilians gunned down since we 'liberated' Baghdad on 9 April.

Here, for the record, are just a few of last week's cull. Hassan Ahmed was twenty-six. At the morgue, his cousin Sadeq produces a photograph of the young man for me. Hassan is smiling, he has a thin, slightly bearded face and is wearing a bright purple shirt. His father, a soldier, was killed in the Iran–Iraq war in 1982, when Hassan was just five years old. At 3 p.m. last Wednesday, he was walking in the street in his home neighbourhood of Al-Biyar in Baghdad when someone – no one knows who or why – shot him twice in the head.

Old Sarhan Daoud is almost toothless and bespectacled and is standing outside the doors of the Baghdad city morgue in a long white 'dishdash' robe. A few hours earlier, his only sons, nineteen-year-old Ahmed and twenty-seven-year-old Ali, were gunned down outside their Baghdad home. There is talk of a revenge killing but the father isn't certain. 'We are just trapped in this tragedy,' Sarhan says. 'There were very few killings like this before. Now everyone uses guns. Please tell about our tragedy.' After half an hour, waiting beside the pool of sewage, shoved aside as other corpses are brought into the morgue – the coffins come from the mosques and are re-used day after day – Ahmed and Ali are brought out in their plywood caskets and roped to the top of a mini-van into which cousins and uncles and the old father climb for the funeral journey to the family's home village near Baquba.

The family of Amr Ibrahim say they know who shot the thirty-year-old construction worker on Wednesday. They even gave the name to the American-paid Iraqi police force. But the police did nothing. 'It is anarchy that we live through,' his uncle Daher says. 'Then, when we get here, they charge us 15,000 dinars (£5) for the autopsy – otherwise we can't have a death certificate. First we are robbed of life. Then they take our money.' For many in Iraq, £5 is a month's wages.

Twenty-six-year-old Fahad Makhtouf was knifed to death near his home on Tuesday night. His uncle speaks slowly. 'No one cares about our tragedy. No one cares about us.'

Up at the Yarmouk, they've had a bad week. Mortada Karim has just received the bodies of three men, all shot dead, from local police stations. All are believed to have been murdered by thieves. 'Four days ago, we had one of the worst cases,' he says. 'A mother and her child. There had been a wedding party and people had been shooting in the air. The Americans opened fire and the woman and her child were hit and killed.' On the same day, they received an Iraqi man, killed by his father because they had quarrelled over the loot they had both stolen in Baghdad.

Last month, a family of nine were brought to the Yarmouk. The mortuary attendants believe the five women were found by their brothers in a brothel and in the subsequent 'honour killings' their brothers were caught up in a gun battle.

On the walls of the city mortuary, families have for weeks left photographs of those who have simply disappeared. 'We lost Mr Abdul-emir al-Noor al-Moussawi last Wednesday, 11 June 2003, in Baghdad,' it says beneath the photograph of a dignified man in suit and tie. 'He is seventy-one years old. Hair white. Wearing a grey dish-dash. A reward will be paid to anyone with information.' Or there is sixteen-year-old Beida Jaffer Sadr, a schoolgirl apparently kidnapped in Baghdad, whose father's telephone number is printed below her picture. 'Blonde hair, brown eyes, wearing a black skirt,' it says.

The occupation powers, the so-called 'Coalition Provisional Authority' (CPA), love statistics when they are useful. They can tell you the number of newly re-opened schools, newly appointed doctors and the previous day's oil production in seconds. The daily slaughter of Iraq's innocents, needless to say, is not among their figures. So here are a few statistics. On Wednesday of last week, the Baghdad city morgue received nineteen corpses, of which eleven were victims of gunfire. The next day, the morticians received eleven dead, of whom five had been killed by bullets. In May, approximately 300 murder victims were brought to the morgue, in June around 500, in July 600, last month about 700. In all of July of last year – under Saddam's regime – Dr Abdullah Razak, the deputy head of the morgue, says that only twenty-one gunshot victims were brought in.

Of course, it's possible to put a gloss on all this. Saddam ruled through terror. If there was security in Baghdad under his regime, there was mass murder in Kurdistan and in the Shia south of Iraq. Tens of thousands have been found in the mass graves of Iraq, men – and women – who had no death certificates, no funerals, no justice. At the Abu Ghraib prison, the head doctor, Hussain Majid – who has been re-appointed by the prison's new American guards – told me that when 'security prisoners' were hanged at night, he was ordered not to issue death certificates.

It might be argued that under the previous regime, the government committed the crimes. Now, the people commit them. How can the Americans be held to account for honour killings? But they are account-able, for it is the duty of the occupying power to protect the people under their control. The mandate of the CPA requires it to care for the people of Iraq. And they don't care.

None of the above statistics takes into account the hundreds of shooting incidents in which the victims are wounded rather than killed. In the Kindi hospital, for example, I come across a man whose father was caretaker of a factory. 'Looters came and he opened fire on them and then the Americans came and shot my father because he was holding his gun,' he said. 'He's had two operations, and he'll live. But no one came to see us. No one came to say sorry. Nobody cared.'

One of the most recent corpses to arrive is that of Saad Mohamed Sultan. He was an official interpreter for the occupying powers and was, incredibly, shot dead by an American soldier on a convoy as he travelled with an Italian diplomat to Mosul. After shooting him, the Americans drove calmly on. They didn't bother to stop to find out whom they'd killed. Saad was thirty-five. He had a wife and two children.

In the yard of the city morgue, a group of very angry young men have gathered. They are Shia and, I suspect, members of the Badr Brigade. They are waiting for the coffin of Taleb Homtoush who was killed by three bullets fired into his head as he stood at the door of his Baghdad home on Wednesday. Taleb had lost his legs in the Iran–Iraq war. Two of his brothers were killed in the same conflict. Another cousin, who will not give his name, a tall man, is spitting in anger as he speaks.

'You must know something,' he shouts at me. 'We are a Muslim country and the Americans want to create divisions among us, between Sunni and Shia. But no civil war will occur here in Iraq. These people are dying because the Americans let this happen. You know that the Americans made many promises before they came here. They promised freedom and security and democracy. We were dreaming of these promises. Now we are just dreaming of blowing ourselves up among the Americans.'

Independent, 21 September 2003

JO WILDING

Eyewitness in Falluja

2004

Falluja, Iraq, 11 April 2004

Trucks, oil tankers, tanks are burning on the highway east to Falluja. A stream of boys and men goes to and from a lorry that's not burnt, stripping it bare. We turn on to the back roads through Abu Ghraib, Nuha and Ahrar, singing in Arabic, past the vehicles full of people and a few possessions heading the other way, past the improvised refreshment posts where boys throw food through the windows into the bus for us and for the people still inside Falluja.

The bus is following a car with the nephew of a local sheikh and a guide who has contacts with the Mujaheddin and has cleared this with them. The reason I'm on the bus is that a journalist I knew turned up at my door at about 11 p.m. telling me things were desperate in Falluja; he'd been bringing out children with their limbs blown off. The US soldiers were going around telling people to leave by dusk or be killed, but then when people fled with whatever they could carry, they were being stopped at the US military checkpoint on the edge of town and not let out; trapped, watching the sun go down.

He said aid vehicles and the media were being turned away. He said there was some medical aid that needed to go in and there was a better chance of it getting there with foreigners, Westerners, to get through the American checkpoints. The rest of the way had been secured with the armed groups who control the roads we'd travel on. We'd take in the medical supplies, see what else we could do to help, and then use the bus to bring out people who needed to leave.

I'll spare you the whole decision-making process, all the questions

we asked ourselves and each other, and you can spare me the accusations of madness, but what it came down to was this: if I don't do
it, who will? Either way, we arrive in one piece.

We pile the stuff in the corridor and the boxes are torn open
straightaway, the blankets most welcomed. It's not a hospital at all
but a clinic, a private doctor's surgery treating people for free since
air strikes destroyed the town's main hospital. Another clinic has been
improvised in a garage. There's no anaesthetic. The blood bags are
in a drinks fridge and the doctors warm them up under the hot tap
in an unhygienic toilet.

Screaming women come in, praying, slapping their chests and faces.
'Ummi, my mother,' one cries. I hold her until Maki, a consultant
and the acting director of the clinic, brings me to the bed where a
child of about ten is lying with a bullet wound to the head. A smaller
child is being treated for a similar injury in the next bed. A US sniper
hit them and their grandmother as they left their home to flee Falluja.

The lights go out, the fan stops and in the sudden quiet someone
holds up the flame of a cigarette lighter for the doctor to carry on
operating by. The electricity to the town has been cut off for days,
and when the generator runs out of petrol they just have to manage
until it comes back on. The children are not going to live.

'Come,' says Maki and ushers me alone into a room where an old
woman has just had an abdominal bullet wound stitched up. Another
in her leg is being dressed, the bed under her foot soaked with blood,
a white flag still clutched in her hand and the same story: I was
leaving my home to go to Baghdad when I was hit by a US sniper.
Some of the town is held by US marines, other parts by local fighters.
Their homes are in the US-controlled area and they are adamant that
the snipers were US marines.

Snipers are causing not just carnage but also the paralysis of the
ambulance and evacuation services. The biggest hospital, after the main
one was bombed, is in US territory and cut off from the clinic by
snipers. The ambulance has been repaired four times after bullet
damage. Bodies are lying in the streets because no one can go to collect
them without being shot.

Some said we were mad to come to Iraq; quite a few said we were
completely insane to come to Falluja; and now there are people telling
me that getting in the back of the pick-up to go past the snipers and
get sick and injured people is the craziest thing they've ever seen. I
know, though, that if we don't, no one will.

He's holding a white flag with a red crescent on; I don't know his name. The men we pass wave us on when the driver explains where we're going. The silence is ferocious in the no man's land between the pick-up at the edge of the Mujaheddin territory, which has just gone from our sight behind the last corner, and the marines' line beyond the next wall: no birds, no music, no indication that anyone is still living until a gate opens opposite and a woman comes out, points.

We edge along to the hole in the wall where we can see the car, spent mortar shells around it. The feet are visible, crossed, in the gutter. I think he's dead already. The snipers are visible, too; two of them on the corner of the building. As yet I think they can't see us so we need to let them know we're here.

'Hello,' I bellow at the top of my voice. 'Can you hear me?' They must. They're about thirty metres from us, maybe less, and it's so still you can hear the flies buzzing at fifty paces. 'We are a medical team. We want to remove this wounded man. Is it OK for us to come out and get him? Can you give us a signal that it's OK?'

I'm sure they can hear me, but they're still not responding. Maybe they didn't understand it all, so I say the same again. Finally I think I hear a shout back. Not sure, I call again.

'Hello.'

'Yeah.'

'Can we come out and get him?'

'Yeah.'

Slowly, our hands up, we go out. The black cloud that rises to greet us carries with it a hot, sour smell. Solidified, his legs are heavy. I leave them to Rana and Dave, our guide lifting under his hips. The Kalashnikov is attached by sticky blood to his hair and hand and we don't want it with us, so I put my foot on it as I pick up his shoulders and his blood falls out through the hole in his back. We heave him into the pick-up as best we can and try to outrun the flies.

I suppose he was wearing flip-flops because he's barefoot now, no more than twenty years old, in imitation Nike pants and a blue and black striped football shirt with a big 28 on the back. As the orderlies from the clinic pull the young fighter out of the pick-up, yellow fluid pours from his mouth and they flip him over, face up, the way into the clinic clearing in front of them, straight up the ramp into the makeshift morgue.

We wash the blood off our hands and get into the ambulance. There are people trapped in the other hospital who need to go to

Baghdad. Siren screaming, lights flashing, we huddle on the floor, passports and ID cards held out of the windows. We pack the ambulance with people, one with his chest taped together and a drip, one on a stretcher, legs jerking violently so I have to hold them down as we wheel him out, lifting him over steps.

The hospital is better able to treat the wounded than the clinic, but hasn't got enough of anything to sort them out properly. The only way to get them to Baghdad is on our bus, which means they have to go to the clinic. We're crammed on the floor of the ambulance in case it's shot at. Nisareen, a woman doctor of about my age, can't stop a few tears once we're out.

The doctor rushes out to meet me: 'Can you go to fetch a lady? She is pregnant and she is delivering the baby too soon.'

Azzam is driving, Ahmed in the middle directing him, and I'm by the window, the visible foreigner, the passport. Something scatters across my hand, simultaneous with the crashing of a bullet through the ambulance, some plastic part dislodged, flying through the window.

We stop, turn off the siren, keep the blue light flashing, wait, eyes on the silhouettes of men in US marine uniforms on the corners of the rooftops. Several shots come. We duck, get as low as possible, and I can see tiny red lights whipping past the window, past my head. Some, it's hard to tell, are hitting the ambulance. I start singing. What else do you do when someone's shooting at you? A tyre bursts with an enormous noise and a jerk of the vehicle.

I'm outraged. We're trying to get to a woman who's giving birth without any medical attention, without electricity, in a city under siege, in a clearly marked ambulance, and you're shooting at us. How dare you?

How dare you?

Azzam grabs the gear stick and gets the ambulance into reverse, another tyre bursting as we go over the ridge in the centre of the road, the shots still coming as we flee around the corner. I carry on singing. The wheels are scraping, burst rubber burning on the road.

The men run for a stretcher as we arrive but I shake my head. They spot the new bullet holes and run to see if we're OK. Is there any other way to get to her, I want to know. *La, maaku tarieq.* There is no other way. They say we did the right thing. They say they've fixed the ambulance four times already and they'll fix it again, but the radiator's gone and the wheels are buckled and she's still at home in the dark giving birth alone. I let her down.

We can't go out again. For one thing there's no ambulance, and besides, it's dark now, and that means our foreign faces can't protect the people who go out with us or the people we pick up. Maki says he hated Saddam but now he hates the Americans more.

We take off the blue gowns as the sky starts exploding somewhere beyond the building opposite. Minutes later a car roars up to the clinic. I can hear him screaming before I can see that there's no skin left on his body. He's burnt from head to foot. For sure, there's nothing they can do. He'll die of dehydration within a few days.

Another man is pulled from the car on to a stretcher. Cluster bombs, they say, although it's not clear whether they mean one or both of them. We set off walking to Mr Yasser's house, waiting at each corner for someone to check the street before we cross. A ball of fire falls from a plane, splits into smaller balls of bright white lights. I think they're cluster bombs, because cluster bombs are in the front of my mind, but they vanish, just magnesium flares, incredibly bright but short-lived, giving a flash picture of the town from above.

Mr Yasser asks us all to introduce ourselves. I tell him I'm training to be a lawyer. One of the other men asks whether I know about international law. They want to know about the law on war crimes, what a war crime is. I tell them I know some of the Geneva Conventions, that I'll bring some information next time I come and we can get someone to explain it in Arabic.

We bring up the matter of Nayoko, one of the hostages. This group of fighters has nothing to do with the ones who are holding the Japanese hostages, but while they're thanking us for what we did this evening, we talk about the things Nayoko did for the street kids, how much they loved her. They can't promise anything but that they'll try to find out where she is and try to persuade the group to let her and the others go. I don't suppose it will make any difference. They're busy fighting a war in Falluja. They're unconnected with the other group. But it can't hurt to try.

The planes are above us all night, so that as I doze I forget I'm not on a long-distance flight, the constant bass note of an unmanned reconnaissance drone overlaid with the frantic thrash of jets and the dull beat of helicopters, interrupted by the explosions.

In the morning I make balloon dogs, giraffes and elephants for the little one, Abdullah Aboudi, who's clearly distressed by the noise of the aircraft and explosions. I blow bubbles, which he follows with his eyes. Finally, finally, I score a smile. The twins, thirteen years old, laugh too, one of them an ambulance driver, both said to be handy with a Kalashnikov.

The doctors look haggard in the morning. None has slept more than a couple of hours a night for a week. One has had only eight hours of sleep in the past seven days, missing the funerals of his brother and aunt because he was needed at the hospital.

'The dead we cannot help,' Jassim said. 'I must worry about the injured.'

We go again, Dave, Rana and I, this time in a pick-up. There are some sick people close to the marines' line who need evacuating. No one dares to come out of their house because the marines are on top of the buildings, shooting at anything that moves. Saad fetches us a white flag and tells us not to worry; he's checked and secured the road, no Mujaheddin will fire at us, that peace is upon us; this eleven-year-old child, his face covered with a keffiyeh but for his bright brown eyes, his AK-47 almost as tall as he is.

We shout again to the soldiers, hold up the flag with a red crescent sprayed on to it. Two come down from the building, cover this side and Rana mutters, '*Allahu akbar*. Please nobody take a shot at them.'

We jump down and tell them we need to get some sick people from the houses and they want Rana to go and bring out the family from the house whose roof they're on. Thirteen women and children are still inside, in one room, without food and water for the past twenty-four hours.

'We're going to be going through soon, clearing the houses,' the senior one says.

'What does that mean, clearing the houses?'

'Going into every one, searching for weapons.' He's checking his watch, can't tell me what will start when, of course, but there are going to be air strikes in support. 'If you're going to do this you gotta do it soon.'

First we go down the street we were sent to. There's a man, face down, in a white dishdasha, a small round red stain on his back. We run to him. Again the flies have got there first. Dave is at his shoulders, I'm by his knees, and as we reach to roll him on to the stretcher, Dave's hand goes through his chest, through the cavity left by the bullet that entered so neatly through his back and blew his heart out.

There's no weapon in his hand. Only when we arrive, his sons come out, crying, shouting. 'He was unarmed,' they scream. 'He was unarmed. He just went out the gate and they shot him.' None of them has dared to come out since. No one had dared to get his body; horrified, terrified, forced to violate the Islamic tradition of burying the body immediately. They couldn't have known we were coming, so it's inconceivable that anyone would have come out and retrieved a weapon, but left the body.

He was unarmed, fifty-five years old, shot in the back.

We cover his face, carry him to the pick-up. There's nothing to cover his body with. A sick woman is helped out of the house, the little girls around her hugging cloth bags to their bodies, whispering, 'Baba. Baba.' Daddy. Shaking, they let us go first, hands up, around the corner, then we usher them to the cab of the pick-up, shielding their heads so they can't see him, the cuddly fat man stiff in the back.

The people seem to pour out of the houses now, in the hope we can escort them safely out of the line of fire; kids, women, men, anxiously asking us whether they can all go, or only the women and children. We go to ask. The young marine tells us that men of fighting age can't leave. What's fighting age, I want to know. He contemplates. Anything under forty-five. No lower limit.

It appals me that all those men will be trapped in a city that is about to be destroyed. Not all of them are fighters, not all are armed. It's going to happen out of the view of the world, out of sight of the media, because most of the media in Falluja is embedded with the marines or turned away at the outskirts. Before we can pass the message on, two explosions scatter the crowd in the side street back into their houses.

Rana's with the marines evacuating the family from the house they're occupying. The pick-up isn't back yet. People are hiding behind their walls. We wait, because there's nothing else we can do. We wait in no man's land. The marines, at least, are watching us through binoculars; maybe the local fighters are, too.

I've got a disappearing hanky in my pocket, so while I'm sitting like a lemon, nowhere to go, gunfire and explosions aplenty all around, I make the hanky disappear, reappear, disappear. It's always best, I think, to seem completely unthreatening and completely unconcerned, so no one worries about you enough to shoot. We can't wait too long, though. Rana's been gone ages. We have to go and get her to hurry. There's a young man in the group. She's talked them into letting him leave, too.

A man wants to use his police car to carry some of the people, a couple of elderly ones who can't walk far, the smallest children. It's missing a door. Who knows if it was really a police car or if the car was reappropriated and just ended up here? It doesn't matter, if it gets people out faster. They creep from their houses, huddle by the wall, follow us out, their hands up too, and walk up the street clutching babies, bags, each other.

The pick-up gets back and we shovel as many into it as we can, as an ambulance arrives from somewhere. A young man waves from the doorway of what's left of a house, his upper body bare, a blood-soaked bandage around his arm, probably a fighter but it makes no difference once someone is wounded and unarmed. Getting the dead isn't essential. As the doctor said, the dead don't need help, but if it's easy enough, then we will. Since we're already OK with the soldiers and the ambulance is here, we run down to fetch them.

The ambulance follows us down. The soldiers start shouting at us in English for it to stop, pointing guns. It's moving fast. We're all yelling, signalling for it to stop, but it seems to take for ever for the driver to hear and see us. It stops. It stops, before they open fire. We haul the dead on to the stretchers and run, shove them in the back. Rana squeezes in the front with the wounded man, and Dave and I crouch in the back beside the bodies. He says he had allergies as a kid and hasn't got much sense of smell. I wish, retrospectively, for childhood allergies, and stick my head out of the window.

The bus is going to leave, taking the injured people back to Baghdad, the man with the burns, one of the women who was shot in the jaw and shoulder by a sniper, several others. Rana says she's staying to help. Dave and I don't hesitate: we're staying, too. 'If I don't do it, who will?' has become an accidental motto, and I'm acutely aware after the last foray how many people, how many women and children, are still in their houses, either because they've got nowhere to go, because they're scared to go out of the door, or because they've chosen to stay.

To begin with it's agreed, then Azzam says we have to go. He hasn't got contacts with every armed group, only with some. There are different issues to square with each one. We need to get these people back to Baghdad as quickly as we can. If we're kidnapped or killed it will cause even more problems, so it's better that we just get on the bus and leave and come back with him as soon as possible.

It hurts to climb on to the bus when the doctor has just asked us to evacuate more people. I hate the fact that a qualified medic can't travel in the ambulance but I can, just because I look like the sniper's sister or one of his mates, but that's the way it is today and the way it was yesterday and I feel like a traitor for leaving, but I can't see that I've got a choice. It's a war now, and as alien as it is to me to do what I'm told, for once I've got to.

Jassim is scared. He harangues Mohammed constantly, tries to pull him out of the driver's seat while we're moving. The woman with the gunshot wound is on the back seat, the man with the burns in front of her, being fanned with cardboard from the empty boxes, his intravenous drip swinging from the rail along the ceiling of the bus. It's hot. It must be unbearable for him.

Saad gets on to the bus to wish us well for the journey. He shakes Dave's hand and then mine. I hold his in both of mine and tell him 'Dir balak,' take care, as if I could say anything more stupid to a pre-teen Mujaheddin with an AK-47 in his other hand, and our eyes meet and stay fixed, his full of fire and fear.

Can't I take him away? Can't I take him somewhere he can be a child? Can't I make him a balloon giraffe and give him some drawing pens and tell him not to forget to brush his teeth? Can't I find the person who put the rifle in the hands of that little boy? Can't I tell someone about what that does to a child? Do I have to leave him here where there are heavily armed men all around him and lots of them are not on his side, however many sides there are in all of this? And, of course, I do. I do have to leave him, like child soldiers everywhere.

The way back is tense, the bus almost getting stuck in a dip in the sand, people escaping in anything, even piled on the trailer of a tractor, lines of cars and pick-ups and buses ferrying people to the dubious sanctuary of Baghdad, lines of men in vehicles, having got their families to safety, queuing to get back into the city, either to fight or to help evacuate more people. The driver, Jassim, the father, ignores Azzam and takes a different road, so that suddenly we're not following the lead car and we're on a road that's controlled by a different armed group than the ones who know us.

A crowd of men waves guns for us to stop. Somehow they seem to believe that there are American soldiers on the bus, as if they wouldn't be in tanks or helicopters, and there are men getting out of their cars with shouts of 'Sahafa Amreeki', American journalists. The passengers shout out of the windows, 'Ana min Falluja,' I am from Falluja. Gunmen run on to the bus and see that it's true, there are sick and injured and old people, Iraqis, and then relax, wave us on.

We stop in Abu Ghraib and swap seats, foreigners in the front,

Iraqis less visible, headscarves off so we look more Western. The American soldiers are so happy to see Westerners, they don't mind too much about the Iraqis we have with us; they search the men and the bus, leave the women unsearched because there are no women soldiers to search us. Mohammed keeps asking me if things are going to be OK.

'*Al-melaach wiyana*,' I tell him. The angels are with us. He laughs.

And then we're in Baghdad, delivering the wounded to the hospitals, Nuha in tears as they take the burnt man off, groaning and whimpering. She puts her arms around me and asks me to be her friend. I make her feel less isolated, she says, less alone.

And the satellite news says the ceasefire is holding and George Bush tells the troops on Easter Sunday, 'I know what we're doing in Iraq is right.' Shooting unarmed men in the back outside their homes is right? Shooting grandmothers with white flags is right? Shooting at women and children who are fleeing is right? Firing at ambulances is right?

Well, George, I know too now. I know what it looks like when you brutalise people so much that they've nothing left to lose. I know what it looks like when an operation is being done without anaesthetic because the hospitals are destroyed or under sniper fire and the city's under siege and aid isn't getting in properly. I know what it sounds like, too. I know what it looks like when tracer bullets are passing your head, even though you're in an ambulance. I know what it looks like when a man's chest is no longer inside him and what it smells like, and I know what it looks like when his wife and children pour out of his house.

It's a crime and it's a disgrace to us all.

EDWARD W. SAID

Covering Islam and Terrorism

1997/2002

This final chapter is a tribute to Edward Said, who died as this collection was under way. It is also fitting that the book ends with such a beacon of journalism; for although Edward Said was a renowned academic, a literary critic, writer, poet and musician, he was, above all, a journalist, inspired by an old-fashioned, fearless humanism which his critics wilfully ignored, along with his honesty and fairness. As a Palestinian exile, he not only stood up to Israel, he was also critical of Arab terrorism; invoking his melancholy irony, he once described himself as 'the last Jewish intellectual', which meant that he was ever wandering, homeless, dispossessed. His enemies never understood that, nor his lifelong affinity with the Jewish people.

Born in Jerusalem in 1935 and forced into exile in 1948, Edward Said wrote tirelessly on the struggle for Palestinian self-determination; his books include the seminal *Orientalism* (1978), *The Question of Palestine* (1979), *The Politics of Dispossession* (1994) and *The End of the Peace Process* (2000). The worst of the press called him a 'professor of terror' and 'Arafat's man in New York'; in fact, Arafat had no more unflagging critic than Edward Said, who was one of the few Palestinians to speak out against the so-called Middle East 'peace process', begun in Oslo in 1993. He argued that the 'Oslo Accords' gave the Palestinians no sovereignty over land that Israel continued to occupy illegally and merely preserved Yassir Arafat's corrupt authority.

I knew Edward for twenty years; the last time I saw him was when we shared a platform in Gothenburg, Sweden, discussing Western journalism, its power and its failure to cover the Middle East and Islam decently. He told me that when he flew from his home in New York to another part of America, he was routinely humiliated because of his name: often strip-searched and told to wait 'over there . . . rather like a recalcitrant dog'. This happened to hundreds of innocent people every day, he said. No journalist would write about it, because 'they have never been as cowed as they are now'.

Sick for much of his life with leukaemia, he was both vulnerable and generous. When I asked him to appear in my film about Palestine, he offered, from his hospital bed in New York, to fly to London especially; I said no. Once, after I had not heard from him for a long time, he wrote, 'I am under siege; please understand.' Few knew that he kept an emergency button in his New York apartment connected to the local police station; his office at Columbia University was once burned down.

The first extract I have chosen is from *Covering Islam*, Edward's 1981 book on the media portrayal of the Muslim world, which today could not be more timely. He wrote it in response to events in Iran in 1979, in particular the occupation of the US embassy in Tehran by students supporting the Islamic revolution that had swept aside Shah Reza Pahlavi. In demanding the extradition of the Shah from the United States, the students held fifty-two Americans hostage for 444 days. The episode led to the defeat of President Jimmy Carter, the election of Ronald Reagan and the Iran–*Contra* affair. It also created a cottage industry of 'terrorism experts', who continue to influence our understanding of the Muslim world. Edward Said was among the first to expose their falsehoods and their veiled racism.

'Malicious generalisations about Islam have become the last accept-able form of denigration of foreign culture in the West,' he wrote; 'what is said about the Muslim mind, or character, or religion, or culture as a whole cannot now be said in mainstream discussion about Africans, Jews, other Orientals, or Asians.' Attacks on Islam as 'stuck in the Middle Ages' were later echoed following September 11, 2001; historical reasons were simply ignored. Just as Americans knew little in 1979 about their government's destruction of democracy in Iran and support for the Shah's vicious regime, so they knew little about the American role in the creation of al-Qaida. Edward Said was warning us all that Western-backed invasions and occupations across the Middle East, from Iraq to Palestine, were building an arc of resistance, and that prejudice and propaganda offered us no protection, let alone peace for all the people of the region.

The following passages are mainly from the introduction that Edward wrote in 1997 for the revised edition of *Covering Islam*. From a range of articles about the current 'war on terror' and Palestine, I have selected one published shortly before his death in 2003.

COVERING ISLAM

In the fifteen years since *Covering Islam* appeared there has been an intense focus on Muslims and Islam in the American and Western media, most of it characterised by a more highly exaggerated stereotyping and belligerent hostility than what I had previously described in my book. Indeed, Islam's role in hijackings and terrorism, descriptions of the way in which overtly Muslim countries like Iran threaten 'us' and our way of life, and speculations about the latest conspiracy to blow up buildings, sabotage commercial airliners, and poison water supplies seem to play increasingly on Western consciousness. A corps of 'experts' on the Islamic world has grown to prominence, and during a crisis they are brought out to pontificate on formulaic ideas about Islam on news programmes or talk shows. There also seems to have been a strange revival of canonical, though previously discredited, Orientalist ideas about Muslim, generally non-white, people – ideas which have achieved a startling prominence at a time when racial or religious misrepresentations of every other cultural group are no longer circulated with such impunity. Malicious generalisations about Islam have become the last acceptable form of denigration of foreign culture in the West; what is said about the Muslim mind, or character, or religion, or culture as a whole cannot now be said in mainstream discussion about Africans, Jews, other Orientals, or Asians.

There *has* been a resurgence of emotion throughout the Islamic world, and there have been a great many incidents of terrorism, organised or not, against Western and Israeli targets. The general state of the Islamic world with its decline in productivity and wellbeing, including such phenomena as censorship, the relative absence of democracy, the dismaying prevalence of dictatorships and fiercely repressive and authoritarian states, some of whom practise and encourage terrorism, torture, genital mutilation, seems backward and cruel; this includes such basically Islamic countries as Saudi Arabia, Egypt, Iraq, Sudan

and Algeria, among others. In addition, the (to me) simplistic reduct-
iveness of some numbers of people who have recourse to a hazy
fantasy of seventh-century Mecca as a panacea for numerous ills in
today's Muslim world makes for an unattractive mix that it would
be rank hypocrisy to deny.

My concern, though, is that the mere use of the label 'Islam',
either to explain or indiscriminately condemn 'Islam', actually ends
up becoming a form of attack, which in turn provokes more hostility
between self-appointed Muslim and Western spokespersons. 'Islam'
defines a relatively small proportion of what actually takes place in
the Islamic world, which numbers a billion people, and includes
dozens of countries, societies, traditions, languages and, of course,
an infinite number of different experiences. It is simply false to try
to trace all this back to something called 'Islam', no matter how
vociferously polemical Orientalists – mainly active in the United
States, Britain and Israel – insisted that Islam regulates Islamic societies from top to bottom, that *dar al-Islam* is a single, coherent
entity, that church and state are really one in Islam, and so forth.
My contention is that most of this is unacceptable generalisation of
the most irresponsible sort, and could never be used for any other
religious, cultural or demographic group on earth. What we expect
from the serious study of Western societies, with its complex theories, enormously variegated analyses of social structures, histories,
cultural formations, and sophisticated languages of investigation,
we should also expect from the study and discussion of Islamic societies in the West.

Instead of scholarship, we often find only journalists making extravagant statements, which are instantly picked up and further drama-
tised by the media. Looming over their work is the slippery concept,
to which they constantly allude, of *'fundamentalism'*, a word that
has come to be associated almost automatically with Islam, although
it has a flourishing, usually elided, relationship with Christianity,
Judaism and Hinduism. The deliberately created associations between
Islam and fundamentalism ensure that the average reader comes to
see Islam and fundamentalism as essentially the same thing. Given
the tendency to reduce Islam to a handful of rules, stereotypes and
generalisations about the faith, its founder and all of its people, then
the reinforcement of every negative fact associated with Islam – its
violence, primitiveness, atavism, threatening qualities – is perpetu-
ated. And all this without any serious effort at defining the term

'fundamentalism', or giving precise meaning either to 'radicalism' or 'extremism', or giving those phenomena some context (for example, saying that 5 per cent, or 10 per cent, or 50 per cent of all Muslims are fundamentalists).

Islam has become a central discussion in many policy-making, as well as media, circles. Most of these discussions elide the fact that the major Islamic groupings today are United States allies and clients, or within the United States orbit – such countries as Saudi Arabia, Indonesia, Malaysia, Pakistan, Egypt, Morocco, Jordan and Turkey, where militant Muslims emerged to some degree because the regimes are openly supported by the United States; these often isolated minority governments, alienated from most of their peoples, have been forced to accept United States tutelage and influence because of a United States, not a Muslim, agenda. The Council on Foreign Relations, a prestigious and influential policy association, has recently set up a Muslim Politics Report and study group which allows a wide range of opinions about Islam, some of them salutary and informative. Yet in such publications as *Foreign Affairs*, the Council's quarterly journal, the debate is often set in polarised terms such as between Judith Miller and Leon Hadar, the latter against, the former for, a positive answer to the question, 'Is Islam a Threat?' (*Foreign Affairs*, spring 1993). With some small degree of empathy it is not difficult to imagine that a Muslim might be made uncomfortable by the relentless insistence – even if it is put in terms of a debate – that her or his faith, culture and people are seen as a source of threat, and that she or he has been deterministically associated with terrorism, violence and 'fundamentalism'.

A steady stream of such characterisations is inflated still more by contributions from pro-Israeli journals and books, in the hope that more Americans and Europeans will see Israel as a victim of Islamic violence. One Israeli government after another has resorted to the propagation of this self-image in the course of the information wars that have gone on since 1948 around the whole question of the Middle East. It is important to insist that such claims about Islam and, most of the time, the Arabs, are designed to obscure what it is that Israel and the United States, as 'Islam's' main opponents, have been doing. Between them, the two countries have bombed and invaded several Islamic countries (Egypt, Jordan, Syria, Libya, Somalia, Iraq), they have (in Israel's case) occupied Arab-Islamic territory in four countries, and in the United States' case are seen in the United Nations as openly supporting the military occupation of these territories; to the overwhelming majority of Muslims and Arabs, Israel is therefore an arrogant regional nuclear power, contemptuous of its neighbours, heedless in the number and frequency of its bombings, killings (which far exceed the number of Israelis killed by Muslims), dispossessions and dislocations, especially so far as the Palestinians are concerned. Defying international law and dozens of United Nations Resolutions, Israel has annexed East Jerusalem and the Golan Heights, has occupied South Lebanon since 1982, has had a policy of treating (and characterising) Palestinians as sub-human – in effect a race apart – and has wielded its power over United States Middle Eastern policy whereby the interests of four million Israelis totally overshadow the interests of two hundred million Arab Muslims.

It is all this, and not Bernard Lewis's quaint formulation that Muslims are enraged at Western 'modernity', that has created an understandable sense of Arab-Islamic grievance against powers who, like Israel and the United States, proclaim that they are liberal democracies but act against lesser peoples according to quite contradictory norms of self-interest and cruelty. When the United States led a coalition of countries against Iraq in 1991, it spoke about the need to reverse aggression and occupation. Had Iraq not been a Muslim country that militarily occupied another such country in an area of huge oil reserves that are considered to be the United States' preserve, the invasion would not have taken place, just as Israel's invasion and occupation of the West Bank and Golan Heights, its annexation of East Jerusalem and the implantation of settlements were not seen by the United States as requiring its intervention.

I am not saying that Muslims have not attacked and injured Israelis and Westerners in the name of Islam. But I am saying that much of what one reads and sees in the media about Islam represents the aggression as coming from Islam because that is what 'Islam' is. Local and concrete circumstances are thus obliterated. In other words, covering Islam is a one-sided activity that obscures what 'we' *do*, and highlights instead what Muslims and Arabs by their very flawed nature *are*.

One of the few recent critical assessments of the damage caused by clichés about Islam in the media, policy journals and academia is by Zachary Karabell (*World Policy Journal*, summer 1995), who starts

from the premise that there has been undue attention paid to 'funda-
mentalist' Islam since the end of the Cold War. The public media,
he says quite rightly, has been filled with negative images of Islam.
'Ask American college students, in the élite universities or elsewhere,
what they think of when the word "Muslim" is mentioned. The
response is inevitably the same: gun-toting, bearded, fanatic terrorists hellbent on destroying the great enemy, the United States.' Karabell
notes, for instance, that ABC's *20/20*, a prestigious, high-profile news
programme, 'broadcast several segments discussing Islam as a
crusading religion inculcating warriors of God; *Frontline* sponsored
an investigation of the tentacles of Muslim terrorists around the
world.' He might also have mentioned Emerson's PBS film *Jihad in
America*, cynically designed and promoted to exploit just this fear;
or even the vogue of books with provocative titles like *Sacred Rage*
or *In the Name of God*, which make the association between Islam
and dangerous irrationalism firmer, more inevitable. 'The same can
be said of the print media,' Karabell continues. 'Stories about the
Middle East are often accompanied by a picture of a mosque or large
crowds praying.'

All this marks a serious deterioration in the situation I described in
the original edition of *Covering Islam*. There is now, for example, a
new wave of large-scale feature films (one of them, *True Lies*, Karabell
reminds us, 'had as its villains classic Arab terrorists, complete with
glinty eyes and a passionate desire to kill Americans') whose main
purpose is first to demonise and dehumanise Muslims in order, second,
to show an intrepid Western, usually American, hero killing them off.
Delta Force (1985) began the trend, but it was carried forward in the
Indiana Jones saga, and innumerable television serials in which Muslims
are uniformly represented as evil, violent and, above all, eminently
killable. One of the changes from an old habit of exoticising the Orient
in Hollywood films is that romance and charm have now been
completely eliminated, as they have also been in the ninja films that
pit a white (or even black) American against endless numbers of black-
masked Orientals, all of whom get their just deserts.

No one, of course, expects journalists or media personalities to spend
a great deal of time being scholarly, reading books, looking for alternative views, or trying to inform themselves in ways that do not
presume that Islam is both monolithic and hostile. But why the
slavish and uncritical adoption of views that stress the unvaryingly

reductive arguments about Islam, and why the extraordinary willingness to accept the official rhetoric emanating from the American
Government in its irresponsible characterisations of Islam: by that I
mean the loose application of the word 'terrorism' to 'Islam', and
the attitude that elevates Israeli views of Islam's 'dangers' to the level
of United States policy?

The answer is in how prevalent age-old views of Islam as an accept-
able competitor to the Christian West still are. Japan-bashing, for
example, exists precisely because Japan is rightly perceived as showing
aggressive resistance to Euro-American economic hegemony. The
tendency to consider the whole world as one country's *imperium* is
very much in the ascendancy in today's United States, the last remaining
superpower. But whereas most other great cultural groupings appear
to have accepted the United States' role, it is only from within the
Islamic world that signs of determined resistance are still strong.
Therefore we have an efflorescence of cultural and religious attacks
on Islam from individuals and groups whose interests are informed
with the idea of the West (and the United States, as its leader) as the
standard for enlightened modernity. Yet far from being an accurate
description of 'the West', such an idea of rightful Western dominance
is in reality an uncritical idolisation of Western *power*.

Judith Miller's book *God Has Ninety-Nine Names: a Reporter's
Journey through a Militant Middle East* (1996) is like a textbook of
the inadequacies and distortions of media coverage of Islam. Much
in evidence on talk shows and seminars on the Middle East, Miller
trades in 'The Islamic Threat', as a *Foreign Affairs* symposium to
which she contributed had it in 1993; her particular mission has been
to advance the millennial thesis that militant Islam is a danger to the
West, the very idea that is at the core of Samuel Huntington's clash
of civilisations diatribe. So in the supposed intellectual vacuum created
by the Soviet Union's dismemberment, the search for a new foreign
devil has come to rest, as it did beginning in the eighth century for
European Christianity, on Islam, a religion whose physical proximity
and unstilled challenge to the West (a vague term used by Bernard
Lewis and Huntington that denotes 'our' civilisation as opposed to
'theirs') seem as diabolical and violent now as they did then. Miller
does not mention that most Islamic countries today are poverty-
stricken, tyrannical and hopelessly inept militarily as well as scientif-
ically to be much of a threat to anyone except their own citizens; and

she doesn't dwell on the fact that the most powerful of them – Saudi Arabia, Egypt, Jordan and Pakistan – are totally within the United States' orbit.

What matters to 'experts' like Miller, Huntington, Martin Kramer, Daniel Pipes and Barry Rubin, plus a whole battery of Israeli academics, is to make sure that the 'threat' is kept before our eyes, the better to excoriate Islam for its terror, despotism and violence, while assuring themselves profitable consultancies, frequent television appearances and book contracts. To a basically indifferent and already poorly informed American clientele the Islamic threat is made to seem disproportionately fearsome, lending support to the thesis (which is an interesting parallel to anti-Semitic paranoia) that there is a worldwide conspiracy behind every explosion.

Political Islam has generally not done well wherever it has tried through Islamist parties to take state power. Iran may be an exception, but neither Sudan, which is in fact an Islamic state, nor Algeria, riven by the contest between Islamic groups and a brutal soldiery, nor Afghanistan, a turbulent and now ultrareactionary country, has done anything but make itself poorer and more marginal on the world stage. Lurking beneath the discourse of Islamic peril in the West is, however, some measure of truth, which is that appeals to Islam among Muslims have fuelled resistance (in the style of what Eric Hobsbawm has called primitive, pre-industrial rebellion) here and there to the *pax Americana-Israelica* throughout the Middle East. Yet neither Hizbollah nor Hamas has presented a serious obstacle to the steamroller of the anything-but-peace process. I would say that most Arab Muslims today are too discouraged and humiliated, and also too anaesthetised by uncertainty and their incompetent and crude dictatorships, to support anything like a vast Islamic campaign against the West. Besides, the élites are for the most part in league with the regimes, supporting martial law which, in Egypt, has endured since 1946, plus various other effective extralegal measures against 'extremists'. So why then the accents of alarm and fear in most discussions of Islam? Of course there have been suicide bombings and outrageous acts of terrorism, but have these accomplished anything except to strengthen the hands of Israel and the United States as well as their client regimes in the Muslim world?

The answer, I think, is that books like Miller's are symptomatic, in that they furnish an additional weapon in the contest to subordinate, beat down, compel and defeat any Arab or Muslim resistance

to United States–Israeli dominance. Moreover, by surreptitiously justifying a policy of single-minded obduracy that links Islamism, however
lamentable it is, to a strategically important, oil-rich part of the world,
the anti-Islam campaign virtually eliminates the possibility of any sort
of equal dialogue between Islam and the Arabs, and the West or Israel.
To demonise and dehumanise a whole culture on the grounds that it
is 'enraged' at modernity is to turn Muslims into the objects of a thera-
peutic, punitive attention. I do not want to be misunderstood here:
the manipulation of Islam, or for that matter Christianity and Judaism,
for retrograde political purposes is catastrophically bad, and must be
opposed, not just in Saudi Arabia, the West Bank and Gaza, Pakistan,
Sudan, Algeria and Tunisia, but also in Israel, among the right-wing
Christians in Lebanon (for whom Miller shows an unseemly sympathy),
and wherever theocratic tendencies appear. And I do not at all believe
that all the ills of Arab Muslim countries are due to Zionism and
imperialism. But this is very far from saying that Israel and the United
States, and their intellectual flacks, have not played a combative, even
incendiary role in stigmatising and heaping invidious abuse on an
abstraction called 'Islam', in order to deliberately stir up feelings of
anger and fear about Islam in Americans and Europeans who are also
enjoined to see in Israel a secular, liberal democracy. Miller says at
the end of her book that right-wing Judaism in Israel is 'the subject
of another book'. It ought actually to be very much a part of the
book that she has written, except that she has suppressed it in order
to go after 'Islam'.

The misrepresentations and distortions committed in the portrayal of
Islam today argue neither a genuine desire to understand nor a willingness to listen and see what there is to see and listen to. Far from
being naïve or pragmatic accounts of Islam, the images and processes
by which the media has delivered Islam for consideration to the Western
consumer of news perpetuate hostility and ignorance for reasons
very well analysed by Noam Chomsky in a long series of books
(*Manufacturing Consent* with Edward S. Herman, *The Culture of
Terrorism* and *Deterring Democracy* in particular). Yet, whatever
motives we attribute to this situation, the fact is that precious little in
the way of dialogue and exchange – both of which occur in scholarly
debate, in artistic production, in the encounters between ordinary human
beings who do business, interact, and generally talk *to*, as opposed to
at, each other – makes it into the public domain so dominated by the

mass media. Sensationalism, crude xenophobia and insensitive belligerence are the order of the day, with results on both sides of the imaginary line between 'us' and 'them' that are extremely unedifying.

On 20 January 1981, the fifty-two Americans held prisoner in the United States embassy for 444 days finally left Iran. A few days later they arrived in the United States to be greeted by the country's genuine happiness in seeing them back. The 'hostage return', as it came to be called, became a week-long media event. There were many frequently intrusive and maudlin hours of live television coverage as the 'returnees' were transported to Algeria, then to Germany, then to West Point, to Washington, and at last to their various home towns. Most newspapers and national weeklies ran supplements on the return, ranging from learned analyses of how the final agreement between Iran and the United States was arrived at, and what it involved, to celebrations of American heroism and Iranian barbarism. Interspersed were personal stories of the hostage ordeal, often embroidered by enterprising journalists and what seemed an alarmingly available number of psychiatrists eager to explain what the hostages were *really* going through. Insofar as there was serious discussion of the past and of the future that went beyond the level of the yellow ribbons designated as symbolic of Iranian captivity, the new Reagan administration set the tone and determined the limits. Analysis of the past was focused on whether the United States should have made (and whether it ought to honour) the agreement with Iran. On 31 January 1981, the *New Republic* predictably attacked 'the ransom', and the Carter administration for giving in to terrorists; then it condemned the whole 'legally controvertible proposition' of dealing with Iranian demands, as well as the use as intermediary of Algeria, a country 'well practised at giving refuge to terrorists and laundering the ransoms they bring'. Discussion of the future was constrained by the Reagan administration's declared war on terrorism; this, not human rights, was to be the new priority of United States policy, even to the extent of supporting 'moderately repressive regimes' if they happen to be allies.

Hints of how the media might responsibly use their enormous capa-

---

[1] Transcript provided courtesy of Veronica Pollard, ABC, New York.

bility for public information were to be found in the three-hour special broadcast by ABC, *The Secret Negotiations*, on 22 and 28 January 1981. In exposing the various methods used to free the hostages, the broadcasts put forth an impressive amount of unknown material, little of it more telling than those moments when unconscious and deep-seated attitudes were suddenly illuminated.

One such moment occurs when Christian Bourguet describes his late March 1980 meeting with Jimmy Carter at the White House. Bourguet, a French lawyer with ties to the Iranians, acted as an intermediary between the United States and Iran; he had come to Washington because, despite an arrangement worked out with the Panamanians to arrest the ex-Shah, the deposed ruler had left suddenly for Egypt. So they were back to square one:

BOURGUET: At a given moment [Carter] spoke of the hostages, saying, you understand that these are Americans. These are innocents. I said to him, yes, Mr President, I understand that you say they are innocent. But I believe you have to understand that for the Iranians they aren't innocent. Even if personally none of them has committed an act, they are not innocent because they are diplomats who represent a country that has done a number of things in Iran.

You must understand that it is not against their person that the action is being taken. Of course, you can see that. They have not been harmed. They have not been hurt. No attempt has been made to kill them. You must understand that it is a symbol, that it is on the plane of symbols that we have to think about this matter.[1]

In fact, Carter does seem to have viewed the embassy seizure in symbolic terms, but unlike the Frenchman, he had his own frame of reference. To him, Americans were by definition innocent and in a sense outside history: Iran's grievances against the United States, he would say on another occasion, were ancient history. What mattered now was that Iranians were terrorists, and Iran perhaps had always been potentially a terrorist nation. Indeed, anyone who disliked America and held Americans captive was dangerous and sick, beyond rationality, beyond humanity, beyond common decency.

Carter's inability to connect what some foreigners felt about the United States' longstanding support for local dictators with what was

happening to the Americans held unlawfully in Tehran is extraordinarily symptomatic. Even if one completely opposes the hostage-
taking, and even if one has only positive feelings about the hostages'
return, there are alarming lessons to be learned from what seems like
the official national tendency to be oblivious to certain realities. All
relationships between people and nations involve two sides. Nothing
at all enjoins 'us' to like or approve of 'them', but we must at least
recognise (a) that 'they' are there, and (b) that so far as 'they' are
concerned, 'we' are what we are, plus what they have experienced
and known of us. This is not a matter of innocence or guilt, or of
patriotism and treason. Neither side commands reality so totally as
to disregard the other. Unless, of course, we believe as Americans that
whereas the other side is ontologically guilty, we are innocent.

Granted that Iran and the United States have undergone wrenching
unpleasantness, and granted too that the embassy seizure turned out
to be an index of an overall Iranian lapse into unproductive, retro-
gressive chaos. Still, there is no need complacently to glean insufficient
wisdom from recent history. The fact is that change is taking place in
'Islam' much as it is taking place in 'the West'. The modes and paces
are different, but some dangers and some uncertainties are similar. As
rallying cries for their constituencies, 'Islam' and 'the West' (or 'America')
provide incitement more than insight. As equal and opposite reactions
to the disorientations of new actualities, 'Islam' and 'the West' can turn
analysis into simple polemic, experience into fantasy. Respect for the
concrete detail of human experience, understanding that arises from
viewing the Other compassionately, knowledge gained and diffused
through moral and intellectual honesty: surely these are better, if not
easier, goals at present than confrontation and reductive hostility. And
if in the process we can dispose finally of both the residual hatred and
the offensive generality of labels like 'the Muslim', 'the Persian', 'the
Turk', 'the Arab' or 'the Westerner', then so much the better.

SAID ON TERRORISM

Aside from the obvious physical discomforts, being ill for a long
period of time fills the spirit with a terrible feeling of helplessness,
but also with periods of analytic lucidity, which, of course, must be

treasured. For the past three months now I have been in and out of the hospital, with days marked by lengthy and painful treatments, blood transfusions, endless tests, hours and hours of unproductive time spent staring at the ceiling, draining fatigue and infection, inability to do normal work, and thinking, thinking, thinking. But there are also the intermittent passages of lucidity and reflection that some-times give the mind a perspective on daily life that allows it to see things (without being able to do much about them) from a different perspective. Reading the news from Palestine and seeing the frightful images of death and destruction on television, it has been my expe-rience to be utterly amazed and aghast at what I have deduced from those details about Israeli government policy, more particularly about what has been going on in the mind of Ariel Sharon. And when, after the recent Gaza bombing by one of his F-16s in which nine children were massacred, he was quoted as congratulating the pilot and boasting of a great Israeli success, I was able to form a much clearer idea than before of what a pathologically deranged mind is capable of, not only in terms of what it plans and orders but, worse, how it manages to persuade other minds to think in the same delusional and criminal way. Getting inside the official Israeli mind is a worthwhile, if lurid, experience.

In the West, however, there's been such repetitious and unedifying attention paid to Palestinian suicide bombing that a gross distortion in reality has completely obscured what is much worse: the official Israeli, and perhaps the uniquely Sharonian, evil that has been visited so deliberately and so methodically on the Palestinian people. Suicide bombing is reprehensible but it is a direct and, in my opinion, a consciously programmed result of years of abuse, powerlessness and despair. It has as little to do with the Arab or Muslim supposed propen-sity for violence as the man in the moon. Sharon wants terrorism, not peace, and he does everything in his power to create the conditions for it. But for all its horror, Palestinian violence, the response of a desperate and horribly oppressed people, has been stripped of its context and the terrible suffering from which it arises: a failure to see that is a failure in humanity, which doesn't make it any less terrible but at least situates it in a real history and real geography.

Yet the location of Palestinian terror – of course it is terror – is never allowed a moment's chance to appear, so remorseless has been the focus on it as a phenomenon apart, a pure, gratuitous evil that Israel, supposedly acting on behalf of pure good, has been virtuously battling in its variously appalling acts of disproportionate violence against a population of three million Palestinian civilians. I am not speaking only about Israel's manipulation of opinion, but its exploitation of the American equivalent of the campaign against terrorism, without which Israel could not have done what it has done. (In fact, I cannot think of any other country on earth that, in full view of nightly TV audiences, has performed such miracles of detailed sadism against an entire society and got away with it.) That this evil has been made consciously part of George W. Bush's campaign against terrorism, irrationally magnifying American fantasies and fixations with extraordinary ease, is no small part of its blind destructiveness. Like the brigades of eager (and, in my opinion, completely corrupt) American intellectuals who spin enormous structures of falsehoods about the benign purpose and necessity of US imperialism, Israeli society has pressed into service numerous academics, policy intellectuals at think-tanks and ex-military men now in defence-related and public-relations businesses, all to rationalise and make convincing inhuman punitive policies that are supposedly based on the need for Israeli security.

Israeli security is now a fabled beast. Like a unicorn it is endlessly hunted and never found, remaining, everlastingly, the goal of future action. That over time Israel has become less secure and more unacceptable to its neighbours scarcely merits a moment's notice. But then who challenges the view that Israeli security ought to define the moral world we live in? Certainly not the Arab and Palestinian leaderships who for thirty years have conceded everything to Israeli security. Shouldn't that ever be questioned, given that Israel has wreaked more damage on the Palestinians and other Arabs relative to its size than any country in the world; Israel with its nuclear arsenal, its air force, navy and army limitlessly supplied by the US taxpayer? As a result, the daily, minute occurrences of what Palestinians have to live through are hidden and, more important, covered over by a logic of self-defence and the pursuit of terrorism (terrorist infrastructure, terrorist nests, terrorist bomb factories, terrorist suspects – the list is infinite) which perfectly suits Sharon and the lamentable George Bush. Ideas about terrorism have thus taken on a life of their own, legitimised and re-legitimised without proof, logic or rational argument.

Consider, for instance, the devastation of Afghanistan, on the one hand, and the 'targeted' assassinations of almost a hundred Palestinians (to say nothing of many thousands of 'suspects' rounded up and still imprisoned by Israeli soldiers) on the other: nobody asks whether all these people killed were in fact terrorists, or proved to be terrorists, or were about to become terrorists. They are all assumed to be dangers by acts of simple, unchallenged affirmation. All you need is an arrogant spokesman or two, like the loutish Ranaan Gissin, Avi Pazner or Dore Gold, and in Washington a non-stop apologist for ignorance and incoherence like Ari Fleischer, and the targets in question are just as good as dead. Without doubts, questions or demurral. No need for proof or any such tiresome delicacy. Terrorism and its obsessive pursuit have become an entirely circular, self-fulfilling murder and slow death of enemies who have no choice or say in the matter.

With the exception of reports by a few intrepid journalists and writers such as Amira Hass, Gideon Levy, Amos Elon, Tanya Leibowitz, Jeff Halper, Israel Shamir and a few others, public discourse in the Israeli media has declined terribly in quality and honesty. Patriotism and blind support for the government has replaced sceptical reflection and moral seriousness. Gone are the days of Israel Shahak, Jakob Talmon and Yehoshua Leibowitch. I can think of few Israeli academics and intellectuals – men like Zeev Sternhell, Uri Avneri and Ilan Pappe, for instance – who are courageous enough to depart from the imbecilic and debased debate about 'security' and 'terrorism' that seems to have overtaken the Israeli peace establishment, or even its rapidly dwindling left opposition. Crimes are being committed every day in the name of Israel and the Jewish people, and yet the intellectuals chatter on about strategic withdrawal, or perhaps whether to incorporate settlements or not, or whether to keep building that monstrous fence (has a crazier idea ever been realised in the modern world, that you can put several million people in a cage and say they don't exist?), in a manner befitting a general or a politician, rather than in ways more suited to intellectuals and artists with independent judgement and some sort of moral standard. Where are the Israeli equivalents of Nadine Gordimer, André Brink, Athol Fugard, those white writers who spoke out unequivocally and with unambiguous clarity against the evils of South African apartheid? They simply don't exist in Israel, where public discourse by writers and academics has sunk to equivocation and the repetition of official propaganda, and where most really first-class writing and thought has disappeared from even the academic establishment.

But to return to Israeli practices and the mind-set that has gripped the country with such obduracy during the past few years, think of

Sharon's plan. It entails nothing less than the obliteration of an entire people by slow, systematic methods of suffocation, outright murder, and the stifling of everyday life. There is a remarkable story by Kafka, 'In the Penal Colony', about a crazed official who shows off a fantastically detailed torture machine whose purpose is to write all over the body of the victim, using a complex apparatus of needles to inscribe the captive's body with minute letters that ultimately cause the prisoner to bleed to death. This is what Sharon and his brigades of willing executioners are doing to the Palestinians, with only the most limited and most symbolic of opposition. Every Palestinian has become a prisoner. Gaza is surrounded by an electrified wire fence on three sides; imprisoned like animals, Gazans are unable to move, unable to work, unable to sell their vegetables or fruit, unable to go to school. They are exposed from the air to Israeli planes and helicopters and are gunned down like turkeys on the ground by tanks and machine guns. Impoverished and starved, Gaza is a human nightmare, each of whose little pieces of episodes – like what takes place at Erez, or near the settlements – involves thousands of soldiers in the humiliation, punishment, intolerable enfeeblement of each Palestinian, without regard for age, gender or illness. Medical supplies are held up at the border, ambulances are fired upon or detained. Hundreds of houses demolished, and hundreds of thousands of trees and agricultural land destroyed in acts of systematic collective punishment against civilians, most of whom are already refugees from Israel's destruction of their society in 1948. Hope has been eliminated from the Palestinian vocabulary so that only raw defiance remains, and still Sharon and his sadistic minions prattle on about eliminating terrorism by an ever-encroaching occupation that has continued now for thirty-five years. That the campaign itself is, like all colonial brutality, futile, or that it has the effect of making Palestinians more, rather than less, defiant simply does not enter Sharon's closed mind.

The West Bank is occupied by 1,000 Israeli tanks whose sole purpose is to fire upon and terrorise civilians. Curfews are imposed for periods of up to two weeks, without respite. Schools and universities are either closed or impossible to get to. No one can travel, not just between the nine main cities, but within the cities. Every town today is a wasteland of destroyed buildings, looted offices, purposely ruined water and electrical systems. Commerce is finished. Malnutrition prevails in half the children. Two-thirds of the population lives below the poverty level of $2 a day. Tanks in Jenin (where the demolition of the refugee camp by Israeli armour, a major war crime, was never investigated because cowardly international bureaucrats such as Kofi Annan back down when Israel threatens) fire upon and kill children, but that is only one drop in an unending stream of Palestinian civilian deaths caused by Israeli soldiers who furnish the illegal Israeli military occupation with loyal, unquestioning service. Palestinians are all 'terrorist suspects'. The soul of this occupation is that young Israeli conscripts are allowed full rein to subject Palestinians at checkpoints to every known form of private torture and abjection. There is the waiting in the sun for hours; then there is the detention of medical supplies and produce until they rot; there are the insulting words and beatings administered at will; the sudden rampage of jeeps and soldiers against civilians waiting their turn by the thousand at the innumerable checkpoints that have made of Palestinian life a choking hell; making dozens of youths kneel in the sun for hours; forcing men to take off their clothes; insulting and humiliating parents in front of their children; forbidding the sick to pass through for no other reason than personal whim; stopping ambulances and firing on them. And the steady number of Palestinian deaths (quadruple that of Israelis) increases on a daily, mostly untabulated basis. More 'terrorist suspects' plus their wives and children, but 'we' regret those deaths very much. Thank you.

Israel is frequently referred to as a democracy. If so, then it is a democracy without a conscience, a country whose soul has been captured by a mania for punishing the weak, a democracy that faithfully mirrors the psychopathic mentality of its ruler, General Sharon, whose sole idea – if that is the right word for it – is to kill, reduce, maim, drive away Palestinians until 'they break'. He provides nothing more concrete as a goal for his campaigns, now or in the past, beyond that, and like the garrulous official in Kafka's story he is most proud of his machine for abusing defenceless Palestinian civilians, all the while monstrously abetted in his grotesque lies by his court advisers and philosophers and generals, as well as by his chorus of faithful American servants. There is no Palestinian army of occupation, no Palestinian tanks, no soldiers, no helicopter gunships, no artillery, no government to speak of. But there are the 'terrorists' and the 'violence' that Israel has invented so that its own neuroses can be inscribed on the bodies of Palestinians, without effective protest from the overwhelming majority of Israel's laggard philosophers, intellectuals, artists, peace activists. Palestinian schools, libraries and universities have ceased normal functioning for months now: and we still wait for the Western freedom-to-write-groups and the vociferous defenders of academic freedom in America to raise their voices in protest. I have yet to see one academic organisation either in Israel or in the West make a declaration about this profound abrogation of the Palestinian right to knowledge, to learning, to attend school.

In sum, Palestinians must die a slow death so that Israel can have its security, which is just around the corner but cannot be realised because of the special Israeli 'insecurity'. The whole world must sympathise, while the cries of Palestinian orphans, sick old women, bereaved communities and tortured prisoners simply go unheard and unrecorded. Doubtless, we will be told, these horrors serve a larger purpose than mere sadistic cruelty. After all, 'the two sides' are engaged in a 'cycle of violence' which has to be stopped, sometime, somewhere. Once in a while, we ought to pause and declare indignantly that there is only one side with an army and a country: the other is a stateless, dispossessed population of people without rights or any present way of securing them. The language of suffering and concrete daily life has either been hijacked, or it has been so perverted as, in my opinion, to be useless except as pure fiction deployed as a screen for the purpose of more killing and painstaking torture – slowly, fastidiously, inexorably. That is the truth of what Palestinians suffer. But in any case, Israeli policy will ultimately fail.

SOURCES

FELICITY ARBUTHNOT: 'Jassim, the Little Poet – R.I.P.' (August 1998) and 'Letter from Basra' (February 1999). Copyright © Felicity Arbuthnot 1998, 1999, 2004. Reproduced by permission of the author.

DAVID ARMSTRONG: 'Dick Cheney's Song of America: Drafting a Plan for Global Dominance', from *Harper's Magazine* (October 2002). Copyright © *Harper's Magazine*, 2002. All rights reserved. Reproduced from the October 2002 issue of *Harper's Magazine* by special permission.

WILFRED BURCHETT: 'The Atomic Plague', from *At the Barricades: Forty Years on the Cutting Edge of History* (New York: New York Times Books, 1981). Copyright © Wilfred Burchett. Reprinted by permission of the Estate of Wilfred Burchett.

JAMES CAMERON: 'Through the Looking-Glass', from *Witness* (London: Victor Gollancz, 1966). Copyright © James Cameron 1965, 1966. Reprinted by permission of David Higham Associates Ltd.

MARK CURTIS: 'Complicity in a Million Deaths', from *Web of Deceit: Britain's Real Role in the World* (London: Vintage, 2003). Copyright © Mark Curtis, 2003. Reprinted by permission of The Random House Group Ltd.

MAX DU PREEZ AND JACQUES PAUW: 'Exposing Apartheid's Death Squads'. Copyright © Max du Preez and Jacques Pauw 2004. Published by permission of the authors.

ROBERT FISK: 'Terrorists', from *Pity the Nation: Lebanon at War* (Oxford: Oxford University Press, 2001). Copyright © Robert Fisk 1990, 1992, 2001. Reprinted by permission of Andre Deutsch Ltd. 'Another War on Terror', from the *Independent* (28 November 2001); 'Baghdad, Blood and Bandages', from the *Independent* (30 March 2003); 'Another Day in the Bloody Death of Iraq', from the *Independent* (21 September 2003). Reprinted by permission of Independent Newspapers (UK) Ltd.

PAUL FOOT: 'The Great Lockerbie Whitewash': the first article, 'Why Weren't We Told?', appeared in the *Daily Mirror*, 21 December 1989; the other pieces appeared in the *Private Eye* issues of 5 January, 8 June, 17 August and 28 September 1990; 22 November and 20 December 1991; 31 January, 13 March and 27 March 1992; 14 January and 30 December 1994; 19 May, 22 September, 6 October and 15 December 1995; 10 January and 31 October 1997; 2 April

Methuen in 1988. This extract translated by Shaun Whiteside, translation copyright © Jonathan Cape 2004. Published by permission of Tanja Howarth Literary Agency.

JO WILDING: 'Eyewitness in Falluja'. Copyright © Jo Wilding 2004. Reprinted by permission of the author.

Every effort has been made to contact all copyright holders. The publishers would be pleased to rectify any omissions or errors brought to their notice at the earliest opportunity.

For permission to reproduce illustrations, the publishers wish to thank the following: AP/Wide World Photos (Martha Gellhorn); Camera Press/Eamonn McCabe (Paul Foot); Corbis (Edward R. Murrow, Seymour Hersh); Bert Hardy (James Cameron); Eric Piper (John Pilger with ATV film crew); Reuters/Alexander Natruskin (Anna Politkovskaya); Rex Features (Edward W. Said); David Silverman/Getty Images (Amira Hass); *Sunday Times*, South Africa (Max du Preez); Stern/Picture Press/SOA (Günter Wallraff); Ted Streshinsky/Time Life Pictures/Getty Images (Jessica Mitford); Times Newspapers Limited (Robert Fisk); and John Pilger (Felicity Arbuthnot).

INDEX